Genealogical & Local History Books in Print

5th Edition

U.S. Sources & Resources Volume

N – W

GENEALOGICAL & LOCAL HISTORY BOOKS IN PRINT

5th Edition

U.S. Sources & Resources Volume

North Carolina – Wyoming

Compiled and Edited by
Marian Hoffman

Published by Genealogical Publishing Co., Inc.
1001 N. Calvert St., Baltimore, MD 21202
Library of Congress Catalogue Card Number 97-70714
International Standard Book Number, Volume N–W: 0-8063-1537-7
Set Number: 0-8063-1535-0
Made in the United States of America

OCLC # 35098313

Contents

How to Use This Book

The entries in this second volume of *U.S. Sources & Resources* are organized alphabetically by state, beginning with North Carolina and ending with Wyoming. For each state, a listing of statewide and regional references appears first, followed by a listing of books dealing with specific counties, towns, and smaller municipalities. This volume includes both an author index and a title index for maximum convenience in your research.

To order any of the listed publications, locate the vendor number at the bottom right of each listing. The names and addresses of these vendors, and any special ordering information, are located on page ix. Send your order to the vendor and include the proper fee. Be sure to mention that you saw their work listed in *Genealogical & Local History Books in Print*. Unless otherwise stated next to the price or in the special ordering information included in the List of Vendors (organized numerically), the prices given in this volume include shipping and handling costs. They do not, however, include sales tax. *You must pay the state sales tax required by the government of the state in which you reside if you order books from vendors operating in your state.*

List of Vendors
(organized numerically)

G0004 William S. Farley, 6592 E. Jackson Court, Highlands Ranch, CO 80126

G0007 Randall C. Maydew, 6908 Brandywine Loop NE, Albuquerque, NM 87111; tel. 505-821-0102

G0009 Virginia Carlisle d'Armand, 3636 Taliluna Ave. Apt. #235, Knoxville, TN 37919

G0010 Genealogical Publishing Co., Inc., 1001 N. Calvert Street, Baltimore, MD 21202-3879; tel. 410-837-8271; Fax: 410-752-8492
Shipping & handling: On orders over $10.00: one book $3.50, each additional book $1.25; on orders totaling $10.00 or less: $1.50. When ordering sets: First volume $3.50, each additional volume, $1.25. MD residents add 5% sales tax; MI residents add 6% sales tax.

G0011 Clearfield Company, 1001 N. Calvert Street, Baltimore, MD 21202; tel. 410-625-9004; Fax: 410-752-8492
Shipping and handling: One item $3.50, each additional item $1.25. MD residents add 5% sales tax, MI residents add 6% sales tax.

G0015 Helen R. Long, 2536 Brockman Street, Manhattan, KS 66502

G0016 Barbara Wisnewski, Coastal Bend Genealogical Society, 2 Bobwhite Trail, Robstown, TX 78380; tel. 512-387-6462

G0019 Carol Cox Bouknecht, 2420 Castletowers Lane, Tallahassee, FL 32301; tel. 904-878-5762

G0021 SFK Genealogy, Mrs. Shirley F. Kinney, 12 Dell Place, Rome, GA 30161-7006; tel. 706-295-2228

G0024 Hilde Shuptrine Farley, 10325 Russell Street, Shawnee Mission, KS 66212-1736

G0028 Susan R. Alexander, PO Box 460614, Houston, TX 77056-8614

G0032 Linda Berg Stafford, PO Box 5261, Bloomington, IN 47407

G0035 James W. Lowry, 13531 Maugansville Road, Hagerstown, MD 21740

G0036 Tallahassee Genealogical Society, Inc., PO Box 4371, Tallahassee, FL 32315

G0039 Mount Holly Cemetery Association, PO Box 250118, Little Rock, AR 72225

G0040 Frances H. Wynne, 104 Gordon Street, Clayton, NC 27520-1746

G0042 Historical & Genealogical Society of Indiana Co., PA, 200 S. Sixth Street, Indiana, PA 15701-2999

G0055 Lorain County Chapter—OGS, PO Box 865, Elyria, OH 44036-0865

G0056 Herman W. Ferguson, 600 Chad Drive, Rocky Mount, NC 27803; tel. 919-443-2258

G0057 S. Worrel, PO Box 6016, Falls Church, VA 22040-6016

G0058 Poestenkill Historical Society, PO Box 140, Poestenkill, NY 12140-0140

G0059 Broken Arrow Genealogical Society, PO Box 1244, Broken Arrow, OK 74013-1244

G0061 Family Publications—Rose Caudle Terry, 5628 60th Drive NE, Marysville, WA 98270-9509; e-mail: cxwp57a@prodigy.com

G0064 Arkansas Research, PO Box 303, Conway, AR 72033; Fax: 501-470-1120

G0067 Arnold Kepple, PO Box 77, Callensburg, PA 16213

G0068 Susan L. Mitchell, 34233 Shawnee Trail, Westland, MI 48185

G0069 Gloucester County Historical Society, 17 Hunter Street, Woodbury, NJ 08096-4605

G0070 Remsen-Steuben Historical Society, PO Box 284, Remsen, NY 13438

G0074 Joan W. Peters, PO Box 144, Broad Run, VA 22014

G0075 Prince George's County Genealogical Society, PO Box 819, Bowie, MD 20718-0819

G0076 Pauline Williams Wright, PO Box 1976, Glenwood, AR 71943

G0077 Roy F. Olson, Jr., 360 Watson Road, Paducah, KY 42003-8978

G0079 Henrietta C. Evans, 638 First Avenue, Gallipolis, OH 45631-1215; tel. 614-446-1775

G0080 Champaign County Genealogical Society, PO Box 680, Urbana, OH 43078

G0081 Genealogical Books in Print, 6818 Lois Drive, Springfield, VA 22150
Shipping and handling: Add $1.75 for first $10.00, $.35 for each additional $10.00.

G0082 Picton Press, PO Box 250, Rockport, ME 04856; tel. 207-236-6565; (sales) 800-742-8667; Fax: 207-236-6713; e-mail: Picton@midcoast.com
Shipping and handling: Add $4.00 for the first book, $2.00 for each additional book.

G0083 Riley County Genealogical Society, 2005 Claflin Road, Manhattan, KS 66502; tel. 913-537-2205

G0084 Dolores Rench, 2508 Airway Road, Muncie, IN 47304

G0085 Buffalo & Erie County Historical Society, 25 Nottingham Court, Buffalo, NY 14216; tel. 716-873-9644

G0087 Don Mills, Inc., PO Box 34, Waynesville, NC 28786; tel. 704-452-7600

G0088 Carter County History Book Committee, c/o Juanita Wilson, Route 7, Box 2085, Elizabethton, TN 37643

G0089 Holston Territory Genealogical Society, PO Box 433, Bristol, VA 24203; tel. 615-787-2228

G0093 Heart of the Lakes Publishing, PO Box 299, Interlaken, NY 14847-0299; tel. 800-782-9687; Fax: 607-532-4684; e-mail: HLP Books@AOL.com
Visa & MasterCard accepted. Shipping additional: $4.00 for the first book, $1.00 for each additional book; most shipping via UPS—provide appropriate delivery address.

G0094 Glyndwr Resources, 43779 Valley Rd, Decatur, MI 49045

G0095 Delaware County Historical Alliance, PO Box 1266, Muncie, IN 47308

G0096 Ronald R. Templin, 2256 River Oak Lane SE, Fort Myers, FL 33905; tel. 813-694-8347

G0103 Elaine Obbink Zimmerman, PO Box 276, Woodstock, MD 21163-0276

G0108 Jane E. Darlington, C.G.R.S., 793 Woodview S Drive, Carmel, IN 46032; tel. 317-848-9002

G0109 Indiana Historical Society, 315 W. Ohio Street, Indianapolis, IN 46202; tel. 317-232-1882
  Shipping and handling: Add $2.75 for first book, $1.00 for the second and other books ordered.

G0110 St. Clair County (IL) Genealogical Society, PO Box 431, Belleville, IL 62222-0431

G0112 W. E. Morrison & Co., Ovid, NY 14521; tel. 607-869-2561

G0113 Nickell Genealogical Books, PO Box 67, West Liberty, KY 41472

G0115 Mrs. Barbara Knott Horsman, 14704 Jefferson Avenue, Chester, VA 23831

G0116 Goodenow Family Association, Route 2, Box 718, Shepherdstown, WV 25443; tel. 304-876-2008

G0117 John T. Humphrey, PO Box 15190, Washington, DC 20003; tel. 202-544-4142

G0118 Scholarly Resources, 104 Greenhill Avenue, Wilmington, DE 19805-1897; tel. 800-772-8937

G0121 Donald Lewis Osborn, 322 SE Willow Way, Lee's Summit, MO 64063-2928; tel. 816-524-5785

G0122 Joan Kusek, 9640 Walmer, Overland Park, KS 66212-1554

G0123 Minnesota Veterinary Historical Museum, 2469 University Avenue, St. Paul, MN 55114

G0126 Catoctin Press, PO Box 505, New Market, MD 21774-0505; tel. 301-620-0157; Fax: 301-620-1817; e-mail: ghmj48b@prodigy.com

G0130 South Carolina Department of Archives and History, PO Box 11669, Columbia, SC 29211; tel. 803-734-8590
  Make checks payable to "Archives and History."

G0131 Jo White Linn, PO Box 1948, Salisbury, NC 28145-1948

G0135 Ohio Genealogy Center, c/o Kenneth Luttner, PO Box 395, St. Peter, MN 56082; tel. 507-388-7158

G0139 Yakima Valley Genealogical Society, PO Box 445, Yakima, WA 98907-0445; tel. 509-248-1328

G0140 Family Line Publications, Rear 63 E Main Street, Westminster, MD 21157; tel. 800-876-6103
  Shipping and handling: First item $2.00, each additional item $.50.

G0145 Mildred S. Wright, 140 Briggs, Beaumont, TX 77707-2329; tel. 409-832-2308

G0148 Archive Publishing/Microform Books, 4 Mayfair Circle, Oxford, MA 01540-2722; tel. 508-987-0881

G0149 Howard County Genealogical Society, PO Box 274, Columbia, MD 21045-0274

G0151 Indian River Genealogical Society, PO Box 1850, Vero Beach, FL 32961

G0154 Pau Hana Press, 1116 Kealaolu Avenue, Honolulu, HI 96816-5419

G0156 Newton County Historical Commission, PO Box 1383, Newton, TX 75966; tel. 409-379-2109

G0157 Diane K. McClure, 105 4th Avenue NE, St. Petersburg, FL 33701

G0160 Hope Farm Press & Bookshop (publishers & distributors), 1708 Route 212, Saugerties, NY 12477; tel. 914-679-6809 (inquiries; 1-6 p.m. eastern time); 800-883-5778 (orders); e-mail: hopefarm@hopefarm.com; website: http://www.hopefarm.com
  Shipping and handling: Add $3.95 for the first book, $1.00 for each additional book. NY residents must pay sales tax.

G0163 Jeffrey L. Haines, 6345 Armindale Avenue, Rural Hall, NC 27045-9753

G0167 Patricia Morrow, PO Box 116, Maplecrest, NY 12454-0116

G0170 Mrs. William H. Counts, 3801 Glenmere Road, North Little Rock, AR 72116

G0172 Nancy Justus Morebeck, 409 Dennis Drive, Vacaville, CA 95688

G0174 Colorado Genealogical Society Inc., Pub. Dir., PO Box 9218, Denver, CO 80209

G0175 Ozarks Genealogical Society, Inc., PO Box 3494, Springfield, MO 65808

G0176 Margaret M. Cowart, 7801 Tea Garden Road SE, Huntsville, AL 35802

G0177 Patricia D. Smith, PO Box 1, Garden City, KS 67846-0001; tel. 316-275-4554

G0180 Hunterdon County Historical Society, 114 Main St, Flemington, NJ 08822; tel. 908- 782-1981

G0181 Frank J. Doherty, 181 Freedom Road, Pleasant Valley, NY 12569

G0182 New York Genealogical and Biographical Society, 122 East 58th Street, New York, NY 10022; tel. 212-755-8532

G0183 Tennessee Valley Publishing, PO Box 52527, Knoxville, TN 37950-2527; tel. 800-762-7079; Fax: 423-584-0113; e-mail: tvp1@ix.netcom.com

G0184 Solano County Genealogical Society, Inc., PO Box 2494, Fairfield, CA 94533

G0187 McCraken County Genealogical & Historical Society, c/o Paducah Public Library, 555 Washington St., Paducah, KY 42003-1735

G0188 Greene County Historical & Genealogical Society, 120 N 12th Street, Paragould, AR 72450

G0190 Worthy-Brandenburg Index, 365 Lake Forrest Lane, Atlanta, GA 30342-3213; tel. 404-255-1471

G0191 The Ancestor Shoppe, 5501 Duncan Road #315, Fort Smith, AR 72903

G0195 Origins, 4327 Milton Avenue, Janesville, WI 53546 608-757-2777

G0197 Ernest Thode, RR 7, Box 306GB, Kern Road, Marietta, OH 45750-9437

G0199 -ana Publishing, Norma R. Lantz, 66543 26th Street, Lawton, MI 49065-9678; tel. 616-624-7324

G0202 The Genealogical Society of Pennsylvania, 1305 Locust Street, Philadelphia, PA 19107-5661; tel. 215-545-0391; Fax: 215-545-0936.
Pennsylvania residents must pay 6% sales tax.

G0238 Family History & Genealogy Center, 1300 E. 109th Street, Kansas City, MO 64131-3585; Fax: 816-943-0477

G0245 Rosamond Houghton Van Noy, 4700 Hwy. K East, Conover, WI 54519; tel. 715-479-5044

G0256 Arthur Louis Finnell Books, 9033 Lyndale Avenue S., Suite 108, Bloomington, MN 55420-3535

G0259 Higginson Book Co., publishers and reprinters of genealogy and local history, 148-BP Washington Street, PO Box 778, Salem, MA 01970 508-745-7170; Fax: 508-745-8025
Complete catalogs are available free with your order, or $4.00 separately. To order: We accept checks or money order, or MC/VISA. Please add $3.50 for the first book and $1.00 for each additional book. We bind our books to order; please allow six to eight weeks for delivery, plus two additional weeks for hardcover books.

G0261 Betty R. Darnell, 204 Hartford Drive, Mount Washington, KY 40047; tel. 502-538-8743; Fax: 502-538-8743

G0274 Clark County Historical Association, PO Box 516, Arkadelphia, AR 71923; tel. 501-245-5332

G0278 Bartlesville Genealogical Society, c/o Public Library, 600 South Johnstone, Bartlesville, OK 74003

G0305 Irish Genealogical Society, Intl., PO Box 16585, St. Paul, MN 55116-0585; Fax: 612-574-0316

G0307 Margaret B. Kinsey, PO Box 459, Lamesa, TX 79331; tel. 806-872-3603

G0312 Michal Martin Farmer, PO Box 140880, Dallas, TX 75214-0880

G0313 Cobb County GA Genealogical Society, Inc., PO Box 1413, Marietta, GA 30061-1413

G0314 William E. Wise, 411 Elm Street, Ravenna, Ky 40472; tel. 606-723-7279

G0319 John H. Stoddard, PO Box 434, Elmhurst, IL 60126; tel. 630-617-4906

G0332 Virginia B. Fletcher, 721 NW 73 Avenue, Ft. Lauderdale, FL 33317-1140; e-mail: VBFletcher@aol.com

G0333 Oscar H. Stroh, Ph.D., 1531 Fishing Creek Valley Road, Harrisburg, PA 17112-9240; tel. 717-599-5117
Add $3.00 for packing and mailing regardless of number of books ordered.

G0335 Warren Co. (OH) Genealogical Society, 300 East Silver Street, Lebanon, OH 45036; tel. 513-933-1144

G0337 Nancie Todd Weber, 22309 Canyon Lake Drive South, Canyon Lake, CA 92587; e-mail: nanciet@inland.net

G0372 Robert Haydon, 12 Fenchley Court, Little Rock, AR 72212 501-224-1313; Fax: 501-224-7081

G0387 Bland Books, Route 5, Box 412 "Dreamwood," Fairfield, IL 62837-8903

G0399 Nathan Mathews, PO Box 1975, Fayetteville, GA 30214; e-mail: Prodigy KNHK84A

G0406 New England Historic Genealogical Society Sales Dept., 160 N. Washington Street, 4th floor, Boston, MA 02114-2120; tel. 617-536-5740; Fax: 617-624-0325; e-mail: nehgs@nehgs.org

G0430 Barbara Stacy Mathews, 1420 D Street, Marysville, CA 95901; tel. 916-741-2967

G0440 Infopreneur Publishing Co., PO Box 4241, Harrisburg, PA 17111-0241

G0450 Kinship, 60 Cedar Heights Road, Rhinebeck, NY 12572; tel. 914-876-4592; e-mail: 71045.1516@compuserve.com
Shipping and handling: Add $1.50 per book. NY residents must add sales tax; 10% discount if 4 or more books ordered.

G0456 Janet Nixon Baccus, 5817 144th Street East, Puyallup, WA 98373-5221; tel. 206-537-8288

G0458 AKB Publications—Annette K. Burgert, 691 Weavertown Road, Myerstown, PA 17067-2642

G0459 Tabernacle Cemetery Trust Fund, 1421 North Fork Road, Black Mountain, NC 28711

G0460 Janice L. Jones, 4839 Towne Centre Drive, St. Louis, MO 63128-2816

G0461 Luxemberg Publications, PO Box 1359, Sutter Creek, CA 95685; Fax: 209-267-5101; e-mail: lensales@cdepot.net

G0462 Grant County Historical Society, 12 Charlotte Heights, Williamstown, KY 41097

G0463 Patricia M. Steele, 10 Cherry Street, Brookville, PA 15825

G0464 M. P. Dolph, 134 E. Goodwin Place, Mundelein, IL 60060

G0465 Jaussi Publications, 284 East 400 South, Orem, Utah 84058-6312; tel. 801-225-7384

G0466 Joyce Martin Murray, 2921 Daniel, Dallas, TX 75205; e-mail: Jmurray785@aol.com
Shipping & handling: Add $3.50 plus $.50 for each additional book/$1.00 each title fiche.

G0467 Judy A. Deeter, 4 Altezza Drive, Mission Viejo, CA 92692-5107

G0468 Mechling Associates, Inc., 203 Pine Tract Road, Butler, PA 16001-8412; tel. 800-941-3735; Fax: 412-285-9231

G0469 Eunice J. Filler, PO Box 251, Burkburnett, TX 76354

G0470 Connie L. Young, 3001 Hillcrest Drive, Irving, TX 75062

G0471 Poplar Grove Press, PO Box 445, Arkadelphia, AR 71923-0445; tel. 501-246-7461; e-mail: swright@iocc.com

G0472 David N. Walters, 1630 N. Buchanan Street, Arlington, VA 22207-2048; tel. 703-525-2551

G0474 Rose Family Association, 1474 Montelegre Drive, San Jose, CA 95120; tel. 408-268-2137

G0476 Old Jail Museum, 326 Thomaston Street, Barnesville, GA 30204; tel. 770-358-0150

G0477 Lincoln-Lancaster County Genealogical Society, PO Box 30055, Lincoln, NE 68503-0055
Please write for price information.

G0478 Ancestor Publishers, 6166 Janice Way, Dept. GBIP96, Arvada, CO 80004-5160; tel. 800-373-0816; Fax: 303-425-9709; e-mail: ancestor@net1comm.com

G0479 Westchester County Historical Society, 2199 Saw Mill River Road, Elmsford, NY 10523; tel. 914-592-4323; Fax: 914-592-4323

G0480 Ms. Connie Jean Casilear, PO Box 611, Winchester, VA 22604-0611

G0482 Bonnie Peters, 3212 Curtis Lane, Knoxville, TN 37918-4003; tel. 423-687-3842

G0483 GenLaw Resources, c/o Patricia Andersen, 9346 Bremerton Way, Gaithersburg, MD 20879-1427; tel. 301-977-8062; Fax: 301-977-8062

G0484 Skipwith Historical & Genealogical Society, PO Box 1382, Oxford, MS 38655

G0486 William B. Bogardus, 1121 Linhof Road, Wilmington, OH 45177-2917

G0487 Woolkoch Publishing, 459 Ross Road, Columbus, OH 43213-1953

G0488 Illinois State Genealogical Society, PO Box 10195, Springfield, IL 62791-0195; tel. 217-789-1968

G0489 Jim W. Faulkinbury, CGRS, PO Box 60727, Sacramento, CA 95860-0727

G0491 Westland Publications, PO Box 117, McNeal, AZ 85617; e-mail: worldrt@primenet.com

G0492 Marietta Publishing Company, 2115 North Denair Avenue, Turlock, CA 95382; tel. 209-634-9473
California residents add 7.375% sales tax.

G0493 Centre County Historical Society, 1001 E. College Avenue, State College, PA 16801; tel. 814-234-4779

G0494 Muskingum County Footprints, 2740 Adamsville Road, Zanesville, OH 43701

G0495 Bedford Historical Society, PO Box 46282, Bedford, OH 44146; tel. 216-232-0796

G0496 TCI Genealogical Resources, PO Box 15839, San Luis Obispo, CA 93406; tel. 805-739-1145

G0497 Camp County Genealogical Society, PO Box 1083, Pittsburg, TX 75686

G0498 Linda Mearse, 2841 Paso del Robles, San Marcos, TX 78666; e-mail: lm@itouch.net

G0499 Connellsville Area Historical Society, 275 South Pittsburgh Street, Connellsville, PA 15425; tel. 412-628-5640

G0500 Maryland Acadian Studies, 11725 Kingtree Street, Wheaton, MD 20902; tel. 301-933-5491

G0501 Illinois State Historical Society, 1 Old State Capitol Plaza, Springfield, IL 62701-1507; tel. 217-782-4286; Fax: 217-524-8042

G0503 Whatcom Genealogical Society, PO Box 1493, Bellingham, WA 98227-1493

G0504 Family History World®, PO Box 22045, Salt Lake City, UT 84122-1045, Publication Division, The Genealogical Institute; tel. 800-377-6058

G0505 Cottage Grove Genealogical Society, PO Box 388, Cottage Grove, OR 97424

G0506 Family Tree, PO Box 4311, Boise, ID 83711

G0507 Betty J. Masley/IDL Research, PO Box 20654, Indianapolis, IN 46220-0654

G0508 James E. Williams, Route 1, Box 864, Milano, TX 76556-9759

G0509 Genealogical Society of North Brevard, Inc., PO Box 897, Titusville, FL 32781-0897

G0510 Library Council of Metropolitan Milwaukee, Inc., 814 W. Wisconsin Avenue, Milwaukee, WI 53233; tel. 414-271-8470; Fax: 414-286-2794

G0511 Rev. Albert H. Ledoux, 11007 Montgomery Road, Beltsville, MD 20705. After June 1998, address is c/o Registrar M.S.M. Seminary, Emmitsburg, MD 21727.

G0512 The Ohio Genealogical Society, PO Box 2625, Mansfield, OH 44406; tel. 419-522-4077; Fax: 419-522-0224; e-mail: OGS@freenet.richland.oh.us

G0514 Fair Printing Company, 10417 Long Meadow Road, Oklahoma City, OK 73162

G0517 InfoServ, Louise K. Pollard, 1497 Cheever Lane, Farmington, UT 84025

G0519 Darlene F. Weaver, 386 Shadwell Drive, Circleville, OH 43113

G0520 Historical Research Associates, PO Box 242, Marshfield Hills, MA 02051; tel. 617-834-7329

G0521 Jean S. Morris, PO Box 8530, Pittsburgh, PA 15220-0530

G0522 The Book Shelf, William R. Snell, 3765 Hillsdale Drive, NE, Cleveland, TN 37312-5133; tel. 423-472-8408

G0524 NCOHA, Inc., PO Box 2811, Dept. GPC, Ponca City, OK 74602; tel. 405-765-7169; website: http://www.brigadoon.com/~nipperb

G0525 Richard H. Taylor, 1211 Seneca Road, Benton Harbor, MI 49022; tel. 616-925-9813

G0526 Mrs. Joyce Ray Lea, 1099 Clay Street, Apt. 1110, Winter Park, FL 32789-5478

G0527 Coiny Publishing Co., PO Box 585, Greenfield, IN 46140; tel. 317-462-7758

G0528 Shirlene Salter, McKinney Memorial Public Library, 220 N. Kentucky Street, McKinney, TX 75069

G0529 GSNOCC, PO Box 706, Yorba Linda, CA 92885-0706; Fax: 801-359-7391

G0530 Audrey Gilbert, 604 State Rt. 503 South, West Alexandria, OH 45381

G0531 The Bookmark, PO Box 90, Knightstown, IN 46148; tel. 800-876-5133, ext. 170; Fax: 1-800-695-8153
Indiana residents must add 5% sales tax.

G0532 Tad Evans, 1506 Stillwood Drive, Savannah, GA 31419; tel. 912-925-1478

G0533 Margaret H. Gentges, 9251 Wood Glade Drive, Great Falls, VA 22066-2209; tel. 703-759-2218; e-mail: mgentges@mindspring.com

G0534 ALDean Enterprises, PO Box 1942, Richmond, IN 47375

G0535 Tom C. Martinet, 82 Hummingbird Lane, Cabot, AR 72023-8883; tel. 501-843-4856; Fax: 501-982-0054

G0536 Closson Press, 1935 Sampson Drive, Apollo, PA 15613-9209; Fax: 412-337-9484; e-mail: rclosson@nauticom.net
Shipping and handling in the Continental U.S.A. is $4.00 for any size order except for special order books where additional shipping/handling is requested.

G0537 Grand Prairie Research, Marilyn Hambrick Sickel, Route 1, PO Box 125A, DeValls Bluff, AR 72041-9753

G0538 Christ Church Parish Preservation Society, Inc., c/o Mary-Julia Royall, 349 Bay View Drive, Mount Pleasant, SC 29464; tel. 803-884-4265

G0539 Minnie Pitts Champ, PO Box 801515, Dallas, TX 75380-1515; tel. 972-562-6543

G0540 Washington County Historical Assoc., PO Box 205, Jonesborough, TN 37659

G0541 Mrs. Thelma S. McManus, C.G.R.S., 507 Vine Street, Doniphan, MO 63935-1466; tel. 573-996-2596
Send SASE to inquire about the availability of any books listed or out of print.

G0542 Altamonte Springs City Library, 281 N. Maitland Avenue, Altamonte Springs, FL 32701; tel. 407-830-3904; Fax: 407-263-3716; e-mail: rmiller@merlin.cflc.lib.fl.us

G0543 Fairfax Genealogical Society, PO Box 2290, Dept. L, Merrifield, VA 22116-2290

G0544 Cemeteries, PO Box 451206, Grove, OK 74345-1206
Shipping and handling: Add $2.50 for the first book, $1.50 for each additional book.

G0545 Donna J. Robertson, 9380 90th Street, North, Largo, FL 34647-2415

G0547 Alma A. Smith, 554 Anna May Drive, Cincinnati, OH 45244; tel. 513-528-1840

G0549 Mountain Press, PO Box 400, Signal Mountain, TN 37377-0400; tel. 423-886-6369; Fax: 423-886-5312

G0551 The Reprint Company, Publishers, PO Box 5401, 601 Hillcrest Offices, Spartanburg, SC 29304; tel. 864-582-0732
Shipping and handling: Add $3.50 for the first book, $1.25 for each additional book. When ordering a multi-volume set, count each volume as one book. South Carolina residents must add 5% sales tax.

G0552 AGLL, PO Box 329, Bountiful, UT 84011-0329; tel. 801-298-5446
Contact vendor for shipping and handling rates.

G0553 The Library Shop, The Library of Virginia, 800 E. Broad Street, Richmond, VA 23219-1905; tel. 804-692-3524; Fax: 804-692-3528
Shipping and handling: Add $4.50 for the first book, $.50 for each additional book. VA residents must add 4.5% sales tax.

G0554 Pennsylvania Historical & Museum Commission, Publications Sales Program, PO Box 11466, Harrisburg, PA 17108-1466; tel. 717-783-2618; Fax: 717-787-8312

G0559 Avotaynu, Inc., PO Box 900, Teaneck, NJ 07666; tel. 201-387-7200; Fax: 201-387-2855; e-mail: infor@avotaynu.com; website: www.avotaynu.com
Shipping and handling in U.S.: Up to $25, $2.50; $25.01 to $35, $3.50; $35.01 to $75, $4.50; $75.01 to $130, $6.50; $130 and above, $8.50. NJ residents add 6% sales tax.

G0561 Hunterdon House, 38 Swan Street, Lambertville, NJ 08530; tel. 609-397-2523

G0567 Florida State Genealogical Society, Inc., John H. Baxley, 1909 W. Hanna Avenue, Tampa, FL 33604

G0569 Dr. George K. Schweitzer, 407 Ascot Court, Knoxville, TN 37923-5807

G0570 Ancestry, Inc., PO Box 476, Salt Lake City, UT 84110-0476; Fax: 801-531-1798
Call for shipping and handling costs. Utah residents add 6.13% sales tax.

G0571 Kansas Statistical Publishing Co., 7609 West 64th Street, Overland Park, KS 66202

G0572 Lancaster County Historical Society, 230 North President Avenue, Lancaster, PA 17603; tel. 717-392-4633; e-mail: jasper@LanClio.org

G0573 Los Banos Genealogical Society, Inc., PO Box 2525, Los Banos, CA 93635

G0574 Ye Olde Genealogie Shoppe, 9605 Vandergriff Road, PO Box 39128, Indianapolis, IN 46239; tel. 317-862-3330; Fax: 317-862-2599
Shipping and handling: Add $4.00 per order. IL, IN, MI, MN, OH, & WI residents add sales tax.

G0577 Byron Sistler & Associates, 1712 Natchez Trace, PO Box 120934, Nashville, TN 37212; Fax: 615-298-2807
Shipping & handling: Add $3.50 per order. Tennessee residents add 8.25% sales tax.

G0578 Connecticut Society of Genealogists, Inc., PO Box 435, Glastonbury, CT 06033

G0581 Henry Z Jones, Jr., F.A.S.G., PO Box 261388, San Diego, CA 92196-1388
California residents pay 6% sales tax.

G0582 Virginia Genealogical Society, 5001 W. Broad Street #115, Richmond, VA 23230-3023
Shipping and handling: Add $3.00 for the first book, $1.00 for each additional book. VA residents add 4.5% tax.

G0583 Park Genealogical Books, PO Box 130968, Roseville, MN 55113-0968; tel. 612-488-4416; Fax: 612-488-2653; e-mail: mbakeman@parkbooks.com

G0585 New Jersey State Archives, 185 W. State Street, CN 307, Trenton, NJ 08625-0307

G0586 North Carolina Division of Archives and History, Historical Publications Section Department of Cultural Resources, 109 East Jones Street, Raleigh, NC 27601-2807; tel. 919-733-7442; Fax: 919-733-1439
Shipping and handling: Add $2.00 for orders of $1.00-$5.00; $3.00 for orders of $6.00-$12.00; $3.00 for orders over $12.00. NC residents add 6% sales tax.

G0587 New York State Archives and Records Administration, 10D45 Cultural Education Center, Albany, NY 12230
Make check payable to New York State Archives.

G0590 Broadfoot Publishing Company, 1907 Buena Vista Circle, Wilmington, NC 28405; tel. 910-686-4816; Fax: 910-686-4379
Shipping & handling: Add $4.00 for the first volume, $1.75 for each additional volume. NC residents add 6% sales tax (before adding shipping).

G0593 Maryland State Archives Publications, 350 Rowe Boulevard, Annapolis, MD 21401

G0594 Martha W. Jackson, 509 Pea Ridge Road, Scottsville, KY 42164

G0595 Cass County Genealogical Society, PO Box 880, Atlanta, TX 75551-0880
Shipping and handling: Add $2.00 for the first book, $.50 for each additional book.

G0596 State Historical Society of Missouri, 1020 Lowry, Columbia, MO 65201-7298

G0597 Delaware Public Archives, Hall of Records, Dover, DE 19901; Fax: 302-739-2578; e-mail: archives@state.de.us

G0598 New Hampshire Society of Genealogists, PO Box 2316, Concord, NH 03302-2316
Shipping and handling: Add $3.00 for each book.

G0599 Mrs. Margaret R. Jenks, 24 Mettowee Street, Granville, NY 12832-1037; tel. 518-642-1894

G0600 Peabody Essex Museum, Museum Shop, East India Square, Salem, MA 01970; Fax: 508-744-6776
Shipping and handling: Orders up to $15.00, $3.50; $15.01-$35.00, $4.50; $35.01-$50.00, $5.50; $50.01-$75.00, $6.95; over $75.00, $7.95.

G0601 Texas State Archives, Texas State Library, PO Box 12927, Austin, TX 78711-1276
Texas residents add 8% sales tax. Add $1.00 to total amount for postage and handling on all orders. Make checks or money orders payable to the Texas State Library.

G0602 Brent H. Holcomb, PO Box 21766, Columbia, South Carolina 29221
Mailing charges: Add $3.00 for the first book, $1.00 for each additional book to the same address.

G0603 John A. Haid, Haid History, 157 E. Fairway Dr., Hamilton, OH 45013; tel. 513-868-1488; Fax: 513-868-1488

G0605 Sonoma County Genealogical Society, Inc. (GP), PO Box 2273, Santa Rosa, CA 95405; website: http://web.wco.com/~hwmiller/genealogy/scgs/htw
Please add $2.00 per item for postage and handling (except postpaid microfiche).

G0606 DuPage County (IL) Genealogical Society, PO Box 133, Lombard, IL 60148

G0607 North Hills Genealogists, c/o E. S. Powell, 720 Highpoint Drive, Wexford, PA 15090-7571; e-mail: Powell@nauticom.net

G0609 T.L.C. Genealogy, PO Box 403369, Miami Beach, FL 33140-1369; tel. 800-858-8558; e-mail: staff@tlc-gen.com; website: http://www.tlc-gen.com/
All prices are postpaid. Florida residents add 6.5% sales tax.

G0610 Southern Historical Press, Inc., PO Box 1267, 275 West Broad Street, Greenville, SC 29602-1267; tel. 864-233-2346
Shipping and handling: Add $3.50 for the first book, $1.50 for each additional book. SC residents add 5% sales tax.

G0611 Frontier Press, PO Box 3715, Suite 3, Galveston, TX 77552; tel. (order line) 800-772-7559; Fax: 409-740-7988; e-mail: kgfrontier@aol.com
Shipping and handling: Add $3.50 for the first book, $1.00 for each additional book. Phone for shipping rates to international and Canadian addresses.

G0612 Hartmann Heritage Productions of Texas, RR 2, Box 148A, 932 East Main Street, Yorktown, TX 78164-9538; tel. 512-564-9200; Fax: 512-564-9200

G0613 Gene L. Williams, Route 2, Box 72, Stephenville, TX 76401; tel. 817-968-5727

G0615 Western Pennsylvania Genealogical Society, 4400 Forbes Avenue, Pittsburgh, PA 15213-4080
Shipping and handling: Add $2.50 for the first item, then $1.00 for each additional item. PA residents must pay sales tax on items & handling.

G0617 Maryland Historical Society, 201 West Monument Street, Baltimore, MD 21201 Non-member and book trade orders to: Alan C. Hood and Co., Inc., PO Box 775, Chambersburg, PA 17201.
Add $3.50 shipping and handling. MD residents add 5% sales tax; PA residents add 6%.

G0618 The Everton Publishers, Inc., PO Box 368, Logan, UT 84323-0368; tel. 800-443-6325; Fax: 801-752-0425
Shipping and handling: Add $1.50 for the first book, $.50 for each additional book.

G0620 General Society of Mayflower Descendants, Mayflower Families, PO Box 3297, Plymouth, MA 02361
Shipping and handling: Add $3.00 for orders under $12.00, $4.00 for orders over $13.00. MA residents add 5% sales tax.

G0622 Hoenstine Rental Library, 414 Montgomery Street, PO Box 208, Hollidaysburg, PA 16648; tel. 814-695-0632

G0623 North Carolina Genealogical Society, PO Box 1492, Raleigh, NC 27502
Shipping and handling: Add $2.00 for the first book, $1.00 for each additional book. NC residents must pay 6% sales tax.

G0624 Laine Sutherland, 2695 North Pebble Beach Drive, Flagstaff, AZ 86004-7419; e-mail: PTPM52A@Prodigy.com

G0625 Tennessee Valley Genealogical Society, PO Box 1568, Huntsville, AL 35807

G0626 Baxter County, Arkansas Historical and Genealogical Society, c/o Mr. Gene Garr, 1505 Mistletoe, Mountain Home, AR 72653

G0627 National Genealogical Society, 4517 17th Street N., Arlington, VA 22207-2399; e-mail: 76702.2417@compuserve.com
Discount given to members.

G0628 California Genealogical Society, 300 Brannon Street, Suite 409, PO Box 77105, San Francisco, CA 94107-0105; tel. 415-777-9936
Shipping and handling: Add $2.00 for each book. CA residents add 8.5% sales tax.

G0629 Family History Library, Salt Lake City Distribution Center, 1999 West 1700 South, Salt Lake City, UT 84104-4233; Fax: 801-240-3685

G0630 Rebecca DeArmond, 1054 Ozment Bluff, Wilmar, AR 71675-9007; tel. 501-367-8712; e-mail: rdea@seark.net

G0631 Lloyd R. Bailey, 4122 Deep Wood Circle, Durham, NC 27707

G0632 Iberian Publishing Company (publishers and distributors), 548 Cedar Creek Drive, Athens, GA 30605-3408; tel. (orders) 800-394-8634

G0633 Genealogical Forum of Oregon, Attn: Publisher, 2130 S.W. Fifth Avenue, Suite 220, Portland, OR 97201-4394; tel. 503-227-2398
Shipping and handling: $2.00 for orders up to $10.00; add $1.00 for each additional $10.00.

G0634 Oregon Genealogical Society, PO Box 10306, Eugene, OR 97440-2306; tel. 503-746-7924

G0635 Lycoming County Genealogical Society, PO Box 3625, Williamsport, PA 17701; e-mail: LCGSgen@aol.com
PA residents add 6% sales tax.

G0636 The Georgia Historical Society, 501 Whitaker Street, Savannah, GA 31499; Fax: 912-651-2831

G0645 Connecticut Historical Society, 1 Elizabeth Street, Hartford, CT 06105; tel. 860-236-5621; Fax: 860-236-2664; website: http://www.hartnet.org/chs/

G0646 Ohio Historical Society, c/o The Museum Store, 1982 Velma Avenue, Columbus, OH 43211; 800-797-2357
Free catalogues are available upon request; we have over 1,000 publications available. Call or write for shipping information.

G0648 Peter Smith Publisher, Inc., 5 Lexington Avneue, Magnolia, MA 01930; Fax: 508-525-3674

G0649 Tazewell County Historical Society, PO Box 916, Tazewell, VA 24651

G0650 Maine State Archives, Station #84, Augusta, ME 04333-0084

G0651 Kentucky Department for Libraries and Archives, Public Records Division, Archives Research Room, PO Box 537, Frankfort, KY 40602-0537
KY residents must add 6% sales tax. Shipping and handling: $2-$15, add $3; $16-$25, add $4; $26-$55, add $8; $56-$100, add $7; $101 and up, add $10. Make check or money order payable to: Kentucky State Treasurer.

G0653 Delaware Genealogical Society, 505 Market Street Mall, Wilmington, DE 19801-3091

G0654 Smoky Mountain Historical Society, PO Box 5078, Sevierville, TN 37864

G0655 Margie Garr, 1505 Mistletoe, Mountain Home, AR 72653

G0656 Southern California Genealogical Society (SCGS), PO Box 4377, Burbank, CA 91503-4377; tel. 818-843-7247
Add $2.50 for postage and handling.

G0659 Institute of Science and Public Affairs, 361 Bellamy Building, Tallahassee, FL 32305-4016

G0660 McClain Printing Company, PO Box 403, 212 Main Street, Parson, West Virginia 26287; Fax: 304-478-4658

G0661 Southwest Oklahoma Genealogical Society, PO Box 148, Lawton, OK 73502-0148
Shipping and handling: Add $2.50 for the first book, $.50 for each additional book.

G0662 Allegheny Regional Family History Society, PO Box 1804, Elkins, West Virginia 26241
WV residents should add 6% sales tax.

G0663 Diane Snyder Ptak, 12 Tice Road, Albany, NY 12203
Shipping and handling: Add $2.00 for the first book, $1.00 for each additional book.

G0664 Barrington Public Library Trustees, Attn: Traditions and Transitions, 39 Province Lane, Barrington, NH 03825
Make check payable to Barrington Public Library.

G0665 Brazos Genealogical Association, PO Box 5493, Bryan, TX 77805

G0666 Joyce Hardy Cates, 4900 Pleasant Avenue, Fairfield, OH 45014

G0667 Rudena Kramer Mallory, 6920 Pennsylvania, Kansas City, MO 64113
MO residents add 6.475% sales tax.

G0668 Idaho Genealogical Society, 4620 Overland Road #204, Boise, ID 83705

G0669 Willow Bend Books, Route 1, Box 15A, Lovettsville, VA 22080-9703

G0670 G. P. Hammond Publishing, Box 546, Strasburg, VA 22657

G0672 Partin Publications, 230 Wedgewood, Nacogdoches, TX 75961-1849

G0673 William T. and Patricia Thomas Martin, 4501 SW 62 Court, Miami, FL 33155-5936

G0674 Genealogical Society of Yuma, Arizona, PO Box 2905, Yuma, AZ 85366

G0675 Arkansas Ancestors, 222 McMahan Drive, Hot Springs, AR 71913-6243

G0676 Hempstead County Genealogical Society, PO Box 1158, Hope, AR 71801

G0677 C. L. Boyd, PO Box 222, Dover, AR 72837

G0678 Laurie Nicklas, 1320 Standiford #4-300, Modesto, CA 95350

G0679 Marin County Genealogical Society, PO Box 1511, Novato, CA 94948
Shipping and handling: Add $2.50 for the first book, $1.00 for each additional book.

G0680 Namaqua Chapter NSDAR, PO Box 697, Loveland, CO 80539-0697

G0681 Mrs. Pauline Martin, 455 Martin Road, Carnesville, GA 30521

G0682 Marion Lavender Reynolds, PO Box 352, Harrisburg, IL 62946-0352

G0683 Joan A. Griffis, 105 Poland Road, Danville, IL 61832
IL residents add sales tax.

G0684 Larry and Cynthia Scheuer Publications, 722 E. Center Street, Warsaw, IN 46580
IN residents add 5% sales tax.

G0685 Elkhart County Genealogical Society, PO Box 1031, Elkhart, IN 46515-1031
IN residents add 5% sales tax.

G0686 Brenda Joyce Jerome, PO Box 325, Newburgh, IN 47629-0325
IN residents add 5% sales tax.

G0687 Simmons Historical Publications, PO Box 66, Melber, KY 42069-0066
Shipping and handling: Add $2.00 per order.

G0688 Laurel County Historical Society, PO Box 816, London, KY 40743
KY residents add 6% sales tax.

G0689 Faye Sea Sanders, 311 Sage Road, Louisville, KY 40207

G0690 Michael R. Olson, 10153 Piney Mountain Road, Frostburg, MD 21532
Make checks payable to Percy Cemetery Commission. MD residents add $1.00 sales tax per book.

G0691 Aceto Bookman, Charles Delmar Townsend, 5721 Antietam Drive, Sarasota, FL 34231

G0692 Northeast Michigan Genealogical and Historical Society, c/o Jesse Besser Museum, 491 Johnson Street, Alpena, MI 49707

G0693 Ben Strickland, PO Box 5147, Moss Point, MS 39563-1147
MS residents add 7% sales tax.

G0694 Janice Soutee Looney, PO Box 231, Walnut Grove, MO 65770

G0695 Nodaway County Genealogical Society, Box 214, Maryville, MO 64468

G0696 The Detroit Society for Genealogical Research, Inc., c/o Burton Historical Collection, Detroit Public Library, 5201 Woodward Avenue, Detroit, MI 48202-4093
MI residents add 6% sales tax.

G0697 Libra Pipecreek Publications, 5179 Perry Road, Mt. Airy, MD 21771

G0698 Historical Data Service, 14 Clark Street, Glens Falls, NY 12804

G0699 Northwest Missouri Genealogical Society, PO Box 382, St. Joseph, MO 64502

G0700 Hyde County Historical and Genealogical Society, Route 1, Box 74, Fairfield, NC 27826

G0701 Joyce M. Gibson, 14921 McFarland Road, Laurel Hill, NC 28351

G0702 Greene County Chapter, OGS, PO Box 706, Xenia, OH 45385
OH residents must add sales tax.

G0703 Lucas County Chapter, OGS, c/o Beverly Todd Reed, 1302 Corry Avenue, Toledo, OH 43624
OH residents must add sales tax.

G0704 Paulding County Chapter, OGS, 205 South Main Street, Paulding, OH 45879
OH residents must add sales tax.

G0705 Williams County Genealogical Society, PO Box 293, Bryan, OH 43506

G0706 Wood County Chapter, OGS, PO Box 722, Bowling Green, OH 43402
OH residents add 6% sales tax.

G0707 Mrs. Helen Tice, 4239 Carolyn Drive, Memphis, TN 38111-8143

G0708 Warrine Hathaway, PO Box 8063, Dothan, AL 36304

G0709 Mahoning County Chapter, OGS, c/o Lois Glasgo, PO Box 9333, Boardman, OH 44513-9333
OH residents add 6% sales tax.

G0710 Bryan County Heritage Association, PO Box 153, Calera, OK 74730-0153
Shipping and handling: Add $2.50 for the first book, $1.00 for each additional book.

G0711 Sandra Tedford, 400 Sherry Lane, Farmersville, TX 75442-1538
TX residents must add sales tax.

G0712 Eldorado Historical Society, Box 234, Eldorado, OK 73537

G0713 Deschutes County Historical Society, PO Box 5252, Bend, OR 97709

G0715 Juanita Davis Cawthon, 944 Acklen Street, Shreveport, LA 71104-3904

G0716 Lewis & Clark County Genealogical Society, PO Box 5313, Helena, MT 59604

G0717 Clark County Genealogical Society, Attn: Rose Marie Harshman, PO Box 2728, Vancouver, WA 98668
WA residents add 7.6% sales tax.

G0718 Irene Martin, PO Box 83, Skamokawa, WA 98647
WA residents must add sales tax.

G0719 Janice Cale Sisler, PO Box 113, Bruceton Mills, WV 26525-0013
WV residents add sales tax.

G0720 West Central Wisconsin Genealogy, W10254 Gaylord Road, Merrilan, WI 54754-7933
Shipping and handling: Add $3.00 for the first book, $1.00 for each additional book.

G0721 Waukesha County Genealogical Society, PO Box 1541, Waukesha, WI 53187-1541

G0722 LaCrosse Public Library Archives, 800 Main Street, LaCrosse, WI 54601-4122

G0723 Illiana Genealogical & Historical Society, Box 207, Danville, IL 61834-0207

G0724 VESCO, Inc., PO Box 1044, Vidalia, GA 30475

G0727 Venango County Historical Society, PO Box 101, Franklin, PA 16323
Shipping and handling: Add $2.00 for the first book, $1.00 for each additional book. PA residents must add sales tax.

G0728 Richland County Genealogical Society, PO Box 3823, Mansfield, OH 44907-0823
OH residents must add sales tax.

G0729 Oklahoma Genealogical Society, Special Publications Chairman, PO Box 12986, Oklahoma City, OK 73157
Shipping and handling: Add $2.50 for the first book, $.50 for each additional book. OK residents add 8.375% sales tax.

G0730 Guilford County Genealogical Society, PO Box 9693 Plaza Station, Greensboro, NC 27429-0093

G0733 Eastern Washington Genealogical Society, PO Box 1826, Spokane, WA 99210-1826
Make check payable to EWGS.

G0734 Dwight Shubert, 8703 Oakhaven Drive, Sherwood, AR 72120

G0736 Paradise Genealogical Society, Inc., PO Box 460, Paradise, CA 95967-0460
Shipping and handling: Add $2.00 for the first book, $.50 for each additional book.

G0737 San Mateo County Genealogical Society, PO Box 5083, San Mateo, CA 94402
Shipping and handling: Add $2.00 for 1 book, $2.50 for 2 books.

G0738 Cemeteries of Oglethorpe County, PO Box 1793, Lexington, GA 30648

G0739 Lake County Genealogical Society, c/o M. P. Dolph, 134 E. Goodwin Place, Mundelein, IL 60060-1896
Make checks payable to Lake County Genealogical Society.

G0740 Macoupin County Illinois Genealogical Society, PO Box 95, Staunton, IL 62088

G0741 Genealogy Society of Southern Illinois, c/o Mrs. Tullyne Oliver, 303 Timothy Lane, Carterville, IL 62918-5021
Make checks payable to Genealogy Society of Southern Illinois.

G0742 Chicago Genealogical Society, PO Box 1160, Chicago, IL 60690
Shipping and handling: Add $2.50 for the first book, $.50 for each additional book.

G0743 South Bend Area Genealogical Society, PO Box 1222, South Bend, IN 46624
IN residents must pay sales tax.

G0744 The Confederate Research Center, Hill College Press, PO Box 619, Hillsboro, TX 76645
TX residents must add sales tax.

G0745 John and Enid Ostertag, 3005 Charles, St. Joseph, MO 64501
MO residents must add sales tax.

G0746 Edna Montgomery Burgin, 4533 Lake Dreamland Road, Louisville, KY 40216

G0747 Loretta E. Burns 1804 Zapp Lane, Pasadena, TX 77502-3123

G0748 Starke County Genealogical Society, c/o Henry F. Schricker Public Library, 152 West Culver Road, Knox, IN 46534
IN residents add 5% sales tax.

G0749 Jeanne Hallgren, 1111 Blue Star Highway, South Haven, MI 49090

G0750 Mrs. Melvin J. Bates, 410 - 20 Mile Road, Cedar Springs, MI 49319-9629

G0751 Shiawassee County Historical Society, 224 Curwood Castle Drive, Owosso, MI 48867

G0752 Fort William Bent Chapter NSDAR, c/o Marcella Swanson, 38724 Co. Rd. T, Walsh, CO 81090-9761

G0753 Mrs. Dean Gransee, RR 2, Box 47, Sanborn, MN 56083-9312

G0754 North Antelope County Genealogical Society, PO Box 56, Orchard, NE 68764
NE residents add 5% sales tax.

G0755 City of Keene Police Department, Attn: PA c/o Capt. Hal G. Brown, 11 Washington Street, Keene, NH 03431

G0756 Catherine Machan Martin, 7195 South Geeck Road, Durand, MI 48429-9102

G0757 Dr. Stephen E. Bradley, Jr., 2001 Jeri Court, Virginia Beach, VA 23464
VA residents add 4.5% sales tax.

G0758 Dee Ann Buck, 10814 Paynes Church Drive, Fairfax, VA 22032

G0759 Historical Publications, Inc., 15705 Hilcroft Cove, Austin, TX 78717-5331; tel. 800-880-6789
TX residents add 8% sales tax.

G0760 N O Inc., c/o Ed Eisley 415 Corrydale Drive, Pensacola, FL 32506
FL residents add 7% sales tax.

G0761 Tammy L. Smallen, 1110 Grove Street, Loudon, TN 37774

G0762 Margaret C. Snider, 633 Lake Spring Road, Franklin, KY 42134

G0763 Nelle J. Berry, Route 1, Box 190, Iron City, TN 38463

G0764 Vandegrift Research, 797 S. 350 W., PO Box 952, Bountiful, UT 84011-0952

G0765 Eve Nicholson, 925 Northwood #9203, Baytown, TX 77521

G0766 Boone County Genealogical Society, PO Box 306, Madison, WV 25130

G0767 W. W. Hoffman, 6364 Cliffside Drive, Florence, KY 41042

G0774 Ashtabula County Genealogical Society, 117 West Main, Geneva, OH 44041-1227
OH residents add 6% sales tax.

G0783 Nebraska State Genealogical Society, PO Box 5608, Lincoln, NE 68505-0608

G0784 Lower Delmarva Genealogical Society, PO Box 3602, Salisbury, Maryland 21802-3602
MD residents add $1.75 sales tax.

G0786 Uptown Press, 2903 Grindon Avenue, Baltimore, MD 21214; tel. 410-254-2294; Fax: 410-254-2395
Shipping and handling: Add $4.50. MD residents must pay 5% sales tax.

G0866 Nadine Billingsley, 706 Pershing, College Station, TX 77840

G0867 Joanne Dominik Glowski, 4131 Bethel, Houston, TX 77092

G0868 Rosemary DePasquale Boykin, 8407 Shadow Oaks, College Station, TX 77845

G0869 Kankakee Valley Genealogical Society, PO Box 442, Bourbonnais, IL 60914
Maximum postage and handling per single order within the continental United States: $4.00.

G0872 Harford County (Maryland) Genealogical Society, PO Box 15, Aberdeen, Maryland 21001
Shipping and handling: $1.50 for the first book, $.50 for each additional book. Make checks payable, in U.S. funds only, to the Harford County Genealogical Society.

List of Vendors
(organized alphabetically)

Aceto Bookman, Vendor G0691
AGLL, Vendor G0552
AKB Publications, Annette K. Burgert, Vendor G0458
ALDean Enterprises, Vendor G0534
Alexander, Susan R., Vendor G0028
Allegheny Regional Family History Society, Vendor G0662
Altamonte Springs City Library, Vendor G0542
-ana Publishing, Norma R. Lantz, Vendor G0199
Ancestor Publishers, Vendor G0478
Ancestor Shoppe, The, Vendor G0191
Ancestry, Inc., Vendor G0570
Archive Publishing/Microform Books, Vendor G0148
Arkansas Research, Vendor G0064
Arkansas Ancestors, Vendor G0675
Ashtabula County Genealogical Society, Vendor G0774
Avotaynu, Inc., Vendor G0559
Baccus, Janet Nixon, Vendor G0456
Bailey, Lloyd R., Vendor G0631
Barrington Public Library Trustees, Vendor G0664.
Bartlesville Genealogical Society, Vendor G0278
Bates, Mrs. Melvin J., Vendor G0750
Baxter County, Arkansas Historical and Genealogical Society, Vendor G0626
Bedford Historical Society, Vendor G0495
Berry, Nelle J., Vendor G0763
Billingsley, Nadine, Vendor G0866
Bland Books, Vendor G0387
Bogardus, William B., Vendor G0486
Bookmark, The, Vendor G0531
Book Shelf, The, Vendor G0522
Boone County Genealogical Society, Vendor G0766
Bouknecht, Carol Cox, Vendor G0019
Boykin, Rosemary DePasquale, Vendor G0868
Boyd, C. L., Vendor G0677
Bradley, Dr. Stephen E., Jr., Vendor G0757
Brazos Genealogical Association, Vendor G0665
Broadfoot Publishing Company, Vendor G0590
Broken Arrow Genealogical Society, Vendor G0059
Bryan County Heritage Association, Vendor G0710
Buck, Dee Ann, Vendor G0758
Buffalo & Erie County Historical Society, Vendor G0085
Burgert, Annette K., Vendor G0458
Burgin, Edna Montgomery, Vendor G0746

Burns, Loretta E., Vendor G0747
California Genealogical Society, Vendor G0628
Camp County Genealogical Society, Vendor G0497
Carter County History Book Committee, Vendor G0088
Casilear, Ms. Connie Jean, Vendor G0480
Cass County Genealogical Society, Vendor G0595
Catoctin Press, Vendor G0126
Cawthon, Juanita Davis, Vendor G0715
Cemeteries of Oglethorpe County, Vendor G0738
Cemeteries [Grove, OK], Vendor G0544
Centre County Historical Society, Vendor G0493
Champ, Minnie Pitts, Vendor G0539
Champaign County Genealogical Society, Vendor G0080
Chicago Genealogical Society, Vendor G0742
Christ Church Parish Preservation Society, Inc., Vendor G0538
City of Keene Police Department, Vendor G0755
Clark County Historical Association, Vendor G0274
Clark County Genealogical Society, Vendor G0717
Clearfield Company, Vendor G0011
Closson Press, Vendor G0536
Coastal Bend Genealogical Society, Vendor G0016
Cobb County GA Genealogical Society, Inc., Vendor G0313
Coiny Publishing Co., Vendor G0527
Colorado Genealogical Society Inc., Vendor G0174
Confederate Research Center, The, Vendor G0744
Connecticut Society of Genealogists, Inc., Vendor G0578
Connecticut Historical Society, Vendor G0645
Connellsville Area Historical Society, Vendor G0499
Cottage Grove Genealogical Society, Vendor G0505
Counts, Mrs. William H,, Vendor G0170
Cowart, Margaret M., Vendor G0176
Darlington, Jane E., Vendor G0108
d'Armand, Virginia Carlisle, Vendor G0009
Darnell, Betty R., Vendor G0261
DeArmond, Rebecca, Vendor G0630
Deeter, Judy A., Vendor G0467
Delaware Genealogical Society, Vendor G0653
Delaware Public Archives, Vendor G0597
Delaware County Historical Alliance, Vendor G0095
Deschutes County Historical Society, Vendor G0713
Detroit Society for Genealogical Research, Inc., Vendor G0696
Doherty, Frank J., Vendor G0181
Dolores Rench, Vendor G0084
Dolph, M. P., Vendor G0464
Don Mills, Inc., Vendor G0087
DuPage County (IL) Genealogical Society, Vendor G0606
Eastern Washington Genealogical Society, Vendor G0733
Eldorado Historical Society, Vendor G0712
Elkhart County Genealogical Society, Vendor G0685
Evans, Henrietta C., Vendor G0079

Evans, Tad, Vendor G0532
Everton Publishers, Inc., Vendor G0618
Fair Printing Company, Vendor G0514
Fairfax Genealogical Society, Vendor G0543
Family History World®, Vendor G0504
Family Line Publications, Vendor G0140
Family Publications, Vendor G0061
Family History & Genealogy Center, Vendor G0238
Family Tree, Vendor G0506
Family History Library, Vendor G0629
Farley, Hilde Shuptrine, Vendor G0024
Farley, William S., Vendor G0004
Farmer, Michal Martin, Vendor G0312
Faulkinbury, Jim W., Vendor G0489
Ferguson, Herman W., Vendor G0056
Filler, Eunice J., Vendor G0469
Finnell, Arthur Louis, Books, Vendor G0256
Fletcher, Virginia B., Vendor G0332
Florida State Genealogical Society, Inc., Vendor G0567
Fort William Bent Chapter NSDAR, Vendor G0752
Frontier Press, Vendor G0611
Garr, Margie, Vendor G0655
Genealogical Publishing Co., Inc., Vendor G0010
Genealogical Society of North Brevard, Inc., Vendor G0509
Genealogical Institute, The, Vendor G0504
Genealogical Society of Pennsylvania, The, Vendor G0202
Genealogical Books in Print, Vendor G0081
Genealogical Forum of Oregon, Vendor G0633
Genealogical Society of Yuma Arizona, Vendor G0674
Genealogy Society of Southern Illinois, Vendor G0741.
General Society of Mayflower Descendants, Vendor G0620
GenLaw Resources, Patricia Andersen, Vendor G0483
Gentges, Margaret H., Vendor G0533
Georgia Historical Society, Vendor G0636
Gibson, Joyce M., Vendor G0701
Gilbert, Audrey, Vendor G0530
Gloucester County Historical Society, Vendor G0069
Glowski, Joanne Dominik, Vendor G0867
Glyndwr Resources, Vendor G0094
Goodenow Family Association, Vendor G0116
Grand Prairie Research, Vendor G0537
Gransee, Mrs. Dean, Vendor G0753
Grant County Historical Society, Vendor G0462
Greene County Historical & Genealogical Society, Vendor G0188
Greene County Chapter, OGS, Vendor G0702
Griffis, Joan A., Vendor G0683
GSNOCC, Vendor G0529
Guilford County Genealogical Society, Vendor G0730
Haid, John A., Vendor G0603
Haines, Jeffrey L., Vendor G0163

Hallgren, Jeanne, Vendor G0749
Hammond, G. P., Publishing, Vendor G0670
Harford County (Maryland) Genealogical Society, Vendor G0872
Hartmann Heritage Productions of Texas, Vendor G0612
Hathaway, Warrine, Vendor G0708
Haydon, Robert, Vendor G0372
Heart of the Lakes Publishing, Vendor G0093
Hempstead County Genealogical Society, Vendor G0676
Higginson Book Co., Vendor G0259
Historical Research Associates, Vendor G0520
Historical Publications, Inc., Vendor G0759
Historical Data Service, Vendor G0698
Historical & Genealogical Society of Indiana Co., PA, Vendor G0042
Hoenstine Rental Library, Vendor G0622
Hoffman, W. W., Vendor G0767
Holcomb, Brent H., Vendor G0602
Holston Territory Genealogical Society, Vendor G0089
Hope Farm Press & Bookshop, Vendor G0160
Horsman, Mrs. Barbara Knott, Vendor G0115
Howard County Genealogical Society, Vendor G0149
Humphrey, John T., Vendor G0117
Hunterdon County Historical Society, Vendor G0180
Hunterdon House, Vendor G0561
Hyde County Historical and Genealogical Society, Vendor G0700
Iberian Publishing Company, Vendor G0632
Idaho Genealogical Society, Vendor G0668
IDL Research, Vendor G0507
Illiana Genealogical & Historical Society, Vendor G0723
Illinois State Genealogical Society, Vendor G0488
Illinois State Historical Society, Vendor G0501
Indian River Genealogical Society, Vendor G0151
Indiana Historical Society, Vendor G0109
Infopreneur Publishing Co., Vendor G0440
InfoServ, Vendor G0517
Institute of Science and Public Affairs, Vendor G0659
Irish Genealogical Society, Intl., Vendor G0305
Jackson, Martha W., Vendor G0594
Jaussi Publications, Vendor G0465
Jenks, Mrs. Margaret R., Vendor G0599
Jerome, Brenda Joyce, Vendor G0686
Jones, Henry Z, Jr., Vendor G0581
Jones, Janice L., Vendor G0460
Joyce Hardy Cates, Vendor G0666
Kankakee Valley Genealogical Society, Vendor G0869
Kansas Statistical Publishing Co., Vendor G0571
Kentucky Department for Libraries and Archives, Vendor G0651
Kepple, Arnold, Vendor G0067
Kinney, Mrs. Shirley F., Vendor G0021
Kinsey, Margaret B., Vendor G0307
Kinship, Vendor G0450

Kusek, Joan, Vendor G0122
LaCrosse Public Library Archives, Vendor G0722
Lake County Genealogical Society, Vendor G0739
Lancaster County Historical Society, Vendor G0572
Lantz, Norma R., Vendor G0199
Laurel County Historical Society, Vendor G0688
Lea, Mrs. Joyce Ray, Vendor G0526
Ledoux, Rev. Albert H., Vendor G0511
Lewis & Clark County Genealogical Society, Vendor G0716
Libra Pipecreek Publications, Vendor G0697
Library of Virginia, The, Vendor G0553
Library Council of Metropolitan Milwaukee, Inc., Vendor G0510
Lincoln-Lancaster County Genealogical Society, Vendor G0477
Linn, Jo White, Vendor G0131
Long, Helen R., Vendor G0015
Looney, Janice Soutee, Vendor G0694
Lorain County Chapter, OGS, Vendor G0055
Los Banos Genealogical Society, Inc., Vendor G0573
Lower Delmarva Genealogical Society, Vendor G0784
Lowry, James W., Vendor G0035
Lucas County Chapter, OGS, Vendor G0703
Luxemberg Publications, Vendor G0461
Lycoming County Genealogical Society, Vendor G0635
Macoupin County Illinois Genealogical Society, Vendor G0740
Mahoning County Chapter, OGS, Vendor G0709
Maine State Archives, Vendor G0650
Mallory, Rudena Kramer, Vendor G0667
Marietta Publishing Company, Vendor G0492
Marin County Genealogical Society, Vendor G0679
Martin, Catherine Machan, Vendor G0756
Martin, Irene, Vendor G0718
Martin, Mrs. Pauline, Vendor G0681
Martin, William T. and Patricia Thomas, Vendor G0673
Martinet, Tom C., Vendor G0535
Maryland Acadian Studies, Vendor G0500
Maryland Historical Society, Vendor G0617
Maryland State Archives Publications, Vendor G0593
Masley, Betty J., Vendor G0507
Mathews, Barbara Stacy, Vendor G0430
Mathews, Nathan, Vendor G0399
Maydew, Randall C., Vendor G0007
McClain Printing Company, Vendor G0660
McClure, Diane K., Vendor G0157
McCraken County Genealogical & Historical Society, Vendor G0187
McKinney Memorial Public Library, Vendor G0528
McManus, Mrs. Thelma S., Vendor G0541
Mearse, Linda, Vendor G0498
Mechling Associates, Inc., Vendor G0468
Minnesota Veterinary Historical Museum, Vendor G0123
Mitchell, Susan L., Vendor G0068

Morebeck, Nancy Justus, Vendor G0172
Morris, Jean S., Vendor G0521
Morrison, W. E., & Co., Vendor G0112
Morrow, Patricia, Vendor G0167
Mount Holly Cemetery Association, Vendor G0039
Mountain Press, Vendor G0549
Murray, Joyce Martin, Vendor G0466
Muskingum County Footprints, Vendor G0494
N O Inc., Vendor G0760
Namaqua Chapter NSDAR, Vendor G0680
National Genealogical Society, Vendor G0627
NCOHA, Inc., Vendor G0524
Nebraska State Genealogical Society, Vendor G0783
New England Historic Genealogical Society, Vendor G0406
New York Genealogical and Biographical Society, Vendor G0182
New Hampshire Society of Genealogists, Vendor G0598
New Jersey State Archives, Vendor G0585
New York State Archives and Records Administration, Vendor G0587
Newton County Historical Commission, Vendor G0156
Nicholson, Eve, Vendor G0765
Nickell Genealogical Books, Vendor G0113
Nicklas, Laurie, Vendor G0678
Nodaway County Genealogical Society, Vendor G0695
North Carolina Genealogical Society, Vendor G0623
North Antelope County Genealogical Society, Vendor G0754
North Hills Genealogists, Vendor G0607
North Carolina Division of Archives and History, Vendor G0586
Northeast Michigan Genealogical and Historical Society, Vendor G0692
Northwest Missouri Genealogical Society, Vendor G0699
Ohio Historical Society, Vendor G0646
Ohio Genealogy Center, Vendor G0135
Ohio Genealogical Society, The, Vendor G0512
Oklahoma Genealogical Society, Vendor G0729
Old Jail Museum, Vendor G0476
Olson, Michael R., Vendor G0690
Olson, Roy F., Jr., Vendor G0077
Oregon Genealogical Society, Vendor G0634
Origins, Vendor G0195
Osborn, Donald Lewis, Vendor G0121
Ostertag, John and Enid, Vendor G0745
Ozarks Genealogical Society, Inc., Vendor G0175
Paradise Genealogical Society, Inc., Vendor G0736
Park Genealogical Books, Vendor G0583
Partin Publications, Vendor G0672
Pau Hana Press, Vendor G0154
Paulding County Chapter, OGS, Vendor G0704
Peabody Essex Museum, Vendor G0600
Pennsylvania Historical & Museum Commission, Vendor G0554
Peters, Bonnie, Vendor G0482
Peters, Joan W., Vendor G0074

Picton Press, Vendor G0082
Poestenkill Historical Society, Vendor G0058
Pollard, Louise K., Vendor G0517
Poplar Grove Press, Vendor G0471
Powell, E. S., Vendor G0607
Prince George's County Genealogical Society, Vendor G0075
Ptak, Diane Snyder, Vendor G0663
Remsen-Steuben Historical Society, Vendor G0070
Reprint Company, The, Vendor G0551
Reynolds, Marion Lavender, Vendor G0682
Richland County Genealogical Society, Vendor G0728
Riley County Genealogical Society, Vendor G0083
Robertson, Donna J., Vendor G0545
Rose Family Association, Vendor G0474
San Mateo County Genealogical Society, Vendor G0737
Sanders, Faye Sea, Vendor G0689
Scheuer Publications, Larry and Cynthia, Vendor G0684
Scholarly Resources, Vendor G0118
Schweitzer, Dr. George K., Vendor G0569
SFK Genealogy, Vendor G0021
Shiawassee County Historical Society, Vendor G0751
Shubert, Dwight, Vendor G0734
Sickel, Marilyn Hambrick, Vendor G0537
Simmons Historical Publications, Vendor G0687
Sisler, Janice Cale, Vendor G0719
Sistler, Byron, & Associates, Vendor G0577
Skipwith Historical & Genealogical Society, Vendor G0484
Smallen, Tammy L., Vendor G0761
Smith, Alma A., Vendor G0547
Smith, Patricia D., Vendor G0177
Smith, Peter, Publisher, Inc., Vendor G0648
Smoky Mountain Historical Society, Vendor G0654
Snell, William R., Vendor G0522
Snider, Margaret C., Vendor G0762
Solano County Genealogical Society, Inc., Vendor G0184
Sonoma County Genealogical Society, Inc., Vendor G0605
South Carolina Department of Archives and History, Vendor G0130
South Bend Area Genealogical Society, Vendor G0743
Southern California Genealogical Society (SCGS), Vendor G0656
Southern Historical Press, Inc., Vendor G0610
Southwest Oklahoma Genealogical Society, Vendor G0661
St. Clair County (IL) Genealogical Society, Vendor G0110
Stafford, Linda Berg, Vendor G0032
Starke County Genealogical Society, Vendor G0748
State Historical Society of Missouri, Vendor G0596
Steele, Patricia M., Vendor G0463
Stoddard, John H., Vendor G0319
Strickland, Ben, Vendor G0693
Stroh, Oscar H., Vendor G0333
Sutherland, Laine, Vendor G0624

T.L.C. Genealogy, Vendor G0609
Tabernacle Cemetery Trust Fund, Vendor G0459
Tallahassee Genealogical Society, Inc., Vendor G0036
Taylor, Richard H., Vendor G0525
Tazewell County Historical Society, Vendor G0649
TCI Genealogical Resources, Vendor G0496
Tedford, Sandra, Vendor G0711
Templin, Ronald R., Vendor G0096
Tennessee Valley Publishing, Vendor G0183
Tennessee Valley Genealogical Society, Vendor G0625
Terry, Rose Caudle, Vendor G0061
Texas State Archives, Vendor G0601
Thode, Ernest, Vendor G0197
Tice, Mrs. Helen, Vendor G0707
Uptown Press, Vendor G0786
Van Noy, Rosamond Houghton, Vendor G0245
Vandegrift Research, Vendor G0764
Venango County Historical Society, Vendor G0727
VESCO, Inc., Vendor G0724
Virginia Genealogical Society, Vendor G0582
Walters, David N., Vendor G0472
Warren Co. (OH) Genealogical Society, Vendor G0335
Washington County Historical Assoc., Vendor G0540
Waukesha County Genealogical Society, Vendor G0721
Weaver, Darlene F., Vendor G0519
Weber, Nancie Todd, Vendor G0337
West Central Wisconsin Genealogy, Vendor G0720
Westchester County Historical Society, Vendor G0479
Western Pennsylvania Genealogical Society, Vendor G0615
Westland Publications, Vendor G0491
Whatcom Genealogical Society, Vendor G0503
Williams County Genealogical Society, Vendor G0705
Williams, Gene L., Vendor G0613
Williams, James E., Vendor G0508
Willow Bend Books, Vendor G0669
Wise, William E., Vendor G0314
Wood County Chapter, OGS, Vendor G0706
Woolkoch Publishing, Vendor G0487
Worrel, S., Vendor G0057
Worthy-Brandenburg Index, Vendor G0190
Wright, Mildred S., Vendor G0145
Wright, Pauline Williams, Vendor G0076
Wynne, Frances H., Vendor G0040
Yakima Valley Genealogical Society, Vendor G0139
Ye Olde Genealogie Shoppe, Vendor G0574
Young, Connie L., Vendor G0470
Zimmerman, Elaine Obbink, Vendor G0103

Genealogical & Local History Books in Print

5th Edition

U.S. Sources & Resources Volume

N – W

North Carolina

Statewide and Regional References

1905 North Carolina Community and Business Directory.
An alphabetical listing of all the small/large communities in the state with the merchants in each given.
Paper. $23.50. .... Vendor G0549

Atlas of North Carolina, 100 county maps.
Includes detailed maps of individual counties, all the back roads, streams, lakes, towns, etc. 11" x 16".
$14.95. .... Vendor G0611

Atlas of North Carolina, Topographical.
This present-day atlas provides the researcher with the detail needed to conduct a proper search. It is the size of a Rand McNally atlas of the entire U.S. 11" x 15½".
$16.95. .... Vendor G0611

Atlases & Gazetteers: North Carolina. Illus.
Paper. $16.95. 80 pp. .... Vendor G0632

Barrett. **The Civil War in North Carolina.** 1963.
The complete story of North Carolina military engagements in the Civil War. Well documented.
Cloth, $22.95. Paper, $16.95. 484 pp. .... Vendor G0611

Bentley, Elizabeth Petty. **Index to the 1800 Census of North Carolina.** (1977) reprint 1995.
Paper. $23.50. 270 pp. .... Vendor G0011

Bentley, Elizabeth Petty. **Index to the 1810 Census of North Carolina.** (1978) reprint 1996.
Cloth. $25.00. 282 pp. .... Vendor G0011

Bernheim, Gotthardt D. **History of the German Settlements and of the Lutheran Church in North and South Carolina.** (1872) reprint 1996. Paper. $40.00. 557 pp. .... Vendor G0011

Bible, Jean P. **Melungeons—Yesterday and Today.** Illus. A full accounting of the lost tribe of Tennessee and North Carolina. Cloth. $12.00. 140 pp. .... Vendor G0549

Bradley, Stephen E., Jr., ed. **North Carolina Confederate Militia Officers Roster.** As Contained in the Adjutant-General's Officers Roster. 1996. Indexed. Illus. Cloth. $35.00. 454 pp. .... Vendor G0590

Broadfoot Publishing Company. **The Colonial and State Records of North Carolina.** 30 vols. 1996. Indexed. Cloth. $1,200.00. Contact vendor for pricing options. .... Vendor G0590

Broughton, Carrie L. **Marriage and Death Notices from *Raleigh Register* and *North Carolina State Gazette*, 1799-1825.** (1942-44) reprint 1995. A valuable record of North Carolina marriages and deaths covering the entire state. Paper. $18.50. 178 pp. .... Vendor G0011

Broughton, Carrie L. **Marriage and Death Notices in *Raleigh Register* and *North Carolina State Gazette*, 1826-1845.** (1947) reprint 1992. A valuable record of North Carolina marriages and deaths covering the entire state. Contact vendor for information. 402 pp. .... Vendor G0011

Broughton, Carrie L. **Marriage and Death Notices in *Raleigh Register* and *North Carolina State Gazette*, 1846-1867** 2 vols. in 1. (1949-50) reprint 1992. A valuable record of North Carolina marriages and deaths covering the entire state. Paper. $20.00. 207 pp. .... Vendor G0011

Burgner, Goldene Fillers. **North Carolina Land Grants in Tennessee, 1778-1791.** 1981. Indexed. This book contains 5,486 land grants issued by the State of North Carolina in the new State of Tennessee. Cloth. $28.50. 214 pp. .... Vendor G0610

Burgner, Goldene Fillers. **North Carolina Land Grants Recorded in Greene County, Tennessee.** 1981. Indexed. Cloth. $25.00. 160 pp. .... Vendor G0610

Butler and Watson, eds. **The North Carolina Experience: An Interpretive and Documentary History.** 1984. A collection of essays with accompanying documentary evidence. Paper. $15.95. 467 pp. .... Vendor G0611

Cain, Barbara T., with Ellen Z. McGrew and Charles E. Morris. **Guide to Private Manuscript Collections in the North Carolina State Archives.** 3rd printing, 1993. Indexed. Description of private papers, microfilmed private papers, and account books in the State Archives. Includes name, place, and subject index. Paper. $25.00. x + 706 pp. .... Vendor G0586

Clark, Walter, ed. **Histories of the Several Regiments and Battalions from North Carolina in the Great War 1861-1865.** 5 vols. Illus. Cloth. $300.00. Contact vendor for pricing options. .... Vendor G0590

Clemens, William Montgomery. **North and South Carolina Marriage Records,** from the Earliest Colonial Days to the Civil War. (1927) reprint 1995. Cloth. $25.00. 295 pp. .... Vendor G0010

Colonial Records of North Carolina [Second Series], Volume I: North Carolina Charters and Constitutions, 1578-1698. Edited by Mattie Erma Edwards Parker. 1963. Indexed. Leather, $20.00. Cloth, $15.00. Add an additional $1.00 shipping charge to the regular p&h charges for each vol. ordered. xxii + 247 pp. .... Vendor G0586

Colonial Records of North Carolina [Second Series], Volume II: North Carolina Higher-Court Records, 1670-1696. Microfilm. $12.00 per reel. Add an additional $1.00 shipping charge to the regular p&h charges for each vol. ordered. .... Vendor G0586

Colonial Records of North Carolina [Second Series], Volume III: North Carolina Higher-Court Records, 1697-1701. Edited by Mattie Erma Edwards Parker. 1971. Indexed. Illus. Cloth. $15.00. Add an additional $1.00 shipping charge to the regular p&h charges for each vol. ordered. lxviii + 620 pp. .... Vendor G0586

Colonial Records of North Carolina [Second Series], Volume IV: North Carolina Higher-Court Records, 1702-1708. Edited by William S. Price, Jr. 1974. Indexed. Illus. Cloth. $16.00. Add an additional $1.00 shipping charge to the regular p&h charges for each vol. ordered. xxxix + 533 pp. .... Vendor G0586

Colonial Records of North Carolina [Second Series], Volume V: North Carolina Higher-Court Minutes, 1709-1723. Edited by William S. Price, Jr. 1977. Indexed. Illus. Cloth. $21.00. Add an additional $1.00 shipping charge to the regular p&h charges for each vol. ordered. xliii + 631 pp. .... Vendor G0586

Colonial Records of North Carolina [Second Series], Volume VI: North Carolina Higher-Court Minutes, 1724-1730. Edited by Robert J. Cain. 1981. Indexed. Illus. Cloth. $30.00. Add an additional $1.00 shipping charge to the regular p&h charges for each vol. ordered. lxi + 791 pp. .... Vendor G0586

Colonial Records of North Carolina [Second Series], Volume VII: Records of the Executive Council, 1664-1734. Edited by Robert J. Cain. 1984. Indexed. Illus. Cloth. $25.00. Add an additional $1.00 shipping charge to the regular p&h charges for each vol. ordered. lxvii + 763 pp. .... Vendor G0586

Colonial Records of North Carolina [Second Series], Volume VIII: Records of the Executive Council, 1735-1754. Edited by Robert J. Cain. 1988. Indexed. Illus. Cloth. $45.00. Add an additional $1.00 shipping charge to the regular p&h charges for each vol. ordered. lxxvii + 723 pp. .... Vendor G0586

Colonial Records of North Carolina [Second Series], Volume IX: Records of the Executive Council, 1755-1775. Edited by Robert J. Cain. 1994. Indexed. Illus.

Cloth. $75.00. Add an additional $1.00 shipping charge to the regular p&h charges for each vol. ordered. lxxix + 870 pp. .... Vendor G0586

Corbitt, David Leroy. **The Formation of the North Carolina Counties, 1663-1943**. 5th printing, 1996. Indexed.
   A basic resource for the study of genealogy and state and local history. Contains date and history of the formation of each county; a description, taken from the laws, of the boundary lines; maps (1700-1912) that show the development of the state from northeast to southeast and then westward; and a chart giving the dates of the formation and the origins of each county.
Paper. $12.00. xxix + 323 pp. .... Vendor G0586

Crow, Jeffrey J. **The Black Experience in Revolutionary North Carolina**. 4th printing, 1996. Illus.
   Includes an appendix of North Carolina blacks who served in the Continental Line or militia.
Paper. $5.00. x + 121 pp. .... Vendor G0586

Crow, Jeffrey J., Paul D. Escott, and Flora J. Hatley. **A History of African Americans in North Carolina**. 2nd printing, 1994. Indexed. Illus.
   Includes an appendix that identifies black legislators who served in the North Carolina General Assembly from 1868 through 1900 and a selected list of suggested readings for further study.
Paper. $10.00. xii + 237 pp. .... Vendor G0586

Cumming, William P. **North Carolina in Maps**. 3rd printing, 1992.
   Maps reproduced in photolithography from original copies; booklet with descriptive and explanatory matter included.
Fifteen maps varying in size, plus booklet. $25.00. viii + 36 pp. .... Vendor G0586

DeMond, Robert O. **The Loyalists in North Carolina During the Revolution**. (1940) reprint 1994. Indexed.
Paper. $25.00. 286 pp. .... Vendor G0011

Dobson, David. **Directory of Scots in The Carolinas, 1680-1830**. (1986) reprint 1994.
Cloth. $25.00. 322 pp. .... Vendor G0010

Douthat, James L. **Robert Armstrong—Plat Book of Those Indians Given Reservations After the 1817 Treaty**. Indexed.
   Over 100 plats are given in their original drawing as presented in Robert Armstrong's Plat Book. The plats are found in North Carolina, Tennessee, and Alabama.
Paper. $10.00. .... Vendor G0549

Draper, L. C. **King's Mountain and Its Heroes:** History of the Battle of King's Mountain, October 7th, 1780. (1881) reprint 1993.
Contact vendor for information. 612 pp. .... Vendor G0010

Family History Library. **Research Outline: North Carolina**.
Leaflet. $.25. 11 pp. .... Vendor G0629

The First Laws of the State of North Carolina. 2 vols. (1791) reprint 1984.
Cloth. $122.50. .... Vendor G0118

Fisher, P. W. **One Dozen Pre-Revolutionary Families of Eastern No. Carolina and Some of Their Descendants**. (1958) reprint 1995.
Cloth. $67.50. 629 pp. .... Vendor G0259

Fulcher, Richard C. **1770-1790 Census of the Cumberland Settlements:** Davidson, Sumner, and Tennessee Counties. 1990.
    These counties, originally a part of North Carolina, now are all or part of Tennessee counties. Abstracted from public records are all references to those living in the jurisdictions between 1770 and 1790.
Cloth. $22.50. 253 pp. .... Vendor G0010

Grimes, J. Bryan. **Abstract of North Carolina Wills:** Compiled from Original and Recorded Wills in the Office of the Secretary of State. (1910) reprint 1985. Indexed.
Cloth. $37.50. 536 pp. .... Vendor G0610

Grimes, J. Bryan. **Abstracts of North Carolina Wills [1663-1760]**. (1910) reprint 1997. Indexed.
Contact vendor for information. 670 pp. .... Vendor G0011

Grimes, J. Bryan. **North Carolina Wills and Inventories**. (1912) reprint 1994. Indexed.
Paper. $40.00. 587 pp. .... Vendor G0011

Guide to Research Materials in the North Carolina State Archives: State Agency Records. 1995. Indexed. Illus.
    Provides detailed information about processed and unprocessed records, microfilmed records, and recently transferred records housed in the state archives.
Paper. $30.00. 855 pp. .... Vendor G0586

Hamrick, David O. **Index to the North Carolina Historical and Genealogical Register (Hathaway's Register), Vol. 1**. 1983. Indexed.
Paper. $15.00. .... Vendor G0632

Hamrick, David O. **Index to the North Carolina Historical and Genealogical Register (Hathaway's Register), Vol. 2**. 1983.
Paper. $15.00. .... Vendor G0632

Hamrick, David O. **Index to the North Carolina Historical and Genealogical Register (Hathaway's Register), Vol. 3**. 1983.
Paper. $10.00. .... Vendor G0632

Hathaway, James Robert Bent. **North Carolina Historical and Genealogical Register**. Vol. I, no. 1-Vol. III, no. 3 (11 nos. all publ.). (1900-1903) reprint 1979.
Paper. $95.00/set, $9.50/no. 1,760 pp. .... Vendor G0010

Hofmann, Margaret. **Colony of North Carolina, 1736-1764: Abstracts of Land Patents, Volume 1**. Indexed.
Cloth. $33.00. 650 pp. .... Vendor G0611

Hofmann, Margaret. **The Granville District of North Carolina, 1748-1763: Abstracts of Land Grants, Volume 1**. Indexed.
    Covers Anson, Beaufort, Bertie, Bladen, Chowan, Cumberland, Currituck, Dobbs, and Edgecombe counties.
Cloth. $24.00. 199 pp. .... Vendor G0611

Hofmann, Margaret. **The Granville District of North Carolina, 1748-1763: Abstracts of Land Grants, Volume 2**. Indexed.
   Covers Granville, Halifax, Hyde, Johnston, Northampton, Orange, and Tyrrell counties.
Cloth. $36.00. .... Vendor G0611

Hofmann, Margaret. **The Granville District of North Carolina, 1748-1763: Abstracts of Land Grants, Volume 3**. Indexed.
   Covers Pasquotank, Perquimans, Pitt, and Rowan counties.
Cloth. $28.00. 164 pp. .... Vendor G0611

Hofmann, Margaret. **The Granville District of North Carolina, 1748-1763: Abstracts of Miscellaneous Land Office Records, Volume 4**. Indexed.
   Covers Anson, Beaufort, Bertie, Bladen, Chowan, Cumberland, Currituck, Dobbs, Edgecombe, and Granville counties.
Cloth. $39.00. 417 pp. .... Vendor G0611

Hunter, C. L. **Sketches of Western North Carolina,** Historical & Biographical, Illustrating Principally the Rev. Period of Mecklenburg, Rowan, Lincoln & Adjoining Cos. (1877) reprint 1992.
Contact vendor for information. 357 pp. .... Vendor G0011

Index to North Carolina Ancestors.
$10.00. Contact vendor for more information. .... Vendor G0623

Jordan, Weymouth T., Jr., ed. **North Carolina Troops, 1861-1865: A Roster**. Volume XII, Infantry (49th-52nd Regiments). 1990. Indexed.
Cloth. $27.00. Add an additional $1.00 shipping charge to the regular p&h charges for each vol. ordered. xx + 565 pp. .... Vendor G0586

Jordan, Weymouth T., Jr., ed. **North Carolina Troops, 1861-1865: A Roster**. Volume XIII, Infantry (53rd-56th Regiments). 1993. Indexed. Illus.
Cloth. $38.00. Add an additional $1.00 shipping charge to the regular p&h charges for each vol. ordered. xx + 752 pp. .... Vendor G0586

Kearney, Timothy. **Abstracts of Letters of Resignation of Militia Officers in North Carolina 1779-1840**. 1992. Indexed.
Paper. $15.00. 144 pp. .... Vendor G0623

Koonts, Russell S. **North Carolina Petitions for Presidential Pardon: 1865-1868 (An Index)**. 1996.
   These records consist of applications for special pardon from some 2,000 North Carolinians who were excluded from the general amnesty proclamations of 29 May 1865.
Paper. $15.00. 76 pp. .... Vendor G0611

Lawson. **A New Voyage to Carolina**. (1709) reprint 1967.
   Arriving in Charleston in 1700, Lawson organized an expedition to chart the Carolina backcountry. This day-by-day journal records descriptions of the land and the early settlements, but is especially rich in the descriptions of the Native Americans of the area.
Paper. $14.95. 305 pp. .... Vendor G0611

Leary, Helen F. M. **North Carolina Research**. 2nd ed. 1996. Indexed.
Cloth. $48.00. 600+ pp. .... Vendor G0623

Liahona Research. **North Carolina Marriages, Early to 1800**. 1990.
Cloth. $95.00. 499 pp. .... Vendor G0552

Liahona Research. **North Carolina Marriages, 1801 to 1825**. 1993.
Cloth. $130.00. 900 pp. .... Vendor G0552

Lucas, Silas Emmett, Jr., and Brent Holcomb. **Marriage and Death Notices from Raleigh, N.C., Newspapers: 1796-1826**. (1977) reprint 1984.
These marriage and death notices are important because they were from all over North Carolina and adjacent states. There are marriage notices included from counties in which marriage bonds are not extant.
Paper. $20.00. 168 pp. .... Vendor G0610

Map Showing the Formation of North Carolina Counties. Drawn by L. Polk Denmark and used in *The Formation of the North Carolina Counties* by D. L. Corbitt. Reprint 1984.
Shows North Carolina counties from 1700 to 1912; illustrates evolution of present county boundaries.
Twelve maps on one sheet. $1.00. .... Vendor G0586

Meyer. **Highland Scots of North Carolina, 1732-1776**.
Examines the migrations of the Highland Scots into North Carolina during the 18th century, and their tendency to remain Loyalist during the Revolution.
Paper. $12.95. 216 pp. .... Vendor G0611

Mitchell, Thornton W. **North Carolina Wills**: A Testator Index, 1665-1900. Corrected and revised edition. (1993) reprint 1996.
Cloth. $49.50. 630 pp. .... Vendor G0010

Newsome, A. R., ed. **Records of Emigrants from England and Scotland to North Carolina, 1774-1775**. 4th printing, 1989.
Contains lists of persons who took passage on ships from Great Britain to North Carolina. The lists include nearly 100 emigrants from England and nearly 500 emigrants, including 100 family groups, from Scotland.
Paper. $3.00. 30 pp. .... Vendor G0586

North Carolina Freedman's Records.
$25.00. Contact vendor for more information. .... Vendor G0623

Oakley, Crestena Jennings. **North Carolina Genealogical Society Journal: A Listing of Journal Articles 1975-1995**. 1995.
Paper. $2.00. .... Vendor G0623

Olds, Fred A. **An Abstract of North Carolina Wills** from About 1760 to About 1800, Supplementing Grimes' Abstract of North Carolina Wills 1663 to 1760. (1925) reprint 1996.
Paper. $27.50. 330 pp. .... Vendor G0011

Pancake. **This Destructive War: The British Campaign in the Carolinas, 1780-1782**. 1985.
The story of the guerrilla warfare fought in the Carolinas. Includes numerous references to weaponry, military organization, and the lives of ordinary soldiers in bo armies.
Paper. $15.95. 293 pp. .... Vendor G0

Peacock, Mary Reynolds. **Silversmiths of North Carolina, 1696-1860**. Rev. ed., 1984. Indexed. Illus.
Lists 273 silversmiths with a biographical sketch of each based on extensive use of primary and secondary sources.
Cloth, $20.00. Paper, $12.00. xxix + 301 pp. .... Vendor G0586

Peden, Henry C., Jr. **Marylanders to Carolina:** Migrations of Marylanders to North and South Carolina Prior to 1800. 1994.
Paper. $17.00. 220 pp. .... Vendor G0140

Powell. **The North Carolina Gazetteer: A Dictionary of Tar Heel Places**. 1968.
Over 20,000 entries that locate the geographical features of North Carolina.
Paper. $16.95. 561 pp. .... Vendor G0611

Powell. **North Carolina Through Four Centuries**. 1989. Illus.
This readable history of the state includes many illustrations, maps, and photographs.
Cloth. $32.50. 652 pp. .... Vendor G0611

Powell. **North Carolina: A History**. 1977.
A concise history of the state, written by its leading historian.
Paper. $10.95. 231 pp. .... Vendor G0611

Powell. **North Carolina: The WPA Guide to the Old North State**. (1939) reprint 1988.
Full of useful information on North Carolina.
Paper. $19.95. 601 pp. .... Vendor G0611

Precision Indexing. **North Carolina 1870 Census Index**. 3 vols. 1989.
Cloth. $350.00. 2,953 pp. .... Vendor G0552

Ramsey. **Carolina Cradle: Settlement of the Northwest Carolina Frontier, 1747-1762**. Reprint 1987.
A fascinating, well-documented account of the first families to move into what was early Rowan County, between the Catawba and Yadkin Rivers. Primary source records document each settler's origin and migration path.
Paper. $16.95. 251 pp. .... Vendor G0611

Ratcliff, Clarence E. **North Carolina Taxpayers, 1679-1790**. (1987) reprint 1996.
Cloth. $25.00. 230 pp. .... Vendor G0010

Ratcliff, Clarence E. **North Carolina Taxpayers, 1701-1786**. (1984) reprint 1993.
Cloth. $20.00. 228 pp. .... Vendor G0010

Ray, Worth S. **Lost Tribes of North Carolina. Part I: Index and Digest to Hathaway's North Carolina Historical and Genealogical Register**. (1945) reprint 1997.
Contact vendor for information. 192 pp. .... Vendor G0011

Ray, Worth S. **Lost Tribes of North Carolina. Part II: Colonial Granville County [North Carolina] and Its People**. (1945) reprint 1996. Indexed. Illus.
Paper. $15.00. 120 pp. .... Vendor G0011

Ray, Worth S. **Lost Tribes of North Carolina. Part III: the Mecklenburg Signers and Their Neighbors**. (1946) reprint 1995. Indexed. Illus.
Paper. $22.50. 246 pp. .... Vendor G0011

Ray, Worth S. **Lost Tribes of North Carolina. Part IV: Old Albemarle and Its Absentee Landlords**. (1947) reprint 1994. Indexed. Illus.
Paper. $15.00. 156 pp. .... Vendor G0011

Register, Alvaretta K. **State Census of North Carolina, 1784-1787**. 2nd ed. (1971) reprint 1993. Indexed.
Cloth. $20.00. 233 pp. .... Vendor G0010

Reichel, Rev. Levin T. **The Moravians in North Carolina**. (1857) reprint 1995.
Paper. $20.00. 206 pp. .... Vendor G0011

Roanoke Island Prisoners—Feb. 1862.
A listing of the prisoners taken at the Battle of Roanoke Island from VA and NC.
Paper. $11.50. .... Vendor G0549

Schweitzer, George K. **North Carolina Genealogical Research**. 1996. Illus.
History of the state, types of records (Bible through will), record locations, research techniques, listings of county records.
Paper. $15.00. 192 pp. .... Vendor G0569

Sifakis. **Compendium of the Confederate Armies: North Carolina**. 1992.
Describes each regiment, the officers, and lists the battles in which they fought.
Cloth. $24.95. 208 pp. .... Vendor G0611

Smith, Dora. **North Carolina 1810 Census Index**.
Cloth. $20.00. 355 pp. .... Vendor G0574

Society of North Carolina Archivists. **Archival and Manuscript Repositories in North Carolina: A Directory**. 1993.
Includes fax and phone numbers, hours and location, and a description of the holdings and services available at each repository.
Paper. $20.00. 149 pp. .... Vendor G0611

Spencer, R. S. **The North Carolina Genealogical Directory: A Listing of Tar Heel Societies and Selected Books for Sale**. 1992. Illus.
Paper. $20.00. 231 pp. .... Vendor G0623

Thompson, Catherine E. **Selective Guide to Women-Related Records in the North Carolina State Archives**. 1977. Indexed.
Description of records in private collections, organization records, and military collections that relate to women.
Paper. $3.00. 77 pp. .... Vendor G0586

Thorndale, William, and William Dollarhide. **County Boundary Map Guides to the U.S. Federal Censuses, 1790-1920: North Carolina, 1790-1920**. 1987.
$5.95. .... Vendor G0552

Toler, Maurice S. **Muster Rolls of the Soldiers of the War of 1812** Detached from the Militia of North Carolina in 1812 and 1814. With an Added Index. (1851, 1976) reprint 1996. Indexed.
Paper. $21.00. 193 pp. .... Vendor G0011

United States Bureau of the Census. **Heads of Families at the First Census of the U.S. Taken in the Year 1790: North Carolina**. (1908) reprint 1992. Indexed.
Paper. $32.50. 292 pp. .... Vendor G0610

United States Bureau of the Census. **Heads of Families at the First Census of the United States Taken in the Year 1790: North Carolina.** (1908) reprint 1992. Indexed. Illus.
Contact vendor for information. 292 pp. .... Vendor G0010

United States Bureau of the Census. **Heads of Families at the First Census of the United States Taken in the Year 1790: North Carolina.**
Cloth, $45.00. Paper, $30.00. .... Vendor G0552

Volunteer Soldiers in the Cherokee War—1836-1839.
An alphabetical listing of over 11,000 volunteers from Tennessee, Georgia, North Carolina, and Alabama who volunteered in the Cherokee Wars and Removal.
$35.00 (perfect bound). 210 pp. .... Vendor G0549

Ware, Lowry. **Associate Reformed Presbyterian Death & Marriage Notices 1843-1863.** 1993. Indexed.
Cloth. $25.00. 209 pp. .... Vendor G0602

Watson, Alan D., comp. & ed. **An Index to North Carolina Newspapers, 1784-1789.** 1992.
Name, place, and subject index to seven existing 18th-century newspapers printed in New Bern, Hillsborough, Edenton, Wilmington, and Fayetteville. Contains an informative introduction, which discusses how newspapers were published in the 18th century and surveys 18th-century newspapers printed in North Carolina.
Paper. $12.00. xxvii + 68 pp. .... Vendor G0586

Wheeler, John Hill. **Historical Sketches of North Carolina from 1584 to 1851.** 2 vols. in 1. (1851) reprint 1993. Indexed.
Paper. $45.00. 138 + 480 pp. .... Vendor G0011

Wheeler, John Hill. **Reminiscences and Memoirs of North Carolina and Eminent North Carolinians.** (1884) reprint 1993. Indexed.
Paper. $42.50. lxxiv + 478 pp. .... Vendor G0011

White, Barnetta McGhee. **Somebody Knows My Name: Marriages of Freed People in North Carolina, County by County.** 3 vols. Indexed.
Paper. $49.95. 1,272 pp. .... Vendor G0632

White, Katherine Keogh. **The King's Mountain Men.** The Story of the Battle, with Sketches of the American Soldiers Who Took Part. (1924) reprint 1996. Indexed.
Paper. $25.00. 271 pp. .... Vendor G0011

Woodmason. **The Carolina Backcountry on the Eve of the Revolution.** 1954.
Probably the fullest and most vivid extant account of the American colonial frontier—the daily life, thoughts, hopes, and fears of the frontier people. First-hand accounts written by an itinerant Anglican minister.
Paper. $12.95. 305 pp. .... Vendor G0611

Yearns and Barrett, eds. **North Carolina Civil War Documentary.** 1980.
Collection of primary source material describes North Carolina from the secession movement through the turbulence of the Civil War.
Cloth. $16.95. 365 pp. .... Vendor G0611

Alamance County

Chiarito, Marian Dodson, scr. **Alamance County, North Carolina 1850 Census with Ancestors & Descendants of Selected Families**. 1987. Indexed. Paper. $23.95. 240 pp. .... Vendor G0632

Albemarle County

Ray, Worth S. **Lost Tribes of North Carolina. Part IV: Old Albemarle and Its Absentee Landlords**. (1947) reprint 1994. Indexed. Illus. Paper. $15.00. 156 pp. .... Vendor G0011

Anson County

1790 Census Series, Anson County. Paper. $3.00. .... Vendor G0549

Anson County Heritage Book Committee. **Anson County Heritage—North Carolina**. 1995. Indexed. Illus.
    Another in the widely acclaimed North Carolina Heritage Book series. An attractive hardbound collector's edition, 9" x 12". Features family genealogies and family histories on nearly 900 different families, with photos accompanying most articles. Other topics in the book include communities, churches, clubs and organizations. Surname index.
Cloth. $59.50. 400 pp. .... Vendor G0087

Holcomb, Brent H. **Anson County, North Carolina Deed Abstracts, 1749-1766, Abstracts of Wills & Estates, 1749-1795**. (1974-1975) reprint 1991. Indexed. Cloth. $20.00. 170 pp. .... Vendor G0010

Medley, Mary L. **A History of Anson County, North Carolina, 1750-1976**. (1976) reprint 1994. Indexed. Illus. Paper. $35.00. 417 pp. .... Vendor G0011

Ashe County

Ingmire, Frances T. **North Carolina Marriage Bonds and Certificates Series: Ashe County, NC, 1819-1871**. Paper. $9.50. 70 pp. .... Vendor G0632

Waters, Evelyn G., comp. **1880 Federal Census of Ashe County**. 1992. Cloth. $39.00. 311 + 67 pp. .... Vendor G0259

Avery County

Bailey, Dr. Lloyd. **Toe River Valley Heritage—North Carolina, Vol. 1**. Indexed. Illus.
  The first in a forthcoming series on Avery, Mitchell, and Yancey counties. Features 632 family genealogies and photos, along with a wealth of information on early history, military (Revolutionary War veterans), and black Americans in the region. Every-name index.
Cloth. $68.00. 556 pp. .... Vendor G0087

Bailey, Lloyd R., ed. **Heritage of the Toe River Valley, Vol. I**. 1994. Indexed. Illus.
  Contains 750 articles on the history and families of Avery, Mitchell, and Yancey counties, North Carolina. A second volume will be available soon—contact vendor for information.
Cloth. $68.00. 550 pp. .... Vendor G0631

Beaufort County

1790 Census Series, Beaufort County.
Paper. $3.00. .... Vendor G0549

Bertie County

1790 Census Series, Bertie County.
Paper. $5.00. .... Vendor G0549

Bell, Mary Best. **Colonial Bertie County, North Carolina, Deed Books A-H, 1720-1757**. (1963) reprint 1980. Indexed. Illus.
Contact vendor for information. 328 pp. .... Vendor G0610

Fouts, Raymond Parker. **Marriages of Bertie County, North Carolina, 1762-1868**. (1982) reprint 1996. Indexed.
Paper. $14.50. 130 pp. .... Vendor G0011

Ingmire, Frances T. **North Carolina Marriage Bonds and Certificates Series: Bertie County, NC, 1759-1866**.
Paper. $9.50. 74 pp. .... Vendor G0632

Watson, Alan D. **Bertie County: A Brief History**. 1982. Illus.
Paper. $5.00. vii + 91 pp. .... Vendor G0586

Bladen County

1790 Census Series, Bladen County.
Paper. $3.00. .... Vendor G0549

Holcomb, Brent H. **Abstracts of Early Deeds, 1738-1804, Bladen County, North Carolina**. (1979) reprint 1992. Indexed.
Paper. $15.00. 88 pp. .... Vendor G0610

Brunswick County

1790 Census Series, Brunswick County.
Paper. $3.00. .... Vendor G0549

Ingmire, Frances T. **North Carolina Marriage Bonds and Certificates Series: Brunswick County, NC, 1804-1867.**
Paper. $9.50. 36 pp. .... Vendor G0632

Buncombe County

Asheville, North Carolina Newspapers.
$15.00. Contact vendor for more information. .... Vendor G0623

Goodson, Robert Benton, Joyce Justus Parris, and Joan Drake Goodson. **Tabernacle Cemetery Listings and Historical Information, 1837-1994, Tabernacle United Methodist Church, Black Mountain, North Carolina.** 1994. Illus.
Cloth. $23.00. 60 pp. .... Vendor G0459

Wooley, James E. **Index to Deeds, 1783-1850, Buncombe County, North Carolina.** 1983. Indexed.
Cloth. $38.50. 565 pp. .... Vendor G0610

Burke County

1790 Census Series, Burke County.
Paper. $5.00. .... Vendor G0549

Huggins, Edith Warren. **Burke County, North Carolina, Land Records, 1778, Vol. 1.** (1977) reprint 1985. Indexed.
Cloth. $28.50. 180 pp. .... Vendor G0610

Huggins, Edith Warren. **Burke County, North Carolina, Land Records, 1779-1790, Vol. 2, and Important Miscellaneous Records, 1777-1800.** (1981) reprint 1985. Indexed.
Cloth. $28.50. 212 pp. .... Vendor G0610

Huggins, Edith Warren. **Burke County, North Carolina, Land Records and More Important Miscellaneous Records, Vol. 3, 1751-1809.** 1987. Indexed.
Cloth. $28.50. 234 pp. .... Vendor G0610

Huggins, Edith Warren. **Burke County, North Carolina, Records, 1755-1821 (Including Wills, Index 1784-1900) Vol. 4.** 1987. Indexed.
Cloth. $28.50. 234 pp. .... Vendor G0610

Ingmire, Frances T. **North Carolina Marriage Bonds and Certificates Series: Burke County, NC, 1781-1868.**
Paper. $9.50. 58 pp. .... Vendor G0632

Phifer, Edward W., Jr. **Burke County: A Brief History**. 1979. Illus.
Paper. $5.00. viii + 144 pp. .... Vendor G0586

Walton, Col. Thomas George. **Sketches of the Pioneers in Burke County History (NC)**. 1984. Indexed.
Paper. $12.50. 96 pp. .... Vendor G0610

White, Emmett R. **Revolutionary War Soldiers of Western North Carolina: Burke County, Vol. 1**. 1984. Indexed.
Cloth. $30.00. 330 pp. .... Vendor G0610

Bute County

Holcomb, Brent H. **Bute County, North Carolina, Minutes of the Court of Pleas and Quarter Sessions, 1767-1779**. 1988. Indexed.
Cloth. $35.00. 377 pp. .... Vendor G0602

Holcomb, Brent H. **Marriages of Bute and Warren Counties, North Carolina 1764-1868**. 1991. Indexed.
Cloth. $24.00. 256 pp. .... Vendor G0011

Cabarrus County

Ingmire, Frances T. **North Carolina Marriage Bonds and Certificates Series: Cabarrus County, NC, 1793-1868**.
Paper. $20.00. 164 pp. .... Vendor G0632

Caldwell County

Alexander, Nancy. **Here Will I Dwell:** The Story of Caldwell County. (1956) reprint 1994.
Cloth. $32.50. 230 pp. .... Vendor G0259

Camden County

1790 Census Series, Camden County.
Paper. $3.50. .... Vendor G0549

Carteret County

1790 Census Series, Carteret County.
Paper. $3.50. .... Vendor G0549

Ingmire, Frances T. **North Carolina Marriage Bonds and Certificates Series: Carteret County, NC, 1755-1868**.
Paper. $15.00. 120 pp. .... Vendor G0632

Simpson, Thelma P., and David R. Taylor. **1850 Federal Census of Carteret County, North Carolina**. 1972. Indexed.
Cloth. $17.50. 227 pp. .... Vendor G0010

Caswell County

1790 Census Series, Caswell County.
Paper. $4.50. .... Vendor G0549

Ingmire, Frances T. **North Carolina Marriage Bonds and Certificates Series: Caswell County, NC, 1778-1876**.
Paper. $22.50. 220 pp. .... Vendor G0632

Kendall, Katharine Kerr. **Caswell County, North Carolina, Deed Books, 1777-1817**.
1989. Indexed.
Cloth. $37.50. 404 pp. + index. .... Vendor G0610

Kendall, Katharine Kerr. **Caswell County, North Carolina, Marriage Bonds, 1778-1868**. (1981) reprint 1990. Indexed.
Cloth. $16.00. 170 pp. .... Vendor G0011

Kendall, Katharine Kerr. **Caswell County, North Carolina, Will Books 1777-1814,** 1784 Tax List, Guardians' Accounts, 1794-1819. (1979) reprint 1989. Indexed.
Paper. $27.50. 183 pp. .... Vendor G0610

Kendall, Katherine Kerr. **Caswell County Will Books, 1814-1843, Guardian Accounts 1819-1847, 1850 & 1860 Census Mortality Schedules, and Powers of Attorney from Deed Books, 1777-1880**. 1983. Indexed.
Paper. $20.00. 226 pp. .... Vendor G0623

Kendall, Katherine Kerr. **Caswell County, North Carolina Will Books, 1843-1868, Guardian's Accounts 1848-1868**. 1986. Indexed.
Paper. $20.00. 211 pp. .... Vendor G0623

T.L.C. Genealogy. **Caswell County, North Carolina Tax Lists, 1777, 1780, & 1784**.
1990. Indexed.
Paper. $10.00. 106 pp. .... Vendor G0609

Chatham County

1790 Census Series, Chatham County.
Paper. $5.50. .... Vendor G0549

Ingmire, Frances T. **North Carolina Marriage Bonds and Certificates Series: Chatham County, NC, 1782-1867**.
Paper. $9.50. 64 pp. .... Vendor G0632

Willis, Laura. **Chatham County, North Carolina Early Deeds Volume Two 1787-1790**. 1995.
Paper. $10.00. .... Vendor G0687

Cherokee County

Douthat, James L. **Hiwassee Reservoir Cemeteries**.
Paper. $20.00. .... Vendor G0549

Chowan County

1790 Census Series, Chowan County.
Paper. $3.50. .... Vendor G0549

Ingmire, Frances T. **North Carolina Marriage Bonds and Certificates Series: Chowan County, NC, 1742-1868**.
Paper. $15.00. 114 pp. .... Vendor G0632

Clay County

Clay County Heritage Book Committee. **Clay County Heritage—North Carolina, Vol. 1**. Indexed. Illus.
  The state's western-most county is included in yet another of the North Carolina County Heritage Book series. An attractive red (imitation) leather hardbound book, 9" x 12". Includes nearly 300 family histories, genealogies, and family photos. Includes churches, clubs, and organizations. Every-name index.
Cloth. $55.50. 156 pp. .... Vendor G0087

Cleveland County

Holcomb, Brent H. **York, South Carolina, Newspapers: Marriage and Death Notices, 1823-1865**. (1981) reprint 1989. Indexed.
  Contains marriage and death notices not only from the York area, but also from Union, Spartanburg, Lancaster, and Chester counties in South Carolina and Cleveland, Gaston, and Mecklenburg counties in North Carolina.
Cloth. $25.00. vi + 129 pp. .... Vendor G0551

Craven County

1790 Census Series, Craven County.
Paper. $6.00. .... Vendor G0549

Ingmire, Frances T. **North Carolina Marriage Bonds and Certificates Series: Craven County, NC, 1780-1867**.
Paper. $27.50. 258 pp. .... Vendor G0632

Cumberland County

1790 Census Series, Cumberland County.
Paper. $5.00. .... Vendor G0549

Ingmire, Frances T. **North Carolina Marriage Bonds and Certificates Series: Cumberland County, NC, 1803-1878.**
Paper. $22.50. 214 pp. .... Vendor G0632

Parker, Roy, Jr. **Cumberland County: A Brief History.** 1990. Illus.
Paper. $8.00. xi + 158 pp. .... Vendor G0586

Currituck County

1790 Census Series, Currituck County.
Paper. $5.00. .... Vendor G0549

Bennett, William Doub. **Currituck County [North Carolina] Eighteenth Century Tax & Militia Records.** 1994. Indexed. Illus.
Paper. $24.00. 134 pp. .... Vendor G0011

Dare County

Stick, David. **Dare County: A Brief History.** 5th printing. 1995. Illus.
Paper. $6.00. x + 64 pp. .... Vendor G0586

Davidson County

Ingmire, Frances T. **North Carolina Marriage Bonds and Certificates Series: Davidson County, NC, 1823-1868.**
Paper. $15.00. 136 pp. .... Vendor G0632

Leonard, Rev. Jacob Calvin. **Centennial History of Davidson County.** (1927) reprint 1995.
Cloth. $55.00. 523 pp. .... Vendor G0259

Davie County

Ingmire, Frances T. **North Carolina Marriage Bonds and Certificates Series: Davie County, NC, 1837-1868.**
Paper. $7.50. 44 pp. .... Vendor G0632

Linn, Jo White. **Davie County, North Carolina, Tax Lists of 1843 and 1847.** 1995. Indexed. Illus.
    Includes maps of county and town lots of Mocksville, county seat.
Paper. $15.00 incl. p&h. 60 pp. .... Vendor G0131

Wall, James W. **Davie County: A Brief History**. 1976.
Paper. $5.00. xiii + 128 pp. .... Vendor G0586

Dobbs County

1790 Census Series, Dobbs County.
Paper. $5.00. .... Vendor G0549

Duplin County

1790 Census Series, Duplin County.
Paper. $4.50. .... Vendor G0549

Draughton, Eleanor Smith. **Duplin County, N.C., Abstracts of Deeds, 1784-1813, Vol. I**. (1983) reprint 1986. Indexed.
Paper. $27.50. 256 pp. .... Vendor G0610

Ingmire, Frances T. **North Carolina Marriage Bonds and Certificates Series: Duplin County, NC, 1755-1868**.
Paper. $9.50. 62 pp. .... Vendor G0632

Murphy, William L. (Bill). **Genealogical Abstracts of Duplin County Wills, 1730-1860**. (1982) reprint 1986. Indexed.
Cloth. $27.50. 280 pp. .... Vendor G0610

Sikes, Leon H. **Duplin County Cemetery Records, Vol. C**. 1986. Indexed. Illus.
Contact vendor for information. 112 pp. .... Vendor G0610

Durham County

Wynne, Frances Holloway. **Durham County, North Carolina; Marriage Register, 1881-1906**. 1983. Indexed.
Paper. $27.75. 260 pp. .... Vendor G0040

Edgecombe County

1790 Census Series, Edgecombe County.
Paper. $6.00. .... Vendor G0549

Bradley, Stephen E., Jr. **Edgecombe County, North Carolina Deeds Volume 3: 1778-1786**. 1996. Indexed.
Paper. $25.00. 128 pp. .... Vendor G0757

Ingmire, Frances T. **North Carolina Marriage Bonds and Certificates Series: Edgecombe County, NC, 1760-1868**.
Paper. $17.00. 146 pp. .... Vendor G0632

Johnston, Hugh Buckner. **Edgecombe County Marriages and Deaths from Tarboro, NC Newspapers, 1824-1865**. 1985. Indexed.
Paper. $20.00. 168 pp. .... Vendor G0610

Turner, J. Kelly, and John L. Bridgers. **History of Edgecombe County, North Carolina**. (1920) reprint 1993. Indexed. Illus.
Contact vendor for information. 544 pp. .... Vendor G0610

Watson, Alan D. **Edgecombe County: A Brief History**. 1979. Illus.
Paper. $5.00. ix + 109 pp. .... Vendor G0586

Watson, Joseph W. **Abstracts of Early Deeds of Edgecombe County, North Carolina, 1759-1772**. (1966) reprint 1993. Indexed.
Cloth. $32.50. vi + 342 pp. .... Vendor G0551

Watson, Joseph W. **Abstracts of Early Deeds of Edgecombe County, North Carolina, 1772-1788, Volume II**. (1967) reprint 1996. Indexed.
Cloth. $32.50. vi + 366 pp. .... Vendor G0551

Watson, Joseph W. **Estate Records of Edgecombe County, North Carolina, 1730-1820**. (1970) reprint 1992. Indexed.
Cloth. $32.50. vi + 321 pp. .... Vendor G0551

Watson, Joseph W. **Estate Records of Edgecombe County, North Carolina, 1820-1850, Volume II**. 1983. Indexed.
Cloth. $25.00. vi + 271 pp. .... Vendor G0551

Franklin County

1790 Census Series, Franklin County.
Paper. $4.50. .... Vendor G0549

Ingmire, Frances T. **North Carolina Marriage Bonds and Certificates Series: Franklin County, NC 1789-1868**.
Paper. $15.00. 122 pp. .... Vendor G0632

Pearce, Thilbert. **They Fought: The Story of Franklin County Men in the Years 1861-1865**. 1996. Indexed. Illus.
Cloth. $30.00. 358 pp. .... Vendor G0590

Watson, Joseph W. **Abstracts of the Early Deeds of Franklin County, North Carolina, 1779-1797**. 1984. Indexed. Illus.
Cloth. $32.50. x + 253 pp. .... Vendor G0551

Gaston County

Holcomb, Brent H. **York, South Carolina, Newspapers: Marriage and Death Notices, 1823-1865**. (1981) reprint 1989. Indexed.
Contains marriage and death notices not only from the York area, but also from Union, Spartanburg, Lancaster, and Chester counties in South Carolina and Cleveland, Gaston, and Mecklenburg counties in North Carolina.
Cloth. $25.00. vi + 129 pp. .... Vendor G0551

Gates County

1790 Census Series, Gates County.
Paper. $4.50. .... Vendor G0549

Ingmire, Frances T. **North Carolina Marriage Bonds and Certificates Series: Gates County, NC 1782-1868**.
Paper. $17.00. 136 pp. .... Vendor G0632

Granville County

1790 Census Series, Granville County.
Paper. $4.50. .... Vendor G0549

Gwynn, Zae Hargett. **Abstracts of the Early Deeds of Granville County, North Carolina, 1746-1765**. Edited by Joseph W. Watson. (1974) reprint 1993. Indexed.
Cloth. $32.50. vii + 322 pp. .... Vendor G0551

Gwynn, Zae Hargett. **Abstracts of the Wills and Estate Records of Granville County, North Carolina, 1808-1833, Volume II**. Edited by Joseph W. Watson. (1976) reprint 1996. Indexed.
Cloth. $32.50. iv + 340 pp. .... Vendor G0551

Gwynn, Zae Hargett. **Kinfolks of Granville County, North Carolina, 1765-1826**. Edited by Joseph W. Watson. (1974) reprint 1992. Indexed.
Cloth. $32.50. vi + 311 pp. .... Vendor G0551

Holcomb, Brent H. **Marriages of Granville County, North Carolina, 1753-1868**. (1981) reprint 1993. Indexed.
Contact vendor for information. 431 pp. .... Vendor G0011

Horsman, Mrs. Barbara Knott. **Reading Backwards On My Knott Heritage**. 1994. Indexed. Illus.
Cloth. $30.00. 432 pp. .... Vendor G0115

Owen, Thomas McAdory. **History and Genealogies of Old Granville, North Carolina, 1746-1800**. 1993. Indexed.
Cloth. $37.50. 300 pp. .... Vendor G0610

Ray, Worth S. **Lost Tribes of North Carolina. Part II: Colonial Granville County [North Carolina] and Its People**. (1945) reprint 1996. Indexed. Illus.
Paper. $15.00. 120 pp. .... Vendor G0011

Guilford County

1790 Census Series, Guilford County.
Paper. $5.50. .... Vendor G0549

Guilford County Genealogical Society. **Guilford County Apprentice Bonds, 1817-1870**. 1996.
Paper. $15.00. 103 pp. .... Vendor G0730

Guilford County Genealogical Society. **Guilford County Cemeteries, Volume 1: Western Section**. 1996. Indexed.
Paper. $25.00. 306 pp. .... Vendor G0730

Ingmire, Frances T. **North Carolina Marriage Bonds and Certificates Series: Guilford County, NC, Vol. 1, A-F**.
Paper. $15.00. 100 pp. .... Vendor G0632

Ingmire, Frances T. **North Carolina Marriage Bonds and Certificates Series: Guilford County, NC, Vol. 2, G-N**.
Paper. $15.00. 116 pp. .... Vendor G0632

Ingmire, Frances T. **North Carolina Marriage Bonds and Certificates Series: Guilford County, NC, Vol. 3, O-Z**.
Paper. $15.00. 120 pp. .... Vendor G0632

Stoesen, Alexander R. **Guilford County: A Brief History**. 1993. Indexed. Illus.
Paper. $5.00. 89 pp. .... Vendor G0586

Webster, Irene B. **Guilford County, N.C., Will Abstracts, 1771-1841**. (1979) reprint 1992.
Paper. $22.50. 190 pp. .... Vendor G0610

Halifax County

1790 Census Series, Halifax County.
Paper. $6.00. .... Vendor G0549

Allen, W. C. **A History of Halifax County, North Carolina**. (1918) reprint 1993. Indexed. Illus.
Cloth. $35.00. 280 pp. .... Vendor G0610

Ingmire, Frances T. **North Carolina Marriage Bonds and Certificates Series: Halifax County, NC, 1818-1867**.
Paper. $17.50. 134 pp. .... Vendor G0632

Haywood County

Haywood County Heritage Book Committee. **Haywood County Heritage—North Carolina, Vol. 1**. Indexed. Illus.
  A gold mine for genealogists! Part of the North Carolina County Heritage Book series; 9" x 12", coffee-table size, rich maroon linen cover with deluxe embossed seal. More than 700 family histories, genealogies, and family photos, along with numerous topical stories of Haywood County places, things, and events. Surname index.
Cloth. $59.50. 380 pp. .... Vendor G0087

Wooley, James E., and Vivian Wooley. **Marriage Bonds of Haywood and Jackson Counties, North Carolina**. (1978) reprint 1991. Indexed.
Contact vendor for information. 324 pp. .... Vendor G0610

Hertford County

1790 Census Series, Hertford County.
Paper. $4.50. .... Vendor G0549

Hyde County

1790 Census Series, Hyde County.
Paper. $4.00. .... Vendor G0549

Harris, Morgan H. **Hyde Yesterdays: A History of Hyde County**. 1995. Indexed.
Cloth. $33.00. xv + 349 pp. .... Vendor G0700

Norris, Allen Wilkinson Hart, comp. **Hyde County, North Carolina Record of Deeds A, 1736-1762**. 1995. Indexed.
Paper. $18.00. xii + 78 pp. .... Vendor G0700

Iredell County

1790 Census Series, Iredell County.
Paper. $4.50. .... Vendor G0549

Jackson County

Wooley, James E., and Vivian Wooley. **Marriage Bonds of Haywood and Jackson Counties, North Carolina.** (1978) reprint 1991. Indexed.
Contact vendor for information. 324 pp. .... Vendor G0610

Johnston County

1790 Census Series, Johnston County.
Paper. $4.50. .... Vendor G0549

Holcomb, Brent H. **Marriages of Johnston County, North Carolina, 1762-1868.** (1985) reprint 1985. Indexed.
Cloth. $13.50. 162 pp. .... Vendor G0011

Ingmire, Frances T. **North Carolina Marriage Bonds and Certificates Series: Johnston County, NC, 1767-1867.**
Paper. $17.50. 154 pp. .... Vendor G0632

Jones County

1790 Census Series, Jones County.
Paper. $3.50. .... Vendor G0549

Lenoir County

Powell, William S. **Annals of Progress: The Story of Lenoir County and Kinston, North Carolina.** 1963. Illus.
Paper. $5.00. x + 107 pp. .... Vendor G0586

Lincoln County

1790 Census Series, Lincoln County.
Paper. $6.00. .... Vendor G0549

Bynum, Curtis. **Marriage Bonds of Tryon and Lincoln Counties, North Carolina.** (1929) reprint 1996. Indexed.
Paper. $18.00. 184 pp. .... Vendor G0011

Bynum, Curtis. **Marriage Bonds of Tryon and Lincoln Counties, North Carolina**. (1929) reprint 1991. Indexed.
Cloth. $27.50. 184 pp. .... Vendor G0610

Holcomb, Brent H. **Deed Abstracts of Tryon, Lincoln and Rutherford Counties, N.C., and Tryon Co. Wills and Estates: 1769-1786**. (1977) reprint 1982. Indexed. Illus.
Cloth. Contact vendor for information. 224 pp. .... Vendor G0610

Ingmire, Frances T. **North Carolina Marriage Bonds and Certificates Series: Lincoln County, NC 1783-1866, Vol. 1 Males; Vol. 2 Females**.
Paper. $35.00/set. 290 pp. .... Vendor G0632

Sherrill, William L. **Annals of Lincoln County, North Carolina . . . 1749 to 1937**. (1937) reprint 1996. Indexed. Illus.
Paper. $42.00. 536 pp. .... Vendor G0011

Macon County

Ingmire, Frances T. **North Carolina Marriage Bonds and Certificates Series: Macon County, NC 1830-1868**.
Paper. $9.50. 58 pp. .... Vendor G0632

McRae, Barbara Sears. **Records of Old Macon County, North Carolina, 1829-1850**. 1991. Indexed.
Cloth. $25.00. 212 pp. .... Vendor G0011

Wooley, James E. **Macon County, North Carolina, Marriages 1829-1939**. 1984. Indexed.
Paper. $22.50. 156 pp. + index. .... Vendor G0610

Madison County

Ingmire, Frances T. **North Carolina Marriage Bonds and Certificates Series: Madison County, NC, 1852-1868**.
Paper. $7.50. 36 pp. .... Vendor G0632

Madison County Heritage Book Committee. **Madison County Heritage—North Carolina, Vol. 1**. 3rd printing. Indexed. Illus.
    This attractive blue, hardbound book is one of the most popular in the North Carolina County Heritage Book series. More than 500 family genealogies, family histories, and photos. Includes information on historical homes and buildings, transportation, medical history, education, communities, and churches. Surname index.
Cloth. $59.50. 262 pp. .... Vendor G0087

Martin County

1790 Census Series, Martin County.
Paper. $4.50. .... Vendor G0549

McDowell County

Crow, Mr. and Mrs. Judson O. **McDowell County, North Carolina Land Entry Abstracts, Volume 1 1843-1869**. 1982. Indexed.
Paper. $25.00. ix + 500 pp. .... Vendor G0551

Ingmire, Frances T. **North Carolina Marriage Bonds and Certificates Series: McDowell County, NC, 1797-1869**.
Paper. $7.50. 34 pp. .... Vendor G0632

Mecklenburg County

1790 Census Series, Mecklenburg County.
Paper. $6.50. .... Vendor G0549

Alexander, J. B. **History of Mecklenburg County, North Carolina, 1740-1900**. (1902) reprint 1993. Indexed.
Cloth. $42.50. 486 pp. .... Vendor G0610

Ferguson, Herman W. **Genealogical Deed Abstracts, Mecklenburg County, NC, Books 10-14**. 1990. Indexed.
Paper. $25.00. 260 pp. .... Vendor G0056

Ferguson, Herman W. **Mecklenburg County, NC Minutes of the Court of Common Pleas & Quarter Sessions, 1780-1800**. 1995. Indexed.
   The index contains 32,000 entries.
Paper. $27.50. x + 276 pp. .... Vendor G0056

Ferguson, Herman W. **Mecklenburg County, NC, Will Abstracts, 1791-1846, Books A-J, and Tax Lists 1797-1799, 1806 & 1807**. 1993. Indexed.
Paper. $30.00. 390 pp. .... Vendor G0056

Holcomb, Brent H. **Deed Abstracts of Mecklenburg County, North Carolina, 1763-1779, Books 1-9**. (1979) reprint 1991. Indexed.
Cloth. $30.00. 288 pp. .... Vendor G0610

Holcomb, Brent H. **Marriages of Mecklenburg County, North Carolina 1783-1868**. (1981) reprint 1995. Indexed.
Paper. $22.50. 284 pp. .... Vendor G0011

Holcomb, Brent H. **Mecklenburg County, North Carolina. Abstracts of Early Wills, 1763-1790 (1749-1790)**. (1980) reprint 1995. Indexed.
Paper. $12.00. 101 pp. .... Vendor G0011

Holcomb, Brent H. **York, South Carolina, Newspapers: Marriage and Death Notices, 1823-1865**. (1981) reprint 1989. Indexed.
   Contains marriage and death notices not only from the York area, but also from Union, Spartanburg, Lancaster, and Chester counties in South Carolina and Cleveland, Gaston, and Mecklenburg counties in North Carolina.
Cloth. $25.00. vi + 129 pp. .... Vendor G0551

Ingmire, Frances T. **North Carolina Marriage Bonds and Certificates Series: Mecklenburg County, NC, 1788-1866**.
Paper. $17.50. 180 pp. .... Vendor G0632

Ray, Worth S. **Lost Tribes of North Carolina. Part III: the Mecklenburg Signers and Their Neighbors**. (1946) reprint 1995. Indexed. Illus.
Paper. $22.50. 246 pp. .... Vendor G0011

Mitchell County

Bailey, Dr. Lloyd. **Toe River Valley Heritage—North Carolina, Vol. 1**. Indexed. Illus.
   The first in a forthcoming series on Avery, Mitchell, and Yancey counties. Features 632 family genealogies and photos, along with a wealth of information on early history, military (Revolutionary War veterans), and black Americans in the region. Every-name index.
Cloth. $68.00. 556 pp. .... Vendor G0087

Bailey, Lloyd R., ed. **Heritage of the Toe River Valley, Vol. I**. 1994. Indexed. Illus.
   Contains 750 articles on the history and families of Avery, Mitchell, and Yancey counties, North Carolina. A second volume will be available soon—contact vendor for information.
Cloth. $68.00. 550 pp. .... Vendor G0631

Montgomery County

1790 Census Series, Montgomery County.
Paper. $4.50. .... Vendor G0549

Ingmire, Frances T. **North Carolina Marriage Bonds and Certificates Series: Montgomery County, NC, 1844-1868**.
Paper. $7.50. 26 pp. .... Vendor G0632

Moore County

1790 Census Series, Moore County.
Paper. $4.50. .... Vendor G0549

Nash County

1790 Census Series, Nash County.
Paper. $5.00. .... Vendor G0549

Ingmire, Frances T. **North Carolina Marriage Bonds and Certificates Series: Nash County, NC 1783-1868**.
Paper. $12.50. 86 pp. .... Vendor G0632

Williams, Ruth Smith, and Margarette Glenn Griffin. **Abstracts of Will Book I, Nash County, North Carolina, 1778-1868.** (1967) reprint 1987. Indexed.
Cloth. $22.50. v + 177 pp. .... Vendor G0551

New Hanover County

1790 Census Series, New Hanover County.
Paper. $3.50. .... Vendor G0549

Ingmire, Frances T. **North Carolina Marriage Bonds and Certificates Series: New Hanover County, NC 1779-1868.**
Paper. $9.50. 72 pp. .... Vendor G0632

Lee, E. Lawrence. **New Hanover County: A Brief History**. 3rd printing, 1984. Illus.
Paper. $5.00. xiv + 124 pp. .... Vendor G0586

Northampton County

1790 Census Series, Northampton County.
Paper. $5.50. .... Vendor G0549

Ingmire, Frances T. **North Carolina Marriage Bonds and Certificates Series: Northampton County, NC 1812-1867.**
Paper. $15.00. 136 pp. .... Vendor G0632

Onslow County

1790 Census Series, Onslow County.
Paper. $4.00. .... Vendor G0549

Ingmire, Frances T. **North Carolina Marriage Bonds and Certificates Series: Onslow County, NC, 1764-1867.**
Paper. $9.50. 66 pp. .... Vendor G0632

Watson, Alan D. **Onslow County: A Brief History**. 1995. Indexed. Illus.
Paper. $8.00. 184 pp. .... Vendor G0586

Orange County

1790 Census Series, Orange County.
Paper. $5.00. .... Vendor G0549

Ingmire, Frances T. **North Carolina Marriage Bonds and Certificates Series: Orange County, NC 1782-1866, Vol. 1, A-F.**
Paper. $15.00. 112 pp. .... Vendor G0632

Ingmire, Frances T. **North Carolina Marriage Bonds and Certificates Series: Orange County, NC, 1782-1868, Vol. 2, G-N.**
Paper. $15.00. 116 pp. .... Vendor G0632

Ingmire, Frances T. **North Carolina Marriage Bonds and Certificates Series: Orange County, NC, 1782-1868, Vol. 3, O-Z.**
Paper. $15.00. 122 pp. .... Vendor G0632

Shields, Ruth Herndon. **Abstracts of Wills Recorded in Orange County, North Carolina, 1752-1800 and 1800-1850.** 2 vols. in 1. (1957, 1966) reprint 1997. Indexed.
Paper. $33.50. 450 pp. in all. .... Vendor G0011

Shields, Ruth Herndon. **Orange County, North Carolina: Abstracts of the Minutes of the Court of Pleas and Quarter Sessions of September 1752-August 1766.** (1965) reprint 1991. Indexed.
Cloth. $22.50. 182 pp. .... Vendor G0610

T.L.C. Genealogy. **Orange County, North Carolina Taxpayers, 1784-1793.** 1991. Indexed.
Paper. $12.00. 97 pp. .... Vendor G0609

Pamlico County

Mobley, Joe A. **Pamlico County: A Brief History.** 1991. Indexed. Illus.
Paper. $8.00. xiv + 144 pp. .... Vendor G0586

Pasquotank County

1790 Census Series, Pasquotank County.
Paper. $4.50. .... Vendor G0549

Ingmire, Frances T. **North Carolina Marriage Bonds and Certificates Series: Pasquotank County, NC, 1776-1868.**
Paper. $9.50. 50 pp. .... Vendor G0632

Perquimans County

1790 Census Series, Perquimans County.
Paper. $4.00. .... Vendor G0549

Ingmire, Frances T. **North Carolina Marriage Bonds and Certificates Series: Perquimans County, NC, 1758-1865.**
Paper. $12.50. 86 pp. .... Vendor G0632

Watson, Alan D. **Perquimans County: A Brief History.** 1987. Illus.
Paper. $5.00. xi + 122 pp. .... Vendor G0586

Winslow, Mrs. Watson. **History of Perquimans County (North Carolina).** (1931) reprint 1990. Indexed. Illus.
Cloth. $27.00. 438 pp. .... Vendor G0011

Person County

Ingmire, Frances T. **North Carolina Marriage Bonds and Certificates Series: Person County, NC, 1792-1868**.
Paper. $15.00. 136 pp. .... Vendor G0632

Kendall, Katharine Kerr. **Person County, North Carolina Deed Books 1792-1825**.
(1994) reprint 1996. Indexed.
Paper. $24.00. 262 pp. .... Vendor G0011

Kendall, Katherine Kerr. **Person County, North Carolina Marriage Records 1792-1868**. 1983. Indexed.
    Includes 3,286 marriage records of Person County, North Carolina, including marriage bonds, licenses, and minister returns.
Paper. $20.00. 96 pp. .... Vendor G0623

Pitt County

1790 Census Series, Pitt County.
Paper. $5.50. .... Vendor G0549

Raleigh

Raleigh, North Carolina Newspapers 1830-1839.
Cloth. $75.00. .... Vendor G0623

Randolph County

1790 Census Series, Randolph County.
Paper. $5.50. .... Vendor G0549

Ingmire, Frances T. **North Carolina Marriage Bonds and Certificates Series: Randolph County, NC, 1785-1868**.
Paper. $22.50. 200 pp. .... Vendor G0632

Richmond County

1790 Census Series, Richmond County.
Paper. $4.50. .... Vendor G0549

Ingmire, Frances T. **North Carolina Marriage Bonds and Certificates Series: Richmond County, NC, 1783-1868**.
Paper. $7.50. 26 pp. .... Vendor G0632

Richmond County Heritage Book Committee. **Richmond County Heritage—North Carolina, Vol. 1**. Indexed. Illus.

Another in the North Carolina County Heritage Book series. A companion volume to *Anson County Heritage*, this book focuses on nearly 700 family histories, genealogies, and family pictures (of both modern and pioneer families). Other topics include military, cemeteries, churches, clubs and organizations, and towns. Rich blue, hardbound, 9" x 12" book with gold embossed seal. Surname index.
Cloth. $59.50. 384 pp. .... Vendor G0087

Robeson County

1790 Census Series, Robeson County.
Paper. $4.50. .... Vendor G0549

Ingmire, Frances T. **North Carolina Marriage Bonds and Certificates Series: Robeson County, NC 1799-1868**.
Paper. $15.00. 98 pp. .... Vendor G0632

Lawrence, R. C. **The State of Robeson**. (1939) reprint 1994.
Cloth. $35.00. 279 pp. .... Vendor G0259

Rockingham County

1790 Census Series, Rockingham County.
Paper. $4.50. .... Vendor G0549

Butler, Lindley S. **Rockingham County: A Brief History**. 1982. Illus.
Paper. $5.00. xiv + 92 pp. .... Vendor G0586

Ingmire, Frances T. **North Carolina Marriage Bonds and Certificates Series: Rockingham County, NC, 1785-1868**.
Paper. $17.50. 160 pp. .... Vendor G0632

James Hunter Chapter, NSDAR of Madison, NC. **Early Families of the North Carolina Counties of Rockingham and Stokes with Revolutionary Service, Vol. 1**. (1977) reprint 1989. Indexed.
    Sketches for 156 families.
Paper. $27.50. 190 pp. .... Vendor G0610

James Hunter Chapter, NSDAR of Madison, NC. **Early Families of the North Carolina Counties of Rockingham and Stokes with Revolutionary Service, Vol. 2**. (1981) reprint 1989. Indexed.
Paper. $27.50. 187 pp. .... Vendor G0610

Webster, Irene B. **Rockingham County, North Carolina Will Abstracts, Vol. 1, 1785-1865**. (1973) reprint 1983. Indexed.
Paper. $18.50. 138 pp. .... Vendor G0610

Webster, Irene B. **Rockingham County, North Carolina Deed Abstracts, 1785-1800**. (1973) reprint 1983. Indexed.
Paper. $18.50. 122 pp. .... Vendor G0610

Rowan County

1790 Census Series, Rowan County.
Paper. $5.50. .... Vendor G0549

Holcomb, Brent H. **Marriages of Rowan County, North Carolina, 1753-1868**. (1981)
reprint 1996. Indexed.
Paper. $37.50. 506 pp. .... Vendor G0011

Ingmire, Frances T. **North Carolina Marriage Bonds and Certificates Series: Rowan
County, NC, 1754-1866, Vol. 1, A-F.**
Paper. $15.00. 112 pp. .... Vendor G0632

Ingmire, Frances T. **North Carolina Marriage Bonds and Certificates Series: Rowan
County, NC, 1754-1866, Vol. 2, G-N.**
Paper. $15.00. 116 pp. .... Vendor G0632

Ingmire, Frances T. **North Carolina Marriage Bonds and Certificates Series: Rowan
County, NC, 1754-1866, Vol. 3, O-Z.**
Paper. $15.00. 122 pp. .... Vendor G0632

Linn, Jo White. **1815 Rowan County, North Carolina, Tax List**. 1987. Indexed. Illus.
Surname index, map. Includes the thirty-seven tax districts with 3,884 white taxables,
even more than are shown on the 1820 tax list.
Paper. $12.00 + $1.00 p&h. 64 pp. .... Vendor G0131

Linn, Jo White. **1850 Census of Rowan County, NC: A Genealogical Compilation
of All Six Schedules**. 1992. Indexed. Illus.
Maps, surname index. This compilation includes statistics for not only the population schedule but also for the mortality schedule, social statistics schedule, slave schedule, agricultural schedule, and manufacturing schedule. Marriage bond information
included.
Paper. $26.00 + $2.00 p&h. 158 pp. .... Vendor G0131

Linn, Jo White. **Abstracts of the Deeds of Rowan County, NC, 1753-1785**. (1972)
reprint 1983. Indexed. Illus.
Includes map; complete-name, topic, and place indexes.
Hard-cover. $30.00 + $3.00 p&h. 276 pp. .... Vendor G0131

Linn, Jo White. **Abstracts of the Minutes of the Court of Pleas & Quarter Ses-
sions, Rowan County, NC:** Volume 1, 1753-1762. Second printing 1977. Indexed.
Includes complete-name, topic, and place indexes.
Hard-cover. $35.00 + $3.00 p&h. 177 pp. .... Vendor G0131

Linn, Jo White. **Abstracts of the Minutes of the Court of Pleas & Quarter Ses-
sions, Rowan County, NC:** Volume 2, 1763-1774. Second printing 1979. Indexed.
Includes complete-name, topic, and place indexes.
Hard-cover. $30.00 + $3.00 p&h. 210 pp. .... Vendor G0131

Linn, Jo White. **Abstracts of the Minutes of the Court of Pleas & Quarter Ses-
sions, Rowan County, NC:** Volume 3, 1775-1789. Second printing 1982. Indexed.
Includes complete-name, topic, and place indexes.
Hard-cover. $35.00 + $3.00 p&h. 240 pp. .... Vendor G0131

Linn, Jo White. **Abstracts of the Wills and Estates Records of Rowan County, NC, 1753-1805 and Rowan County Tax Lists of 1759 and 1778** [includes the unrecorded wills and translations of wills recorded in German]. (1970) reprint 1995. Indexed.
Includes complete-name index and slave indexes.
Hard-cover. $30.00 + $3.00 p&h. 220 pp. .... Vendor G0131

Linn, Jo White. **First Presbyterian Church, Salisbury, North Carolina, and Its People, 1821-1995**. 1996. Indexed. Illus.
Includes complete-name, topic, place, and slave indexes. A genealogical, social, and church history in an ancient southern town. Membership and baptismal lists, session minutes, family histories and connections.
Hard-cover. $45.00 + $3.50 p&h. 540 pp. .... Vendor G0131

Linn, Jo White. **Rowan County, North Carolina, Tax Lists 1757-1800: Annotated Transcriptions**. 1995. Indexed. Illus.
Map by Herman Ferguson; introduction by William D. Bennett; bibliography; complete-name, topic, and slave indexes; 163 lists.
Hard-cover. $40.00 + $3.00 p&h. 444 pp. .... Vendor G0131

Linn, Jo White. **Rowan County Register**.
A quarterly genealogical magazine centering on Rowan County, featuring unpublished Rowan County source materials of a historical and genealogical nature. This publication continues (but does not repeat) the records of deeds, wills, and court minutes abstracted in the hard-cover volumes listed above for this vendor and provides abstracts of the following records: Salisbury District Superior Court Minutes, Rowan County Divisions of Estates, Rowan County tax lists, naturalization lists, guardian bonds, bibliographies, maps, profiles of families and individuals, articles on methodology, announcements of general interest to genealogists, book reviews, queries from subscribers, etc. Annual complete-name, place, and topic indexes. Back issues available: 1986-1988 issues at $21.00 per year; 1989-1996 issues at $25.00 per year.
Subscription: $25.00/yr. 240 pp./yr. .... Vendor G0131

Rowan County, North Carolina—Guards for Salisbury Gaol 1778-1779.
Paper. $8.50. .... Vendor G0549

Rutherford County

1790 Census Series, Rutherford County.
Paper. $3.50. .... Vendor G0549

Holcomb, Brent H. **Deed Abstracts of Tryon, Lincoln and Rutherford Counties, N.C., and Tryon Co. Wills and Estates: 1769-1786**. (1977) reprint 1982. Indexed. Illus.
Cloth. Contact vendor for information. 224 pp. .... Vendor G0610

Holcomb, Brent H. **Marriages of Rutherford County, North Carolina, 1779-1868**. 1986. Indexed.
Cloth. $20.00. 205 pp. .... Vendor G0010

Ingmire, Frances T. **North Carolina Marriage Bonds and Certificates Series: Rutherford County, NC, 1799-1867**.
Paper. $20.00. 190 pp. .... Vendor G0632

Wooley, James E., and Vivian Wooley. **Rutherford County, NC, Wills and Miscellaneous Records, 1783-1868**. 1984. Indexed.
Paper. $25.00. 184 pp. .... Vendor G0610

Sampson County

1790 Census Series, Sampson County.
Paper. $4.50. .... Vendor G0549

Scotland County

Gibson, Joyce M. **Scotland County Emerging 1750-1900**. The History of a Small Section of North Carolina. 1995. Indexed.
Cloth. $39.50. 316 pp. .... Vendor G0701

Stokes County

1790 Census Series, Stokes County.
Paper. $3.50. .... Vendor G0549

Absher, Mrs. W. O. **Stokes County, N.C., Deeds, Vols. 1-2**. 1985. Indexed.
Paper. $22.50. Approx. 200 pp. + index .... Vendor G0610

Absher, Mrs. W. O. **Stokes County, N.C., Wills, Vols. 1-4, 1790-1864**. 1985. Indexed.
Paper. $21.50. 181 pp. + index. .... Vendor G0610

Ingmire, Frances T. **North Carolina Marriage Bonds and Certificates Series: Stokes County, NC 1783-1868, Vol. 1, Males; Vol. 2, Females**.
Paper. $30.00/set. 232 pp. .... Vendor G0632

James Hunter Chapter, NSDAR of Madison, NC. **Early Families of the North Carolina Counties of Rockingham and Stokes with Revolutionary Service, Vol. 1**. (1977) reprint 1989. Indexed.
   Sketches for 156 families.
Paper. $27.50. 190 pp. .... Vendor G0610

James Hunter Chapter, NSDAR of Madison, NC. **Early Families of the North Carolina Counties of Rockingham and Stokes with Revolutionary Service, Vol. 2**. (1981) reprint 1989. Indexed.
Paper. $27.50. 187 pp. .... Vendor G0610

Surry County

1790 Census Series, Surry County.
Paper. $3.50. .... Vendor G0549

Absher, Mrs. W. O. **Surry County, N.C., Court Minutes, Vols. 1 and 2, 1768-1789**. 1985. Indexed.
Paper. $18.50. 168 pp. + index. .... Vendor G0610

Absher, Mrs. W. O. **Surry County, N.C., Deed Books A, B, & C: 1768-1789**. (1981) reprint 1987. Indexed.
Cloth. $22.50. 128 pp. .... Vendor G0610

Absher, Mrs. W. O. **Surry County, N.C., Deeds, Books D, E, & F: 1779-1797**. 1985. Indexed.
Paper. $15.00. 128 pp. + index. .... Vendor G0610

Holcomb, Brent H. **Marriages of Surry County, North Carolina 1779-1868**. (1982) reprint 1993. Indexed.
Contact vendor for information. 272 pp. .... Vendor G0011

Ingmire, Frances T. **North Carolina Marriage Bonds and Certificates Series: Surry County, NC, 1783-1868, Vol. 1 Males; Vol. 2, Females**.
Paper. $30.00/set. 220 pp. .... Vendor G0632

Linn, Jo White. **Surry County, North Carolina, Wills, 1771-1827:** Annotated Genealogical Abstracts. 1992. Indexed. Illus.
Map; complete-name, slave, and topic index. Includes information from court minutes, unpublished tax lists, marriage bonds, and additional material from the author's files.
Cloth. $25.00. 215 pp. .... Vendor G0010

Tryon County

Bynum, Curtis. **Marriage Bonds of Tryon and Lincoln Counties, North Carolina**. (1929) reprint 1996. Indexed.
Paper. $18.00. 184 pp. .... Vendor G0011

Bynum, Curtis. **Marriage Bonds of Tryon and Lincoln Counties, North Carolina**. (1929) reprint 1991. Indexed.
Cloth. $27.50. 184 pp. .... Vendor G0610

Holcomb, Brent H. **Deed Abstracts of Tryon, Lincoln and Rutherford Counties, N.C., and Tryon Co. Wills and Estates: 1769-1786**. (1977) reprint 1982. Indexed. Illus.
Cloth. Contact vendor for information. 224 pp. .... Vendor G0610

Holcomb, Brent H. **Tryon County, North Carolina, Minutes of the Court of Pleas and Quarter Sessions, 1769-1779**. 1993. Indexed.
Cloth. $27.50. 234 pp. .... Vendor G0602

Tyrrell County

1790 Census Series, Tyrrell County.
Paper. $4.00. .... Vendor G0549

Ingmire, Frances T. **North Carolina Marriage Bonds and Certificates Series: Tyrrell County, NC, 1761-1862**.
Paper. $15.00. 96 pp. .... Vendor G0632

Wake County

1790 Census Series, Wake County.
Paper. $6.00. .... Vendor G0549

Ingmire, Frances T. **North Carolina Marriage Bonds and Certificates Series: Wake County, NC, 1781-1867: Vol. 1, A-F; Vol. 2, L-N; Vol. 3, O-Y.**
Paper. $30.00/set. 343 pp. .... Vendor G0632

Wynne, Frances Holloway. **Abstract of Record of Wills, Inventories, Settlements of Estates 1771-1802, Wake County, North Carolina**. 1985. Indexed.
Cloth. $32.75. 283 pp. .... Vendor G0040

Wynne, Frances Holloway. **Abstract of Record of Wills, Inventories, Settlements of Estates 1802-1812, Wake County, North Carolina**. 1993. Indexed.
Cloth. $32.75. 223 pp. .... Vendor G0040

Wynne, Frances Holloway. **Wake County, North Carolina, Census and Tax Lists 1830 and 1840**. 1985. Indexed.
Cloth. $32.75. 312 pp. .... Vendor G0040

Warren County

1790 Census Series, Warren County.
Paper. $4.50. .... Vendor G0549

Holcomb, Brent H. **Marriages of Bute and Warren Counties, North Carolina 1764-1868**. 1991. Indexed.
Cloth. $24.00. 256 pp. .... Vendor G0011

Ingmire, Frances T. **North Carolina Marriage Bonds and Certificates Series: Warren County, NC, 1780-1867**.
Paper. $17.50. 162 pp. .... Vendor G0632

Wayne County

1790 Census Series, Wayne County.
Paper. $4.50. .... Vendor G0549

Watson, Joseph W. **Kinfolks of Wayne County, North Carolina, 1739-1832**. 1986. Indexed.
Cloth. $25.00. vi + 274 pp. .... Vendor G0551

Wilkes County

1790 Census Series, Wilkes County.
Paper. $6.00. .... Vendor G0549

Absher, Mrs. W. O. **Some Pioneers from Wilkes County, North Carolina**. 1989. Indexed.
Cloth. $35.00. 292 pp. .... Vendor G0610

Absher, Mrs. W. O. **Wilkes County Court Minutes, 1778-1788, Volumes I & II**. 1989. Indexed.
Paper. $23.50. Approx. 120 pp. .... Vendor G0610

Absher, Mrs. W. O. **Wilkes County Court Minutes: 1789-1797, Volumes III & IV**. 1989. Indexed.
Paper. $23.50. 132 pp. .... Vendor G0610

Absher, Mrs. W. O. **Wilkes County, North Carolina, Deed Books A-1, B-1 & C-1: 1778-1803**. 1989. Indexed.
Paper. $25.00. 152 pp. + index. .... Vendor G0610

Absher, Mrs. W. O. **Wilkes County, North Carolina, Deed Books D, F-1, G-H: 1795-1815**. 1989. Indexed.
Paper. $27.50. 200 pp. + index. .... Vendor G0610

Absher, Mrs. W. O. **Wilkes County, N.C., Land Entry Book: 1778-1781**. 1989. Indexed.
Paper. $23.50. 130 pp. .... Vendor G0610

Absher, Mrs. W. O. **Wilkes County, North Carolina, Will Abstracts, Books 1 and 2: 1778-1811**. 1989. Indexed.
Paper. $23.50. 116 pp. .... Vendor G0610

Holcomb, Brent H. **Marriages of Wilkes County, North Carolina 1778-1868**. (1983) reprint 1993. Indexed.
Contact vendor for information. 243 pp. .... Vendor G0011

Ingmire, Frances T. **North Carolina Marriage Bonds and Certificates Series: Wilkes County, NC, 1779-1868**.
Paper. $22.50. 202 pp. .... Vendor G0632

Yadkin County

Ingmire, Frances T. **North Carolina Marriage Bonds and Certificates Series: Yadkin County, NC, 1851-1868**.
Paper. $9.50. 52 pp. .... Vendor G0632

Yancey County

Bailey, Dr. Lloyd. **Toe River Valley Heritage—North Carolina, Vol. 1**. Indexed. Illus.
The first in a forthcoming series on Avery, Mitchell, and Yancey counties. Features 632 family genealogies and photos, along with a wealth of information on early history, military (Revolutionary War veterans), and black Americans in the region. Every-name index.
Cloth. $68.00. 556 pp. .... Vendor G0087

Bailey, Lloyd R., ed. **Heritage of the Toe River Valley, Vol. I**. 1994. Indexed. Illus. Contains 750 articles on the history and families of Avery, Mitchell, and Yancey counties, North Carolina. A second volume will be available soon—contact vendor for information.
Cloth. $68.00. 550 pp. .... Vendor G0631

North Dakota

Statewide and Regional References

Aberle, Monseigneur George P. **Pioneers & Their Sons:** One Hundred Sixty-Five Family Histories (Vol. I only, but contains all 165 families).
Cloth. $49.50. 471 pp. .... Vendor G0259

Compendium of History & Biography of North Dakota. (1900) reprint 1994.
Cloth. $145.00. 1,410 pp. .... Vendor G0259

Family History Library. **Research Outline: North Dakota.**
Leaflet. $.25. 6 pp. .... Vendor G0629

History of the Red River Valley, Past & Present. 2 vols. (1909) reprint 1994.
Cloth. $115.00. 1,165 pp. .... Vendor G0259

Pensioners on the Rolls As of January 1883 in Dakota Territory. 1996. Indexed.
Paper. $10.50. .... Vendor G0583

Thorndale, William, and William Dollarhide. **County Boundary Map Guides to the U.S. Federal Censuses, 1790-1920: North Dakota, 1850-1920.** 1987.
$5.95. .... Vendor G0552

Dickey County

Black, R. M., ed. **History of Dickey County.** (1930) reprint 1993.
Cloth. $37.50. 333 pp. .... Vendor G0259

Ransom County

Arnold, H. V. **Early History of Ransom County,** Including References to Sargent County, 1835-1885. (1918) reprint 1995.
Paper. $15.00. 74 pp. .... Vendor G0259

Sargent County

Arnold, H. V. **Early History of Ransom County,** Including References to Sargent County, 1835-1885. (1918) reprint 1995.
Paper. $15.00. 74 pp. .... Vendor G0259

Wells County

Spokesfield, Walter E. **History of Wells County & Its Pioneers,** with a Sketch of No. Dakota History & the Origin of the Place Names. (1929) reprint 1993. Cloth. $82.50. 804 pp. .... Vendor G0259

Ohio

Statewide and Regional References

Atlas of Ohio, 88 county maps.
   Includes detailed maps of individual counties, all the back roads, streams, lakes, towns, etc. 11" x 16".
$14.95. .... Vendor G0611

Atlas of Ohio, Detailed Back Roads.
   This present-day atlas provides the researcher with the detail needed to conduct a proper search. It is the size of a Rand McNally atlas of the entire U.S. 11" x 15½".
$16.95. .... Vendor G0611

Atlases & Gazetteers: Ohio. Illus.
Paper. $16.95. 80 pp. .... Vendor G0632

Bell, Carol. **Abstracts from Biographies in John Struthers Stewart's History of Northeastern Ohio.**
Paper. $5.00. 7 pp. .... Vendor G0574

Bell, Carol W. **Ohio Guide to Genealogical Sources.** (1988) reprint 1993.
Cloth. $30.00. 372 pp. .... Vendor G0010

Bell, Carol Willsey. **Ohio Divorces: The Early Years.**
Paper. $35.00. 166 pp. .... Vendor G0512

Bell, Carol Willsey. **Ohio Genealogical Guide, 6th Edition.**
Paper. $18.00. 130 pp. .... Vendor G0512

Bell, Carol Willsey. **Ohio Wills and Estates to 1850: An Index.** 1981.
Cloth. $55.00. 400 pp. .... Vendor G0512

Berry, Ellen, and David Berry. **Early Ohio Settlers Purchasers of Land in East and East Central Ohio, 1800-1840.** 1989. Illus.
Cloth. $25.00. 330 pp. .... Vendor G0010

Berry, Ellen, and David Berry. **Early Ohio Settlers Purchasers of Land in Southwestern Ohio, 1800-1840.** (1986) reprint 1993. Illus.
Cloth. $30.00. 372 pp. .... Vendor G0010

Biographical Encyclopedia of Ohio of the 19th Century. (1876) reprint 1995.
   Many portraits.
Cloth. $74.00. 672 pp. + illus. .... Vendor G0259

KENTUCKY BOOKS IN PRINT, 1996 Edition

Collected & Compiled by Betty Masley, of IDL Research

In its second printing & now published by IDL Research, this help-ful 202-page catalog of **Kentucky** Genealogy Resource Materials lists 150 vendors, 1500 publications, plus resources for each county. Sources are locating: cemetery & funeral home records; 100+ family histories; microfilm of vital statistics, newspaper abstracts, census records, tax lists, manuscripts; military personnel & veterans' burial records; naturalization petitions; church records; African American genealogy, biographies & case studies; Records of the Bureau of Refugees, Freedmen & Abandoned Lands; Indian genealogy & Cherokee records. Also information about local & state societies' newsletters & publications.

202 pages $23.00 ppd.

OHIO BOOKS IN PRINT, 1994 Edition

Collected & Compiled by Betty Masley, of IDL Research

A helpful 125-page catalog of **Ohio** Genealogy Resource Materials listing 110 vendors, 1000 publications, and a resource directory for each county. Sources are shown for locating: cemetery & funeral home records; church records; Dutch, Italian & German emigrants' lists; Indian census rolls; microfilm of vital statistics, newspaper abstracts, census records, tax lists, manuscripts; military personnel records; veterans' burial records; naturalization petitions; plus valu-able information for researching biographies of African Americans in the US Army. Forty individual family histories & contacts for local & state societies.

125 pages $15.75 ppd.

**Order from IDL Research, Betty Masley,
PO Box 20654, Indianapolis, IN 46220-0654**

Bowers, Ruth, and Anita Short. **Gateway to The West**. 2 vols. (1967-1978) reprint 1989. Indexed.
A reprint of a magazine published from 1967 to 1978, it has the most important genealogical records of seventy-six of Ohio's eighty-eight counties.
Cloth. $150.00. 2,000 pp. .... Vendor G0010

Bowman, Mary L. **Abstracts & Extracts of the Legislative Acts and Resolutions of the State of Ohio: 1803-1821**. 1994. Indexed.
Cloth. $39.95. 359 pp. .... Vendor G0512

Broglin, Jana Sloan. **Index to the Official Roster of Ohio Soldiers in the War with Spain**. 1990. Indexed.
Cloth. $23.00. 78 pp. .... Vendor G0512

Broglin, Jana Sloan. **Roster of the Soldiers of Ohio in the War with Mexico**. (1897) reprint 1991. Indexed.
Cloth. $30.00. 275 pp. .... Vendor G0512

Burton, Ann, and Conrad Burton. **Born in Ohio & Living In Southwest Michigan 1860**. (1986) reprint 1993. Indexed.
One Microfiche. $5.00. 78 pp. .... Vendor G0094

Butterfield, C. W. **Historical Account of the Expedition Against Sandusky** Under Col. William Crawford in 1782, with Biographical Sketches, Personal Reminiscences & Descriptions of Interesting Localities. (1873) reprint 1993.
The Battle of Sandusky and the surrounding events comprised one of the most notable campaigns of the Western Border War of the Revolution. However, little had been written about it when this interesting book, which relied almost exclusively on original sources, was first published.
Cloth. $45.00. 403 pp. .... Vendor G0259

Butterfield, Consul Willshire. **History of the Girtys,** a Concise Acct. of the Girty Bros.—Thomas, Simon, James & George, & Their Half-Brother John Turner—Also of the Part Taken by Them in Lord Dunsmore's War, the Western Border War of the Revolution, and the Indian War, 1790-95. (1905) reprint 1995.
Cloth. $42.50. 425 pp. .... Vendor G0259

Caccamo, James F. **Marriage Notices from the** *Ohio Observer* Series. Indexed.
Although the primary focus is northeast Ohio, other marriages are noted from areas west where former Western Reserve residents had emigrated or New England where relatives of Western Reserve residents were located. Ohio's Western Reserve counties: Ashland (part), Ashtabula, Cuyahoga, Erie, Geauga, Huron, Lake, Lorain, Mahoning (part), Medina, Ottawa (part), Portage, Summit (part), and Trumbull.
Paper. $19.95. 208 pp. .... Vendor G0536

Canfield, Capt. S. S. **History of the 21st Regiment, Ohio Volunteer Infantry, in the War of the Rebellion**. (1893) reprint 1995.
Cloth. $32.50. 192 + 47 pp. .... Vendor G0259

Cayton. **The Frontier Republic: Ideology and Politics in the Ohio Country, 1780-1825**. 1986.
Studies the political formation of the state: land policies, government, and ideological conflicts.
Paper. $9.50. 197 pp. .... Vendor G0611

Darlington, William M. **An Account of the Remarkable Occurrences in the Life & Travels of Col. James Smith,** During His Captivity with the Indians, in the Years 1755-1759. (1870) reprint 1993.
Cloth, $29.00. Paper, $19.00. 190 pp. .... Vendor G0259

Dyer, Albion M. **First Ownership of Ohio Lands.** (1911) reprint 1997.
Contact vendor for information. 85 pp. .... Vendor G0011

Family History Library. **Research Outline: Ohio.**
Leaflet. $.25. 10 pp. .... Vendor G0629

Francy, Leila S. **Surname Index to History of the Upper Ohio Valley** with Family History and Biog. Sketches, A Statement of Its Resources, Industrial Growth and Commercial Advantages, Grant & Fuller, 1890. 2 vols.
Paper. $6.00. 46 pp. .... Vendor G0536

Green. **Pioneer Ohio Newspapers, 1793-1810 and 1802-1818:** Genealogical and Historical Abstracts. 2 vols. 1986, 1988. Indexed.

Two volumes of abstracts of the earliest Ohio newspapers include over 88,000 references to both ordinary people (farmers, merchants, and artisans) and prominent Ohioans. Volume II does not duplicate material from the first, but includes more early newspapers. Info. on marriages, obits, court and probate records, early ads, heirs, militia, land disputes, occupations, former residences, estate settlements, divorce, local events and disputes, military expeditions, and much more. Each abstract contains enough information to explain the context of the advertisement or article. Complete index (persons, place names, subjects).
Cloth. $26.00/vol., $52.00/set. 383 + 362 pp. .... Vendor G0611

Haid, John A. **The Historical Bibliography of Hamilton, Ohio, and Butler County, Ohio.** 2nd ed. 1994. Indexed. Illus.

This historical and genealogical reference work includes 90 pages on Butler County Courthouse, immigration, cemetery, church, birth, and death records, as well as a detailed 33-page index. It also covers the prehistory and history of the region, from the frontier days of Fort Hamilton to the present day.
Paper. $17.25. 325 pp. .... Vendor G0603

Hall. **The Shane Manuscript Collection: A Genealogical Guide to the Kentucky and Ohio Papers.** 1990.

While many genealogists and historians are familiar with the collection of Rev. John Dabney Shane's papers in the Draper Manuscripts, it often comes as a surprise that half of Shane's papers are located at the Presbyterian Historical Association in Philadelphia, and not in Draper's collection. The collection (36 reels of microfilm) reflects his interest in the history of the Presbyterian Church in very early KY and OH, and the migration of congregations into IL, IN, MO.
Paper. $12.00. 133 pp. .... Vendor G0611

Hatcher. **The Western Reserve: The Story of New Connecticut in Ohio.** 1991.

Describes this region's evolution from frontier community to industrial center—from Moses Cleveland's first surveying party and early settlement to the construction of the Ohio-Erie canal.
Paper. $14.00. 328 pp. .... Vendor G0611

Hayden, A. S. **The Disciples Early History in Western Reserve 1875**. (1875) reprint 1979. Indexed.
Cloth. $14.00. 476 pp. .... Vendor G0531

Heisey, John W. **Ohio Genealogical Research Guide**.
Paper. $12.00. 35 pp. .... Vendor G0574

Hildreth, S. P. **Memoirs of the Early Pioneer Settlers of Ohio,** with Narratives of Incidents and Occurrences in 1775. (1854) reprint 1995.
Paper. $35.00. 539 pp. .... Vendor G0011

Historical Account of Bouquet's Expedition Against the Indians in 1764. Preface by Francis Parkman, with a Biographical Sketch of General Bouquet. (1868) reprint 1993.
    This authentic and reliable narrative of one of the earliest British military expeditions into the "Northwest Territory" was originally published in English in 1765 and in French in 1769.
Cloth, $28.00. Paper, $18.00. xxiii + 162 pp. .... Vendor G0259

Howe, Henry. **Historical Collections of Ohio**. With 177 Engravings. (1848) reprint 1993.
Cloth. $59.50. 599 pp. .... Vendor G0259

Howe, Henry. **Historical Collections of Ohio**. 2 vols. (Rev. ed. 1888-1908) reprint 1994.
Cloth. $95.00/vol., $179.00/set. 992 + 911 pp. .... Vendor G0259

Hulbert, Archer Butler. **The Ohio River: A Course of Empire**. (1906) reprint 1996.
    The history of the territory along the Ohio, especially Pittsburgh, Wheeling, Marietta, Cincinnati, and Louisville.
Cloth. $45.00. 378 pp. .... Vendor G0259

Hutslar. **Log Construction in the Ohio Country, 1750-1850**. 1992.
    A rich source of social history as well as a practical source of building techniques, this extensive study of early log buildings includes archival research of diaries, local histories, traveler's accounts, and site photographs.
Paper. $19.95. 270 pp. .... Vendor G0611

Kilbourne, John. **1833 Ohio Gazetteer**. (1833) reprint 1981.
Cloth. $29.00. 494 pp. .... Vendor G0531

Masley, Betty J., comp. **Ohio Books in Print, 1994 Edition**.
    An 125-page catalogue of Ohio genealogy resource materials from 110 vendors. Advertisement on page 40.
Paper. $22.75. 125 pp. .... Vendor G0507

Maxwell, Fay. **Northwest Territory 1800 Census (Before Ohio's Statehood)**. Plus Index of Washington County, Ohio 1791-1803 Marriages and Thomas Summers *History of Marietta* Index, Plus Wm. P. Cutler's List of Signers of July 13, 1787 Ordinance. 1973. Indexed.
    ISBN 1-885463-20-0.
Paper. $13.25. 51 pp. .... Vendor G0135

Maxwell, Fay. **Ohio Charles Galbreath's** *History of Ohio* Index. 1973.
  ISBN 1-885463-23-5. Leaders of 1900s.
Paper. $6.75. 7 pp. .... Vendor G0135

Maxwell, Fay. **Ohio Indian, Revolutionary War, and War of 1812 Trails.** 1974.
Indexed. Illus.
  ISBN 1-885463-22-7.
Paper. $9.75. 59 pp. .... Vendor G0135

Maxwell, Fay. **Ohio Revolutionary War Soldiers 1840 Census and Grave Locations.** 1985. Indexed.
  ISBN 1-885463-24-3. Carries a four-way listing of both 1840 living and burials.
Paper. $13.50. 69 pp. .... Vendor G0135

Maxwell, Fay. **Ohio's Virginia Military Tract Settlers, Also 1801 Tax List.** 1991.
Indexed.
  ISBN 1-885463-25-1.
Paper. $12.25. 25 pp. .... Vendor G0135

Ohio Adjutant General's Department. **Roster of Ohio Soldiers in the War of 1812.**
(1968) reprint 1989.
Cloth. $18.00. 157 pp. .... Vendor G0011

Ohio Cemetery Records Extracted from the "Old Northwest" Genealogical Quarterly. (1984) reprint 1989. Indexed.
Cloth. $30.00. 495 pp. .... Vendor G0010

Ohio Genealogical Society. **1880 Ohio Census Index: Heads of Households and Other Surnames in Households Index.** 3 vols. 1991.
Cloth. $395.00. 3,252 pp. .... Vendor G0552

Ohio Genealogical Society. **First Families of Ohio, Official Roster, Vol. 2.** 1988.
  Key to 6,113 pre-1820 Ohio settlers applications.
Paper. $20.00. .... Vendor G0512

Ohio Genealogical Society. **The Ohio Genealogical Society Chapter Directory and Publications List.** 1996.
Paper. $10.00. 75 pp. .... Vendor G0512

Ohio Genealogical Society. **Ohio Source Records** from The Ohio Genealogical Quarterly. (1937-1944, 1986) reprint 1993. Indexed.
Cloth. $40.00. 666 pp. .... Vendor G0010

Ohio Historical Society. **Guide to Manuscripts at the Ohio Historical Society.**
Paper. $10.00. .... Vendor G0646

Ohio Historical Society. **Guide to Ohio City and Municipal Records.**
Paper. $4.00. .... Vendor G0646

Ohio Historical Society. **Guide to Primary Sources in Ohio.**
Paper. $3.95. .... Vendor G0646

Powell, Esther Weygandt. **Early Ohio Tax Records.** Reprinted with "The Index to Early Ohio Tax Records." 2 vols. in 1. (1971, 1973, 1985) reprint 1993.
Cloth. $40.00. 632 pp. total. .... Vendor G0010

Rerick, Rowland H. **State Centennial History of Ohio,** Covering the Periods of Indian, French and British Dominion, the Territory Northwest, and the Hundred Years of Statehood. (1902) reprint 1995.
Cloth. $45.00. 425 pp. .... Vendor G0259

Riegel, Mayburt Stephenson. **Early Ohioans' Residences from the Land Grant Records**.
Paper. $12.00. 62 pp. .... Vendor G0512

Schweitzer, George K. **Ohio Genealogical Research**. 1995. Illus.
History of the state, types of records (Bible through will), record locations, research techniques, listings of county records.
Paper. $15.00. 216 pp. .... Vendor G0569

Scott, Carol A. **Marriage and Death Notices of Wheeling, Western Virginia, and the Tri-State Area, 1818-1857**. 3 vols.
Extracted paid marriage and death notices from major newspapers published in Wheeling, WV. The newspapers carried notices of the people from West Virginia, western Pennsylvania, and southeastern Ohio. Volume I covers records from 1818 to 1857. Volume II covers records from 1858 to 1865. Volume III covers 1866 through 1870.
Paper. $9.50/vol. 90 + 104 + 110 pp. .... Vendor G0536

Smith, Clifford N. **Early Nineteenth-Century German Settlers in Ohio, Kentucky, and Other States**. German-American Genealogical Research Monograph Number 20. Parts 1-4C.
Part 1 (1984; iv + 36 pp. double-columned). ISBN 0-915162-22-9.
Part 2 (1988; ii + 56 pp. double-columned). ISBN 0-915162-23-7.
Part 3 (1988; ii + 60 pp. double-columned). ISBN 0-915162-25-5.
Part 4A: Surnames A Through J (1991; ii + 34 pp. double-columned). ISBN 0-915162-84-9.
Part 4B: Surnames K Through Z (1991; ii + 37 pp. double-columned). ISBN 0-915162-85-7.
Part 4C: Appendices (1991; ii + 26 pp. double-columned). ISBN 0-915162-85-7.
Contact vendor for information about additional parts.
Paper. $20.00/part. .... Vendor G0491

T.L.C. Genealogy. **The 1812 Census of Ohio: A State-Wide Index of Taxpayers**. 1992. Indexed.
A single, alphabetical list of all resident land owners in Ohio, as found in the Ohio Tax Duplicate for the year 1812.
Paper. $18.00. 221 pp. .... Vendor G0609

Templin, Ronald R. **The Templins of Ohio**. 1995. Indexed. Illus.
Contact vendor for information. .... Vendor G0096

Thomson, Peter G. **Bibliography of the State of Ohio,** Being a Catalog of the Books & Pamphlets Relating to the History of the State, the West & Northwest. With Complete Subject Index. (1880) reprint 1993.
Cloth. $55.00. 427 + 108 pp. .... Vendor G0259

Thorndale, William, and William Dollarhide. **County Boundary Map Guides to the U.S. Federal Censuses, 1790-1920: Ohio, 1790-1920**. 1987.
$5.95. .... Vendor G0552

Upton, Harriet T. **History of the Western Reserve**. With Biographies & Every-name Index Included in Vol. III. 3 vols. Edited by H. G. Cutler. Every-name Index by Lake Co. (OH) Genealogical Soc. (1910; Index, 1988) reprint 1995.
Cloth. $67.50/vol., $189.50/set. Index only: $19.50 (paper). 1,874 pp.; Index, 184 pp.
Vendor G0259

Walling, H. F. **1868 Ohio Atlas**. (1868) reprint 1995. Illus.
Paper. $26.50. 68 pp. .... Vendor G0531

Western Pennsylvania Genealogical Society. **Marriages & Deaths from Pittsburgh Dispatch 1858-1860**. 1993.
Over 4,500 names listed from a time before vital records were recorded in PA. Names from all over western PA, Ohio, West Virginia.
Paper. $15.00. .... Vendor G0615

Workman, Marjean Holmes, comp. **Index to the History of Northwestern Ohio, History of Paulding County by Everett A. Budd and Township and Personal Histories of Paulding County**. Originally published by H. H. Hardesty & Co. (1882) reprint 1995.
Paper. $12.00. .... Vendor G0704

Adams County

Evans, N. W., and E. B. Stivers. **History of Adams County,** from Its Earliest Settlement to the Present Time, Including Character Sketches of the Prominent Persons Identified with the First Century of the County's Growth. (1900) reprint 1994.
Cloth. $96.50. 946 pp. .... Vendor G0259

T.L.C. Genealogy. **Adams County, Ohio Deeds, 1797-1806**. 1990. Indexed.
Paper. $12.00. 165 pp. .... Vendor G0609

T.L.C. Genealogy. **Adams County, Ohio Deeds, 1806-1812**. 1990. Indexed.
Paper. $14.00. 198 pp. .... Vendor G0609

Allen County

Miller, Charles C., ed., with Dr. Samuel A. Baxter. **History of Allen County & Representative Citizens**. (1906) reprint 1993.
Cloth. $89.50. 872 pp. .... Vendor G0259

Ashland County

Baughman, A. J. **History of Richland & Ashland Counties**. (1901) reprint 1993.
Cloth. $86.00. 831 pp. .... Vendor G0259

Hill, George William, M.D. **History of Ashland County,** with Illustrations & Biographical Sketches. (1880) reprint 1993.
Cloth. $44.50. 408 pp. .... Vendor G0259

Ashtabula County

Ashtabula County Genealogical Society. **Birth Records 1867-1909 Ashtabula County, Ohio.**
Contact vendor for information. 565 pp. .... Vendor G0774

Ashtabula County Index to Microfilm of Marriage Returns from Ashtabula County, Ohio (1811-1900).
Paper. $27.50. 704 pp. .... Vendor G0536

Griswold, Glenn E. **Ohio Inscriptions: Ashtabula County (Windsor and Windsor Mills).** 1994.
Paper. $10.00. 39 pp. .... Vendor G0691

Sargent, M. P. **Pioneer Sketches: Scenes & Incidents of Former Days.** (1891) reprint 1993.
An entertaining & very useful account of the early days of Crawford Co., Pa., & Ashtabula Co., including biographical sketches of early settlers.
Cloth. $54.00. 512 pp. .... Vendor G0259

Williams, William W. **History of Ashtabula County,** with Illustrations & Biographical Sketches of Its Pioneers & Most Prominent Men. (1878) reprint 1993. Illus.
This originally oversized history has been reduced slightly to an 8½" x 11" format, in order to be more convenient to use. The type & illustrations are still clear & legible.
Cloth. $37.50. 256 pp. + illus. .... Vendor G0259

Athens County

1833 Citizens Records: Athens County, Ohio.
Taken from official government documents detailing the petitions sent to Congress in 1833 from the citizens of each county requesting that the government keep their Federal Banks within the boundaries of the county.
Paper. $4.00. .... Vendor G0549

Blower, James Girard. **Athens County, Ohio—Trimble Twp.—Ohio History.** Indexed by Fay Maxwell. 1964. Illus.
ISBN 1-885463-00-6. Many complete family histories from 1797-1960. Area now Burr Oaks, a vast fishing, boating, and recreation playground.
Paper. $23.50. 211 pp. .... Vendor G0135

Kocher, L. Richard. **A Listing of Entrymen on Lands in Athens Co., OH.** 1994. Indexed.
Acetate cover, GBC spiral bound. $21.00. 72 pp. .... Vendor G0487

Mitchell, Susan L. **The Hewitts of Athens County, Ohio.** 1989. Indexed. Illus.
History of county; genealogy of Hewitt and allied lines.
Cloth. $42.50. 455 pp. .... Vendor G0068

Auglaize County

Spear, Elmer C., comp. **Auglaize County Marriage Records, Books 1-7 (1848-1899).**
Paper. $24.95. 380 pp. .... Vendor G0536

Belmont County

1833 Citizens Records: Belmont County, Ohio.
  Taken from official government documents detailing the petitions sent to Congress in 1833 from the citizens of each county requesting that the government keep their Federal Banks within the boundaries of the county.
Paper. $4.00. .... Vendor G0549

Hanna, C. A. **Ohio Valley Genealogies,** Relating Chiefly to Families in Harrison, Belmont & Jefferson Cos., Oh., & Washington, Westmoreland & Fayette Cos., Pa. (1900) reprint 1990.
Contact vendor for information. 172 pp. .... Vendor G0010

McKelvey, A. T., ed. **Centennial History of Belmont County, & Representative Citizens.** (1903) reprint 1994.
Cloth. $85.00. 833 pp. .... Vendor G0259

Butler County

Haid, John A. **The Historical Bibliography of Hamilton, Ohio, and Butler County, Ohio.** 2nd ed. 1994. Indexed. Illus.
  This historical and genealogical reference work includes 90 pages on Butler County Courthouse, immigration, cemetery, church, birth, and death records, as well as a detailed 33-page index. It also covers the prehistory and history of the region, from the frontier days of Fort Hamilton to the present day.
Paper. $17.25. 325 pp. .... Vendor G0603

History & Biographical Cyclopedia of Butler County, with Illustrations & Sketches of Its Representative Men & Pioneers. (1882) reprint 1995.
Cloth. $69.50. 666 pp. .... Vendor G0259

Hover, Wright, Barnes, et al. **Memoirs of the Miami Valley.** 2 vols. (1919) reprint 1993.
Cloth. $63.00/Vol. I. $66.00/Vol. II. $124.50/set. 636 + 670 pp. .... Vendor G0259

Rerick Bros. **1895 Landowner Atlas and Art Folio.** (1895) reprint 1978-79. Indexed.
  Four pages of history added from Howe's 1890 Collection.
Cloth, $28.00. Paper, $17.00. 96 pp. .... Vendor G0531

Whitesell, Martha. **Abstracts of Biographies from a History of Butler Co.**
Paper. $5.00. 12 pp. .... Vendor G0574

Carroll County

Commemorative & Biographical Records of the Counties of Harrison & Carroll, Containing Biographical Sketches of Prominent & Representative Citizens & Many of the Early Settled Families. (1891) reprint 1994.
Cloth. $109.00. 1,150 pp. .... Vendor G0259

Hardesty, H. H. **1874 Historical and Landowner Atlas**. (1874) reprint 1979. Indexed. Illus.
Paper. $11.00. 108 pp. .... Vendor G0531

Harrison, Joseph T. **The Story of the "Dining Fork."** (1927) reprint 1994.
The "Dining Fork" is a region in northern Harrison and southern Carroll counties, including the town of Scio; this book is an entertaining and informative account of the lives of the pioneer families, especially the Harrisons, and includes a great deal of biographical information.
Cloth. $39.50. 370 pp. .... Vendor G0259

Maxwell, Fay. **Carroll & Harrison County, Ohio**. *Eckley & Perry 1921 History Index*. 1983.
ISBN 1-885463-01-4. Many migrated from Augusta County, Virginia into Carroll and Harrison counties and on to Athens, Morgan, and Perry counties, Ohio.
Paper. $12.25. 24 pp. .... Vendor G0135

Champaign County

Champaign County Genealogical Society. **Champaign County Guardianships to 1850**. 1993. Indexed.
Paper. $16.00. 70 pp. .... Vendor G0080

Champaign County Genealogical Society. **Champaign County Ohio**. 1991. Indexed. Illus.
County and biographical history.
Cloth. $69.00. 368 pp. .... Vendor G0080

Champaign Democrat—Centennial 15 June 1905. (1905) reprint 1987. Illus.
Centennial newspaper with histories and photos.
Paper. $5.00. 8 pp. .... Vendor G0080

History of Champaign County, Containing a History of the County, Its Cities, Towns, Etc.; General & Local Statistics, Portraits of Early Settlers & Prominent Men, Etc. (1881) reprint 1992.
Cloth. $89.50. 921 pp. .... Vendor G0259

Ridder, Edgar A., and Champaign County Genealogical Society. **An Atlas of Champaign County Landmarks**. (1987) reprint 1992. Indexed. Illus.
Lists all early schools, cemeteries, and churches.
Paper. $10.00. 85 pp. .... Vendor G0080

Clark County

1833 Citizens Records: Clark County, Ohio.
Taken from official government documents detailing the petitions sent to Congress in 1833 from the citizens of each county requesting that the government keep their Federal Banks within the boundaries of the county.
Paper. $4.00. .... Vendor G0549

History of Clark County, Containing a History of Its Cities, Towns, Etc. (1881) reprint 1993.
Cloth. $99.50. 1,085 pp. .... Vendor G0259

Clermont County

History of Clermont County, with Illustrations & Biographical Sketches of Its Prominent Men & Pioneers. With Index comp. by the Clermont Co. Genealogical Society. (1880) reprint 1993.
Cloth. $68.00. 557 + 121 pp. .... Vendor G0259

Smith. **Clermont County, OH, Land Records, 1787-1812: Surveys, Patents, Deeds & Mortgages**. 1990.
Thousands of persons listed.
Paper. $20.00. 168 pp. .... Vendor G0611

Smith. **Virginia Military Surveys of Clermont and Hamilton Counties, Ohio, 1787-1849**. 1985. Indexed. Illus.
Abstracted entries and surveys of the Virginia Military District of Ohio satisfying bounty warrants of Revolutionary War soldiers. Maps, historical background, photographs, a bibliography, and three indexes.
Cloth. $32.00. 253 pp. .... Vendor G0611

Smith, Alma Aicholtz, C.G.R.S. **Clermont County, Ohio Deeds and Mortgages: An Index 1791-1830**. 1991. Indexed. Illus.
Cloth. $37.50. 304 pp. .... Vendor G0547

Smith, Alma Aicholtz, C.G.R.S. **Clermont County, Ohio Land Records 1787-1812**. 1990. Indexed. Illus.
Cloth, $30.00. Paper, $20.00. 168 pp. .... Vendor G0547

Smith, Alma Aicholtz, C.G.R.S. **The Virginia Military Surveys of Clermont and Hamilton Counties, Ohio 1787-1849**. 1985. Indexed. Illus.
Cloth. $30.00. 253 pp. .... Vendor G0547

Whitt, Aileen M. **Clermont County, Ohio, Revolutionary War Veterans, Vol. II**. 1990. Indexed.
Transcripts of depositions, photographs of documents, and a complete index.
Cloth, $30.00. Paper, $20.00. 198 pp. .... Vendor G0611

Whitt, Aileen M. **Clermont County, Ohio, Revolutionary War Veterans, Vol. III**. 1991.
A continuation of Volume II described above.
Cloth, $30.00. Paper, $20.00. 196 pp. .... Vendor G0611

Whitt, Aileen M. **Clermont County, Ohio, Wills, Estates, and Guardianships, 1851-1900: An Index**. 1987.
  More of an annotated index, since the endnotes often supply important information above and beyond the usual scope of an index.
Cloth, $30.00. Paper, $20.00. 171 pp. .... Vendor G0611

Clinton County

History of Clinton County, Containing a History of Its Townships, Cities, Etc. (1882) reprint 1993.
Cloth. $105.00. 1,180 pp. .... Vendor G0259

Columbiana County

History of Columbiana County, with Illustrations & Biographical Sketches of Some of Its Prominent Men & Pioneers. (1879) reprint 1994.
Cloth. $39.50. 334 pp. .... Vendor G0259

Hunt, George D. **History of Salem & the Immediate Vicinity, Columbiana Co.** (1898) reprint 1993.
Cloth. $29.50. 241 pp. .... Vendor G0259

McCord, William B., ed. **History of Columbiana County, and Representative Citizens**. With Every-name Index. (1905) reprint 1994.
Cloth. $89.50. 848 + 49 pp. .... Vendor G0259

Coshocton County

Bahmer, William J. **Centennial History of Coshocton County**. 2 vols. (1909) reprint 1993.
  Volume I: History.
  Volume II: Biography.
Cloth. $52.50/vol., $95.00/set. 531 + 488 pp. .... Vendor

Hill, N. N., Jr. **History of Coshocton County, Its Past & Present, 1740-1881**. (1881) reprint 1993.
Cloth. $86.00. 838 pp. .... Vendor G0259

Hunt, William E. **Supplement to History of Coshocton County**. Compiled by Miriam C. Hunter for the Coshocton Public Library. (1903-4, 1964) reprint 1993.
Cloth. $28.00. 208 pp. typescript. .... Vendor G0259

Hunt, William E. **Historical Collections of Coshocton County**. A Complete Panorama of the County, from the Time of the Earliest Known Occupants Until the Present Time, 1764-1876. (1876; Index, 1964) reprint 1993.
Cloth. $32.00. 264 + 27 pp. index. .... Vendor G0259

Crawford County

Fisher, Jane, comp. **Crawford County, Ohio Court Records**.
Paper. $16.50. 210 pp. .... Vendor G0536

Perrin, William H., et al. **History of Crawford County & Ohio, Containing . . .**
Biographical Sketches & Portraits of Some Early Settlers & Prominent Men. (1881)
reprint 1993.
Cloth. $99.50. 1,047 pp. .... Vendor G0259

Sargent, M. P. **Pioneer Sketches: Scenes & Incidents of Former Days**. (1891) re-
print 1993.
  An entertaining & very useful account of the early days of Crawford Co., Pa., &
Ashtabula Co., including biographical sketches of early settlers.
Cloth. $54.00. 512 pp. .... Vendor G0259

Cuyahoga County

1833 Citizens Records: Cuyahoga County, Ohio.
  Taken from official government documents detailing the petitions sent to Congress
in 1833 from the citizens of each county requesting that the government keep their
Federal Banks within the boundaries of the county.
Paper. $4.00. .... Vendor G0549

Johnson, Crisfeld, comp. **History of Cuyahoga County, with Portraits & Biographical Sketches of Some of Its Prominent Men & Pioneers**. (1879) reprint 1993.
Cloth. $57.00. 534 pp. .... Vendor G0259

Squire, Dick. **Bedford Vignettes**. 1982. Indexed. Illus.
  See description under the following book.
Cloth. $32.50. 360 pp. .... Vendor G0495

Squire, Dick. **Bedford Village Views**. 1992. Indexed. Illus.
  Bedford Village Views and the preceding book, *Bedford Vignettes*, are two com-
pletely different books, portraying the history and genealogy of an early Western
Reserve village, with more than 200 photographs and maps in each volume.
Cloth. $26.50. 375 pp. .... Vendor G0495

Wickham, Gertrude Van Rensselaer. **Pioneer Families of Cleveland, 1796-1840**. 2
vols. in 1. (1914) reprint 1993.
  An invaluable work that establishes a connecting link between the genealogy of
New England & Ohio, through 400 family sketches.
Cloth. $69.50. 694 pp. .... Vendor G0259

Darke County

History of Darke County, Containing a History of the County, Its Cities, Towns,
Etc.; Portraits of Early Settlers & Prominent Men, Etc. (1880) reprint 1993.
Cloth. $79.50. 772 pp. .... Vendor G0259

Short, Anita, and Ruth Bowers. **Darke County, Ohio Cemetery Inscriptions: Greenville Township**. (1973) reprint 1995. Indexed.
Paper. $18.00. 178 pp. .... Vendor G0011

Short, Anita, and Ruth Bowers. **Darke County, Ohio Common Pleas Court Records, 1817-1860**. (1972) reprint 1995. Indexed.
Paper. $16.50. 148 pp. .... Vendor G0011

Short, Anita, and Ruth Bowers. **Darke County, Ohio Deed Records, 1817-1834**. (1977) reprint 1993. Indexed.
Paper. $17.50. 170 pp. .... Vendor G0011

Short, Anita, and Ruth Bowers. **Darke County, Ohio Marriages, 1817-1840 & Darke County, Ohio Will Abstracts, 1818-1857**. 2 vols. in 1. (c. 1965, 1966) reprint 1995. Indexed.
Paper. $17.00. 144 pp. in all. .... Vendor G0011

Whitesell, Martha. **Abstract from Biographies Printed in the History of Darke County, Ohio**.
Paper. $5.00. 11 pp. .... Vendor G0574

Delaware County

History of Delaware County & Ohio, with Biographical Sketches. (1880) reprint 1993.
Cloth. $89.50. 885 pp. .... Vendor G0259

Erie County

Aldrich, Lewis Cass, ed. **History of Erie County,** with Illustrations & Biographical Sketches of Some of Its Prominent Men & Pioneers. (1889) reprint 1993.
Cloth. $68.00. 653 pp. .... Vendor G0259

Fairfield County

Graham, A. A., comp. **History of Fairfield & Perry Counties,** Their Past & Present (reprinted without the History of the NW Territories and Ohio). (1883) reprint 1994.
Cloth. $99.50. 994 pp. .... Vendor G0259

Kocher, L. Richard. **A Listing of Entrymen on Lands in Fairfield Co., OH**. 1993. Indexed.
Acetate cover, GBC spiral bound. $19.00. 58 pp. .... Vendor G0487

Kocher, L. Richard. **Section Maps with Entrymen on Lands in Fairfield Co., OH, Vol. I**. 1994. Indexed. Illus.
Acetate cover, GBC spiral bound. $57.50. 316 pp. .... Vendor G0487

Kocher, L. Richard. **Section Maps with Entrymen on Lands in Fairfield Co., OH, Vol. II**. 1994. Indexed. Illus.
Acetate cover, GBC spiral bound. $47.50. 230 pp. .... Vendor G0487

Maxwell, Fay. **Fairfield County, Ohio Index of Hervey Scott's** *1795-1876 History* **Index &** *C. M. L. Wiseman History* **Index Plus Fairfield County, Lancaster 1803-1865 Will Index**. 1971.
  ISBN 1-885463-02-2.
Paper. $18.50. 102 pp. .... Vendor G0135

Scott, Hervey. **A Complete History of Fairfield County, 1795-1876**. (1877) reprint 1994.
Cloth. $35.00. 304 pp. .... Vendor G0259

Fayette County

Dills, R. S. **History of Fayette County,** Together with Historic Notes on the Northwest & the State of Ohio. (1891) reprint 1993.
Cloth. $99.50. 1,039 pp. .... Vendor G0259

Franklin County

Bareis, George F. **History of Madison Township,** Including Groveport & Canal Winchester, Franklin County. (1902) reprint 1993.
Cloth. $55.00. 515 pp. .... Vendor G0259

Martin, William T. **Franklin County, Ohio History (1858 Edition Reprint)**.
Cloth. $13.00. 460 pp. .... Vendor G0512

Martin, William T. **History of Franklin County:** A Collection of Reminiscences of the Early County with Biographical Sketches & a Complete History of the County to [1858]. (1858) reprint 1993.
Cloth. $49.00. 449 pp. .... Vendor G0259

Maxwell, Fay. **The 1880 Franklin and Pickaway Counties, Ohio History Illustrations Index**. 1984.
  ISBN 1-885463-12-X.
Paper. $5.00. 4 pp. .... Vendor G0135

Maxwell, Fay. **Franklin County, Ohio 1826, 1832, and 1842 Chattels**. 1978.
  ISBN 1-885463-05-7.
Paper. $33.25. 120 pp. .... Vendor G0135

Maxwell, Fay. **Franklin County, Ohio 1860 Mortality Schedules, Complete Death Records**. 1977.
  ISBN 1-885463-09-X.
Paper. $6.50. 24 pp. .... Vendor G0135

Maxwell, Fay. **Franklin County, Ohio 1864 Civil War Military Roster Index**. 1984.
  ISBN 1-885463-06-5.
Paper. $28.50. 98 pp. .... Vendor G0135

Maxwell, Fay. **Franklin County, Ohio, Columbus 1843 City Directory Indexed Including Important Events in Columbus 1797-1843**. Plus Franklin County Death Records 1811-1832 from Area Newspapers. 1977.
  ISBN 1-885463-03-0.
Paper. $13.25. 55 pp. .... Vendor G0135

Maxwell, Fay. **Franklin County, Ohio Franklinton Cemetery Records**. 1985.
  ISBN 1-885463-10-3.
Paper. $4.75. 14 pp. .... Vendor G0135

Maxwell, Fay. **Franklin County, Ohio German Village and Brewery History Including Index**. 1971.
  ISBN 1-885463-07-3. Village sits upon Colonel John McGowan's 1816 South Columbus Patent.
Paper. $10.00. 57 pp. .... Vendor G0135

Maxwell, Fay. **Franklin County, Ohio Living in a Landmark**. A Pictorial of German Village. 1971. Illus.
  ISBN 1-885463-08-1.
Paper. $6.25. 54 pp. .... Vendor G0135

Maxwell, Fay. **Franklin County, Ohio Scotch-Irish Nova Scotia Acadians Refugee Tract History**. 1974. Indexed.
  ISBN 1-885463-11-1. This is a first. The Scotch-Irish Protestant refugees from General Washington and the Revolutionary War. Coverage includes migratory and military service to the King, their refusal to change Protestant beliefs, and finally settling in the 48½-mile strip called the Refugee Tract in Franklin County, Ohio. Congress waited to eve of War of 1812 before fulfilling land grant promise.
Paper. $35.00. 160 pp. .... Vendor G0135

Maxwell, Fay. **Franklin County, Ohio Taxables of 1806, 1810, and 1814**. Plus Franklin County 1803-1865 Will Index. 1976. Indexed.
  ISBN 1-885463-04-9.
Paper. $12.25. 43 pp. .... Vendor G0135

Moore, Opha. **History of Franklin County**. 3 vols. (1930) reprint 1993.
Cloth. $50.00/vol., $139.00/set. 1,424 pp. .... Vendor G0259

Studer, Jacob J. **Columbus: Its History, Resources & Progress, with Numerous Illustrations**. (1873) reprint 1993.
Cloth. $61.00. 585 pp. .... Vendor G0259

Taylor, William Alexander. **Centennial History of Columbus & Franklin County**. 2 vols. (1909) reprint 1993.
Cloth. $85.00/vol., $159.50/set. 839 + 824 pp. .... Vendor G0259

Williams Bros. **1880 History of Franklin and Pickaway Counties**. (1880) reprint 1978.
  Includes 158-page index.
Cloth. $41.00. 591 pp. .... Vendor G0531

Gallia County

Evans, Henrietta C. **1819 Gallia County, OH Tax List**. (1984) reprint 1989.
Paper. $3.75. 10 pp. .... Vendor G0079

Evans, Henrietta C., and Mary P. Wood. **Abstracts of Gallia County Chancery Records, 1835-1852**. (1988) reprint 1993. Indexed.
Paper. $16.25. 75 pp. .... Vendor G0079

Evans, Henrietta C., and Mary P. Wood. **Death Notices, Obituaries and Marriage Notices Taken from the Gallia County, Ohio Newspapers from 1825 to 1875**. (1986) reprint 1990. Indexed.
Paper. $30.25. 277 pp. .... Vendor G0079

Evans, Henrietta C., and Mary P. Wood. **Early Gallia Court Records, 1846-1900**. (1984) reprint 1989.
    Naturalizations, licenses, minors, divorces.
Paper. $6.25. 24 pp. .... Vendor G0079

Evans, Henrietta C., and Mary P. Wood. **Gallipolis, Pictorial History**. 1990. Illus.
    Over 550 photos and copy.
Paper. $27.50. 174 pp. .... Vendor G0079

Evans, Henrietta C., and Mary P. Wood. **Index of Gallia County, Ohio 1900 Census**. 1981. Indexed.
Paper. $9.25. 45 pp. .... Vendor G0079

Kocher, L. Richard. **A Listing of Entrymen on Lands in Gallia Co., OH**. 1995. Indexed.
Acetate cover, GBC spiral bound. $21.00. 121 pp. .... Vendor G0487

Geauga County

1833 Citizens Records: Geauga County, Ohio.
    Taken from official government documents detailing the petitions sent to Congress in 1833 from the citizens of each county requesting that the government keep their Federal Banks within the boundaries of the county.
Paper. $4.00. .... Vendor G0549

Geauga County Historical Society, comp. **Pioneer & General History of Geauga County**. (1953) reprint 1994.
Cloth. $79.50. 783 pp. .... Vendor G0259

Pioneer & General History of Geauga County, with Sketches of Some of Its Pioneers & Prominent Men, 1798-1880. (1880) reprint 1993.
Cloth. $85.00. 832 pp. .... Vendor G0259

Greene County

Greene County, 1803-1908. Edited by a Committee of the Homecoming Assoc. (1908) reprint 1993.
Cloth. $29.50. 190 + 38 pp. .... Vendor G0259

Overton, Julie, ed. **Revolutionary War Veterans of Greene County, Ohio**. 1995. Indexed.
Paper. $30.50. 262 pp. .... Vendor G0702

Robinson, George F. **History of Greene County** Embracing the Organization of the County, Its Division into Townships . . . also a Roster of Ten Thousand of the Early Settlers . . . to 1840. (1902) reprint 1994.
Cloth. $89.50. 927 pp. .... Vendor G0259

Guernsey County

Portrait & Biographical Record of Guernsey County, Containing Biographical Sketches of Prominent and Representaative Citizens of the County. (1895) reprint 1995.
Cloth. $57.50. 541 pp. .... Vendor G0259

Hamilton County

Alexander, Susan R., comp. **The Diaries of John M. Miller of Westwood/Cincinnati, Ohio: Excerpts from 1869-1870 and 1881-1894**. 1993. Indexed. Illus.
John M. Miller (1822-1894) was the son of Mary (Ludlow) and George Carter Miller. His wife was the former Huldah Woodhull Nicholas, daughter of Sarah (Woodhull) and Elias Nicholas. Huldah and John Miller had 13 children. John Miller's diaries reflect his busy life as a devoted family man, staunch Presbyterian, carriage-manufacturing company president, and involved citizen. His first-person account vividly evokes the horse-and-buggy days of late 19th-century Westwood (where he lived) and Cincinnati (where he worked). Other frequently mentioned surnames include Applegate, Bruce, Burnham, Davis, Drake, Ernst, Gamble, Gibson, Glasby, Hazen, Hedges, Hinsch, Kugler, Lawrence, Logan, McMicken, Moore, Mussey, Oehlman, Peterson, Powell, Ricketts, Rowland, Sanders, Sayre, Walker, Ward, Williams, Wilson, and Wise.
Besides the 34-page name index, supplementary material consists of pictures of people, carriages, and buildings; maps; family notes and charts; and a table of notable events and items.
Cloth. $54.95. 634 pp. .... Vendor G0028

Ford, Henry A., and Kate B. Ford, comps. **History of Hamilton County,** with Illustrations & Biographical Sketches. (1881) reprint 1993.
Cloth. $48.00. 432 pp. .... Vendor G0259

Hall. **Cincinnati City Directory for 1825**. 1988.
A transcription of the original. Unlike other directories that only list prominent citizens, this one lists every head of household (male and female) residing in Cincinnati in 1825, along with their address, their occupation, and their place of birth! The birthplaces are especially helpful for this period preceding the 1850 census.
Paper. $9.00. 90 pp. .... Vendor G0611

Hamilton County Biographical Sketches Vol. III of *Memoirs of the Miami Valley*. (1919) reprint 1995.
Cloth. $56.50. 537 pp. .... Vendor G0259

History of Cincinnati & Hamilton County: Their Past & Present . . . Including Biographies & Portraits of Pioneers & Representative Citizens. (1894) reprint 1994.
Cloth. $99.50. 1,056 pp. .... Vendor G0259

Hover, Wright, Barnes, et al. **Memoirs of the Miami Valley**. 2 vols. (1919) reprint 1993.
Cloth. $63.00/Vol. I. $66.00/Vol. II. $124.50/set. 636 + 670 pp. .... Vendor G0259

Smith. **Virginia Military Surveys of Clermont and Hamilton Counties, Ohio, 1787-1849**. 1985. Indexed. Illus.
   Abstracted entries and surveys of the Virginia Military District of Ohio satisfying bounty warrants of Revolutionary War soldiers. Maps, historical background, photographs, a bibliography, and three indexes.
Cloth. $32.00. 253 pp. .... Vendor G0611

Smith, Alma Aicholtz, C.G.R.S. **Ohio Lands: Hamilton County Deed Book A 1787-1797**. 1992. Indexed. Illus.
Paper. $19.95. 87 pp. .... Vendor G0547

Smith, Alma Aicholtz, C.G.R.S. **The Virginia Military Surveys of Clermont and Hamilton Counties, Ohio 1787-1849**. 1985. Indexed. Illus.
Cloth. $30.00. 253 pp. .... Vendor G0547

Hancock County

Beardsley, D. B. **History of Hancock County,** from Its Earliest Settlement to the Present Time, Together with Reminiscences of Pioneer Life . . . and Biographical Sketches. (1881) reprint 1993.
Cloth. $49.50. 472 pp. .... Vendor G0259

History of Hancock County, Containing a History of the County, Its Townships, Villages . . . Biographies, Etc. (1886) reprint 1993.
Cloth. $89.50. 880 pp. .... Vendor G0259

Hardin County

Blue, Herbert T. O. **Centennial History of Hardin County, 1833-1933,** Including Centennial Celebration Program. (1933) reprint 1994.
Cloth. $27.00. 180 pp. .... Vendor G0259

History of Hardin County Containing a History of the County; Its Townships, Towns, Churches, Schools, Etc. . . . With biographical sketches. (1883) reprint 1995.
Cloth. $99.50. 1,064 pp. .... Vendor G0259

Harrison County

Commemorative & Biographical Records of the Counties of Harrison & Carroll, Containing Biographical Sketches of Prominent & Representative Citizens & Many of the Early Settled Families. (1891) reprint 1994.
Cloth. $109.00. 1,150 pp. .... Vendor G0259

Hanna, C. A. **Ohio Valley Genealogies,** Relating Chiefly to Families in Harrison, Belmont & Jefferson Cos., Oh., & Washington, Westmoreland & Fayette Cos., Pa. (1900) reprint 1990.
Contact vendor for information. 172 pp. .... Vendor G0010

Hanna, Charles A. **Historical Collections of Harrison County,** in the State of Ohio [Comprising Ohio Valley Genealogies]. (1900) reprint 1994. Indexed. Paper. $46.50. 636 pp. .... Vendor G0011

Harrison, Joseph T. **The Story of the "Dining Fork."** (1927) reprint 1994. The "Dining Fork" is a region in northern Harrison and southern Carroll counties, including the town of Scio; this book is an entertaining and informative account of the lives of the pioneer families, especially the Harrisons, and includes a great deal of biographical information. Cloth. $39.50. 370 pp. .... Vendor G0259

Maxwell, Fay. **Carroll & Harrison County, Ohio.** *Eckley & Perry 1921 History* **Index.** 1983. ISBN 1-885463-01-4. Many migrated from Augusta County, Virginia into Carroll and Harrison counties and on to Athens, Morgan, and Perry counties, Ohio. Paper. $12.25. 24 pp. .... Vendor G0135

Highland County

History of Ross & Highland Counties, with Illustrations & Biographical Sketches. (1880) reprint 1993. Cloth. $56.00. 532 pp. .... Vendor G0259

Whitesell, Martha. **Abstracts of Biographies Taken from the History of Ross and Highland Cos.** Paper. $3.00. 3 pp. .... Vendor G0574

Hocking County

Kocher, L. Richard. **A Listing of Entrymen on Lands in Hocking Co., OH.** 1993. Indexed. Acetate cover, GBC spiral bound. $21.00. 98 pp. .... Vendor G0487

Kocher, L. Richard. **Section Maps with Entrymen on Lands in Hocking Co., Oh., Vol. I.** 1993. Indexed. Illus. Acetate cover, GBC spiral bound. $47.50. 234 pp. .... Vendor G0487

Kocher, L. Richard. **Section Maps with Entrymen on Lands in Hocking Co., Oh., Vol. II.** 1993. Indexed. Illus. Acetate cover, GBC spiral bound. $47.50. 260 pp. .... Vendor G0487

Jackson County

Kocher, L. Richard. **A Listing of Entrymen on Lands in Jackson Co., OH.** 1995. Indexed. Acetate cover, GBC spiral bound. $23.00 164 pp. .... Vendor G0487

Maxwell, Fay. **Jackson County, Ohio Romain Aten Jones** *1842 History* **Index.** 1976. ISBN 1-885463-13-8. Includes early taxes. Paper. $5.00. 14 pp. .... Vendor G0135

Jefferson County

Doyle, Joseph B. **Twentieth Century of Steubenville & Jefferson County & Representative Citizens.** (1910) reprint 1993.
Cloth. $109.00. 1,196 pp. .... Vendor G0259

Francy, Leila S. **Genealogical Selections from the Steubenville Weekly Gazette, 1887.** Indexed.
Paper. $9.50. 96 pp. .... Vendor G0536

Francy, Leila S. **Genealogical Selections from the Steubenville Weekly Gazette, 1888.** Indexed.
Paper. $8.50. 89 pp. .... Vendor G0536

Francy, Leila S. **Genealogical Selections from the Steubenville Weekly Gazette, 1889.** Indexed.
Paper. $9.50. 130 pp. .... Vendor G0536

Francy, Leila S. **Genealogical Selections from the Steubenville Weekly Gazette, 1890.** Indexed.
Paper. $9.50. 139 pp. .... Vendor G0536

Francy, Leila S., comp. **Jefferson County Deaths Recorded in Steubenville, Ohio Newspapers (ca. 1875-79).** Indexed.
Paper. $16.95. 254 pp. .... Vendor G0536

Francy, Leila S. **Marriage Records of Jefferson County, Ohio Book 7 (1850-1866).** Indexed.
Paper. $21.95. 274 pp. .... Vendor G0536

Francy, Lelia S. **Marriage Records of Jefferson County, Ohio, Book 8, Pt. I (1865-1874).** Indexed.
Paper. $14.95. 159 pp. .... Vendor G0536

Francy, Leila S. **Marriage Records of Jefferson County, Ohio, Book 8, Pt. II (1874-1883).** Indexed.
    Also includes some later entries.
Paper. $14.95. 167 pp. .... Vendor G0536

Hanna, C. A. **Ohio Valley Genealogies,** Relating Chiefly to Families in Harrison, Belmont & Jefferson Cos., Oh., & Washington, Westmoreland & Fayette Cos., Pa. (1900) reprint 1990.
Contact vendor for information. 172 pp. .... Vendor G0010

Hunter, W. H., comp. **The Pathfinders of Jefferson County.** (1898) reprint 1993.
Cloth. $37.50. 311 pp. .... Vendor G0259

Ohio Historical Society. **Mt. Pleasant & Early Quakers.**
Paper. $4.00. .... Vendor G0646

Knox County

Caldwell and Starr. **1871 Landowner Atlas Including History and Business Directories**. (1871) reprint 1971. Illus.
Paper. $12.00. 33 pp. .... Vendor G0531

Hill, N. N., Jr., comp. **History of Knox County:** Its Past & Present. (1881) reprint 1993.
Cloth. $88.00. 854 pp. .... Vendor G0259

Norton, A. Banning. **History of Knox County,** from 1779 to 1862, Comprising Biographical Sketches, Anecdotes & Incidents of Men Connected with the County from Its First Settlement. (1862) reprint 1993.
Cloth. $45.00. Index to above, 240 pp., $25.00. 424 pp. .... Vendor G0259

Lake County

Maxwell, Fay. **Lake County, Ohio 1940 History Index**. 1975.
  ISBN 1-885463-14-6.
Paper. $4.00. 7 pp. .... Vendor G0135

Lawrence County

Kocher, L. Richard. **A Listing of Entrymen on Lands in Lawrence Co., OH**. 1995. Indexed.
Acetate cover, GBC spiral bound. $23.00. 162 pp. .... Vendor G0487

Licking County

Bushnell, Rev. Henry. **History of Granville, Licking Co**. (1889) reprint 1993.
Cloth. $42.00. 372 pp. .... Vendor G0259

Hill, N. N., Jr., comp. **History of Licking County:** Its Past & Present. (1881) reprint 1993.
Cloth. $85.00. 822 pp. .... Vendor G0259

Maxwell, Fay. **Licking County, Ohio Records Indexes to Licking County 1808-1822 Marriages and Isaac Smucker's** *Centennial History* **Index**. 1984.
  ISBN 1-885463-16-2.
Paper. $23.25. 117 pp. .... Vendor G0135

Logan County

History of Logan County & Ohio, Containing a History of the State . . . and Biographical Sketches. (1880) reprint 1993.
Cloth. $87.00. 840 pp. .... Vendor G0259

Hover, Wright, Barnes, et al. **Memoirs of the Miami Valley**. 2 vols. (1919) reprint 1993.
Cloth. $63.00/Vol. I. $66.00/Vol. II. $124.50/set. 636 + 670 pp. .... Vendor G0259

Lorain County

Brothers, Williams. **History of Lorain County, Ohio. With Illustrations & Biographical Sketches**. (1879) reprint 1993. Indexed. Illus.
Cloth. $51.00. 435 pp. .... Vendor G0055

Lorain County Chapter—OGS. **Index to the Census of 1870 for Lorain County, Ohio**. 1989. Indexed.
Paper. $9.50. 64 pp. .... Vendor G0055

Lorain County Chapter—OGS. **Index to the Census of 1880 for Lorain County, Ohio**. 1992. Indexed.
Paper. $11.50. 74 pp. .... Vendor G0055

Webber, A. R. **Early History of Elyria & Her People**. (1930) reprint 1993.
Cloth. $39.50. 326 pp. .... Vendor G0259

Webster, Frederick. **Legends of the Indian Hollow Road (Lorain County, Ohio)**. (1912/13) reprint 1987. Indexed.
Paper. $6.50. 40 pp. .... Vendor G0055

Wright, G. F., ed. **Standard History of Lorain County**. 2 vols. (1916) reprint 1994.
Cloth. $55.00/vol., $105.00/set. 1,062 pp. .... Vendor G0259

Lucas County

Killits, John M., ed. **History of Toledo & Lucas County, 1623-1923**. 3 vols. in 2. (1923) reprint 1993.
Cloth. $75.00/Vol. I. $125.00/Vols. II & III. $195.00/set. 762 +
1,383 pp. .... Vendor G0259

Lucas County Chapter OGS. **Index of Certificates of Naturalization from the Board of Election, Lucas County, Ohio**. Indexed.
Spiral binding. $23.00. 267 pp. .... Vendor G0703

Mahoning County

History of Trumbull & Mahoning Counties, with Illustrations & Biographical Sketches. 2 vols. (1882) reprint 1992.
Cloth. $54.50/vol., $99.50/set. 504 + 566 pp. .... Vendor G0259

Joseph, Lois J., and Sara Jay Joseph. **Saint Joseph's Church Cemetery and Rose Hill Cemetery Burial Records, Youngstown, Ohio**. 1995. Indexed.
Paper. $7.00. 37 pp. .... Vendor G0709

Twentieth Century History of Youngstown & Mahoning County & Representative Citizens. (1907) reprint 1994.
Cloth. $99.50. 1,030 pp. .... Vendor G0259

Marion County

History of Marion County, Containing a History of the County; Its Townships, Towns . . . Etc.; Portraits of Early Settlers and Prominent Men; Etc. With Biographies. (1883) reprint 1996.
Cloth. $105.00. 1,031 pp. .... Vendor G0259

Wilson, Sylvia D., and Ruth E. Wilson. **Biographies of Many Residents of Marion Co.,** & Review of the History of Marion Co. (1950) reprint 1993.
Cloth. $42.00. 370 pp. .... Vendor G0259

Maumee Region

Slocum, Charles E. **History of the Maumee River Basin,** from the Earliest Account to Its Organization into Counties. (1905) reprint 1993.
    The Maumee River Basin was organized into the counties of Allen, Fulton, Hancock, Hardin, Henry, Lucas, Mercer, Paulding, Putnam, Seneca, Van Wert, Williams, and Wood. This rare book covers the earliest history of the territory and makes fascinating and informative reading.
Cloth. $68.50. 638 + xx pp. .... Vendor G0259

Van Tassel, Charles Sumner. **Story of the Maumee Valley, Toledo and the Sandusky Region.** 4 vols. (1929) reprint 1995.
    Volumes I & II: History. 2,092 pp., $195.00.
    Volumes III & IV: Biography. 670 + 688 pp., $69.50/vol.
Cloth. $299.50/set. .... Vendor G0259

Medina County

Kraynek, Sharon L. D. **Births, Marriages, Deaths from 1886-1887 Medina Co. Gazette.** Indexed.
Paper. $9.50. 92 pp. .... Vendor G0536

Kraynek, Sharon L. D. **Births, Marriages, Deaths from 1892-1893 Medina Co. Gazette.** Indexed.
Paper. $9.95. 116 pp. .... Vendor G0536

Kraynek, Sharon L. D. **Births, Marriages, Deaths from 1896-1897**. Indexed.
Paper. $9.95. 128 pp. .... Vendor G0536

Kraynek, Sharon L. D. **Early Twentieth Century Chatham**. Indexed.
Paper. $9.50. 112 pp. .... Vendor G0536

Kraynek, Sharon L. D. **Event-Full:** Chippewa Lake Correspondence to Medina County [Ohio] Gazette Jan-Dec 1900. Indexed.
The Chippewa Lake area (located in Lafayette Township) had their own scribes who wrote a column for this newspaper in 1900. This book contains a whole year's correspondence showing the progression of events for the entire year.
Paper. $6.00. 58 pp. .... Vendor G0536

Kraynek, Sharon L. D. **Life and Times in Brunswick, Ohio**. Indexed.
Paper. $16.95. 199 pp. .... Vendor G0536

Kraynek, Sharon L. D. **Local Chips and Splinters, 1886-1888**. Indexed.
From the column in the *Medina County Gazette*.
Paper. $12.00. 140 pp. .... Vendor G0536

Kraynek, Sharon L. D. **Local Chips and Splinters**. Indexed.
A column from the 1889 *Medina County Gazette*. Mentions births, deaths, community events.
Paper. $5.00. 49 pp. .... Vendor G0536

Kraynek, Sharon L. D. **Local Happenings of Chippewa Lake**. Indexed.
Covers Jan. 1892-Dec. 1893.
Paper. $5.00. 55 pp. .... Vendor G0536

Kraynek, Sharon L. D. **Marriages, Deaths and Divorces, 1870, 1872-1875, Medina Co. Gazette**. Indexed.
Paper. $9.95. 124 pp. .... Vendor G0536

Kraynek, Sharon L. D. **Medina Co. Gazette Births, Marriages, Deaths from 1894-1895**. Indexed.
Paper. $9.95. 123 pp. .... Vendor G0536

Kraynek, Sharon L. D. **Medina County Gazette Happenings (1878-1898)**. Indexed.
Paper. $8.00. 113 pp. .... Vendor G0536

Kraynek, Sharon L. D. **Medina County Gazette Happenings (1899)**. Indexed.
Paper. $5.00. 54 pp. .... Vendor G0536

Kraynek, Sharon L. D. **Medina County, Ohio Civil War Veterans**. Indexed.
Paper. $6.00. 64 pp. .... Vendor G0536

Kraynek, Sharon L. D. **Medina County, Ohio Gleanings**. Indexed.
Includes a list of soldiers buried in Medina from the Civil War, transfers of Real Estate (1886-1887), a directory of Medina businesses from a listing in the *Gazette*, and 1886 Medina Village Officers.
Paper. $5.00. 34 pp. .... Vendor G0536

Kraynek, Sharon L. D. **Pioneer Folks**. Indexed.
In 1891 Chas. D. Neil, editor and publisher of the *Medina County Gazette* ran a

series of articles entitled "Pioneer Folks" in the weekly newspaper. Early settlers of the county recall their arrival to the county and name parents, siblings, place of origin, who received pensions from the War of the Rebellion, what they did for a living, etc. Paper. $6.00. 59 pp. .... Vendor G0536

Kraynek, Sharon L. D. **A Pioneer Perspective of Early Medina**. Indexed. Paper. $8.95. 89 pp. .... Vendor G0536

Kraynek, Sharon L. D. **Years Ago Now, Medina County [OH] Gazette 1854-1895**. Indexed.
Over 3,500 Medina County names mentioned.
Paper. $9.50. 129 pp. .... Vendor G0536

Medina County Historical Society. **History of Medina County**. (1948) reprint 1993. Cloth. $45.00. 419 pp. .... Vendor G0259

Meigs County

Kocher, L. Richard. **A Listing of Entrymen on Lands in Meigs Co., OH**. 1995. Indexed.
Acetate cover, GBC spiral bound. $19.00 49 pp. .... Vendor G0487

Larkin, Stillman Carter. **Pioneer History of Meigs County**. (1908) reprint 1994. Cloth. $32.50. 208 pp. .... Vendor G0259

Miami County

Hill, Leonard U., ed. **History of Miami County (1807-1953)**. (1953) reprint 1993. Cloth. $45.00. xii + 403 pp. .... Vendor G0259

History of Miami County. (1880) reprint 1993. Cloth. $89.50. 880 pp. .... Vendor G0259

Hover, Wright, Barnes, et al. **Memoirs of the Miami Valley**. 2 vols. (1919) reprint 1993.
Cloth. $63.00/Vol. I. $66.00/Vol. II. $124.50/set. 636 + 670 pp. .... Vendor G0259

Montgomery County

Drury, Rev. A. W. **History of the City of Dayton & Montgomery County**. 2 vols. (1909) reprint 1993.
Volume I: History.
Volume II: Biography.
Cloth. $95.00/vol., $185.00/set. 941 + 1,078 pp. .... Vendor

Edgar, John F. **Pioneer Life in Dayton & Vicinity**. (1896) reprint 1993. Cloth. $37.00. 289 pp. .... Vendor G0259

Hover, Wright, Barnes, et al. **Memoirs of the Miami Valley**. 2 vols. (1919) reprint 1993. Cloth. $63.00/Vol. I. $66.00/Vol. II. $124.50/set. 636 + 670 pp. .... Vendor G0259

Morgan County

Kocher, L. Richard. **A Listing of Entrymen on Lands in Morgan Co., OH**. 1993. Indexed.
Acetate cover, GBC spiral bound. $19.00. 64 pp. .... Vendor G0487

Robertson, Charles. **History of Morgan County,** with Portraits & Biographical Sketches of Some of the Pioneers & Prominent Men. With Modern Every-name Index. (1886) reprint 1996.
Cloth. $59.50. 538 + 57 pp. .... Vendor G0259

Muskingum County

Bell, Carol. **Muskingum Co. Genealogical Guide**.
Paper. $8.00. 46 pp. .... Vendor G0574

Everhart, J. F. **History of Muskingum County, 1794-1882,** with Illustrations & Biographical Sketches of Prominent Men & Pioneers. (1882) reprint 1992.
Cloth. $49.50. 481 pp. .... Vendor G0259

Hargrove, Sylvia, and Hilda E. Yinger. **Muskingum County Footprints, Vol. 2** (Vol. 1 is out of print). 1984. Indexed.
  Early guardianships and jurors, 1850 Mortality Schedule, Asbury Chapel baptisms, and more.
Paper. $9.00 + $.59 sales tax to OH residents. 60 pp. .... Vendor G0494

Hargrove, Sylvia, and Hilda E. Yinger. **Muskingum County Footprints, Vol. 3**. 1985. Indexed.
  Earliest land transfers, 1860 Mortality Schedule, 1900 death records, newspaper abstracts, and more.
Paper. $9.00 + $.59 sales tax to OH residents. 58 pp. .... Vendor G0494

Hargrove, Sylvia, and Hilda E. Yinger. **Muskingum County Footprints, Vol. 4**. 1985. Indexed.
  Will Record Index 1804-1831, church records, 1870 census and 1866 Atlas Index for some townships, church records, court records, and newspaper abstracts.
Paper. $9.00 + $.59 sales tax to OH residents. 60 pp. .... Vendor G0494

Hargrove, Sylvia, and Hilda E. Yinger. **Muskingum County Footprints, Vol. 5**. 1986. Indexed.

Muskingum County Genealogical Society
Chapter of OGS

P.O. Box 3066 • Zanesville, OH 43702-3066
Send SASE for current list of publications.
NEW: Birth and Death Record Indexes 1908-1970.

Naturalizations 1860-1875, more township indexes as in Vol. 4, Salt Creek Baptist and Muskingum Presbyterian Church records, newspaper abstracts from 1814.
Paper. $9.00 + $.59 sales tax to OH residents. 60 pp. .... Vendor G0494

Hargrove, Sylvia, and Hilda E. Yinger. **Muskingum County Footprints, Vol. 6**. 1986. Indexed.
Will Records Index beginning 1832, Probate Appearance Docket abstractions, interment records from St. Thomas Catholic Church, newspaper abstracts.
Paper. $9.00 + $.59 sales tax to OH residents. 62 pp. .... Vendor G0494

Hargrove, Sylvia, and Hilda E. Yinger. **Muskingum County Footprints, Vol. 7**. 1987. Indexed.
Conclusion of St. Thomas Church interments, Muskingum Chapter DAR members and ancestors, Trinity Church baptisms, will record, atlas and census indexes continued.
Paper. $9.00 + $.59 sales tax to OH residents. 70 pp. .... Vendor G0494

Hargrove, Sylvia, and Hilda E. Yinger. **Muskingum County Footprints, Vol. 8**. 1987. Indexed.
Greenwood cemetery inscriptions before 1895.
Paper. $13.25 + $.86 sales tax to OH residents. 132 pp. .... Vendor G0494

Hargrove, Sylvia, and Hilda E. Yinger. **Muskingum County Footprints, Vol. 9**. 1988. Indexed.
1820 census of Muskingum County. Complete copy of the census.
Paper. $11.25 + $.73 sales tax to OH residents. 163 pp. .... Vendor G0494

Maxwell, Fay. **Muskingum County, Ohio *J. F. Everhart History* Index and Muskingum County Duplicate Tax Lists of 1807**. 1976. Indexed.
ISBN 1-885463-19-7.
Paper. $10.75. 53 pp. .... Vendor G0135

Maxwell, Fay. **Muskingum County, Ohio Marriages 1804-1818 and Some of 1818-1835**. 1977. Indexed.
ISBN 1-885463-18-9.
Paper. $18.25. 86 pp. .... Vendor G0135

Mitchener, C. H., ed. **Tuscarawas and Muskingum Valley Ohio History 1775-1840 *Ohio Annals* Reprint**. Indexed by Fay Maxwell. (1876) reprint 1975.
ISBN 1-885463-27-8. Carries many land sales made prior to arrival in Ohio. Much early history not found in other county histories. Home of murdered Christian Indians.
Paper. $20.25. 392 pp. .... Vendor G0135

Muskingum County Footprints
Hilda E. Yinger
2740 Adamsville Road, Zanesville, Ohio 43701
If your ancestor was in this area, I can help. SASE for rates.

New Lisbon

Speaker, C. S., C. C. Connell, and George T. Farrell. **Historical Sketch of the Old Village of New Lisbon,** with Biographical Notes of Its Citizens Prominent in the Affairs of the Village, State & Nation. (1903) reprint 1996.
Cloth. $32.00. 203 pp. .... Vendor G0259

Paulding County

Ray, Keck (indexed by). **Paulding County, Ohio Census Index 1830, 1840, 1850, 1860**. 1996. Indexed.
Paper. $12.00. .... Vendor G0704

Workman, Marjean Holmes, comp. **Index to the History of Northwestern Ohio, History of Paulding County by Everett A. Budd and Township and Personal Histories of Paulding County**. Originally published by H. H. Hardesty & Co. (1882) reprint 1995.
Paper. $12.00. .... Vendor G0704

Perry County

Graham, A. A., comp. **History of Fairfield & Perry Counties,** Their Past & Present (reprinted without the History of the NW Territories and Ohio). (1883) reprint 1994.
Cloth. $99.50. 994 pp. .... Vendor G0259

Kocher, L. Richard. **A Listing of Entrymen on Lands in Perry Co., OH**. 1993. Indexed.
Acetate cover, GBC spiral bound. $21.00. 60 pp. .... Vendor G0487

Kocher, L. Richard. **Section Maps with Entrymen on Lands in Perry Co., OH, Vol. I**. 1993. Indexed. Illus.
Includes Hopewell, Jackson, Monday Creek, Reading, and Thorn Townships. Contains county map showing the survey ranges, townships, and sections, along with the current township boundaries.
Acetate cover, GBC spiral bound. $47.50. 203 pp. .... Vendor G0487

Kocher, L. Richard. **Section Maps with Entrymen on Lands in Perry Co., OH., Vol. II**. 1994. Indexed. Illus.
Includes Madison, Clayton, Pike, Salt Lick, Coal, Harrison, Bearfield, Pleasant, and Monroe Townships.
Acetate cover, GBC spiral bound. $47.50. 236 pp. .... Vendor G0487

Maxwell, Fay. **Perry County Ohio Clement L. Martzolff *1902 History* Index**. 1983. ISBN 1-885463-26-X.
Paper. $9.00. 18 pp. .... Vendor G0135

Pickaway County

Kocher, L. Richard. **A Listing of Entrymen on Lands East of the Scioto River in Pickaway Co., OH**. 1993. Indexed.
Acetate cover, GBC spiral bound. $17.00. 29 pp. .... Vendor G0487

Kocher, L. Richard. **Section Maps with Entrymen on Lands in Pickaway Co., OH East of the Scioto River**. 1993. Indexed. Illus.
Acetate cover, GBC spiral bound. $47.50. 253 pp. .... Vendor G0487

Maxwell, Fay. **The 1880 Franklin and Pickaway Counties, Ohio History Illustrations Index**. 1984.
   ISBN 1-885463-12-X.
Paper. $5.00. 4 pp. .... Vendor G0135

Van Cleaf, Aaron R., ed. **History of Pickaway County & Representative Citizens**. (1906) reprint 1993.
Cloth. $88.00. 882 pp. .... Vendor G0259

Weaver, Darlene F. **Pickaway County, Ohio Probate Court Abstracts—From Order Book I 1852-1858**. 1995. Indexed.
Paper. $14.00. 108 pp. .... Vendor G0519

Williams Bros. **1880 History of Franklin and Pickaway Counties**. (1880) reprint 1978.
   Includes 158-page index.
Cloth. $41.00. 591 pp. .... Vendor G0531

Pike County

Kocher, L. Richard. **A Listing of Entrymen on Lands East of the Scioto River in Pike Co., OH**. 1995. Indexed.
Acetate cover, GBC spiral bound. $21.00. 67 pp. .... Vendor G0487

Portage County

Holm, James B., assisted by Lucille Dudley. **Portage Heritage. History of Portage County:** Its Towns & Townships, & the Men & Women Who Have Developed Them; Its Life, Institutions & Biographies, Facts & Lore. (1957) reprint 1992.
Cloth. $85.00. 824 pp. .... Vendor G0259

Portraits & Biographical Record of Portage & Summit Counties, Containing Biographical Sketches of Many Prominent & Representative Citizens. (1898) reprint 1994.
Cloth. $95.00. 988 pp. .... Vendor G0259

Preble County

Gilbert, Audrey. **Obituary Abstracts—Preble Co. OH Newspapers Vol. V**. 1995. Indexed.
Paper. $36.00. 331 pp. .... Vendor G0530

Gilbert, Audrey. **Preble County OH Land Records Vol. VII**. 1996. Indexed.
Paper. $41.00. 389 pp. .... Vendor G0530

Gilbert, Audrey. **Twin Valley Tidbits Vol. II**. 1996. Indexed.
Paper. $20.50. 165 pp. .... Vendor G0530

Shilt, Rose. **Preble County, Ohio 1850 Census**. Indexed.
Cloth. $17.00. 195 pp. .... Vendor G0512

Short, Anita, and Ruth Bowers. **Preble County, Ohio Cemetery Inscriptions**. (1969) reprint 1994. Indexed.
Paper. $15.00. 106 pp. .... Vendor G0011

Short, Anita, and Ruth Bowers. **Preble County, Ohio Common Pleas Court Records, 1810-1850**. (1970) reprint 1995. Indexed.
Paper. $16.00. 142 pp. .... Vendor G0011

Short, Anita, and Ruth Bowers. **Preble County, Ohio Deed Records, 1808-1821**. (1978) reprint 1993. Indexed.
Paper. $15.00. 108 pp. .... Vendor G0011

Short, Anita, and Ruth Bowers. **Preble County, Ohio Marriage Records, 1808-1840**. 2 vols. in 1. (1966, 1967) reprint 1994. Indexed.
Paper. $17.50. 148 pp. in all. .... Vendor G0011

Short, Anita, and Ruth Bowers. **Preble County, Ohio Will Abstracts, 1806-1854**. 2 vols. in 1. (1967, 1973) reprint 1995. Indexed.
Paper. $14.00. 93 pp. in all. .... Vendor G0011

Richland County

Baughman, A. J. **History of Richland & Ashland Counties**. (1901) reprint 1993.
Cloth. $86.00. 831 pp. .... Vendor G0259

Brinkerhoff, Gen. Roeliff. **A Pioneer History of Richland County, Ohio**. 1993.
Cloth. $29.45. 195 pp. .... Vendor G0728

Graham, A. A., comp. **History of Richland County** (Including the Original Boundaries): Its Past & Present, Containing . . . Its Cities, Towns, & Villages . . . & Biographies & Histories. (1880) reprint 1993.
Cloth. $95.00. 941 pp. .... Vendor G0259

Henney, M. J., comp. **From the Annals of Richland County, Ohio**. 1996.
Cloth. $29.00. 240 pp. .... Vendor G0728

Ohio Genealogical Society. **Marlow-Patterson Cemetery, Springfield Twp., Richland Co., Ohio**. 1960.
Paper. $4.00. 10 pp. .... Vendor G0512

Richland County Genealogical Society. **1870 Richland County Ohio Federal Census Index**.
Paper. $10.00. 83 pp. .... Vendor G0728

Richland County Genealogical Society. **Richland County, Ohio Marriage Records 1813-1871**. 1993.
Cloth. $32.95. 430 pp. .... Vendor G0728

Ross County

Bennett, Henry Holcomb, ed. **The County of Ross:** A History of Ross County from the Earliest Days . . . with Biographical Sketches. (1902) reprint 1995.
Cloth. $76.00. 736 pp. .... Vendor G0259

History of Ross & Highland Counties, with Illustrations & Biographical Sketches. (1880) reprint 1993.
Cloth. $56.00. 532 pp. .... Vendor G0259

Kocher, L. Richard. **A Listing of Entrymen on Lands East of the Scioto River in Ross Co., OH**. 1994. Indexed.
Acetate cover, GBC spiral bound. $17.00. 50 pp. .... Vendor G0487

Portrait & Biographical Record of the Scioto Valley. (1894) reprint 1993.
Cloth. $47.00. 429 pp. .... Vendor G0259

Whitesell, Martha. **Abstracts of Biographies Taken from the History of Ross and Highland Cos**.
Paper. $3.00. 3 pp. .... Vendor G0574

Sandusky County

Meek, Basil, ed. & comp. **Twentieth Century History of Sandusky County** & Representative Citizens. (1909) reprint 1993.
Cloth. $95.00. 934 pp. .... Vendor G0259

Sandusky Region

Van Tassel, Charles Sumner. **Story of the Maumee Valley, Toledo and the Sandusky Region**. 4 vols. (1929) reprint 1995.
    Volumes I & II: History. 2,092 pp., $195.00.
    Volumes III & IV: Biography. 670 + 688 pp., $69.50/vol.
Cloth. $299.50/set. .... Vendor G0259

Scioto County

Kocher, L. Richard. **A Listing of Entrymen on Lands East of the Scioto River in Scioto Co., OH**. 1995. Indexed.
Acetate cover, GBC spiral bound. $21.00 105 pp. .... Vendor G0487

Seneca County

Burton, Conrad. **Descendants of Abraham and Elizabeth Electa Payne Burton of Seneca Co., OH and Koscuisko/Wabash Cos. IN**. 1991. Indexed. Illus.
Paper. $10.00. 77 pp. .... Vendor G0094

Butterfield, Consul W. **History of Seneca County,** Containing a Detailed Narrative of the Principal Events That Have Occurred Since Its First Settlement . . . with Biographical Sketches. (1848) reprint 1995.
Cloth. $35.00. 252 pp. .... Vendor G0259

A Centennial Biographical History of Seneca County. (1902) reprint 1995.
Cloth. $77.50. 757 pp. .... Vendor G0259

Shelby County

Hover, Wright, Barnes, et al. **Memoirs of the Miami Valley**. 2 vols. (1919) reprint 1993.
Cloth. $63.00/Vol. I. $66.00/Vol. II. $124.50/set. 636 + 670 pp. .... Vendor G0259

Stark County

Perrin, William H., ed. **History of Stark County,** with an Outline Sketch of Ohio. (1881) reprint 1995.
Cloth. $97.50. 1,010 pp. .... Vendor G0259

Summit County

Grismer, Karl H. **Akron & Summit County**. (1952) reprint 1993.
Cloth. $85.00. 834 pp. .... Vendor G0259

Perrin, William H., ed. **History of Summit County**. (1881) reprint 1993.
Cloth. $99.50. 1,056 pp. .... Vendor G0259

Portraits & Biographical Record of Portage & Summit Counties, Containing Biographical Sketches of Many Prominent & Representative Citizens. (1898) reprint 1994.
Cloth. $95.00. 988 pp. .... Vendor G0259

Trumbull County

History of Trumbull & Mahoning Counties, with Illustrations & Biographical Sketches. 2 vols. (1882) reprint 1992.
Cloth. $54.50/vol., $99.50/set. 504 + 566 pp. .... Vendor G0259

Upton, Harriet Taylor. **Twentieth Century History of Trumbull County:** A Narrative Account of Its Historical Progress, Its People & Its Principal Interests. 2 vols. (1909) reprint 1993.
Cloth. $54.50/vol., $99.50/set. 643 + 436 pp. .... Vendor G0259

Tuscarawas County

History of Tuscarawas County. (1884) reprint 1994.
Cloth. $99.50. 1,007 pp. .... Vendor G0259

Lowry, James W. **Haskins Genealogy: The Descendants of Jonas Haskins (1788-1837) of Dutchess Co., New York, and Uhrichsville, Ohio.** 1992. Indexed. Illus.
    Includes Tuscarawas and Harrison Co., Ohio, local history.
Cloth. $29.95. 350 pp. .... Vendor G0035

Mitchener, C. H., ed. **Tuscarawas and Muskingum Valley Ohio History 1775-1840** *Ohio Annals* Reprint. Indexed by Fay Maxwell. (1876) reprint 1975.
    ISBN 1-885463-27-8. Carries many land sales made prior to arrival in Ohio. Much early history not found in other county histories. Home of murdered Christian Indians.
Paper. $20.25. 392 pp. .... Vendor G0135

Vinton County

Kocher, L. Richard. **A Listing of Entrymen on Lands in Vinton Co., OH.** 1994. Indexed.
Acetate cover, GBC spiral bound. $21.00. 125 pp. .... Vendor G0487

Ogan, Lew. **History of Vinton County,** Wonderland of Ohio. (1952) reprint 1993.
Cloth. $39.50. 314 pp. .... Vendor G0259

Warren County

Bogan, Dallas R. **Early Transportation in Warren County (OH).** 1992. Indexed. Illus.
Paper. $16.95. 196 pp. .... Vendor G0335

Bogan, Dallas R. **Warren County's Involvement in the Civil War.** 1991. Indexed.
Paper. $17.00. 228 pp. .... Vendor G0335

Carlisle Citizens. **Carlisle, the Jersey Settlement in Ohio 1800-1990.** Edited by Harriet E. Foley. 1980. Indexed. Illus.
Cloth. $39.75. 221 pp. .... Vendor G0335

Chamberlain, Charles E., and Martha B. Chamberlain. **New Jersey Presbyterian Church 1813-1988, Carlisle, Ohio, 175 Years**. 1988. Illus.
Cloth, $27.50. Paper, $22.50. 187 pp. .... Vendor G0335

Dunn, Chester L., and Jessie Van Meter. **Late Birth Records—Probate Court 1876-1933**. 3 vols. 1980, 1991. Indexed.
    Vol. 1: Books 1-7.
    Vol. 2: Books 8-12.
    Vol. 3: Recorded 1953-1959.
Paper. $9.00/vol. 43 + 63 + 146 pp. .... Vendor G0335

Dunn, Chester L., comp., and Warren Co. (OH) Genealogical Society. **Warren Co. Births 1909-1919, by Townships**. 1992. Indexed.
Paper. $37.00. 388 pp. .... Vendor G0335

Dunn, Chester L. **Warren County Death Records**. 3 vols. 1991.
    Vol. 1: 1909-1915.
    Vol. 2: 1916-1920.
    Vol. 3: 1921-1925.
Paper. $12.00/vol. .... Vendor G0335

History of Warren County, Containing a History of the County; Its Townships, Towns, Etc. . . . With biographies. (1882) reprint 1995.
Cloth. $105.00. 1,070 pp. .... Vendor G0259

Hover, Wright, Barnes, et al. **Memoirs of the Miami Valley**. 2 vols. (1919) reprint 1993.
Cloth. $63.00/Vol. I. $66.00/Vol. II. $124.50/set. 636 + 670 pp. .... Vendor G0259

Warren Co. (OH) Genealogical Society. **Heir Lines—WCGS Quarterly**. Edited by Harriet Foley. 1981.
Subscription $10.00/yr. $3.00 for back issues. Approx. 120 pp./yr. .... Vendor G0335

Warren Co. (OH) Genealogical Society. **Warren Co. Cemeteries, Vol. 1. Morrow Cemetery**. 1983. Indexed.
Paper. $7.00. 84 pp. .... Vendor G0335

Warren Co. (OH) Genealogical Society. **Warren Co. Cemeteries, Vol. 2. Harlan Twp. Cemeteries**. 1985. Indexed.
Paper. $7.00. 44 pp. .... Vendor G0335

Warren Co. (OH) Genealogical Society. **Warren Co. Cemeteries, Vol. 3. Union Twp. Cemeteries of Deerfield & Fellowship**. 1985. Indexed.
Paper. $7.50. 53 pp. .... Vendor G0335

Warren Co. (OH) Genealogical Society. **Warren Co. Cemeteries, Vol. 4. Springboro Cemetery, Clearcreek Township**. 1986. Indexed. Illus.
Paper. $12.00. 110 pp. .... Vendor G0335

Warren Co. (OH) Genealogical Society. **Warren Co. Cemeteries, Vol. 5. Hamilton Twp.: Hopkinsville, Maineville, Murdock**. 1986. Indexed.
Paper. $9.25. 72 pp. .... Vendor G0335

Warren Co. (OH) Genealogical Society. **Warren Co. Cemeteries, Vol. 6. Old Cemeteries in Eight Townships**. 1988. Indexed.
Paper. $11.50. 97 pp. .... Vendor G0335

Warren Co. (OH) Genealogical Society. **Warren Co. Cemeteries, Vol. 7. Thirteen Cemeteries: Lebanon Pioneer & Washington Twp**. 1988. Indexed.
Paper. $12.00. 105 pp. .... Vendor G0335

Dunn, Chester, and Dorothy Linkous. **Warren Co. Cemeteries, Vol. 8. Miami Cemetery at Corwin**. 1990. Indexed. Illus.
Paper. $26.00. 191 pp. .... Vendor G0335

Marshall, Russell M., Sr., and Warren Co. (OH) Genealogical Society. **Warren Co. Cemeteries, Vol. 9. Woodhill Cemetery at Franklin**. 1990. Indexed.
Paper. $24.00. 179 pp. .... Vendor G0335

Warren Co. (OH) Genealogical Society. **Warren Co. Cemeteries, Vol. 10. Lebanon Cemetery**. 1993. Indexed.
Paper. $27.00. 214 pp. .... Vendor G0335

Washington County

1833 Citizens Records: Washington County, Ohio.
Taken from official government documents detailing the petitions sent to Congress in 1833 from the citizens of each county requesting that the government keep their Federal Banks within the boundaries of the county.
Paper. $4.00. .... Vendor G0549

Dickinson, C. E. **History of Belpre, Washington Co**. (1920) reprint 1996.
Cloth. $34.00. 243 pp. .... Vendor G0259

Eldridge, Carrie. **Washington County, Ohio Tax List, 1817, and Non-Resident Taxes**. 1801. Indexed. Illus.
Paper. $20.00. 102 pp. .... Vendor G0632

Graham, Bernice, and Elizabeth S. Cottle. **Abstract of Probate Records, Washington County, Ohio**. Wills, Estates & Guardianships [1789-1855]. (1982) reprint 1995.
Paper. $16.00. 154 pp. .... Vendor G0011

Graham, Bernice, and Elizabeth S. Cottle. **Washington County, Ohio Marriages, 1789-1840**. (1976) reprint 1989. Indexed.
Paper. $14.00. 117 pp. .... Vendor G0011

Maxwell, Fay. **Northwest Territory 1800 Census (Before Ohio's Statehood)**. Plus Index of Washington County, Ohio 1791-1803 Marriages and Thomas Summers *His-*

tory of Marietta Index, Plus Wm. P. Cutler's List of Signers of July 13, 1787 Ordinance. 1973. Indexed.
  ISBN 1-885463-20-0.
Paper. $13.25. 51 pp. .... Vendor G0135

Maxwell, Fay. **Washington County, Ohio Marriages 1804-1823 Indexed**. 1974. Illus.
  ISBN 1-885463-29-4.
Paper. $7.75. 26 pp. .... Vendor G0135

Thode, Ernest. **Index to Naturalization Records of Washington County, OH**. 1988.
Paper. $14.00 postpaid ($14.91 in OH). 66 pp. .... Vendor G0197

Zenglein, Dieter, et al. **To the Banks of the Ohio**. Translated from German by Ernest Thode. 1988. Index available. Illus.
  Fascinating German letters; history of migration from Kusel, Palatinate, Germany, to Fearing Twp., Washington County, OH.
Paper. $14.00 postpaid ($14.91 in OH). 64 pp. .... Vendor G0197

Wayne County

Commemorative Biographical Record of Wayne County, Containing Biographical Sketches of Prominent & Representative Citizens & Many of the Early Families. (1889) reprint 1994.
Cloth. $64.00. 608 pp. .... Vendor G0259

Douglass, Ben. **History of Wayne County,** from the Days of the Pioneers & First Settlers. (1878) reprint 1993.
Cloth. $87.50. 868 pp. .... Vendor G0259

Williams County

Goodspeed, Weston A., and Charles Blanchard, eds. **County of Williams, Historical & Biographical,** with an Outline Sketch of the N.W. Territory, the State & Miscellaneous Matters. (1882) reprint 1993.
Cloth. $85.00. 820 pp. .... Vendor G0259

Williams County Genealogical Society. **Madison Township, Williams County, Ohio Cemetery Records (Inclusive to August 1995)**. 1996. Indexed.
Spiral binding. $17.00. 274 pp. .... Vendor G0705

Wood County

Commemorative Historical & Biographical Record of Wood County; Its Past & Present, Early Settlement & Development. (1897) reprint 1993.
Cloth. $129.50. 1,386 pp. .... Vendor G0259

Wood County Chapter OGS. **Lake Township Cemetery, Wood County, Ohio**. 1995. Indexed. Illus.
Paper. $16.50. xviii + 194 pp. .... Vendor G0706

Wood County Chapter OGS. **Probate Death Records, Wood County, Ohio, Volume I, 1867-1887**. 1995. Indexed. Illus.
Paper. $7.50. xviii + 194 pp. .... Vendor G0706

Wyandot County

History of Wyandot County. With Biographical Sketches. (1884) reprint 1993.
Cloth. $99.00. 1,056 pp. .... Vendor G0259

Oklahoma

Statewide and Regional References

Baker, T. Lindsay, and Julie P. Baker. **The WPA Oklahoma Slave Narratives**.
The Bakers have collected all the known WPA Oklahoma "slave narratives" in this volume, including fourteen never published before. An important resource for Oklahoma and Southwest historians.
Paper. $24.95. 544 pp. .... Vendor G0611

Bicha. **The Czechs in Oklahoma**. 1980.
Paper. $4.95. 81 pp. .... Vendor G0611

Bivins, Murphy, and Tankersley, eds. **SW Oklahoma Keys**. Indexed. Illus.
An index-type pedigree summary, which lists more than 7,400 names in alphabetical order with vital statistics and links with parents and spouses.
Cloth. $30.00. 552 pp. .... Vendor G0661

Bolt, Helen Deister. **Kiowa Agency Mission Schools of Oklahoma 1881-1914**.
An extraction of names and pertinent information from the mission records located at the Oklahoma Historical Society Indian Archives in Oklahoma City.
Paper. $10.00. 47 pp. .... Vendor G0661

North Central Oklahoma
Rooted In The Past-Growing For The Future

1996 Winner of Prestigious Certificate of Commendation by the American Association For State and Local History

Limited first edition published December, 1995 by North Central Oklahoma Historical Association, Inc. in a 1,088 page, two-volume hardbound, illustrated, indexed book. Eight documented chapters include the Cherokee Strip Land Run of 1893, the native Americans, cowboys and settlers, the oil boom, family, church and school histories. **$75.25 per set plus $8.00 S&H.** Send check or money orders to: **NCOHA, Inc., P.O. Box 2811, Dept. GPC, Ponca City, OK 74602.** Include name, street address, city, state, zip, and telephone. See index on http://www.brigadoon.com/~nipperb.

Clevenger, Anna B., comp. **100 Ancestor Charts**. 6 vols. Indexed.
Paper. $12.50/vol. 111 pp. ea. .... Vendor G0661

Clevenger, Anna B., comp. **Surname Index to the Federal Land Tract Books of Oklahoma Territory**. 22 vols.
   The land tract books are the records of the first owners of land, showing name, legal description, and date of entry for all of Oklahoma Territory. Contact vendor for information regarding the contents of each volume.
Paper. $10.00/vol. .... Vendor G0661

Family History Library. **Research Outline: Oklahoma**.
Leaflet. $.25. 10 pp. .... Vendor G0629

Garrison, Linda Norman, comp. **1890 Oklahoma & Indian Territory Census of Union Veterans and Widows**. 1991. Indexed.
Paper. $15.00. 61 pp. .... Vendor G0661

Garrison, Linda Norman, ed. **Successful Bidders of the Big Pasture Land Opening 1906**. 1992. Indexed.
   Compiled from a list published in *The Temple Tribune* in 1907. Lists the name of the bidders and their post office address.
Paper. $10.00. 24 pp. .... Vendor G0661

Index to Applications for Registration for Registration for Homestead Entry Within the Kiowa, Comanche and Apache Ceded Lands.
   List of registrants for the land lottery for the opening of the Kiowa-Comanche-Apache Lands (now Comanche, Cotton, Tillman, Caddo, and Kiowa counties) at Ft. Sill. Does not include list of registrants at El Reno for same lands.
Paper. $10.00. 24 pp. .... Vendor G0661

Morris, et al. **Historical Atlas of Oklahoma**. 1986.
   Historical atlases are invaluable to the genealogist.
Paper. $19.95. Approx. 200 pp. .... Vendor G0611

North Central Oklahoma Historical Association, Inc. **North Central Oklahoma: Rooted in the Past—Growing for the Future**. 2 vols. 1995. Indexed. Illus.
   Limited first edition. Eight documented chapters include the Cherokee Strip Land Run of 1893, the Native Americans, cowboys and settlers, the oil boom, family, church, and school histories.
Cloth. $83.25/set. 1,088 pp. .... Vendor G0524

Oklahoma Genealogical Society. **1880 and 1890 Census, Canadian District, Cherokee Nation, Indian Territory**.
Paper. $8.50. .... Vendor G0729

Oklahoma Genealogical Society. **Records of the Choctaw Nation**.
   Choctaw census of 1896; miscellaneous cemetery, church, and marriage records.
16 mm microfilm. $17.00. .... Vendor G0729

Oklahoma Genealogical Society. **Subject Index to the Oklahoma Genealogical Society Quarterly, 1955-1990**.
   By county; by name; alphabetical.
Paper. $10.00. .... Vendor G0729

Olsen, Monty, comp. **Choctaw Emigration Records 1831-1856, Volume I**. 1990.
Paper. $15.00. 281 pp. .... Vendor G0710

Olsen, Monty, comp. **Choctaw Emigration Records 1831-1856, Volume II**. 1990.
Paper. $15.00. 106 pp. .... Vendor G0710

Portrait & Biographical Record of Oklahoma, Commemorating the Achievements
of Citizens Who Have Contributed to the Progress of Oklahoma & the Development
of Its Resources. (1901) reprint 1994.
Cloth. $119.00. 1,298pp. .... Vendor G0259

Southern California Genealogical Society. **Land! Georgia Land Lotteries; Oregon
Donation Land; Oklahoma Land Rushes**.
Paper. $2.00. 10 pp. .... Vendor G0656

Southern California Genealogical Society. **Sources of Genealogical Help in
Oklahoma**.
Paper. $1.50. 10 pp. .... Vendor G0656

Strickland. **The Indians in Oklahoma**. 1980. Illus.
   An interesting history, with many pictures.
Paper. $11.95. 176 pp. .... Vendor G0611

Tankersley, Jewell R., comp. **1910 Township Maps of 23 Southwest Oklahoma
Counties**.
Paper. $7.00. 39 pp. .... Vendor G0661

Tedford, Sandra. **Chickasaw Nation, Indian Territory (Oklahoma) Marriage Book
D**. 1996. Indexed.
Paper. $17.50. 100 pp. .... Vendor G0711

Thorndale, William, and William Dollarhide. **County Boundary Map Guides to the
U.S. Federal Censuses, 1790-1920: Oklahoma, 1820-1920**. 1987.
$5.95. .... Vendor G0552

Wright. **A Guide to the Indian Tribes of Oklahoma**. 1986.
   Oklahoma is home to sixty-seven Indian tribes, and this guide gives detailed infor-
mation on the customs, location, and history of each.
Paper. $14.95. 300 pp. .... Vendor G0611

Bryan County

Bryan County Heritage Association. **Bryan County, Oklahoma Cemeteries Volume
I**. 1985. Indexed.
Paper. $15.00. 176 pp. .... Vendor G0710

Bryan County Heritage Association. **Bryan County, Oklahoma Cemeteries Volume
II**. 1986. Indexed.
Paper. $15.00. 173 pp. .... Vendor G0710

Bryan County Heritage Association. **Bryan County, Oklahoma Cemeteries Volume
III**. Edited by Wanda Shelton. 1987. Indexed.
Paper. $15.00. 144 pp. .... Vendor G0710

Bryan County Heritage Association. **Bryan County, Oklahoma Cemeteries Volume IV**. Edited by Wanda Shelton. 1992. Indexed.
Paper. $25.00. 305 pp. .... Vendor G0710

Ellis, Wanda M. **Bryan County, Oklahoma Pre-Statehood Marriages July 1902-November 1907**. 1995. Indexed.
Paper. $20.00. 216 pp. .... Vendor G0710

Manery, Phyllis J., comp. **Ancestor Charts Preserving Yesterday for Tomorrow, Volumes 1 and 2**. 1991. Indexed.
Paper. $15.00/vol. 200+ pp./vol. .... Vendor G0710

Caddo County

Garrison, Linda Norman. **1917 Census of the Comanche Indian Tribe, Kiowa Indian Agency, Anadarko, OK**. Indexed by Polly Lewis Murphy. Indexed.
Paper. $12.00. 71 pp. .... Vendor G0661

Washburn, Faye. **1895 Census of the Comanche Indian Tribe, Kiowa Indian Agency, Anadarko, Okla. Terr**. 1994. Indexed.
Paper. $12.00. 59 pp. .... Vendor G0661

Washburn, Faye. **1905 Census of the Comanche Indian Tribe, Kiowa Indian Agency, Anadarko, Okla. Terr**. Indexed.
Paper. $12.00. 57 pp. .... Vendor G0661

Choctaw County

Olsen, Monty. **1885 Choctaw Census Kiamitia County**. 1996.
Paper. $10.00. 65 pp. .... Vendor G0710

Cleveland County

Cleveland County Genealogical Society. **First Families of Cleveland County, OK—A Lineage Society**. 1993. Indexed. Illus.
Cloth. $22.40. 360 pp. .... Vendor G0183

Comanche County

English, Darold, comp. **Index to *The Chronicles of Comanche County***. 1990.
  The Chronicles of Comanche County was a periodical from 1955 to 1961 of the Comanche County Historical Society, which no longer exists.
Paper. $8.00. 126 pp. .... Vendor G0661

Goodin, Barbara, and Kenneth Goodin. **An Index to Area Indian Cemeteries**. 1994.
  Lists alphabetically the names of approximately 1,700 persons buried in eight separate cemeteries located predominately in Comanche County.
Paper. $15.00. 103 pp. .... Vendor G0661

Goodin, Barbara. **Relocation of Post Oak Cemetery, Fort Sill, Oklahoma, 1959**.
Paper. $12.00. 46 pp. .... Vendor G0661

Irwin, Jay E., and Judy Ray, comps. **Index to Deaths, *Lawton Constitution* Newspaper Vol. I, 1905-1917**.
Paper. $10.00. 34 pp. .... Vendor G0661

Lawton Monument Company Sales Records [Lawton, Comanche Co., OK].
List of sales for monuments with name of deceased and dates of birth and death.
Paper. $12.00. 47 pp. .... Vendor G0661

Murphy, Polly Lewis. **Brief History of Geronimo School**.
Includes school board members, teachers, superintendents, list of pupils 1907-08, scholastic census from County Superintendent.
Paper. $5.00. 19 pp. .... Vendor G0661

Murphy, Polly Lewis, comp. **Comanche County, OK Marriage Records, Books 1 and 2, Aug. 1901-25 Feb. 1906**. 1984. Indexed.
Paper. $15.00. 143 pp. .... Vendor G0661

Murphy, Polly Lewis, comp. *The Geronimo Advocate* **[Comanche Co., OK] Vol. 1: 1906**. Vol. 2: 1907-1912.
Excerpts of marriages, deaths, births, social and business news from the newspaper of Geronimo, OK.
Paper. $15.00/vol. 146 + 160 pp. .... Vendor G0661

Murphy, Polly Lewis, comp. **Owners of Cattle Brands Recorded at the Red Store, Lawton Okla. Terr., 1891-1908**. Compiled from records of Cynthia Wilson. 1983.
Paper. $15.00. 128 pp. .... Vendor G0661

Murphy, Polly Lewis, comp. **Records of Medical History of Fort Sill, Indian Territory, Feb. 1873-May 1880 and of Fort Sill, OK, 1903-1913**. 1984.
Includes information on soldiers on sick call and in the hospital and of daily reports of the medical units on the post and on scouting parties. Interesting accounts of military life on the frontier in the late 1880s.
Paper. $15.00. 81 pp. .... Vendor G0661

Murphy, Polly Lewis, comp. **So Lingers Memory—Inventories of Ft. Sill and Old Ft. Reno, OK Cemeteries**.
Includes Ft. Sill Main Post, Apache Indian, Comanche Indian, and Comanche Mission cemeteries.
Paper. $25.00. 321 pp. .... Vendor G0661

Poli, Twila (transcriber and indexer). **Cache Cemetery, 1902-1995, Comanche County, OK**. 1995. Indexed.
Paper. $15.00. 117 pp. .... Vendor G0661

Tankersley, Jewell R., comp. **Index to Tax Lists of Comanche County, OK, 1911**. 1984.
Paper. $15.00. 111 pp. .... Vendor G0661

Cotton County

Garrison, Linda Norman, comp. **Cotton County, Oklahoma, Birth Records 1912-1918**. Indexed.
Paper. $12.00. 41 pp. .... Vendor G0661

Delaware County

Delaware County Cemetery Readers. **Cemeteries and Burial Places of Delaware County, Oklahoma**. 1995+. Indexed. Illus.
   Four volumes, each indexed, and consolidated index.
Cloth, $30.00/vol. Paper, price varies per vol. .... Vendor G0544

Grady County

Murphy, Polly Lewis. **Full Name Index to** *History of Rush Springs* [Grady Co., OK].
Paper. $5.00. 12 pp. .... Vendor G0661

Greer County

Martin, Jodean McGuffin. **The Mangum Star Weekly 1898-1900**. 1994. Indexed.
Paper. $30.00. 230 pp. .... Vendor G0712

Murphy, Polly Lewis (extracted by). **Blooming #3 Precinct, Greer County, OK, Register 1912-1946**.
   Includes full names, school district, date of district, date of registration, age, residence, occupation, political party, and notes.
Paper. $5.00. 19 pp. .... Vendor G0661

Harmon County

Murphy, Polly Lewis (copied and indexed by). **Spooner Funeral Home Records 1926-1938 [Hollis, Harmon County, OK]**. Indexed.
Paper. $12.00. 135 pp. .... Vendor G0661

Jackson County

Bolt, Helen Deister, comp. **Jackson County (OK) Marriage Index 1907-1910**.
Paper. $5.00. 20 pp. .... Vendor G0661

Kiowa County

Garrison, Linda Norman (abstracted by). **Abstracts from** *The Mountain Parker*, Mountain Park, Kiowa Co., OK, 1935-1944.
   Marriages, deaths, births, family visits, etc.
Paper. $12.00. 81 pp. .... Vendor G0661

Oklahoma County

Oklahoma Genealogical Society. **Index to Probate, Oklahoma County, Oklahoma, 1895-1920**.
Paper. $12.00. .... Vendor G0729

Oklahoma Genealogical Society. **Marriage Records, Oklahoma County, Oklahoma Territory, 1889-1907**.
Paper. $15.00. .... Vendor G0729

Tulsa County

Apsley, Marmie, Jack McGinty, and Donald A. Wise. **1910 Federal Census Schedules for Broken Arrow, Tulsa County, Oklahoma and Adjoining Townships**. 1993. Indexed.
   Includes townships of Boles, Fry, Lynn Lane, and Willow Springs.
Paper. $12.50. 146 pp. .... Vendor G0059

Apsley, Marmie, Jerrie Townsend, and Donald A. Wise, eds. **The Broken Arrow Chronicles**. 1987.
   History of Historical Society; profiles of early settlers and historic homes.
Paper. $6.50. 69 pp. .... Vendor G0059

Broken Arrow Genealogical Society. **Broken Arrow Funeral Home Records 1912-1939, with Addenda**. 1996. Indexed.
   Covers the first three volumes of early funeral home records with additional information from city cemetery records, 1910 federal census, and tombstone records.
Paper. Contact vendor for price. Est. 200 pp. .... Vendor G0059

Broken Arrow Genealogical Society. **Oklahoma Green Country Cemeteries, Broken Arrow & Coweta**. 1984. Indexed.
Unbound. $14.00. 180 pp. .... Vendor G0059

Wise, Donald A. **First Census of Broken Arrow, Oklahoma, 1904**. 1994. Indexed. Illus.
Paper. $6.50. 28 pp. .... Vendor G0059

Wise, Donald A., comp. **Tracking Through Broken Arrow, Oklahoma**. 1987. Illus.
    Early history of the town and KATY railroad.
Paper. $6.50. 69 pp. .... Vendor G0059

Wagoner County

Broken Arrow Genealogical Society. **Oklahoma Green Country Cemeteries, Volume II, Western Wagoner County**. 1989. Indexed.
Unbound. $17.00. 226 pp. .... Vendor G0059

Washington County

Bartlesville Genealogical Society. **Washington County, Oklahoma Index of Marriage Records 1907-1920**. 1988.
    Book is organized in alphabetical order by grooms and brides.
Paper. $22.00. 258 pp. .... Vendor G0278

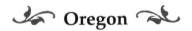

Oregon

Statewide and Regional References

Banvard, Theodore James Fleming. **Goodenows Who Originated in Sudbury, Massachusetts 1638 A.D.** 1994. Indexed. Illus.
Cloth. $78.50. 952 pp. .... Vendor G0116

Cottage Grove Genealogical Society. **1890 Civil War Veterans & Widows Census, State of Oregon**. Indexed.
Paper. $39.00. 459 pp. .... Vendor G0505

Cottage Grove Genealogical Society. **Honor Roll of Oregon Grand Army of Republic 1881-1935**.
Paper. $11.00. 96 pp. .... Vendor G0505

Dilts, Bryan Lee, comp. **1860 Oregon Census Index: Heads of Household and Other Surnames in Household Index**. 1985.
Cloth. $33.00. 68 pp. .... Vendor G0552

Dilts, Bryan Lee, comp. **1870 Oregon Census Index: Heads of Household and Other Surnames in Household Index**. 1985.
Cloth. $47.00. 119 pp. .... Vendor G0552

Family History Library. **Research Outline: Oregon**.
Leaflet. $.25. 7 pp. .... Vendor G0629

Genealogical Forum of Oregon. **Lone Fir Cemetery, Early Sexton Records**.
Paper. $10.75. .... Vendor G0633

Genealogical Forum of Oregon. **Oregon Guide to Genealogical Sources**. 1994.
Paper. $25.00. .... Vendor G0633

Lenzen, Connie Miller. **Research in Oregon**.
Paper. $6.50. 29 pp. .... Vendor G0627

Military Casualties and MIA's, Oregon WWII.
Paper. $17.50. .... Vendor G0633

Oregon Genealogical Society. **Abstracts of the Gate City Journal**.
Paper. $22.00. .... Vendor G0634

Oregon Genealogical Society. **Oregon Pioneers, Volume 1 (OGS Pio. Cert.)**.
Paper. $10.00. .... Vendor G0634

Oregon Genealogical Society. **Oregon Pioneers, Volume 2 (OGS Pio. Cert.)**.
Paper. $9.00. .... Vendor G0634

Oregon Genealogical Society. **Oregon Pioneers, Volume 3 (A-B)**.
Paper. $17.00. .... Vendor G0634

Oregon Genealogical Society. **Oregon Pioneers, Volume 3 (C-D-E)**.
Paper. $22.00. .... Vendor G0634

Oregon Genealogical Society. **Oregon Pioneers, Volume 3 (F-G-H)**.
Paper. $17.00. .... Vendor G0634

Oregon Genealogical Society. **Register Guard Obits. Vol. 1 1962-72**.
Paper. $22.00. .... Vendor G0634

Oregon Genealogical Society. **Register Guard Obits. Vol. 2 1973-79**.
Paper. $22.00. .... Vendor G0634

Oregon Genealogical Society. **Register Guard Obits. Vol. 3 1980-81**.
Paper. $22.00. .... Vendor G0634

Oregon Genealogical Society. **Register Guard Obits. Vol. 4 1982-83**.
Paper. $22.00. .... Vendor G0634

Oregon Genealogical Society. **Register Guard Obits. Vol. 5 1984-85**.
Paper. $22.00. .... Vendor G0634

Oregon Genealogical Society. **Register Guard Obits. Vol. 6 1986-87**.
Paper. $22.00. .... Vendor G0634

Oregon Provisional Land Claims, Vols. I-VIII.
Paper. $13.50. .... Vendor G0633

Southern California Genealogical Society. **Land! Georgia Land Lotteries; Oregon Donation Land; Oklahoma Land Rushes**.
Paper. $2.00. 10 pp. .... Vendor G0656

Thorndale, William, and William Dollarhide. **County Boundary Map Guides to the U.S. Federal Censuses, 1790-1920: Oregon, 1850-1920**. 1987.
$5.95. .... Vendor G0552

Baker County

Genealogical Forum of Oregon. **Yesterday's Roll Call, Vol. I 1860-1910: Baker, Sherman & Umatilla County Cemetery Records**.
Paper. $14.00. .... Vendor G0633

Columbia County

Genealogical Forum of Oregon. **Columbia County, Oregon Marriage Records, 1855-1900**.
Paper. $6.00. .... Vendor G0633

Coos County

Genealogical Forum of Oregon. **Some Cemetery Records of Coos & Curry County, Oregon**.
Paper. $17.00. .... Vendor G0633

Curry County

Genealogical Forum of Oregon. **Some Cemetery Records of Coos & Curry County, Oregon**.
Paper. $17.00. .... Vendor G0633

Deschutes County

Summers, Barbara, Betty Bennett, and Ray Bennett. **Oregon 1920 Deschutes County Census**. 1995. Indexed.
Spiral binding. $20.00. 115 pp. + index. .... Vendor G0713

Douglas County

Cottage Grove Genealogical Society. **Comstock Cemetery**.
Paper. $5.00. 12 pp. .... Vendor G0505

Lane County

Cottage Grove Genealogical Society. **1905 Military Census of Lane County, Oregon**. 2 vols in 1. Indexed.
Paper. $25.00. 258 pp. .... Vendor G0505

Cottage Grove Genealogical Society. **Funeral Register, Cottage Grove, Oregon**.
Paper. $23.00. 100 pp. .... Vendor G0505

Cottage Grove Genealogical Society. **Lane County, Oregon, Marriage Records, Vol. I 1852-1869**. Indexed.
Paper. $7.00. 65 pp. .... Vendor G0505

Cottage Grove Genealogical Society. **Lane County, Oregon, Marriage Records, Vol. II 1870-1879**. Indexed.
Paper. $10.00. 91 pp. .... Vendor G0505

Cottage Grove Genealogical Society. **Lane County, Oregon, Marriage Records, Vol. III 1880-1889**. Indexed.
Paper. $10.00. 88 pp. .... Vendor G0505

Cottage Grove Genealogical Society. **Lane County, Oregon, Marriage Records, Vol. IV 1890-1900**. Indexed.
Paper. $15.50. 130 pp. .... Vendor G0505

Cottage Grove Genealogical Society. **Masonic Records of Cottage Grove Lodge #51 A.F. & A.M. 1895-1991**.
Paper. $15.00. 203 pp. .... Vendor G0505

Oregon Genealogical Society. **1860 Lane Co., OR Census**.
Paper. $12.00. .... Vendor G0634

Oregon Genealogical Society. **1870 Lane Co., OR Census**.
Paper. $12.00. .... Vendor G0634

Oregon Genealogical Society. **1880 Lane Co., OR Census**.
Paper. $17.00. .... Vendor G0634

Oregon Genealogical Society. **1900 Lane Co., OR Census**.
Paper. $10.00. .... Vendor G0634

Oregon Genealogical Society. **1910 Lane Co., OR Census, Vol. 1**.
Paper. $17.00. .... Vendor G0634

Oregon Genealogical Society. **1910 Lane Co., OR Census, Vol. 2**.
Paper. $17.00. .... Vendor G0634

Oregon Genealogical Society. **1910 Lane Co., OR Census, Vol. 3**.
Paper. $17.00. .... Vendor G0634

Oregon Genealogical Society. **1910 Lane Co., OR Census, Vol. 4**.
Paper. $17.00. .... Vendor G0634

Oregon Genealogical Society. **1910 Lane Co., OR Census, Vol. 5**.
Paper. $22.00. .... Vendor G0634

Oregon Genealogical Society. **1910 Lane Co., OR Master Index**.
Paper. $10.00. .... Vendor G0634

Walling, Albert G., comp. & pub. **Illustrated History of Lane County**. (1884) reprint 1993.
Cloth. $53.00. 508 pp. .... Vendor G0259

Lincoln County

Oregon Genealogical Society. **1900 Lincoln Co., OR Census Index**.
Paper. $7.00. .... Vendor G0634

Oregon Genealogical Society. **1910 Lincoln Co., OR Census Index**.
Paper. $21.00. .... Vendor G0634

Oregon Genealogical Society. **At Rest in Lincoln Co., Index**.
Paper. $5.00. .... Vendor G0634

Oregon Genealogical Society. **Lincoln Co., OR Marriages**.
Paper. $21.00. .... Vendor G0634

Malheur County

Oregon Genealogical Society. **1900 Malheur Co., OR Census Index**.
Paper. $8.00. .... Vendor G0634

Oregon Genealogical Society. **Malheur Co., OR Cemetery Book**.
Paper. $25.00. .... Vendor G0634

Oregon Genealogical Society. **Malheur Co., OR Marriages**.
Paper. $12.00. .... Vendor G0634

Multnomah County

Marriage Records of Multnomah County, Oregon, 1855-1873.
Paper. $6.25. .... Vendor G0633

Marriage Records of Multnomah County, Oregon, 1873-1883.
Paper. $12.00. .... Vendor G0633

Marriage Records of Multnomah County, Oregon, 1883-1885.
Paper. $12.00. .... Vendor G0633

Marriage Records of Multnomah County, Oregon, 1885-1888.
Paper. $12.00. .... Vendor G0633

Marriage Records of Multnomah County, Oregon, 1888-1890.
Paper. $12.00. .... Vendor G0633

Portland Area

Genealogical Forum of Oregon. **Portland Area Census Records**. 1994.
Paper. $3.50. .... Vendor G0633

Sherman County

Genealogical Forum of Oregon. **Yesterday's Roll Call, Vol. I 1860-1910: Baker, Sherman & Umatilla County Cemetery Records**.
Paper. $14.00. .... Vendor G0633

Umatilla County

Genealogical Forum of Oregon. **Yesterday's Roll Call, Vol. I 1860-1910: Baker, Sherman & Umatilla County Cemetery Records**.
Paper. $14.00. .... Vendor G0633

Union County

Oregon Genealogical Society. **Union Co., OR Misc. Records**.
Paper. $10.00. .... Vendor G0634

Wasco County

Genealogical Forum of Oregon. **Some Cemetery Records of Wasco County, Oregon**.
Paper. $13.25. .... Vendor G0633

Washington County

Genealogical Forum of Oregon. **Records of Washington County, Oregon, Vols. I & II, 1842-1896**.
Paper. $10.50. .... Vendor G0633

Genealogical Forum of Oregon. **Records of Washington County, Oregon, Vol. III (Cemetery)**.
Paper. $10.25. .... Vendor G0633

Wheeler County

Genealogical Forum of Oregon. **Records of Wheeler County, Oregon Marriages, 1899-1920**.
Paper. $7.50. .... Vendor G0633

Genealogical Forum of Oregon. **Records of Wheeler County, Oregon, 1890-1910 Census**.
Paper. $9.00. .... Vendor G0633

❧ Pennsylvania ❦

Statewide and Regional References

1820 PA Pension List.
Paper. $5.00. 22 pp. .... Vendor G0536

1840 Census of PA Pensioners for Revolutionary and Military Service.
   Index taken from special 1840 census. Includes name, age, and place of residence as well as name of family with whom the pensioner resided as of June 1, 1840. Does not include actual information from the census microfilm readings.
Paper. $4.50. 36 pp. .... Vendor G0536

Atlas of Pennsylvania, Topographical.
   This present-day atlas provides the researcher with the detail needed to conduct a proper search. It is the size of a Rand McNally atlas of the entire U.S. 11" x 15½".
$16.95. .... Vendor G0611

Atlas of Pennsylvania, 67 county maps.
   Includes detailed maps of individual counties, all the back roads, streams, lakes, towns, etc. 11" x 16".
$14.95. .... Vendor G0611

Atlases & Gazetteers: Pennsylvania. Illus.
Paper. $16.95. 80 pp. .... Vendor G0632

Balderston, Marion. **James Claypoole's Letter Book: London and Philadelphia, 1681-1684**. 1967.
   A fresh, absorbing picture of the early years of the American colony of Pennsylvania seen through the letters of the London Quaker merchant James Claypoole.
Cloth. $12.00. 258 pp. .... Vendor G0611

Banvard, Theodore James Fleming. **Goodenows Who Originated in Sudbury, Massachusetts 1638 A.D.** 1994. Indexed. Illus.
Cloth. $78.50. 952 pp. .... Vendor G0116

Bates, Samuel P. **History of Pennsylvania Volunteers**. 14 vols. Indexed.
Cloth. $700.00. Contact vendor for pricing options. .... Vendor G0590

Browning, Charles H. **Welsh Settlement of Pennsylvania**. (1912) reprint 1993.
Indexed.
Paper. $42.50. 631 pp. .... Vendor G0011

Burgert, Annette K. **Brethren from Gimbsheim in the Palatinate to Ephrata and Bermudian in Pennsylvania**. 1994. Indexed. Illus.
Paper. $14.00. 39 pp. .... Vendor G0458

Burgert, Annette K. **Eighteenth Century Emigrants from Pfungstadt, Hessen-Darmstadt to Pennsylvania**. 1995. Indexed. Illus.
Paper. $17.00. 50 pp. .... Vendor G0458

Carousso, Dorothee Hughes. **How to Search for Your Revolutionary Patriot in Pennsylvania**. n. d.
Paper. $3.00 + $1.00 p&h. 12 pp. .... Vendor G0202

Claar. **Obituary Clippings: Vol. 1, 1933 A to Z 1933**. 1989. Indexed.
   From newspapers in Bedford, Blair, Cambria, Centre, Clearfield, Huntington, Somerset, and other Pennsylvania counties. Some of the later volumes include clippings from northern West Virginia as well (see below listings).
Paper. $44.00. 200 pp. .... Vendor G0622

Claar. **Obituary Clippings: Vol. 2, 1934 A to Z 1934**. 1989. Indexed.
Paper. $44.00. 204 pp. .... Vendor G0622

Claar. **Obituary Clippings: Vol. 3, 1935 A to Z 1935**. 1989. Indexed.
Paper. $44.00. 180 pp. .... Vendor G0622

Claar. **Obituary Clippings: Vol. 4, 1936 A to H 1936**. 1989. Indexed.
Paper. $44.00. 179 pp. .... Vendor G0622

Claar. **Obituary Clippings: Vol. 5, 1936 H to R 1936**. 1989. Indexed.
Paper. $44.00. 180 pp. .... Vendor G0622

Claar. **Obituary Clippings: Vol. 6, 1936 R to Z 1937**. 1989. Indexed.
Paper. $44.00. 123 pp. .... Vendor G0622

Claar. **Obituary Clippings: Vol. 7, 1937 A to L 1937**. 1989. Indexed.
Paper. $44.00. 266 pp. .... Vendor G0622

Claar. **Obituary Clippings: Vol. 8, 1937 M to W 1937**. 1989. Indexed.
Paper. $44.00. 223 pp. .... Vendor G0622

Claar. **Obituary Clippings: Vol. 9, 1937 W to D 1938**. 1989. Indexed.
Paper. $44.00. 180 pp. .... Vendor G0622

Claar. **Obituary Clippings: Vol. 10, 1938 D to M 1938**. 1989. Indexed.
Paper. $44.00. 270 pp. .... Vendor G0622

Claar. **Obituary Clippings: Vol. 11, 1938 M to S 1938**. 1990. Indexed.
Paper. $44.00. 202 pp. .... Vendor G0622

Claar. **Obituary Clippings: Vol. 12, 1938 S to B 1939**. 1990. Indexed.
Paper. $44.00. 223 pp. .... Vendor G0622

Claar. **Obituary Clippings: Vol. 13, 1939 B to H 1939**. 1990. Indexed.
Paper. $44.00. 224 pp. .... Vendor G0622

Claar. **Obituary Clippings: Vol. 14, 1939 H to P 1939**. 1990. Indexed.
Paper. $44.00. 267 pp. .... Vendor G0622

Claar. **Obituary Clippings: Vol. 15, 1939 P to Z 1939**. 1990. Indexed.
Paper. $44.00. 269 pp. .... Vendor G0622

Claar. **Obituary Clippings: Vol. 16, 1939 Z to E 1940**. 1990. Indexed.
Paper. $44.00. 228 pp. .... Vendor G0622

Claar. **Obituary Clippings: Vol. 17, 1940 E to K 1940**. 1990. Indexed.
Paper. $44.00. 226 pp. .... Vendor G0622

Claar. **Obituary Clippings: Vol. 18, 1940 L to R 1940**. 1990. Indexed.
Paper. $44.00. 237 pp. .... Vendor G0622

Claar. **Obituary Clippings: Vol. 19, 1940 R to W 1940**. 1990. Indexed.
Paper. $44.00. 214 pp. .... Vendor G0622

Claar. **Obituary Clippings: Vol. 20, 1940 W to C 1941**. 1990. Indexed.
Paper. $44.00. 242 pp. .... Vendor G0622

Claar. **Obituary Clippings: Vol. 21, 1941 C to H 1941**. 1990. Indexed.
Paper. $44.00. 222 pp. .... Vendor G0622

Claar. **Obituary Clippings: Vol. 22, 1941 H to M 1941**. 1990. Indexed.
Paper. $44.00. 222 pp. .... Vendor G0622

Claar. **Obituary Clippings: Vol. 23, 1941 M to R 1941**. 1990. Indexed.
Paper. $44.00. 176 pp. .... Vendor G0622

Claar. **Obituary Clippings: Vol. 24, 1941 R to T 1941**. 1992. Indexed.
Paper. $44.00. 199 pp. .... Vendor G0622

Claar. **Obituary Clippings: Vol. 25, 1941 T to B 1942**. 1992. Indexed.
Paper. $44.00. 199 pp. .... Vendor G0622

Claar. **Obituary Clippings: Vol. 26, 1942 B to C 1942**. 1992. Indexed.
Paper. $44.00. 200 pp. .... Vendor G0622

Claar. **Obituary Clippings: Vol. 27, 1942 C to G 1942**. 1992. Indexed.
Paper. $44.00. 200 pp. .... Vendor G0622

Claar. **Obituary Clippings: Vol. 28, 1942 G to K 1942**. 1992. Indexed.
Paper. $44.00. 200 pp. .... Vendor G0622

Claar. **Obituary Clippings: Vol. 29, 1942 K to M 1942**. 1992. Indexed.
Paper. $44.00. 200 pp. .... Vendor G0622

Claar. **Obituary Clippings: Vol. 30, 1942 M to S 1942**. 1992. Indexed.
Paper. $44.00. 201 pp. .... Vendor G0622

Claar. **Obituary Clippings: Vol. 31, 1942 S to W 1942**. 1994. Indexed.
Paper. $44.00. 194 pp. .... Vendor G0622

Claar. **Obituary Clippings: Vol. 32, 1942 W to B 1943**. 1994. Indexed.
Paper. $44.00. 194 pp. .... Vendor G0622

Claar. **Obituary Clippings: Vol. 33, 1943 B to F 1943**. 1994. Indexed.
Paper. $44.00. 194 p. .... Vendor G0622

Claar. **Obituary Clippings: Vol. 34, 1943 F to H 1943**. 1994. Indexed.
Paper. $44.00. 195 pp. .... Vendor G0622

Claar. **Obituary Clippings: Vol. 35, 1943 H to M 1943**. 1995. Indexed.
Paper. $44.00. 194 pp. .... Vendor G0622

Claar. **Obituary Clippings: Vol. 36, 1943 M to P 1943**. 1995. Indexed.
Paper. $44.00. 194 pp. .... Vendor G0622

Claar. **Obituary Clippings: Vol. 37, 1943 P to S 1943**. 1995. Indexed.
Paper. $44.00. 194 pp. .... Vendor G0622

Claar. **Obituary Clippings: Vol. 38, 1943 S to Y 1943**. 1995. Indexed.
Paper. $44.00. 194 pp. .... Vendor G0622

Claar. **Obituary Clippings: Vol. 39, 1943 Y to C 1944**. 1995. Indexed.
Paper. $44.00. 195 pp. .... Vendor G0622

Claar. **Obituary Clippings: Vol. 40, 1944 C to G 1944**. 1995. Indexed.
Paper. $44.00. 194 pp. .... Vendor G0622

Claar. **Obituary Clippings: Vol. 41, 1944 G to K 1944**. 1995. Indexed.
Paper. $44.00. 104 pp. .... Vendor G0622

Claar. **Obituary Clippings: Vol. 42, 1944 K to M 1944**. 1995. Indexed.
Paper. $44.00. 195 pp. .... Vendor G0622

Claar. **Obituary Clippings: Vol. 43, 1944 M to R 1944**. 1995. Indexed.
Paper. $44.00. 195 pp. .... Vendor G0622

Claar. **Obituary Clippings: Vol. 44, 1944 R to T 1944**. 1995. Indexed.
Paper. $44.00. 195 pp. .... Vendor G0622

Claar. **Obituary Clippings: Vol. 45, 1944 T to B 1945**. 1995. Indexed.
Paper. $44.00. 194 pp. .... Vendor G0622

Claar. **Obituary Clippings: Vol. 46, 1945 B to D 1945**. 1995. Indexed.
Paper. $44.00. 194 pp. .... Vendor G0622

Claar. **Obituary Clippings: Vol. 47, 1945 D to H 1945**. 1995. Indexed.
Paper. $44.00. 195 pp. .... Vendor G0622

Claar. **Obituary Clippings: Vol. 48, 1945 H to L 1945**. 1995. Indexed.
Paper. $44.00. 194 pp. .... Vendor G0622

Claar. **Obituary Clippings: Vol. 49, 1945 L to P 1945**. 1995. Indexed.
Paper. $44.00. 194 pp. .... Vendor G0622

Claar. **Obituary Clippings: Vol. 50, 1945 P to S 1945**. 1995. Indexed.
Paper. $44.00. 194 pp. .... Vendor G0622

Claar. **Obituary Clippings: Vol. 51, 1945 S to Y 1945**. 1995. Indexed.
Paper. $44.00. 193 pp. .... Vendor G0622

Claar. **Obituary Clippings: Vol. 52, 1945 Y to C 1946**. 1995. Indexed.
Paper. $44.00. 194 pp. .... Vendor G0622

Claar. **Obituary Clippings: Vol. 53, 1946 C to F 1946**. 1995. Indexed.
Paper. $44.00. 193 pp. .... Vendor G0622

Claar. **Obituary Clippings: Vol. 54, 1946 F to H 1946**. 1995. Indexed.
Paper. $44.00. 194 pp. .... Vendor G0622

Claar. **Obituary Clippings: Vol. 55, 1946 H to M 1946**. 1995. Indexed.
Paper. $44.00. 194 pp. .... Vendor G0622

Claar. **Obituary Clippings: Vol. 56, 1946 M to P 1946**. 1995. Indexed.
Paper. $44.00. 194 pp. .... Vendor G0622

Claar. **Obituary Clippings: Vol. 57, 1946 P to S 1946**. 1995. Indexed.
Paper. $44.00. 194 pp. .... Vendor G0622

Claar. **Obituary Clippings: Vol. 58, 1946 S to W 1946**. 1995. Indexed.
Paper. $44.00. 194 pp. .... Vendor G0622

Claar. **Obituary Clippings: Vol. 59, 1946 W to B 1947**. 1995. Indexed.
Paper. $44.00. 194 pp. .... Vendor G0622

Claar. **Obituary Clippings: Vol. 60, 1947 B to D 1947**. 1995. Indexed.
Paper. $44.00. 200 pp. .... Vendor G0622

Claar. **Obituary Clippings: Vol. 61, 1947 D to H 1947**. 1995. Indexed.
Paper. $44.00. 200 pp. .... Vendor G0622

Claar. **Obituary Clippings: Vol. 62, 1947 H to K 1947**. 1995. Indexed.
Paper. $44.00. 195 pp. .... Vendor G0622

Claar. **Obituary Clippings: Vol. 63, 1947 K to M 1947**. 1995. Indexed.
Paper. $44.00. 195 pp. .... Vendor G0622

Claar. **Obituary Clippings: Vol. 64, 1947 M to R 1947**. 1995. Indexed.
Paper. $44.00. 195 pp. .... Vendor G0622

Claar. **Obituary Clippings: Vol. 65, 1947 R to S 1947**. 1995. Indexed.
Paper. $44.00. 195 pp. .... Vendor G0622

Claar. **Obituary Clippings: Vol. 66, 1947 S to Z 1947**. 1995. Indexed.
Paper. $44.00. 194 pp. .... Vendor G0622

Clark, Dennis. **The Irish in Pennsylvania: A People Share a Commonwealth**. 1991. Illus.

A well-written and concise account of the history of the Irish in Pennsylvania and their many contributions to the Commonwealth.
Paper. $4.95. 56 pp. .... Vendor G0554

Collins, Patricia Wainwright. **Marriages and Deaths from Cambria Tribune, Vol. 1, 1853-1858**. Indexed.

Although most persons lived in either Cambria or Somerset County, many others are included from neighboring localities and a few other states. Includes a locality index, as well as an every-name index to the marriage and death notices.

Paper. $7.00. 32 pp. .... Vendor G0536

Collins, Patricia Wainwright. **Marriages and Deaths from Cambria Tribune, Vol. 2, 1859-1865**. Indexed.

See description for Vol. 1, above.

Paper. $8.00. 61 pp. .... Vendor G0536

Collins, Patricia Wainwright. **Marriages and Deaths from Cambria Tribune, Vol. 3, 1866-1875**. Indexed.

See description for Vol. 1, above.

Paper. $13.00. 126 pp. .... Vendor G0536

Collins, Patricia Wainwright. **Marriages and Deaths from Cambria Tribune, Vol. 4, 1876-1880**. Indexed.

See description for Vol. 1, above.

Paper. $18.00. 242 pp. .... Vendor G0536

Collins, Patricia Wainwright. **Marriages and Deaths from Cambria Tribune, Vol. 5, 1881-1885**. Indexed.

Contains over 6,500 names of residents of many counties and states. Includes index to names only.

Paper. $23.00. 302 pp. .... Vendor G0536

Comfort, William Wistar. **The Quakers**. Revised by Edwin B. Bronner. 1986. Illus.

A look at the beginnings of Quakerism in the mid-17th century, followed by details of Quaker life, institutions, and contributions to Pennsylvania history.

Paper. $5.95. 65 pp. .... Vendor G0554

Cuff, Young, Muller, Zelinsky, and Abler, eds. **The Atlas of Pennsylvania**. 1989.

Includes the complete historical atlas that has been printed separately as *A Concise Historical Atlas of Pennsylvania*, as well as virtually any fact or statistic you'd like to know about Pennsylvania.

Cloth. $120.00. 288 pp. .... Vendor G0611

Day, Reed B. **Whiskey Insurrection**.

Paper. $6.00. 33 pp. .... Vendor G0536

Day, Sherman. **Historical Collections of the State of Pennsylvania,** Containing a Copious Selection of the Most Interesting Facts, Traditions, Biographical, Anecdotes, Etc., Relating to the History and Antiquities . . . with Topographical Descriptions of Every County. (1843) reprint 1995.

Cloth. $74.00. 705 pp. .... Vendor G0259

Diffenderffer, Frank R. **The German Immigration into Pennsylvania** Through the Port of Philadelphia, from 1700 to 1775, and the Redemptioners. (1900) reprint 1988. Indexed. Illus.

Cloth. $21.50. 328 pp. .... Vendor G0010

Draper, Lyman. **Pennsylvania Manuscripts 1747 to 1827—Part I**. Transcribed by Phyllis Slater. Indexed.
   Deals with the early military records, camp life, court martials, Indian affairs, and pioneer life.
Paper. $8.95. 85 pp. .... Vendor G0536

Duer, Clara, comp. *Pittsburgh Gazette* **Abstracts**. 5 vols. Indexed.
   A valuable reference tool for all of western PA during this time period.
   Volume 1 covers years 1787-1797: publ. (1985) reprint 1988, 331 pp., $15.00.
   Volume 2 covers years 1797-1803: publ. 1986, 430 pp., $15.00.
   Volume 3 covers years 1806-1811: publ. 1989, 366 pp., $18.00.
   Volume 4 covers years 1812-1816: publ. 1991, 489 pp., $20.00.
   Volume 5 covers years 1817-1820: publ. 1996, 464 pp., $22.50.
Paper. $85.00/set. .... Vendor G0615

Duffin, James M., comp. **Guide to the Mortgages of the General Loan Office of the Province of Pennsylvania 1724-1756**. 1995.
Paper. $17.95 + $2.60 p&h. 160 pp. .... Vendor G0202

Dunaway, Wayland F. **The Scotch-Irish of Colonial Pennsylvania**. (1944) reprint 1997. Indexed.
Contact vendor for information. 273 pp. .... Vendor G0010

Dunn, Mary. **Index to Pennsylvania's Colonial Records Series**. (1992) reprint 1996.
Cloth. $20.00. 228 pp. .... Vendor G0010

Eddy, Henry Howard, and Martha L. Simonetti, ed. **Guide to the Published Archives of Pennsylvania**. 1976.
   A guide to the Pennsylvania State Archives, a 138-volume collection of printed source materials.
Paper. $4.95. 91 pp. .... Vendor G0554

Egle, William Henry. **Early Pennsylvania Land Records**. Minutes of the Board of Property of the Province of Pennsylvania. With a New Foreword by Dr. George E. McCracken. (1893) reprint 1997. Indexed.
Paper. $55.00. 787 pp. .... Vendor G0011

Egle, William Henry. **Pennsylvania Genealogies,** Chiefly Scotch-Irish and German. 2nd ed. (1896) reprint 1997. Indexed.
Paper. $49.95. 798 pp. .... Vendor G0011

Egle, William Henry. **Some Pennsylvania Women During the War of the Revolution**. (1898) reprint 1993.
Paper. $21.50. 208 pp. .... Vendor G0011

Eshleman, H. Frank. **Historic Background and Annals of the Swiss and German Pioneer Settlers** of Southeastern Pennsylvania, and of Their Remote Ancestors. (1917) reprint 1991. Indexed.
Cloth. $25.00. 386 pp. .... Vendor G0010

Espenshade, A. Howry. **Pennsylvania Place Names**. (1925) reprint 1995.
Paper. $32.50. 375 pp. .... Vendor G0011

Eyster, Anita L., comp. **Notices by German and Swiss Settlers Seeking Informa-tion of Members of Their Families, Kindred, or Friends** Between the Years 1742 and 1761 in the Pennsylvania Berichte and between the Years 1762 and 1779 in the State of Pennsylvania. Reprint. Indexed.
Paper. $7.00. 41+ pp. .... Vendor G0536

Family Genealogies in the Carnegie Library. 1993.
An index to a collection of over 2,000 family genealogies accumulated by the Carnegie Library in Oakland, PA, since its founding. Includes family name, author, publication date, and number of pages for most books or records. Listings are national in scope, but primarily cover PA heritage.
Paper. $6.00. 43 pp. .... Vendor G0536

Family History Library. **Research Outline: Pennsylvania**.
Leaflet. $.25. 14 pp. .... Vendor G0629

Felldin, Jeanne Robey, and Gloria Kay Vandiver Inman. **Index to the 1800 Census of Pennsylvania**. (1984) reprint 1996.
Paper. $36.00. 453 pp. .... Vendor G0011

Fields, S. Helen, ed. **Register of Marriages and Baptisms Performed By Rev. John Cuthbertson, Covenanter Minister, 1751-1791**. (1934) reprint 1996. Indexed. Illus.
In his capacity as missionary of the Reformed Presbyterian Church from 1751 to 1791, principally in Lancaster County but also throughout the entire region of the Cumberland Valley, Rev. Cuthbertson kept a meticulous account of his ministrations.
Paper. $28.50. 301 pp. .... Vendor G0011

The First Laws of the Commonwealth of Pennsylvania. (1779) reprint 1984.
Cloth. $62.50. 527 pp. .... Vendor G0118

Fisher, Charles A. **Central Pennsylvania Marriages, 1700-1896**. (1946) reprint 1993.
Cloth. $8.00. 449 pp. .... Vendor G0010

Fisher, Charles A. **Early Pennsylvania Births, 1675-1875**. (1947) reprint 1996.
Paper. $9.00. 107 pp. .... Vendor G0010

Freeble, Charles R., Jr. **Toscape Death**—A Novelized Version of the Life of Herman Husband, a Forgotten Early American Original.
The life story of Herman Husband, who was sentenced to death for treason by the Royal Governor but eluded capture by traveling backwoods to Western Pennsylvania, where he lived using the alias Toscape Death.
Paper. $7.95. 61 pp. .... Vendor G0536

Genealogical Society of Pennsylvania. **Pennsylvania Will Abstracts**. Indexed.
Pennsylvania will abstracts dating from 1682 to 1850 are available for Berks, Bucks, Chester, Cumberland, Delaware, Lancaster, Montgomery, and Philadelphia counties by special order.
Contact vendor for information. .... Vendor G0202

Genealogical Society of Pennsylvania. **Philadelphia Newspaper Abstracts 1791-1870**.
Numerous volumes containing marriage and death notices, and items of genealogi-cal interest, are available by special order only.
Hard-bound with gold lettering. Contact vendor for details. .... Vendor G0202

Genealogies of Pennsylvania Families. From the Pennsylvania Genealogical Magazine. 3 vols. 1982. Indexed. Illus.
> Vol. I: Arnold-Hertzel. 945 pp.
> Vol. II: Hinman-Sotcher. 921 pp.
> Vol. III: Stauffer-Zerbe. 1,028 pp.
Cloth. $45.00/vol., $135.00/set. 2,894 pp. .... Vendor G0010

Glatfelter, Charles H. **Pennsylvania Germans: A Brief Account of Their Influence on Pennsylvania**. 1990.
> Covers the entire period of the Germans in Pennsylvania with emphasis on their religion, schooling, and craftsmanship.
Paper. $5.95. 80 pp. .... Vendor G0554

Glenn, Thomas Allen. **Merion in the Welsh Tract**. With Sketches of the Townships of Haverford and Radnor. Historical and Genealogical Collections Concerning the Welsh Barony in the Province of Pennsylvania Settled by the Cymric Quakers in 1682. Partially indexed. (1896) reprint 1994. Illus.
Paper. $32.50. 394 pp. .... Vendor G0011

Glenn, Thomas Allen. **Welsh Founders of Pennsylvania**. 2 vols. in 1. (1911, 1913) reprint 1991. Indexed. Illus.
Cloth. $31.50. 356 pp. in all. .... Vendor G0011

Gordon, T. F. **A Gazetteer of the State of Pennsylvania**. (1832) reprint 1989.
Cloth. $57.50. 63 + 508 pp. .... Vendor G0259

Grifo, Richard D., and Anthony F. Noto. **Italian Presence in Pennsylvania**. 1990.
> A stimulating account of the contributions of Italians in Pennsylvania, and their rich heritage in the Commonwealth.
Paper. $4.95. 38 pp. .... Vendor G0554

Grubb, Farley. **Runaway Servants, Convicts, and Apprentices** Advertised in the Pennsylvania Gazette, 1728-1796. 1992.
Cloth. $18.50. 198 pp. .... Vendor G0011

Hanna, Charles. **The Wilderness Trails**. 2 vols. Reprint 1995. Illus.
> An examination of the influence of both Indian history and colonial trading practices on the developing American colonies. Traces the early development and expansion of the young American colonies westward across the Great Pennsylvania Frontier.
Cloth. $79.95/set. 840 pp. .... Vendor G0554

Heckethorn, Paul Keith. **The Chronological Beginnings of the Christian Church in Western PA, 1743-1793**. Indexed.
Paper. $6.00. 54 pp. .... Vendor G0536

Heisey, John W. **Handbook for Genealogical Research in Pennsylvania**.
Paper. $12.00. 32 pp. .... Vendor G0574

Herrick, Cheesman A. **White Servitude in Pennsylvania,** Indentured and Redemption Labor in Colony and Commonwealth. (1926) reprint 1996. Indexed. Illus.
Paper. $35.00. 340 pp. .... Vendor G0011

Hocker, Edward W. **Genealogical Data Relating to the German Settlers of Pennsylvania** and Adjacent Territory. From Advertisements in German Newspapers Published in Philadelphia and Germantown, 1743-1800. 1989. Indexed.
Cloth. $17.50. 242 pp. .... Vendor G0010

Hoenstine. **1955 Yearbook, Pennsylvania Society, S.A.R**. 1956. Indexed.
Cloth. $25.00. 784 pp. .... Vendor G0622

Hoenstine. **Guide to Genealogical and Historical Research in Pennsylvania**. 4th ed. 1978. Indexed.
    Lists over 2,600 items available as rentals, with a cumulative index listing over 50,000 names, with over 200,000 references.
Cloth. $24.50. Also available as a set with 3 supplements (see listings below) for $75.00. 606 pp. .... Vendor G0622

Hoenstine. **Guide to Genealogical and Historical Research in Pennsylvania: Supplement I**. 1985. Indexed.
Paper. $16.00. 216 pp. .... Vendor G0622

Hoenstine. **Guide to Genealogical and Historical Research in Pennsylvania: Supplement II**. 1990. Indexed.
Paper. $18.00. 127 pp. .... Vendor G0622

Hoenstine. **Guide to Genealogical and Historical Research in Pennsylvania: Supplement III**. 1995. Indexed.
Paper. $20.00. 112 pp. .... Vendor G0622

Hulbert, Archer Butler. **The Ohio River:** A Course of Empire. (1906) reprint 1996.
    The history of the territory along the Ohio, especially Pittsburgh, Wheeling, Marietta, Cincinnati, and Louisville.
Cloth. $45.00. 378 pp. .... Vendor G0259

Hull, William I. **William Penn and the Dutch Quaker Migration to Pennsylvania**. (1935) reprint 1990. Indexed. Illus.
Cloth. $30.00. 460 pp. .... Vendor G0011

Index to the Encyclopedia of Pennsylvania Biography. Two Volumes in One. Frederick A. Godcharles, Index to Volumes I-XX. Walter D. Stock, Index to Volumes XXI-XXXII. 1932, 1996.
Paper. $35.00. 189 + 277 pp. .... Vendor G0011

Jordan, John W. **Colonial and Revolutionary Families of Pennsylvania**. In Three Volumes. (1911) reprint 1994. Indexed.
Paper. $125.00. 1,706 pp. .... Vendor G0011

Jordan, John W., ed. **Genealogical & Personal History of the Allegheny Valley.** 3 vols. (1913) reprint 1996.
Cloth. $42.50/vol., $115.00/set. 1,162 pp. .... Vendor G0259

Keith, Charles P. **The Provincial Councillors of Pennsylvania Who Held Office Between 1733 and 1776,** and Those Earlier Councillors Who Were Some Time Chief Magistrates of the Province, and Their Descendants. (1883) reprint 1997. Indexed.
   Covers many of the leading families of the mid-Atlantic region and includes the entire progeny of the councillors.
Cloth. $45.00. 628 pp. .... Vendor G0010

Kieffer, Henry Martyn. **Some of the First Settlers of "The Forks of the Delaware" and Their Descendants,** Being a Translation from the German of the Record Books of the First Reformed Church of Easton, Penna. from 1760 to 1852. (1902) reprint 1995. Illus.
Paper. $31.50. 404 pp. .... Vendor G0011

Kriebel, Howard W. **The Schwenkfelders in Pennsylvania:** A Historical Sketch. (1904) reprint 1995.
Cloth. $35.00. 246 pp. .... Vendor G0259

Kriebel, Rev. Reuben. **Genealogical Record of the Descendants of the Schwenkfelders** Who Arrived in Pennsylvania in 1733, 1734, 1736, 1737. From the German of the Rev. Balthasar Heebner and from Other Sources. (1879) reprint 1993. Indexed.
Paper. $24.50. 371 pp. .... Vendor G0011

Lacock, John Kennedy. **Braddock Road.**
   Reprint of scarce booklet originally published about 1908 outlines expeditions of Major-Gen. Edward Braddock and his army. Map of Braddock's Military Road from Cumberland, Maryland to Braddock, Pennsylvania, 1755, denoting encampments.
Paper. $6.00. 38 pp. .... Vendor G0536

Ledoux, Rev. Albert H. **Catholic Vital Records of Central Pennsylvania, Vol. I (1793-1839).** 1993. Indexed.
Cloth. $29.50 (PA & MD residents must pay tax). 318 pp. .... Vendor G0511

Ledoux, Rev. Albert H. **Catholic Vital Records of Central Pennsylvania, Vol. II (1840-1849).** 1994. Indexed.
Cloth. $29.50 (PA & MD residents must pay tax). 328 pp. .... Vendor G0511

Ledoux, Rev. Albert H. **Catholic Vital Records of Central Pennsylvania, Vol. III (1850-1857).** 1994. Indexed.
Cloth. $40.50 (PA & MD residents must pay tax). 539 pp. .... Vendor G0511

Ledoux, Rev. Albert H. **Catholic Vital Records of Central Pennsylvania, Vol. IV (1858-1864).** 1996. Indexed.
Cloth. $43.50 (PA & MD residents must pay tax). 602 pp. .... Vendor G0511

Levy. **Quakers and the American Family: British Settlement in the Delaware Valley.** 1988.
   An important social history, this book examines the reasons for the migration of Quaker families from 17th-century England into colonial southeastern Pennsylvania,

as well as their life once they arrived there. Many early families mentioned. Extensive footnotes.
Paper. $18.95. 340 pp. .... Vendor G0611

Linn, John B., and William H. Egle. **Muster Rolls of the Pennsylvania Volunteers in the War of 1812-1814** (from the Pennsylvania Archives, Second Series, Volume XII, 1890). (1890) reprint 1994. Indexed.
Paper. $39.95. 560 pp. .... Vendor G0011

Linn, John B., and William H. Egle, eds. **Names of Persons Who Took the Oath of Allegiance to the State of Pennsylvania, 1776-1794**. (1890) reprint 1995. Indexed.
Paper. $10.00. 118 pp. .... Vendor G0140

Linn, John B., and William H. Egle. **Pennsylvania Marriages Prior to 1790**. Names of Persons for Whom Marriage Licenses Were Issued in the Province of Pennsylvania Previous to 1790. (1890, 1908, 1915, 1960) reprint 1994.
Cloth. $25.00. 376 pp. .... Vendor G0010

Linn, John B., and William H. Egle. **Persons Naturalized in the Province of Pennsylvania, 1740-1773**. With an Added Index. (1890) reprint 1995.
Paper. $16.00. 139 pp. .... Vendor G0011

Linn, John B., and William H. Egle. **Record of Pennsylvania Marriages Prior to 1810**. 2 vols. (1980) reprint 1987.
Cloth. $75.00. 790 + 601 pp. .... Vendor G0010

Magda, Matthew S. **Polish Presence in Pennsylvania**. 1992.
    Community building, Polish-American institutions, Polish Protestantism and Roman Catholicism, labor and politics, and ethnic decline and revival.
Paper. $4.95. 65 pp. .... Vendor G0554

Maps Showing the Development of Pennsylvania.
Paper. $5.00. 12 pp. .... Vendor G0574

McBride, David. **The Afro-American in Pennsylvania: A Critical Guide to Sources in the Pennsylvania State Archives**. 1979. Illus.
Paper. $2.95. 36 pp. .... Vendor G0554

Metzgar, Thomas J., and James B. Whisker, comps. **Clockmakers and Watchmakers, Goldsmiths and Silversmiths—A Checklist**.
    Excellent list of Pennsylvania tradesmen including genealogical facts, documentation, and a section of nostalgic ads and clippings from newspapers.
Paper. $19.95. .... Vendor G0536

Morris, Jean S. **Library Research in Pennsylvania with Map**. 7th ed. 1996.
Paper. $9.00. 15 pp. .... Vendor G0521

Morris, Jean S. **Locating Your Pennsylvania French & Indian War Ancestor 1754-1763 Sources & Maps**. 1996.
Paper. $9.00. 14 pp. .... Vendor G0521

Morris, Jean S. **Maps Showing the Development of Pennsylvania 1681-1920 with County Chronology & Map**. (1920) reprint 1996.
Paper. $7.50. 14 pp. .... Vendor G0521

Morris, Jean S. **Pennsylvania Quaker Research: A Bibliography & Guide with Maps**. 1996.
Paper. $13.00. 18 pp. .... Vendor G0521

Muller, Edward K. **A Concise Historical Atlas of Pennsylvania**. 1981.
This book consists of the historical chapter reprinted from *The Atlas of Pennsylvania*. Extremely useful to genealogists.
Paper. $29.95. 115 pp. .... Vendor G0611

Munger, Donna Bingham. **Pennsylvania Land Records: A History and Guide for Research**. 1991. Indexed. Illus.
Describes how to use Pennsylvania'a land records and provides history of settlement. "A magnificent finding aid . . . Highly recommended."—*NY Genealogical and Biographical Record*
Cloth, $77.50. Paper, $32.45. 240 pp. .... Vendor G0118

Munger, Donna Bingham. **Pennsylvania Land Records: A History and Guide for Research**. 1991.
The first history of and research guide to the land records of Pennsylvania, which are among the most complete in the nation, stretching back to the 1680s.
Cloth, $75.00. Paper, $29.95. 240 pp. .... Vendor G0554

Myers, Albert Cook. **Immigration of the Irish Quakers into Pennsylvania, 1682-1750**. With Their Early History in Ireland. (1902) reprint 1994. Indexed. Illus.
Cloth. $30.00. xxii + 477 pp. .... Vendor G0010

Myers, Paul W. **PA Soldiers of the Revolutionary War** (Living in States Other than PA).
An alphabetical compilation of 1,400 Pennsylvania soldiers of the Revolutionary War who qualified for pension benefits under the Acts of March 18, 1818, and June 7, 1832, and who were living in states other than Pennsylvania.
Paper. $5.00. 30 pp. .... Vendor G0536

175 SW PA Marriages performed by Rev. Abraham Boyd during the years 1802-1849 (Presbyterian).
Paper. $2.50. 7 pp. .... Vendor G0536

Parker, J. Carlyle. **Pennsylvania and Middle Atlantic States Genealogical Manuscripts:** A User's Guide to the Manuscript Collections of the Genealogical Society of Pennsylvania as Indexed in Its Manuscript Materials Index; Microfilmed by the Genealogical Department, Salt Lake City. 1986.
Strongest in coverage of eastern Pennsylvania and southern New Jersey.
Paper. $16.95. 45 pp. .... Vendor G0492

Pennsylvania German Church Records. Births, Baptisms, Marriages, Burials, Etc. from the Pennsylvania German Society Proceedings and Addresses. With an introduction by Don Yoder. 3 vols. 1983. Indexed. Illus.
Cloth. $135.00/set, $45.00/vol. 900 + 700 + 771 pp. .... Vendor G0010

Pennsylvania Historical Survey. Works Projects Administration. **Inventory of Church Archives Society of Friends in Pennsylvania**. (1941) reprint 1996.
Paper. $35.00. 397 pp. .... Vendor G0011

Pennsylvania State Library. **Index to Main Families, Persons, Places and Subjects in Egle's Notes and Queries**. 1970.
Cloth. $15.00. 81 pp. .... Vendor G0011

Precision Indexing. **1870 Pennsylvania East Census Index: Heads of Households and Other Surnames in Households Index**. 2 vols.
Cloth. $395.00. .... Vendor G0552

Precision Indexing. **1870 Pennsylvania West Census Index: Heads of Households and Other Surnames in Households Index**. 2 vols.
Cloth. $350.00. .... Vendor G0552

Reamy, Martha. **Newspaper Abstracts of South Central Pennsylvania: 1785-1800**. 3 vols. 1988. Indexed.
 Volume 1: 1785-1790.
 Volume 2: 1791-1795.
 Volume 3: 1796-1800.
Paper. $16.00/vol, $35.00/set. 177 + 190 + 183 pp. .... Vendor G0140

Register of Invalid Pensions, Rev. Service, 1789.
 A list of wounded and disabled officers and soldiers of the Revolution residing in Pennsylvania in 1789. Includes names of Revolutionary War soldiers, dates when they were paid, which may be regarded as approximate to their death.
Paper. $2.50. 16 pp. .... Vendor G0536

Retzer, Henry J. **German Regiment of Maryland and Pennsylvania**. 1991. Rev. ed. 1996. Indexed.
 Gives information on a little-known unit of Gen. Washington's army.
Paper. $15.00. 183 pp. .... Vendor G0140

Rev. Pensioners—A Transcript of the Pension List of PA for 1813.
Paper. $1.00. 5 pp. .... Vendor G0536

Roach, Hannah Benner. **The Pennsylvania Militia in 1777**. (ca. 1980) reprint 1994. Indexed.
Paper. $4.00 + $1.00 p&h. 80 pp. .... Vendor G0202

Romig, Nancy, comp. **WPGS 1991-1992 Members Family Name Index**. 1992.
Paper. $4.00. .... Vendor G0615

Rupp, Israel Daniel. **A Collection of Upwards of Thirty Thousand Names of German, Swiss, Dutch, French and Other Immigrants in Pennsylvania from 1727 to 1776**. (1876, 1931) reprint 1994. Indexed. Illus.
Cloth. $30.00. 583 pp. .... Vendor G0010

Schuylkill Roots. **Circuit and Circuit Riders**. 2 vols. Indexed.
 Collection of pastoral acts of various preachers as they traveled through Eastern Pennsylvania.
Paper. $49.95/set. 323 + 315 pp. .... Vendor G0536

Schweitzer, George K. **Pennsylvania Genealogical Research**. 1997. Illus.
 History of the state, types of records (Bible through will), record locations, research techniques, listings of county records.
Paper. $15.00. 227 pp. .... Vendor G0569

Scott, Carol A. **Marriage and Death Notices of Wheeling, Western Virginia, and the Tri-State Area, 1818-1857**. 3 vols.

Extracted paid marriage and death notices from major newspapers published in Wheeling, WV. The newspapers carried notices of the people from West Virginia, western Pennsylvania, and southeastern Ohio. Volume I covers records from 1818 to 1857. Volume II covers records from 1858 to 1865. Volume III covers 1866 through 1870.

Paper. $9.50/vol. 90 + 104 + 110 pp. .... Vendor G0536

Scott, Kenneth. **Genealogical Abstracts from *The American Weekly Mercury*, 1719-1746**. (1974) reprint 1995. Indexed. Illus.

Paper. $20.00. 180 pp. .... Vendor G0011

Scott, Kenneth. **Genealogical Data from the Pennsylvania Chronicle, 1764-1774**. Indexed.

Cloth. $17.00. 170 pp. .... Vendor G0627

Smylie, James H. **Scotch-Irish Presence in Pennsylvania**. 1990.

Focuses on the immigration and life of the Scotch-Irish in Pennsylvania, as well as on their important contributions to Pennsylvania.

Paper. $4.95. 38 pp. .... Vendor G0554

Southern California Genealogical Society. **Using the Printed Pennsylvania Archives: A Guide**.

Paper. $5.00. 20 pp. .... Vendor G0656

Stapleton, Ammon. **Memorials of Huguenots in America**. With Special Reference to Their Emigration to Pennsylvania. (1901) reprint 1996. Indexed.

Paper. $18.50. 164 pp. .... Vendor G0011

Strassburger, Ralph Beaver, and William John Hinke. **Pennsylvania German Pioneers. A Publication of the Original Lists of Arrivals in the Port of Philadelphia from 1727 to 1808, Signature Volume**. (1934) reprint 1992.

This set, which is commonly known as "Strassburger & Hinke," is the time-honored reference for arrival of German emigrants to America before 1800. It is one of the basic works for genealogical libraries. Volumes 1 and 3 have been reprinted a number of times, but this is the first time this volume (which shows the actual signatures of the emigrants) has been reprinted.

Cloth. $55.00. 909 pp. .... Vendor G0081

Strassburger, Ralph Beaver. **Pennsylvania German Pioneers: A Publication of the Original Lists of Arrivals in the Port of Philadelphia from 1727 to 1808**. 2 vols. (1934) reprint 1992. Indexed.

Cloth. $75.00. 1,485 pp. total .... Vendor G0010

Strassburger, Ralph Beaver, and William John Hinke. **Pennsylvania German Pioneers**. 3 vols. (1937) reprint 1992. Indexed.

Book #1345.

Cloth. $175.00. 2,560 pp. .... Vendor G0082

Tepper, Michael. **Emigrants to Pennsylvania, 1641-1819**. A Consolidation of Ship Passenger Lists from the Pennsylvania Magazine of History and Biography. (1877-1934) reprint 1992. Indexed.

Cloth. $20.00. 302 pp. .... Vendor G0010

Thorndale, William, and William Dollarhide. **County Boundary Map Guides to the U.S. Federal Censuses, 1790-1920: Pennsylvania, 1790-1920**. 1987. $5.95. .... Vendor G0552

Treese, Lorett. **The Storm Gathering: The Penn Family and the American Revolution**. 1992.
Recounts the fascinating saga of the Penn family, focusing primarily on Thomas and John Penn, two of the last members of the family to figure significantly in pre-Revolutionary Pennsylvania history.
Contact vendor for information. 245 pp. .... Vendor G0554

Trussell, John B. B., comp. **Pennsylvania Historical Bibliography I—Additions Through 1970**. 1979. Indexed.
Paper. $6.95. 108 pp. .... Vendor G0554

Trussell, John B. B., comp. **Pennsylvania Historical Bibliography II—Additions Through 1973**. 1980. Indexed.
Paper. $6.95. 87 pp. .... Vendor G0554

Trussell, John B. B., comp. **Pennsylvania Historical Bibliography III—Additions Through 1976**. 1980. Indexed.
Paper. $6.95. 119 pp. .... Vendor G0554

Trussell, John B. B., comp. **Pennsylvania Historical Bibliography IV—Additions Through 1979**. 1983. Indexed.
Paper. $6.95. 121 pp. .... Vendor G0554

Trussell, John B. B., comp. **Pennsylvania Historical Bibliography V—Additions Through 1982**. 1986. Indexed.
Paper. $6.95. 138 pp. .... Vendor G0554

Trussell, John B. B., comp. **Pennsylvania Historical Bibliography VI—Additions Through 1985**. 1989. Indexed.
Paper. $7.95. 136 pp. .... Vendor G0554

United States Bureau of the Census. **Heads of Families at the First Census of the United States Taken in the Year 1790: Pennsylvania**. (1908) reprint 1992. Indexed. Illus.
Contact vendor for information. 426 pp. .... Vendor G0010

United States Bureau of the Census. **Heads of Families at the First Census of the United States Taken in the Year 1790: Pennsylvania**.
Cloth, $56.50. Paper, $41.50. .... Vendor G0552

Veech, James. **The Monongahela of Old:** Or, Historical Sketches of South-Western Pennsylvania to the Year 1800. (1910) reprint 1996. Indexed. Illus.
Paper. $22.00. 272 pp. .... Vendor G0011

Wall, Carol A. **Bibliography of Pennsylvania History: A Supplement**. 1976.
Cloth. $8.95. 252 pp. .... Vendor G0554

Wallace, Paul A. W. **Daniel Boone in Pennsylvania**. Rev. ed. 1987.
Recounts the story of Daniel Boone's early life in Pennsylvania and his later activ-

ity in Kentucky, describing his Quaker family and the popular traditions that have survived the years.
Paper. $1.95. 21 pp. .... Vendor G0554

Weinberg et al. **Index to 1759 Warrants and Surveys of Province of Pennsylvania Including Three Lower Counties (Delaware).** (1965) reprint 1975. Indexed.
Paper. $9.00. 91 pp. .... Vendor G0531

Welchley, Mark. **Pittsburgh, PA Gazette Genealogical Gleanings, 1786-1820, Volume I.**
News items, advertisements, and public notices containing genealogical information of a local nature from Western Pennsylvania and parts of Ohio and Virginia.
Paper. $11.00. 81 pp. .... Vendor G0536

Westcott, Thompson. **Names of Persons Who Took the Oath of Allegiance to the State of Pennsylvania Between the Years 1777 and 1789,** with a History of the "Test Laws" of Pennsylvania. (1865) reprint 1996. Indexed.
Paper. $20.00. 192 pp. .... Vendor G0011

Western Pennsylvania Genealogical Society. **Marriages & Deaths from Pittsburgh Dispatch 1858-1860.** 1993.
Over 4,500 names listed from a time before vital records were recorded in PA. Names from all over western PA, Ohio, West Virginia.
Paper. $15.00. .... Vendor G0615

Western Pennsylvania Genealogical Society. **Pensioners in Western Pennsylvania in 1883.** 4 vols.
Volume I: Allegheny, Beaver, and Lawrence counties.
Volume II: Armstrong, Fayette, Greene, Indiana, Washington, and Westmoreland counties.
Volume III: Bedford, Blair, Cambria, Cameron, Clearfield, Elk, Forest, Jefferson, McKean, Somerset, and Warren counties.
Volume IV: Butler, Clarion, Crawford, Erie, Mercer, and Venango counties.
Paper. $8.00/vol., $27.00/set. .... Vendor G0615

Woodroofe, Helen Hutchison, comp. **A Genealogist's Guide to Pennsylvania Records.** 1979-87.
Originally published over seventeen issues of the *Pennsylvania Genealogical Magazine.*
Paper. $39.95 + $4.00 p&h. 464 pp. .... Vendor G0202

Yoder, Don, ed. **Pennsylvania German Immigrants, 1709-1786** Lists Consolidated from Yearbooks of The Pennsylvania German Folklore Society. (1984) reprint 1989. Indexed. Illus.
Cloth. $25.00. 394 pp. .... Vendor G0010

Adams County

Barnes, Robert. **Guide to Research in York and Adams Counties, Pennsylvania.** 1996. Illus.
Paper. $18.00. 121 pp. .... Vendor G0140

Day, Sherman, and Wayne E. Morrison, Sr. **History of Adams County, Penn'a**. 1843. Indexed. Illus.
Cloth. $30.00. 96 pp. .... Vendor G0112

History of Cumberland & Adams Counties. With Biographies. (1886) reprint 1994.
Cloth. $119.50. 132 + 588 + 516 pp. .... Vendor G0259

Hopkins, G. M. **1858 Landowner Atlas Printed in Atlas Form from Original Wall Map**. 1994. Illus.
Business directories, many lithographic drawings.
Paper. $22.00. 62 pp. .... Vendor G0531

Rupp, I. Daniel. **History & Topography of Dauphin, Cumberland, Franklin, Bedford, Adams & Perry Counties**. (1846) reprint 1994.
Cloth. $65.00. 606 pp. .... Vendor G0259

Wright, F. Edward. **Adams County Church Records of the 18th Century**. Indexed.
Paper. $24.00. 305 pp. .... Vendor G0140

Allegheny County

1790 Pennsylvania Census: Allegheny County.
Paper. $6.00. .... Vendor G0549

Atlas of the City of Pittsburgh, Pennsylvania 1911. 1992.
In 1906 Allegheny City was annexed to Pittsburgh, and two years later the pattern of Wards was modified and many street names changed because of duplication. This atlas was published to illustrate these changes. Maps show both old and new wards, and the street index lists both old and new names of streets.
Paper. $16.00. 50 pp. .... Vendor G0615

Braden, Dorothy B., comp. **Presbyterian Churches in Allegheny County, Pennsylvania**.
Contains all known Presbyterian churches, past or present.
Paper. $16.00. .... Vendor G0615

Crumrine, Boyd. **Virginia Court Records in Southwestern Pennsylvania**. Records of the District of West Augusta and Ohio and Yohogania Counties, Virginia 1775-1780. (1902, 1905) reprint 1997. Indexed. Illus.
The minute books of the old Virginia courts herein transcribed cover the District of West Augusta and Yohogania and Ohio counties during the period when Virginia claimed and exercised jurisdiction over what are now the Pennsylvania counties of Washington, Greene, Fayette, Westmoreland, and Allegheny.
Contact vendor for information. 542 pp. .... Vendor G0011

Cushing, Thomas, et al. **A Genealogical and Biographical History of Allegheny County, Pennsylvania**. (1889) reprint 1993. Indexed.
Paper. $43.50. 578 pp. .... Vendor G0011

Davison, E. M., and E. B. McKee. **Annals of Old Wilkinsburg & Vicinity, the Village, 1788-1888**. (1940) reprint 1995.
Cloth. $57.50. 549 pp. .... Vendor G0259

Directory of 1815, Pittsburgh and Vicinity.
   Typewritten reproduction of original 1815 directory. Includes name, address, and occupation of early residents of Pittsburgh, Birmingham, and Lawrenceville, Bayard's Town, etc.
Paper. $6.00. 29 pp. .... Vendor G0536

Duer, Clara, comp. **Pittsburgh Gazette Abstracts. Volume 1: 1787-1797**. (1985) reprint 1988. Indexed.
Paper. $15.00 (also available as a 5-vol. set for $85.00—see listings for other vols.).
331 pp. .... Vendor G0615

Duer, Clara, comp. **Pittsburgh Gazette Abstracts. Volume 2: 1797-1803**. 1986. Indexed.
Paper. $15.00 (also available as a 5-vol. set for $85.00—see listings for other vols.).
430 pp. .... Vendor G0615

Duer, Clara, comp. **Pittsburgh Gazette Abstracts. Volume 3: 1806-1811**. 1989. Indexed.
Paper. $18.00 (also available as a 5-vol. set for $85.00—see listings for other vols.).
366 pp. .... Vendor G0615

Duer, Clara, comp. **Pittsburgh Gazette Abstracts. Volume 4: 1812-1816**. 1991. Indexed.
Paper. $20.00 (also available as a 5-vol. set for $85.00—see listings for other vols.).
489 pp. .... Vendor G0615

Duer, Clara, comp. **Pittsburgh Gazette Abstracts. Volume 5: 1817-1820**. 1996. Indexed.
Paper. $22.50 (also available as a 5-vol. set for $85.00—see listings for other vols.).
464 pp. .... Vendor G0615

Fishman, Joel, ed. **Lists and Indexes to the Legal, Court, and Municipal Records of Allegheny County, PA**. Volume 1. 1982.
   Includes tavern licenses for Pittsburgh 1818-1827; law students in Allegheny County 1831-1900; births and deaths in Allegheny City Home 1871-1904; nurses' discharge paper 1917-1946.
Paper. $5.00. 109 pp. .... Vendor G0615

Harriss, Helen, and Eden Harriss. **Courthouse Research in Allegheny County**. 1993.
   Gives locations of documents in the Allegheny County Courthouse; shows examples of the documents and how to use them. Includes director for all Pennsylvania courthouses.
Paper. $5.00. .... Vendor G0615

History of Allegheny County, with Illustrations. (1876) reprint 1996.
The original book is oversized. It has been reduced approximately 25 percent to fit an 8½" x 11" format; the print is small but quite legible.
Cloth. $32.00. 242 pp. .... Vendor G0259

History of Allegheny County. Including Its Early Settlement & Progress; a Description of Its Historical & Interesting Localities; Its Cities, Towns, & Villages; Portraits of Some Prominent Men & Biogr. of Many Citizens. 2 vols. (1889) reprint 1992.
Cloth. $79.00/vol., $149.00/set. 762 + 786 pp. .... Vendor G0259

Kraynek, Sharon L. D. **Allegheny County, PA Cemetery Records, Vol. 1**. Indexed.
Paper. $9.00. 51 pp. .... Vendor G0536

Kraynek, Sharon L. D. **Allegheny County, PA Cemetery Records, Vol. 2**. Indexed.
Paper. $9.00. 82 pp. .... Vendor G0536

Kraynek, Sharon L. D. **Allegheny County, PA Cemetery Records, Vol. 3**. Indexed.
Paper. $7.00. 70 pp. .... Vendor G0536

Kraynek, Sharon L. D. **Allegheny County, PA Cemetery Records, Vol. 4**. Indexed.
Paper. $10.00. 143 pp. .... Vendor G0536

Kraynek, Sharon L. D. **Allegheny County, PA Cemetery Records, Vol. 5**. Indexed.
Paper. $7.00. 69 pp. .... Vendor G0536

Kraynek, Sharon L. D. **Allegheny County, PA Cemetery Records, Vol. 6**. Indexed.
Paper. $14.00. 173 pp. .... Vendor G0536

Kraynek, Sharon L. D. **Allegheny County, PA Cemetery Records, Vol. 7**. Indexed.
Paper. $9.00. 118 pp. .... Vendor G0536

Kraynek, Sharon L. D. **Allegheny County, PA Cemetery Records, Vol. 8**. Indexed.
Paper. $9.00. 115 pp. .... Vendor G0536

Kraynek, Sharon L. D. **Allegheny County, PA Cemetery Records, Vol. 9**. Indexed.
Paper. $14.00. 185 pp. .... Vendor G0536

Kraynek, Sharon L. D. **Allegheny County, PA Cemetery Records, Vol. 10**. Indexed.
Paper. $9.00. 106 pp. .... Vendor G0536

Kraynek, Sharon L. D. **Allegheny County, PA Cemetery Records, Vol. 11**. Indexed.
Paper. $10.00. 147 pp. .... Vendor G0536

Kraynek, Sharon L. D. **Allegheny County, PA Cemetery Records, Vol. 12**. Indexed.
Paper. $10.00. 137 pp. .... Vendor G0536

Kraynek, Sharon L. D. **Allegheny County, PA Cemetery Records, Vol. 13**. Indexed.
Paper. $9.00. 112 pp. .... Vendor G0536

Long, Nancy. **Greentree/German United Evangelical/Vierhellers/West End United Church of Christ Cemetery**. 1988.
The original church was located in the then Temperanceville, now West End section, about 1864.
Paper. $5.50. 53 pp. .... Vendor G0615

Long, Nancy, and Eden Harriss, comps. **St. Phillip's Roman Catholic Church Cemetery, Crafton, Allegheny County**. 1991. Indexed.
Paper. $3.50. 22 pp. .... Vendor G0615

McFarland, Kenneth, comp. **Allegheny County, PA Archives, Volume 1. Orphans' Court Docket I, 1789-1820**. Indexed.
Cloth. $19.95. 185 pp. .... Vendor G0536

McFarland, Kenneth, comp. **Allegheny County, PA Archives, Volume 2. Deed Books 1 & 2, 1788-1792**. Indexed.
Cloth. $19.95. 136 pp. .... Vendor G0536

McFarland, Kenneth, comp. **Allegheny County, PA Archives, Volume 3. Orphans' Court Docket 2, 1821-1831**. Indexed.
   Continuation of Volume 1.
Cloth. $19.95. 174 pp. .... Vendor G0536

McFarland, Kenneth, comp. **Allegheny County, PA Archives, Volume 4. Orphans' Court Docket 4, 1831-1838**. Indexed.
Cloth. $19.95. 157 pp. .... Vendor G0536

McFarland, Kenneth, comp. **Allegheny County, PA Archives, Volume 5. Orphans' Court Docket 3, 1838-1843**. Indexed.
Cloth. $19.95. 117 pp. .... Vendor G0536

McFarland, Kenneth, comp. **Allegheny County, PA Archives, Volume 6. Orphans' Court Docket 5 & 6, 1843-1847**. Indexed.
Cloth. $19.95. 167 pp. .... Vendor G0536

McFarland, Kenneth, comp. **Allegheny County, PA Archives, Volume 7. Partition Dockets 1, 2 & 3, 1858-1873**. Indexed.
   Starting in 1858, this became the record of distribution of real estate among the heirs in intestate (and some testate) situations. Usually names children of the decedent, gives names of some spouses and places of residence.
Cloth. $19.95. 121 pp. .... Vendor G0536

McFarland, Kenneth, comp. **Allegheny County, PA Archives, Volume 8. Partition Dockets 4-7, 1873-1884**. Indexed.
Cloth. $19.95. 127 pp. .... Vendor G0536

McFarland, Kenneth. **Allegheny County, PA Cemetery Records: Union Dale Cemetery Records, Volume 1**. Indexed.
   Union Dale Cemetery was formed by the merging of two earlier cemeteries, Mount Union and Hillsdale. While other nationalities and religious groups are represented, Scots-Irish names predominate. Each of this eight-volume set contains a division of the cemetery. Includes all interments up to 1986; 23,000 inscription readings. Arrangement is in burial order.
Paper. $11.95. 109 pp. .... Vendor G0536

McFarland, Kenneth. **Allegheny County, PA Cemetery Records: Union Dale Cemetery Records, Volume 2**. Indexed.
   Primarily Scotch-Irish burials.
Paper. $11.95. 112 pp. .... Vendor G0536

McFarland, Kenneth. **Allegheny County, PA Cemetery Records: Union Dale Cemetery Records, Volume 3**. Indexed.
Considerable German presence plus a sizable Welsh contingent.
Paper. $11.95. 126 pp. .... Vendor G0536

McFarland, Kenneth. **Allegheny County, PA Cemetery Records: Union Dale Cemetery Records, Volume 4**. Indexed.
Primarily German and Welsh.
Paper. $13.95. 141 pp. .... Vendor G0536

McFarland, Kenneth. **Allegheny County, PA Cemetery Records: Union Dale Cemetery Records, Volume 5**. Indexed.
Paper. $15.95. 175 pp. .... Vendor G0536

McFarland, Kenneth. **Allegheny County, PA Cemetery Records: Union Dale Cemetery Records, Volume 6**. Indexed.
Paper. $13.95. 149 pp. .... Vendor G0536

McFarland, Kenneth. **Allegheny County, PA Cemetery Records: Union Dale Cemetery Records, Volume 7**. Indexed.
Paper. $13.95. 153 pp. .... Vendor G0536

McFarland, Kenneth. **Allegheny County, PA Cemetery Records: Union Dale Cemetery Records, Volume 8**. Indexed.
Paper. $13.95. 166 pp. .... Vendor G0536

McFarland, Kenneth. **Inscriptions from Chartiers Cemetery, I**.
Paper. $11.95. 118 pp. .... Vendor G0536

McFarland, Kenneth. **Inscriptions from Chartiers Cemetery, II**.
Paper. $16.95. 247 pp. .... Vendor G0536

McFarland, Kenneth. **Inscriptions from Highwood Cemetery, I,** Allegheny (now Pittsburgh), PA. Indexed.
Paper. $11.95. 138 pp. .... Vendor G0536

McFarland, Kenneth. **Inscriptions from Highwood Cemetery, II**. Indexed.
Paper. $16.95. 229 pp. .... Vendor G0536

McFarland, Kenneth. **Inscriptions from Two German Protestant Cemeteries** Allegheny (now Pittsburgh), PA—St. John's Lutheran Cemetery (Spring Hill), Voegtly Cemetery (Troy Hill).
If your ancestor was German or Swiss, you should look for them in this record.
Paper. $11.95. 132 pp. .... Vendor G0536

Myers, Paul W. **Allegheny County, PA Revolutionary War Soldiers**.
Alphabetical list of about 630 Revolutionary War soldiers who lived, and in most cases died, in Allegheny County.
Paper. $9.00. 112 pp. .... Vendor G0536

North Hills Genealogists (of Pittsburgh, PA). **Pioneer Cemeteries of Hampton Township: Tombstone Readings and Cemetery Guide**. 1997. Indexed. Illus.
Please write for price and publication date of this unique resource with three read-

ings (including lot ownership) and a guide to all cemeteries in Hampton Township, Allegheny County, PA.

Contact vendor for information. 150 pp. .... Vendor G0607

Pittsburgh, PA Marriages 1803-1867.

Records first extracted in 1938 by the PA Society of Colonial Dames of America. They represent marriages officiated by clergy of Trinity Episcopal Church, Pittsburgh. Excellent source of early Allegheny County and surrounding area marriages, not necessarily of this church membership.

Paper. $7.50. 37 pp. .... Vendor G0536

Sadler, Charlotte, comp. **Letters from the Past**. Indexed.

Compilation of letters to and from the Wainwright family of England written in the Pittsburgh Area between July 1805-October 1866. Valuable as a first-hand account of things as they were in the Pittsburgh area during this time period.

Paper. $7.50. 73 pp. .... Vendor G0536

Stewart, Reid W. **Scottish Dissenting Presbyterian Churches in Allegheny County, Pennsylvania**. 1994. Indexed. Illus.

Paper. $10.00. 41 pp. .... Vendor G0615

Warner & Co. **History of Allegheny County, Pennsylvania**. 4 vols. 1889. Indexed. Illus.

Describes early settlement and evolution of county to 1889.

Paper. $80.00/set. 1,548 pp. .... Vendor G0615

Western Pennsylvania Genealogical Society. **Allegheny County Naturalizations**. 7 vols. (Vols. 1 & 2 are out of print).

Volume 3: 1856-1869 (4,600 names).
Volume 4: 1870-1879 (7,550 names).
Volume 5: 1880-1887 (6,250 names).
Volume 6: 1888-1891 (6,500 names).
Volume 7: 1892-1906 (8,650 names).

Cloth. $10.00/vol. .... Vendor G0615

Western Pennsylvania Genealogical Society. **Pittsburgh and Some Allegheny County Marriages 1875-1885, Ministers Marriage Returns**.

Microfilm. $30.00/fiche. 52 fiche + index. .... Vendor G0615

Armstrong County

Barth, Margaret. **Freeport Journal, 1876-1900**. Indexed.

The Freeport Journal, a gossipy little newspaper that came out each Friday and was published from 1876 until the 1930s. One feature of this paper was the year-end summarization of the events of the year.

Paper. $16.95. 228 pp. .... Vendor G0536

Cramer, Peggy C. **Complete Records of Emmanuel Evangelical Lutheran Church, Freeport, Armstrong, PA, 1875-1920**. Indexed.

Paper. $12.95. 152 pp. .... Vendor G0536

Cramer, Peggy C. **Complete Records of St. Matthew's Lutheran Church 1844-1932**. Indexed.
Paper. $16.95. 175 pp. .... Vendor G0536

Cramer, Peggy C. **Records of Clinton Lutheran Church,** Clinton, South Buffalo Township. Indexed.
Records cover period 1852-1860.
Paper. $5.00. 17 pp. .... Vendor G0536

Hidinger, Nancy Hill, comp. **The Armstrong Democrat & Sentinel, Published in Kittanning, Armstrong County, PA—Genealogical Abstracts July 1889-Dec. 1891, Vol. 1**. Indexed.
Very complete newspaper abstractions including jury lists, legal notices, gossip columns, deaths, marriages, visitors, lodge members, prisoners, real estate transactions, elections, retirements, even murder trials.
Paper. $22.95. 277 pp. .... Vendor G0536

Hidinger, Nancy Hill. **The Armstrong Democrat & Sentinel, Jan. 1892-Dec. 1894, Vol. 2**. Indexed.
Paper. $39.95. 539 pp. .... Vendor G0536

Mechling, Allen R., and Marla K. Mechling. **Burials in the Kittanning Cemetery, Kittanning, PA, 1811-1995**. 1996. Illus.
Includes 30,000 names; 10,500 burials. Birth, death, and burial dates and places; parents, spouse, and marriage date. Burial lot maps; cross-referenced; alphabetical.
Cloth, $63.95. Paper, $53.95. 675 pp. .... Vendor G0468

Mechling, Allen R. **History of the Old Kittanning Cemetery (1811-1960)**. Indexed.
Paper. $14.95. 113 pp. .... Vendor G0536

Mechling, Allen R., and Marla K. Mechling. **Patients with Communicable Diseases in the Borough of Kittanning, PA 1907-1955**. Illus.
Provides valuable information that may not be available elsewhere regarding the parent or guardian of each patient, as well as the street and house number where each lived, and information about the disease and attending physician. Includes a short biographical account of most of the attending physicians.
Paper. $10.95. 136 pp. .... Vendor G0536

Rupert, Don W. **Cemetery Listings of Armstrong County, PA**. Indexed.
Thirty-nine cemetery compilations.
Paper. $35.00. 470 pp. .... Vendor G0536

Smith, Robert Walter. **History of Armstrong Co., Pennsylvania**. Reprint of 1883 edition. Indexed.
Over 6,000 dates and 50,000 names of Armstrong County residents.
Cloth. $60.00. 696 pp. .... Vendor G0536

Wiley, Samuel T. **Biographical & Historical Cyclopedia of Indiana and Armstrong Counties, PA**. Indexed.
Reprint of 1891 work. Over 2,000 surnames and vast amount of historical research.
Cloth. $60.00. 658 pp. .... Vendor G0536

Beaver County

Bausman, J. H. **History of Beaver Co**. 2 vols. (1904) reprint 1989.
Cloth. $139.00. 612 + 703 pp. .... Vendor G0259

Beaver County, PA Cemetery Records, Vol. 1. By the Resource and Research Center for Beaver County. Indexed.
Paper. $11.00. 85 pp. .... Vendor G0536

Beaver County, PA Cemetery Records, Vol. 2. By the Resource and Research Center for Beaver County. Indexed.
  Twenty-one cemeteries.
Paper. $11.00. 109 pp. .... Vendor G0536

Beaver County, PA Cemetery Records, Vol. 3. By David and Elsa Hays.
Paper. $11.00. 91 pp. .... Vendor G0536

Beaver County, PA Cemetery Records, Vol. 4. By the Resource and Research Center for Beaver County. Indexed.
Paper. $11.00. 58 pp. .... Vendor G0536

Book of Biographies: Biographical Sketches of Leading Citizens of Beaver Co. (1899) reprint 1995.
Cloth. $47.00. 435 pp. .... Vendor G0259

History of Beaver County, Including Its Early Settlement. (1888) reprint 1992.
Cloth. $99.50. 908 + 123 pp. .... Vendor G0259

Lutes, Margt. Dilworth (shared by). **Excerpts from the Diary of the Rev. Robert Dilworth and His Cousin, Blacksmith Dilworth, Nov. 19, 1789-1865.** Indexed.
  Rev. Dilworth was licensed to preach by the Presbytery of Hartford in 1824 and served as a missionary among the churches of western PA and eastern Ohio. He was the pastor of the Church of Little Beaver for thirty years, beginning in 1836. Notations of deaths, marriages, and other bits of genealogical information primarily for the years 1836, 1856 on through October 1866, and some entries for 1821-1823.
Paper. $5.00. 17 pp. .... Vendor G0536

Warner, A. **History of Beaver County, Pennsylvania.** Reprint of 1888 edition. Indexed.
  Includes about 300 pages of family biographies.
Cloth. $60.00. 1,031 pp. .... Vendor G0536

Welchley, Mark H. **Beaver Argus Genealogical Gleanings, 1830-58.** Indexed.
Paper. $11.00. 130 pp. .... Vendor G0536

Welchley, Mark H. **Beaver County, PA Church History Data Base.**
  This book is set up as a data base of the churches and synagogues in Beaver County.
Paper. $11.00. 143 pp. .... Vendor G0536

Welchley, Mark H. **Beaver County, PA Marriages, 1830-1873.**
Paper. $11.00. 99 pp. .... Vendor G0536

Bedford County

1790 Pennsylvania Census: Bedford County.
Paper. $7.50. .... Vendor G0549

Bedford County, PA Archives, Vol. 1. Indexed.
Paper. $16.00. 133 pp. .... Vendor G0536

Bedford County, PA Archives, Vol. 2. Indexed.
Paper. $16.00. 142 pp. .... Vendor G0536

Bedford County, PA Archives, Vol. 3. Indexed.
Paper. $16.00. 148 pp. .... Vendor G0536

Bedford County, PA Archives, Vol. 4. Indexed.
Paper. $16.00. 153 pp. .... Vendor G0536

Bedford County, PA Archives, Vol. 5. Indexed.
Paper. $16.00. 158 pp. .... Vendor G0536

Bedford County, PA Archives, Vol. 6. Indexed.
Paper. $16.00. 227 pp. .... Vendor G0536

Bedford County, PA Archives, Vol. 7. Indexed.
Paper. $16.00. 151 pp. .... Vendor G0536

Hengst, Michael A., comp. **Bedford County, PA Marriage Records, Oct. 1885-April 1890**. Indexed.
Paper. $24.95. 221 pp. .... Vendor G0536

Hickok, Dr. Charles N., comp. **Bedford in Ye Olden Times**. Indexed.
   Dr. Charles N. Hickok compiled this Bedford County information to deliver as two lectures at the Bedford County Courthouse in 1886. Includes historical stories, events, poems, and letters of the 1700s pertaining to that area.
Paper. $5.00. 86 pp. .... Vendor G0536

History of Bedford, Somerset & Fulton Counties. (1884) reprint 1991. Illus.
Cloth. $87.50. 672 pp. + illus. .... Vendor G0259

Hoenstine. **Abstracts of Bedford County Wills, Unrecorded & Volume 1 (1770-1819)**. 1990. Indexed.
Paper. $27.00. 62 pp. .... Vendor G0622

Hoenstine. **Abstracts of Bedford County Wills, Vols. 2 & 3, 1819-1849**. 1990. Indexed.
Paper. $27.00. 80 pp. .... Vendor G0622

Rupp, I. Daniel. **History & Topography of Dauphin, Cumberland, Franklin, Bedford, Adams & Perry Counties**. (1846) reprint 1994.
Cloth. $65.00. 606 pp. .... Vendor G0259

Saylor, E. C., comp. **Church Records of Berlin, Somerset Co., PA**. Indexed.
Since Somerset County was formed from the westernmost part of Bedford County in 1795, a portion of these records cover Bedford County. They represent one of the earliest and most complete sets of vital records of western PA.
Paper. $19.95. 195 pp. .... Vendor G0536

Spielman, Margaret Aaron. **Bedford Co. Unrecorded Bible Records.**
Paper. $5.00. 38 pp. .... Vendor G0536

Whisker, James B., ed. **Bedford Co., PA in the American Revolution**. Indexed.
Documents the soldiers who served in Bedford County during the Revolution, Indian attacks, pay scales for soldiers, historical overview, battles, genealogical facts about the men, and more.
Paper. $22.00. 219 pp. .... Vendor G0536

Whisker, James B. **Early Distillers of Bedford County, PA**.
Paper. $2.50. 13 pp. .... Vendor G0536

Whisker, James B. **Early Occupations of Bedford Co., PA People**.
Paper. $3.50. 28 pp. .... Vendor G0536

Whisker, James B. **Gunsmiths and Gunmakers of Bedford and Somerset County**.
Paper. $2.50. 12 pp. .... Vendor G0536

Whisker, James B. **St. Thomas the Apostle Roman Catholic Church**. Indexed.
Paper. $8.50. 90+ pp. .... Vendor G0536

Whisker, James B. **Tavern- & Innkeepers of Bedford County, PA**.
Paper. $4.00. 38 pp. .... Vendor G0536

Berks County

1790 Pennsylvania Census: Berks County.
Paper. $10.00. .... Vendor G0549

Beers & Co., J. H. **Historical and Biographical Annals of Berks Co., Pennsylvania**. 1909. Indexed.
Order no. 420-421—Vol. 1, $54.00; order no. 975-977—Vol. 2, $68.00. 784 + 939 pp.
Vendor G0478

Bern Church Record. Bern Township, Berks Co., PA, 1739-1835. Made available through Schuylkill Roots. Indexed.
Paper. $5.00. 39 pp. .... Vendor G0536

Daniel Schumacher's Baptismal Register, 1754-1773. 1994. Indexed.
Book #1425.
Cloth. $29.50. 320 pp. .... Vendor G0082

Dix, Katharine F., comp. **1767 Berks Co., PA Archives**. Indexed.
Index of information extracted from the PA Archives, Third Series, Vol. 18, which contains information from 1767 to 1785.
Paper. $6.00. 33 pp. .... Vendor G0536

Dix, Katharine F., comp. **1784 Berks Co., PA Archives**. Indexed.
Paper. $8.00. 95 pp. .... Vendor G0536

Early, Rev. J. W., trans. **Trinity Lutheran Church of Reading, Part I (Baptisms 1751-1790)**. Indexed.
This and the following three books were all translated from the original records by Rev. J. W. Early ca. 1906.
Paper. $14.00. 122 pp. .... Vendor G0536

Early, Rev. J. W., trans. **Trinity Lutheran Church of Reading, Part 2 (Baptisms 1790-1812)**. Indexed.
Paper. $14.00. 123 pp. .... Vendor G0536

Early, Rev. J. W., trans. **Trinity Lutheran Church of Reading, Part 3 (Marriages 1754-1812)**. Indexed.
Paper. $8.50. 72 pp. .... Vendor G0536

Early, Rev. J. W., trans. **Trinity Lutheran Church of Reading, Part 4 (Burials 1754-1812)**. Indexed.
Paper. $8.50. 74 pp. .... Vendor G0536

Kistler, John L. **Baptismal Records of Jerusalem Lutheran and Reformed Church, Berks County, Pennsylvania**.
English translation of entries dating between 1768-1863 from the church's first record book. The church served an area including parts of Berks and Lehigh counties.
Paper. $7.00. 62 pp. .... Vendor G0627

Martin, Jacob, and John P. Smith. **Abstracts of Berks County Wills: 1752-1785**.
Paper. $16.00. 216 pp. .... Vendor G0140

Martin, Jacob, and John P. Smith. **Abstracts of Berks County Wills: 1785-1800**.
Paper. $19.50. 237 pp. .... Vendor G0140

Martin, Jacob, and John P. Smith. **Abstracts of Berks County Wills: 1800-1825**.
Paper. $29.00. 364 pp. .... Vendor G0140

Montgomery, Morton L. **Historical & Biographical Annals of Berks Co.:** A Concise History of the Co., & Genealogical & Biographical Records of Representative Families. 2 vols. (1909) reprint 1992.
Cloth. $155.00. 1,700 pp. .... Vendor G0259

Montgomery, Morton L. **History of Berks County, Pennsylvania in the Revolution, from 1774 to 1783**. (1894) reprint 1995. Indexed. Illus.
Paper. $25.00. 295 pp. .... Vendor G0011

Rupp, I. Daniel. **History of the Counties of Berks & Lebanon**. (1844) reprint 1992.
Cloth. $55.00. 512 pp. .... Vendor G0259

Schuylkill Roots. **Church Record of the Christ (Maxatawny or DeLong's) Reformed Church at Bowers, Berks County, PA**.
Paper. $8.00. 68 pp. .... Vendor G0536

Schuylkill Roots. **Collected Church Records of Berks County, PA.** 2 vols. Indexed.
Paper. $49.95/set. 587 pp. in all. .... Vendor G0536

Schuylkill Roots. **Host Tulpehocken Church at Marion Township** (actually the church is in Tulpehocken Twp.).
Paper. $14.25. 128 pp. .... Vendor G0536

Schuylkill Roots. **Private Records of Rev. Johannes H. Helfrich (1790-1810).** Indexed.
   Rev. Helfrich was one of the fathers of the Reformed Church movement in America. He served congregations in Lehigh and Berks counties. This book contains marriage records from 1790-1810 and burial records 1790-1795.
Paper. $5.00. 38 pp. .... Vendor G0536

Wright, F. Edward. **Berks County, Pennsylvania Church Records of the 18th Century.** 4 vols. Indexed.
   Volume 1, 340 pp., $27.00.
   Volume 2, 391 pp., $32.00.
   Volume 3, 360 pp., $28.50.
   Volume 4, 320 pp., $26.50.
Paper. .... Vendor G0140

Blair County

Africa, J. Simpson. **History of Huntingdon & Blair Counties.** (1883) reprint 1992.
Cloth. $79.50. 500 + 261 pp. .... Vendor G0259

Davis, Tarring S., ed., with Lucile Schenk. **History of Blair County.** 2 vols. in 1. (1931) reprint 1995.
Cloth. $56.00. 527 pp. .... Vendor G0259

Hoenstine. **Soldiers of Blair County Pennsylvania.** 1940.
Paper. $22.00. 426 pp. .... Vendor G0622

McFarland, Kenneth T. H. **Hollidaysburg Records.** Indexed.
   Marriages, deaths, and partitions from weekly newspapers of Hollidaysburg (Huntingdon/Blair counties) for the years 1836-1852.
Paper. $12.95. 129 pp. .... Vendor G0536

Bradford County

Bradsby, H. C. **History of Bradford County,** with Biographical Selections. (1891) reprint 1993.
Cloth. $125.00. 1,320 pp. .... Vendor G0259

Perkins, Mrs. George A. **Early Times on the Susquehanna (Athens, Bradford Co.).** (1906) reprint 1996.
Cloth. $35.00. 285 pp. .... Vendor G0259

Bucks County

1790 Pennsylvania Census: Bucks County.
Paper. $12.00. .... Vendor G0549

Allen, Ruth. **Early Pennsylvania Reformed Church and Cemetery Records**.
Indexed.
Paper. $24.95. 276+ pp. .... Vendor G0536

Bucks County, PA Church Records of the 18th Century: Vol. 1, German Church
Records. By F. Edward Wright. 1993. Indexed.
Paper. $27.00. 340 pp. .... Vendor G0140

Bucks County, PA Church Records of the 18th Century: Vol. 2, Quaker Records:
Falls and Middletown Monthly Meetings. By Anna Miller Watring. 1993. Indexed.
Paper. $32.00. 395 pp. .... Vendor G0140

Bucks County, Pennsylvania Church Records of the 18th Century: Vol. 3, Quaker
Records: Wrightstown, Richland, Buckingham, Makefield, and Solebury Monthly
Meetings. By Anna Miller Watring. 1994. Indexed.
Paper. $18.00. 233 pp. .... Vendor G0140

Davis, W. W. H. **History of Bucks Co. from the Discovery of the Delaware to the
Present Time**. (1876) reprint 1993.
Cloth. $95.00. 875 + 54 pp. .... Vendor G0259

Davis, William W. H. **A Genealogical and Personal History of Bucks County,
Pennsylvania**. 2 vols. (1905) reprint 1994. Indexed. Illus.
Paper. $65.00. 751 pp. .... Vendor G0011

Green, Doron. **A History of Bristol Borough, in the Co. of Bucks,** State of Penna.,
Anciently Known as "Buckingham," Being the Third Oldest Town & Second Chartered Borough in Penna., from Its Earliest Times to the Present Year. (1911) reprint
1995.
Cloth. $45.00. 370 pp. .... Vendor G0259

Historical Society of Pennsylvania. **Abstracts of Bucks County, Pennsylvania Wills,
1685-1785**. 1995. Indexed.
Paper. $14.00. 184 pp. .... Vendor G0140

Humphrey, John T. **Pennsylvania Births, Bucks County**. 1993. Indexed.
    Over 12,000 births.
Cloth. $34.00. 352 pp. .... Vendor G0117

Meier, Judith A. H., comp. **Advertisements and Notices of Interest from Norristown,
PA Newspapers, Volume I (1799-1821)**. Indexed.
    Because the Norristown newspapers served such a large area, news of Chester,
Bucks, Delaware, and even more distant counties appear. See also volumes II-VI
under Montgomery County.
Paper. $19.95. 166 pp. .... Vendor G0536

Meldrum, Charlotte D. **Abstracts of Bucks County, Pennsylvania Land Records,
1684-1723**. 1995. Indexed. Illus.
Paper. $12.00. 155 pp. .... Vendor G0140

Roberts, Clarence V. **Early Friends Families of Upper Bucks** with Some Account of Their Descendants. (1925) reprint 1995. Indexed. Illus.
Paper. $49.95. 680 pp. .... Vendor G0011

T.L.C. Genealogy. **Bucks County, Pennsylvania Deed Book 5 (1713-1731)**. 1991. Indexed.
Paper. $14.00. 89 pp. .... Vendor G0609

Butler County

Bowden, Rev. George S. **Souvenir History of Slippery Rock**. (1925) reprint 1994.
Paper. $13.00. 117 pp. .... Vendor G0259

History of Butler County, Embracing . . . Early Settlement & Subsequent Growth . . . Sketches of Boroughs, Townships & Villages . . . Biographies & Portraits of Pioneers & Representative Citizens, Etc. (1895) reprint 1995.
Cloth. $129.50. 1,360 pp. .... Vendor G0259

McKee, James A. **Twentieth Century of Butler & Butler Co**. (1909) reprint 1994.
Cloth. $139.50. 1,487 pp. .... Vendor G0259

Myers, Paul W. **Revolutionary War Veterans Who Settled in Butler, PA**.
Paper. $5.00. 21 pp. .... Vendor G0536

Romig, Nancy. **Surname Index to 1874 Atlas of Butler County, PA**. 1993.
    A landowner atlas of Butler County in 1874. Those who find their name in the Index can write to the vendor for a copy of the map.
Paper. $10.00. 27 pp. .... Vendor G0615

Cambria County

Oyler, Phyllis M., comp. **Sandyvale Cemetery, Johnstown, Pennsylvania**.
    Alphabetized listings of burials (1850-1906) plus a cross index of maiden names, early lot owners, a chronology of the cemetery, some short family histories, lists of lots held by the City of Johnstown, and a map of the cemetery.
Paper. $30.00. 362 pp. .... Vendor G0536

Storey, Henry Wilson. **History of Cambria County.** With Genealogical Memoirs. 3 vols. (1907) reprint 1993.
    Volume I: History.
    Volume II: History, with Genealogical Memoirs.
    Volume III: Biography.
Cloth. $59.50/Vols. I & II. $69.50/Vol. III. $155.00/set. 590 + 575 + 679 pp. .... Vendor G0259

Warzel, Des. **Cambria Co. Cemeteries, Vol. I**. Indexed.
Paper. $10.95. 115 pp. .... Vendor G0536

Warzel, Des. **Cambria Co. Cemeteries, Vol. II**. Indexed.
Paper. $19.95. 250 pp. .... Vendor G0536

Cameron County

History of the Counties of McKean, Elk, Cameron & Potter, with Biographical Selections. (1890) reprint 1989.
Cloth. $126.50. 1,261 pp. .... Vendor G0259

Carbon County

Brenckman, Fred. **History of Carbon County**. With Biographical Sketches. (1913) reprint 1994.
Cloth. $65.00. 626 pp. .... Vendor G0259

Mathews, Alfred, and A. Hungerford. **History of the Counties of Lehigh & Carbon**. (1884) reprint 1993.
Cloth. $82.50. 802 pp. .... Vendor G0259

Rupp, I. D. **History of Northampton, Lehigh, Monroe, Carbon, and Schuylkill Counties**. (1845) reprint 1991.
Cloth. $59.00. 568 pp. .... Vendor G0259

Centre County

A. Pomeroy & Co. **Atlas of Centre County, Pennsylvania**. (1874) reprint 1986. Indexed. Illus.
Cloth. $35.50. 60 pp. .... Vendor G0493

Centre County Heritage, 1956-1975. 1975. Indexed.
Paper. $8.00. 233 pp. .... Vendor G0493

Heathcote, C. W., and Lucile Shenk, eds. **History of Centre & Clinton Counties.** With Biographies. (1932) reprint 1994.
Cloth. $52.00. 478 pp. .... Vendor G0259

Linn, John Blair. **History of Centre and Clinton Counties, Pennsylvania**. (1883) reprint 1990. Indexed. Illus.
Cloth. $80.00. 1,052 pp. .... Vendor G0493

Macneal, Douglas, ed. **Centre County Heritage, 1976-1985**. 1996. Indexed. Illus.
Cloth. $18.00. 424 pp. .... Vendor G0493

Stevens, Sylvester K. Revised and expanded by Philip S. Klein. **The Centre Furnace Story: A Return to Our Roots**. 1985. Indexed. Illus.
Cloth, $20.50. Paper, $15.00. 68 pp. .... Vendor G0493

Williams, Harry M. Edited by Betty F. Johnson. **The Story of Scotia**. 1992. Illus.
Cloth. $33.00. 128 pp. .... Vendor G0493

Chester County

1790 Pennsylvania Census: Chester County.
Paper. $12.50. .... Vendor G0549

Cope, Gilbert, and Henry G. Ashmead, eds. **Historic Homes & Institutions, & Genealogical & Personal Memoirs of Chester & Delaware Counties.** 2 vols. (1904) reprint 1993.
   Volume I: Chester County.
   Volume II: Delaware County.
Cloth. $62.50/vol., $119.00/set. 600 + 598 pp. .... Vendor G0259

Dix, Katharine F. **1765 Chester County, PA Archives.**
   Over 5,700 names.
Paper. $8.00. 105 pp. .... Vendor G0536

Futhey, J. S., and G. Cope. **History of Chester Co.,** with Genealogical & Biographical Sketches. (1881) reprint 1990.
   The 226-page Index is available in paperback or bound with this book.
Cloth. $91.50. 782 + xliv pp. .... Vendor G0259

Heathcote, C. W., and Lucile Shenk, eds. **History of Chester County. With Biographies.** (1932) reprint 1994.
Cloth. $51.00. 478 pp. .... Vendor G0259

Humphrey, John T. **Pennsylvania Births, Chester County 1682-1800**. 1994. Indexed.
   Over 9,000 births.
Cloth. $30.00. 245 pp. .... Vendor G0117

Martin, Joseph. **Abstracts of the Wills of Chester County: 1713-1748**. 1993. Indexed.
Paper. $15.00. 188 pp. .... Vendor G0140

Martin, Joseph. **Abstracts of the Wills of Chester County: 1748-1776**. 1994. Indexed.
Paper. $16.00. 204 pp. .... Vendor G0140

Meier, Judith A. H., comp. **Advertisements and Notices of Interest from Norristown, PA Newspapers, Volume I (1799-1821)**. Indexed.
   Because the Norristown newspapers served such a large area, news of Chester, Bucks, Delaware, and even more distant counties appear. See also volumes II-VI under Montgomery County.
Paper. $19.95. 166 pp. .... Vendor G0536

Reamy, Martha. **Early Church Records of Chester County.** Vol. 1: Quaker Records of Bradford Monthly Meeting. 1995. Indexed.
Paper. $20.00. 260 pp. .... Vendor G0140

Thompson, Wilmer W., ed. **Chester County and Its People**. (1898) reprint 1993.
Cloth. $95.00. 982 pp. .... Vendor G0259

Wiley, Samuel T. **Biographical & Portrait Cyclopedia of Chester County**. (1893) reprint 1994.
Cloth. $89.50. 879 pp. .... Vendor G0259

Clarion County

Kepple, Arnold. **Callensburg, a Small Community—History of Callensburg & Licking Township, 3rd Edition**. (1975) reprint 1991. Indexed. Illus.
Includes 370 pictures.
Paper. $23.00. 399 pp. .... Vendor G0067

Clinton County

Heathcote, C. W., and Lucile Shenk, eds. **History of Centre & Clinton Counties**. With Biographies. (1932) reprint 1994.
Cloth. $52.00. 478 pp. .... Vendor G0259

Linn, John Blair. **History of Centre and Clinton Counties, Pennsylvania**. (1883) reprint 1990. Indexed. Illus.
Cloth. $80.00. 1,052 pp. .... Vendor G0493

Columbia County

Battle, J. H., ed. **History of Columbia & Montour Counties,** Containing a History of Each County, Their Townships, Towns & Villages . . . & Biographies. (1887) reprint 1993.
Cloth. $88.00. 132 + 542 + 220 pp. .... Vendor G0259

Freeze, John G. **History of Columbia County,** from the Earliest Times. (1883) reprint 1996.
Cloth. $59.00. 566 pp. .... Vendor G0259

Rice, Phillip A., comp. **Cemeteries of Centralia**. Indexed.
Paper. $9.50. 78 pp. .... Vendor G0536

Schuylkill Roots. **Miscellaneous Church and Cemetery Records from Columbia County, PA**. Indexed.
Paper. $9.50. 80 pp. .... Vendor G0536

Crawford County

History of Crawford Co., Containing a Hist. of the Co.; Its Twps., Towns . . . Etc., Portraits of Early Settlers & Prominent Men, Biogr., Etc. (1885) reprint 1990.
Cloth. $119.50. 1,186 pp. .... Vendor G0259

Sargent, M. P. **Pioneer Sketches: Scenes & Incidents of Former Days**. (1891) reprint 1993.
An entertaining and very useful account of the early days of Crawford Co., Pa., & Ashtabula, Oh., including biographical sketches of early settlers.
Cloth. $54.00. 512 pp. .... Vendor G0259

Cumberland County

1790 Pennsylvania Census: Cumberland County.
Paper. $11.00. .... Vendor G0549

Cumberland County, Pennsylvania, Marriages, 1761-1800. From the collection of J. Zeamer. Organized alphabetically. (1926) reprint ca. 1990.
Paper. $4.00 + $1.00 p&h. 40 pp. .... Vendor G0202

Fralish, John C., Jr. **Cumberland County Archives: Records of the Office of the Recorder of Deeds, Deed Abstracts and Mortgage Book 1750-1785.** 1995. Indexed. Illus.
Paper. $85.00. 697 pp. .... Vendor G0440

History of Cumberland & Adams Counties. With Biographies. (1886) reprint 1994.
Cloth. $119.50. 132 + 588 + 516 pp. .... Vendor G0259

Rupp, I. Daniel. **History & Topography of Dauphin, Cumberland, Franklin, Bedford, Adams & Perry Counties.** (1846) reprint 1994.
Cloth. $65.00. 606 pp. .... Vendor G0259

Warner, Beers & Co. **1886 History Taken from History of Cumberland and Adams Counties.** (1856) reprint 1977. Illus.
  Includes 92-page index.
Cloth. $26.00. 588 pp. .... Vendor G0531

Wright, F. Edward. **Abstracts of Cumberland County Wills, 1750-1785.** 1992. Indexed.
Paper. $9.00. 110 pp. .... Vendor G0140

Wright, F. Edward. **Cumberland County Church Records of the 18th Century.** 1994. Indexed.
Paper. $14.00. 170 pp. .... Vendor G0140

Dauphin County

1790 Pennsylvania Census: Dauphin County.
Paper. $11.00. .... Vendor G0549

Burgert, Annette K. **Early Marriage Evidence from the Court Records of Dauphin County, Pennsylvania (including Lebanon Co.) 1785-1815.** (1986) reprint 1993.
  Alphabetically arranged.
Cloth. $21.95. 91 pp. .... Vendor G0458

Egle, W. H. **History of the Counties of Dauphin & Lebanon** in the Commonwealth of Pennsylvania, Biogr. & Genealogical. (1883) reprint 1990.
Cloth. $103.50. 616 + 360 pp. .... Vendor G0259

Kelker, Luther Reily. **History of Dauphin Co., with Genealogical Memoirs.** 3 vols. in 2. (1907) reprint 1989.

Volumes I & II, History.
Volume III, Genealogy.
Cloth. $109.00/Vols. I & II. $73.00/Vol. III. 1,136 + 727 pp. .... Vendor G0259

Rupp, I. Daniel. **History & Topography of Dauphin, Cumberland, Franklin, Bedford, Adams & Perry Counties**. (1846) reprint 1994.
Cloth. $65.00. 606 pp. .... Vendor G0259

Schuylkill Roots. **Oakdale Church Record,** Berrysburg Circuit, East PA Conf. Evangelical Association (1863-1968). Indexed.
Paper. $8.00. 64 pp. .... Vendor G0536

Schuylkill Roots. **Salem Evangelical Lutheran Church, Killinger, Upper Paxton Township (1770-1859)**. Indexed.
Covers Dauphin and very early Lancaster County (Dauphin was formed from Lancaster County March 4, 1785). Majority of records transcribed from German.
Paper. $6.00. 57 pp. .... Vendor G0536

Schuylkill Roots. **Salem's Union Church Lutheran and Reformed**—now Peace United Church of Christ Berrysburg, Mifflin Township, Dauphin County, PA. Indexed.
Paper. $6.50. 48 pp. .... Vendor G0536

Schuylkill Roots. **St. Matthew's (Coleman's) Evang. Lutheran Church and Cemetery Records (1872-1966), Lykens Township**.
Paper. $7.50. 52 pp. .... Vendor G0536

Schuylkill Roots. **St. Peter's (Fetterhoff's) Evangelical Lutheran and German Reformed (now: United Church of Christ) Church Record** at Armstrong Valley, Upper Paxton Twp.; now Halifax Twp. Indexed.
Paper. $12.75. 112 pp. .... Vendor G0536

Stroh, Oscar H. **Dauphin County Tombstone Inscriptions, Vol. I**. 1985. Indexed.
Cloth, $35.00. Paper, $20.00. 202 pp. .... Vendor G0333

Stroh, Oscar H. **Dauphin County Tombstone Inscriptions, Vol. II**. 1987. Indexed.
Cloth, $35.00. Paper, $18.00. 169 pp. .... Vendor G0333

Stroh, Oscar H. **Dauphin County Tombstone Inscriptions, Vol. III**. Indexed.
Paper. $16.00. 108 pp. .... Vendor G0536

Wright, F. Edward. **Early Church Records of Dauphin County**. 1995. Indexed.
Records of the 1700s.
Paper. $12.00. 140 pp. .... Vendor G0140

Delaware County

1790 Pennsylvania Census: Delaware County.
Paper. $6.00. .... Vendor G0549

Ashmead, Henry Graham. **History of Delaware County**. (1884) reprint 1993.
Cloth. $78.00. 767 pp. .... Vendor G0259

Cope, Gilbert, and Henry G. Ashmead, eds. **Historic Homes & Institutions, & Genealogical & Personal Memoirs of Chester & Delaware Counties.** 2 vols. (1904) reprint 1993.
>   Volume I: Chester County.
>   Volume II: Delaware County.
Cloth. $62.50/vol., $119.00/set. 600 + 598 pp. .... Vendor G0259

Humphrey, John T. **Pennsylvania Births, Delaware County, 1682-1800**. 1995. Indexed.
>   Over 4,500 births.
Cloth. $21.50. 117 pp. .... Vendor G0117

Jordan, John W., ed. **A History of Delaware County and Its People**. 3 vols. in 2. (1914) reprint 1995.
>   Part I: History.
>   Part II: Biography.
Cloth. $59.50/vol., $109.00/set. 558 + 596 pp. .... Vendor G0259

Martin, John Hill. **Chester & Its Vicinity, Delaware Co.,** with Gen. Sketches of Some Old Families. (1877) reprint 1990.
Cloth. $57.00. 530 pp. .... Vendor G0259

Meier, Judith A. H., comp. **Advertisements and Notices of Interest from Norristown, PA Newspapers, Volume I (1799-1821)**. Indexed.
>   Because the Norristown newspapers served such a large area, news of Chester, Bucks, Delaware, and even more distant counties appear. See also volumes II-VI under Montgomery County.
Paper. $19.95. 166 pp. .... Vendor G0536

Palmer, Charles, ed., with Lucile Schenk. **History of Delaware County**. 2 vols. (1932) reprint 1995.
>   Volume I: History.
>   Volume II: Biography.
Cloth. $42.00/Vol. I. $22.00/Vol. II. Both volumes in one, $52.00.
352 + 100 pp. .... Vendor G0259

Wiley, S. T. **Biographical & Historical Cyclopedia of Delaware Co.,** Comprising an Historical Sketch of the County. Edited by W. S. Garner. (1894) reprint 1992.
Cloth. $54.50. 500 pp. .... Vendor G0259

Elk County

History of the Counties of McKean, Elk, Cameron & Potter, with Biographical Selections. (1890) reprint 1989.
Cloth. $126.50. 1,261 pp. .... Vendor G0259

Erie County

Miller, John. **A Twentieth Century History of Erie Co.:** A Narrative Acct. of Its Historical Progress, Its People, & Its Principal Interests. 2 vols. (1909) reprint 1990.
>   Volume I: History.
>   Volume II: Biography.
Cloth. $91.00/Vol. I. $74.50/Vol. II. 897 + 712 pp. .... Vendor G0259

Reed, John Elmer. **History of Erie County**. 2 vols. (1925) reprint 1993. Cloth. $67.50/vol., $119.00/set. 1,288 pp. .... Vendor G0259

Fayette County

1790 Pennsylvania Census: Fayette County. Paper. $8.00. .... Vendor G0549

Connellsville Area Historical Society. **Cemetery Records—Hill Grove Cemetery Connellsville, Fayette County Pennsylvania**. (1984) reprint 1994. Paper. $13.00. 232 pp. .... Vendor G0499

Crumrine, Boyd. **Virginia Court Records in Southwestern Pennsylvania**. Records of the District of West Augusta and Ohio and Yohogania Counties, Virginia 1775-1780. (1902, 1905) reprint 1997. Indexed. Illus.
 The minute books of the old Virginia courts herein transcribed cover the District of West Augusta and Yohogania and Ohio counties during the period when Virginia claimed and exercised jurisdiction over what are now the Pennsylvania counties of Washington, Greene, Fayette, Westmoreland, and Allegheny.
Contact vendor for information. 542 pp. .... Vendor G0011

Dull, Keith A. **Early Families of Somerset and Fayette Counties, Pennsylvania**. 1996. Indexed. Paper. $10.00. 120 pp. .... Vendor G0140

Ellis, Franklin. **History of Fayette County, Pennsylvania 1882**. (1882) reprint 1995. Indexed. Cloth. $70.00. 1,074 pp. .... Vendor G0499

Ellis, Franklin. **History of Fayette County,** with Biographical Sketches of Many of Its Prominent Men. (1882) reprint 1994. Cloth. $87.00. 841 pp. .... Vendor G0259

Gresham, John M., ed and Sam'l T. Wiley. **Biographical & Portrait Cyclopedia of Fayette Co**. (1889) reprint 1995. Cloth. $63.50. 602 pp. .... Vendor G0259

Hadden, James. **A History of Uniontown 1913**. (1913) reprint 1987. Indexed. Cloth. $50.00. 877 pp. .... Vendor G0499

Hadden, James. **Washington's and Braddock's Expeditions**. (1910) reprint 1991. Cloth. $16.00. 139 pp. .... Vendor G0499

Hanna, C. A. **Ohio Valley Genealogies,** Relating Chiefly to Families in Harrison, Belmont & Jefferson Cos., Oh., & Washington, Westmoreland & Fayette Cos., Pa. (1900) reprint 1990. Paper. $19.00. 172 pp. .... Vendor G0259

A History of Uniontown, the County Seat of Fayette County. (1913) reprint 1992. Cloth. $85.00. 824 pp. .... Vendor G0259

Hopkins, G. M. & Co. **Atlas of the County of Fayette and the State of Pennsylvania 1872**. (1872) reprint 1987. Illus. Cloth. $26.50. 68 pp. .... Vendor G0499

Jordan, John W., and James Hadden. **Genealogical & Personal History of Fayette County**. 3 vols. (1912) reprint 1994.
Cloth. $32.50/vol., $95.00/set. 922 pp. .... Vendor G0259

McClenathan, J. C., William A. Edie, et al. **Centennial History of the Borough of Connellsville, 1806-1906**. (1906) reprint 1995.
Cloth. $59.00. 564 pp. .... Vendor G0259

McClenathan, J. C. **Centennial History of the Borough of Connellsville, Pennsylvania, 1806-1906**. (1906) reprint 1982. Indexed.
Cloth. $29.00. 564 pp. .... Vendor G0499

Miller, Kathryn Cooley. **Fayette Co., PA Gleanings**. Indexed.
   Death records (1891-1947), cemetery records, complete Farmington-Ohiopyle, PA records.
Paper. $9.00. 114 pp. .... Vendor G0536

Miller, Kathryn Cooley. **Some Fayette Co., PA Cemeteries**. Indexed.
Paper. $19.95. 239 pp. .... Vendor G0536

Rentmeister, Jean. **Marriage and Death Notices Extracted from the Genius of Liberty and Fayette Advertiser of Uniontown, PA, 1805 [1809]-1854**. Indexed.
Paper. $8.50. 52 pp. .... Vendor G0536

T.L.C. Genealogy. **Fayette County, Pennsylvania Taxpayers, 1785-1799**. 1991. Indexed.
Paper. $14.00. 175 pp. .... Vendor G0609

Veech, James. **The Monongahela of Old:** Or, Historical Sketches of South-Western Pennsylvania to the Year 1800. (1910) reprint 1996. Indexed. Illus.
Paper. $22.00. 272 pp. .... Vendor G0011

Franklin County

1790 Pennsylvania Census: Franklin County.
Paper. $8.00. .... Vendor G0549

Biographical Annals of Franklin County. (1905) reprint 1994.
Cloth. $74.00. 706 pp. .... Vendor G0259

M'Cauley, I. H. **Historical Sketch of Franklin County**. (1878) reprint 1994.
Cloth. $32.50. 294 pp. .... Vendor G0259

Park, Miriam, and Harold Park. **Fannettsburg Presbyterian Records, 1851-1970**. Indexed.
Paper. $39.95. 446 pp. .... Vendor G0536

Richard, J. F. **History of Franklin County,** Containing a History of the County, Its Townships, Towns, Etc. . . . & Biographies. (1887) reprint 1993.
Cloth. $97.00. 968 pp. .... Vendor G0259

Rupp, I. Daniel. **History & Topography of Dauphin, Cumberland, Franklin, Bedford, Adams & Perry Counties**. (1846) reprint 1994.
Cloth. $65.00. 606 pp. .... Vendor G0259

Fulton County

History of Bedford, Somerset & Fulton Counties. (1884) reprint 1991. Illus. Cloth. $87.50. 672 pp. + illus. .... Vendor G0259

Greene County

Bates, Samuel P. **A Biographical History of Greene County, Pennsylvania**. (1888) reprint 1993.
Contact vendor for information. 338 pp. .... Vendor G0011

Crumrine, Boyd. **Virginia Court Records in Southwestern Pennsylvania**. Records of the District of West Augusta and Ohio and Yohogania Counties, Virginia 1775-1780. (1902, 1905) reprint 1997. Indexed. Illus.
   The minute books of the old Virginia courts herein transcribed cover the District of West Augusta and Yohogania and Ohio counties during the period when Virginia claimed and exercised jurisdiction over what are now the Pennsylvania counties of Washington, Greene, Fayette, Westmoreland, and Allegheny.
Contact vendor for information. 542 pp. .... Vendor G0011

Hanna, Rev. William. **History of Greene Co., PA**. Reprint of works published in 1882. Indexed.
Paper. $16.20. 357 pp. .... Vendor G0536

Huntingdon County

1790 Pennsylvania Census: Huntingdon County.
Paper. $4.50. .... Vendor G0549

Africa, J. Simpson. **History of Huntingdon & Blair Counties**. (1883) reprint 1992. Cloth. $79.50. 500 + 261 pp. .... Vendor G0259

Hoenstine. **Abstracts of Huntingdon County Wills, Vols. 1 & 2, 1787-1822**. 1990. Indexed.
Paper. $27.00. 71 pp. .... Vendor G0622

Hoenstine. **Abstracts of Huntingdon County Wills, Vol. 3, 1822-1835**. 1990. Indexed.
Paper. $27.00. 100 pp. .... Vendor G0622

Hoenstine. **Abstracts of Huntingdon County Wills, Vol. 4, 1835-1847**. 1990. Indexed.
Paper. $27.00. 86 pp. .... Vendor G0622

Lytle, M. S. **History of Huntingdon Co.,** from Earliest Times to the Centennial Anniversary of American Independence. (1876) reprint 1989.
Cloth. $42.00. 360 pp. .... Vendor G0259

McFarland, Kenneth T. H. **Hollidaysburg Records**. Indexed.
  Marriages, deaths, and partitions from weekly newspapers of Hollidaysburg (Huntingdon/Blair counties) for the years 1836-1852.
Paper. $12.95. 129 pp. .... Vendor G0536

Whisker, Jim. **Gunsmiths of Huntingdon County, PA**.
Paper. $2.00. 9 pp. .... Vendor G0536

Indiana County

History of Indiana County, 1745-1880. (1880) reprint 1993.
  The print of this oversized original has been reduced to fit an 8½" x 11" format, but is clear and legible. See Index listing below.
Cloth. $59.50. 543 pp. .... Vendor G0259

Index to History of Indiana County, 1745-1880. Compiled by the Indiana Co. Historical Society. 1993.
  May be ordered bound with *History of Indiana County* (see above listing).
Paper. $11.00. 52 pp. .... Vendor G0259

Stephenson, Clarence D. **Indiana County 175th Anniversary History, Vol. I**. 1978. Indexed.
  Chronological-topical narrative, prehistoric to 1865. Extensive source notes. Table of Contents; 146 illustrations, 18 color.
Cloth. $27.50. 736 pp. .... Vendor G0042

Stephenson, Clarence D. **Indiana County 175th Anniversary History, Vol. II**. 1989. Indexed.
  Continuing chronological-topical narrative, 1866-1988. 82 illustrations, 54 color. (Also available: paperback list of source notes; write for price.)
Cloth. $35.00. 809 pp. .... Vendor G0042

Stephenson, Clarence D. **Indiana County 175th Anniversary History, Vol. III**. 1979. Indexed.
  Personal narratives, letters, journals, newspapers and pamphlets concerning the society, economy, politics, life and times of Indiana County, 1758-1978. 172 illustrations, 21 color.
Cloth. $27.50. 650 pp. .... Vendor G0042

Stephenson, Clarence D. **Indiana County 175th Anniversary History, Vol. IV**. 1983. Indexed. Illus.
  Biographical sketches of 801 Indiana County notables, past and present. Table of Surnames.
Cloth. $27.50. 637 pp. .... Vendor G0042

Stephenson, Clarence D. **Indiana County 175th Anniversary History, Vol. V**. 1995.
  Indexes to all volumes, bibliography, gazetteer of place names, errata, and appendices. Pennsylvania residents add 6% sales tax for above volumes (less $2.50 postage).
Cloth. $35.00. .... Vendor G0042

Warzel, Des. **Indiana Co., PA Cemeteries plus History of Brush Valley Lutheran Church, Volume I**. Indexed.
Paper. $17.95. 189 pp. .... Vendor G0536

Wiley, Samuel T. **Biographical & Historical Cyclopedia of Indiana and Armstrong Counties, PA**. Indexed.
Reprint of 1891 work. Over 2,000 surnames and vast amount of historical research.
Cloth. $60.00. 658 pp. .... Vendor G0536

Jefferson County

McKnight, W. J. **Jefferson Co., Pennsylvania:** Her Pioneers & People, 1800-1915. 2 vols. (1917) reprint 1990.
Volume I: History.
Volume II: Gen.-Bio.
Cloth. $57.00/Vol. I. $75.00/Vol. II. 542 + 701 pp. .... Vendor G0259

McKnight, W. J. **A Pioneer History of Jefferson Co., 1755-1844**. (1898) reprint 1989.
Cloth. $69.50. 670 pp. .... Vendor G0259

Steele, Patricia M. **Who, When, and Where, Vol. I, Jefferson Co., PA**. 1987. Indexed.
Deaths 1852-1855, 1893-1906. Marriages 1852-1855.
Hard-cover. $32.50. 191 pp. .... Vendor G0463

Steele, Patricia M. **Who, When, and Where, Vol. II, Jefferson Co., PA**. 1988. Indexed.
Newspaper items, 1834-1837, 1854-1889.
Hard-cover. $22.50. 117 pp. .... Vendor G0463

Steele, Patricia M. **Who, When, and Where, Vol. III, Jefferson Co., PA**. 1991. Indexed.
Marriage licenses, 1885-1890.
Hard-cover. $27.50. 141 pp. .... Vendor G0463

Steele, Patricia M. **Tombstone Hoppin', Volume I** Cemetery Inscriptions of Jefferson Co., PA. 1980. Indexed. Illus.
Seventy-five cemeteries.
Hard-cover, $42.50. 300 pp. .... Vendor G0463

Steele, Patricia M. **Tombstone Hoppin', Volume II** Cemetery Inscriptions of Jefferson Co., PA. 1981. Indexed. Illus.
Eighty-three cemeteries.
Hard-cover, $42.50. 300 pp. .... Vendor G0463

Juniata County

Historical Book of Berrysburg & Mifflin Twp., 1819-1969. (1969) reprint 1995.
Cloth. $42.50. 363 pp. .... Vendor G0259

History of That Part of the Susquehanna & Juniata Valleys, Embraced in the Counties of Mifflin, Juniata, Perry, Union & Snyder. 2 vols. (1886) reprint 1992.
Cloth. $125.00. 1,601 pp. .... Vendor G0259

Jones, U. C. **History of the Early Settlement of the Juniata Valley,** Embracing an Account of the Early Pioneers. (1855) reprint 1993.
Cloth. $47.50. 440 pp. .... Vendor G0259

Lackawanna County

Stephens, J. B. **History & Directory of Newton & Ransom Twps., Lackawanna Co.,** Including a History of the Wyoming Valley . . . Also Many Biographical Sketches. (1912) reprint 1994.
Cloth. $29.50. 247 pp. .... Vendor G0259

Lackawanna Valley

Hayden, Horace E., et al., eds. **Genealogical & Family History of the Wyoming & Lackawanna Valleys.** 2 vols. (1906) reprint 1995.
Cloth. $65.00/vol., $119.50/set. 582 + 627 pp. .... Vendor G0259

Lancaster County

1790 Pennsylvania Census: Lancaster County.
Paper. $15.00. .... Vendor G0549

Clare, Israel Smith. **Brief History of Lancaster County**. (1892) reprint 1994.
Cloth. $36.00. 317 pp. .... Vendor G0259

Dix, Katharine F. **1771 Lancaster County, PA Archives**.
  An alphabetical listing of taxpayers/land owners.
Paper. $8.00. 104 pp. .... Vendor G0536

Ellis, Franklin, and Samuel Evans. **History of Lancaster County,** with Biographical Sketches of Many of Its Prominent Men & Pioneers. 1883.
Cloth. $105.00. 1,101 pp. .... Vendor G0259

Index to History of Lancaster County. Compiled by Lancaster County Historical Society. Repr. by permission. 1993.
Cloth. $39.50. 337 + 12 pp. .... Vendor G0259

Fulton, Eleanore J., and Barbara K. Mylin. **An Index to the Will Books and Intestate Records of Lancaster County, Pennsylvania, 1729-1850**. (1936) reprint 1994. Illus.
Cloth. $15.00. 136 pp. .... Vendor G0010

Harris, Alexander. **A Biographical History of Lancaster County [Pennsylvania]:** Being a History of Eminent Men of the County. (1872) reprint 1997.
Contact vendor for information. 638 pp. .... Vendor G0011

Historical Society of Pennsylvania. **Abstracts of Lancaster County, Pennsylvania Wills, 1732-1785**. 1996. Indexed.
Paper. $26.00. 327 pp. .... Vendor G0140

Historical Society of Pennsylvania. **Abstracts of Lancaster County, Pennsylvania Wills, 1786-1820**. 1996. Indexed.
Paper. $27.00. 337 pp. .... Vendor G0140

Journal of the Lancaster County Historical Society. 1896-present. Indexed.
 Local history, genealogy, and biography.
Paper. $8.00. .... Vendor G0572

Kelker, Luther R., trans. **Baptismal and Marriage Records, Rev. John Waldschmidt: Cocalico, Moden Krick, Weisseichen Land and Seltenreich Gemeinde Lancaster County, Penna., 1752-1786**. (1906) reprint 1996.
Paper. $16.00. 164 pp. .... Vendor G0011

Lancaster County, PA Cemetery Surname Index.
 A listing of all surnames found in over 600 cemeteries encompassing just about every township and hamlet as well as the larger towns of the county.
Paper. $10.50. 118 pp. .... Vendor G0536

Mayhill, R. Thomas. **Deed Abstracts and Oaths of Allegiance, Deed Books A through M, 1729-1770**. rev. ed. 1973. Indexed.
 With adjoining landowners and witnesses.
Cloth. $34.00. 276 pp. .... Vendor G0531

Mombert, J. I. **An Authentic History of Lancaster County in the State of Pennsylvania**. (1969) reprint 1994.
Cloth. $79.50. 617 + 175 pp. .... Vendor G0259

Portrait & Biographical Record of Lancaster County. (1894) reprint 1994.
Cloth. $72.50. 685 pp. .... Vendor G0259

Rineer, A. Hunter, Jr. **Churches and Cemeteries of Lancaster County, PA. A Complete Guide**. 1993. Indexed.
 Churches and cemeteries listed by municipality. Location of available records listed.
Cloth. $43.95. 560 pp. .... Vendor G0572

Rupp, I. Daniel. **History of Lancaster Co.,** To Which is Prefixed a Brief Sketch of the Early History of Pa. (1844) reprint 1992.
Cloth. $55.00. 524 pp. .... Vendor G0259

Schuylkill Roots. **Salem Evangelical Lutheran Church, Killinger, Upper Paxton Township (1770-1859)**. Indexed.
 Covers Dauphin and very early Lancaster County (Dauphin was formed from Lancaster County March 4, 1785). Majority of records transcribed from German.
Paper. $6.00. 57 pp. .... Vendor G0536

Smith, Debra D., and Frederick S. Weiser, eds. **Trinity Lutheran Church Records, Vol. 1, 1730-1767**. Indexed.
 One of pre-Revolutionary America's most influential Protestant congregations. Includes complete and accurate church records (baptisms, marriages, communicants, confirmands, pew rents). A necessity for anyone searching German Lancaster Co. heritage.
Cloth. $39.95. 487 pp. .... Vendor G0536

Smith, Debra D., and Frederick S. Weiser, eds. **Trinity Lutheran Church Records, Vol. 2, 1767-1782**. Indexed.
Cloth. $39.95. 578 pp. .... Vendor G0536

Wood, Stacy B. C., Jr. **Clockmakers & Watchmakers of Lancaster County, Pennsylvania**. 1995. Indexed. Illus.
  Includes biographical listings, maps, photos, and old advertisements.
Cloth. $27.95. 75 pp. .... Vendor G0572

Wright, F. Edward. **Lancaster County Church Records of the 18th Century. Vol. 1**. 1994. Indexed.
  Includes Blaser's Reformed, Cocalico Ref., Manheim, Maytown, Muddy Creek, Pequea, Reiher's, Seltenreich, Swamp Reformed, White Oaks Congregation, Elizabethtown Luth., and Bergstrasse Lutheran.
Paper. $21.50. 270 pp. .... Vendor G0140

Wright, F. Edward. **Lancaster County Church Records of the 18th Century, Vol. 2: First Reformed Church of the City of Lancaster**. 1994. Indexed.
Paper. $26.00. 325 pp. .... Vendor G0140

Wright, F. Edward. **Lancaster County Church Records of the 18th Century, Vol. 3**. 1994. Indexed.
  Births, marriages, and deaths from Sadsbury Monthly Meeting (also abstracts of minutes), St. James Episcopal, St. Mary's Catholic, the pastoral records of Rev. Cuthbertson (Presby.) and Casper Stoever (Lutheran), and lists of names for Donegal Presbyterian.
Paper. $22.50. 279 pp. .... Vendor G0140

Xakellis, Martha J., comp. **Grave Undertakings 1, Elizabeth Township, Lancaster**.
  Contents include map of Elizabeth Township with cemetery locations and tombstone inscriptions from a number of cemeteries.
Paper. $12.00. 96 pp. .... Vendor G0536

Xakellis, Martha J., comp. **Grave Undertakings 2, Warwick Township**.
  Includes 28 cemeteries.
Paper. $14.95. 160 pp. .... Vendor G0536

Grave Undertakings 3, Clay Township (Old Warwick Twp). By Martee's.
Paper. $8.00. 41 pp. .... Vendor G0536

Lawrence County

Copper, Dwight Edward. **Cemeteries of Lawrence County, Pennsylvania, Book 1 (Scott Township)**.
  All twelve books in this series include tombstone inscriptions.
Paper. $8.00. 29 pp. .... Vendor G0536

Copper, Dwight Edward. **Cemeteries of Lawrence County, Pennsylvania, Book 2 (Hickory Township)**.
Paper. $8.00. 36 pp. .... Vendor G0536

Copper, Dwight Edward. **Cemeteries of Lawrence County, Pennsylvania, Book 3 (Slippery Rock Twp.—A).**
Paper. $8.00. 31 pp. .... Vendor G0536

Copper, Dwight Edward. **Cemeteries of Lawrence County, Pennsylvania, Book 4 (Slippery Rock Twp.—B).**
Paper. $8.00. 31 pp. .... Vendor G0536

Copper, Dwight Edward. **Cemeteries of Lawrence County, Pennsylvania, Book 5 (Slippery Rock Twp.—C).**
Paper. $8.00. 39 pp. .... Vendor G0536

Copper, Dwight Edward. **Cemeteries of Lawrence County, Pennsylvania, Book 6 (Pulaski Township).**
Paper. $8.00. 41 pp. .... Vendor G0536

Copper, Dwight Edward. **Cemeteries of Lawrence County, Pennsylvania, Book 7 (Wayne Township).** Indexed.
Paper. $8.00. 77 pp. .... Vendor G0536

Copper, Dwight Edward. **Cemeteries of Lawrence County, Pennsylvania, Book 8 (Perry and Washington Twp).**
Paper. $8.00. 28 pp. .... Vendor G0536

Copper, Dwight Edward. **Cemeteries of Lawrence County, Pennsylvania, Book 9 (Plaingrove Township).** Indexed.
Paper. $8.00. 49 pp. .... Vendor G0536

Copper, Dwight Edward. **Cemeteries of Lawrence County, Pennsylvania, Book 10 (Shenango Twp).** Indexed.
Paper. $8.00. 70 pp. .... Vendor G0536

Copper, Dwight Edward. **Cemeteries of Lawrence County, Pennsylvania, Book 11 (Mahoning Twp.).**
Paper. $8.00. 45 pp. .... Vendor G0536

Copper, Dwight Edward. **Cemeteries of Lawrence County, Pennsylvania, Book 12 (New Beaver Boro).**
Paper. $8.00. 113 pp. .... Vendor G0536

Hazen, Aaron L., ed. & comp. **Twentieth Century History of New Castle & Lawrence County,** & Representative Citizens. (1908) reprint 1992.
Cloth. $99.00. 1,015 pp. .... Vendor G0259

Myers, Paul. **Lawrence Co., PA Soldiers** (Rev. War, War of 1812, Civil War).
Paper. $9.00. 91 pp. .... Vendor G0536

Lebanon County

Burgert, Annette K. **Early Marriage Evidence from the Court Records of Dauphin County, Pennsylvania (including Lebanon Co.) 1785-1815**. (1986) reprint 1993.
Alphabetically arranged.
Cloth. $21.95. 91 pp. .... Vendor G0458

Egle, W. H. **History of the Counties of Dauphin & Lebanon** in the Commonwealth of Pennsylvania, Biogr. & Genealogical. (1883) reprint 1990.
Cloth. $103.50. 616 + 360 pp. .... Vendor G0259

Humphrey, John T. **Pennsylvania Births, Lebanon County, 1714-1800**. 1996. Indexed.
  Over 7,500 births.
Cloth. $29.50. 267 pp. .... Vendor G0117

Rupp, I. Daniel. **History of the Counties of Berks & Lebanon**. (1844) reprint 1992.
Cloth. $55.00. 512 pp. .... Vendor G0259

Wright, F. Edward. **Early Church Records of Lebanon County, PA**. 1995. Indexed.
Paper. $40.00. 511 pp. .... Vendor G0140

Lehigh County

Daniel Schumacher's Baptismal Register, 1754-1773. 1994. Indexed.
  Book #1425.
Cloth. $29.50. 320 pp. .... Vendor G0082

Humphrey, John T. **Pennsylvania Births, Lehigh County, 1734-1800**. 1992. Indexed.
  Over 11,000 births.
Cloth. $32.50. 327 pp. .... Vendor G0117

Kistler, John L. **Baptismal Records of Jerusalem Lutheran and Reformed Church, Berks County, Pennsylvania**.
  English translation of entries dating between 1768-1863 from the church's first record book. The church served an area including parts of Berks and Lehigh counties.
Paper. $7.00. 62 pp. .... Vendor G0627

Mathews, Alfred, and A. Hungerford. **History of the Counties of Lehigh & Carbon**. (1884) reprint 1993.
Cloth. $82.50. 802 pp. .... Vendor G0259

Roberts, Stoudt, Krick, and Dietrich. **History of Lehigh County,** with a Genealogical & Biographical Record of Its Families. 3 vols. (1914) reprint 1993.
  Volume I: History.
  Volumes II & III: Genealogy & Biography.
Cloth. $105.00/Vol. I. $72.50/Vols. II & III. $225.00/set. 1,101 + 780 +
690 pp. .... Vendor G0259

Rupp, I. D. **History of Northampton, Lehigh, Monroe, Carbon, and Schuylkill Counties**. (1845) reprint 1991.
Cloth. $59.00. 568 pp. .... Vendor G0259

Schuylkill Roots. **Church Records of the Upper Milford Reformed Congregation Now Zion's Reformed Church at Zionsville, Lehigh County, PA**. Indexed.
Paper. $5.00. 36 pp. .... Vendor G0536

Schuylkill Roots. **Private Records of Rev. Johannes H. Helfrich (1790-1810)**. Indexed.
  Rev. Helfrich was one of the fathers of the Reformed Church movement in America.

He served congregations in Lehigh and Berks counties. This book contains marriage records from 1790-1810 and burial records 1790-1795.
Paper. $5.00. 38 pp. .... Vendor G0536

Lehigh Valley

Jordan, Breen, and Ettinger. **Historic Homes & Institutions, & Genealogical & Personal Memoirs of the Lehigh Valley.** 2 vols. (1905) reprint 1992.
Cloth. $56.00/vol., $99.00/set. 516 + 528 pp. .... Vendor G0259

Luzerne County

1790 Pennsylvania Census: Luzerne County.
Paper. $4.00. .... Vendor G0549

Bradsby, H. C., ed. **History of Luzerne County,** with Biographical Selections. (1893) reprint 1992.
Cloth. $145.00. 1,509 pp. .... Vendor G0259

Drasher, Norm, and Peggy Drasher. **Tombstone Inscriptions Part I.** Indexed.
Paper. $14.95. 139 pp. .... Vendor G0536

Drasher, Norm, and Peggy Drasher. **Tombstone Inscriptions Part II.** Indexed.
A tombstone inscription inventory of two large Luzerne County cemeteries: Conyngham Lutheran and Black Creek United Methodist Cemetery.
Paper. $14.95. 157 pp. .... Vendor G0536

Drasher, Norm, and Peggy Drasher. **Tombstone Inscriptions Part III.** Indexed.
Contains the cemetery records of the Conyngham Cemetery and Mountain View Cemetery.
Paper. $19.95. 236 pp. .... Vendor G0536

Drasher, Norm, and Peggy Drasher, comps. **Tombstone Inscriptions St. John's Lutheran and Reformed Cemetery St. John's (formerly Hughesville).** Indexed.
Information from the early 1800s until October 1992.
Paper. $19.95. 202 pp. .... Vendor G0536

Kulp, George B. **Families of the Wyoming Valley,** with Biographical, Genealogical & Historical Sketches of the Bench & Bar of Luzerne County. 3 vols. (1885) reprint 1994.
Cloth. $135.00. 1,423 pp. .... Vendor G0259

Pearce, Stewart. **Annals of Luzerne County:** A Record of Interesting Events, Traditions, and Anecdotes from the First Settlement in Wyoming Valley to 1866. 2nd ed., with notes, corrections, and additions. (1866) reprint 1995.
Cloth. $59.50. 564 pp. .... Vendor G0259

Plumb, H. B. **History of Hanover Township,** Including Sugar Notch, Ashley & Nanticoke Boroughs: Also a Hist. of Wyoming Val. in Luzerne Co. (1885) reprint 1990.

Includes genealogical tables for seventy-three Hanover Twp. families.
Cloth. $53.00. 498 pp. .... Vendor G0259

Winans, Donald L. **Index to Part II, Biographical Sketches of the History of Luzerne Co., Pennsylvania**. 1996.
Contact vendor for information. .... Vendor G0140

Wright, H. B. **Historical Sketches of Plymouth, Luzerne Co.,** Including Genealogical Information on the Founding Families. (1873) reprint 1988.
Cloth. $45.00. 404 pp. .... Vendor G0259

Lycoming County

Brass, Lucas. **Muncy Cemetery Records**. 1996. Indexed.
Hard-cover. $35.00. .... Vendor G0635

Brass, Lucas. **Turbotville & Edgewood Cemetery Records**. 1996. Indexed.
Hard-cover. $20.00. .... Vendor G0635

Leidhecker, Robin, comp. **Otzinachson Index**.
Complete every-name index of the 1889 edition of *Otzinachson: A History of the West Branch Valley* by John Meginness.
Paper. $5.00. .... Vendor G0635

Lloyd, Col. Thomas W. **History of Lycoming County**. With Biographical Sketches. 2 vols. (1929) reprint 1994.
Cloth. $65.00/vol., $125.00/set. 600 + 618 pp. .... Vendor G0259

Lycoming County Genealogical Society. **Kelchner Funeral Home Records, 1901-1933, Jersey Shore, PA**. 1996. Indexed.
Hard-cover. $20.00. 269 pp. .... Vendor G0635

Lycoming County Genealogical Society. **Lycoming County Cemetery Series, Vol. 1: Anthony, Armstrong, Bastress, Brady, Brown, Cascade, Clinton Twps**. 1996.
Hard-cover. $32.50. .... Vendor G0635

Lycoming County Genealogical Society. **Lycoming County Cemetery Series, Vol. 2: Cogan House, Cummings, Eldred, Fairfield, Franklin Twps**. 1996.
Cloth, $32.50. Paper, $25.00. .... Vendor G0635

Lycoming County Genealogical Society. **Lycoming County Cemetery Series, Vol. 3: Gamble, Hepburn, Jackson, Jordan Twps**. 1996.
Hard-cover. $32.50. .... Vendor G0635

Lycoming County Genealogical Society. **Lycoming County Cemetery Series, Vol. 4: Lewis, Limestone, Loyalsock, Lycoming Twps**.
Hard-cover. $32.50. .... Vendor G0635

Lycoming County Genealogical Society. **Records of Pleasant Hill Cemetery, Hughesville, PA**. 1996. Indexed.
Hard-cover. $35.00. .... Vendor G0635

Lycoming County Genealogical Society. **Surname Index to History of Lycoming County** (see next listing). 1996.
Paper. $5.25. .... Vendor G0635

Meginness, John. **History of Lycoming County**. (1892) reprint 1996.
Hard-cover. $88.00. 1,200 pp. .... Vendor G0635

Warzel, Des. **Lycoming Co. Cemeteries, Vol. I**. Indexed.
Paper. $15.95. 161 pp. .... Vendor G0536

McKean County

Hatch, Vernelle A. **Illustrated History of Bradford, McKean Co**. (1901) reprint 1994.
Cloth. $32.00. 261 pp. .... Vendor G0259

History of the Counties of McKean, Elk, Cameron & Potter, with Biographical Selections. (1890) reprint 1989.
Cloth. $126.50. 1,261 pp. .... Vendor G0259

Kilmer, Lawrence W. **Bradford & Foster Brook—The Peg Leg Railroad**. 1993. Illus.
   Information on five railroads in Cattaraugus Co., NY and McKean Co., PA; includes the history of the men that built them. Maps.
Paper. $20.00. 206 pp. .... Vendor G0093

Mercer County

History of Mercer Co., Its Past & Present. (1888) reprint 1989.
Cloth. $119.00. 1,210 pp. .... Vendor G0259

Myers, Paul W. **Mercer County, PA Soldiers (Revolutionary War, War of 1812, and Civil War)**. Indexed.
Paper. $8.50. 78 pp. .... Vendor G0536

Painter, Mark S. **Mercer County Archives, Volume 1 (Deeds)**. Indexed. Illus.
Paper. $12.00. 122 pp. + 7 maps. .... Vendor G0536

Painter, Mark S. **Mercer County Archives, Volume 2 (Naturalizations)**.
Paper. $19.95. 258 pp. .... Vendor G0536

Sewall, Dr. James K. **Mercer County Archives, Volume 3 (Orphan's Court)**. Indexed.
Paper. $9.95. .... Vendor G0536

Mifflin County

1790 Pennsylvania Census: Mifflin County.
Paper. $5.00. .... Vendor G0549

History of That Part of the Susquehanna & Juniata Valleys, Embraced in the Counties of Mifflin, Juniata, Perry, Union & Snyder. 2 vols. (1886) reprint 1992.
Cloth. $125.00. 1,601 pp. .... Vendor G0259

Monroe County

Jones, Robert J., comp. **Place Names of Monroe County, PA**.
Contains the history of each of Monroe County's traditional village or local community names.
Paper. $6.00. 50 pp. .... Vendor G0536

Kimler, Kim Pryse. **Tannersville Circuit Church Records (1859-1884)**. Indexed.
Paper. $14.95. 160 pp. .... Vendor G0536

Mathews, Alfred. **History of Wayne, Pike & Monroe Counties**. (1886) reprint 1993.
Cloth. $119.50. 1,283 pp. .... Vendor G0259

Rupp, I. D. **History of Northampton, Lehigh, Monroe, Carbon, and Schuylkill Counties**. (1845) reprint 1991.
Cloth. $59.00. 568 pp. .... Vendor G0259

Montgomery County

1790 Pennsylvania Census: Montgomery County.
Paper. $12.00. .... Vendor G0549

Bean, T. W. **History of Montgomery Co**. (1884) reprint 1989.
Cloth. $129.50. 1,197 + 98 pp. .... Vendor G0259

Cramer, Peggy C. **(Index) Marriage Notices from the Norristown Herald 1843-1899**.
Index to marriage notices from the *Norristown Herald*, a countywide newspaper that began publication in 1799.
Paper. $24.95. 272 pp. .... Vendor G0536

Humphrey, John T. **Pennsylvania Births, Montgomery County 1682-1800**. 1993. Indexed.
Over 18,000 births.
Cloth. $42.50. 536 pp. .... Vendor G0117

Johnson, Ralph L. **(Collegeville) Genealogical Studies of Some Providence Families (& Their Connections)**. (1934) reprint 1994.
Paper. $19.50. 181 pp. .... Vendor G0259

Meier, Judith A. H., comp. **Advertisements and Notices of Interest from Norristown, PA Newspapers, Volume I (1799-1821)**. Indexed.
Because the Norristown newspapers served such a large area, news of Chester, Bucks, Delaware, and even more distant counties appear. See also volumes II-VI below.
Paper. $19.95. 166 pp. .... Vendor G0536

Meier, Judith A. H., comp. **Advertisements and Notices of Interest from Norristown, PA Newspapers, Volume II (1822-1827)**. Indexed.
Contains abstracts of newspaper notices of marriages and deaths, sales of houses, farms, mills, and taverns, and announcements of meetings.
Paper. $19.95. 187 pp. .... Vendor G0536

Meier, Judith A. H., comp. **Advertisements and Notices of Interest from Norristown, PA Newspapers, Volume III (1828-1832)**. Indexed.
Paper. $19.95. 196 pp. .... Vendor G0536

Meier, Judith A. H., comp. **Advertisements and Notices of Interest from Norristown, PA Newspapers, Volume IV (1833-1838)**. Indexed.
Paper. $19.95. 227 pp. .... Vendor G0536

Meier, Judith A. H., comp. **Advertisements and Notices of Interest from Norristown, PA Newspapers, Volume V (1839-1843)**. Indexed.
Paper. $19.95. 242 pp. .... Vendor G0536

Meier, Judith A. H., comp. **Advertisements and Notices of Interest from Norristown, PA Newspapers, Volume VI (1844-1848)**. Indexed.
Paper. $22.95. 324 pp. .... Vendor G0536

Roberts, Ellwood. **Biographical Annals of Montgomery County.** 2 vols. 1904.
Cloth. $55.00/vol., $105.00/set. 544 + 542 pp. .... Vendor G0259

Sachse, Julius Friedrich. **Augustus Evangelical Lutheran Congregation at Trappe (Perkiomen Valley)**. Indexed.
Paper. $9.00. 77 pp. .... Vendor G0536

Wiley, Samuel T. **Biographical & Portrait Cyclopedia of Montgomery County.** (1895) reprint 1994.
Cloth. $69.50. 652 pp. .... Vendor G0259

Montour County

Battle, J. H., ed. **History of Columbia & Montour Counties,** Containing a History of Each County, Their Townships, Towns & Villages . . . & Biographies. (1887) reprint 1993.
Cloth. $88.00. 132 + 542 + 220 pp. .... Vendor G0259

Northampton County

1790 Pennsylvania Census: Northampton County.
Paper. $12.50. .... Vendor G0549

Daniel Schumacher's Baptismal Register, 1754-1773. 1994. Indexed.
Book #1425.
Cloth. $29.50. 320 pp. .... Vendor G0082

Griffiths, Gaylord, comp. **An Alphabetized Listing of Those Subscribers to the Oaths of Allegiance, 1777-1784 (also Oaths of Office 1789-1804)**.
Lists 4,172 white male inhabitants of Northampton County over 18 years of age who subscribed to the Oath of Allegiance to the Commonwealth of Pennsylvania between 1777 and 1784.
Paper. $12.00. 91 pp. .... Vendor G0536

History of Northampton County, 1752-1877, with Illustrations Descriptive of Its Scenery. (1877) reprint 1995.
Cloth. $39.00. 293 pp. .... Vendor G0259

Humphrey, John T. **Pennsylvania Births, Northampton County, 1733-1800**. 1991. Indexed.
   Over 7,000 births.
Cloth. $28.00. 239 pp. .... Vendor G0117

Kieffer, Henry Martyn. **Some of the First Settlers of the Forks of the Delaware, and Their Descendants**. (1902) reprint 1990. Indexed.
Paper. $35.00. 500 pp. .... Vendor G0140

Rupp, I. D. **History of Northampton, Lehigh, Monroe, Carbon, and Schuylkill Counties**. (1845) reprint 1991.
Cloth. $59.00. 568 pp. .... Vendor G0259

Northumberland County

1790 Pennsylvania Census: Northumberland County.
Paper. $12.00. .... Vendor G0549

Bell, Herbert C., ed. **History of Northumberland County**. (1891) reprint 1993.
Cloth. $109.00. 1,256 pp. .... Vendor G0259

Eisley, Ed. **Sunbury, Pennsylvania: An Alphabetical Guide to the Newspapers**. Includes: Marriages, Deaths, and Estate Notes Volume 24, 1895.
   Paper. $50.50. Contact vendor for information about other volumes in this series.
324 pp. .... Vendor G0760

Fisher, Charles A. **Wills and Administrations of Northumberland County, Pennsylvania, 1772-1849**. Reprint on microfiche.
Order no. 311, $10.00. 77 pp. .... Vendor G0478

Fisher, Charles A. **Wills and Administrations of Northumberland County, Pennsylvania,** Including Wills and Administrations of Union, Mifflin, and Indiana Counties. (1950) reprint 1996. Indexed.
Paper. $10.00. 77 pp. .... Vendor G0011

Myers, Paul W., comp. **Frontier Rangers from Northumberland County**.
   Chronicles the names of close to 3,000 men who devoted themselves to the protection of the frontier settlements in Pennsylvania from Iroquois Indians.
Paper. $6.00. 59 pp. .... Vendor G0536

Schuylkill Roots. **Church Records of St. David's Lutheran & Reformed Church Hebe, Jordan Twp., Northumberland County**. Indexed.
Paper. $9.95. 74 pp. .... Vendor G0536

Schuylkill Roots. **Mount Carmel Cemetery,** Located at Mount Carmel. Indexed.
   Located just outside of Mt. Carmel in the section known as "Alaska," this is a very

large interdenominational cemetery, composed of 13 sections bounded by paved roads.
Paper. $16.00. 145 pp. .... Vendor G0536

Schuylkill Roots, comp. **Oakhill (O. of I.A.) Cemetery at Mt. Carmel (Alaska).**
Indexed.
Paper. $5.00. 27 pp. .... Vendor G0536

Pennsylvania County

Pennsylvania County Willbook Indices.
   Allegheny, 1789-1869; Armstrong, 1805-1900; Beaver, 1800-1900; Bedford, 1771-
1900; Butler, 1800-1900; Cambria, 1804-1900; Fayette, 1783-1900; Fulton, 1850-
1900; Greene, 1796-1900; Indiana, 1803-1900; Jefferson, 1852-1906; Mercer, 1804-
1900; Northampton, 1752-1802; Somerset, 1795-1900; Washington, 1781-1900;
Westmoreland, 1773-1896; York, 1749-1900.
Any 1 index, $9.50. Any 3 indexes, $25.00. Each additional index
over 3, $7.00. .... Vendor G0536

Perry County

Hain, H. H. **History of Perry Co.,** Including Descriptions of Indian & Pioneer Life,
from the Time of Earliest Settlement, with Sketches of Its Noted Men & Women, and
Many Professional Men. (1922) reprint 1992.
Cloth. $98.00. 1,088 pp. .... Vendor G0259

History of That Part of the Susquehanna & Juniata Valleys, Embraced in the
Counties of Mifflin, Juniata, Perry, Union & Snyder. 2 vols. (1886) reprint 1992.
Cloth. $125.00. 1,601 pp. .... Vendor G0259

Rupp, I. Daniel. **History & Topography of Dauphin, Cumberland, Franklin,
Bedford, Adams & Perry Counties.** (1846) reprint 1994.
Cloth. $65.00. 606 pp. .... Vendor G0259

30 Perry County, PA Cemeteries. Indexed.
Paper. $30.00. 348 pp. .... Vendor G0536

Wright, Silas. **History of Perry County in Pennsylvania,** from the Earliest Settlement to the Present Time. (1873) reprint 1993.
Cloth. $34.00. 290 pp. .... Vendor G0259

Philadelphia County

1790 Pennsylvania Census: Philadelphia County.
Paper. $25.00. .... Vendor G0549

Adams, Raymond D. **Ulster Emigrants to Philadelphia, 1803-1850.** (1992) reprint
1996.
Paper. $15.00. 102 pp. .... Vendor G0011

Birkett, Oda Katherine. **Records of the Tioga Presbyterian Church.** Indexed.
In 1859 the Kenderton Presbyterian Church merged with the McDowell Presbyterian Church and changed its name to Tioga. Church records for period Jan. 16, 1859-April 2, 1905.
Paper. $10.95. 85 pp. .... Vendor G0536

Dixon, Ruth Priest, and Katherine George Eberly. **Index to Seamen's Protection Certificate Applications, Port of Philadelphia, 1796-1823.** 1995.
Paper. $16.50. 152 pp. .... Vendor G0011

Dixon, Ruth Priest. **Index to Seamen's Protection Certificate Applications, Port of Philadelphia, 1824-1861.** (1994) reprint 1997.
Contact vendor for information. 170 pp. .... Vendor G0011

Guide to Records of Sale of Commonwealth Property in the County of Philadelphia, 1780-1798. 1996.
Paper. $17.95 + $3.50 p&h. .... Vendor G0202

Hildeburn, Charles R. **Baptisms and Burials** from the Records of Christ Church, Philadelphia, 1709-1760. (1877-83, 1888-93) reprint 1995.
Paper. $24.00. 231 pp. .... Vendor G0011

Humphrey, John T. **Pennsylvania Births, Philadelphia County 1644-1765.** 1994. Indexed.
Over 17,000 births.
Cloth. $42.00. 567 pp. .... Vendor G0117

Humphrey, John T. **Pennsylvania Births, Philadelphia County, 1766-1780.** 1995. Indexed.
Over 17,000 births.
Cloth. $42.00. 570 pp. .... Vendor G0117

Martindale, Joseph C., rev. ed. by Albert W. Dudley. **A History of the Townships of Byberry & Moreland in Philadelphia,** from Their Earliest Settlements to the Present Time. n. d.
Cloth. $46.00. 416 pp. .... Vendor G0259

Meier, Judith Ann Highley. **Runaway Women—Elopements and Other Miscreant Deeds** as Advertised in The Pennsylvania Gazette, 1728-1789. Indexed.
Paper. $10.95. 113 pp. .... Vendor G0536

Myers, Albert Cook. **Quaker Arrivals at Philadelphia 1682-1750.** Being a List of Certificates of Removal Received at Philadelphia Monthly Meeting of Friends. (1902) reprint 1997. Indexed.
Paper. $15.00. 131 pp. .... Vendor G0011

Philadelphia Maps, 1682-1982: Townships-Districts-Wards. 1996.
Paper. $18.95 + $4.00 p&h. 112 pp. .... Vendor G0202

Precision Indexing. **Philadelphia, Pennsylvania 1870 Census Index.** 2 vols. 1989. Indexed. Illus.
Cloth. $250.00. 2,192 pp. .... Vendor G0552

Record of Indentures [1771-1773] of Individuals Bound Out as Apprentices, Servants, Etc. and of German and Other Redemptioners in the Office of the Mayor of the City of Philadelphia, October 3, 1771, to October 5, 1773 (Excerpted from The Pennsylvania-German Society Proceedings and Addresses, XVI, 1907). (1907, 1973) reprint 1995. Indexed.

The vast majority of the passengers cited herein sailed from British, Irish, or Dutch ports, though some passengers were of German origin. Information given for each individual includes the port of embarkation, exact date of arrival, name of person to whom apprenticed or indentured, residence here, occupation, term of service, and exact price of apprenticeship or indenture.
Paper. $30.00. 364 pp. .... Vendor G0011

Roach, Hannah Benner, comp. **Taxables in the City of Philadelphia**. Organized alphabetically. (1961) reprint 1990.
Paper. $6.00 + $1.00 p&h. 41 pp. .... Vendor G0202

T.L.C. Genealogy. **Philadelphia City & County, Pennsylvania Taxpayers 1779**. 1991. Indexed.
Paper. $12.00. 144 pp. .... Vendor G0609

Tepper, Michael H., ed. **Passenger Arrivals at the Port of Philadelphia, 1800-1819**. Transcribed by Elizabeth P. Bentley. 1986.
Cloth. $45.00. xvii + 913 pp. .... Vendor G0010

Whisker, Jim. **Armsmakers of Philadelphia**.
Paper. $4.00. 32 pp. .... Vendor G0536

Wright, F. Edward. **Abstracts of Philadelphia County Wills, 1682-1726**. 1995. Indexed.
Paper. $24.00. 297 pp. .... Vendor G0140

Wright, F. Edward. **Abstracts of Philadelphia County Wills, 1726-1747**. 1995. Indexed.
Paper. $24.00. 297 pp. .... Vendor G0140

Wright, F. Edward. **Early Records of the First Reformed Church of Philadelphia: Vol. 1, 1748-1780**. 1994. Indexed.
Paper. $22.00. 275 pp. .... Vendor G0140

Wright, F. Edward. **Early Records of the First Reformed Church of Philadelphia: Vol. 2, 1781-1800**. 1994. Indexed.
Paper. $22.00. 275 pp. .... Vendor G0140

Wright, F. Edward. **18th Century Records of the Germantown Reformed Church of Pennsylvania**. 1994.
Paper. $12.50. 160 pp. .... Vendor G0140

Pike County

Mathews, Alfred. **History of Wayne, Pike & Monroe Counties**. (1886) reprint 1993.
Cloth. $119.50. 1,283 pp. .... Vendor G0259

Potter County

History of the Counties of McKean, Elk, Cameron & Potter, with Biographical Selections. (1890) reprint 1989.
Cloth. $126.50. 1,261 pp. .... Vendor G0259

Schuylkill County

Daniel Schumacher's Baptismal Register, 1754-1773. 1994. Indexed.
  Book #1425.
Cloth. $29.50. 320 pp. .... Vendor G0082

Dellock, Stephen J. **Schuylkill County Death Records**. Indexed.
Paper. $19.95. 201 pp. .... Vendor G0536

History of Schuylkill County, with Illustrations & Biographical Sketches of Some of Its Prominent Men & Pioneers. (1881) reprint 1993.
Cloth. $49.50. 390 + 60 pp. .... Vendor G0259

Moser, H. O. **History of Delano, 1861-1931**. With Biographical Sketches. (1931) reprint 1993.
Cloth. $32.00. 227 pp. .... Vendor G0259

Rice, Phillip A. **Church Records of the Bethany Evangelical Congregational Church,** formerly Bethany United Evangelical, 13th and Market Street, Ashland. Indexed.
Paper. $22.95. 197 pp. .... Vendor G0536

Rice, Phillip A. **Early and Later Records of the Church of the Holy Apostles (Episcopal)** at Saint Clair, Schuylkill County, PA.
Paper. $18.50. 168 pp. .... Vendor G0536

Rice, Phillip A. **Early Records of Christ Protestant Episcopal Church at Frackville**.
Paper. $7.50. 63 pp. .... Vendor G0536

Rice, Phillip A. **Early Records of St. Paul's Episcopal Church at Minersville, Schuylkill County**. Indexed.
Paper. $13.50. 120 pp. .... Vendor G0536

Rice, Phillip A. **Early Records of Trinity Episcopal Church**. Indexed.
  Located at Centre Street and Howard Avenue, Pottsville.
Paper. $18.50. 170 pp. .... Vendor G0536

Rice, Phillip A. **More Early Records of Trinity Episcopal Church, Pottsville, Schuylkill County, PA**. Indexed.
  Church volumes 3, 4, and 5 of baptisms, marriages, and burials covering approximately years 1871-1895.
Paper. $14.50. 131 pp. .... Vendor G0536

Rice, Phillip A. **German Protestant Cemetery of Mahanoy City**.
Paper. $16.95. 152 pp. .... Vendor G0536

Rice, Phillip A. **Gilberton United Methodist Church, Gilberton, W. Mahanoy Twp.** Indexed.
Includes baptisms 1872-1938 and marriages 1872-1946.
Paper. $12.50. 109 pp. .... Vendor G0536

Rice, Phillip A. **Greenwood Cemetery.** Indexed.
Paper. $9.95. 85 pp. .... Vendor G0536

Rice, Phillip A. **Index to the Obituaries as Found in the Pottsville Republican and Various Other Periodicals of the Region for the Year 1990.**
Covering Schuylkill as well as adjoining counties.
Paper. $7.50. 56 pp. .... Vendor G0536

Rice, Phillip A. **Index to the Obituaries as Found in the Pottsville Republican and Various Other Periodicals of the Region for the Year 1991.**
Covering Schuylkill as well as adjoining counties.
Paper. $8.50. 71 pp. .... Vendor G0536

Rice, Phillip A. **Index to the Obituaries as Found in the Pottsville Republican and Various Other Periodicals of the Region for the Year 1992.**
Covering Schuylkill as well as adjoining counties.
Paper. $9.75. 82 pp. .... Vendor G0536

Rice, Phillip A. **Odd Fellows Cemetery, Pottsville, Schuylkill County, PA.** Indexed.
Paper. $16.50. 156 pp. .... Vendor G0536

Rice, Phillip A. **Odd Fellows (I.O.O.F.) Cemetery, Shenandoah Heights, West Mahonoy Twp.** Indexed.
Paper. $14.50. 135 pp. .... Vendor G0536

Rice, Phillip A., and Jean Dellock. **St. Paul's (White Church) and Ref. Congregation Records (1874-1913) with Collected Cemeteries of Union Twp. and N. Union Twp.** Indexed.
Paper. $24.95. 280 pp. .... Vendor G0536

Rupp, I. D. **History of Northampton, Lehigh, Monroe, Carbon, and Schuylkill Counties.** (1845) reprint 1991.
Cloth. $59.00. 568 pp. .... Vendor G0259

Schuylkill Roots. **Charles Baber Cemetery at Pottsville, Schuylkill County.**
Paper. $23.50. 218 pp. .... Vendor G0536

Schuylkill Roots. **Early History of St. Paul's (Summer Hill) Lutheran and Reformed Church Including Tombstone Inscriptions and Burial Record.** Indexed.
Paper. $7.50. 56 pp. .... Vendor G0536

Schuylkill Roots. **Early Records of the Memorial Church of St. John (Episcopal) at Ashland.** Indexed.
Includes baptisms, marriages, and burials (ca. 1856-1895 and as recent as 1979)
Paper. $16.50. 151 pp. .... Vendor G0536

Schuylkill Roots. **Schuylkill County, PA Archives, Vol. I.** Indexed.
Cloth. $39.95. 560 pp. .... Vendor G0536

Schuylkill Roots. **Schuylkill County, PA Archives, Vol. II**. Indexed.
Paper. $39.95. 577 pp. .... Vendor G0536

Schuylkill Roots. **Schuylkill County, PA Archives, Vol. III**. Indexed.
Paper. $39.95. 573 pp. .... Vendor G0536

Schuylkill Roots. **St. Andrew's United Methodist Church Formerly Evangelical United Brethren Church, Pt. One,** Valley View, Hegins Twp. Compiled by Dr. Glenn P. Schwalm from the original records. Indexed.
Paper. $8.50. 74 pp. .... Vendor G0536

Schuylkill Roots. **St. Andrew's United Methodist Church, Pt. Two**. Edited by Dr. Glenn P. Schwalm.
Compiled from the personal records of the Rev. Harry M. Mentzer; 2,175 baptisms, 700 marriages, 888 burials (1913-1958).
Paper. $21.95. 206 pp. .... Vendor G0536

Schuylkill Roots, comp. **St. Joseph/St. Mauritus Cemetery at Ashland**. Indexed.
Paper. $8.50. 65 pp. .... Vendor G0536

Schwalm, Dr. Glenn P., and Schuylkill Roots, comps. **Minersville Evangelical Lutheran Congregation,** Branch Twp., Schuylkill Co., PA. Indexed.
Compiled from the private record of Rev. Daniel Sanner. Includes baptisms, deaths, and marriages from 1859 to 1866.
Paper. $5.00. 34 pp. .... Vendor G0536

Schwalm, Dr. Glenn P. **St. Paul's or "White" Church at Ringtown, Union Twp**. Indexed.
Earlier records of the "Old White Church."
Paper. $15.00. 135 pp. .... Vendor G0536

Schwalm, Dr. Glenn P., comp. **Zion's Evangelical German Lutheran Church Records**. Indexed.
Located in Girardville, this church held its first service June 1, 1880.
Paper. $8.50. 74 pp. .... Vendor G0536

St. John's Evangelical Lutheran Church of Tremont. Indexed.
Includes baptisms 1861-1903, marriages 1863-1903, and deaths 1861-1902.
Paper. $16.50. 154 pp. .... Vendor G0536

Wiley, S. T., and H. W. Ruoff. **Biographical & Portrait Cyclopedia of Schuylkill County,** Comprising a Historical Sketch of the County. (1893) reprint 1993.
Over 550 biographical sketches.
Cloth. $75.00. 752 pp. .... Vendor G0259

Snyder County

Fisher, Charles A. **Probate and Orphans Court Records of Snyder County, Pennsylvania, 1772-1855**. (1940) reprint 1991. Indexed.
Paper. $10.00. 87 pp. .... Vendor G0011

History of That Part of the Susquehanna & Juniata Valleys, Embraced in the Counties of Mifflin, Juniata, Perry, Union & Snyder. 2 vols. (1886) reprint 1992.
Cloth. $125.00. 1,601 pp. .... Vendor G0259

Somerset County

Collins, Pat. **Nominal Index to N. Leroy Baldwin's 200 Years in Shade Twp., PA, 1762-1962.**
Paper. $2.50. 9 pp. .... Vendor G0536

Dull, Keith A. **Early Families of Somerset and Fayette Counties, Pennsylvania.** 1996. Indexed.
Paper. $10.00. 120 pp. .... Vendor G0140

History of Bedford, Somerset & Fulton Counties. (1884) reprint 1991. Illus.
Cloth. $87.50. 672 pp. + illus. .... Vendor G0259

Palmer, Mary Pyle. **Beam German Reformed Church Records** (now Mt. Laurel United Church of Christ), Jenner Township, and Joint Consistory of the Beam's Charge. Indexed.
Paper. $8.50. 95 pp. .... Vendor G0536

Saylor, E. C., comp. **Church Records of Berlin, Somerset Co., PA**. Indexed.
Since Somerset County was formed from the westernmost part of Bedford County in 1795, a portion of these records cover Bedford County. They represent one of the earliest and most complete sets of vital records of western PA.
Paper. $19.95. 195 pp. .... Vendor G0536

Whisker, James B. **Gunsmiths and Gunmakers of Bedford and Somerset County**.
Paper. $2.50. 12 pp. .... Vendor G0536

Sullivan County

Streby. **Index to History of Sullivan County**. 1996.
Unbound. $3.25. .... Vendor G0635

Susquehanna County

Blackman, Emily C. **History of Susquehanna Co.,** from a Period Preceding Its Settlement to Recent Times. (1873) reprint 1992.
Cloth. $68.00. 640 pp. .... Vendor G0259

Harrington, Jeanne E. S. **Marriage and Death Records Copied from Susquehanna Pennsylvania Newspapers, 1815-1849**. Reprint on microfiche.
Order no. 292, $10.00. 147 pp. .... Vendor G0478

Hawley, D. P., comp. **Silver Lake Twp. (Susquehanna Co.) Tax Rolls, 1878-1879**. 1994.
Paper. $13.00. 64 pp. .... Vendor G0259

Stocker, Rhamanthus M. **Centennial History of Susquehanna County**. (1887) reprint 1993.
Cloth. $87.50. 851 pp. .... Vendor G0259

Tioga County

History of Tioga County, with Illustrations, Portraits & Sketches of Prominent Families & Individuals. (1883) reprint 1992.
Cloth. $45.00. 366 + 35 pp. .... Vendor G0259

Maginess, Meagher, et al., comps. **The History of Tioga County**. (1897) reprint 1988.
Cloth. $109.00. 1,186 pp. .... Vendor G0259

Murray, Louis Welles. **History of Old Tioga Point & Early Athens**. (1908) reprint 1994.
Cloth. $69.00. 656 pp. .... Vendor G0259

Union County

History of That Part of the Susquehanna & Juniata Valleys, Embraced in the Counties of Mifflin, Juniata, Perry, Union & Snyder. 2 vols. (1886) reprint 1992.
Cloth. $125.00. 1,601 pp. .... Vendor G0259

Venango County

Babcock, Charles A. **Venango County, Her Pioneers & People**. 2 vols. (1919) reprint 1994.
　　Volume I: History.
　　Volume II: Biography.
Cloth. $55.00/vol., $105.00/set. 560 + 527 pp. .... Vendor G0259

Hanson, Joan (Search), and Kenneth L. Hanson. **Marriages from Venango County Sources 1795-1885 (All Inclusive), 1886-1921 (Outside the County)**. Indexed. Illus.
Cloth, $45.95. Paper, $35.95. 381 pp. .... Vendor G0536

Hanson, Ken, and Joan (Search) Hanson. **Venango Co., PA Death Book Summary & Index**.
Paper. $9.95. 1,105 pp. .... Vendor G0536

History of Venango County: Its Past & Present, Including Its Aboriginal History . . . Its Early Settlement & Subsequent Growth . . . Its Historic & Interesting Localities . . . Family History, Etc. (1890) reprint 1992.
Cloth. $108.50. 1,164 pp. .... Vendor G0259

Myers, Paul W., comp. **Venango Co., PA Soldiers**. Indexed.
Paper. $8.50. 73 pp. .... Vendor G0536

Romig, Nancy Byers. **Scrips & Scraps—Scrapbook Abstracts—Venango and Surrounding Counties**. Indexed.
　Abstracts from scrapbooks kept by Porter and Sarah Phipps, Nannie Cross, and their families. Includes obituaries, weddings, birthdays, and other social and political events, primarily concerning families in the Clintonville-Kennerdell area, oil men, Civil War friends, and then Pittsburgh friends after 1900.
Paper. $24.95. 318 pp. .... Vendor G0536

Venango County Historical Society. **Venango County, Pennsylvania Cemetery Records and Early Church Histories, Volume I** (Irwin, Mineral and Victory Twps.). Paper. $15.00. 190 pp. .... Vendor G0536

Venango County Historical Society. **Venango County, Pennsylvania Cemetery Records and Early Church Histories, Volume 3: Scrubgrass Township.** Paper. $15.00. .... Vendor G0727

Warren County

Schenk, J. S., and W. S. Rann, eds. **History of Warren Co.,** with Illustrations & Biogr. Sketches of Some of Its Prominent Men & Pioneers. (1887) reprint 1992. Cloth. $82.00. 807 pp. .... Vendor G0259

Washington County

1790 Pennsylvania Census: Washington County. Paper. $11.50. .... Vendor G0549

Abstracts of Washington County, PA Will Books 1-5. Recompiled by Bob and Mary Closson by permission of Citizens Library. Indexed. Cloth. $39.95. 769 pp. .... Vendor G0536

Beers' 1893 (reprint) Commemorative Biographical Record of Washington County, PA. Biographical Sketches of Prominent and Representative Citizens and Many of the Early Settled Families. 2 vols. Indexed. Cloth. $80.00. 1,628 pp. .... Vendor G0536

Commemorative Biographical Record of Washington County, Containing Biographical Sketches of Prominent & Representative Citizens & Many of the Early Settled Families. (1893) reprint 1993. Cloth. $137.50. 1,486 pp. .... Vendor G0259

Creigh, Alfred. **History of Washington County from Its First Settlement.** (1870) reprint 1993. Cloth. $53.50. 386 + 121 pp. .... Vendor G0259

Crumrine, Boyd, ed. **History of Washington County,** with Biographical Sketches of Many of Its Pioneers & Prominent Men. (1882) reprint 1993. Cloth. $94.50. 1,002 pp. .... Vendor G0259

Crumrine, Boyd. **Virginia Court Records in Southwestern Pennsylvania.** Records of the District of West Augusta and Ohio and Yohogania Counties, Virginia 1775-1780. (1902, 1905) reprint 1997. Indexed. Illus.
   The minute books of the old Virginia courts herein transcribed cover the District of West Augusta and Yohogania and Ohio counties during the period when Virginia claimed and exercised jurisdiction over what are now the Pennsylvania counties of Washington, Greene, Fayette, Westmoreland, and Allegheny. Contact vendor for information. 542 pp. .... Vendor G0011

Dixon, Glen. **Records of Coal Center Methodist Church, 1873-1938**. Indexed.
Paper. $8.50. 75 pp. .... Vendor G0536

Hanna, C. A. **Ohio Valley Genealogies,** Relating Chiefly to Families in Harrison, Belmont & Jefferson Cos., Oh., & Washington, Westmoreland & Fayette Cos., Pa. (1900) reprint 1990.
Paper. $19.00. 172 pp. .... Vendor G0259

Harris, Edgar. **Highland Cemetery, California, Washington Co., PA**. Indexed.
Paper. $24.95. 292 pp. .... Vendor G0536

Historical Magazine of Monongahela's Old Home Coming Week, 1908. (1908) reprint 1993.
　Includes a history of the city, as well as reminiscences, illustrations, and miscellany.
Cloth. $32.50. 267 pp. .... Vendor G0259

Malmat, Bonnie, comp. **Abstracts of the Washington County Reporter, 1808-1814**. Indexed.
Paper. $19.95. 323 pp. .... Vendor G0536

Malmat, Bonnie, comp. **Abstracts of the Washington County Reporter, 1814-1816— Bk. 2**. Indexed.
Paper. $19.95. 222 pp. .... Vendor G0536

McFarland, Joseph F. **20th Century History of the City of Washington & Washington Co.,** & Representative Citizens. (1910) reprint 1993.
　A comprehensive history of the city and county, with over 800 pages of biography.
Cloth. $125.00. 1,369 pp. .... Vendor G0259

Myers, Paul W., comp. **Washington County, PA Frontier Rangers, 1781-1782**.
　Lists names, ranks, companies, and the PA Archives numerical code for men who served during the American Revolution as Frontier Rangers from Washington County, PA.
Paper. $7.00. 53 pp. .... Vendor G0536

Washington County, PA Marriages, 1780-1857.
　There is only one 1780 marriage and the majority of the marriages were performed from the early 1800s on.
Paper. $5.00. 16 pp. .... Vendor G0536

Wayne County

Mathews, Alfred. **History of Wayne, Pike & Monroe Counties**. (1886) reprint 1993.
Cloth. $119.50. 1,283 pp. .... Vendor G0259

Westmoreland County

1790 Pennsylvania Census: Westmoreland County.
Paper. $9.00. .... Vendor G0549

Albert, George D., ed. **History of the County of Westmoreland,** with Biographical Sketches of Its Many Pioneers & Prominent Men. (1882) reprint 1995.
Cloth. $53.00. 496 pp. .... Vendor G0259

Beers', S. N., and D. G. Beers'. **Atlas of Westmoreland County, PA.** (1867) reprint 1981. Indexed.
Paper. $25.00. .... Vendor G0536

Boucher, John N., and John W. Jordan. **History of Westmoreland County.** 3 vols. in 2. (1906) reprint 1994.
Cloth. $68.00/Vol. I. $127.50/Vols. II & III. $189.50/set. 678 +
1,308 pp. .... Vendor G0259

Crumrine, Boyd. **Virginia Court Records in Southwestern Pennsylvania.** Records of the District of West Augusta and Ohio and Yohogania Counties, Virginia 1775-1780. (1902, 1905) reprint 1997. Indexed. Illus.
    The minute books of the old Virginia courts herein transcribed cover the District of West Augusta and Yohogania and Ohio counties during the period when Virginia claimed and exercised jurisdiction over what are now the Pennsylvania counties of Washington, Greene, Fayette, Westmoreland, and Allegheny.
Contact vendor for information. 542 pp. .... Vendor G0011

Hanna, C. A. **Ohio Valley Genealogies,** Relating Chiefly to Families in Harrison, Belmont & Jefferson Cos., Oh., & Washington, Westmoreland & Fayette Cos., Pa. (1900) reprint 1990.
Paper. $19.00. 172 pp. .... Vendor G0259

Myers, Paul W., comp. **Westmoreland County in the American Revolution.** Indexed.
Paper. $24.00. 263 pp. .... Vendor G0536

Seven Westmoreland Co., Pennsylvania Cemeteries. Indexed. Illus.
Paper. $7.50. 67 pp. .... Vendor G0536

Speece, Jody. **Everyname Index for Fort Ligonier and Its Time.**
Paper. $3.00. 54 pp. .... Vendor G0536

Surname Index to 52 Westmoreland County, PA Cemeteries, Volume I.
Paper. $6.50. Also sold as set with Volume 2 (see next listing), $15.00/set. 51 pp. .... Vendor G0536

Surname Index to 43 Westmoreland County, PA Cemeteries, Volume 2.
Paper. $9.50. Also sold as set with Volume 1 (see above listing), $15.00/set. 127 pp. .... Vendor G0536

T.L.C. Genealogy. **Westmoreland County, Pennsylvania, Deeds, 1773-1784.** 1995. Indexed.
Paper. $16.00. 200 pp. .... Vendor G0609

Welsh, Nancy, comp. **Four Westmoreland County, PA Cemeteries.**
Paper. $15.00. 119 pp. .... Vendor G0536

Wyoming Valley

Hayden, Horace E., et al., eds. **Genealogical & Family History of the Wyoming & Lackawanna Valleys**. 2 vols. (1906) reprint 1995.
Cloth. $65.00/vol., $119.50/set. 582 + 627 pp. .... Vendor G0259

Kulp, George B. **Families of the Wyoming Valley,** with Biographical, Genealogical & Historical Sketches of the Bench & Bar of Luzerne County. 3 vols. (1885) reprint 1994.
Cloth. $135.00. 1,423 pp. .... Vendor G0259

Stephens, J. B. **History & Directory of Newton & Ransom Twps., Lackawanna Co.,** Including a History of the Wyoming Valley . . . Also Many Biographical Sketches. (1912) reprint 1994.
Cloth. $29.50. 247 pp. .... Vendor G0259

York County

1790 Pennsylvania Census: York County.
Paper. $15.00. .... Vendor G0549

Barnes, Robert. **Guide to Research in York and Adams Counties, Pennsylvania**. 1996. Illus.
Paper. $18.00. 121 pp. .... Vendor G0140

Bates, Marlene S., and F. Edward Wright. **York County, Pennsylvania Church Records of the 18th Century**. 3 vols. 1991. Indexed.
Paper. $32.00/vol. 396 + 380 + 380 pp. .... Vendor G0140

Bowman, Diana L. **The Pennsylvania Herald & York Advertiser, Book 1 1789-1793**. Indexed.
Paper. $19.95. 214 pp. .... Vendor G0536

Bowman, Diana L. **The Pennsylvania Herald & York Advertiser, Book 2 1794-1798**.
Paper. $12.95. 132 pp. .... Vendor G0536

Carter, W. C., and A. J. Glossbrenner. **History of York County, Pa. [1729-1834]**. (1930) reprint 1996.
Paper. $24.00. 235 pp. .... Vendor G0011

Dull, Keith A. **Early Families of York County, Pennsylvania**. 2 vols. 1995.
Paper. $22.00/set. 131 + 150 pp. .... Vendor G0140

Gibson, John. **A Biographical History of York County, Pennsylvania**. (1886) reprint 1996. Illus.
Paper. $23.50. 207 pp. .... Vendor G0011

Historical Society of Pennsylvania. **Abstracts of York County, Pennsylvania, Wills, 1749-1819**. 1995. Indexed.
Paper. $32.00. 407 pp. .... Vendor G0140

Prowell, George R. **History of York County**. With Modern Subject Index. 3 vols. (1907) reprint 1993.
Volume I: History. $105.00.
Volume II: Biography. $99.50.
Volume III: Subject Index. $49.50.
Cloth. $229.00/set. $195.00/set of Vols. I & II only. 1,118+ 1,058 + 474 pp. .... Vendor G0259

Records of St. Matthews Evangelical Church 1741-1831. 1994. Indexed. Illus. Book #1463.
Cloth. $24.50. 160 pp. .... Vendor G0082

 Rhode Island

Statewide and Regional References

Arnold, James N., comp. **Records of the Proprietors of the Narragansett,** Otherwise Called the "Fones Record." (1894) reprint 1992.
These records are the very valuable Land Evidences of the founders & settlers of Rhode Island.
Paper. $21.50. 199 pp. .... Vendor G0259

Arnold, James N. **Vital Records of Rhode Island, First Series, 1636-1850**. Vols. 1, 2, 3, 7, and 8. 1895. Reprint on microfiche. Indexed.
Order no. 374—Vol. 1, $14.00; order no. 731—Vol. 2, $24.00; order no. 923—Vol. 3, $24.00; order no. 402—Vol. 7, $36.00; order no. 409—Vol. 8, $44.00. Vendor G0478

Arnold, James N. **Vital Records of Rhode Island, 1636-1850**. Births, Marriages & Deaths: A Family Register for the People. Volume VII, "Friends" & Ministers. (1891-1912) reprint 1994.
Cloth. $64.00. 634 pp. .... Vendor G0259

Arnold, James N. **Vital Records of Rhode Island, 1636-1850**. Births, Marriages & Deaths: A Family Register for the People. Volume VIII, Episcopal & Congregational. (1891-1912) reprint 1994.
Cloth. $63.50. 631 pp. .... Vendor G0259

Arnold, James N. **Vital Records of Rhode Island, 1636-1850**. Births, Marriages & Deaths: A Family Register for the People. Volume X, Town & Church Records. 1891-1912.
Cloth. $51.00. 510 pp. .... Vendor G0259

Arnold, James N. **Vital Records of Rhode Island, 1636-1850**. Births, Marriages & Deaths: A Family Register for the People. Volume XI, Church Records. (1891-1912) reprint 1994.
Cloth. $59.00. 590 pp. .... Vendor G0259

Arnold, James N. **Vital Records of Rhode Island, 1636-1850**. Births, Marriages & Deaths: A Family Register for the People. Volume XII, Revolutionary Rolls & Newspapers. (1891-1912) reprint 1994.
Cloth. $62.00. 616 pp. .... Vendor G0259

Arnold, James N. **Vital Records of Rhode Island, 1636-1850**. Births, Marriages & Deaths: A Family Register for the People. Volume XV, Providence Gazette Marriages, D-Z, U.S. Chronicle Deaths A-Z. 1891-1912.
Cloth. $63.50. 632 pp. .... Vendor G0259

Arnold, James N. **Vital Records of Rhode Island, 1636-1850**. Births, Marriages & Deaths: A Family Register for the People. Volume XVI, Marriages & Deaths. (1891-1912) reprint 1994.
Cloth. $60.00. 601 pp. .... Vendor G0259

Arnold, James N. **Vital Records of Rhode Island, 1636-1850**. Births, Marriages & Deaths: A Family Register for the People. Volume XVII, Providence "Patriot" & Columbian "Phenix." (1891-1912) reprint 1994.
Cloth. $59.50. 599 pp. .... Vendor G0259

Arnold, James N. **Vital Records of Rhode Island, 1636-1850**. Births, Marriages & Deaths: A Family Register for the People. Volume XVIII, Marriages & Deaths from the Providence "Phenix," the "Patriot," & Columbian "Phenix"; Marriages S-Z; Deaths A-M.
Cloth. $60.00. 605 pp. .... Vendor G0259

Arnold, James N. **Vital Records of Rhode Island, 1636-1850**. Births, Marriages & Deaths: A Family Register for the People. Volume XX, Rhode Island "American" Marriages, H-Z; Deaths A-B. (1891-1912) reprint 1994.
Cloth. $74.00. 737 pp. .... Vendor G0259

Arnold, James N. **Vital Records of Rhode Island, 1636-1850**. Births, Marriages & Deaths: A Family Register for the People. Volume XXI, Rhode Island "American," Deaths C-S. (1891-1912) reprint 1994.
Contact vendor for information. .... Vendor G0259

Austin, J. O. **Ancestry of 33 Rhode Islanders,** Born in the 18th Century; Also 27 Charts of Roger Williams' Descendants to the 5th Generation. (1889) reprint 1991.
Paper. $17.00. 139 pp. .... Vendor G0259

Austin, John Osborne. **Genealogical Dictionary of Rhode Island** Comprising Three Generations of Settlers Who Came Before 1690. With Additions & Corrections by G. Andrews Moriarty, 1943-1963, and a new Foreword. (1887) reprint 1995. Indexed.
Cloth. $50.00. 496 pp. .... Vendor G0010

Bartlett, John R. **Census of the Inhabitants of the Colony of Rhode Island and Providence Plantations 1774**. (1858, 1954) reprint 1990. Indexed.
Cloth. $25.00. 359 pp. .... Vendor G0011

Bartlett, John R. **Census of the Inhabitants of the Colony of Rhode Island and Providence Plantations, 1774**. (1858) Reprinted.
All towns are included with the exception of New Shoreham.
Paper. $12.00. 246 pp. .... Vendor G0561

Chamberlain, Mildred M., scr. **The Rhode Island 1777 Military Census**. 1985. Indexed.
Cloth. $20.00. 181 pp. .... Vendor G0010

Chapin, Howard M. **Rhode Island in the Colonial Wars**. A List of Rhode Island Soldiers and Sailors in King George's War, 1740-1748, and A List of Rhode Island Soldiers and Sailors in the Old French & Indian War, 1755-1762. (1918, 1920) reprint 1994.
Cloth. $15.00. 193 pp. .... Vendor G0011

Cowell, Benjamin. **Spirit of '76 in Rhode Island,** or Sketches of the Efforts of the Government and People in the War of the Revolution, Together with the Names of Those Who Belonged to R.I. Regiments in the Army, with Biogr. Notices, Etc. (1850) reprint 1996.
Contact vendor for information. 560 pp. .... Vendor G0010

Dilts, Bryan Lee, comp. **1860 Rhode Island Census Index: Heads of Household and Other Surnames in Household Index**. 1985.
Cloth. $91.00. 251 pp. .... Vendor G0552

Dilts, Bryan Lee, comp. **1870 Rhode Island Census Index: Heads of Household and Other Surnames in Household Index**. 1985.
Cloth. $91.00. 272 pp. .... Vendor G0552

Family History Library. **Research Outline: Rhode Island**.
Leaflet. $.25. 10 pp. .... Vendor G0629

The First Laws of the State of Rhode Island. 2 vols. (1798) reprint 1983.
Cloth. $122.50. .... Vendor G0118

Genealogies of Rhode Island Families. From Rhode Island Periodicals. 2 vols. 1983. Indexed. Illus.
    Vol. I: Adams-Slack. 862 pp.
    Vol. II: Smith-Yates. 914 pp.
Contact vendor for information. .... Vendor G0010

Hazard, Caroline. **The Narragansett Friends' Meeting in the XVIII Century,** with a Chapter on Quaker Beginnings in R. I. (1899) reprint 1992.
Paper. $21.00. 197 pp. .... Vendor G0259

Holbrook, Jay Mack. **Rhode Island 1782 Census**. 1979.
Cloth. $30.00. 241 pp. .... Vendor G0148

Ledogar, Edwin Richard. **Vital Statistics of Eastern Connecticut, Western Rhode Island, South Central Massachusetts**. 2 vols. 1995. Reprint on microfiche.
    Organized alphabetically.
Order no. 867-868, $38.00/each or $69.00/set. 540 + 537 pp. .... Vendor G0478

Long, John H., ed. **Connecticut, Maine, Massachusetts, and Rhode Island Atlas of Historical County Boundaries**. 1994.
    A beautiful and extremely useful book detailing the changes in county boundaries from colonial times to 1990. 8½" x 11".
Cloth. $92.00. 412 pp. .... Vendor G0611

Parker, J. Carlyle. **Rhode Island Biographical and Genealogical Sketch Index.** 1991.
Cloth. $32.45. 272 pp. .... Vendor G0492

Pease, J., and J. Niles. **Gazetteer of the States of Connecticut & R.I.** Consisting of Two Parts: I, Geogr. & Statistical Desc. of Each State; II, General Geogr. View of Each County, & a Minute & Ample Topographical Desc. of Each Town, Village, Etc. (1819) reprint 1990.
Paper. $35.00. 339 pp. .... Vendor G0259

Peirce, Ebenezer Weaver. **Peirce's Colonial Lists.** Civil, Military and Professional Lists of Plymouth and Rhode Island Colonies . . . 1621-1700. (1881) reprint 1995. Indexed.
Paper. $17.00. 156 pp. .... Vendor G0011

Potter, Elisha R. **Memoir Concerning the French Settlements and French Settlers in the Colony of Rhode Island.** (1879) reprint 1996. Illus.
Paper. $14.00. 138 pp. .... Vendor G0011

Rhode Island Historical Society. **Rhode Island Land Evidences.** Volume I. 1648-1696, Abstracts (all published). With a Preface by Albert T. Klyberg. (1921, 1970) reprint 1996. Indexed. Illus.
Cloth. $25.00. 271 pp. .... Vendor G0011

Southern California Genealogical Society. **Sources of Genealogical Help in Rhode Island.**
Paper. $1.75. 10 pp. .... Vendor G0656

Sperry, Kip. **Rhode Island Sources for Family Historians and Genealogists.**
Paper. $9.95. 146 pp. .... Vendor G0618

Taylor, Maureen A. **Rhode Island Passenger Lists** Port of Providence, 1798-1808, 1820-1872; Ports of Bristol and Warren 1820-1871. 1995.
Cloth. $25.00. 232 pp. .... Vendor G0010

Thorndale, William, and William Dollarhide. **County Boundary Map Guides to the U.S. Federal Censuses, 1790-1920: Connecticut, Massachusetts, Rhode Island, 1790-1920.** 1987.
Paper. $5.95. .... Vendor G0552

United States Bureau of the Census. **Heads of Families at the First Census of the United States Taken in the Year 1790: Rhode Island.** (1908) reprint 1992. Indexed. Illus.
Contact vendor for information. 71 pp. .... Vendor G0010

United States Bureau of the Census. **Heads of Families at the First Census of the United States Taken in the Year 1790: Rhode Island.**
Cloth, $27.50. Paper, $12.50. .... Vendor G0552

Volkel, Lowell. **Rhode Island 1800 Census Index.**
Paper. $10.00. 75 pp. .... Vendor G0574

Bristol County

Arnold, James N. **Vital Records of Rhode Island, 1636-1850**. Births, Marriages & Deaths: A Family Register for the People. Volume VI, Bristol County. (1891-1912) reprint 1994.
Cloth. $35.00. 312 pp. .... Vendor G0259

Bicknell, Thomas Williams. **History of Barrington**. (1898) reprint 1993.
Cloth. $64.50. 619 pp. .... Vendor G0259

Munro, W. H. **The History of Bristol:** The Story of the Mount Hope Lands, from the Visit of the Northmen to the Present Time. (1880) reprint 1988.
Cloth. $44.00. 396 pp. .... Vendor G0259

Kent County

Arnold, James N. **Vital Records of Rhode Island, 1636-1850**. Births, Marriages & Deaths: A Family Register for the People. Volume I, Kent County. (1891-1912) reprint 1994.
Cloth. $59.50. 610 pp. .... Vendor G0259

Arnold, James N. **Vital Records of Warwick, Rhode Island**. Originally published as *Vital Records of Rhode Island*, Volume 1, Part 1. Reprinted.
Cloth. $16.00. 234 pp. .... Vendor G0561

Cole, J. R. **History of Washington & Kent Counties**. (1889) reprint 1993.
Cloth. $129.50. 1,324 pp. .... Vendor G0259

Greene, D. H. **History of the Town of East Greenwich & Adjacent Territory, 1677-1877**. (1877) reprint 1987.
Cloth. $32.50. 263 pp. .... Vendor G0259

The Rhode Island Historical Society, ed. **Early Records of the Town of Warwick**. (1926) reprint 1993.
Cloth. $42.00. 361 pp. .... Vendor G0259

Newport County

Arnold, James N. **Vital Records of Rhode Island, 1636-1850**. Births, Marriages & Deaths: A Family Register for the People. Volume IV, Newport County. (1891-1912) reprint 1994.
Cloth. $75.00. 759 pp. .... Vendor G0259

Bayles, Richard M., ed. **History of Newport County**. (1880) reprint 1991.
Cloth. $99.00. 1,060 pp. .... Vendor G0259

Brigham, C. S., ed. **Early Records of the Town of Portsmouth**. (1901) reprint 1991.
Cloth. $49.50. 462 pp. .... Vendor G0259

Channing, G. G. **Early Recollections of Newport, from 1793 to 1811**. (1868) reprint 1987.
Cloth. $31.00. 248 pp. .... Vendor G0259

Mason, George C. **Reminiscences of Newport**. (1884) reprint 1990.
A charming history of Newport as a "watering-place," from the earliest days as a vacation spot.
Cloth. $44.00. 407 pp. .... Vendor G0259

Providence County

Arnold, James N. **Vital Records of Cranston, Johnston and North Providence, Rhode Island**. Originally published as *Vital Records of Rhode Island*, Volume 2, Parts 2, 3, and 4. Reprinted.
Cloth. $14.00. 148 pp. .... Vendor G0561

Arnold, James N. **Vital Records of Providence, Rhode Island**. Originally published as *Vital Records of Rhode Island*, Volume 2, Part 1. Reprinted.
Cloth. $21.00. 310 pp. .... Vendor G0561

Arnold, James N. **Vital Records of Rhode Island, 1636-1850**. Births, Marriages & Deaths: A Family Register for the People. Volume IX, Seekonk (Including E. Providence) & Pawtucket. (1891-1912) reprint 1994.
Cloth. $59.50. 595 pp. .... Vendor G0259

Arnold, James N. **Vital Records of Rhode Island, 1636-1850**. Births, Marriages & Deaths: A Family Register for the People. Volume XIII, Deaths, Providence, 1762-1830. (1891-1912) reprint 1994.
Contact vendor for information. .... Vendor G0259

Arnold, James N. **Vital Records of Rhode Island, 1636-1850**. Births, Marriages & Deaths: A Family Register for the People. Volume XIV, Providence Gazette Deaths, K-Z; Marriages, ABC, 1762-1825. (1891-1912) reprint 1994.
Cloth. $62.00. 616 pp. .... Vendor G0259

Arnold, James N. **Vital Records of Rhode Island, 1636-1850**. Births, Marriages & Deaths: A Family Register for the People. Volume XV, Providence Gazette Marriages, D-Z, U.S. Chronicle Deaths A-Z. 1891-1912.
Cloth. $63.50. 632 pp. .... Vendor G0259

Bayles, Richard M., et al., eds. **History of Providence County**. 2 vols. (1891) reprint 1992.
Cloth. $82.00/Vol. I. $64.00/Vol. II. $135.00/set. 821 + 639 pp. .... Vendor G0259

Chapin, Charles V., M.D. **Providence Births, 1871 to 1880, Inclusive**. Vol. IX, Alphabetical Index of the Births, Marriages & Deaths. (1903) reprint 1995.
Cloth. $57.00. 545 pp. .... Vendor G0259

Hopkins, Charles Wyman. **The Home Lotts of the Early Settlers of the Providence Plantations,** with Notes and Plats. (1886) reprint 1997. Indexed. Illus.
Contact vendor for information. 78 pp. .... Vendor G0011

Kimball, Gertrude S. **Providence in Colonial Times**. 1912. Illus.
Cloth. $45.00. 392 pp. + illus. .... Vendor G0259

Register of Seamen's Protection Certificates from the Providence, Rhode Island Customs District, 1796-1870, from the Custom House Papers in the Rhode Island Historical Society. With an Introduction by Maureen A. Taylor. 1995.
Paper. $26.50. 309 pp. .... Vendor G0011

Richardson, E. **History of Woonsocket**. (1876) reprint 1990.
Cloth. $32.50. 264 pp. .... Vendor G0259

Snow, Edwin M. **Alphabetical Index to Births Recorded in Providence from 1851-1870**. (1882) reprint 1993.
  Gives volume and page of city records where birth is recorded for 29,768 births.
Cloth. $59.50. 615 pp. .... Vendor G0259

Snow, Edwin M. **Alphabetical Index to Marriages Recorded in Providence from 1851-1870**. (1880) reprint 1993.
  Gives volume and page of city records where marriage is recorded for 13,135 marriages.
Cloth. $58.00. 547 pp. .... Vendor G0259

Snow, Edwin M., M.D. **Providence Deaths from 1851 to 1870, Inclusive**. Vol. III, Alphabetical Index of the Births, Marriages and Deaths Recorded in Providence. (1881) reprint 1996.
Cloth. $65.00. 627 pp. .... Vendor G0259

Staples, William R. **Annals of the Town of Providence** from Its First Settlement to June, 1832. (1843) reprint 1993.
Cloth. $69.50. 670 pp. .... Vendor G0259

Steere, T. **History of the Town of Smithfield,** from Its Organization in 1730 to Its Division in 1871. (1881) reprint 1987.
Cloth. $29.00. 230 pp. .... Vendor G0259

Washington County

Arnold, James N. **The Records of the Proprietors of the Narragansett,** Otherwise Called The Fones Record. (1894) reprint 1990. Indexed.
  One of the oldest surviving documents of Washington County, Rhode Island, the so-called Fones Record commences with a 1659 land grant from Doginaquond, Sachem of the Narragansetts, to a group of proprietors consisting of prominent New England officials.
Cloth. $13.50. 199 pp. .... Vendor G0011

Arnold, James N. **Vital Records of Rhode Island, 1636-1850**. Births, Marriages & Deaths: A Family Register for the People. Volume V, Washington County. (1891-1912) reprint 1994.
Cloth. $47.50. 465 pp. .... Vendor G0259

Cole, J. R. **History of Washington & Kent Counties**. (1889) reprint 1993.
Cloth. $129.50. 1,324 pp. .... Vendor G0259

Crandall, Earl P., comp. & ed. **Charlestown in the Mid-19th Century,** As Seen Through the Eyes of "Uncle Phineas" (Nelson Byron Vars). 1992. Paper. $16.00. 79 pp. .... Vendor G0259

Crandall, Earl P. **Five Families of Charlestown (Bliven, Crandall, Macomber, Money, Taylor Families),** with Appendix. 1993. Cloth. $35.00. 165 + 120 pp. .... Vendor G0259

Denison, Frederic. **Westerly & Its Witnesses, for Two Hundred & Fifty Years, 1626-1876,** Including Charlestown, Hopkinton & Richmond Until Their Separate Organization. With index by Sallie E. Coy. (1878) reprint 1994. Cloth. $37.00. 314 + 28 pp. .... Vendor G0259

Gardiner, George W. **Lafayette: A Few Phases of Its History from the Ice Age to the Atomic.** (1949) reprint 1993. Cloth. $35.00. 267 pp. .... Vendor G0259

Griswold, S. S. **Historical Sketch of the Town of Hopkinton, 1757-1876.** (1876) reprint 1993. Paper. $18.00. 93 pp. .... Vendor G0259

# South Carolina

Statewide and Regional References

1905 South Carolina Communities and Business Directory.
    An alphabetical listing of the communities in South Carolina showing the businesses in each.
Paper. $18.50. .... Vendor G0549

Atlas of South Carolina, 46 county maps.
    Includes detailed maps of individual counties, all the back roads, streams, lakes, towns, etc. 11" x 16".
$14.95. .... Vendor G0611

Baldwin, Agnes Leland. **First Settlers of South Carolina, 1670-1700.** 1985. Indexed. Cloth. $20.00. 262 pp. .... Vendor G0610

Begley, Paul R., and Steven D. Tuttle. **African American Genealogical Research**. 1991. Illus.
Lists genealogical guidebooks and departmental records available at the South Carolina Department of Archives and History.
Paper. $2.00. 24 pp. .... Vendor G0130

Bernheim, Gotthardt D. **History of the German Settlements and of the Lutheran Church in North and South Carolina**. (1872) reprint 1996.
Paper. $40.00. 557 pp. .... Vendor G0011

Bhatia, Sharmila. **Vital Records**. 1993.
A booklet published by the South Carolina Department of Archives and History listing state and county vital records.
Paper. $1.75. 8 pp. .... Vendor G0130

Bond, Col. O. J. **The Story of the Citadel**. (1936) reprint 1989. Indexed.
Cloth. $27.50. 282 pp. .... Vendor G0610

Brinsfield, John W. **Religion and Politics in Colonial South Carolina**. 1983. Indexed. Illus.
Cloth. $25.00. 204 pp. .... Vendor G0610

Burgess, James M. **Chronicles of St. Mark's Parish, Santee Circuit, and Williamsburg Township, South Carolina, 1731-1885**. 1888.
Paper. $12.50. 108 pp. .... Vendor G0610

Clemens, William Montgomery. **North and South Carolina Marriage Records,** from the Earliest Colonial Days to the Civil War. (1927) reprint 1995.
Cloth. $25.00. 295 pp. .... Vendor G0010

Clute, Robert F. **The Annals and Parish Register of St. Thomas and St. Denis Parish, in South Carolina, from 1680 to 1884**. (1884) reprint 1989.
A collection of parish registers containing "vital records" of the French Huguenot settlement of South Carolina known as the Orange Quarter.
Cloth. $15.00. 111 pp. .... Vendor G0011

Corley, Ge Lee, and Morn McKoy Lindsay. **The Jury Lists of South Carolina, 1778-1779**. (1975) reprint 1980.
Cloth. $11.50. 131 pp. .... Vendor G0011

Cote, Richard N., and Patricia H. Williams, eds. **The Dictionary of South Carolina Biography, Vol. 1**. 1985. Indexed.
Cloth. $30.00. 404 pp. + index. .... Vendor G0610

Cote, Richard N. **Local and Family History in South Carolina: A Bibliography**. (1981) reprint 1991. Indexed.
Paper. $32.50. 520 pp. .... Vendor G0610

Dilts, Bryan Lee, comp. **1860 South Carolina Census Index: Heads of Household and Other Surnames in Household Index**. 2 vols. 1993.
Cloth. $199.00. .... Vendor G0552

Dobson, David. **Directory of Scots in The Carolinas, 1680-1830**. 1986.
Cloth. $25.00. 322 pp. .... Vendor G0010

Edgar. **South Carolina: The WPA Guide to the Palmetto State**. (1941) reprint 1988.
  A guide to the state as it was in 1941. The descriptions of places, historical sites, and geographic features are especially helpful.
Paper. $16.95. 531 pp. .... Vendor G0611

Elliott, Colleen M., ed. **The Marriage and Death Notices, Keowee Courier: 1849-1851; 1857-1861 and 1865-1871**. 1979. Indexed.
Cloth. Out of Print. iv. + 210 pp. .... Vendor G0610

Ervin, Sara Sullivan. **South Carolinians in the Revolution** . . . Also Abstracts of Wills, Laurens County (Ninety-Six District) 1775-1855. (1949) reprint 1997. Indexed. Illus.
Contact vendor for information. 230 pp. .... Vendor G0011

Family History Library. **Research Outline: South Carolina**.
Leaflet. $.25. 11 pp. .... Vendor G0629

Federal Writers' Project. **Palmetto Place Names**. (1941) reprint 1992. Illus.
  Explores the history of South Carolina place names.
Paper. $20.00. 158 pp. .... Vendor G0551

The First Laws of the State of South Carolina. 2 vols. (1790) reprint 1984.
Cloth. $122.50. .... Vendor G0118

Flynn, Jean Martin. **The Militia in Antebellum South Carolina Society**. 1991. Indexed. Illus.
Cloth. $25.00. xiv + 200 pp. .... Vendor G0551

Garrett, W. R. **History of the South Carolina Cession and the Northern Boundary of Tennessee**. Illus.
Paper. $5.00. .... Vendor G0549

Gregg, Alexander. **History of the Old Cheraws [South Carolina]**. With Notices of Families and Sketches of Individuals. With Addenda Comprising Additional Facts Concerning the Eight Pedee Counties and Sketches of the Persons for Whom They Are Named by John J. Dargan. (1867, 1925) reprint 1994. Indexed. Illus.
  A history of the Old Cheraw District of South Carolina and of the settlement of the territory now part of the eight Pedee counties of Chesterfield, Darlington, Florence, Georgetown, Horry, Marion, Marlboro, and Williamsburg, from their first settlement in the 1730s down to 1810.
Paper. $49.95. 629 pp. .... Vendor G0011

Helsley, Alexia J., and Michael E. Stauffer. **South Carolina Court Records: An Introduction for Genealogists**. 1993. Illus.
  Sketches the background of South Carolina's judicial system prior to 1868 and lists the colonial, early state, and antebellum court records held by the South Carolina Department of Archives and History.
Paper. $4.75. 30 pp. .... Vendor G0130

Hendrix, Ge Lee Corley. **Research in South Carolina**.
Paper. $6.50. 32 pp. .... Vendor G0627

Hirsch, Arthur Henry. **The Huguenots of Colonial South Carolina**. (1928) reprint 1991. Indexed. Illus.
Contact vendor for information. 347 pp. .... Vendor G0011

Holcomb, Brent H., and Elmer Parker. **Camden District, South Carolina Wills & Administrations: 1781-1787**. (1978) reprint 1981. Indexed.
Contact vendor for information. 120 pp. .... Vendor G0610

Holcomb, Brent H. **A Guide to South Carolina Genealogical Research and Records**. 1991. Indexed.
Paper. $15.00. 58 pp. .... Vendor G0602

Holcomb, Brent H. **Index to the 1800 Census of South Carolina**. (1980) reprint 1997.
Contact vendor for information. 264 pp. .... Vendor G0011

Holcomb, Brent H. **Index to the 1850 Mortality Schedule of S.C**. 1980.
Contact vendor for information. 56 pp. .... Vendor G0610

Holcomb, Brent H. **Marriage and Death Notices from Baptist Newspapers of South Carolina 1835-1865**. (1981) reprint 1993. Indexed.
   Contains marriage and death notices from the three Baptist newspapers which were published in South Carolina before and during the Civil War. Notices are not limited to Baptists.
Cloth. $25.00. vi + 143 pp. .... Vendor G0551

Holcomb, Brent H. **Marriage and Death Notices from Baptist Newspapers of South Carolina, Volume 2: 1866-1887**. 1996. Indexed.
Cloth. $35.00. 354 pp. .... Vendor G0602

Holcomb, Brent H. **Marriage and Death Notices from Camden, S.C., Newspapers, 1816-1865**. 1978. Indexed.
   Notices included in this book are from Camden, Kershaw District, Fairfield, and also from Chester, York, Darlington, Newberry, Marlboro, Orangeburg, and Charleston District, as well as the border counties of N.C.
Contact vendor for information. 192 pp. + index .... Vendor G0610

Holcomb, Brent H. **Marriage and Death Notices from Columbia, South Carolina Newspapers, 1792-1839**. 1982. Indexed.
   These notices are from all over South Carolina, but particularly from the counties of Richland, Kershaw, Lexington, Newberry, Orangeburg, and Edgefield.
Cloth. $20.00. 114 pp. .... Vendor G0610

Holcomb, Brent H. **Marriage and Death Notices from *The Pendleton Messenger*, 1807-1851**. (1977) reprint 1991. Indexed.
   These notices of marriages and deaths are from the entire state of South Carolina as well as from counties in Georgia and North Carolina.
Cloth. $25.00. 123 pp. .... Vendor G0610

Holcomb, Brent H. **Marriage and Death Notices from the Up-Country of South Carolina As Taken from Greenville Newspapers 1826-1863**. 1983. Indexed.
Cloth. $30.00. .... Vendor G0602

Holcomb, Brent H. **Marriage and Death Notices from Upper S.C. Newspapers, 1843-1865**. (1977) reprint 1990. Indexed.
Cloth. $25.00. 176 pp. .... Vendor G0610

Holcomb, Brent H. **Marriage, Death, and Estate Notices from Georgetown, S.C., Newspapers: 1791-1861**. (1978) reprint 1994. Indexed.

These notices cover the counties of Georgetown District: Horry, Williamsburg, Georgetown, and Marion. Also notices are to be found from neighboring counties of Darlington, Sumter, and Charleston.
Cloth. $35.00. iv + 236 pp. .... Vendor G0610

Holcomb, Brent H., and Marguerite Clark. **Ninety-Six District, S.C.: Journal of the Court of Ordinary, Inventory Book, Will Book, 1781-1786**. (1978) reprint 1992. Indexed.
Paper. $12.50. 80 pp. .... Vendor G0610

Holcomb, Brent H. **Petitions for Land from the South Carolina Council Journals Vol. I: 1734/5-1748**. 1996. Indexed.
Cloth. $40.00. 341 pp. .... Vendor G0602

Holcomb, Brent H. **Probate Records of S.C., Vol. 1. An Index to Inventories, 1746-1785**. 1977. Indexed. Illus.
Cloth. $20.00. x + 72 pp. .... Vendor G0610

Holcomb, Brent H. **Probate Records of S.C., Vol. 2**. (1978) reprint 1992. Indexed.
Cloth. $30.00. 336 pp. .... Vendor G0610

Holcomb, Brent H. **Probate Records of S.C., Vol. 3.: Journal of the Court of Ordinary, 1764-1771**. (1979) reprint 1992. Indexed.
Cloth. $25.00. vi + 154 pp. .... Vendor G0610

Holcomb, Brent H., and Silas Emmett Lucas, Jr. **Some South Carolina County Records, Vol. 1**. (1976) reprint 1992. Indexed. Illus.
See "Lucas, Silas Emmett, Jr." for Volume 2.
Cloth. $25.00. 162 pp. .... Vendor G0610

Holcomb, Brent H. **South Carolina Deed Abstracts 1773-1778**. 1993. Indexed.
Cloth. $35.00. 300 pp. .... Vendor G0602

Holcomb, Brent H. **South Carolina Deed Abstracts 1776-1783**. 1994. Indexed.
Cloth. $35.00. 300 pp. .... Vendor G0602

Holcomb, Brent H. **South Carolina Deed Abstracts 1783-1788**. 1996. Indexed.
Cloth. $50.00. 560 pp. .... Vendor G0602

Holcomb, Brent H. **South Carolina Marriages, 1688-1779**. (1980) reprint 1995. Indexed.
Cloth. $25.00. 349 pp. .... Vendor G0010

Holcomb, Brent H. **South Carolina Marriages, 1800-1820**. (1981) reprint 1995. Indexed.
Cloth. $20.00. 171 pp. .... Vendor G0010

Holcomb, Brent H. **South Carolina Naturalizations 1783-1850**. (1985) reprint 1997. Indexed.
Contact vendor for information. 255 pp. .... Vendor G0011

Holcomb, Brent H. **Supplement to South Carolina Marriages, 1688-1820**. (1984) reprint 1995. Indexed.
Paper. $9.00. 57 pp. .... Vendor G0010

Holt, Thomas. **Black Over White: Negro Political Leadership in South Carolina During Reconstruction**. (1977) reprint 1979.
   Studies not only the identities of the black politicians who gained power in South Carolina during Reconstruction, but also how they functioned within the political system.
Paper. $11.95. 269 pp. .... Vendor G0611

Houston, Martha L. **Indexes to the County Wills of South Carolina**. (1939) reprint 1996.
Paper. $25.00. 261 pp. .... Vendor G0011

Howe, George. **The Scotch-Irish and Their First Settlements on the Tyger River,** and Other Neighboring Precincts in South Carolina, A Centennial Discourse. (1861) reprint 1981. Indexed.
Paper. $10.00. 31 pp. .... Vendor G0610

Joyner. **Down by the Riverside: A South Carolina Slave Community**. 1984.
   A fascinating reconstruction of antebellum plantation life in All Saints Parish. Extensive footnotes.
Paper. $11.95. 324 pp. .... Vendor G0611

Klein. **Unification of a Slave State: The Rise of the Planter Class in the South Carolina Backcountry, 1760-1808**. 1990.
   Extensive footnotes in this excellent study of this area between 1760 and 1808.
Paper. $14.95. 331 pp. .... Vendor G0611

Landrum, John B. O. **Colonial and Revolutionary History of Upper South Carolina**. (1897) reprint 1996. Indexed. Illus.
Cloth. $35.00. 364 pp. .... Vendor G0551

Langley, Clara B. **Deed Abstracts 1719-1772, South Carolina**. Vol. 1, 1719-1740, Books A-T. 1983. Indexed.
Contact vendor for information. 392 pp. + index. .... Vendor G0610

Langley, Clara B. **Deed Abstracts 1719-1772, South Carolina**. Vol. 2, 1740-1755, Books V-PP. 1984. Indexed.
Cloth. $37.50. 370 pp. + index. .... Vendor G0610

Langley, Clara B. **Deed Abstracts 1719-1772, South Carolina**. Vol. 3, 1755-1768, Books QQ-HHH. 1983. Indexed.
Cloth. $37.50. 386 pp. + index. .... Vendor G0610

Langley, Clara, B. **Deed Abstracts 1719-1772, South Carolina**. Vol. 4, 1768-1772, Books III-ZZZ. 1984. Indexed.
Cloth. $37.50. Approx. 400 pp. .... Vendor G0610

Lippy. **Religion in South Carolina**. 1993.
   Fourteen essays written by distinguished religious studies scholars illuminate the intricacies of organized religion in South Carolina.
Cloth. $24.95. 233 pp. .... Vendor G0611

Littlefield, Daniel C. **Rice and Slaves: Ethnicity and the Slave Trade in Colonial South Carolina**. (1981) reprint 1991.

Studies the early slave trade in colonial South Carolina and shows how that led to significant contributions made by African slaves to the development of American institutions. Casts "the enslaved Africans as creative, dynamic forces shaping American culture."—*Georgia Historical Quarterly*
Paper. $15.95. 199 pp. .... Vendor G0611

Logan, John H. **A History of the Upper Country of S.C., Vol. 2**. (1910) reprint 1980. Indexed.
Cloth. $17.50. 126 pp. .... Vendor G0610

Lucas, Silas Emmett, Jr., and Brent Holcomb. **An Index to Deeds of the Province and State of South Carolina, 1719-1785, and Charleston District, 1785-1800**. (1977) reprint 1980.
Contact vendor for information. 848 pp. .... Vendor G0610

Lucas, Silas Emmett, Jr., ed. **Quakers in South Carolina,** Wateree and Bush River, Crane Creek, Piney Grove, and Charleston Meetings. 1892, 1905, 1936. Reprinted in consolidated format 1991. Indexed. Illus.
Paper. $20.00. 150 pp. .... Vendor G0610

Lucas, Silas Emmett, Jr. **Some South Carolina County Records, Vol. 2**. 1989. Indexed. (See page 166 for Vol. 1.)
Cloth. $40.00. 480 pp. + index. .... Vendor G0610

Mackintosh, Robert H., Jr. **Selected Bibliography of County, City, and Town Histories and Related Published Records in the South Carolina Archives Reference Library**. 1994.
Paper. $2.00. 43 pp. .... Vendor G0130

Mayer, O. B. **The Dutch Fork**. Edited by Brent H. Holcomb and James E. Kibler, Ph.D. 1980. Indexed.
Cloth. $20.00. 139 pp. .... Vendor G0602

McCawley, Patrick J. **Guide to Civil War Records:** A Guide to the Records in the South Carolina Department of Archives & History. 1994. Indexed. Illus.
Paper. $6.75. 81 pp. .... Vendor G0130

McKain, James D. **Index to the Two Volumes *The History of the Presbyterian Church in South Carolina*.** 1995.
Paper. $12.00. 92 pp. .... Vendor G0602

Mills, Robert. **Atlas of the State of South Carolina,** Prefaced with a Geographical, Statistical, and Historical Map of the State. (1825) reprint 1980. Indexed. Illus.
Cloth. $50.00. 44 pp. + 29 maps. .... Vendor G0610

Moss, Bobby Gilmer. **Roster of South Carolina Patriots in the American Revolution**. (1985) reprint 1994. Illus.
Cloth. $50.00. 1,023 pp. .... Vendor G0010

Motes, Jesse Hogan, and Margaret Peckham Motes. **South Carolina Memorials: Abstracts of Land Titles, Vol. 1, 1774-1776**. 1996. Indexed.
Cloth. $35.00. 434 pp. .... Vendor G0610

Pancake. **This Destructive War: The British Campaign in the Carolinas, 1780-1782**. 1985.

The story of the guerrilla warfare fought in the Carolinas. Includes numerous references to weaponry, military organization, and the lives of ordinary soldiers in both armies.
Paper. $15.95. 293 pp. .... Vendor G0611

Peden, Henry C., Jr. **Marylanders to Carolina:** Migrations of Marylanders to North and South Carolina Prior to 1800. 1994.
Paper. $17.00. 220 pp. .... Vendor G0140

Precision Indexing. **South Carolina 1870 Census Index**. 2 vols. 1989. Illus.
Cloth. $195.00. 1,983 pp. .... Vendor G0552

Ravenel, Daniel. **[List of French and Swiss] . . . settled in Charleston, on the Santee, and at the Orange Quarter in Carolina . . .** (1888) reprint 1990. Indexed. Illus.
One of the earliest lists of Huguenot emigrants to South Carolina.
Paper. $8.50. 77 pp. .... Vendor G0011

Revill, Janie. **A Compilation of the Original Lists of Protestant Immigrants to South Carolina, 1763-1773**. (1939) reprint 1996. Indexed.
Paper. $17.50. 163 pp. .... Vendor G0011

Revill, Janie. **Original Index Book Showing the Revolutionary Claims Filed in South Carolina** Between August 20, 1783 and August 31, 1786. (1941) reprint 1990.
Cloth. $30.00. 387 pp. .... Vendor G0011

Revill, Janie. **Some South Carolina Genealogical Records**. 1985. Indexed.
Cloth. $35.00. 456 pp. .... Vendor G0610

Salley, A. S., Jr . **Death Notices in the *South-Carolina* Gazette 1732-1775**. [Published with] **Death Notices in *The South Carolina Gazette*, 1766-1774** by Mabel L. Webber. 2 vols. in 1. (1917, 1933) reprint 1996. Indexed.
Paper. $12.00. 35 + 39 pp. .... Vendor G0011

Salley, Alexander S., Jr. **Marriage Notices in the *South-Carolina and American General Gazette*, 1766 to 1781 and *The Royal Gazette*, 1781-1782**. (1914) reprint 1990. Indexed.
Paper. $5.00. 52 pp. .... Vendor G0011

Salley, Alexander S., Jr. **Marriage Notices in the *South-Carolina Gazette* and Its Successors, 1732-1801**. (1902) reprint 1989. Indexed.
Cloth. $17.95. 174 pp. .... Vendor G0011

Schweitzer, George K. **South Carolina Genealogical Research**. 1994. Illus.
History of the state, types of records (Bible through will), record locations, research techniques, listings of county records.
Paper. $15.00. 190 pp. .... Vendor G0569

Sifakis. **Compendium of the Confederate Armies: South Carolina and Georgia**. 1995.
Describes each regiment, the officers, and lists the battles in which they fought.
Cloth. $29.95. 311 pp. .... Vendor G0611

South Carolina Department of Archives and History. **A Guide to Local Government Records in the South Carolina Archives**. 1988. Indexed.
Paper. $11.75. viii + 315 pp. .... Vendor G0130

South Carolina Historical Society. **The Historical Writings of Henry Augustus Middleton Smith**. Reprinted from the *South Carolina Historical and Genealogical Magazine*, with an introduction and indexes by Alexander Moore. 1988. Indexed. Illus.
   Includes studies of the towns, plantations, baronies, and river communities of the early colonial period. Working from land records, Smith traced ownership of land, constructed genealogies of the planter families, and devised an unusual series of large maps to illustrate his articles. See below for individual volumes.
Cloth. $75.00/set. 888 pp. .... Vendor G0551

South Carolina Historical Society. **The Historical Writings of Henry Augustus Middleton Smith: The Baronies of South Carolina, Volume 1**. Indexed. Illus.
Cloth. $25.00. xx + 199 pp. .... Vendor G0551

South Carolina Historical Society. **The Historical Writings of Henry Augustus Middleton Smith: Cities and Towns of Early South Carolina, Volume II**. Indexed. Illus.
Cloth. $25.00. xx + 249 pp. .... Vendor G0551

South Carolina Historical Society. **The Historical Writings of Henry Augustus Middleton Smith: Rivers and Regions of Early South Carolina, Volume III**. Indexed. Illus.
Cloth. $25.00. xx + 380 pp. .... Vendor G0551

South Carolina Historical Society. **South Carolina Genealogies,** Volume 1: Alston-Colcock. 1983. Illus.
   Reprinted from the *South Carolina Historical and Genealogical Magazine.*
Cloth. $35.00. xi + 439 pp. .... Vendor G0551

South Carolina Historical Society. **South Carolina Genealogies,** Volume II: Colleton-Izard. 1983. Illus.
Cloth. $35.00. xi + 455 pp. .... Vendor G0551

South Carolina Historical Society. **South Carolina Genealogies,** Volume III: Jenkins-Quattlebaum. 1983. Illus.
Cloth. $35.00. xi + 458 pp. .... Vendor G0551

South Carolina Historical Society. **South Carolina Genealogies,** Volume IV: Rhett-Wragg. 1983. Illus.
Cloth. $25.00. ix + 437 pp. .... Vendor G0551

South Carolina Historical Society. **South Carolina Genealogies,** Volume V: New Every-Name Index. 1983.
Cloth. $25.00. vi + 198 pp. .... Vendor G0551

Southern California Genealogical Society. **Sources of Genealogical Help in South Carolina**.
Paper. $.50. 2 pp. .... Vendor G0656

Stauffer, Michael E. **The Formation of Counties in South Carolina**. 1994. Illus.

Examines how the state's counties were formed and provides maps showing the changing face of the state as the counties were established.
Paper. $4.75. 22 pp. .... Vendor G0130

Stewart, William C. **Gone to Georgia**. Indexed.
    Continuation of 1800 Census of Pendleton District, South Carolina. Examines people who followed the Great Road from Virginia and North Carolina's Yadkin country into South Carolina and northeastern Georgia.
Paper. $18.00. 326 pp. .... Vendor G0627

Thorndale, William, and William Dollarhide. **County Boundary Map Guides to the U.S. Federal Censuses, 1790-1920: South Carolina, 1790-1920**. 1987.
$5.95. .... Vendor G0552

Townsend, Leah. **South Carolina Baptists, 1670-1805**. (1935) reprint 1990. Indexed.
Cloth. $23.50. 391 pp. .... Vendor G0011

Tuttle, Steven D. **Census Records at the Archives [South Carolina Department of Archives and History]**. 1994.
Paper. $2.00. 10 pp. .... Vendor G0130

Tuttle, Steven D. **Sources for Genealogists**. 1994. Illus.
    Provides a selected checklist of useful records and publications for genealogical research at the South Carolina Department of Archives and History.
Paper. $1.75. 8 pp. .... Vendor G0130

United States Bureau of the Census. **Heads of Families at the First Census of the United States Taken in the Year 1790: South Carolina**. (1908) reprint 1992. Indexed. Illus.
Contact vendor for information. 150 pp. .... Vendor G0010

United States Bureau of the Census. **Heads of Families at the First Census of the United States Taken in the Year 1790: South Carolina**.
Cloth, $35.00. Paper, $20.00. .... Vendor G0552

Ware, Lowry. **Associate Reformed Presbyterian Death & Marriage Notices 1843-1863**. 1993. Indexed.
Cloth. $25.00. 209 pp. .... Vendor G0602

Warren, Mary Bondurant. **South Carolina Jury Lists: 1718-1783**. Illus.
Hard-cover. $15.00. 130 pp. .... Vendor G0632

White, Katherine Keogh. **The King's Mountain Men**. The Story of the Battle, with Sketches of the American Soldiers Who Took Part. (1924) reprint 1996. Indexed.
Paper. $25.00. 271 pp. .... Vendor G0011

Wooley, James E, ed. **A Collection of Upper South Carolina Genealogical and Family Records** (From the Private Files of the Late Pauline Young). 3 vols. 1980. Indexed.
Cloth. $37.50/Vol. 1. $40.00/Vol. 2. Contact vendor for Vol. 3 price. 416 + 408 + 354 pp. .... Vendor G0610

Young, Pauline. **A Genealogical Collection of South Carolina Wills and Records, Vol. 1**. (1955) reprint 1981. Indexed.
Cloth. $35.00. 266 pp. .... Vendor G0610

Young, Pauline. **A Genealogical Collection of South Carolina Wills and Records, Vol. 2**. 1984. Indexed.
Cloth. $28.50. 328 pp. .... Vendor G0610

Abbeville County

1790 South Carolina Census, Abbeville County.
Paper. $4.00. .... Vendor G0549

Abbeville County Heritage Book Committee. **Abbeville County Heritage—South Carolina**. 1995. Indexed. Illus.
One of the County Heritage Book series. More than 300 family stories, genealogies, and family photos are included. Printed on acid free paper in the deluxe 9" x 12", hardbound format, this book features chapters on towns, clubs and organizations, churches, business and industry, schools, historic homes and buildings, and other subjects. Surname index.
Cloth. $55.50. 168 pp. .... Vendor G0087

Lucas, S. Emmett, Jr. **Abbeville District, S.C., Marriages, 1777-1852**. (1980) reprint 1988. Indexed.
Paper. $17.50. 76 pp. .... Vendor G0610

South Carolina WPA. **Some Cemetery Records of Abbeville County, South Carolina**. (1982) reprint 1993. Indexed.
Paper. $10.00. 105 pp. .... Vendor G0011

Ware, Lowry. **Old Abbeville** (a history of the town). 1992. Indexed.
Cloth. $25.00. 260 pp. .... Vendor G0602

Young, Pauline. **Abstracts of (Old) Ninety-Six and Abbeville District, S.C., Wills and Bonds**. (1950) reprint 1977. Indexed.
Cloth. $50.00. 797 pp. .... Vendor G0610

Aiken County

McClearen, H. Addison, and S. Owen Sheetz. **St. Thaddeus of Aiken: A Church and Its City**. 1994. Indexed. Illus.
Discusses both the history of the town and of the church. Appendices include a list of rectors, burial records, Aiken accommodations in the 19th century, thoroughbred horse stables and trainers, and winter cottage owners.
Cloth. $37.50. xxi + 286 pp. .... Vendor G0551

Toole, Gasper Loren, II. **Ninety Years in Aiken County:** Memories of Aiken County & Its People. (1959) reprint 1993.
Cloth. $44.50. 404 pp. .... Vendor G0259

Anderson County

Alexander, Virginia, Colleen M. Elliott, and Betty Willie. **Pendleton District and Anderson County, S.C., Wills, Estates, and Legal Records (1793-1857)**. (1980) reprint 1994. Indexed.
Cloth. $45.00. 512 pp. .... Vendor G0610

Simpson, R. W. **History of the Old Pendleton District,** with a Genealogy of the Leading Families of the District. (1913) reprint 1993.
Cloth. $28.00. 226 pp. .... Vendor G0259

Stewart, William C. **1800 Census of Pendleton District, South Carolina**.
  Pendleton District included present-day Pickens, Anderson, and Oconee counties.
Paper. $13.00. 178 pp. .... Vendor G0627

Wilkinson, Tom C. **Early Anderson County, S.C., Newspapers, Marriages & Obituaries, 1841-1882**. (1978) reprint 1994.
Cloth. $35.00. iv + 268 pp. .... Vendor G0610

Barnwell County

Holcomb, Brent H. **Winton (Barnwell) Co., S.C., Minutes of the County Ct. & Will Book 1, 1785-1791**. (1978) reprint 1989. Indexed.
Cloth. $32.50. 184 pp. .... Vendor G0610

Holcomb, Brent H. **Winton (Barnwell) County, South Carolina, Minutes of County Court and Will Book I 1785-1791**. 1989. Indexed.
Cloth. $30.00. 179 pp. .... Vendor G0602

Beaufort County

1790 South Carolina Census, Beaufort County.
Paper. $5.00. .... Vendor G0549

Holmgren, Virginia C. **Hilton Head Island**. A Sea Island Chronicle. (1957) reprint 1985. Indexed.
Cloth. $15.00. 176 pp. .... Vendor G0610

Salley, Alexander, Jr. **Minutes of the Vestry of St. Helena's Parish, South Carolina, 1726-1812**. (1919) reprint 1958. Indexed.
Cloth. $20.00. 296 pp. .... Vendor G0610

Berkeley County

Heitzler, Michael J., Ph.D. **Historic Goose Creek, South Carolina, 1670-1980**. Edited by Richard N. Cote. 1982. Indexed. Illus.
Contact vendor for information. 302 pp. .... Vendor G0610

Charleston County

Charleston Free Library. **Index to Wills of Charleston County, South Carolina, 1671-1868**. (1950) reprint 1993.
Paper. $26.00. 324 pp. .... Vendor G0011

Charleston, South Carolina, 1670-1883: The Centennial of Incorporation. (1883) reprint 1994. Illus.
    A general history of the city.
Cloth. $37.50. 259 pp. + 9 fold-out maps. .... Vendor G0259

Cote, Richard N. **The Genealogists' Guide to Charleston County, South Carolina**. (1978) reprint 1982.
Paper. $10.00. vi + 46 pp. .... Vendor G0610

Fraser. **Charleston! Charleston!: The History of a Southern City**. 1989.
    A comprehensive history of this colorful city.
Paper. $19.95. 542 pp. .... Vendor G0611

Fraser. **Patriots, Pistols and Petticoats: "Poor Sinful CharlesTown" During the American Revolution**. (1945) reprint 1993.
    Portrays the lively (at times bawdy) atmosphere in Charleston during the Revolutionary era.
Paper. $14.95. 166 pp. .... Vendor G0611

Hagy, James W. **City Directories for Charleston, South Carolina for the Years 1803, 1806, 1807, 1809, and 1813**. 1995.
Paper. $18.00. 170 pp. .... Vendor G0011

Hagy, James W. **Charleston, South Carolina City Directories for the Years 1816, 1819, 1822, 1825, and 1829**. 1996.
Paper. $18.00. 169 pp. .... Vendor G0011

Hagy, James W. **Charleston, South Carolina City Directories for the Years 1830-1841**. 1997.
Paper. $16.00. 132 pp. .... Vendor G0011

Hagy, James W. **People and Professions of Charleston, South Carolina, 1782-1802**. (1992) reprint 1995.
Paper. $17.50. 112 pp. .... Vendor G0011

Holcomb, Brent H. **Marriage and Death Notices from the (Charleston)** *Times*, 1800-1821. 1979. Indexed.
Cloth. $18.50. 374 pp. .... Vendor G0011

Holcomb, Brent H., comp. **Passenger Arrivals at the Port of Charleston, 1820-1829**. 1994. Indexed.
Cloth. $25.00. 188 pp. .... Vendor G0010

King, Susan L. **History and Records of the Charleston Orphan House, 1790-1860**. 1984. Indexed.
    The Charleston Orphan House was the first municipal orphanage in the United States. Many of the orphans were children of Revolutionary soldiers. Contains the records of approximately 1,800 children.
Cloth. $25.00. 204 pp. .... Vendor G0610

King, Susan L. **History and Records of the Charleston Orphan House, Volume 2, 1860-1899**. 1994. Indexed.
Paper. $20.00. 183 pp. .... Vendor G0602

Mazyck, Arthur, and Gene Waddell. **Charleston in 1883**. (1883) reprint 1984. Indexed. Illus.
Paper. $15.00. 176 pp. .... Vendor G0610

McIver, Petrona Royall. **History of Mount Pleasant**. (1960 & 1970) reprint 1995. Indexed. Illus.
Cloth. $15.00. 165 pp. .... Vendor G0538

Ravenel, Mrs. St. Julien. **Charleston, the Place and the People**. (1906) reprint 1982. Indexed.
Paper. Contact vendor for information. 560 pp. .... Vendor G0610

Salley, A. S., Jr., ed. **Register of St. Philips, Charles Town, 1720-1758**. (1904) reprint 1992.
Cloth. $39.00. 355 pp. .... Vendor G0259

Salley, Alexander S. **Marriage Notices in Charleston Courier, 1803-1808**. (1919) reprint 1994. Indexed.
Paper. $10.00. 83 pp. .... Vendor G0011

Stockton, Robert P. **The Great Shock:** The Effects of the 1886 Earthquake on the Built Environment of Charleston, South Carolina. 1986. Indexed. Illus.
Cloth. $15.00. 184 pp. .... Vendor G0610

Cheraw District

Holcomb, Brent H. **St. David's Parish, (Cheraw) S.C.: Minutes of the Vestry, 1768-1832, and Parish Register, 1819-1924**. (1979) reprint 1991. Indexed.
Cloth. $25.00. 165 pp. .... Vendor G0610

Cherokee County

Malone, Samuel Lorenzo. **Black Families in Cherokee County, South Carolina as Taken from 1910-1920 Federal Census**. 1983. Illus.
Paper. $25.00. xvi + 93 pp. .... Vendor G0551

Chester County

1790 South Carolina Census, Chester County.
Paper. $5.00. .... Vendor G0549

Holcomb, Brent H. **Chester County, S.C. Minutes of the County Court, 1785-1799**. (1979) reprint 1996. Indexed.
Cloth. $35.00. 456 pp. .... Vendor G0610

Holcomb, Brent H. **York, South Carolina, Newspapers: Marriage and Death Notices, 1823-1865**. (1981) reprint 1989. Indexed.
　Contains marriage and death notices not only from the York area, but also from

Union, Spartanburg, Lancaster, and Chester counties in South Carolina and Cleveland, Gaston, and Mecklenburg counties in North Carolina.
Cloth. $25.00. vi + 129 pp. .... Vendor G0551

Claremont County

1790 South Carolina Census, Claremont County.
Paper. $3.50. .... Vendor G0549

Clarendon County

1790 South Carolina Census, Clarendon County.
Paper. $3.50. .... Vendor G0549

Daufuskie Island

Burn, Billie. **An Island Named Daufuskie**. 1991. Indexed. Illus.
    The story of a small island between Hilton Head Island, South Carolina, and Tybee Island, Georgia. The first comprehensive study of the island from the 1700s to the present.
Cloth. $24.95. xxiv + 592 pp. .... Vendor G0551

Edgefield County

1790 South Carolina Census, Edgefield County.
Paper. $6.50. .... Vendor G0549

Burton. **In My Father's House Are Many Mansions: Family and Community in Edgefield, South Carolina**. 1987.
    While this social history is especially important to genealogists interested in Edgefield, all genealogists will gain from reading this book. The extensive footnotes and bibliography provide additional sources to investigate.
Paper. $20.95. 480 pp. .... Vendor G0611

Chapman, John A. **History of Edgefield County,** from the Earliest Settlements to 1897, Biographical & Anecdotal. Incl. Saluda Co., Which Separated from Edgefield. (1897) reprint 1993.
Cloth. $55.00. 521 + 6 pp. .... Vendor G0259

Chapman, John A. **History of Edgefield County, S.C.** (1897) reprint 1994. Indexed.
    The history begins with the colonial settlement and goes through 1897. Saluda County was formed from Edgefield County.
Hard-cover. $40.00. 521 pp. .... Vendor G0610

Hendrix, Ge Lee Corley. **Edgefield County, South Carolina, Abstracts of Deed Books 1-12, 1786-1796**. 1985. Indexed.
Cloth. $30.00. Approx. 300 pp. .... Vendor G0610

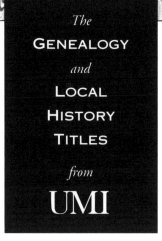

Holcomb, Brent H. **Edgefield County, S.C., Minutes of the County Court, 1785-1795**. 1979. Indexed.
Cloth. $25.00. 220 pp. + index. .... Vendor G0610

Holcomb, Brent H. **Journal of the Reverend Godfrey Drehr, 1819-1851**. 1978. Indexed.
  Contains many baptisms, marriages, deaths, and burials, as well as the churches and other places where Drehr, a well-known Lutheran minister, preached in Lexington, Newberry, Orangeburg, and Edgefield districts.
Cloth. $15.00. 104 pp. .... Vendor G0610

Revill, Janie. **Edgefield County, South Carolina, Records**. 1984. Indexed.
Cloth. $30.00. 246 pp. .... Vendor G0610

Wooley, James E., and Vivian Wooley. **Edgefield County, S.C., Wills 1787-1836**. 1991.
Cloth. $30.00. Approx. 238 pp. + index. .... Vendor G0610

Fairfield County

1790 South Carolina Census, Fairfield County.
Paper. $6.00. .... Vendor G0549

Holcomb, Brent H. **Fairfield County, S.C., Minutes of the County Court, 1785-1799**. 1981. Indexed.
Cloth. $22.50. 177 pp. .... Vendor G0610

Georgetown County

Holcomb, Brent H. **Parish Registers of Prince George Winyah Church, Georgetown, South Carolina 1815-1936**. 1996. Indexed.
Cloth. $30.00. 200 pp. .... Vendor G0602

Rogers, George C., Jr. **The History of Georgetown County, South Carolina**. (1970) reprint 1995. Indexed. Illus.
Cloth. $37.50. xviii + 566 pp. .... Vendor G0551

Greenville County

1790 South Carolina Census, Greenville County.
Paper. $4.50. .... Vendor G0549

McCuen, Anne K. **Abstracts of Some Greenville County, South Carolina, Records Concerning Black People, Free and Slave, 1791-1861, Vol. 1**. 1991. Indexed.
Cloth. $25.00. x + 228 pp. .... Vendor G0551

Richardson, James M. **History of Greenville County, South Carolina**. 1930. Indexed.
Cloth. $32.50. 342 pp. + index. .... Vendor G0610

Kershaw County

Holcomb, Brent H. **Kershaw County, SC, Minutes of the County Court 1791-1799**. 1986. Indexed.
Cloth. $20.00. 159 pp. .... Vendor G0602

Kirkland, Thomas J., and Robert M. Kennedy. **Historic Camden: Part II, Nineteenth Century**. (1926) reprint 1995.
Cloth. $52.50. 485 pp. .... Vendor G0259

McKain, James D. **Index to the Two Volumes of *Historic Camden***. 1995.
Cloth. $17.50. 88 pp. .... Vendor G0602

Lancaster County

1790 South Carolina Census, Lancaster County.
Paper. $5.50. .... Vendor G0549

Holcomb, Brent H. **Lancaster County, S.C., Deed Abstracts, 1787-1811**. 1981. Indexed.
Contact vendor for information. 240 pp. .... Vendor G0610

Holcomb, Brent H. **York, South Carolina, Newspapers: Marriage and Death Notices, 1823-1865**. (1981) reprint 1989. Indexed.
  Contains marriage and death notices not only from the York area, but also from Union, Spartanburg, Lancaster, and Chester counties in South Carolina and Cleveland, Gaston, and Mecklenburg counties in North Carolina.
Cloth. $25.00. vi + 129 pp. .... Vendor G0551

Laurens County

1790 South Carolina Census, Laurens County.
Paper. $6.50. .... Vendor G0549

Elliott, Colleen. **Laurens County, South Carolina, Wills, 1784-1840**. 1988. Indexed.
Cloth. $38.50. 336 pp. .... Vendor G0610

Ingmire, Frances. **Laurens County, South Carolina Will Book A 1840-1853**.
Paper. $40.00. 184 pp. .... Vendor G0549

Motes, Jesse Hogan, and Margaret Peckham Motes. **Laurens and Newberry Counties, S.C.: Little River Settlement 1749-1775**. 1994. Indexed.
Hard-cover. $32.50. Approx. 230 pp. .... Vendor G0610

Lexington County

Holcomb, Brent H. **Journal of the Reverend Godfrey Drehr, 1819-1851**. 1978. Indexed.
  Contains many baptisms, marriages, deaths, and burials, as well as the churches and

other places where Drehr, a well-known Lutheran minister, preached in Lexington, Newberry, Orangeburg, and Edgefield districts.
Cloth. $15.00. 104 pp. .... Vendor G0610

Holcomb, Brent H. **Memorialized Records of Lexington District, South Carolina 1814-1825**. 1989. Indexed.
Cloth. $25.00. 167 pp. .... Vendor G0602

Marion County

Sellers, W. W. **History of Marion County,** from Its Earliest Times to the Present, 1901. With Family Sketches. (1902) reprint 1992.
Contact vendor for information. 647 pp. .... Vendor G0011

Marlboro County

Holcomb, Brent H. **Marlborough County, South Carolina, Minutes of the County Court 1785-1799 and Minutes of the Court Ordinary 1791-1821**. 1982. Indexed.
Cloth. $20.00. 152 pp. .... Vendor G0610

Thomas, Rev. J. A. W. **A History of Marlboro County [South Carolina]**. With Traditions and Sketches of Numerous Families. (1897, 1978) reprint 1992. Illus.
Paper. $21.50. 325 pp. .... Vendor G0011

Newberry County

1790 South Carolina Census, Newberry County.
Paper. $5.50. .... Vendor G0549

Chapman, John A., and John B. O'Neall. **The Annals of Newberry [South Carolina]**. (1892) reprint 1995. Illus.
Paper. $55.00. 823 pp. .... Vendor G0011

Holcomb, Brent H. **Journal of the Reverend Godfrey Drehr, 1819-1851**. 1978. Indexed.
    Contains many baptisms, marriages, deaths, and burials, as well as the churches and other places where Drehr, a well-known Lutheran minister, preached in Lexington, Newberry, Orangeburg, and Edgefield districts.
Cloth. $15.00. 104 pp. .... Vendor G0610

Holcomb, Brent H. **Newberry County, S.C., Minutes of the County Court, 1785-1798**. 1977. Indexed.
Contact vendor for information. 356 pp. .... Vendor G0610

Motes, Jesse Hogan, and Margaret Peckham Motes. **Laurens and Newberry Counties, S.C.: Little River Settlement 1749-1775**. 1994. Indexed.
Hard-cover. $32.50. Approx. 230 pp. .... Vendor G0610

O'Neall, John Belton, and John A. Chapman. **The Annals of Newberry, South Carolina**. (1892) reprint 1994. Indexed.
Hard-cover. $48.50. 816 pp. + index. .... Vendor G0610

Summer, George Leland. **Newberry County, South Carolina:** Historical and Genealogical Annals. 1950. Indexed.
Paper. $37.50. 483 pp. .... Vendor G0011

Oconee County

Oconee County Heritage Book Committee (B.R.A.C.). **The Heritage of Oconee County, South Carolina, Vol. 1, 1868-1995**. Indexed. Illus.
　Another in the prestigious County Heritage Book series. Nearly 400 family stories, genealogies, and family photos, along with numerous topics of interest to researchers: churches, organizations, communities, and businesses. Printed on acid free, non-glare paper, 9" x 12" format. Surname index.
Cloth. $55.50. 242 pp. .... Vendor G0087

Stewart, William C. **1800 Census of Pendleton District, South Carolina**.
　Pendleton District included present-day Pickens, Anderson, and Oconee counties.
Paper. $13.00. 178 pp. .... Vendor G0627

Orangeburg County

1790 South Carolina Census, Orangeburg County.
Paper. $8.50. .... Vendor G0549

Culler, Daniel Marchant. **Orangeburgh District, 1768-1868, History and Records**. 1995. Indexed. Illus.
Cloth. $50.00. xxvi + 738 pp. .... Vendor G0551

Haigler, Anne Martin. **The Church Records of Saint Matthews Lutheran Church, Orangeburg Co., S.C., Beginning in 1799, Giving Births, Christenings, Confirmations, Marriages and Burials: And "The Red Church," 1767-1838**. 1985. Indexed. Illus.
Cloth. $20.00. 126 pp. + index. .... Vendor G0610

Holcomb, Brent H. **Journal of the Reverend Godfrey Drehr, 1819-1851**. 1978. Indexed.
　Contains many baptisms, marriages, deaths, and burials, as well as the churches and other places where Drehr, a well-known Lutheran minister, preached in Lexington, Newberry, Orangeburg, and Edgefield districts.
Cloth. $15.00. 104 pp. .... Vendor G0610

Holcomb, Brent H. **Orangeburg District, South Carolina, Estate Partitions from the Court of Equity 1824-1837**. 1995. Indexed.
Paper. $20.00. 96 pp. .... Vendor G0602

Salley, Alexander S., Jr. **The History of Orangeburg County, South Carolina,** from Its First Settlement to the Close of the Revolutionary War. (1898) reprint 1994. Indexed. Illus.
Paper. $45.00. 572 pp. .... Vendor G0011

Salley, Alexander S. **History of Orangeburg County, S.C. from Its First Settle-ment to the Close of the Revolutionary War, 1704-1782**. (1898) reprint 1994. In-dexed.
Hard-cover. $40.00. 572 pp. .... Vendor G0610

Pee Dee Area

Cook, Harvey Toliver. **Rambles in the Pee Dee Basin, S.C.** (1926) reprint 1991. Indexed. Illus.
Cloth. $37.50. 512 pp. .... Vendor G0610

Dargan, John J. **History of the Old Cheraws,** With Notices of Families and Sketches of Individuals, The Rt. Rev. Alexander Gregg. (With:) Addenda Comprising Addi-tional Facts Concerning the Eight Pee Dee Counties and Sketches of the Persons for Whom They Are Named. (1867) reprint 1991. Indexed. Illus.
Cloth. $38.50. 704 pp. .... Vendor G0610

Gregg, Alexander. **History of the Old Cheraws**. (1867) reprint 1991. Indexed. Illus.
A history of the upper Pee Dee country from 1730 to 1810, this book gives an account of the Indians of the Pee Dee, the first white settlements, subsequent growth and progress of the region, and the changes brought about by the Revolution. Includes an addendum in which is found information on the eight Pee Dee counties with sketches of the persons for whom they are named. Also contains a new every-name index.
Cloth. $38.50. 629 pp. .... Vendor G0551

National Association Colonial Dames of America. **Prince Frederick Winyaw, The Register Book for the Parish**. Ann: Dom: 1713. (1916) reprint 1982. Indexed. Illus.
This book is a must for people with ancestry in the Pee Dee area of South Carolina and border North Carolina (Anson-Bladen County) area.
Cloth. $25.00. 270 pp. .... Vendor G0610

Pendleton County

1790 South Carolina Census, Pendleton County.
Paper. $6.50. .... Vendor G0549

Alexander, Virginia, Colleen M. Elliott, and Betty Willie. **Pendleton District and Anderson County, S.C., Wills, Estates, and Legal Records (1793-1857)**. (1980) reprint 1994. Indexed.
Cloth. $45.00. 512 pp. .... Vendor G0610

Simpson, R. W. **History of (Old) Pendleton District and Genealogy of Leading Families**. (1913) reprint 1978, 1981. Indexed.
Cloth. $35.00. 264 pp. .... Vendor G0610

Van Clayton, Frederick. **Settlement of Pendleton District, 1777-1800**. 1988. Indexed. Illus.
Paper. $20.00. 112 pp. .... Vendor G0610

Willie, Betty. **Pendleton District, S.C., Deeds, 1790-1806**. 1982. Indexed.
Contact vendor for information. 479 pp. .... Vendor G0610

Pendleton District

Stewart, William C. **1800 Census of Pendleton District, South Carolina**.
Pendleton District included present-day Pickens, Anderson, and Oconee counties.
Paper. $13.00. 178 pp. .... Vendor G0627

Pickens County

Pickens County Heritage Book Committee. **Pickens County Heritage—South Carolina**. 1995. Indexed. Illus.
Another in the South Carolina County Heritage Book series. More than 350 family genealogies, stories, and family photos. Printed on acid free paper, 9" x 12" format. Features a special photo album of early life in Pickens County with dozens of photos of the early days. Also included are chapters on towns, clubs and organizations, and churches. Surname index.
Cloth. $55.50. 200 pp. .... Vendor G0087

Stewart, William C. **1800 Census of Pendleton District, South Carolina**.
Pendleton District included present-day Pickens, Anderson, and Oconee counties.
Paper. $13.00. 178 pp. .... Vendor G0627

Richland County

1790 South Carolina Census, Richland County.
Paper. $3.50. .... Vendor G0549

Holcomb, Brent H. **Record of Deaths in Columbia and Other Places As Recorded by John Glass 1859-1877**. 1986. Indexed.
Cloth. $20.00. 223 pp. .... Vendor G0602

Saluda County

Chapman, John A. **History of Edgefield County,** from the Earliest Settlements to 1897, Biographical & Anecdotal. Incl. Saluda Co., Which Separated from Edgefield. (1897) reprint 1993.
Cloth. $55.00. 521 + 6 pp. .... Vendor G0259

Chapman, John A. **History of Edgefield County, S.C.** (1897) reprint 1994. Indexed.
The history begins with the colonial settlement and goes through 1897. Saluda County was formed from Edgefield County.
Hard-cover. $40.00. 521 pp. .... Vendor G0610

Spartanburg County

1790 South Carolina Census, Spartanburg County.
Paper. $5.50. .... Vendor G0549

Bailey, J. D. **History of Grindal Shoals**. (1923) reprint 1981.
A history of Grindal Shoals, which is located on the Pacolet River between Spartanburg and Union.
Paper. $10.00. 86 pp. .... Vendor G0610

Holcomb, Brent H. **Spartanburg County, S.C., Minutes of the County Court, 1785-1799**. (1979) reprint 1994.
Hard-cover. $35.00. 325 pp. .... Vendor G0610

Holcomb, Brent H. **Spartanburg County, South Carolina, Will Abstracts 1787-1849**. 1983. Indexed.
Cloth. $25.00. 179 pp. .... Vendor G0602

Holcomb, Brent H. **York, South Carolina, Newspapers: Marriage and Death Notices, 1823-1865**. (1981) reprint 1989. Indexed.
Contains marriage and death notices not only from the York area, but also from Union, Spartanburg, Lancaster, and Chester counties in South Carolina and Cleveland, Gaston, and Mecklenburg counties in North Carolina.
Cloth. $25.00. vi + 129 pp. .... Vendor G0551

Landrum, John B. O. **History of Spartanburg County**. (1900) reprint 1996. Indexed. Illus.
Cloth. $45.00. xii + 790 pp. .... Vendor G0551

Pruitt, Albert Bruce. **Spartanburg County/District, South Carolina, Deed Abstracts, Book A-T, 1785-1827 (1752-1827)**. 1989. Indexed.
Cloth. $55.00. 872 pp. .... Vendor G0610

Spartanburg Unit of the Writer's Program of the WPA in the State of SC. **A History of Spartanburg County**. (1940) reprint 1996. Indexed. Illus.
Cloth. $37.50. 304 pp. .... Vendor G0551

Union County

1790 South Carolina Census, Union County.
Paper. $4.50. .... Vendor G0549

Bailey, J. D. **History of Grindal Shoals**. (1923) reprint 1981.
A history of Grindal Shoals, which is located on the Pacolet River between Spartanburg and Union.
Paper. $10.00. 86 pp. .... Vendor G0610

Holcomb, Brent H. **Union County, S.C., Minutes of the County Court, 1785-1799**. (1979) reprint 1994. Indexed.
Cloth. $40.00. 523 pp. + index. .... Vendor G0610

Holcomb, Brent H. **Union County, South Carolina, Will Abstracts 1787-1849**. 1987. Indexed.
Cloth. $25.00. 183 pp. .... Vendor G0602

Holcomb, Brent H. **York, South Carolina, Newspapers: Marriage and Death Notices, 1823-1865**. (1981) reprint 1989. Indexed.

Contains marriage and death notices not only from the York area, but also from Union, Spartanburg, Lancaster, and Chester counties in South Carolina and Cleveland, Gaston, and Mecklenburg counties in North Carolina.
Cloth. $25.00. vi + 129 pp. .... Vendor G0551

Waccamaw Peninsula

Bull, Henry DeSaussure. **All Saints Church, Waccamaw, 1739-1968:** With Updates to Which Have Been Added Additional Text, Parish Register Updates, Appendices, and Index, 1948/1968-1992. Illus.
Cloth. $37.50. ix, (vi), 1-128, (16), 129-349 pp. .... Vendor G0551

Michie, James L. **Richmond Hill Plantation, 1810-1868: The Discovery of Antebellum Life on a Waccamaw Rice Plantation**. 1990. Indexed. Illus.
Cloth. $24.95. 204 pp. .... Vendor G0551

Williamsburg County

Boddie, William Willis. **History of Williamsburg**. Something About the People of Williamsburg County, South Carolina, from the First Settlement by Europeans About 1705 Until 1923. (1923) reprint 1995. Indexed.
Paper. $45.00. 620 pp. .... Vendor G0011

Boddie, William Willis. **History of Williamsburg**. Something About the People of Williamsburg County, South Carolina, from the First Settlement by Europeans About 1705 Until 1923. (1923) reprint 1992. Indexed. Illus.
Cloth. $37.50. ix + 611 pp. .... Vendor G0551

Boddie, William Willis. **History of Williamsburg**. Something About the People of Williamsburg County, South Carolina, from the First Settlement by Europeans About 1705 until 1923. (1923) reprint 1992. Indexed. Illus.
Cloth. $35.00. 620 pp. .... Vendor G0610

Winton County

Holcomb, Brent H. **Winton (Barnwell) Co., S.C., Minutes of the County Ct. & Will Book 1, 1785-1791**. (1978) reprint 1989. Indexed.
Cloth. $32.50. 184 pp. .... Vendor G0610

Holcomb, Brent H. **Winton (Barnwell) County, South Carolina, Minutes of County Court and Will Book I 1785-1791**. 1989. Indexed.
Cloth. $30.00. 179 pp. .... Vendor G0602

York County

1790 South Carolina Census, York County.
Paper. $5.50. .... Vendor G0549

Holcomb, Brent H. **York, South Carolina, Newspapers: Marriage and Death Notices, 1823-1865**. (1981) reprint 1989. Indexed.
   Contains marriage and death notices not only from the York area, but also from Union, Spartanburg, Lancaster, and Chester counties in South Carolina and Cleveland, Gaston, and Mecklenburg counties in North Carolina.
Cloth. $25.00. vi + 129 pp. .... Vendor G0551

Wells, Laurence K. **York County, SC, Minutes of the County Court 1786-1797**. 1996. Indexed.
Cloth. $30.00. 199 pp. .... Vendor G0602

South Dakota

Statewide and Regional References

Family History Library. **Research Outline: South Dakota**.
Leaflet. $.25. 7 pp. .... Vendor G0629

Pensioners on the Rolls As of January 1883 in Dakota Territory. 1996. Indexed.
Paper. $10.50. .... Vendor G0583

Sanford, Rev. J. I. **The Black Hills Souvenir,** a Pictorial & Historic Description of the Black Hills. (1902) reprint 1994.
Cloth. $29.95. 223 pp. .... Vendor G0259

Tallent, Annie D. **The Black Hills, or, the Last Hunting Ground of the Dakotas**. (1899) reprint 1994.
   Heavily illustrated.
Cloth. $69.95. 713 pp. .... Vendor G0259

Thorndale, William, and William Dollarhide. **County Boundary Map Guides to the U.S. Federal Censuses, 1790-1920: South Dakota, 1790-1920**. 1987.
$5.95. .... Vendor G0552

Faulk County

Ellis, Capt. C. H. **History of Faulk County,** Together with Biographical Sketches of Pioneers & Prominent Citizens. (1909) reprint 1994.
Cloth. $53.00. 508 pp. .... Vendor G0259

Jerauld County

Dunham, Niles J. **History of Jerauld County,** from Its Earliest Settlement to Jan. 1st, 1909. (1910) reprint 1993.
Cloth. $48.50. 441 pp. .... Vendor G0259

Minnehaha County

Bailey, Dana R. **History of Minnehaha County,** Containing an Account of Its Settlements, Growth, Development & Resource . . . and Biographical Sketches. (1899) reprint 1993.
Cloth. $99.50. 1,099 + xii pp. .... Vendor G0259

Smith, Charles A. **Comprehensive History of Minnehaha County**. (1949) reprint 1994.
Cloth. $54.50. 504 pp. .... Vendor G0259

Tennessee

Statewide and Regional References

1814 Court Martial of Tennessee Militiamen. A Report from the War Department to the House of Representatives in the 20th Congress Numbered 140.
$28.50 (perfect bound). 181 pp. .... Vendor G0549

1905 Tennessee Community and Business Directory.
An alphabetical listing by county of each community with the merchants in each.
Paper. $35.00. .... Vendor G0549

Acklen, Jeannette Tillotson, et al. **Tennessee Records: Bible Records and Marriage Bonds**. (1933) reprint 1995. Indexed.
Paper. $36.00. 521 pp. .... Vendor G0011

Acklen, Jeannette Tillotson, et al. **Tennessee Records: Tombstone Inscriptions and Manuscripts**. (1933) reprint 1995. Indexed.
Paper. $36.00. 517 pp. .... Vendor G0011

Allen, Penelope Johnson. **Leaves from the Family Tree**. 1982. Indexed.
A collection of family histories primarily in East Tennessee, which Mrs. Allen compiled and wrote for the *Chattanooga Times* Sunday magazine from December 3, 1933 to March 21, 1937.
Cloth. $45.00. 464 pp. .... Vendor G0610

Allison, John, ed. **Notable Men of Tennessee, Personal and Genealogical,** with Portraits. 2 vols. (1905) reprint 1995.
Cloth. $69.50. 332 + 335 pp. .... Vendor G0259

Armstrong, Zella. **Some Tennessee Heroes of the Revolution**. (1933) reprint 1996. Indexed.
Paper. $18.00. 162 pp. .... Vendor G0011

Armstrong, Zella. **Twenty-four Hundred Tennessee Pensioners:** Revolution and War of 1812. (1937) reprint 1996.
Paper. $9.00. 121 pp. .... Vendor G0010

Atlas of Tennessee, 95 county maps.
Includes detailed maps of individual counties, all the back roads, streams, lakes, towns, etc. 11" x 16".
$14.95. .... Vendor G0611

Atlas of Tennessee, Topographical.
This present-day atlas provides the researcher with the detail needed to conduct a proper search. It is the size of a Rand McNally atlas of the entire U.S. 11" x 15½".
$16.95. .... Vendor G0611

Atlases & Gazetteers: Tennessee. Illus.
Paper. $16.95. 80 pp. .... Vendor G0632

Bailey. **Class and Tennessee's Confederate Generation**. 1987.
Brings to life a long-neglected group in the history of the South: the non-slaveholders. Excellent social history taken from the Tennessee Civil War Veterans Questionnaires.
Cloth. $24.95. 205 pp. .... Vendor G0611

Baker, Russell P. **Marriages and Obituaries from The Tennessee Baptist, 1844-1862**. (1979) reprint 1981. Indexed.
Cloth. $18.50. 137 pp. .... Vendor G0610

Bamman, Gale Williams. **Research in Tennessee**.
Paper. $6.50. 31 pp. .... Vendor G0627

Bentley, Elizabeth Petty. **Index to the 1820 Census of Tennessee**. (1981) reprint 1996.
Paper. $25.00. 287 pp. .... Vendor G0011

Bible, Jean P. **Melungeons—Yesterday and Today**. Illus.
A full accounting of the lost tribe of Tennessee and North Carolina.
Cloth. $12.00. 140 pp. .... Vendor G0549

Burgner, Goldene Fillers. **North Carolina Land Grants in Tennessee, 1778-1791**. 1981. Indexed.
This book contains 5,486 land grants issued by the State of North Carolina in the new State of Tennessee. The counties in which the land fell were: Davidson, Greene, Hawkins, Sullivan, Sumner, Tennessee, Washington, and the Eastern, Middle, and Western districts.
Cloth. $28.50. 214 pp. .... Vendor G0610

Creekmore, Pollyanna. **Early East Tennessee Taxpayers (1778-1839)**. 1980, 1988. Indexed. Illus.
Cloth. $38.50. 328 pp. .... Vendor G0610

Daniel. **Soldiering in the Army of Tennessee: A Portrait of Life in a Confederate Army**. 1991.
Written from the enlisted man's perspective from journals and letters. Gives a unique glimpse into this experience.
Cloth. $22.50. 231 pp. .... Vendor G0611

Dickinson, J. M. **The Centennial of the Admission**.
An address given in Nashville on 1 June 1896 at the centennial of the admission of the State of Tennessee into the Union. This is a brief overview of the history of the state.
Paper. $7.50. .... Vendor G0549

Douthat, James L. **Robert Armstrong—Plat Book of Those Indians Given Reservations After the 1817 Treaty**. Indexed.

Over 100 plats are given in their original drawing as presented in Robert Armstrong's Plat Book. The plats are found in North Carolina, Tennessee, and Alabama.
Paper. $10.00. .... Vendor G0549

Douthat, James L. **Kentucky Lake Reservoir Cemeteries**. 3 vols.

Volume 1 covers the Kentucky portion of the lake and includes Calloway and Lyon, Livingston, Marshall, and Trigg counties. Volume 2 covers the upper west Tennessee areas of Benton, Henry, Houston, Humphreys, and Stewart counties. Volume 3 involves the southern part of west Tennessee with the areas of Decatur, Hardin, Henderson, McNairy, Perry, and Wayne counties plus the reinterment sites for the entire Kentucky Lake Reservoir.
Paper. $35.00/vol., $90.00/set. .... Vendor G0549

Douthat, James L. **Roster of Upper East Tennessee Confederate Veterans**.

The roster of the Upper East TN Confederate Veterans Association is given in detail with comments on the war from the veterans themselves.
Paper. $10.00. 42 pp. .... Vendor G0549

Douthat, James L. **Tennessee Today—1796**.
Paper. $24.00. .... Vendor G0549

Family History Library. **Research Outline: Tennessee**.
Leaflet. $.25. 9 pp. .... Vendor G0629

Fischer, Marjorie Hood. **Tennessee Tidbits, 1778-1914, Vol. 1**. 1985. Indexed.

Includes records from Blount, Davidson, Dickson, Fayette, Giles, Green, Hardin, Haywood, Hickman, Humphreys, Lincoln, Putnam, Rutherford, Washington, and Williamson counties.
Cloth. $38.50. 420 pp. .... Vendor G0610

Fischer, Marjorie Hood, and Ruth Burns. **Tennessee Tidbits, 1778-1914, Vol. II**. 1985-1989. Indexed.

Abstracts of County, Circuit, and Chancery Court minutes, counties of Bedford, Claiborne, Dyer, Fentress, Jackson, Madison, McMinn, Obion, Roane, Robertson, Sevier, Stewart, Washington, and Wilson.
Cloth. $32.50. 400 pp. .... Vendor G0577

Fischer, Marjorie Hood, and Ruth Burns. **Tennessee Tidbits, 1778-1914, Vol. III**. 1985-1989. Indexed.

Similar to Vol. II above for counties of Anderson, Bradley, Carroll, Decatur, Grainger, Johnson, Macon, Marion, Monroe, Rhea, Tipton, and Warren. About 19,000 names.
Cloth. $35.00. 540 pp. .... Vendor G0577

Foster, Austin P. **Counties of Tennessee**. (1923) reprint 1990. Illus.
Cloth. $30.00. 124 pp. .... Vendor G0522

Foster, Austin P. **Maps of Tennessee from 1790-1920: (The Formation of) Counties of Tennessee**. (1923) reprint 1989.

Data is given on the formation of each county and the counties from which each was formed with dates and other pertinent data.
Cloth. $28.50. 124 pp. .... Vendor G0610

Fulcher, Richard C. **Guide to County Records and Genealogical Resources in Tennessee**. (1987) reprint 1989.
Cloth. $20.00. 199 pp. .... Vendor G0010

G.A. Ogle & Company. **Biographical Sketches of the Cumberland Region of Tennessee, Part II**. Memoirs & Biographical Records, An Illustrated Compendium of Biography. (1898) reprint 1980. Indexed. Illus.
Cloth. $35.00. 291 pp. + index. .... Vendor G0610

Garrett, Jill Knight. **Obituaries from Tennessee Newspapers**. 1980. Indexed.
Cloth. $38.50. 476 pp. .... Vendor G0610

Garrett, W. R. **History of the South Carolina Cession and the Northern Boundary of Tennessee**. Illus.
Paper. $5.00. .... Vendor G0549

Goodspeed Publishing Company. **The History of Thirty East Tennessee Counties**. (1887) reprint 1991. Indexed.
Cloth. $42.50. 526 pp. .... Vendor G0610

Horn. **The Army of Tennessee**. (1941) reprint 1993.
A study of this tragic army during the Civil War.
Paper. $17.95. 503 pp. .... Vendor G0611

Killebrew, Joseph B. **Introduction to the Resources of Tennessee**. (1874) reprint 1974. Indexed. Illus.
Cloth. $40.00. viii + 1,193 pp. .... Vendor G0551

Liahona Research. **Tennessee Marriages, Early to 1800**. 1990. Illus.
Cloth. $25.00. 69 pp. .... Vendor G0552

Liahona Research. **Tennessee Marriages, 1801 to 1825**. 1993. Illus.
Cloth. $105.00. .... Vendor G0552

Lindsley, John Berrien, ed. **The Military Annals of Tennessee: Confederate**. 2 vols. 1996. Indexed. Illus.
Cloth. $75.00. 1,167 pp. .... Vendor G0590

Lucas, Silas Emmett, Jr. **Marriages from Early Tennessee Newspapers, 1794-1851**. (1978) reprint 1980.
Contact vendor for information. 544 pp. .... Vendor G0610

Lucas, Silas Emmett, Jr. **Obituaries from Early Tennessee Newspapers, 1794-1851**. (1978) reprint 1980.
Contact vendor for information. 432 pp. .... Vendor G0610

Lucas, Silas Emmett, Jr. **35,000 Tennessee Marriage Records & Bonds**. 3 vols. 1981.
  Volume 1: A-F. Contact vendor for information.
  Volume 2: G-N. 610 pp., including full-name index.
  Volume 3: O-Z. 580 pp., including full-name index.
Cloth. $45.00/vol., $90.00/set. .... Vendor G0610

Marsh, Helen C., and Timothy R. Marsh. **1850 Mortality Schedule of Tennessee (Entire State)**. 1982. Indexed.
Contact vendor for information. 368 pp. .... Vendor G0610

Marsh, Helen C., and Timothy R. Marsh. **Tennesseans in Texas:** As Found in the 1850 Census of Texas. 1986. Indexed.
Hard-cover. $37.50. 416 pp. .... Vendor G0610

McCammon, Charles S., ed. **Loyal Mountain Troopers: The 2nd & 3rd Volunteer Cavalry (Union) in the Civil War**. 1992. Indexed.
Memoirs of Cavalry officers written in 1878. Includes complete official roster published 1866.
Cloth. $32.00. .... Vendor G0204

Moore, John Trotwood. **Biographical Questionnaires of 150 Prominent Tennesseans**. Edited by Elliott Colleen Morse. 1982. Indexed.
Cloth. $20.00. 148 pp. .... Vendor G0610

Moore, John Trotwood. **Tennessee Civil War Veterans Questionnaires**. Edited by Colleen Morse Elliott and Louise Armstrong Moxley. 5 vols. 1985. Indexed.
In 1914 and 1915 and again in 1920, questionnaire forms were sent to all known living Tennessee Civil War veterans. Some 1,600 were returned by 1922. Vol. 1 contains Federal veterans (161 veterans) and Confederate veterans A-B (204 veterans); Vol. 2 contains Confederates C-F (307 veterans); Vol. 3 contains Confederates G-K (325 veterans); Vol. 4 contains Confederates L-Q (317 veterans); and Vol. 5 contains Confederates P-Y (373 veterans).
Cloth. $30.00/vol., $150.00/set. 472 + 479 + 487 + 510 + 525 pp. .... Vendor G0610

History of Tennessee, from the Earliest Time . . . Together with an Historical & Biographical Sketch of from Twenty-five to Thirty Cos. of East Tenn., Etc. East Tennessee ed. (1887) reprint 1994.
Cloth. $125.00. 1,317 pp. .... Vendor G0259

Potter, Johnny L. T. N. **Vidette Cavalry**. Illus.
The roster of the First Tennessee and Alabama Independent Vidette Cavalry is listed alphabetically, with the addition of the *Official Records* entries for the unit.
$12.50 (perfect bound). 42 pp. .... Vendor G0549

Ramsey, J. G. M. **Annals of Tennessee to the End of the 18th Century,** Comprising Its Settlement as the Watauga Assoc. from 1769 to 1777 . . . to the State of Tennessee, 1796 to 1800. (1853) reprint 1995.
Cloth. $77.50. 743 pp. .... Vendor G0259

Ray, Worth Stickley. **Tennessee Cousins:** A History of Tennessee People. (1950) reprint 1994. Indexed. Illus.
Cloth. $40.00. 819 pp. .... Vendor G0010

Roster of Upper East Tennessee CSA.
Paper. $10.00. 42 pp. .... Vendor G0549

Schweitzer, George K. **Tennessee Genealogical Research**. 1994. Illus.
History of the state, types of records (Bible through will), record locations, research techniques, listings of county records.
Paper. $15.00. 138 pp. .... Vendor G0569

Sifakis. **A Compendium of the Confederate Armies: Tennessee**. 1992.
  Describes each regiment, the officers, and lists the battles in which they fought.
Cloth. $24.95. 208 pp. .... Vendor G0611

Sistler, Barbara, and Byron Sistler. **Early East Tennessee Marriages**. 2 vols. (1987)
reprint 1993, 1996.
  Volume 1 arranged by grooms, Volume 2 arranged by brides. About 76,000 marriages including all extant antebellum records from East TN.
Cloth. $120.00. 800 pp. .... Vendor G0577

Sistler, Byron, and Barbara Sistler. **1830 Census—Tennessee**. 3 vols. (1969-71) reprint 1993.
  Volume 1: East. Volume 2: Middle. Volume 3: West. Volume 2 covers counties of Bedford, Davidson, Franklin, Jackson, Lincoln, Maury, Robertson, Rutherford, Smith, Sumner, Warren, White, Williamson, and Wilson. Volume 1 covers counties east of these, Volume 3 covers counties west of these.
Vol. 1, paper, $32.00. Vol. 2, cloth, $35.00. Vol. 3, paper, $33.00. .... Vendor G0577

Sistler, Byron, and Barbara Sistler. **1840 Census—Tennessee**. 1986.
  A statewide alphabetical listing of all household heads, with statistical detail showing composition of the family by sex and age groups. About 107,000 names.
Cloth. $93.00. 600 pp. .... Vendor G0577

Sistler, Byron, and Barbara Sistler. **1850 Census—Tennessee**. 8 vols. in 4. (1974-76) reprint 1991.
  Arranged by head of household, with names and ages of all members included, with county of residence, household and schedule page numbers, and place of birth of the first two members of the household.
Cloth. $300.00/set. .... Vendor G0577

Sistler, Byron, and Barbara Sistler. **1860 Census—Tennessee**. 5 vols. 1982.
  Volume 1: A-Crag.
  Volume 2: Crai-Haynes.
  Volume 3: Hayney-McKee.
  Volume 4: McKeehan-Sexton.
  Volume 5: Sexus-Z.
Cloth. $52.00/vol. .... Vendor G0577

Sistler, Byron, and Barbara Sistler. **1870 Census—Tennessee**. 2 vols. 1985.
  A statewide head of household index with age, sex, race, county of residence, and schedule page number.
Cloth. $120.00/set. .... Vendor G0577

Sistler, Byron, and Barbara Sistler. **1890 Civil War Veterans Census—Tennesseans in Texas**. 1978.
  About 550 men living in Texas in 1890 who served in Tennessee units during the Civil War, mostly Union veterans.
Paper. $7.00. .... Vendor G0577

Sistler, Byron, and Barbara Sistler. **1890 Civil War Veterans Census—Tennessee**. 1978.
  A listing of all known veterans as enumerated in the 1890 U.S. Census.
Cloth. $45.00. .... Vendor G0577

Sistler, Byron, and Barbara Sistler. **Early Middle Tennessee Marriages**. 2 vols. 1988.
Arranged alphabetically first by grooms, and then by brides. About 109,000 marriages including virtually all antebellum marriages.
Cloth. $170.00/set. 1,200 pp. .... Vendor G0577

Sistler, Byron, and Barbara Sistler. **Early Tennessee Tax Lists**. (1977) reprint 1993.
A single index to sixty-seven county tax lists, petitions, voter lists, and newspaper lists of inhabitants in thirty-three TN counties; about 46,000 entries in all.
Cloth. $33.00. .... Vendor G0577

Sistler, Byron, and Barbara Sistler. **Early West Tennessee Marriages**. 2 vols. 1989.
Arranged alphabetically, first by grooms and then by brides. About 57,000 marriages including virtually all antebellum marriages.
Cloth. $118.00/set. 670 pp. .... Vendor G0577

Sistler, Byron and Barbara Sistler. **Early West Tennessee Marriages**. 2 vols. 1989.
Indexed.
Hard-cover. $118.00. vii + 670 pp. .... Vendor G0632

Sistler, Byron, and Barbara Sistler. **Index to Tennessee Wills and Administrations 1779-1861**. 1990.
A statewide index with 41,500 entries covering all 62 counties for which antebellum estate records have survived.
Cloth. $47.00. 416 pp. .... Vendor G0577

Sistler, Byron, and Samuel Sistler. **Tennesseans in the War of 1812**. 1992.
Cloth. $40.00. 549 pp. .... Vendor G0577

Sistler, Byron, and Barbara Sistler. **Tennesseans in the War of 1812**. 1992.
Hard-cover. $40.00. Approx. 550 pp. .... Vendor G0610

Sistler, Byron, and Barbara Sistler. **Tennessee Mortality Schedules, 1850, 1860 & 1880**. (1984) reprint 1993.
A statewide listing, alphabetically by surname, of these three schedules combined (1870 schedules were lost).
Cloth. $40.00. .... Vendor G0577

Sistler, Byron, and Barbara Sistler. **Vital Statistics from 19th Century Tennessee Church Records, Vol. 2**. 1978.
Births, baptisms, marriages, deaths, and burials from 55 churches and/or church associations in TN (Volume 1 is out of print).
Cloth. $33.50. .... Vendor G0577

Sistler, Samuel. **Index to Tennessee Confederate Pension Applications**. 1994.
Essential information from over 28,000 files, including applications of soldiers, widows, and "colored" soldiers.
Cloth. $36.50. 400 pp. .... Vendor G0577

Sistler, Samuel. **Index to Tennessee Confederate Pension Applications**. Rev. ed. 1995. Indexed.
Cloth. $36.50. Approx. 400 pp. .... Vendor G0632

Speer, William S. **Sketches of Prominent Tennesseans**. (1888) reprint 1978. Indexed. Illus.
Contact vendor for information. 728 pp. .... Vendor G0610

The Story of the General.
A brief accounting of the General and the escape of Andrew's Raiders with their final capture and imprisonment.
Paper. $3.50. .... Vendor G0549

Survey of the Tennessee River 1826-1846. A Report Sent to the House of Representatives of the 29th Congress, First Session in March of 1846.
Paper. $20.00. .... Vendor G0549

Thorndale, William, and William Dollarhide. **County Boundary Map Guides to the U.S. Federal Censuses, 1790-1920: Tennessee, 1790-1920**. 1987.
$5.95. .... Vendor G0552

Volunteer Soldiers in the Cherokee War—1836-1839.
An alphabetical listing of over 11,000 volunteers from Tennessee, Georgia, North Carolina, and Alabama who volunteered in the Cherokee Wars and Removal.
$35.00 (perfect bound). 210 pp. .... Vendor G0549

Ware, Lowry. **Associate Reformed Presbyterian Death & Marriage Notices 1843-1863**. 1993. Indexed.
Cloth. $25.00. 209 pp. .... Vendor G0602

Whitley, Edythe Rucker. **Tennessee Genealogical Records:** Records of Early Settlers from State and County Archives. (1985) reprint 1997. Indexed.
Contact vendor for information. 393 pp. .... Vendor G0010

Wiefering. **Tennessee's Confederate Widows and Their Families**. 1992.
Abstracts of 11,190 Confederate widows' pension applications.
Cloth. $45.00. 479 pp. .... Vendor G0611

Williams, Mike K. **Virginians in Tennessee 1850**.
Paper. $25.00. .... Vendor G0549

Anderson County

Douthat, James L. **1836 Civil Districts and Tax Lists (Anderson Co., TN)**. Indexed.
Paper. $8.00. .... Vendor G0549

Douthat, James L. **John McClellan's Survey Book**. Indexed.
The plat survey book of the period for the counties of Roane, Rhea, Overton, Campbell, Anderson, and Bledsoe counties. Plat maps of each survey given.
Paper. $18.50. .... Vendor G0549

Pedersen, Diane E. **Entry Book—5th Survey District Book A—Grants Number 1-800**.
Covers the land sales and tracts in Anderson, Grainger, Jefferson, Claiborne, Knox, and Sevier counties.
Paper. $25.00. .... Vendor G0549

Sistler, Byron, and Barbara Sistler. **1880 Census—Tennessee**. Anderson County.
Paper. $13.00. .... Vendor G0577

Whitley, Edythe Rucker, comp. **Tennessee Marriage Records: Anderson County, 1838-1858**. 1983. Indexed.
Cloth. $12.00. 85 pp. .... Vendor G0011

Bedford County

Goodspeed Publishing Company. **History of Tennessee Illustrated, Historical and Biographical Sketches of the Counties of Maury, Williamson, Rutherford, Wilson, Bedford, and Marshall**. (1887) reprint 1988. Indexed.
Cloth. $42.50. 536 pp. .... Vendor G0610

Marsh, Helen C., and Timothy R. Marsh. **Bedford County, Tennessee, Bible Records, Vol. 1**. 1977. Indexed.
Paper. Contact vendor for information. 222 pp. .... Vendor G0610

Marsh, Helen C., and Timothy R. Marsh. **Bedford County, Tennessee, Bible Records, Vol. 2**. 1985. Indexed.
Paper. $22.50. 192 pp. .... Vendor G0610

Marsh, Helen C., and Timothy R. Marsh. **Bedford County, Tennessee Wills, 1854-1910**. (1984) reprint 1985. Indexed.
Contact vendor for information. 290 pp. .... Vendor G0610

Marsh, Helen C., and Timothy R. Marsh. **Cemetery Records of Bedford County, Tennessee**. Rev. ed. 1986. Indexed.
Contact vendor for information. 352 pp. .... Vendor G0610

Marsh, Helen C., and Timothy R. Marsh. **Chancery Court Records, Bedford County, Tennessee, 1830-1865**. 1987. Indexed.
Cloth. $37.50. 336 pp. .... Vendor G0610

Marsh, Helen C., and Timothy R. Marsh. **Earliest County Records of Bedford County, Tennessee**. 1986. Indexed.
Paper. $22.50. 184 pp. .... Vendor G0610

Marsh, Helen C., and Timothy R. Marsh. **Hoover Funeral and Burial Records, Bedford County, Tennessee**. 1989. Indexed.
Cloth. $32.50. 260 pp. .... Vendor G0610

Marsh, Helen C., and Timothy R. Marsh. **Land Deed Genealogy of Bedford County, Tennessee**. 1987. Indexed. Illus.
Cloth. $40.00. 484 pp. .... Vendor G0610

Marsh, Helen C., and Timothy R. Marsh. **Newspaper Vital Records of Bedford County, Tennessee**. 1984. Indexed.
Contact vendor for information. 250 pp. .... Vendor G0610

Marsh, Helen C., and Timothy R. Marsh. **Revolutionary War Soldiers of Bedford County, Tennessee**. 1989. Indexed.
Cloth. $32.50. Approx. 320 pp. .... Vendor G0610

Sistler, Byron, and Barbara Sistler. **1870 Census—Tennessee**. Bedford County.
Paper. $20.50. .... Vendor G0577

Sistler, Byron, and Samuel Sistler. **Every Name Index to 18 Middle Tennessee County Record Books**. 1992.

A single integrated index to eighteen inadequately indexed books: Bedford Co. (9 titles), Giles Co. (8), Lincoln Co. (1). About 165,000 entries.

Cloth. $52.00. 800 pp. .... Vendor G0577

WPA. **Bedford County, Tennessee Will Book 1—1847-1881**.

Paper. $15.00. .... Vendor G0549

Benton County

Douthat, James L. **Benton County, Tennessee Marriages—Book 1, 1846-1850**.

Paper. $7.50. .... Vendor G0549

Douthat, James L. **Kentucky Lake Reservoir Cemeteries. Volume 2**.

Covers the upper west Tennessee areas of Benton, Henry, Houston, Humphreys, and Stewart counties. Also available as a set with Volumes 1 and 3 (see Tennessee, Statewide and Regional References).

Paper. $35.00. .... Vendor G0549

Goodspeed Publishing Company. **Carroll, Henry, and Benton Counties**. (1886) reprint 1978. Indexed. Illus.

Contact vendor for information. 176 pp. .... Vendor G0610

Sistler, Byron, and Barbara Sistler. **1870 Census—Tennessee**. Benton County.

Paper. $13.00. .... Vendor G0577

Smith, Jonathan K. T. **Benton County (Tennessee)**. 1979. Indexed. Illus.

Cloth. $17.50. 136 pp. .... Vendor G0522

WPA. **Benton County, Tennessee—Administration, Guardian, Clerks and Trustees Probate of Deeds and Records of Wills 1836-1855**. Indexed.

Paper. $35.00. 200 pp. .... Vendor G0549

Bledsoe County

1830 Bledsoe County, Tennessee Census.

Paper. $7.50. .... Vendor G0549

1840 Bledsoe County, Tennessee Census.

Paper. $7.50. .... Vendor G0549

1850 Bledsoe County, Tennessee Census.

Paper. $20.00. .... Vendor G0549

Abstract of Bledsoe County Court Minutes 1841-1846.

Paper. $18.50. .... Vendor G0549

Bledsoe County, Tennessee Biographies.

Paper. $8.00. .... Vendor G0549

Douthat, James L. **1836 Bledsoe County, Tennessee Civil Districts and Tax Lists**. Indexed.
Paper. $8.00. .... Vendor G0549

Douthat, James L. **John McClellan's Survey Book**. Indexed.
The plat survey book of the period for the counties of Roane, Rhea, Overton, Campbell, Anderson, and Bledsoe counties. Plat maps of each survey given.
Paper. $18.50. .... Vendor G0549

Douthat, James L. **Sequatchie Families**.
A collection of eighty-one biographical sketches of families who are found in Sequatchie Valley prior to 1850.
Paper. $15.00. .... Vendor G0549

Douthat, James L. **Sequatchie Valley Bible Records**. Indexed.
Since most records of the marriages, births, and deaths are no longer existent for each of the counties in the valley, this book is an invaluable research tool.
Paper. $10.00. .... Vendor G0549

Robnett, Elizabeth Parham. **Bledsoe County, Tennessee—A History**. Indexed. Illus.
Cloth. $28.50. 294 pp. .... Vendor G0549

Sistler, Byron, and Barbara Sistler. **1870 Census—Tennessee**. Bledsoe County.
Paper. $11.00. .... Vendor G0577

Stephens, Miriam Rose. **Methodism in Bledsoe County**.
Paper. $6.00. .... Vendor G0549

WPA. **Bledsoe County, Tennessee Chancery Court Minutes 1836-1847**. Indexed.
Paper. $45.00. 272 pp. .... Vendor G0549

WPA. **Bledsoe County, Tennessee Circuit Court Minutes 1834-1841**. Indexed.
Paper. $55.00. 398 pp. .... Vendor G0549

Blount County

Blount County Heritage Book Committee. **Blount County, TN and Its People**. 1992. Indexed. Illus.
Part of the prestigious County Heritage Book series! More than 800 family histories, genealogies, and family photos. Hardbound, 9" x 12" book, with chapters on military, forts, religion, clubs, organizations, and communities. Surname index.
Cloth. $59.95 (incl. postage & tax). 432 pp. .... Vendor G0087

Dockter, Albert, Jr. **Blount County Chancery Court Records 1852-1865**. 1992. Indexed.
Paper. $19.50. 172 pp. .... Vendor G0204

Dockter, Albert, Jr. **Blount County Chancery Court Records 1866-1869 Including Divorce Proceedings 1860-1937**. 1994. Indexed.
Paper. $26.00. 267 pp. .... Vendor G0204

Douthat, James L. **1836 Blount County, Tennessee Civil Districts and Tax Lists**. Indexed.
Paper. $10.00. .... Vendor G0549

Douthat, James L. **Fort Loudon Reservoir Cemeteries**.
Paper. $18.50. .... Vendor G0549

Friendsville Academy.
   Friendsville Academy was begun by the Society of Friends (Quakers) about 1855. This is the 38th annual catalogue, which includes the roster of alumni as well as those attending in 1893.
Paper. $3.50. .... Vendor G0549

Parham, Will E. **Blount County, Tennessee, Marriages, 1795-1865**. 1982. Indexed.
Cloth. $25.00. iv + 422 pp. .... Vendor G0610

Sistler, Byron, and Barbara Sistler. **1870 Census—Tennessee**. Blount County.
Paper. $16.00. .... Vendor G0577

Smith, Lorene, and Elgin Kintner, comps. **Blount County Remembered: The 1980s Photography of W. O. Garner**. 1991.
Cloth. $27.00. .... Vendor G0204

Thomas, Jane Kizer. **Blount County, Tennessee, Deeds: 1795-1819**. 1990. Indexed.
Paper. $20.00. 119 pp. .... Vendor G0204

Thomas, Jane Kizer. **Blount County, Tennessee, Deeds: 1819-1833**. 1993. Indexed.
Paper. $26.00. 283 pp. .... Vendor G0204

Thomas, Jane Kizer, comp. **Our Ancestry: Family Records of Members of Blount County Genealogical & Historical Society**. 1988.
Cloth. $32.00. 355 pp. .... Vendor G0204

Whitley, Edythe Rucker, comp. **Tennessee Marriage Records: Blount County, 1795-1859**. 1982. Indexed.
Cloth. $12.00. 102 pp. .... Vendor G0011

WPA. **Blount County, Tennessee—County Court Minutes 1795-1804**.
$37.50 (perfect bound). 242 pp. .... Vendor G0549

WPA. **Blount County, Tennessee—County Court Minutes 1814-1817**.
$40.00 (perfect bound). 265 pp. .... Vendor G0549

WPA. **Blount County, Tennessee—County Court Records 1804-1807**.
$30.00 (perfect bound). 195 pp. .... Vendor G0549

WPA. **Blount County, Tennessee—County Court Records 1808-1811**.
$30.00 (perfect bound). 192 pp. .... Vendor G0549

WPA. **Blount County, Tennessee Entry Taker's Book 1824-1826**.
$23.50 (perfect bound). 110 pp. .... Vendor G0549

WPA. **Blount County, Tennessee—Tombstone Inscriptions**. Indexed.
Paper. $55.00. 448 pp. .... Vendor G0549

WPA. **Blount County, Tennessee Will Book 1, 1799-1856**.
$35.00 (perfect bound). 242 pp. .... Vendor G0549

Bradley County

Bradley County Genealogical Society. **Bradley County, Tennessee: Pre-Civil War Settlement Map**.
Parchment. $12.50. .... Vendor G0549

Douthat, James L. **1836 Bradley County, Tennessee Civil Districts and Tax Lists**. Indexed.
Paper. $12.50. .... Vendor G0549

Hurlburt, J. S. **The History of the Rebellion in Bradley County, East Tennessee**. (1866) reprint 1988. Indexed. Illus.
Cloth. $32.50. 289 pp. .... Vendor G0522

McClure, Lucille. **Abstracts of Ocoee District Early Land Records—Entries**. Illus.
   The Ocoee Land Office was opened in October 1838 to sell the lands formerly owned by the Cherokee Indians prior to their removal to the western lands. The lands are in present Hamilton, Bradley, Marion, Polk, and parts of McMinn and Monroe counties.
Paper. $25.00. 134 pp. .... Vendor G0549

Randolph, Sheridan C., and William R. Snell. **Bradley County, Tennessee, 1840 Federal Census**. 1987. Indexed.
Paper. $12.00. 85 pp. .... Vendor G0522

Sistler, Byron, and Barbara Sistler. **1870 Census—Tennessee**. Bradley County.
Paper. $14.00. .... Vendor G0577

Snell, William R. **1860 Federal Census (index) Bradley County, Tennessee**. 1983. Indexed.
Paper. $12.00. 41 pp. .... Vendor G0522

Snell, William R., Rena Jones, and Kent Hawkins. **Bradley County Tax Lists (TN) 1837, 1838, 1839**. 1978.
Paper. $10.00. 30 pp. .... Vendor G0522

Snell, William R. **Bradley County, Tennessee, Post Offices, 1836-1994**. 1994.
Paper. $8.00. 32 pp. .... Vendor G0522

Snell, William R. **Cleveland, the Beautiful: A History of Cleveland, Tennessee 1842-1931**. 1986. Indexed. Illus.
Cloth. $30.00. 458 pp. .... Vendor G0522

Snell, William R., and Virginia Faye Taylor. **Death Notices in the Cleveland Banner (Tennessee) 1865-1883**. (1981) reprint 1991. Indexed.
Paper. $8.00. 27 pp. .... Vendor G0522

Snell, William R., and Robert L. George, eds. **From War to Peace: World War II and the Postwar Years, Bradley County, Tennessee, 1940-1950**. 1986. Indexed. Illus.
Paper. $12.00. 176 pp. .... Vendor G0522

Snell, William R., and Virginia Faye Taylor. **Marriage Notices in the Cleveland Banner, 1865-1883, Cleveland, Tennessee.** (1982) reprint 1995. Indexed.
Paper. $8.00. 32 pp. .... Vendor G0522

Campbell County

Douthat, James L. **1836 Campbell County, Tennessee Civil Districts and Tax Lists.** Indexed.
Paper. $10.00. .... Vendor G0549

Douthat, James L. **John McClellan's Survey Book.** Indexed.
　The plat survey book of the period for the counties of Roane, Rhea, Overton, Campbell, Anderson, and Bledsoe counties. Plat maps of each survey given.
Paper. $18.50. .... Vendor G0549

Goodspeed Publishing Co. **Campbell County, Tennessee Biographies.** 1887. Reprinted. Indexed.
Paper. $4.00. 14 pp. .... Vendor G0549

Jones, Janice L. **Campbell Co., TN Will & Probate Records, Vol. 1, 1806-1841.** 1995. Indexed.
Paper. $49.00. 257 pp. .... Vendor G0460

Jones, Janice L. **Tax List Addendum, Campbell Co., TN 1806-1841.** 1995.
Paper. $19.50. 67 pp. .... Vendor G0460

Pedersen, Diane E. **Entry Book—5th Survey District Book C 1816-1823—Grants Numbered 1601-2548.**
Paper. $29.50. .... Vendor G0549

Sistler, Byron, and Barbara Sistler. **1870 Census—Tennessee.** Campbell County.
Paper. $13.00. .... Vendor G0577

Sistler, Byron, and Barbara Sistler. **Campbell County, TN Marriages 1838-1881.** 1984.
　About 3,000 marriages, arranged alphabetically by both bride and groom.
Paper. $12.00. .... Vendor G0577

Whitley, Edythe Rucker. **Marriages of Claiborne County, Tennessee, 1838-1850 & Campbell County, Tennessee, 1838-1853.** (1983) reprint 1996. Indexed.
Paper. $12.50. 112 pp. .... Vendor G0011

WPA. **Campbell County, Tennessee Deed Book D, 1820-1826.** Indexed.
Paper. $16.00. .... Vendor G0549

Cannon County

Carlson, Gladys. **Abstract of Cannon County, Tennessee Will Book Volume A, 1836-1895.** Indexed.
Paper. $12.50. 427 pp. .... Vendor G0549

Goodspeed Publishing Company. **White, Warren, DeKalb, Coffee and Cannon Counties**. (1886) reprint 1979. Indexed.
Cloth. $28.50. 195 pp. .... Vendor G0610

Rogers, Helen L. **Cannon County, Tennessee Marriage Records**.
Paper. $35.00. 262 pp. .... Vendor G0549

Sistler, Byron, and Barbara Sistler. **1870 Census—Tennessee**. Cannon County.
Paper. $14.00. .... Vendor G0577

Sistler, Byron, and Barbara Sistler. **Cannon County, TN Marriages 1838-1873**. 1985.
  About 3,000 marriages, arranged alphabetically by both bride and groom.
Paper. $12.00. .... Vendor G0577

WPA. **Cannon County, Tennessee Minute Book A—1836-1841**. Indexed.
Paper. $40.00. 323 pp. .... Vendor G0549

Carroll County

Goodspeed Publishing Company. **Carroll, Henry, and Benton Counties**. (1886) reprint 1978. Indexed. Illus.
Contact vendor for information. 176 pp. .... Vendor G0610

Sistler, Byron, and Barbara Sistler. **1870 Census—Tennessee**. Carroll County.
Paper. $19.00. .... Vendor G0577

Sistler, Byron, and Barbara Sistler. **Carroll County, TN Marriages 1860-1873**. 1988.
  About 2,400 marriages, arranged alphabetically by both bride and groom.
Paper. $12.00. .... Vendor G0577

Carter County

Burgner, Goldene Fillers. **Carter County, Tennessee, Marriages, 1796-1870**. 1987. Indexed.
Paper. $25.00. 150 pp. .... Vendor G0610

Carter County, TN and Its People 1796-1993. By more than 1,300 past and present Carter Co. family historians/genealogists. 1993. Indexed. Illus.
  More than 1,300 family stories/genealogies and pictures are included in this comprehensive history of Carter County, TN. Also included in this collector's edition are nearly 180 pages of topical stories and pictures, including articles on communities, military (rosters from all wars), religion, education, etc. Every-name index.
Cloth. $67.00. 736 pp .... Vendor G0088

Douthat, James L. **1836 Carter County, Tennessee Civil Districts and Tax Lists**. Indexed.
Paper. $10.00. .... Vendor G0549

Douthat, James L. **Carter County, Tennessee Wills and Inventories 1794-1847**.
Paper. $7.50. .... Vendor G0549

Douthat, James L. **Watauga Reservoir Cemeteries**.
Paper. $28.50. 160 pp. .... Vendor G0549

Sistler, Byron, and Barbara Sistler. **1870 Census—Tennessee**. Carter County.
Paper. $13.00. .... Vendor G0577

Sistler, Byron, and Barbara Sistler. **Carter County, TN Marriages 1850-1876**. 1987.
   About 3,000 marriages, arranged alphabetically by both bride and groom.
Paper. $12.00. .... Vendor G0577

WPA. **Carter County, Tennessee Minutes of County Court—Volume 4 1826-1829**.
Paper. $35.00. 235 pp. .... Vendor G0549

WPA. **Sinking Creek Baptist Church Records, 1783-1905**.
Paper. $35.00. .... Vendor G0549

Cheatham County

Goodspeed Publishing Company. **Montgomery, Robertson, Humphreys, Stewart, Dickson, Cheatham, and Houston Counties**. (1886) reprint 1979. Indexed.
Contact vendor for information. 653 pp. .... Vendor G0610

Sistler, Byron, and Barbara Sistler. **1870 Census—Tennessee**. Cheatham County.
Paper. $13.00. .... Vendor G0577

Sistler, Byron, and Barbara Sistler. **Cheatham County, TN Marriages 1856-1881**. 1988.
   Copied from microfilm of the original marriage books. Arranged alphabetically by bride and groom.
Paper. $10.00. .... Vendor G0577

WPA. **Cheatham County, Tennessee Wills and Inventories—Vol. A 1856-1871**. Indexed.
Paper. $45.00. .... Vendor G0549

WPA. **Marriage Records of Cheatham County, Tennessee—Vol. A 1856-1897**. Indexed.
Paper. $12.50. .... Vendor G0549

Chester County

Goodspeed Publishing Company. **Henderson, Chester, McNairy, Decatur and Hardin Counties**. (1886) reprint 1978. Indexed.
Contact vendor for information. 136 pp. .... Vendor G0610

Claiborne County

Douthat, James L. **1836 Claiborne County, Tennessee Civil Districts and Tax Lists**. Indexed.
Paper. $10.00. .... Vendor G0549

Fletcher, Virginia B. **Index to the First Deed Books of Claiborne Co., TN 1801-1865**. 1996. Indexed.
Paper. $30.00. 250 pp. .... Vendor G0332

Fletcher, Virginia B. **Index to the Probate Court Records of Claiborne Co., TN 1844-1865**. 1993. Indexed.
Paper. $12.50. 100 pp. .... Vendor G0332

Holt, Edgar A. **Claiborne County (Tennessee)**. 1981. Indexed. Illus.
Cloth. $17.50. 134 pp. .... Vendor G0522

Pedersen, Diane E. **Entry Book—5th Survey District Book A—Grants Number 1-800**.
Covers the land sales and tracts in Anderson, Grainger, Jefferson, Claiborne, Knox, and Sevier counties.
Paper. $25.00. .... Vendor G0549

Pedersen, Diane E. **Entry Book—5th Survey District Book C, 1816-1823—Grants Number 1601-2548**.
Early land records from the present counties of Knox, Jefferson, Union, Grainger, Hamblen, Claiborne, Hancock, and Hawkins counties.
Paper. $29.50. .... Vendor G0549

Sistler, Byron, and Barbara Sistler. **1870 Census—Tennessee**. Claiborne County.
Paper. $15.00. .... Vendor G0577

Sistler, Byron, and Barbara Sistler. **Claiborne County, TN Marriages 1838-1868**. 1983.
About 3,000 marriages, arranged alphabetically by both bride and groom.
Paper. $12.00. .... Vendor G0577

Sistler, Byron, and Barbara Sistler. **Claiborne County, TN Marriages 1868-1891**. 1984.
About 3,000 marriages, arranged alphabetically by both bride and groom.
Paper. $12.00. .... Vendor G0577

Whitley, Edythe Rucker. **Marriages of Claiborne County, Tennessee, 1838-1850 & Campbell County, Tennessee, 1838-1853**. (1983) reprint 1996. Indexed.
Paper. $12.50. 112 pp. .... Vendor G0011

WPA. **Claiborne County, Tennessee Court of Pleas and Quarter Session Minute Book 1819-1821**. Indexed.
Paper. $35.00. .... Vendor G0549

WPA. **Claiborne County, Tennessee Will Book A, 1837-1846**. Indexed.
$35.00 (perfect bound). 271 pp. .... Vendor G0549

Cocke County

Cocke Co. Heritage Book Committee. **Cocke County, TN and Its People 1992**. 1992. Indexed. Illus.
Part of the prestigious County Heritage Book series! An attractive, hardbound collector's edition, 9" x 12" size. More than 700 family stories, genealogies, and

photos are the highlight of this most comprehensive Cocke County history ever. Other topics include clubs, chuches, education, and military. Surname index.
Cloth. $63.50. 422 pp. .... Vendor G0087

O'Dell, Ruth Webb. **Over the Misty Blue Hills**. The Story of Cocke County, Tennessee. (1951) reprint 1985. Indexed.
Contact vendor for information. 436 pp. .... Vendor G0610

Sistler, Barbara, and Byron Sistler. **1880 Census, Cocke Co., TN**. 1996.
Paper. $16.00. .... Vendor G0577

Coffee County

Goodspeed Publishing Company. **White, Warren, DeKalb, Coffee and Cannon Counties**. (1886) reprint 1979. Indexed.
Cloth. $28.50. 195 pp. .... Vendor G0610

Sistler, Byron, and Barbara Sistler. **1870 Census—Tennessee**. Coffee County.
Vendor G0577

Cooke County

Douthat, James L. **1836 Cooke County. Tennessee Civil Districts and Tax Lists**. Indexed.
Paper. $8.00. .... Vendor G0549

Crockett County

Goodspeed Publishing Company. **Lauderdale, Tipton, Haywood, and Crockett Counties**. (1886) reprint 1978. Indexed.
Contact vendor for information. 208 pp. .... Vendor G0610

Sistler, Byron, and Barbara Sistler. **1870 Census—Tennessee**. Crockett County.
Paper. $16.00. .... Vendor G0577

Cumberland County

Sistler, Byron, and Barbara Sistler. **1870 Census—Tennessee**. Cumberland County.
Paper. $10.00. .... Vendor G0577

WPA. **Cumberland County, Tennessee Entry Takers Book 2 1856-1891**.
Paper. $7.50. .... Vendor G0549

WPA. **Cumberland County, Tennessee Journal B—1856-1860**.
Paper. $8.50. .... Vendor G0549

Davidson County

Clayton, W. Woodford. **History of Davidson County,** with Illustrations & Biographical Sketches of Its Prominent Men & Pioneers. (1880) reprint 1993.
Cloth. $52.50. 499 pp. .... Vendor G0259

Crew, H. W. **History of Nashville**. (1890) reprint 1993.
Cloth. $68.00. 656 pp. .... Vendor G0259

Elliott, Lizzie P. **Early History of Nashville**. (1911) reprint 1993.
Cloth. $35.00. 286 pp. .... Vendor G0259

Fulcher, Richard C. **1779-1790 Census of the Cumberland Settlements:** Davidson, Sumner, and Tennessee Counties. 1990.
These counties, originally a part of North Carolina, now are all or part of Tennessee counties. Abstracted from public records are all references to those living in the jurisdictions between 1770 and 1790.
Cloth. $22.50. 253 pp. .... Vendor G0010

Gambill, Nell M. **The Kith & Kin of Captain James Leeper & Susan Drake, His Wife**. 1946.
A most useful book for any researcher with early Davidson Co. connections. History of the first couple to be married in Nashville (1780) and their descendants.
Cloth. $7.50. 200 pp. .... Vendor G0577

Lucas, Silas Emmett, Jr. **Davidson County Marriage Record Book I, 1789-1837**. 1979. Indexed.
Cloth. $28.00. 166 pp. + index. .... Vendor G0610

Marsh, Helen C., and Timothy R. Marsh. **Davidson County, Tennessee, Wills & Inventories 1784-1832**. 2 vols. 1989. Indexed.
Cloth. $37.50/vol. 272 pp./vol. .... Vendor G0610

Marsh, Helen C., and Timothy R. Marsh. **Land Deed Genealogy of Davidson County, Tennessee, 1783-1803:** Vol. 1 (1783-1792) Deed Books A-B. 1992. Indexed.
Cloth. $32.50. 290 pp. .... Vendor G0610

Marsh, Helen C., and Timothy R. Marsh. **Land Deed Genealogy of Davidson County, Tennessee, 1783-1803:** Vol. 2 (1792-1797) Deed Books C-D. 1992. Indexed.
Cloth. $32.50. 300 pp. .... Vendor G0610

Marsh, Helen C., and Timothy R. Marsh. **Land Deed Genealogy of Davidson County, Tennessee, 1783-1803:** Vol. 3 (1797-1803) Deed Books D-E. 1992. Indexed.
Cloth. $32.50. 258 pp. .... Vendor G0610

Sistler, Byron, and Barbara Sistler. **Davidson County, TN Marriages 1838-1863**. 1985.
About 7,000 marriages, arranged alphabetically by both bride and groom.
Cloth. $26.00. .... Vendor G0577

Sistler, Byron, and Barbara Sistler. **Davidson County, TN Wills & Administrations to 1861: An Index**. 1989.
About 3,300 enties.
Paper. $12.00. .... Vendor G0577

Whitley, Edythe R. **Pioneers of Davidson County, Tennessee**. (1965) reprint 1996. Indexed.
Paper. $10.00. 84 pp. .... Vendor G0011

Whitley, Edythe Rucker, comp. **Tennessee Marriage Records: Davidson County, 1789-1847**. 1981. Indexed.
Cloth. $16.50. 277 pp. .... Vendor G0011

Decatur County

Carter, William S., comp. **An Every-Name Index to the History of Decatur County Tennessee,** by Lillye Younger. 1990.
Paper. $14.95. 57 pp. .... Vendor G0656

Douthat, James L. **Kentucky Lake Reservoir Cemeteries. Volume 3**.
    Covers the southern part of west Tennessee with the areas of Decatur, Hardin, Henderson, McNairy, Perry, and Wayne counties plus the reinterment sites for the entire Kentucky Lake Reservoir. Also available as a set with Volumes 1 and 2 (see Tennessee, Statewide and Regional References).
Paper. $35.00. .... Vendor G0549

Goodspeed Publishing Company. **Henderson, Chester, McNairy, Decatur and Hardin Counties**. (1886) reprint 1978. Indexed.
Contact vendor for information. 136 pp. .... Vendor G0610

Sistler, Byron, and Barbara Sistler. **1870 Census—Tennessee**. Decatur County.
Paper. $14.00. .... Vendor G0577

Younger, Lillye. **Decatur County (Tennessee)**. 1979. Indexed. Illus.
Cloth. $17.50. 136 pp. .... Vendor G0522

DeKalb County

Goodspeed Publishing Company. **White, Warren, DeKalb, Coffee and Cannon Counties**. (1886) reprint 1979. Indexed.
Cloth. $28.50. 195 pp. .... Vendor G0610

Hale, Will T. **History of DeKalb County**. (1915) reprint 1993.
Cloth. $32.50. xii + 254 pp. .... Vendor G0259

Majors, Betty Moore. **DeKalb County, Tennessee Genealogy from Administrator's Settlement Books 1846-1907**. Indexed.
Paper. $13.50. 86 pp. .... Vendor G0549

Sistler, Byron, and Barbara Sistler. **1870 Census—Tennessee**. DeKalb County.
Paper. $14.00. .... Vendor G0577

Sistler, Byron. **DeKalb County, Tennessee, Marriages, 1848-1880**. 1985. Indexed.
Paper. $14.00. 123 pp. .... Vendor G0610

Sistler, Byron, and Barbara Sistler. **DeKalb County, TN Marriages 1848-1880**. 1985.
About 3,800 marriages arranged alphabetically by both bride and groom.
Paper. $14.00. .... Vendor G0577

Dickson County

Corlew, Robert E. **History of Dickson County,** from the Earliest Times to the Present.
(1956) reprint 1994.
Cloth. $32.00. 243 pp. .... Vendor G0259

Garrett, Jill Knight. **Dickson County, Tennessee, Handbook**. 1984. Indexed.
Cloth. $37.50. 460 pp. .... Vendor G0610

Goodspeed Publishing Company. **Montgomery, Robertson, Humphreys, Stewart, Dickson, Cheatham, and Houston Counties**. (1886) reprint 1979. Indexed.
Contact vendor for information. 653 pp. .... Vendor G0610

Kilgore, Sherry J. **Dickson County, TN Marriages 1817-1856**. 1988.
A combination of the earliest marriage books and loose bonds and licenses. About 1,600 marriages.
Paper. $11.00. .... Vendor G0577

Sistler, Byron, and Barbara Sistler. **1870 Census—Tennessee**. Dickson County.
Paper. $14.00. .... Vendor G0577

Sistler, Byron, and Barbara Sistler. **Dickson County, TN Marriages 1857-1870**. 1988.
Copied from microfilm of the original marriage books.
Paper. $9.00. .... Vendor G0577

Dyer County

Goodspeed Publishing Company. **Gibson, Obion, Weakley, Dyer and Lake Counties**. (1886) reprint 1988. Indexed.
Cloth. $37.50. 352 pp. .... Vendor G0610

Sistler, Byron, and Barbara Sistler. **Dyer County, TN Marriages 1860-1879**.
About 2,900 marriages copied from the original marriage books and arranged alphabetically by bride and groom.
Paper. $12.00. 1989 .... Vendor G0577

Fayette County

Goodspeed Publishing Company. **Fayette and Hardeman Counties**. (1887) reprint 1979. Indexed.
Cloth. $25.00. 167 pp. .... Vendor G0610

Ingmire, Frances. **Fayette County, Tennessee Marriages 1838-1857**.
Paper. $16.00. 58 pp. .... Vendor G0549

Sistler, Byron, and Barbara Sistler. **Fayette County, TN Marriages 1838-1871**. 1989.
    About 4,300 marriages copied from original marriage books and arranged alphabetically by bride and groom.
Paper. $16.00. .... Vendor G0577

Fentress County

1860 Fentress County, Tennessee Census.
Paper. $35.00. .... Vendor G0549

1870 Fentress County, Tennessee Census.
Paper. $10.00. .... Vendor G0549

1880 Fentress County, Tennessee Census.
Paper. $21.00. .... Vendor G0549

1900 Fentress County, Tennessee Census.
Paper. $35.00. .... Vendor G0549

1910 Fentress County, Tennessee Census.
Paper. $28.50. .... Vendor G0549

1920 Fentress County, Tennessee Census.
Paper. $45.00. .... Vendor G0549

Hatfield, Wanda S. **1872 Fentress County, Tennessee Tax List**. Indexed.
Paper. $18.50. .... Vendor G0549

Hatfield, Wanda S. **Early Settlers of Fentress County, Tennessee**. Indexed.
Paper. $25.00. .... Vendor G0549

Hatfield, Wanda S. **Entry Books of Fentress County, Tennessee, Volumes A, B & C, 1824-1901**.
Paper. $24.00. 97 pp. .... Vendor G0549

Hogue, Albert R. **History of Fentress County, Tennessee**. (1916, 1920) reprint 1994.
Indexed. Illus.
Paper. $20.00. 197 pp. .... Vendor G0011

Sistler, Byron, and Barbara Sistler. **1870 Census—Tennessee**. Fentress County.
Paper. $12.00. .... Vendor G0577

WPA. **Fentress County, Tennessee Deed Books A & B, 1824-1838**.
$16.50 (perfect bound). .... Vendor G0549

WPA. **Fentress County, Tennessee Minute Book 1, 1842-1844**.
$35.00 (perfect bound). 231 pp. .... Vendor G0549

Franklin County

1837 Tennessee Volunteers. Indexed.
    A report to the 25th Congress of the U.S. with regard to the Militia of Tennessee
called up for service in Florida against the Indians. Most of the men did not serve but
this roster was drawn up from those who volunteered from Franklin County, TN.
$8.50 (perfect bound). 54 pp. .... Vendor G0549

1900 Franklin County, Tennessee Census Index.
Paper. $9.50. .... Vendor G0549

Franklin County, Tennessee Wills 1876-1891.
Paper. $12.50. .... Vendor G0549

Goodspeed Publishing Company. **Giles, Lincoln, Franklin, and Moore Counties**. (1886) reprint 1979. Indexed.
Contact vendor for information. 181 pp. .... Vendor G0610

Ingmire, Frances. **1860 Franklin County, Tennessee Census—Annotated**.
Paper. $50.00. 222 pp. .... Vendor G0549

Ingmire, Frances. **Franklin County, Tennessee Abstract of Wills 1808-1875**.
Paper. $32.50. 116 pp. .... Vendor G0549

Partlow, Thomas E. **Franklin County, Tennessee, Wills and Deeds, 1800-1876**. 1991. Indexed.
Cloth. $28.50. 244 pp. .... Vendor G0610

Sistler, Byron, and Barbara Sistler. **1870 Census—Tennessee**. Franklin County.
Paper. $18.00. .... Vendor G0577

Sistler, Byron, and Barbara Sistler. **Franklin County, TN Marriages 1838-1874**. 1985.
    About 4,000 marriages, arranged alphabetically by bride and groom.
Paper. $15.00. .... Vendor G0577

WPA. **Franklin County, Tennessee—County Court Minutes 1832-1837**. Indexed.
$45.00 (perfect bound). 285 pp. .... Vendor G0549

Gibson County

Goodspeed Publishing Company. **Gibson, Obion, Weakley, Dyer and Lake Counties**. (1886) reprint 1988. Indexed.
Cloth. $37.50. 352 pp. .... Vendor G0610

Whitley, Edythe Rucker, comp. **Tennessee Marriage Records: Gibson County, 1824-1860**. 1982. Indexed.
Cloth. $15.00. 173 pp. .... Vendor G0011

Giles County

Goodspeed Publishing Company. **Giles, Lincoln, Franklin, and Moore Counties**. (1886) reprint 1979. Indexed.
Contact vendor for information. 181 pp. .... Vendor G0610

Lyons, Sherri H. **Giles County, Tennessee Early Marriage Records 1810-1849**. 1996. Indexed.
Spiral binding. $14.83. 10 pp. .... Vendor G0672

McCallum, James. **Giles County, Tennessee History**.
$28.50 (perfect bound). 140 pp. .... Vendor G0549

McCallum, James. **The History of Giles County, Tennessee**. A Brief Sketch of the
Settlement and Early History. (1876) reprint 1983. Indexed.
Paper. $15.00. 135 pp. .... Vendor G0610

Murray, Joyce Martin. **Williamson County, Tennessee Deed Abstracts, 1799-1811**.
Indexed.
   Present Maury, Giles, and Lawrence counties. Includes full-name, location, and
slave indexes.
Cloth. $25.00. 202 pp. .... Vendor G0466

Sistler, Byron, and Samuel Sistler. **Every Name Index to 18 Middle Tennessee County
Record Books**. 1992.
   A single integrated index to eighteen inadequately indexed books: Bedford Co. (9
titles), Giles Co. (8), Lincoln Co. (1). About 165,000 entries.
Cloth. $52.00. 800 pp. .... Vendor G0577

WPA. **Giles County, Tennessee County Court Minutes Book H, 1823-1825**.
Indexed.
Paper. $50.00. 443 pp. .... Vendor G0549

WPA. **Giles County, Tennessee Miscellaneous Wills 1830-1857**.
Paper. $20.00. 134 pp. .... Vendor G0549

Grainger County

Douthat, James L. **1836 Grainger County, Tennessee Civil Districts and Tax Lists**.
Indexed.
Paper. $10.00. .... Vendor G0549

Douthat, James L. **Grainger County, Tennessee Various Records**. Indexed.
   Records taken from Guardian Bonds 1796-1835; Orphan Records from County
Court Minutes 1802-1812; Administrative Bonds 1798-1832; Scholastic Population
1848; Merchant Licenses; and 1830 Voters Listing.
$15.00 (perfect bound). .... Vendor G0549

Miller, Alan N., II. **Grainger County, Tennessee Apprenticeships 1797-1875**.
Indexed.
$7.50 (perfect bound). 32 pp. .... Vendor G0549

Pedersen, Diane E. **Entry Book—5th Survey District Book A—Grants Number 1-800**.
   Covers the land sales and tracts in Anderson, Grainger, Jefferson, Claiborne, Knox,
and Sevier counties.
Paper. $25.00. .... Vendor G0549

Pedersen, Diane E. **Entry Book—5th Survey District Book C, 1816-1823—Grants
Number 1601-2548**.
   Early land records from the present counties of Knox, Jefferson, Union, Grainger,
Hamblen, Claiborne, Hancock, and Hawkins counties.
Paper. $29.50. .... Vendor G0549

Reeves, Mary E. **Grainger County Inventories of Estates and Wills, 1833-1852**. 1989. Indexed.
Cloth. $28.50. 180 pp. .... Vendor G0610

Sheffield, Ella Lee, ed. **Grainger County, Tennessee, Court of Pleas and Quarter Session Record Book No. 3, 1812-1816**. 1983. Indexed.
Paper. $21.50. 240 pp. .... Vendor G0610

Sheffield, Ella Lee., and Silas Emmett Lucas, Jr., eds. **Grainger County, Tennessee, Records, Letters of Administrations, 1842-1854**. 1983. Indexed.
Paper. $16.50. 96 pp. .... Vendor G0610

Sistler, Byron, and Barbara Sistler. **1870 Census—Tennessee**. Grainger County.
Paper. $15.00. .... Vendor G0577

Whitley, Edythe Rucker. **Marriages of Grainger County, Tennessee, 1796-1837**. (1982) reprint 1996. Indexed.
Paper. $13.00. 116 pp. .... Vendor G0011

WPA. **Grainger County, Tennessee Loose Will Book**.
$18.50 (perfect bound). 106 pp. .... Vendor G0549

WPA. **Grainger County, Tennessee Minutes of Court of Pleas & Quarter Sessions—Vol. 2, 1802-1812**.
Paper. $55.00. 390 pp. .... Vendor G0549

WPA. **Grainger County, Tennessee Tax Listing 1814-1815**.
Paper. $11.00. .... Vendor G0549

Greene County

Burgner, Goldene Fillers. **Greene County Minutes of the Court of Common Pleas, 1783-1795**. 1982. Indexed.
Contact vendor for information. 280 pp. .... Vendor G0610

Burgner, Goldene Fillers. **Greene County Tax Digests, 1809-1817**. 1986. Indexed.
Cloth. $27.50. Approx. 250 pp. .... Vendor G0610

Burgner, Goldene Fillers. **Greene County, Tennessee, Chancery Court Minutes, 1825-1876**. 1987. Indexed.
Cloth. $38.50. 371 pp. .... Vendor G0610

Burgner, Goldene Fillers. **Greene County, Tennessee, Marriages, 1783-1868**. (1981) reprint 1991. Indexed.
Cloth. $35.00. vi + 390 pp. .... Vendor G0610

Burgner, Goldene Fillers. **Greene County, Tennessee, Wills: 1783-1890**. 1981. Indexed.
Cloth. $27.50. 150 pp. .... Vendor G0610

Burgner, Goldene Fillers. **North Carolina Land Grants Recorded in Greene County, Tennessee**. 1981. Indexed.
Cloth. $25.00. 160 pp. .... Vendor G0610

Douthat, James L. **1836 Greene County, Tennessee Civil Districts and Tax Lists**. Indexed.
Paper. $10.00. .... Vendor G0549

Greene Co. Heritage Book Committee. **Historic Greene County, TN and Its People 1783-1992**. 1993. Indexed. Illus.
   Part of the prestigious County Heritage Book series! 9" x 12" hardbound, collector's edition. The first and most comprehensive history of Greene County, TN. It features more than 700 family genealogies, histories, and pictures, along with numerous topics, including communities, churches, and cemeteries. Surname index.
Cloth. $63.50. 440 pp. .... Vendor G0087

Houston, Sandra Kelton. **Greene County Minutes of the Court of Common Pleas, 1797-1807**. 1981. Indexed.
Cloth. $30.00. 333 pp. + index. .... Vendor G0610

Houston, Sandra Kelton. **Greene County, Tennessee, Guardians and Orphans Court Records 1783-1870; and 1830 Tax List**. 1983. Indexed.
Paper. $25.00. 144 pp. + index. .... Vendor G0610

Murray, Joyce Martin. **Green County, Tennessee Deed Abstracts, 1785-1810**. Indexed.
   Includes full-name, location, and slave indexes.
Paper. $25.00. 199 pp. .... Vendor G0466

Murray, Joyce Martin. **Greene County, Tennessee Deed Abstracts, 1810-1822**. 1996. Indexed.
   Includes full-name, location, and slave indexes.
Paper. $25.00. 200 pp. .... Vendor G0466

Sistler, Byron, and Barbara Sistler. **1870 Census—Tennessee**. Greene County.
Paper. $20.00. .... Vendor G0577

WPA. **Greene County, Tennessee—Court of Pleas 1826-1827**.
Paper. $22.50. 169 pp. .... Vendor G0549

WPA. **Greene County, Tennessee Marriage Licenses and Bonds 1780-1837**. Indexed.
Paper. $35.00. 440 pp. .... Vendor G0549

WPA. **Greene County, Tennessee Tombstone Records**.
$55.00 (perfect bound). 458 pp. .... Vendor G0549

Grundy County

Douthat, James L. **Grundy County, Tennessee Marriages 1850-1874**.
Paper. $10.00. .... Vendor G0549

Sistler, Byron, and Barbara Sistler. **1870 Census—Tennessee**. Grundy County.
Paper. $10.00. .... Vendor G0577

WPA. **Grundy County Court Minutes 1844-1855**.
Paper. $25.00. 171 pp. .... Vendor G0549

WPA. **Grundy County, Tennessee Will Book 1838-1874**.
Paper. $15.00. 51 pp. .... Vendor G0549

WPA. **Grundy County, Tennessee WPA Records**. Indexed.
Paper. $18.00. .... Vendor G0549

Hamblen County

Douthat, James L. **Marriage Books 1-5, 1870-1888**. Indexed.
Paper. $10.00. .... Vendor G0549

Hamblen County Heritage Book Committee. **A History of Hamblen County, TN and Its People**. 1996. Indexed. Illus.
One of many in the well-known County Heritage Book series. Features nearly 300 family histories, genealogies, and family photos. Hardbound, 9" x 12" book, with a large section on religion and churches in Hamblen County; other topics include communities, landmarks, clubs, and organizations. Surname index.
Cloth. $58.50 (incl. postage & tax). 156 pp. .... Vendor G0087

Pedersen, Diane E. **Entry Book—5th Survey District Book C, 1816-1823—Grants Number 1601-2548**.
Early land records from the present counties of Knox, Jefferson, Union, Grainger, Hamblen, Claiborne, Hancock, and Hawkins counties.
Paper. $29.50. .... Vendor G0549

Sistler, Byron, and Barbara Sistler. **1870 Census—Tennessee**. Hamblen County.
Paper. $14.00. .... Vendor G0577

WPA. **Hamblen County, Tennessee Tombstone Records**.
$37.50 (perfect bound). 282 pp. .... Vendor G0549

Hamilton County

Chattanooga [TN] 1885.
Paper. $17.50. .... Vendor G0549

Douthat, James L. **1836 Hamilton County, Tennessee Civil Districts and Tax Lists**. Indexed.
Paper. $10.00. .... Vendor G0549

Douthat, James L. **1860 Hamilton County, Tennessee Census**. Indexed.
Paper. $20.00. .... Vendor G0549

Douthat, James L. **Along the Pike—The History of Walden's Ridge Along Anderson Pike**. Indexed. Illus.
Anderson Pike was one of the oldest roads from Sequatchie Valley to Chattanooga, begun in 1840 and completed in 1852. Sketches of the communities, Civil War impact, and families comprise this history.
Cloth. $24.50. 206 pp. .... Vendor G0549

Douthat, James L. **Chickamauga Reservoir Cemeteries**.
Paper. $20.00. .... Vendor G0549

Douthat, James L. **Early Settlers of Hamilton County, Tennessee**.
Paper. $25.00. .... Vendor G0549

Douthat, James L. **Hamilton County, Tennessee Marriage Book 1, 1853-1870**.
Paper. $20.00. .... Vendor G0549

Douthat, James L. **Hamilton County, Tennessee Marriage Book 2, 1864-1874**.
Paper. $20.00. .... Vendor G0549

Douthat, James L. **Hamilton County, Tennessee Marriage Book 3, 1874-1880**.
Paper. $20.00. .... Vendor G0549

Hamilton County, Tennessee Will Book 1, 1862-1892.
Paper. $35.00. .... Vendor G0549

Lea, Joyce Ray. **So Great a Cloud—A Part of the History of Brainerd United Methodist Church and Cemetery and the Brainerd Area**. 1995. Indexed.
Church organized 1895. Cemetery much older. Public cemetery many years prior to 1952. Earliest *marked* grave 1861. Lists all persons known buried there, birth/death dates if known. Obituary abstracts of most.
Cloth. $28.00. 234 pp. .... Vendor G0526

McClure, Lucille. **Abstracts of Ocoee District Early Land Records—Entries**. Illus.
The Ocoee Land Office was opened in October 1838 to sell the lands formerly owned by the Cherokee Indians prior to their removal to the western lands. The lands are in present Hamilton, Bradley, Marion, Polk, and parts of McMinn and Monroe counties.
Paper. $25.00. 134 pp. .... Vendor G0549

Roster of CSA Soldiers Buried in Chattanooga. 1894. Reprinted.
Listing of men from various states who are not buried in the area.
Paper. $3.50. .... Vendor G0549

Sistler, Barbara, and Byron Sistler. **1880 Census, Hamilton Co., TN**. 1996.
Arranged alphabetically by head of household, with names and ages of all individuals.
Paper. $22.00. 236 pp. .... Vendor G0577

The Story of the General.
A brief accounting of the General and the escape of Andrew's Raiders with their final capture and imprisonment.
Paper. $3.50. .... Vendor G0549

WPA. **Hamilton County, Tennessee Entry Takers Book 1824-1897**. Indexed.
Paper. $35.00. 257 pp. .... Vendor G0549

Hancock County

Bible, Jean P. **Melungeons—Yesterday and Today**. Illus.
A full accounting of the lost tribe of Tennessee and North Carolina.
Cloth. $12.00. 140 pp. .... Vendor G0549

Pedersen, Diane E. **Entry Book—5th Survey District Book C, 1816-1823—Grants Number 1601-2548**.
Early land records from the present counties of Knox, Jefferson, Union, Grainger,

Hamblen, Claiborne, Hancock, and Hawkins counties.
Paper. $29.50. .... Vendor G0549

Sistler, Barbara, and Byron Sistler. **1880 Census, Hancock Co., TN**. 1996.
Paper. $13.00. 63 pp. .... Vendor G0577

Hardeman County

Goodspeed Publishing Company. **Fayette and Hardeman Counties**. (1887) reprint
1979. Indexed.
Cloth. $25.00. 167 pp. .... Vendor G0610

Sistler, Byron, and Barbara Sistler. **Hardeman County, TN Marriages 1823-1861**.
1986.
 About 3,700 marriages, arranged alphabetically by bride and groom.
Paper. $14.00. .... Vendor G0577

WPA. **Hardeman County, Tennessee Cemetery Check List**.
Paper. $5.00. .... Vendor G0549

WPA. **Hardeman County, Tennessee County Court Minutes Vol. 2, 1827-1829**.
Indexed.
Paper. $28.50. 235 pp. .... Vendor G0549

Hardin County

Douthat, James L. **Kentucky Lake Reservoir Cemeteries. Volume 3**.
 Covers the southern part of west Tennessee with the areas of Decatur, Hardin,
Henderson, McNairy, Perry, and Wayne counties plus the reinterment sites for the
entire Kentucky Lake Reservoir. Also available as a set with Volumes 1 and 2 (see
Tennessee, Statewide and Regional References).
Paper. $35.00. .... Vendor G0549

Douthat, James L. **Pickwick Landing Reservoir Cemeteries**.
 Cemeteries found in Hardin County, TN; Tishomingo County, MS; and Lauderdale
and Colbert counties, AL.
Paper. $12.00. .... Vendor G0549

Goodspeed Publishing Company. **Henderson, Chester, McNairy, Decatur and Hardin
Counties**. (1886) reprint 1978. Indexed.
Contact vendor for information. 136 pp. .... Vendor G0610

Hays, Thomas A. **Hardin County, Tennessee, Records 1820-1860**. 1985. Indexed.
Cloth. $27.50. 272 pp. .... Vendor G0610

Hawkins County

Douthat, James L. **1836 Hawkins County, Tennessee Civil Districts and Tax Lists**.
Indexed.
Paper. $10.00. .... Vendor G0549

Lucas, Silas Emmett, Jr., and Ella Lee Sheffield, eds. **The Hawkins County Circuit Court Minutes, 1822-1825, and Fragment for the Period, November 1827-August 1828**. 1984. Indexed.
Paper. $21.50. 176 pp. .... Vendor G0610

Lucas, Silas Emmett, Jr., and Ella E. Lee Sheffield, eds. **The Hawkins County Minutes of the Court of Common Pleas, 1810-1821**. 1990.
Contact vendor for information. .... Vendor G0610

Messick, Eugenia L. **Hawkins County, Tennessee Will Book 1786-1864**. Indexed.
Paper. $30.00. .... Vendor G0549

Pedersen, Diane E. **Entry Book—5th Survey District Book C, 1816-1823—Grants Number 1601-2548**.
 Early land records from the present counties of Knox, Jefferson, Union, Grainger, Hamblen, Claiborne, Hancock, and Hawkins counties.
Paper. $29.50. .... Vendor G0549

Sistler, Barbara, and Byron Sistler. **1880 Census, Hawkins Co., TN**. 1996.
Paper. $20.00. 146 pp. .... Vendor G0577

WPA. **Hawkins County, Tennessee Circuit Court Minutes 1810-1821**.
$45.00 (perfect bound). 310 pp. .... Vendor G0549

WPA. **Hawkins County, Tennessee Circuit Court Minutes 1822-1825**.
$22.50 (perfect bound). 150 pp. .... Vendor G0549

WPA. **Hawkins County, Tennessee Court Minutes Nov. 1827-Aug. 1828**.
$12.50 (perfect bound). 59 pp. .... Vendor G0549

WPA. **Hawkins County, Tennessee Deed Book 1, 1788-1800**. Indexed.
Paper. $45.00. .... Vendor G0549

WPA. **Hawkins County, Tennessee General Index of Deeds Volume 1, 1788-1861**.
Paper. $55.00. .... Vendor G0549

WPA. **Hawkins County, Tennessee Miscellaneous Records**.
$15.00 (perfect bound). 84 pp. .... Vendor G0549

Haywood County

Goodspeed Publishing Company. **Lauderdale, Tipton, Haywood, and Crockett Counties**. (1886) reprint 1978. Indexed.
Contact vendor for information. 208 pp. .... Vendor G0610

WPA. **Haywood County, Tennessee County Court Minutes 1834-1840**. Indexed.
Paper. $40.00. 352 pp. .... Vendor G0549

WPA. **Haywood County, Tennessee Miscellaneous Records**.
$18.00 (perfect bound). 72 pp. .... Vendor G0549

Henderson County

Douthat, James L. **Kentucky Lake Reservoir Cemeteries. Volume 3**.
Covers the southern part of west Tennessee with the areas of Decatur, Hardin, Henderson, McNairy, Perry, and Wayne counties plus the reinterment sites for the entire Kentucky Lake Reservoir. Also available as a set with Volumes 1 and 2 (see Tennessee, Statewide and Regional References).
Paper. $35.00. .... Vendor G0549

Goodspeed Publishing Company. **Henderson, Chester, McNairy, Decatur and Hardin Counties**. (1886) reprint 1978. Indexed.
Contact vendor for information. 136 pp. .... Vendor G0610

Stewart, G. Tillman. **Henderson County (Tennessee)**. 1979. Indexed. Illus.
Cloth. $17.50. 133 pp. .... Vendor G0522

Henry County

Douthat, James L. **Kentucky Lake Reservoir Cemeteries. Volume 2**.
Covers the upper west Tennessee areas of Benton, Henry, Houston, Humphreys, and Stewart counties. Also available as a set with Volumes 1 and 3 (see Tennessee, Statewide and Regional References).
Paper. $35.00. .... Vendor G0549

Goodspeed Publishing Company. **Carroll, Henry, and Benton Counties**. (1886) reprint 1978. Indexed. Illus.
Contact vendor for information. 176 pp. .... Vendor G0610

Hickman County

Goodspeed Publishing Company. **Lawrence, Wayne, Perry, Hickman and Lewis Counties**. (1886) reprint 1979. Indexed.
Cloth. $22.50. 129 pp. .... Vendor G0610

Spence, W. Jerome, and David L. Spence. **History of Hickman County**. (1900) reprint 1993.
Cloth. $53.00. 509 pp. .... Vendor G0259

Spence, W. Jerome, and David L. Spence. **The History of Hickman County, Tennessee**. (1900) reprint 1982. Indexed.
Contact vendor for information. 532 pp. .... Vendor G0610

Houston County

Douthat, James L. **Kentucky Lake Reservoir Cemeteries. Volume 2**.
Covers the upper west Tennessee areas of Benton, Henry, Houston, Humphreys, and Stewart counties. Also available as a set with Volumes 1 and 3 (see Tennessee, Statewide and Regional References).
Paper. $35.00. .... Vendor G0549

Goodspeed Publishing Company. **Montgomery, Robertson, Humphreys, Stewart, Dickson, Cheatham, and Houston Counties**. (1886) reprint 1979. Indexed.
Contact vendor for information. 653 pp. .... Vendor G0610

Humphreys County

Douthat, James L. **Kentucky Lake Reservoir Cemeteries. Volume 2**.
Covers the upper west Tennessee areas of Benton, Henry, Houston, Humphreys, and Stewart counties. Also available as a set with Volumes 1 and 3 (see Tennessee, Statewide and Regional References).
Paper. $35.00. .... Vendor G0549

Fischer, Marjorie, and Ruth Burns. **Bakerville Review, Vol. II**. 1985. Indexed.
Abstracts from this rural Humphreys Co. newspaper for the years 1897-1898 (Vol. 1 is out of print).
Cloth. $20.00. 322 pp. .... Vendor G0577

Fischer, Marjorie, and Ruth Burns. **Bakerville Review, Vol. III**. 1988. Indexed.
Abstracts from this rural Humphreys Co. newspaper for the years 1898-1899.
Cloth. $20.00. 217 pp. .... Vendor G0577

Fischer, Marjorie, and Ruth Burns. **Humphreys County, Tennessee Marriage Records 1861-1888**. 1984.
Arranged alphabetically by grooms. Brides & bondsmen separately indexed.
Paper. $15.00. .... Vendor G0577

Fischer, Marjorie, and Ruth Burns. **Humphreys County, Tennessee Records**. 1987.
Tax lists 1837-43; marriages 1888-1900.
Paper. $18.00. .... Vendor G0577

Goodspeed Publishing Company. **Montgomery, Robertson, Humphreys, Stewart, Dickson, Cheatham, and Houston Counties**. (1886) reprint 1979. Indexed.
Contact vendor for information. 653 pp. .... Vendor G0610

Jackson County

1837 Tennessee Volunteers. Indexed.
The report to the 25th Congress of the U.S. of the Tennessee Militia called into service against the Indians in Florida in 1837 from Jackson County and others. Most of these men did not serve but the roster shows those who volunteered.
Paper. $8.50. .... Vendor G0549

Sistler, Byron, and Barbara Sistler. **1870 Census—Tennessee**. Jackson County.
Paper. $14.00. .... Vendor G0577

WPA. **Jackson County, Tennessee WPA Records**. Indexed.
Paper. $20.00. .... Vendor G0549

James County

Douthat, James L. **James County, Tennessee Marriages 1913-1919**.
Paper. $10.00. .... Vendor G0549

Sistler, Byron, and Barbara Sistler. **1870 Census—Tennessee**. James County.
Paper. $11.00. .... Vendor G0577

Jefferson County

d'Armand, Virginia Carlisle. **Jefferson County, Tennessee Marriages 1792 through 1870**. 1983.
Paper. $30.00. 252 pp. .... Vendor G0009

Douthat, James L. **1836 Jefferson County, Tennessee Civil Districts and Tax Lists**. Indexed.
Paper. $10.00. .... Vendor G0549

Douthat, James L. **Jefferson County, Tennessee Grant Book 1: 1792-1794**. Indexed.
Paper. $7.50. .... Vendor G0549

Douthat, James L. **Jefferson County, Tennessee Will Book 1, 1792-1810**. Indexed.
See "Prevost, Toni Jollay" for Will Books 3 and 4.
Paper. $7.50. .... Vendor G0549

Douthat, James L. **Jefferson County, Tennessee Will Book 2, 1811-1826**. Indexed.
See "Prevost, Toni Jollay" for Will Books 3 and 4.
Paper. $12.50. .... Vendor G0549

Holdaway, Boyd J. **Land Deeds of Jefferson County, Tennessee, 1792-1814**. 1991. Indexed.
Cloth. $30.00. 306 pp. .... Vendor G0610

Jefferson County Genealogical Society. **Jefferson County, TN Families and History 1792-1996**. Indexed. Illus.
    Part of the prestigious County Heritage Book series. Printed in a rich blue imitation leather. Features 460 pioneer and modern family histories, genealogies, and family photos. Includes chapters on communities, early court records, religion, education, clubs, and organizations. 9" x 12" format. Surname index.
Cloth. $58.50. 272 pp. .... Vendor G0087

Jefferson County, Tennessee Marriages 1792 through 1870
By Virginia Carlisle d'Armand
$30.00 plus $2.00 postage

Virginia Carlisle d'Armand
3636 Taliluna Avenue, Apt. 235 • Knoxville, TN 37919

Jefferson County Guardian Bonds 1805-1832. Indexed.
$10.00 (perfect bound). 48 pp. .... Vendor G0549

Pedersen, Diane E. **Entry Book—5th Survey District Book A—Grants Number 1-800**.
Covers the land sales and tracts in Anderson, Grainger, Jefferson, Claiborne, Knox, and Sevier counties.
Paper. $25.00. .... Vendor G0549

Pedersen, Diane E. **Entry Book—5th Survey District Book C, 1816-1823—Grants Number 1601-2548**.
Early land records from the present counties of Knox, Jefferson, Union, Grainger, Hamblen, Claiborne, Hancock, and Hawkins counties.
Paper. $29.50. .... Vendor G0549

Prevost, Toni Jollay. **Jefferson County, Tennessee Will Book 3, 1826-1833**. Indexed.
See "Douthat, James L." for Will Books 1 and 2.
Paper. $15.00. .... Vendor G0549

Prevost, Toni Jollay. **Jefferson County, Tennessee Will Book 4, 1833-1840**. Indexed.
See "Douthat, James L." for Will Books 1 and 2.
Paper. $20.00. .... Vendor G0549

Sistler, Byron, and Barbara Sistler. **1870 Census—Tennessee**. Jefferson County.
Paper. $16.00. .... Vendor G0577

Whitley, Edythe Rucker. **Marriages of Jefferson County, Tennessee, 1792-1836**. (1982) reprint 1993. Indexed.
Contact vendor for information. 110 pp. .... Vendor G0011

WPA. **Jefferson County, Tennessee Court Minutes 1792-1795**. Indexed.
Paper. $17.50. .... Vendor G0549

Johnson County

Douthat, James L. **1836 Johnson County, Tennessee Civil Districts and Tax Lists**. Indexed.
Paper. $10.00. .... Vendor G0549

Douthat, James L. **Johnson County, Tennessee Marriage Book 1, 1838-1858**. Indexed.
Paper. $12.50. .... Vendor G0549

Douthat, James L. **Johnson County, Tennessee Tax Lists 1836-1839**. Indexed.
Paper. $15.00. .... Vendor G0549

Douthat, James L. **Johnson County Will Book 1, 1827-1860**.
Paper. $7.50. .... Vendor G0549

Douthat, James L. **Watauga Reservoir Cemeteries**.
Paper. $28.50. 160 pp. .... Vendor G0549

Sistler, Byron, and Barbara Sistler. **1870 Census—Tennessee**. Johnson County.
Paper. $13.00. .... Vendor G0577

WPA. **Johnson County, Tennessee Bible & Tombstone Records**.
Paper. $8.00. .... Vendor G0549

Knox County

d'Armand, Roscoe Carlisle, and Virginia Carlisle d'Armand. **Knox County, Tennessee Marriages 1792 through 1900**. (1970) reprint 1986.
Paper. $59.00. 1,144 pp. .... Vendor G0009

Douthat, James L. **1836 Knox County, Tennessee Civil Districts and Tax Lists**. Indexed.
Paper. $10.00. .... Vendor G0549

Douthat, James L. **Fort Loudon Reservoir Cemeteries**.
Paper. $18.50. .... Vendor G0549

Goodspeed Publishing Company. **Knox County, Tennessee**. (1887) reprint 1982. Indexed.
Cloth. $27.50. 299 pp. .... Vendor G0610

Pedersen, Diane E. **Entry Book—5th Survey District Book A—Grants Number 1-800**.
  Covers the land sales and tracts in Anderson, Grainger, Jefferson, Claiborne, Knox, and Sevier counties.
Paper. $25.00. .... Vendor G0549

Pedersen, Diane E. **Entry Book—5th Survey District Book C, 1816-1823—Grants Number 1601-2548**.
  Early land records from the present counties of Knox, Jefferson, Union, Grainger, Hamblen, Claiborne, Hancock, and Hawkins counties.
Paper. $29.50. .... Vendor G0549

WPA. **1836 Knox County Tennessee Estate Book 1, 1792-1811**.
$45.00 (perfect bound). 336 pp. .... Vendor G0549

WPA. **Knox County, Tennessee Estate Book 1 1792-1811**.
$28.50 (perfect bound). 272 pp. .... Vendor G0549

WPA. **Knox County, Tennessee Marriages 1792-1837**.
$35.00 (perfect bound). 235 pp. .... Vendor G0549

Knox County, Tennessee Marriages 1792 through 1900

By Roscoe Carlisle d'Armand and Virginia Carlisle d'Armand
$59.00 plus $4.25 postage

Virginia Carlisle d'Armand
3636 Taliluna Avenue, Apt. 235 • Knoxville, TN 37919

Lake County

Goodspeed Publishing Company. **Gibson, Obion, Weakley, Dyer and Lake Counties**. (1886) reprint 1988. Indexed.
Cloth. $37.50. 352 pp. .... Vendor G0610

Lauderdale County

Goodspeed Publishing Company. **Lauderdale, Tipton, Haywood, and Crockett Counties**. (1886) reprint 1978. Indexed.
Contact vendor for information. 208 pp. .... Vendor G0610

WPA. **Lauderdale County, Tennessee County Court Minutes, Vol. A 1836-1844**. Indexed.
Paper. $25.00. 212 pp. .... Vendor G0549

WPA. **Lauderdale County, Tennessee Marriages 1844-1860**. Indexed.
Paper. $5.00. .... Vendor G0549

Lawrence County

Goodspeed Publishing Company. **Lawrence, Wayne, Perry, Hickman and Lewis Counties**. (1886) reprint 1979. Indexed.
Cloth. $22.50. 129 pp. .... Vendor G0610

Murray, Joyce Martin. **Williamson County, Tennessee Deed Abstracts, 1799-1811**. Indexed.
  Present Maury, Giles, and Lawrence counties. Includes full-name, location, and slave indexes.
Cloth. $25.00. 202 pp. .... Vendor G0466

Whitley, Edythe Rucker, comp. **Tennessee Marriage Records: Lawrence County, 1818-1854**. 1982. Indexed.
Cloth. $12.00. 110 pp. .... Vendor G0011

Lewis County

Goodspeed Publishing Company. **Lawrence, Wayne, Perry, Hickman and Lewis Counties**. (1886) reprint 1979. Indexed.
Cloth. $22.50. 129 pp. .... Vendor G0610

WPA. **Lewis County, Tennessee WPA Records**. Indexed.
Paper. $15.00. .... Vendor G0549

Lincoln County

1820 Lincoln County, Tennessee Census.
Paper. $12.50. .... Vendor G0549

Goodspeed Publishing Company. **Giles, Lincoln, Franklin, and Moore Counties**. (1886) reprint 1979. Indexed.
Contact vendor for information. 181 pp. .... Vendor G0610

Ingmire, Frances. **Lincoln County, Tennessee Wills & Inventories 1809-1824**.
Paper. $25.00. 90 pp. .... Vendor G0549

Marsh, Helen C, and Timothy Marsh. **Cemetery Records of Lincoln-Moore Counties, Tennessee, 1820-1826**. 1983. Indexed.
Contact vendor for information. 452 pp. .... Vendor G0610

Marsh, Helen C., and Timothy Marsh. **First County Court Minutes of Lincoln County, Tennessee, 1809-1819**. 1989. Indexed.
Cloth. $37.50. Approx. 292 pp. .... Vendor G0610

Marsh, Helen C., and Timothy R. Marsh. **First County Court Minutes of Lincoln County, Tennessee 1820-1826, Vol. 2**. 1991. Indexed.
Cloth. $35.00. 270 pp. .... Vendor G0610

Marsh, Helen C., and Timothy R. Marsh. **Lincoln County, Tennessee Early Unpublished Court Records**. 1993. Indexed.
Cloth. $35.00. 262 pp. .... Vendor G0610

Marsh, Timothy, and Helen Marsh. **Lincoln County, Tennessee, Official Marriages, 1838-1880**. (1974) reprint 1986. Indexed.
Paper. $30.00. 320 pp. .... Vendor G0610

Sistler, Byron, and Samuel Sistler. **Every Name Index to 18 Middle Tennessee County Record Books**. 1992.
   A single integrated index to eighteen inadequately indexed books: Bedford Co. (9 titles), Giles Co. (8), Lincoln Co. (1). About 165,000 entries.
Cloth. $52.00. 800 pp. .... Vendor G0577

Wills of Lincoln County, Tennessee, 1810-1921.
Cloth. $32.50. .... Vendor G0610

WPA. **Lincoln County, Tennessee Marriages 1838-1860**. Indexed.
Paper. $35.00. 281 pp. .... Vendor G0549

Loudon County

Douthat, James L. **Fort Loudon Reservoir Cemeteries**.
Paper. $18.50. .... Vendor G0549

Smallen, Tammy L., scr. **1910 Loudon County, Tennessee Census**. 1995. Indexed.
Spiral binding. $27.50. 396 pp. .... Vendor G0761

Macon County

Goodspeed Publishing Company. **Sumner, Smith, Macon and Trousdale Counties**. (1886) reprint 1979. Indexed.
Cloth. $28.50. 194 pp. .... Vendor G0610

Sistler, Byron, and Barbara Sistler. **1870 Census—Tennessee**. Macon County.
Paper. $14.00. .... Vendor G0577

Madison County

Goodspeed Publishing Company. **Madison County**. (1887) reprint 1979. Indexed.
Cloth. $22.50. 120 pp. .... Vendor G0610

Sistler, Byron, and Barbara Sistler. **Madison County, TN Marriages 1838-1871**. 1983.
About 3,000 marriages, arranged alphabetically by both bride and groom.
Paper. $12.00. .... Vendor G0577

WPA. **Madison County, Tennessee County Court Minutes Vol. 1, 1821-1825**. Indexed.
Paper. $45.00. 320 pp. .... Vendor G0549

WPA. **Madison County, Tennessee Loose Marriage Bonds 1823-1832**. Indexed.
Paper. $5.00. .... Vendor G0549

WPA. **Madison County, Tennessee Marriage Book 2, 1838-1847**. Indexed.
Paper. $10.00. .... Vendor G0549

Marion County

1830 Marion County, Tennessee Census.
A part of the 1830 Sequatchie Valley Census.
Paper. $7.50. .... Vendor G0549

1840 Marion County, Tennessee Census.
A part of the 1840 Sequatchie Valley Census.
Paper. $7.50. .... Vendor G0549

1850 Marion County, Tennessee Census.
Paper. $12.50. .... Vendor G0549

Douthat, James L. **1836 Marion County, Tennessee Civil Districts and Tax Lists**. Indexed.
Paper. $10.00. .... Vendor G0549

Douthat, James L. **Sequatchie Families**.
A collection of eighty-one biographical sketches of families who are found in Sequatchie Valley prior to 1850.
Paper. $15.00. .... Vendor G0549

Douthat, James L. **Sequatchie Valley Bible Records**. Indexed.
Since most records of the marriages, births, and deaths are no longer existent for each of the counties in the valley, this book is an invaluable research tool.
Paper. $10.00. .... Vendor G0549

McClure, Lucille. **Abstracts of Ocoee District Early Land Records—Entries**. Illus.
The Ocoee Land Office was opened in October 1838 to sell the lands formerly owned by the Cherokee Indians prior to their removal to the western lands. The lands are in present Hamilton, Bradley, Marion, Polk, and parts of McMinn and Monroe counties.
Paper. $25.00. 134 pp. .... Vendor G0549

Sistler, Barbara, and Byron Sistler. **1880 Census, Marion Co., TN**.
All individuals named, including ages, arranged alphabetically by household head.
Paper. $13.00. .... Vendor G0577

WPA. **Marion County, Tennessee County Court Minutes 1842-1847**. Indexed.
Paper. $20.00. .... Vendor G0549

WPA. **Marion County, Tennessee Deed Book A, 1817-1826**. Indexed.
Paper. $18.50. 205 pp. .... Vendor G0549

WPA. **Marion County, Tennessee Deed Book B 1827-1830**. Indexed.
Paper. $28.50. 144 pp. .... Vendor G0549

Marshall County

Goodspeed Publishing Company. **History of Tennessee Illustrated, Historical and Biographical Sketches of the Counties of Maury, Williamson, Rutherford, Wilson, Bedford, and Marshall**. (1887) reprint 1988. Indexed.
Cloth. $42.50. 536 pp. .... Vendor G0610

Marsh, Helen, and Timothy Marsh. **Cemetery Records of Marshall County, Tennessee**. 1981. Indexed. Illus.
Contact vendor for information. 338 pp. .... Vendor G0610

Maury County

Alexander, Virginia Wood. **Maury County, Tennessee Deed Books A-F, 1807-1817**. 2 vols. in 1. (1965) reprint 1981. Indexed.
Paper. $27.50. 248 pp. .... Vendor G0610

Garrett, Jill Knight, and Marise Parrish Lightfoot. **Maury County, Tennessee, Will Books A, B, C-1, D and E: 1807-1832**. (1964) reprint 1984. Indexed.
Paper. $30.00. 288 pp. .... Vendor G0610

Goodspeed Publishing Company. **History of Tennessee Illustrated, Historical and Biographical Sketches of the Counties of Maury, Williamson, Rutherford, Wilson, Bedford, and Marshall**. (1887) reprint 1988. Indexed.
Cloth. $42.50. 536 pp. .... Vendor G0610

Murray, Joyce Martin. **Williamson County, Tennessee Deed Abstracts, 1799-1811**. Indexed.
Present Maury, Giles, and Lawrence counties. Includes full-name, location, and slave indexes.
Cloth. $25.00. 202 pp. .... Vendor G0466

Robbins, D. P. **Century Review of Maury County, Tennessee, 1807-1907**. (1905) reprint 1980. Indexed.
Contact vendor for information. 426 pp. .... Vendor G0610

Sistler, Byron,. **1870 Census—Tennessee**. Maury County.
Paper. $27.00. .... Vendor G0577

Sistler, Byron, and Barbara Sistler. **Index to Maury Co., TN Wills & Administrations, 1807-1861**. 1990.
About 2,000 entries. Includes name of deceased, year of probate or administration, where to find the information.
Paper. $10.00. 28 pp. .... Vendor G0577

Sistler, Byron, and Barbara Sistler. **Maury County, TN Marriages 1852-1867**. 1986.
About 2,700 marriages, arranged alphabetically by both bride and groom.
Paper. $12.00. .... Vendor G0577

Whitley, Edythe Rucker, comp. **Tennessee Marriage Records: Maury County, 1808-1852**. 1982. Indexed.
Cloth. $16.00. 245 pp. .... Vendor G0011

WPA. **Maury County, Tennessee Chancery Court Minutes #2, 1820-1839**. Indexed.
Paper. $55.00. 474 pp. .... Vendor G0549

WPA. **Maury County, Tennessee County Court Minutes Book 1, 1808-1809**. Indexed.
Paper. $16.50. 112 pp. .... Vendor G0549

WPA. **Maury County, Tennessee Wills Vol. 1 Book B, 1810-1825**. Indexed.
$55.00 (perfect bound). 470 pp. .... Vendor G0549

McMinn County

Boyer, Reba Bayless. **McMinn County, Tennessee, Marriages, 1820-1870**. (1964) reprint 1983. Indexed.
Paper. $25.00. 256 pp. .... Vendor G0610

Boyer, Reba Bayless. **Wills and Estate Records of McMinn County, Tennessee, 1820-1870**. (1966) reprint 1983. Indexed.
Paper. $25.00. 202 pp. .... Vendor G0610

McClure, Lucille. **Abstracts of Ocoee District Early Land Records—Entries**. Illus.
The Ocoee Land Office was opened in October 1838 to sell the lands formerly owned by the Cherokee Indians prior to their removal to the western lands. The lands are in present Hamilton, Bradley, Marion, Polk, and parts of McMinn and Monroe counties.
Paper. $25.00. 134 pp. .... Vendor G0549

Sistler, Barbara, and Byron Sistler. **1880 Census, McMinn Co., TN**.
All individuals named, including ages, arranged alphabetically by household head.
Paper. $16.00. .... Vendor G0577

Whitley, Edythe Rucker, comp. **Tennessee Marriage Records: McMinn County, 1821-1864**. 1983. Indexed.
Cloth. $12.00. 121 pp. .... Vendor G0011

WPA. **McMinn County, Tennessee WPA Records**. Indexed.
Paper. $10.00. .... Vendor G0549

McNairy County

Douthat, James L. **Kentucky Lake Reservoir Cemeteries. Volume 3**.
Covers the southern part of west Tennessee with the areas of Decatur, Hardin, Henderson, McNairy, Perry, and Wayne counties plus the reinterment sites for the entire Kentucky Lake Reservoir. Also available as a set with Volumes 1 and 2 (see Tennessee, Statewide and Regional References).
Paper. $35.00. .... Vendor G0549

Goodspeed Publishing Company. **Henderson, Chester, McNairy, Decatur and Hardin Counties**. (1886) reprint 1978. Indexed.
Contact vendor for information. 136 pp. .... Vendor G0610

Meigs County

1840 Meigs County, Tennessee Census.
Paper. $10.00. .... Vendor G0549

1850 Meigs County, Tennessee Census.
Paper. $10.00. .... Vendor G0549

Allen, V. C. **Rhea & Meigs County, Tennessee in the Civil War**. Indexed.
Paper. $13.50. 56 pp. .... Vendor G0549

Douthat, James L. **Chickamauga Reservoir Cemeteries**.
Paper. $20.00. .... Vendor G0549

Douthat, James L. **Watts Bar Reservoir Cemeteries**.
Paper. $20.00. .... Vendor G0549

Lillard, Stewart. **Meigs County, Tennessee: A Documented Account of Its European Settlement and Growth**. (1975) reprint 1982. Indexed. Illus.
Cloth. $32.50. 211 pp. .... Vendor G0522

Lillard, Stewart. **Meigs County, Tennessee: A Documented Account of Its European Settlement and Growth**. (1975) reprint 1983. Indexed. Illus.
Cloth. $20.00. 202 pp. .... Vendor G0610

Sistler, Byron, and Barbara Sistler. **1870 Census—Tennessee**. Meigs County.
Paper. $13.00. .... Vendor G0577

Sistler, Byron, and Barbara Sistler. **Meigs County, Tenn. Marriages 1851-1865**. 1988.
   Copied from microfilm of the original marriage books. Arranged alphabetically by
bride and groom.
Paper. $9.00. .... Vendor G0577

Monroe County

1840 Monroe County, Tennessee Census.
Paper. $10.00. .... Vendor G0549

Boyer, Reba Bayless. **Monroe County, Tennessee, Records, 1820-1870, Vol. 1**. (1969)
reprint 1983. Indexed.
Paper. $25.00. 198 pp. .... Vendor G0610

Boyer, Reba Bayless. **Monroe County, Tennessee, Records, 1820-1870, Vol. 2**. (1970)
reprint 1983. Indexed.
Paper. $25.00. 198 pp. .... Vendor G0610

Douthat, James L. **Chickamauga Reservoir Cemeteries**.
Paper. $20.00. .... Vendor G0549

Hayes, Sallie. **Monroe County, Tennessee Deed Books A-D, 1820-1834**. Indexed.
$20.00 (perfect bound). 106 pp. .... Vendor G0549

Lenoir, William B. **History of Sweetwater Valley, Tennessee.** With a New Index.
(1916) reprint 1994. Indexed.
Paper. $34.00. 419 pp. .... Vendor G0011

McClure, Lucille. **Abstracts of Ocoee District Early Land Records—Entries**. Illus.
   The Ocoee Land Office was opened in October 1838 to sell the lands formerly
owned by the Cherokee Indians prior to their removal to the western lands. The lands
are in present Hamilton, Bradley, Marion, Polk, and parts of McMinn and Monroe
counties.
Paper. $25.00. 134 pp. .... Vendor G0549

Sistler, Byron, and Barbara Sistler. **1870 Census—Tennessee.** Monroe County.
Paper. $15.00. .... Vendor G0577

WPA. **Christianburg Church Minutes 1822-1872**. Indexed.
$33.50 (perfect bound). 225 pp. .... Vendor G0549

WPA. **Monroe County, Tennessee Chancery Court Minute Book 1832-1842**.
Indexed.
$37.00 (perfect bound). .... Vendor G0549

WPA. **Monroe County, Tennessee Deed Books E-H, 1834-1836**. Indexed.
$20.00 (perfect bound). 96 pp. .... Vendor G0549

WPA. **Monroe County, Tennessee Tombstones**.
   A collection of the many cemeteries and tombstone inscriptions in the county.
Paper. $60.00. .... Vendor G0549

WPA. **Monroe County, Tennessee Will Book A, 1825-1869**. Indexed.
Paper. $24.50. 152 pp. .... Vendor G0549

Montgomery County

Goodspeed Publishing Company. **Montgomery, Robertson, Humphreys, Stewart, Dickson, Cheatham, and Houston Counties**. (1886) reprint 1979. Indexed.
Contact vendor for information. 653 pp. .... Vendor G0610

Sistler, Byron, and Barbara Sistler. **Index to Montgomery County, TN Wills and Administrations, 1795-1861**. 1990.
    About 2,200 entries. Includes name of deceased, year of probate or administration, where to find the information.
Paper. Contact vendor for price. 30 pp. .... Vendor G0577

Sistler, Byron, and Barbara Sistler. **Montgomery County, Tennessee Marriages 1838-1867**. 1986.
    About 4,000 marriages, arranged alphabetically by bride and groom.
Paper. $15.00. .... Vendor G0577

Whitley, Edythe Rucker. **Red River Settlers.** Records of the Settlers of Northern Montgomery, Robertson, and Sumner Counties, Tennessee. (1980) reprint 1995. Indexed.
Paper. $18.50. 189 pp. .... Vendor G0011

Willis, Laura. **Montgomery County, Tennessee Wills and Administrations, Vol. Four (1814-1817)**. 1995. Indexed.
Paper. $10.00. 105 pp. .... Vendor G0687

WPA. **Montgomery County, Tennessee County Court Minutes Vol. 12, 1822-1824**. Indexed.
Paper. $30.00. 253 pp. .... Vendor G0549

Moore County

Goodspeed Publishing Company. **Giles, Lincoln, Franklin, and Moore Counties**. (1886) reprint 1979. Indexed.
Contact vendor for information. 181 pp. .... Vendor G0610

Marsh, Helen C, and Timothy Marsh. **Cemetery Records of Lincoln-Moore Counties, Tennessee, 1820-1826**. 1983. Indexed.
Contact vendor for information. 452 pp. .... Vendor G0610

Morgan County

Dickinson, W. Calvin. **Morgan County (Tennessee)**. 1987. Indexed. Illus.
Cloth. $17.50. 136 pp. .... Vendor G0522

Douthat, James L. **Morgan County, Tennessee Marriages 1862-1886**.
Paper. $15.00. .... Vendor G0549

WPA. **Morgan County, Tennessee Bible and Cemetery Records**. Indexed.
Paper. $10.00. .... Vendor G0549

Obion County

Goodspeed Publishing Company. **Gibson, Obion, Weakley, Dyer and Lake Counties**. (1886) reprint 1988. Indexed.
Cloth. $37.50. 352 pp. .... Vendor G0610

WPA. **Obion County, Tennessee Court of Pleas & Quarter Session 1834-1835**. Indexed.
Paper. $20.00. .... Vendor G0549

WPA. **Obion County, Tennessee Marriages 1825-1860**. Indexed.
Paper. $15.00. .... Vendor G0549

Overton County

1820 Overton County, Tennessee Census.
Paper. $8.00. .... Vendor G0549

1837 Tennessee Volunteers. Indexed.
   The report to the 25th Congress of the U.S. of the Tennessee Militia called up for the Indian wars in Florida. This is the roster of each county sending volunteers, most of whom did not serve.
Paper. $8.50. .... Vendor G0549

Douthat, James L. **John McClellan's Survey Book**. Indexed.
   The plat survey book of the period for the counties of Roane, Rhea, Overton, Campbell, Anderson, and Bledsoe counties. Plat maps of each survey given.
Paper. $18.50. .... Vendor G0549

Sistler, Byron, and Barbara Sistler. **1870 Census—Tennessee**. Overton County.
Paper. $15.00. .... Vendor G0577

WPA. **Overton County, Tennessee Deed Book A, 1792-1808**. Indexed.
Paper. $8.00. .... Vendor G0549

Perry County

Douthat, James L. **Kentucky Lake Reservoir Cemeteries. Volume 3**.
   Covers the southern part of west Tennessee with the areas of Decatur, Hardin, Henderson, McNairy, Perry, and Wayne counties plus the reinterment sites for the entire Kentucky Lake Reservoir. Also available as a set with Volumes 1 and 2 (see Tennessee, Statewide and Regional References).
Paper. $35.00. .... Vendor G0549

Goodspeed Publishing Company. **Lawrence, Wayne, Perry, Hickman and Lewis Counties**. (1886) reprint 1979. Indexed.
Cloth. $22.50. 129 pp. .... Vendor G0610

Young, Connie Copeland, and Francine Sullivan Copeland. **Perry County, Tennessee Land Survey Abstracts 1820-1890**. 1995. Indexed. Illus.
Cloth. $40.00. 153 pp. .... Vendor G0470

Polk County

McClure, Lucille. **Abstracts of Ocoee District Early Land Records—Entries**. Illus.
The Ocoee Land Office was opened in October 1838 to sell the lands formerly owned by the Cherokee Indians prior to their removal to the western lands. The lands are in present Hamilton, Bradley, Marion, Polk, and parts of McMinn and Monroe counties.
Paper. $25.00. 134 pp. .... Vendor G0549

Sistler, Byron, and Barbara Sistler. **1870 Census—Tennessee.** Polk County.
Paper. $13.00. .... Vendor G0577

WPA. **Polk County, Tennessee County Court Minutes 1840-1843**. Indexed.
Paper. $18.50. .... Vendor G0549

Powell Valley

Davis, Joy Edwards. **More Speedwell Families**. 1988. Indexed. Illus.
Powell Valley, of which Speedwell is a part, was a major thoroughfare for early pioneers.
Cloth. $37.50. Approx. 616 pp. .... Vendor G0610

Edwards, Lawrence, and Joy Edwards Davis. **Old Speedwell Families,** Revised and Updated. (1980) reprint 1983. Indexed.
Cloth. $40.00. 760 pp. + index. .... Vendor G0610

Putnam County

Sistler, Byron, and Barbara Sistler. **1870 Census—Tennessee**. Putnam County.
Paper. $13.00. .... Vendor G0577

WPA. **Putnam County, Tennessee Bible Records**. Indexed.
$18.00 (perfect bound). 154 pp. .... Vendor G0549

WPA. **Putnam County, Tennessee Diaries, Letters, Wills and Other Records**. Indexed.
$20.00 (perfect bound). 166 pp. .... Vendor G0549

WPA. **Richard F. Cook's Survey Book 1825-1839**. Indexed.
$55.00 (perfect bound). 426 pp. .... Vendor G0549

Rhea County

1850 Rhea County, Tennessee Census.
Paper. $15.00. .... Vendor G0549

Allen, V. C. **Rhea & Meigs County, Tennessee in the Civil War**. Indexed.
Paper. $13.50. 56 pp. .... Vendor G0549

Douthat, James L. **Chickamauga Reservoir Cemeteries**.
Paper. $20.00. .... Vendor G0549

Douthat, James L. **John McClellan's Survey Book**. Indexed.
The plat survey book of the period for the counties of Roane, Rhea, Overton, Campbell, Anderson, and Bledsoe counties. Plat maps of each survey given.
Paper. $18.50. .... Vendor G0549

Douthat, James L. **Watts Bar Reservoir Cemeteries**.
Paper. $20.00. .... Vendor G0549

Gray, David, and Bettye J. Broyles. **1850 Rhea County Deed Books A, B, C, D, & E 1806-1831**. Indexed.
An abstraction with notes that tell more about the county than found anywhere else.
Paper. $30.00. 256 pp. .... Vendor G0549

Sistler, Byron, and Barbara Sistler. **1870 Census—Tennessee**. Rhea County.
Paper. $13.00. .... Vendor G0577

Whitley, Edythe Rucker, comp. **Tennessee Marriage Records: Rhea County, 1808-1859**. 1983. Indexed.
Cloth. $12.00. 89 pp. .... Vendor G0011

Roane County

1830 Roane County, Tennessee Census.
Paper. $7.50. .... Vendor G0549

Douthat, James L. **Colonel Return Jonathan Meigs—Day Book 2**. Indexed.
Col. Return Jonathan Meigs served as the Indian Agent for the Cherokee from 1801 to 1823 when he died. This Day Book is the daily accounts and correspondence he kept between 1801and 1807 while a resident of Roane County.
Paper. $20.00. .... Vendor G0549

Douthat, James L. **John McClellan's Survey Book**. Indexed.
The plat survey book of the period for the counties of Roane, Rhea, Overton, Campbell, Anderson, and Bledsoe counties. Plat maps of each survey given.
Paper. $18.50. .... Vendor G0549

Douthat, James L. **Watts Bar Reservoir Cemeteries**.
Paper. $20.00. .... Vendor G0549

Douthat, Marilee. **Revolutionary War Pension Applications from Roane County, Tennessee**.
Paper. $12.50. .... Vendor G0549

Roane County, Tennessee Witness Docket Book 1802-1815. Indexed.
Paper. $9.50. .... Vendor G0549

Sistler, Byron, and Barbara Sistler. **1870 Census—Tennessee**. Roane County.
Paper. $16.00. .... Vendor G0577

Sistler, Byron, and Barbara Sistler. **Roane County, TN Marriages 1856-1875**. 1988. Copied from microfilm of the original marriage books. Arranged alphabetically by bride and groom.
Paper. $11.00. .... Vendor G0577

Wells, Emma Middleton. **The History of Roane County, Tennessee, 1801-1870.** With a New Index. (1927) reprint 1994. Indexed.
Contact vendor for information. 352 pp. .... Vendor G0011

WPA. **Roane County, Tennessee Court Minute Book 1807-1809**. Indexed.
$20.00 (perfect bound). 132 pp. .... Vendor G0549

WPA. **Roane County, Tennessee Court Minute Book 1816-1818**. Indexed.
$30.00 (perfect bound). 200 pp. .... Vendor G0549

WPA. **Roane County, Tennessee County Court Minutes 1819-1821**. Indexed.
$35.00 (perfect bound). 231 pp. .... Vendor G0549

WPA. **Roane County, Tennessee Land Entry Book A, 1807-1808**. Indexed.
Paper. $12.50. 104 pp. .... Vendor G0549

WPA. **Roane County, Tennessee Minute Book A, 1801-1805**. Indexed.
Paper. $24.50. 202 pp. .... Vendor G0549

WPA. **Roane County, Tennessee Trial Docket Book 1810-1830**. Indexed.
Paper. $15.00. .... Vendor G0549

Robertson County

Goodspeed Publishing Company. **Montgomery, Robertson, Humphreys, Stewart, Dickson, Cheatham, and Houston Counties**. (1886) reprint 1979. Indexed.
Contact vendor for information. 653 pp. .... Vendor G0610

Whitley, Edythe Rucker. **Red River Settlers.** Records of the Settlers of Northern Montgomery, Robertson, and Sumner Counties, Tennessee. (1980) reprint 1995. Indexed.
Paper. $18.50. 189 pp. .... Vendor G0011

Whitley, Edythe Rucker, comp. **Tennessee Marriage Records: Robertson County, 1839-1861**. 1981. Indexed.
Cloth. $12.00. 135 pp. .... Vendor G0011

Rutherford County

1837 Tennessee Volunteers. Indexed.
The report to the 25th Congress of the U.S. of the Tennessee Militia called up for the Indian wars in Florida. This is the roster of each county sending volunteers, most of whom did not serve.
Paper. $8.50. .... Vendor G0549

Goodspeed Publishing Company. **History of Tennessee Illustrated, Historical and Biographical Sketches of the Counties of Maury, Williamson, Rutherford, Wilson, Bedford, and Marshall.** (1887) reprint 1988. Indexed.
Cloth. $42.50. 536 pp. .... Vendor G0610

Sistler, Byron, and Barbara Sistler. **Index to Rutherford County, TN Wills & Administrations, 1804-1861.** 1990.
    About 2,500 entries. Includes name of deceased, year of probate or administration, where to find the information.
Paper. $10.00. 34 pp. .... Vendor G0577

Scott County

1860 Scott County, Tennessee Census.
Paper. $15.00. .... Vendor G0549

Sistler, Byron, and Barbara Sistler. **1870 Census—Tennessee.** Scott County.
Paper. $12.00. .... Vendor G0577

Sistler, Byron, and Barbara Sistler. **Scott County, Tenn. Marriages 1854-1880.** 1988.
    Copied from microfilm of the original marriage books. Arranged alphabetically by bride and groom.
Paper. $10.00. .... Vendor G0577

WPA. **Scott County, Tennessee County Court Minutes 1850-1855.** Indexed.
Paper. $20.00. 152 pp. .... Vendor G0549

Sequatchie County

1830 Sequatchie Valley Census.
Paper. $7.50. .... Vendor G0549

1840 Sequatchie Valley Census.
Paper. $7.50. .... Vendor G0549

1860 Sequatchie Valley Census.
Paper. $7.50. .... Vendor G0549

Douthat, James L. **Along the Pike—The History of Walden's Ridge Along Anderson Pike.** Indexed. Illus.
    Anderson Pike was one of the oldest roads from Sequatchie Valley to Chattanooga, begun in 1840 and completed in 1852. Sketches of the communities, Civil War impact, and families comprise this history.
Cloth. $24.50. 206 pp. .... Vendor G0549

Douthat, James L. **Sequatchie County, Tennessee Marriages 1858-1881.**
Paper. $7.50. .... Vendor G0549

Douthat, James L. **Sequatchie Families.**
    A collection of eighty-one biographical sketches of families who are found in Sequatchie Valley prior to 1850.
Paper. $15.00. .... Vendor G0549

Douthat, James L. **Sequatchie Valley Bible Records**. Indexed.

Since most records of the marriages, births, and deaths are no longer existent for each of the counties in the valley, this book is an invaluable research tool.

Paper. $10.00. .... Vendor G0549

Sistler, Byron, and Barbara Sistler. **1870 Census—Tennessee.** Sequatchie County.

Paper. $10.00. .... Vendor G0577

Sevier County

Pedersen, Diane E. **Entry Book—5th Survey District Book A—Grants Number 1-800**.

Covers the land sales and tracts in Anderson, Grainger, Jefferson, Claiborne, Knox, and Sevier counties.

Paper. $25.00. .... Vendor G0549

Smoky Mountain Historical Society. **Gentle Winds of Change:** The History of Sevier County, Tennessee, 1900-1930. 1996.

$21.20. .... Vendor G0654

Smoky Mountain Historical Society. **In the Shadow of the Smokies:** Sevier County, Tennessee Cemetery Records. Rev. ed. 1996.

$49.00. 800+ pp. .... Vendor G0662

WPA. **Sevier County, Tennessee Marriages 1856-1873**. Indexed.

Paper. $22.50. 156 pp. .... Vendor G0549

Shelby County

Tice, Helen. **Early Settlers of Shelby County, Tenn. and Adjoining Counties**. Indexed. Illus.

Cloth. $20.00. 193 pp. .... Vendor G0707

Whitley, Edythe Rucker. **Tennessee Marriage Records: Shelby County, 1820-1858**. 1982. Indexed.

Cloth. $12.00. 139 pp. .... Vendor G0011

WPA. **Shelby County, Tennessee WPA Records**. Indexed.

Paper. $30.00. .... Vendor G0549

Smith County

Goodspeed Publishing Company. **Sumner, Smith, Macon and Trousdale Counties**. (1886) reprint 1979. Indexed.

Cloth. $28.50. 194 pp. .... Vendor G0610

Partlow, Thomas E. **Smith County, Tennessee Deed Books B-M, 1800-1835**. 1993. Indexed.

Cloth. $38.50. 402 pp. .... Vendor G0610

Sistler, Byron, and Barbara Sistler. **1870 Census—Tennessee.** Smith County.
Paper. $22.00. .... Vendor G0577

WPA. **Smith County, Tennessee Deed Book B 1801-1807—Index.**
Paper. $15.00. .... Vendor G0549

WPA. **Smith County, Tennessee Deed Book C 1807-1811—Index.**
Paper. $12.00. .... Vendor G0549

WPA. **Smith County, Tennessee Marriages 1838, 1845-1854.** Indexed.
Paper. $12.00. .... Vendor G0549

Stewart County

Douthat, James L. **Kentucky Lake Reservoir Cemeteries. Volume 2.**
    Covers the upper west Tennessee areas of Benton, Henry, Houston, Humphreys, and Stewart counties. Also available as a set with Volumes 1 and 3 (see Tennessee, Statewide and Regional References).
Paper. $35.00. .... Vendor G0549

Goodspeed Publishing Company. **Montgomery, Robertson, Humphreys, Stewart, Dickson, Cheatham, and Houston Counties.** (1886) reprint 1979. Indexed.
Contact vendor for information. 653 pp. .... Vendor G0610

Whitley, Edythe Rucker, comp. **Tennessee Marriage Records: Stewart County, 1838-1866.** 1982. Indexed.
Cloth. $12.00. 105 pp. .... Vendor G0011

WPA. **Stewart County, Tennessee Deeds—Vol. 3, 1789-1818.** Indexed.
Paper. $14.00. .... Vendor G0549

WPA. **Stewart County, Tennessee Deeds—Vol. 4, 1810-1813.** Indexed.
Paper. $25.00. .... Vendor G0549

Sullivan County

Allen, Penelope Johnson. **Tennessee Soldiers in The Revolution.** A Roster of Soldiers Living During the Revolutionary War in the Counties of Washington and Sullivan. (1935) reprint 1996.
Paper. $7.50. 71 pp. .... Vendor G0010

Holston Territory Genealogical Society (and approx. 1,000 Bristol Co., TN contributors). **History & Families of Sullivan Co., TN 1779-1992.** 1993. Indexed. Illus.
    Beautiful, hardbound collector's edition; 9" x 12". Nearly 1,000 family stories, genealogies, and photos are the highlights of this only complete 20th-century history of Sullivan County, TN. Also included are stories about communities, clubs, organizations, military histories/casualties, and deeds and other court records.
Cloth. $60.00 in VA, $58.00 elsewhere. 686 pp. .... Vendor G0089

Sistler, Byron, and Barbara Sistler. **1870 Census—Tennessee.** Sullivan County.
Paper. $18.00. .... Vendor G0577

Sullivan County, Tennessee Deed Book 3, 1795-1802. Indexed.
$30.00 (perfect bound). .... Vendor G0549

Sullivan County, Tennessee Deed Book 4, 1802-1807. Indexed.
$26.00 (perfect bound). 130 pp. .... Vendor G0549

Sullivan County, Tennessee Deed Book 5, 1807-1808, 1834-1838. Indexed.
$18.50 (perfect bound). 112 pp. .... Vendor G0549

Sullivan County, Tennessee Deed Book 6, 1809-1815. Indexed.
$35.00 (perfect bound). .... Vendor G0549

Sullivan County, Tennessee Deed Book 8, 1819-1820, 1837-1840. Indexed.
$15.50 (perfect bound). 70 pp. .... Vendor G0549

Sullivan County, Tennessee Deed Book 10, 1824-1835. Indexed.
$27.50 (perfect bound). 126 pp. .... Vendor G0549

WPA. **Sullivan County, Tennessee Marriages 1861-1870**.
$20.00 (perfect bound). 120 pp. .... Vendor G0549

WPA. **Sullivan County, Tennessee Will Book 1, 1830-1870**.
Paper. $25.00. 159 pp. .... Vendor G0549

Sumner County

1837 Tennessee Volunteers. Indexed.
The report to the 25th Congress of the U.S. of the Tennessee Militia called up for the Indian wars in Florida. This is the roster of each county sending volunteers, most of whom did not serve.
Paper. $8.50. .... Vendor G0549

Cisco, Jay Guy. **Historic Sumner County,** with Genealogies of the Bledsoe, Cage & Douglass Families & Genealogical Notes of Other County Families. (1909) reprint 1993.
Cloth. $38.00. 319 pp. .... Vendor G0259

Fulcher, Richard C. **1779-1790 Census of the Cumberland Settlements:** Davidson, Sumner, and Tennessee Counties. 1990.
These counties, originally a part of North Carolina, now are all or part of Tennessee counties. Abstracted from public records are all references to those living in the jurisdictions between 1770 and 1790.
Cloth. $22.50. 253 pp. .... Vendor G0010

Goodspeed Publishing Company. **Sumner, Smith, Macon and Trousdale Counties**. (1886) reprint 1979. Indexed.
Cloth. $28.50. 194 pp. .... Vendor G0610

Murray, Joyce Martin. **Sumner County, Tennessee Deed Abstracts, 1793-1805**. Indexed.
All or part of fourteen present north-central Tennessee counties. Includes full-name, location, and slave indexes.
Paper. $30.00. Microfiche, $7.00. 176 pp. .... Vendor G0466

Murray, Joyce Martin. **Sumner County, Tennessee Deed Abstracts, 1806-1817**. Indexed.
Includes full-name, location, and slave indexes.
Paper. $30.00. Microfiche, $7.00. 176 pp. .... Vendor G0466

Restoration of Maple Hill Cemetery, Inc. **Maple Hill Cemetery [Portland, Sumner County, Tennessee]**. 1995. Indexed.
Paper. $11.50. 120 pp. .... Vendor G0762

Sistler, Byron, and Barbara Sistler. **1870 Census—Tennessee**. Sumner County.
Paper. $20.00. .... Vendor G0577

Whitley, Edythe Rucker. **Marriages of Sumner County, Tennessee, 1787-1838**. 1981. Indexed.
Cloth. $17.50. 150 pp. .... Vendor G0010

Whitley, Edythe Rucker. **Red River Settlers**. Records of the Settlers of Northern Montgomery, Robertson, and Sumner Counties, Tennessee. (1980) reprint 1995. Indexed.
Paper. $18.50. 189 pp. .... Vendor G0011

Whitley, Edythe Rucker. **Sumner County, Tennessee Abstracts of Will Books 1 and 2 (1788-1842)**. (1956) reprint 1995. Indexed.
Paper. $12.50. 84 pp. .... Vendor G0011

Tennessee County

Fulcher, Richard C. **1779-1790 Census of the Cumberland Settlements:** Davidson, Sumner, and Tennessee Counties. 1990.
These counties, originally a part of North Carolina, now are all or part of Tennessee counties. Abstracted from public records are all references to those living in the jurisdictions between 1770 and 1790.
Cloth. $22.50. 253 pp. .... Vendor G0010

Tipton County

Goodspeed Publishing Company. **Lauderdale, Tipton, Haywood, and Crockett Counties**. (1886) reprint 1978. Indexed.
Contact vendor for information. 208 pp. .... Vendor G0610

Hayes, Sallie. **Tipton County, Tennessee Miscellaneous Records (WPA Records)**. Indexed.
$27.50 (perfect bound). 140 pp. .... Vendor G0549

Sistler, Byron, and Barbara Sistler. **1870 Census—Tennessee**. Tipton County.
Paper. $19.00. .... Vendor G0577

Sistler, Byron, and Barbara Sistler. **Tipton County, TN Marriages 1840-1874**. 1987.
About 3,000 marriages, arranged alphabetically by bride and groom.
Paper. $12.00. .... Vendor G0577

Trousdale County

Goodspeed Publishing Company. **Sumner, Smith, Macon and Trousdale Counties**. (1886) reprint 1979. Indexed.
Cloth. $28.50. 194 pp. .... Vendor G0610

Unicoi County

Unicoi County Heritage Book Committee. **Unicoi County, TN and Its People 1875-1995**. Indexed. Illus.
One of the prestigious County Heritage Book series. More than 400 family histories, genealogies, and family photos, combined with dozens of topical articles and photos. Hardbound, 9" x 12", collector's edition. Surname index.
Cloth. $58.50 (incl. postage & tax). 238 pp. .... Vendor G0087

Union County

Hayes, Sallie. **Union County, Tennessee Cemeteries (WPA Records)**. Indexed.
$15.00 (perfect bound) 68 pp. .... Vendor G0549

Pedersen, Diane E. **Entry Book—5th Survey District Book C, 1816-1823—Grants Number 1601-2548**.
Early land records from the present counties of Knox, Jefferson, Union, Grainger, Hamblen, Claiborne, Hancock, and Hawkins counties.
Paper. $29.50. .... Vendor G0549

Peters, Bonnie Heiskell, and Winnie Palmer McDonald. **Our Union County (TN) Families, A Pictorial History with Genealogical Summaries**. 1993. Indexed. Illus.
Cloth. $50.00 + $6.00 p&h. 420 pp. .... Vendor G0482

Peters, Bonnie Heiskell, and Winnie Palmer McDonald. **Union County Faces of War, A Pictorial Military History**. 1995. Indexed. Illus.
Cloth. $35.00 + $5.00 p&h. 256 pp. .... Vendor G0482

Warren County

1837 Tennessee Volunteers. Indexed.
The report to the 25th Congress of the U.S. of the Tennessee Militia called up for the Indian wars in Florida. This is the roster of each county sending volunteers, most of whom did not serve.
Paper. $8.50. .... Vendor G0549

1870 Warren County, Tennessee Census.
Paper. $31.00. .... Vendor G0549

1880 Warren County, Tennessee Census.
Paper. $40.00. .... Vendor G0549

1900 Warren County, Tennessee Census.
Paper. $40.00. .... Vendor G0549

1910 Warren County, Tennessee Census.
Paper. $40.00. .... Vendor G0549

Cunningham, Almetia, and Martha Holt. **Warren County, Tennessee Cemetery Book 1—Cemeteries A-F.** Edited by Betty M. Majors. Indexed.
$38.50 (perfect bound). 236 pp. .... Vendor G0549

Cunningham, Almetia, and Martha Holt. **Warren County, Tennessee Cemetery Book 2—Cemeteries G-L.** Edited by Betty M. Majors. Indexed.
$38.50 (perfect bound). 312 pp. .... Vendor G0549

Goodspeed Publishing Company. **White, Warren, DeKalb, Coffee and Cannon Counties**. (1886) reprint 1979. Indexed.
Cloth. $28.50. 195 pp. .... Vendor G0610

Hillis, Robert A. C., Jr. **Warren County, Tennessee Marriages 1900-1950**. Indexed.
Paper. $45.00. .... Vendor G0549

Hillis, Robert A. C., Jr. **Warren County, Tennessee Marriages 2, 1951-1975**. Indexed.
Paper. $35.00. .... Vendor G0549

Majors, Betty M. **Warren County, Tennessee Deed Book A, 1808-1818**. Indexed.
Paper. $10.00. 46 pp. .... Vendor G0549

Majors, Betty M. **Warren County, Tennessee Will Books 1-3: Volume 1, 1827-1858**. Indexed.
Cloth. $28.50. 212 pp. .... Vendor G0549

Majors, Betty M. **Warren County, Tennessee Will Books 4-7, 1858-1887**. Indexed.
Cloth. $28.50. 220 pp. .... Vendor G0549

Majors, Betty M. **Warren County, Tennessee—Wills & Settlements (Vol. 3) 1887-1910**. Indexed.
$28.50 (perfect bound). 220 pp. .... Vendor G0549

Sistler, Byron, and Barbara Sistler. **Warren County, TN Marriages 1852-1865**. 1986. About 1,000 marriages, arranged alphabetically by bride and groom.
Paper. $8.00. .... Vendor G0577

Washington County

Allen, Penelope Johnson. **Tennessee Soldiers in The Revolution**. A Roster of Soldiers Living During the Revolutionary War in the Counties of Washington and Sullivan. (1935) reprint 1996.
Paper. $7.50. 71 pp. .... Vendor G0010

Burgner, Goldene Fillers. **Washington County, Tennessee, Marriages 1780-1870**. 1985. Indexed. Illus.
Cloth. $27.50. 224 pp. .... Vendor G0610

Burgner, Goldene Fillers. **Washington County, Tennessee, Wills, 1777-1872**. (1983) reprint 1992. Indexed. Illus.
Paper. $25.00. 144 pp. .... Vendor G0610

Fischer, Marjorie Hood. **Tennesseans Before 1800: Washington County**. 1996.
   A powerful finding aid listing 72,203 individual entries from records of the county created between 1778 and 1800. Included here is every name in every Washington County record available on microfilm from the Tennessee State Archives. Records indexed include: inventories, marriages, court minutes (County Court, Superior Court, County Pleas, Circuit Court), administrator's and executor's settlements, wills, deeds, and tax lists. The entries give the name, type of record, book number or other identifying information (i.e. militia unit in the case of tax lists), and the Tennessee State Library microfilm number. 8½" x 11".
Cloth. $49.50. 344 pp. .... Vendor G0611

Grammer, Norma Rutledge, and Marion Day Mullins. **Marriage Record of Washington County, Tennessee, 1787-1840**. (1949) reprint 1991. Indexed.
Paper. $6.00. 55 [13 index] pp. .... Vendor G0010

Kozsuch, Mildred S., ed. **Washington County Historical Assoc. Speeches 1987-1988**. 1993. Indexed. Illus.
   Covers historic sites and districts, genealogical sources, Washington County Court, State of Franklin, pioneer routeways and entertainment 100 years ago in Johnson City.
Paper. $10.50. 158 pp. .... Vendor G0540

Rae, Lorraine. **Washington County, Tennessee Deeds, 1777-1800**. 1991. Indexed.
Cloth. $30.00. 180 pp. .... Vendor G0610

Rae, Lorraine. **Washington County, Tennessee Deeds, 1797-1817, Vol. 2**. 1993. Indexed. Illus.
Cloth. $30.00. Approx. 200 pp. .... Vendor G0610

Sistler, Byron, and Barbara Sistler. **1870 Census—Tennessee.** Washington County.
Paper. $18.00. .... Vendor G0577

Wayne County

Berry, Nelle J. **Wayne County [Tennessee] Chancery Court Loose Records 1880-1889 Volume III**. 1996.
Paper. $27.00. 298 pp. .... Vendor G0763

Douthat, James L. **Kentucky Lake Reservoir Cemeteries. Volume 3**.
   Covers the southern part of west Tennessee with the areas of Decatur, Hardin, Henderson, McNairy, Perry, and Wayne counties plus the reinterment sites for the entire Kentucky Lake Reservoir. Also available as a set with Volumes 1 and 2 (see Tennessee, Statewide and Regional References).
Paper. $35.00. .... Vendor G0549

Goodspeed Publishing Company. **Lawrence, Wayne, Perry, Hickman and Lewis Counties**. (1886) reprint 1979. Indexed.
Cloth. $22.50. 129 pp. .... Vendor G0610

Weakley County

Goodspeed Publishing Company. **Gibson, Obion, Weakley, Dyer and Lake Counties**. (1886) reprint 1988. Indexed.
Cloth. $37.50. 352 pp. .... Vendor G0610

Hayes, Sallie. **Weakley County, Tennessee Miscellaneous Records**. Indexed.
$22.50 (perfect bound). 106 pp. .... Vendor G0549

Martin, Pat. **Weakley County, Tennessee Marriage Records, Volume One 1843-1854**. 1996.
Paper. $5.50. 46 pp. .... Vendor G0687

White County

Goodspeed Publishing Company. **White, Warren, DeKalb, Coffee and Cannon Counties**. (1886) reprint 1979. Indexed.
Cloth. $28.50. 195 pp. .... Vendor G0610

Murray, Joyce Martin. **White County, Tennessee Deed Abstracts, 1801-1820**. Indexed.
   Parts present Putnam, Van Buren, Cumberland, and DeKalb counties. Includes full-name, location, and slave indexes.
Paper. $25.00. Microfiche, $7.00. 158 pp. .... Vendor G0466

Murray, Joyce Martin. **White County, Tennessee Deed Abstracts, 1820-1834**. Indexed.
   Includes full-name, location, and slave indexes.
Paper. $25.00. Microfiche, $7.00. 150 pp. .... Vendor G0466

Seals, Monroe. **History of White County, Tennessee**. (1935) reprint 1988. Indexed.
Cloth. $25.00. viii + 191 pp. .... Vendor G0551

WPA. **White County, Tennessee Court Minutes 1814-1817**. Indexed.
$65.00 (perfect bound). 542 pp. .... Vendor G0549

WPA. **White County, Tennessee County Court Minutes 1819-1820**.
Paper. $15.00. .... Vendor G0549

WPA. **White County, Tennessee Court of Pleas 1835-1841**. Indexed.
$55.00 (perfect bound). 473 pp. .... Vendor G0549

WPA. **White County, Tennessee Minute Book 1820**. Indexed.
$10.00 (perfect bound). 55 pp. .... Vendor G0549

WPA. **White County, Tennessee Minute Book 1820-1823**. Indexed.
$70.00 (perfect bound). 596 pp. .... Vendor G0549

WPA. **White County, Tennessee Minute Book 1824-1827**. Indexed.
$85.00 (perfect bound). 762 pp. .... Vendor G0549

WPA. **White County, Tennessee Wills & Inventories 1831-1840**. Indexed.
$30.00 (perfect bound). 250 pp. .... Vendor G0549

Williamson County

Goodspeed Publishing Company. **History of Tennessee Illustrated, Historical and Biographical Sketches of the Counties of Maury, Williamson, Rutherford, Wilson, Bedford, and Marshall**. (1887) reprint 1988. Indexed.
Cloth. $42.50. 536 pp. .... Vendor G0610

Lynch, Louise. **Williamson County, Tennessee Deeds, Books A1, A2 & B, 1800-1811, Volume 1**. 1992. Indexed.
Paper. $26.50. 178 pp. .... Vendor G0610

Lynch, Louise. **Williamson County, Tennessee Deeds, Books C, D & E, 1812-1818, Vol. 2**. 1992. Indexed.
Paper. $26.50. Approx. 178 pp .... Vendor G0610

Lynch, Louise. **Williamson County, Tennessee Wills, 1800-1818, Books 1 & 2**. Rev. ed. 1992. Indexed. Illus.
Paper. $25.00. 144 pp. .... Vendor G0610

Murray, Joyce Martin. **Williamson County, Tennessee Deed Abstracts, 1799-1811**. Indexed.
   Present Maury, Giles, and Lawrence counties. Includes full-name, location, and slave indexes.
Cloth. $25.00. 202 pp. .... Vendor G0466

Sistler, Byron, and Barbara Sistler. **Williamson County, TN Wills & Administrations, 1800-1861**. 1989.
   About 2,400 entries. Includes name of deceased, year of probate or administration, where to find the information in the original will books.
Paper. $10.00. .... Vendor G0577

Wilson County

Goodspeed Publishing Company. **History of Tennessee Illustrated, Historical and Biographical Sketches of the Counties of Maury, Williamson, Rutherford, Wilson, Bedford, and Marshall**. (1887) reprint 1988. Indexed.
Cloth. $42.50. 536 pp. .... Vendor G0610

Partlow, Thomas E. **The People of Wilson County, Tennessee, 1800-1899**. 1983. Indexed.
Contact vendor for information. 158 pp. .... Vendor G0610

Partlow, Thomas E. **Wilson County, Tennessee, Circuit Court Records, 1810-1855**. 1989. Indexed.
Paper. $24.50. 144 pp. .... Vendor G0610

Partlow, Thomas E. **Wilson County, Tennessee, Deed Books C-M, 1793-1829**. 1984. Indexed.
Cloth. $25.00. 248 pp. + index .... Vendor G0610

Partlow, Thomas E. **Wilson County, Tennessee Deed Books N-Z, 1829-1853**. 1984. Indexed.
Cloth. $35.00. 464 pp. .... Vendor G0610

Partlow, Thomas E. **Wilson County, Tennessee, Deeds, Marriages and Wills, 1800-1902**. 1987. Indexed.
Paper. $32.50. 244 pp. .... Vendor G0610

Partlow, Thomas E. **Wilson County, Tennessee, Miscellaneous Records, 1800-1875**. 1982. Indexed.
Cloth. $25.00. 270 pp. .... Vendor G0610

Partlow, Thomas E. **Wilson County, Tennessee, Wills, Books 1-13 (1802-1850)**. 1981. Indexed.
Contact vendor for information. 222 pp. .... Vendor G0610

Sistler, Byron, and Barbara Sistler. **1870 Census—Tennessee.** Wilson County.
Paper. $23.00. .... Vendor G0577

Sistler, Byron, and Barbara Sistler. **Index to Wilson Co., TN Wills & Administrations, 1802-1861**. 1990.
   About 2,500 entries. Includes name of deceased, year of probate or administration, where to find the information.
Paper. $10.00. 32 pp. .... Vendor G0577

Whitley, Edythe Rucker, comp. **Tennessee Marriage Records: Wilson County, 1802-1850**. 1981. Indexed.
Cloth. $18.50. 306 pp. .... Vendor G0011

✒ Texas ✒

Statewide and Regional References

Atlas of Texas, Topographical.
   This present-day atlas provides the researcher with the detail needed to conduct a proper search. It is the size of a Rand McNally atlas of the entire U.S. 11" x 15½".
$24.95. .... Vendor G0611

Atlases & Gazetteers: Texas. Illus.
Paper. $24.95. 80 pp. .... Vendor G0632

Banvard, Theodore James Fleming. **Goodenows Who Originated in Sudbury, Massachusetts 1638 A.D.** 1994. Indexed. Illus.
Cloth. $78.50. 952 pp. .... Vendor G0116

F. A. Battley & Company. **The Biographical Souvenir of the State of Texas**. (1889) reprint 1978. Indexed.
Contact vendor for information. 950 pp. .... Vendor G0610

Births, Deaths & Marriages from El Paso Newspapers, Through 1886. By the El Paso Genealogical Society. 1982. Indexed.
Cloth. $22.50. 226 pp. + index. .... Vendor G0610

Births, Deaths & Marriages from El Paso Newspapers, 1886-1890. By the El Paso Genealogical Society. 1992. Indexed.
Cloth. $35.00. 410 pp. + index. .... Vendor G0610

Births, Deaths, and Marriages from El Paso Area Newspapers, 1891-1895, Vol. III By Mrs. Jane A. Beard. 1995. Indexed.
Cloth. 42.50. 408 pp.+ index. .... Vendor G0610

Bockstruck, Lloyd. **Research in Texas**.
Paper. $6.50. 36 pp. .... Vendor G0627

Bolton, Herbert E. **The Spanish Borderlands: A Chronicle of Old Florida and the Southwest**. (1921) reprint 1996.
    In narrative prose, Bolton recounts the Spanish exploration and the permanent settlement of Old Florida, New Mexico, Texas, Louisiana, and California.
Paper. $22.50. 320 pp. .... Vendor G0611

Bowen, Alberta Wright. **Death of Chas. B. McKinney: A Poem of South Texas.** Edited by Chuck Parsons. 1993. Illus.
Paper. $7.50. 24 pp. .... Vendor G0612

Brown, John Henry. **Indian Wars and Pioneers of Texas, 1822-1874**. (1880) reprint 1994. Indexed. Illus.
Cloth. $65.00. 1,152 pp. .... Vendor G0610

Connor, Seymour V. **Kentucky Colonization in Texas.** A History of the Peters Colony. (1953-54) reprint 1994.
Paper. $15.00. 153 pp. .... Vendor G0011

Dilts, Bryan Lee, comp. **1890 Texas Veterans Census Index.** 2nd ed. 1992. Illus.
Cloth. $19.00. 74 pp. .... Vendor G0552

Family History Library. **Research Outline: Texas**.
Leaflet. $.25. 11 pp. .... Vendor G0629

Galveston County Genealogical Society. **Port of Galveston, Texas, Ships Passenger List, 1846-1871**. 1984. Indexed.
Cloth. $28.00. 272 pp. .... Vendor G0610

Geue, Chester W., and Ethel H. Geue. **A New Land Beckoned.** German Immigration to Texas, 1844-1847. (1972) reprint 1982.
Contact vendor for information. .... Vendor G0011

Geue, Ethel H. **New Homes in a New Land.** German Immigration to Texas, 1847-1861. (1970) reprint 1994. Indexed. Illus.
    Contains information gleaned from the passenger lists of ships that arrived at Galveston between the years 1847 and 1861, with a history of the German immigration to Texas during this formative period.
Paper. $18.50. 175 pp. .... Vendor G0011

Goodspeed Publishing Company. **Memorial and Genealogical Record of (East) Texas**. (1895) reprint 1982. Indexed. Illus.
Cloth. $42.50. 465 pp. + index. .... Vendor G0610

Goodspeed Publishing Company. **Memorial and Genealogical Record of Southwest Texas**. (1884) reprint 1994. Indexed. Illus.
Cloth. $50.00. 688 pp. .... Vendor G0610

Hall-Little, Marianne E., and Charles N. "Chuck" Parsons. **Texas Ranger Captain Leander H. McNelly**. 1997. Indexed. Illus.
Cloth. Contact vendor for price. Est. 260 pp. .... Vendor G0612

Hogan. **The Texas Republic: A Social and Economic History**. Reprint 1986.
An interesting account of early Texas from independence to statehood.
Paper. $14.95. 338 pp. .... Vendor G0611

Hunter, J. Marvin. **Index to Frontier Times Volume 1.** Extractions by Vandegrift Research.
Includes issues from January 1923 to March 1942.
Hard-cover. $45.00. 394 pp. .... Vendor G0764

Jordan. **Texas Graveyards: A Cultural Legacy**. 1982.
Not only marks the distinct ethnic and racial traditions in burial practices, but also preserves a Texas legacy endangered by changing customs, rural depopulation, vandalism, and the erosion of time.
Paper. $13.95. 147 pp. .... Vendor G0611

Kennedy, Imogene, and Leon Kennedy. **Genealogical Records in Texas**. (1987) reprint 1992.
Cloth. $35.00. 248 pp. .... Vendor G0010

Liahona Research. **Texas Marriages, Early to 1850**. 1990. Illus.
Cloth. $60.00. 241 pp. .... Vendor G0552

Marsh, Helen C., and Timothy R. Marsh. **Tennesseans in Texas:** As Found in the 1850 Census of Texas. 1986. Indexed.
Hard-cover. $37.50. 416 pp. .... Vendor G0610

McComb, David. **Texas: A Modern History**. 1989.
An interesting and well-written history.
Paper. $12.95. 197 pp. .... Vendor G0611

McIntire, Jim. **Early Days in Texas: A Trip to Heaven and Hell**. 1996.
Gentleman, reprobate, killer, lawman—Jim McIntire was all of these, and more. A life story rich with notable characters from early Texas life.
Paper. $12.95. 192 pp. .... Vendor G0611

Mearse, Linda. **Confederate Indigent Families Lists of Texas, 1863-1865**. 1995. Indexed.
Transcript of lists for 110 counties. These lists were created as a result of an "Act to Support the Families and Dependents of Texas Soldiers" passed by the Texas Legislature in 1863. Contains the name of soldier or head of household, and total number of dependents. Some lists give additional information: dependents' family relationships, MIA, wounded, deceased, name of unit . . . .

Also available by region in six softcover volumes. Contact vendor for list of counties in each volume.

Cloth. $57.00. 499 pp. .... Vendor G0498

Mullins, Marion Day. **First Census of Texas, 1829 to 1836**.
Paper. $10.25. 63 pp. .... Vendor G0627

Mullins, Marion Day. **Republic of Texas Poll Lists for 1846**. (1974) reprint 1995.
Paper. $19.50. 189 pp. .... Vendor G0011

Newcomb. **The Indians of Texas**. 1990.
An anthropologist's comprehensive survey of the Indians of Texas.
Paper. $12.95. 404 pp. .... Vendor G0611

Nicklas, Linda Cheves. **Abstracts of Early East Texas Newspapers, 1839-1856**.
1994. Indexed.
Cloth. $30.00. 168 pp. .... Vendor G0610

Parsons, Chuck. **Bowen and Hardin**. 1991. Indexed. Illus.
Cloth. $29.95. 159 pp. .... Vendor G0612

Parsons, Chuck. **James Madison Brown, Texas Sheriff, Texas Turfman**. 1993. Indexed. Illus.
Cloth. $39.95. 182 pp. .... Vendor G0612

Parsons, Chuck, and Gary Fitterer. **Captain C. B. McKinney—The Law in South Texas**. 1993. Indexed. Illus.
Cloth. $39.95. 159 pp. .... Vendor G0612

Parsons, Charles N. "Chuck," Marianne E. Hall-Little, and Donaly Brice. **Texas Ranger N. O. Reynolds**. 1997. Indexed. Illus.
Cloth. Contact vendor for price. Est. 250 pp. .... Vendor G0612

Peters, James Stephen. Charles N. "Chuck" Parsons, and Marianne E. Hall-Little.
Mace Bowman—Texas Feudist—Western Lawman. 1996. Indexed. Illus.
Contains previously unpublished photographs of Clay Allison and Allison family members. John and wife, Kate; Jeremiah; Saluda and husband, Louis Coleman. Also, previously unprinted photographs of Mace Bowman, Clay Allison, and friends.
Cloth. $39.95. Collector edition, $79.95. 228 pp. .... Vendor G0612

Sidney Sherman Chapter, Daughters of the Republic of Texas. **Texas Heroes Buried on Galveston Island**. 1982. Indexed.
Paper. $12.50. 88 pp. .... Vendor G0610

Sifakis. **Compendium of the Confederate Armies: Texas**. 1995.
Describes the regiments, officers, and battles.
Cloth. $24.95. 147 pp. .... Vendor G0611

Sistler, Byron, and Barbara Sistler. **1890 Civil War Veterans Census—Tennesseans in Texas**. 1978.
About 550 men living in Texas in 1890 who served in Tennessee units during the Civil War, mostly Union veterans.
Paper. $7.00. .... Vendor G0577

Smith, Mary Fay. **War of 1812 Veterans in Texas—Revised**. (1979) reprint 1994. Indexed.
Cloth, $42.50. Paper, $35.00. Approx. 468 pp. .... Vendor G0610

Stephens and Holmes. **Historical Atlas of Texas**. 1988.
The history of Texas illustrated by 64 maps.
Paper. $19.95. 168 pp. .... Vendor G0611

Sumner, Jane, Alice Gracy, and Emma S. Gentry. **Early Texas Birth Records, 1838-1878**. (1869) reprint 1991.
Cloth. $25.00. 150 pp. .... Vendor G0610

Texas State Archives. **1880-1930 Index to Probate Birth Records, Vols. 1-40**.
Microfilm (16 mm). $17.50/roll. 5 rolls. .... Vendor G0601

Texas State Archives. **1903-1940 Index to Probate Birth Records**.
Microfilm (16 mm). $17.50/roll. 7 rolls. .... Vendor G0601

Texas State Archives. **1903-1976 Index to Birth Records**.
Microfilm (16 mm). $17.50/roll. 50 rolls. .... Vendor G0601

Texas State Archives. **1920 Index to Birth Records**.
Microfilm (16 mm). $17.50. 1 roll. .... Vendor G0601

Texas State Archives. **1930-1945 Index to Probate Birth Records**.
Microfilm (16 mm). $17.50/roll. 2 rolls. .... Vendor G0601

Texas State Archives. **1941-1973 Index to Death Records, Texas**.
Microfilm (16 mm). $17.50/roll. 11 rolls. .... Vendor G0601

Texas State Archives. **Compiled Index to Elected and Appointed Officials of the Republic of Texas, 1836-1846**.
Paper. $3.00. .... Vendor G0601

Texas State Archives. **Genealogical Resources at the Texas State Library**. 1996.
Brochure. Contact vendor for information. .... Vendor G0601

Texas State Archives. **Journals of the Ninth Legislature of the State of Texas (1861)**.
Volume 2: Senate Journal, Called Session.
Volume 3: House Journal, Regular Session.
Volume 4: House Journal, Called Session.
(Volume 1 is no longer available.)
Cloth. $4.50 each/Vols. 2 & 4. $3.75/Vol. 3. .... Vendor G0601

Texas State Archives. **Journals of the Tenth Legislature of the State of Texas (1863)**.
Volume 1: Senate Journal, Regular Session.
Volume 2: House Journal, Regular Session.
Volume 3: Senate and House Journals, First Called Session.
Volume 4: Senate and House Journals, Second Called Session.
Paper. $5.00/Vol. 1. $5.50/Vol. 2. $4.75/Vol. 3. $3.50/Vol. 4. .... Vendor G0601

Texas State Archives. *The Liberty Gazette* **Newspaper, 1855-1869**.
Microfilm (35 mm). $17.50/roll. Contact vendor for information. .... Vendor G0601

Texas State Archives. *The Liberty Vindicator* **Newspaper, 1925-1935**.
Microfilm (35 mm). $17.50/roll. Contact vendor for information. ...... Vendor G0601

Texas State Archives. **Nacagdoches Archives**.
Selected records of Spanish and Mexican colonial government in East Texas.
Microfilm (35 mm). $17.50/roll. 27 rolls. .... Vendor G0601

Texas State Archives. **Post Office Department Records, Republic of Texas 1835-1841**.
Microfilm (16 mm). $17.50. 1 roll. .... Vendor G0601

Texas State Archives. **Post Office Papers of the Republic of Texas**.
Volume I: 1835-1836.
Volume II: 1836-1841.
Volume III: 1841-1846.
Paper. $4.00/Vol. I. $11.75 each/Vols. II & III. .... Vendor G0601

Texas State Archives. **Roster of Confederate Home, Austin, Texas**.
Microfilm (35 mm). $17.50. 1 roll. .... Vendor G0601

Texas State Archives. **Taxes Collected from Railroads in Texas: 1874-1875**.
Microfilm (16 mm). $17.50. 1 roll. .... Vendor G0601

Texas State Archives. **Texas Confederate Military Service Records**.
Alphabetical lists of company commanders with muster rolls, of counties containing company commanders with muster rolls, and of Texas Confederate soldiers.
Microfilm (16 mm). $17.50/roll. 8 rolls. .... Vendor G0601

Texas State Archives. **Texas County Records: A Guide to the Holdings of the Texas State Library of County Records on Microfilm**.
$20.00. .... Vendor G0601

Texas State Archives. **Texas Rangers Records: 1919 Ranger Investigation**.
Microfilm (16 mm). $17.50. 1 roll. .... Vendor G0601

Texas State Archives. **Texas Rangers Records: 1919-1920 Loyalty Rangers**.
Microfilm (16 mm). $17.50. 1 roll. .... Vendor G0601

Texas State Archives. **Texas Rangers Records: 1919-1935 Regular Rangers**.
Microfilm (16 mm). $17.50/roll. 2 rolls. .... Vendor G0601

Texas State Archives. **Texas Rangers Records: 1919-1935 Special Rangers**.
Microfilm (16 mm). $17.50/roll. 7 rolls. .... Vendor G0601

Texas State Archives. **Texas Rangers Records: 1920 Railroad Rangers**.
Microfilm (16 mm). $17.50/roll. 3 rolls. .... Vendor G0601

Texas State Archives. **Texas Rangers Service Records**.
Service records for Texas Rangers and associated groups, 1830-1900, and of the Minute Men, 1841. Note: Reel no. 8 of the Texas Confederate Military Service Records is combined with reel no. 1 of the Ranger service records.
Microfilm (16 mm). $17.50/roll. 2 rolls. .... Vendor G0601

Texas State Archives. **Texas State Library Circulating Genealogy Duplicates List**.
Contact vendor for information. .... Vendor G0601

Texas State Archives. **Texas Tax Rolls.** Early 1800s Through 1981. Microfilm (1960-1974 on 35 mm microfilm; all other yrs. on 16 mm). $17.50/roll. Contact vendor for details. .... Vendor G0601

Texas State Archives. **U.S. Census of Texas: 1850-1860 Mortality.** Microfilm (35 mm). $17.50/roll. 7 rolls. .... Vendor G0601

Texas State Archives. **U.S. Census of Texas: 1850-1860 State of Texas Index.** Microfilm (35 mm). $17.50/roll. 11 rolls. .... Vendor G0601

Texas State Archives. **U.S. Census of Texas: 1850-1870 Products of Industry.** Microfilm (35 mm). $17.50/roll. 3 rolls. .... Vendor G0601

Texas State Archives. **U.S. Census of Texas: 1850-1870 Social Statistics.** Microfilm (35 mm). $17.50/roll. 2 rolls. .... Vendor G0601

Texas State Archives. **U.S. Census of Texas: 1850-1880 Texas Agricultural Statistics.** Microfilm (35 mm). $17.50/roll. 43 rolls. .... Vendor G0601

Texas State Archives. **U.S. Census of Texas: 1880 Manufacturers' Statistics.** Microfilm (35 mm). $17.50/roll. 3 rolls. .... Vendor G0601

Texas State Archives. **U.S. Census of Texas: Defective, Dependent and Delinquent Class.** Microfilm (35 mm). $17.50/roll. 5 rolls. .... Vendor G0601

Texas State Archives. **Valentine Overton King's Index to Books about Texas before 1889.** Paper. $17.00. .... Vendor G0601

Texas State Archives. **Voter Registers, 1867-1869.** Microfilm (35 mm). $17.50/roll. 12 rolls. .... Vendor G0601

Texas State Archives. **Wheat, Postmasters, and Post Offices of Texas, 1846-1930.** Microfilm (16 mm). $11.50/roll. Contact vendor for information. ...... Vendor G0601

Thorndale, William, and William Dollarhide. **County Boundary Map Guides to the U.S. Federal Censuses, 1790-1920: Texas, 1840-1920.** 1987. $5.95. .... Vendor G0552

Von-Maszewski. **Handbook and Registry of German-Texan Heritage.** 1989.
    Useful collection of German churches, societies, businesses, more.
Paper. $9.00. 193 pp. .... Vendor G0611

White, Gifford. **Character Certificates in the General Land Office of Texas.** (1985) reprint 1996. Indexed.
Paper. $25.00. 266 pp. .... Vendor G0011

Williams, Villamae. **Stephen F. Austin's Register of Families.** (1984) reprint 1996. Indexed.
    In 1811 Mexico declared its independence from Spain and established itself as a republic. The new government made contracts with Empresarios (contractors) to bring specific numbers of families into the State of Coahuila and Texas. Stephen Austin was the first and most successful of the Empresarios, and he began granting land to settlers

in 1824. These records provide information on about 3,000 Anglo-American settlers
of Mexican Texas.
Cloth. $20.00. 198 pp. .... Vendor G0011

ALVARADO, TEXAS GLENWOOD CEMETERY: A CENSUS, 1890-1990

Compiled by ANNIE BILL and SAM A. KELLEY. Edited by LOUISE K. POLLARD. 1990.
Only known listing of this Johnson Co. pioneer cemetery. Dates of death: 1874 - 1990.
Indexed by NAME (birth date, death date, block #, row #, relationship) and by
ROW (name and block # within row). Plot maps of rows and blocks. iii + 138.
INFOSERV, L. K. POLLARD, - 1497 CHEEVER LANE- FARMINGTON, UT 84025
$27.50 Prepaid - Shipping included ($30 U.S. international)

Anderson County

Anderson County, Texas Land Titles 1831-1878.
Paper. $10.00. .... Vendor G0549

Andrews County

Andrews and Archer Counties, Texas Land Titles 1831-1878.
Paper. $10.00. .... Vendor G0549

Archer County

Andrews and Archer Counties, Texas Land Titles 1831-1878.
Paper. $10.00. .... Vendor G0549

Austin County

Austin and Bandera Counties, Texas Land Titles 1831-1878.
Paper. $10.00. .... Vendor G0549

Murray, Joyce Martin. **Austin County, Texas Deed Abstracts, 1837-1852.** Indexed.
Includes full-name, location, and slave indexes.
Microfiche. $7.00. 190 pp. .... Vendor G0466

Bandera County

Austin and Bandera Counties, Texas Land Titles 1831-1878.
Paper. $10.00. .... Vendor G0549

Bastrop County

Ray, Worth S. **Austin [Texas] Colony Pioneers,** Including History of Bastrop, Fayette, Grimes, Montgomery and Washington Counties, Texas. (1949) reprint 1995. Indexed. Illus.
Cloth. $22.50. 378 pp. .... Vendor G0011

Baylor County

Baylor County, Texas Land Titles 1831-1878.
Paper. $8.50. .... Vendor G0549

Bee County

Bee and Borden Counties, Texas Land Titles 1831-1878.
Paper. $11.50. .... Vendor G0549

Bell County

Bell County, Texas Land Titles 1831-1878.
Paper. $10.00. .... Vendor G0549

Tyler, George W. **History of Bell County.** Edited by Charles W. Ramsdell. (1936) reprint 1992.
Cloth. $48.00. xxiii + 425 pp. .... Vendor G0259

Bexar County

Bexar County, Texas Land Titles 1831-1878.
Paper. $10.00. .... Vendor G0549

Blanco County

Calhoun and Blanco Counties, Texas Land Titles 1831-1878.
Paper. $11.00. .... Vendor G0549

Borden County

Bee and Borden Counties, Texas Land Titles 1831-1878.
Paper. $11.50. .... Vendor G0549

Brazos County

Billingsley, Nadine. **Recorded Births in Brazos County, Texas 1850-1910**. Indexed. Contact vendor for information. 328 pp. .... Vendor G0866

Boykin, Rosemary DePasquale. **Italians of Steele's Store, Texas**. Contact vendor for information. .... Vendor G0868

Brazos County Cemetery Book. Contact vendor for information. .... Vendor G0665

Brazos County, Texas District Court Case Abstracts. Contact vendor for information. .... Vendor G0665

Brazos County, Texas Index to Probate Cases 1841-1939. Paper. $12.50. .... Vendor G0549

Brazos County, Texas Probate Packet Abstracts. Contact vendor for information. .... Vendor G0665

Glowski, Joanne Dominik, comp. **Index to Birth, Marriage, and Death Records, 1876-1909, St. Joseph Catholic Church, Bryan, Brazos Co., Texas**. Indexed. Contact vendor for information. 96 pp. .... Vendor G0867

Glowski, Joanne Dominik, comp. **Marriage and Death Records, 1877-1909, St. Joseph Catholic Church, Bryan, Brazos Co., Texas**.
Includes list of birthplaces.
Contact vendor for information. 83 pp. .... Vendor G0867

Murray, Joyce Martin. **Washington County, Texas Deed Abstracts, 1834-1841**. Indexed.
Parts of Walker, Burleson, Brazos, Lee, Grimes, Montgomery, Milam, and San Jacinto counties. Includes full-name index.
Cloth. $25.00. 160 pp. .... Vendor G0466

Page, Bill, comp. **Brazos County, Texas: Annotated Adoption Records, 1862-1933**. Indexed.
Identifies fifty-four deeds listing the adoption of sixty-two Brazos County children.
Contact vendor for information. 26 pp. .... Vendor G0665

Page, Bill, comp. **Butchers, Bakers, and Candlestick Makers: Notes on Bryan Businesses, 1867-1889**. Indexed.
Contact vendor for information. 45 pp. .... Vendor G0665

Page, Bill, comp. **The Other Pioneers: Notes on Slaves and Slavery in Brazos County**. Indexed.
Contact vendor for information. 40 pp. .... Vendor G0665

Brown County

Brown County, Texas Inventory of County Archives.
An inventory of the records of the various offices in the courthouse.
Paper. $42.50. 151 pp. .... Vendor G0549

Burleson County

Murray, Joyce Martin. **Washington County, Texas Deed Abstracts, 1834-1841**. Indexed.

Parts of Walker, Burleson, Brazos, Lee, Grimes, Montgomery, Milam, and San Jacinto counties. Includes full-name index.

Cloth. $25.00. 160 pp. .... Vendor G0466

Caldwell County

Callahan, Caldwell and Cameron Counties, Texas Land Titles 1831-1878.
Paper. $11.00. .... Vendor G0549

Calhoun County

Calhoun and Blanco Counties, Texas Land Titles 1831-1878.
Paper. $11.00. .... Vendor G0549

Callahan County

Callahan, Caldwell and Cameron Counties, Texas Land Titles 1831-1878.
Paper. $11.00. .... Vendor G0549

Cameron County

Callahan, Caldwell and Cameron Counties, Texas Land Titles 1831-1878.
Paper. $11.00. .... Vendor G0549

Camp County

Camp County Genealogical Society. **Camp County Texas Marriages 1874-1978, Books 1-13**. 1996.

6" x 9", acid-free paper. Alphabetized by grooms, then brides, each containing 13,255 names.

Hard-cover. $41.00. 477 pp. .... Vendor G0497

Cass County

Cass County Genealogical Society. **Cass County Connections**. Published quarterly.
Dues, $12.00/yr. .... Vendor G0595

Cass County Genealogical Society. **Cass County Records of 1890**. Indexed.
Paper. $20.00. 201 pp. .... Vendor G0595

Cass County Genealogical Society. **Cemeteries with Cass County Connections, Volume 1**. 1996. Indexed.
This is the first of several volumes. Contact vendor for more information.
Paper. $18.00. 343 pp. .... Vendor G0595

Cass County Genealogical Society. **History of Cass County People**. Indexed. Illus.
Includes surname index.
Paper. $20.00. 249 pp. .... Vendor G0595

Cass County Genealogical Society. **Pedigrees, Volume 1 and Supplement**. Reprint 1995. Indexed.
Paper. $15.00. 180 pp. .... Vendor G0595

Cass County Genealogical Society. **Pedigrees, Volume 2**. Reprint 1993.
Paper. $28.00. 430 pp. .... Vendor G0595

Cass County Genealogical Society. **People of Cass County: Atlanta, Queen City, Texas, Vol. 1**. Indexed.
Paper. $25.00. 272 pp. .... Vendor G0595

Cass County Genealogical Society. **Volume 2, Records of Cass County People, Queen City, Cass County, Texas**. Indexed.
Paper. $10.00. 100 pp. .... Vendor G0595

Cass County Genealogical Society. **Spirit of '76: Queen City, Texas 1876-1976**. Reprint 1992. Indexed.
Paper. $20.00. 236 pp. .... Vendor G0595

Cawthon, Juanita. **Marriage & Death Notices, Cass County, Texas 1883-1939**. Indexed.
Includes full-name index.
Paper. $15.00. 179 pp. .... Vendor G0595

Hanes, John D. **A History of Queen City, Texas.** Index added by CCGS. Indexed.
Paper. $12.00. 127 pp. .... Vendor G0595

Collin County

McKinney Memorial Public Library Volunteers, comps. **Newspaper Obituaries, Collin County, Texas 1884-1899**.
Index of obituaries for Collin County, Texas.
Paper. $11.00. 25 pp. .... Vendor G0528

McKinney Memorial Public Library Volunteers, comps. **Newspaper Obituaries, Collin County, Texas 1900-1909**.
Index of obituaries for Collin County, Texas.
Paper. $16.00. 103 pp. .... Vendor G0528

McKinney Memorial Public Library Volunteers, comps. **Newspaper Obituaries, Collin County, Texas 1910-1919**.
Index of obituaries for Collin County, Texas.
Paper. $16.00. 77 pp. .... Vendor G0528

McKinney Memorial Public Library Volunteers, comps. **Newspaper Obituaries, Collin County, Texas 1920-1929**.
Index of obituaries for Collin County, Texas.
Paper. $16.00. 99 pp. .... Vendor G0528

McKinney Memorial Public Library Volunteers, comps. **Newspaper Obituaries, Collin County, Texas 1930-1939**.
Index of obituaries for Collin County, Texas.
Paper. $16.00. .... Vendor G0528

Pitts, Alice Ellison, Wanda O'Roark, and Doris Posey. **Collin County, Texas, Cemetery Inscriptions. Volume I**. 1975. Indexed.
Includes four pages of county sectional maps with each cemetery plotted by number for quick location.
Cloth. $35.00. Also available as a set with Vol. II for $49.50 + postage.
746 pp. .... Vendor G0539

Pitts, Alice Ellison, Wanda O'Roark, and Doris Posey. **Collin County, Texas, Cemetery Inscriptions. Volume II**. 1975.
Inventories of thirty-five public and private cemeteries. Abstracted obituaries for 1974-76 from the McKinney Courier-Gazette and Sherman Democrat.
Cloth. $30.00. Also available with above book for $49.50 + postage.
161 pp. .... Vendor G0539

Pitts, Alice Ellison, and Minnie Pitts Champ. **Collin County, Texas, Families**. 1994. Illus.
Includes 548 family stories and 330 pictures.
Hard-cover. $66.00. 397 pp. .... Vendor G0539

Dawson County

Lamesa Area Genealogical Society. **Dawson County, Texas Marriage Records, Books I & II**. 1994. Indexed. Illus.
Paper. $14.50. 134 pp. .... Vendor G0307

Lamesa Area Genealogical Society. **Index to the Dawson County, Texas 1910 Census: An Every-Name Index Including Ages and States of Birth**. 1991.
Paper. $5.00. 35 pp. .... Vendor G0307

Delta County

Delta County, Texas Index to Probate Cases 1870-1939.
Paper. $14.50. .... Vendor G0549

Denton County

Denton County, Texas Marriage 1875-1891.
Paper. $22.50. .... Vendor G0549

DeWitt County

DeWitt County, Texas Inventory of County Archives.
An inventory of records of each of the county offices.
Paper. $35.00. 129 pp. .... Vendor G0549

Hall-Little, Marianne E. **Clemens Georg Ludwig Gottlieb "C. G." Hartmann: DeWitt County, Texas, County Surveyor**. 1996. Indexed. Illus.
Cloth. $39.95. 100 pp. .... Vendor G0612

Hall-Little, Marianne E. **Fred House: Cattle Baron of Davy, DeWitt County, Texas**. 1993. Indexed. Illus.
Also, of Gonzales County, Bee County, Karnes County, and Wilson County, TX. He was grandfather of John Wesley Hardin, Jr., & sold horses to John Wesley Hardin, the gunfighter.
Cloth. $39.95. 100 pp. .... Vendor G0612

Ellis County

Kinsey, Margaret B. **Ebenezer Baptist of Ellis County, Texas; 1880-1892 Church Records with Genealogies**. 1990. Indexed. Illus.
Cloth. $25.00. 338 pp. .... Vendor G0307

Murray, Joyce Martin. **Ellis County, Texas Deed Abstracts, 1841-18__?**.
In progress.
Contact vendor for details. .... Vendor G0466

Erath County

Williams, Gene. **Hurrah for Morgan Mill**. 1996. Illus.
Includes the beginnings of Morgan Mill, Texas, life in the early days, the families of Morgan Mill (genealogies of about seventy-five families), stores and businesses, schools, churches, cemeteries and lodges, Morgan Mill today, and names to be remembered.
Cloth. $25.00 incl. tax & shipping. 320 pp. .... Vendor G0613

Fannin County

1850 Fannin County, Texas Census & Consorts.
Paper. $25.00. .... Vendor G0549

Fannin County, Texas Land Titles 1831-1878.
Paper. $16.50. .... Vendor G0549

Fannin County, Texas Log Book 1885-1889—Maddrey & Hunter Livery Stable.
Paper. $20.00. .... Vendor G0549

Fayette County

Fayette County, Texas Inventory of County Archives.
An inventory record of each of the holdings of every county office as of 1939.
Paper. $48.00. 174 pp. .... Vendor G0549

Ray, Worth S. **Austin [Texas] Colony Pioneers,** Including History of Bastrop, Fayette, Grimes, Montgomery and Washington Counties, Texas. (1949) reprint 1995. Indexed. Illus.
Cloth. $22.50. 378 pp. .... Vendor G0011

Franklin County

Franklin County, Texas Index to Probate Records.
Paper. $10.00. .... Vendor G0549

Galveston County

Galveston County Genealogical Society. **St. Joseph Catholic Church, Galveston, Texas, Baptismal, Confirmation, Marriage and Death Records 1860-1952**. 1984. Indexed.
If you have German ancestors who came to Texas, or through Texas to the Midwest, in the mid-1800s, this book is a must. Many Germans came to the Republic of Texas on German land contracts through the port of Galveston and stayed to raise their families. By 1855, Galveston's population was close to one-half German. It was at this time that the Catholic Diocese tried to build a church in Galveston so services could be held in German.
Paper. $27.50. 168 pp. .... Vendor G0610

Partin, SheRita Kae Vaughn, comp. & ed. **Galveston County, Texas 1890 Mortality Schedule**. 1996.
Paper. $21.27. 9 pp. .... Vendor G0672

Weber, Retta Lou, and Gayle Weber Strange. **Lively Stones: A History of the People Who Built First Presbyterian Church, Galveston, Texas, 1840-1990**. 1993. Indexed.
This beautiful book is a complete history of the First Presbyterian Church and the families who worshipped there. Includes lists of members and hundreds of photographs.
Cloth. $40.00. 340 pp. .... Vendor G0611

Grayson County

Grayson County, Texas Marriage Records 1846-1877.
Paper. $23.00. .... Vendor G0549

Holder, Charlotte, and Catherine Overturff. **Grayson County, Texas Miscellaneous Wills and Probates 1833-1923**. 1993.
Paper. $15.00. 151 pp. .... Vendor G0710

Gregg County

Gregg County, Texas Inventory of County Archives.
An inventory of the records in each of the county offices through 1939.
Paper. $49.00. 182 pp. .... Vendor G0549

Grimes County

Murray, Joyce Martin. **Washington County, Texas Deed Abstracts, 1834-1841**. Indexed.
Parts of Walker, Burleson, Brazos, Lee, Grimes, Montgomery, Milam, and San Jacinto counties. Includes full-name index.
Cloth. $25.00. 160 pp. .... Vendor G0466

Ray, Worth S. **Austin [Texas] Colony Pioneers,** Including History of Bastrop, Fayette, Grimes, Montgomery and Washington Counties, Texas. (1949) reprint 1995. Indexed. Illus.
Cloth. $22.50. 378 pp. .... Vendor G0011

Harris County

Dreyer, Dorothy Williams, with Eveann Ramsey Nicholson. **Paul U. Lee Funeral Home Records, Baytown, Texas 1923-1951.** Published by Baytown Genealogical Society.
Spiral binding. $27.50. .... Vendor G0765

Hays County

Hays County, Texas Inventory of County Archives.
An inventory of the records in each of the county offices through 1939.
Paper. $30.00. 110 pp. .... Vendor G0549

Mearse, Linda. **Marriage Records, Hays County, Texas, Volumes A-C, 1848-1881**. 1996. Indexed.
Lists groom, bride, marriage date, page, minister, and notes such as witnesses, consents. . . .
Paper. $13.50. 68 pp. .... Vendor G0498

Mearse, Linda. **Marriage Records, Hays County, Texas, Volumes D-G, 1881-1900**. In progress.
Contact vendor for information. .... Vendor G0498

Mearse, Linda. **Obituaries, Hays County, Texas**. In progress. Indexed.
Contact vendor for information. .... Vendor G0498

Hood County

Hood County, Texas Inventory of County Archives.
An inventory of the records in each of the county offices through 1939.
Paper. $21.50. 74 pp. .... Vendor G0549

Houston County

Farley, Hilde Shuptrine. **The Harrisons from Houston County, Texas, 1835-1993**.
1994. Indexed. Illus.
Cloth. $28.00. 297 pp. .... Vendor G0024

Howard County

Knight, Eunice J. **Howard County, Texas—Marriages and Will and Probate Proceedings, 1882-1930**. 1992. Indexed.
Cloth. $55.00. 408 pp. .... Vendor G0469

Hunt County

Thompson, Robert Lee, and Kathy Lynn Penson. **Hunt County, Texas Cemeteries Volume 1**.
Seventy-four cemeteries; maps.
Paper. $45.00. 228 pp. .... Vendor G0549

Thompson, Robert Lee, and Kathy Lynn Penson. **Hunt County, Texas Cemeteries Volume 2**.
Nineteen cemeteries; maps.
Paper. $45.00. 230 pp. .... Vendor G0549

Thompson, Robert Lee, and Kathy Lynn Penson. **Hunt County, Texas Cemeteries Volume 3**.
Eleven cemeteries; maps.
Paper. $45.00. 230 pp. .... Vendor G0549

Jackson County

Jackson County, Texas Inventory of County Archives.
An inventory of the records held in each of the county offices through 1939.
Paper. $30.00. 109 pp. `.. Vendor G0549

Jefferson County

Wright, Mildred S. **Jefferson County, Texas Cemeteries, Part I: Oak Bluff, Port Neches**. 1979. Indexed.
Paper. $17.00. 130 pp. .... Vendor G0145

Wright, Mildred S. **Jefferson County, Texas Cemeteries, Part III: Rural, Family and Ethnic**. 1981. Indexed.
Seventy sites including lost and/or moved, tombstone inscriptions when present.
Paper. $22.50. 104 pp. .... Vendor G0145

Johnson County

Kelley, Annie Bill, and Sam A. Kelley, comps. **Alvarado Texas Glenwood Cemetery: A Census 1890-1990.** Edited by Louise K. Pollard. 1990. Indexed.
Paper. $27.50. iii + 138 pp. .... Vendor G0517

Lee County

Murray, Joyce Martin. **Washington County, Texas Deed Abstracts, 1834-1841**. Indexed.
Parts of Walker, Burleson, Brazos, Lee, Grimes, Montgomery, Milam, and San Jacinto counties. Includes full-name index.
Cloth. $25.00. 160 pp. .... Vendor G0466

Liberty County

Liberty County, Texas Index to Probate Cases 1850-1939.
Paper. $14.00. .... Vendor G0549

Marion County

Cawthon, Juanita Davis. **Some Early Citizens of Marion County, Texas**. 1996.
Paper. $17.00. 111 pp. .... Vendor G0715

Medina County

Medina County, Texas Cemeteries Volume 2.
Paper. $10.50. .... Vendor G0549

Milam County

Crawford, Dorothy Brown. **Easy Search for Milam Ancestors: Milam Co. Censuses for 1850, 1860 and 1870**. (1985) reprint 1994.
Cloth, $42.50. Paper, $32.50. 322 pp. .... Vendor G0259

Murray, Joyce Martin. **Washington County, Texas Deed Abstracts, 1834-1841**. Indexed.
   Parts of Walker, Burleson, Brazos, Lee, Grimes, Montgomery, Milam, and San Jacinto counties. Includes full-name index.
Cloth. $25.00. 160 pp. .... Vendor G0466

Williams, James E. **Milam County, Texas in the Civil War**. 1993. Indexed.
   Service records; government employees; petitions.
Paper. $14.00. 68 pp. .... Vendor G0508

> **Milam County, Texas in the Civil War**
> *Confederate Service Records
> *Roster of Texas State Troops
> *List of Government Employees
> *Citizens' Petitions
> *Bibliography & Complete Index
> Send $14 (TX residents add 95¢ sales tax) to:
>   James E. Williams
>   Rt. 1 Box 864
>   Milano, TX 76556-9759

Montgomery County

Murray, Joyce Martin. **Washington County, Texas Deed Abstracts, 1834-1841**. Indexed.
   Parts of Walker, Burleson, Brazos, Lee, Grimes, Montgomery, Milam, and San Jacinto counties. Includes full-name index.
Cloth. $25.00. 160 pp. .... Vendor G0466

Ray, Worth S. **Austin [Texas] Colony Pioneers,** Including History of Bastrop, Fayette, Grimes, Montgomery and Washington Counties, Texas. (1949) reprint 1995. Indexed. Illus.
Cloth. $22.50. 378 pp. .... Vendor G0011

Newton County

Hines, Pauline M. **Glimpses of Newton County History**. 1982. Indexed. Illus.
Hard-cover. $20.00. 271 pp. .... Vendor G0156

Hines, Pauline M., comp. **Newton County Nuggets—A Collection of True Stories by Newton County Folk**. 1986. Indexed. Illus.
Hard-cover. $20.00. 479 pp. .... Vendor G0156

Newton County, Texas Historical Commission. **Crosscuts—An Anthology of Memoirs by Newton County Folk**. 1984. Indexed. Illus.
Hard-cover. $20.00. 356 pp. .... Vendor G0156

Newton County, Texas Historical Commission. **Newton County, Texas 1860 Census**. Indexed.
Paper. $13.00. 66 pp. .... Vendor G0156

Newton County, Texas Historical Commission. **Newton County, Texas 1870 Census**. (1978) reprint 1993. Indexed.
Paper. $13.00. 55 pp. .... Vendor G0156

Newton County, Texas Historical Commission. **Newton County, Texas 1880 Census**. 1980. Indexed.
Paper. $13.00. 117 pp. .... Vendor G0156

Newton County, Texas Historical Commission. **Newton County, Texas Marriage Records, 1900-1940**. 1991. Indexed.
Paper. $18.00. 87 pp. .... Vendor G0156

Newton County, Texas Index to Probate Cases 1846-1939.
Paper. $10.00. .... Vendor G0549

Smith, Robert Edd., Sr., and Tonia R. Smith. **1850 Census of Newton County, Texas with Maiden Names and Marriages**. 1985. Indexed.
Paper. $13.00. 58 pp. .... Vendor G0156

WPA History of Newton County, Texas. Copied by Newton County, Texas Historical Commission. 1991. Indexed.
Paper. $13.00. 125 pp. .... Vendor G0156

Nueces County

Ward, Charles A., and Brooks Noel, comps. **Cemetery Data of Nueces County, Texas Supplemented and Expanded with Other Death Records**. 1991. Indexed. Illus.
Paper. $32.50. 322 pp. .... Vendor G0016

Orange County

Orange County, Texas Index to Probate Cases 1852-1939.
Paper. $11.50. .... Vendor G0549

Orange County, Texas Inventory of County Archives.
An inventory of the holdings of each of the county offices as of 1939.
Paper. $50.00. 194 pp. .... Vendor G0549

Panola County

Panola County, Texas Marriages 1846-1889.
Paper. $16.50. .... Vendor G0549

Red River County

Murray, Joyce Martin. **Red River County, Texas Deed Abstracts, Volume I (to 1846)**. Indexed.
Includes full-name, location, and slave indexes.
Cloth. $30.00. Microfiche, $7.00. 188 pp. .... Vendor G0466

Murray, Joyce Martin. **Red River County, Texas Deed Abstracts, Volume II (1846-1855)**. Indexed.
Includes full-name, location, and slave indexes.
Cloth. $25.00. 192 pp. .... Vendor G0466

Robertson County

Robertson County, Texas Index to Probate Cases.
Paper. $24.50. .... Vendor G0549

Robertson County, Texas Marriages 1838-1875.
Paper. $14.50. .... Vendor G0549

San Jacinto County

Murray, Joyce Martin. **Washington County, Texas Deed Abstracts, 1834-1841**. Indexed.
Parts of Walker, Burleson, Brazos, Lee, Grimes, Montgomery, Milam, and San Jacinto counties. Includes full-name index.
Cloth. $25.00. 160 pp. .... Vendor G0466

San Saba County

San Saba County, Texas Index to Probate Cases.
Paper. $8.50. .... Vendor G0549

Shelby County

Shelby County, Texas Index to Probate Cases.
Paper. $15.50. .... Vendor G0549

Travis County

Sumner, Jane. **Travis County, Texas, Early Records**. 1978. Indexed.
Cloth. $25.00. 196 pp. .... Vendor G0610

Tyler County

Tyler County, Texas Marriages 1847-1888.
Paper. $10.00. .... Vendor G0549

Van Zandt County

Van Zandt County, Texas Marriages 1855-1880.
Paper. $15.00. .... Vendor G0549

Victoria County

Victoria County, Texas Marriages 1838-1890.
Paper. $16.00. .... Vendor G0549

Walker County

Murray, Joyce Martin. **Washington County, Texas Deed Abstracts, 1834-1841**.
Indexed.
   Parts of Walker, Burleson, Brazos, Lee, Grimes, Montgomery, Milam, and San
Jacinto counties. Includes full-name index.
Cloth. $25.00. 160 pp. .... Vendor G0466

Washington County

Murray, Joyce Martin. **Washington County, Texas Deed Abstracts, 1834-1841**.
Indexed.
   Parts of Walker, Burleson, Brazos, Lee, Grimes, Montgomery, Milam, and San
Jacinto counties. Includes full-name index.
Cloth. $25.00. 160 pp. .... Vendor G0466

Ray, Worth S. **Austin [Texas] Colony Pioneers,** Including History of Bastrop, Fayette,
Grimes, Montgomery and Washington Counties, Texas. (1949) reprint 1995. Indexed.
Illus.
Cloth. $22.50. 378 pp. .... Vendor G0011

Utah

Statewide and Regional References

Dilts, Bryan Lee, comp. **1856 Utah Census Index: An Every-Name Index**. 1983.
Cloth. $99.00. 292 pp. .... Vendor G0552

Family History Library. **Family History Centers: Nevada and Utah**.
Free. 2 pp. .... Vendor G0629

Family History Library. **Research Outline: Utah**.
Leaflet. $.25. 22 pp. .... Vendor G0629

Jaussi, Laureen R., and Gloria D. Chaston. **Genealogical Records of Utah**. 1974.
Indexed. Illus.
Cloth. $8.95. 312 pp. .... Vendor G0465

Kent, Allan, ed. **Utah History Encyclopedia**. 1994. Illus.
Cloth. $50.00. 674 pp. .... Vendor G0611

May, Dean L. **Utah: A People's History**. 1987.
   A very engaging history of the state of Utah based on the author's television series
of the same name.
Paper. $15.95. 210 pp. .... Vendor G0611

Thorndale, William, and William Dollarhide. **County Boundary Map Guides to the
U.S. Federal Censuses, 1790-1920: Utah, 1851-1920**. 1987.
$5.95. .... Vendor G0552

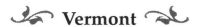

Vermont

Statewide and Regional References

Atlas of Vermont, Detailed Back Roads.
   This present-day atlas provides the researcher with the detail needed to conduct a
proper search. It is the size of a Rand McNally atlas of the entire U.S. 11" x 15½".
$16.95. .... Vendor G0611

Bartley, Scott A. **Vermont Families in 1791 Volume 1**. 1992. Indexed.
   Book #1395.
Cloth. $30.00. 311 pp. .... Vendor G0082

Benedict, G. G. **Vermont in the Civil War.** A History of the Part Taken by the
Vermont Soldiers & Sailors in the War for the Union, 1861-5. 2 vols. (1886-88)
reprint 1995.
Cloth. $65.00/Vol. I. $82.00/Vol. II. $135.00/set. 620 + 808 pp. .... Vendor G0259

Clark, Byron N. **A List of Pensioners of the War of 1812 [Vermont Claimants]**. (1904) reprint 1996. Illus.
Paper. $18.00. 171 pp. .... Vendor G0011

Crockett, Walter H. **Soldiers of the Revolutionary War Buried in Vermont.** And Anecdotes and Incidents Relating to Some of Them. (1903-04 and 1905-06) reprint 1991.
Contact vendor for information. 77 pp. .... Vendor G0011

Dodge, Nancy L. **Settlement & Cemeteries in Vermont's Northeast Kingdom**. 1986.
    Includes indexed transcripts from gravesites in Canaan, Lemington, Bloomfield, Brunswick & Maidstone, Vt., & Hereford, Quebec.
Cloth. $39.00. 197 pp. .... Vendor G0259

Family History Library. **Research Outline: Vermont**.
Leaflet. $.25. 9 pp. .... Vendor G0629

Gilman, M. D. **Bibliography of Vermont;** or, a List of Books & Pamphlets Relating in Any Way to the State. With Biographical & Other Notes. (1897) reprint 1991.
Cloth. $45.00. 349 pp. .... Vendor G0259

Goodrich, John E., ed. **Rolls of the Soldiers in the Revolutionary War, 1775-1783**. (1904) reprint 1993.
Cloth. $85.00. 927 pp. .... Vendor G0259

Holbrook, Jay Mack. **Vermont 1771 Census**. 1982.
Cloth. $25.00. 130 pp. .... Vendor G0148

Holbrook, Jay Mack. **Vermont Land Grantees 1749-1803**. 1986.
    About 15,000 grantees received land under the VT Charters or the NH Land Grants.
Microfiche. $6.00. 276 pp. on 1 fiche. .... Vendor G0148

Johnson, Herbert T. **State of Vermont.** Roster of Soldiers in the War of 1812-14. (1933) reprint 1995.
Paper. $37.50. 474 pp. .... Vendor G0011

Long, John H., ed. **New Hampshire and Vermont Atlas of Historical Boundaries**. 1993.
    A beautiful and extremely useful book detailing the changes in county boundaries from colonial times to 1990. 8½" x 11".
Cloth. $57.00. 216 pp. .... Vendor G0611

Revised Roster of Vermont Volunteers and Lists of Vermonters Who Served in the Army and Navy of the United States During the War of the Rebellion, 1861-66. Compiled under the supervision of Theodore S. Peck. (1892) reprint 1995.
Cloth. $87.50. 862 pp. .... Vendor G0259

Rollins, Alden M. **Vermont Warnings at 1779-1817, Vol. 1**. 1995.
    Book #1619.
Cloth. $39.50. 448 pp. .... Vendor G0082

Rollins, Alden M. **Vermont Warnings at 1779-1817, Vol. 2**.
    Book #1749.
Cloth. $39.50. 448 pp. .... Vendor G0082

Southern California Genealogical Society. **Sources of Genealogical Help in Vermont**.
Paper. $1.50. 8 pp. .... Vendor G0656

Thorndale, William, and William Dollarhide. **County Boundary Map Guides to the U.S. Federal Censuses, 1790-1920: New Hampshire, Vermont, 1790-1920**. 1987.
$5.95. .... Vendor G0552

U.S. Bureau of the Census. **Vermont: Heads of Families** at the Second Census of the United States Taken in the Year 1800. (1938) reprint 1995. Indexed. Illus.
Paper. $32.50. 233 pp. .... Vendor G0011

United States Bureau of the Census. **Heads of Families at the First Census of the United States Taken in the Year 1790: Vermont**. (1907) reprint 1992. Indexed. Illus.
Contact vendor for information. 95 pp. .... Vendor G0010

United States Bureau of the Census. **Heads of Families at the First Census of the United States Taken in the Year 1790: Vermont**.
Cloth, $27.50. Paper, $12.50. .... Vendor G0552

Addison County

Hemenway, Abby Maria, ed. **Vermont Historical Gazetteer, Vol. I**. A Magazine Embracing a History of Each Town, Civil, Ecclesiastical, Biographical & Military: Addison, Bennington, Caledonia, Chittenden & Essex Cos. (1868) reprint 1994.
Cloth. $105.00. 1,092 pp. .... Vendor G0259

Matthews, Rev. Lyman. **History of the Town of Cornwall**. (1862) reprint 1993.
Cloth. $39.50. xii + 356 pp. .... Vendor G0259

Smith, H. P. **History of Addison County**, with Illustrations & Biographical Sketches of Its Prominent Men & Pioneers. (1886) reprint 1992.
Cloth. $85.00. 774 + 62 pp. .... Vendor G0259

Bennington County

Aldrich, Lewis C., ed. **History of Bennington County**, with Illustrations & Biographical Sketches of Some of Its Prominent Men & Pioneers. (1889) reprint 1993.
Cloth. $59.50. 584 pp. .... Vendor G0259

Child, Hamilton, comp. **Gazetteer and Business Directory of Bennington Co. for 1880-81**. (1880) reprint 1996.
Cloth. $53.00. 500 pp. .... Vendor G0259

Hemenway, Abby Maria, ed. **Vermont Historical Gazetteer, Vol. I**. A Magazine Embracing a History of Each Town, Civil, Ecclesiastical, Biographical & Military: Addison, Bennington, Caledonia, Chittenden & Essex Cos. (1868) reprint 1994.
Cloth. $105.00. 1,092 pp. .... Vendor G0259

History of Bennington. From Vermont Historical Gazetteer, Volume V. (1891) reprint 1994.
Paper. $19.50. 108 pp. .... Vendor G0259

Caledonia County

Fairbanks, E. T. **The Town of St. Johnsbury:** A Review of 125 Years. (1914) reprint 1991.
Cloth. $59.00. 592 pp. .... Vendor G0259

Hemenway, Abby Maria, ed. **Vermont Historical Gazetteer, Vol. I.** A Magazine Embracing a History of Each Town, Civil, Ecclesiastical, Biographical & Military: Addison, Bennington, Caledonia, Chittenden & Essex Cos. (1868) reprint 1994.
Cloth. $105.00. 1,092 pp. .... Vendor G0259

History of Sutton. From Vermont Historical Gazetteer, Volume V. (1891) reprint 1994.
Paper. $11.00. 54 pp. .... Vendor G0259

Miller, E., and F. P. Wells. **History of Ryegate,** from Its Settlement by Scotch-American Farmers to 1912. (1913) reprint 1987.
Cloth. $62.00. 604 pp. .... Vendor G0259

Wells, Frederic Palmer. **History of Barnet,** from the Outbreak of the French & Indian Wars to the Present. With Genealogical Records of Many Families. (1923) reprint 1993.
Cloth. $71.50. 691 pp. .... Vendor G0259

Chittenden County

Auld, Joseph. **Picturesque Burlington:** A Handbook of Burlington & Lake Champlain, with One Hundred & Sixty-Four Illustrations. (1894) reprint 1993.
Cloth. $29.50. 190 pp. .... Vendor G0259

Hayden, Chauncy H., et al., eds. **History of Jericho.** With Family Histories. (1916) reprint 1991.
Cloth. $67.00. 665 pp. .... Vendor G0259

Hemenway, Abby Maria, ed. **Vermont Historical Gazetteer, Vol. I.** A Magazine Embracing a History of Each Town, Civil, Ecclesiastical, Biographical & Military: Addison, Bennington, Caledonia, Chittenden & Essex Cos. (1868) reprint 1994.
Cloth. $105.00. 1,092 pp. .... Vendor G0259

Research Pub. Co., comp. **Marriages of Montpelier (through 1852), Burlington (through 1833), Berlin (through 1876).** (1903) reprint 1993.
Paper. $18.00. 92 pp. .... Vendor G0259

Essex County

Benton, Everett Chamberlin. **History of Guildhall,** Containing Some Account of the . . . First Settlement in 1764 . . . and Events to 1886. With Genealogical Records. (1886) reprint 1993.
Cloth. $32.50. 270 pp. .... Vendor G0259

Dodge, Nancy L. **Gravestones of Guildhall, Vt. & Northumberland, N.H**. 1987.
Cloth. $39.00. 185 pp. .... Vendor G0259

Hemenway, Abby Maria, ed. **Vermont Historical Gazetteer, Vol. I.** A Magazine
Embracing a History of Each Town, Civil, Ecclesiastical, Biographical & Military:
Addison, Bennington, Caledonia, Chittenden & Essex Cos. (1868) reprint 1994.
Cloth. $105.00. 1,092 pp. .... Vendor G0259

Franklin County

Aldrich, L. C., ed. **History of Franklin & Grand Isle Counties**. (1891) reprint 1991.
Cloth. $82.50. 821 pp. .... Vendor G0259

Dutcher, L. L., with H. R. Whitney. **History of St. Albans,** Civil, Religious, Biographical & Statistical. With History of Sheldon. From Vermont Gazetteer. (1872)
reprint 1991.
Paper. $16.00. 107 pp. .... Vendor G0259

Hemenway, Abby Maria, ed. **Vermont Historical Gazetteer, Vol. II:** Franklin, Grand
Isle, LaMoille, Orange Counties. (1863?) reprint 1994.
Cloth. $117.50. 1,200 pp. .... Vendor G0259

Grand Isle County

Aldrich, L. C., ed. **History of Franklin & Grand Isle Counties**. (1891) reprint 1991.
Cloth. $82.50. 821 pp. .... Vendor G0259

Hemenway, Abby Maria, ed. **Vermont Historical Gazetteer, Vol. II:** Franklin, Grand
Isle, LaMoille, Orange Counties. (1863?) reprint 1994.
Cloth. $117.50. 1,200 pp. .... Vendor G0259

LaMoille County

Hemenway, Abby Maria, ed. **Vermont Historical Gazetteer, Vol. II:** Franklin, Grand
Isle, LaMoille, Orange Counties. (1863?) reprint 1994.
Cloth. $117.50. 1,200 pp. .... Vendor G0259

History of the Town of Johnson, 1784-1907. Compiled under the direction of Oread
Lit. Club. (1908) reprint 1996.
Cloth, $25.00. Paper, $15.00. 83 pp. .... Vendor G0259

Orange County

Comstock, John Moore. **Chelsea: The Origin of Chelsea and a Record of Its Institutions and Individuals.** (1944) reprint 1996.
Paper. $12.00. 62 pp. .... Vendor G0259

Hemenway, Abby Maria, ed. **Vermont Historical Gazetteer, Vol. II:** Franklin, Grand Isle, LaMoille, Orange Counties. (1863?) reprint 1994.
Cloth. $117.50. 1,200 pp. .... Vendor G0259

McKeen, S. **History of Bradford,** Containing Some Account of the Place from Its First Settlement in 1765 & the Principal Improvements & Events to 1874. With Genealogical Records. (1875) reprint 1987.
Cloth. $46.00. 459 pp. .... Vendor G0259

Wells, F. **History of Newbury,** from the Discovery of Coos Co. to 1902. With Genealogical Records. (1902) reprint 1987.
Cloth. $79.00. 779 pp. .... Vendor G0259

Orleans County

Hamilton, Esther B. **History of the Town Charleston (Named "Navy," 1803-1825).** (1955) reprint 1993.
Cloth. $21.00. 129 pp. .... Vendor G0259

Hemenway, Abby Maria, ed. **Vermont Historical Gazetteer, Vol. III:** Orleans & Rutland Cos. (1877) reprint 1994.
Cloth. $119.50. 1,245 pp. .... Vendor G0259

Rutland County

Adams, Andrew N. **History of the Town of Fair Haven**. (1870) reprint 1990.
Cloth. $52.00. 516 pp. .... Vendor G0259

Batcheller, Birney C. **People of Wallingford**. (1937) reprint 1995.
Cloth. $39.50. 317 pp. .... Vendor G0259

Caverly, A. M. **History of the Town of Pittsford,** with Biographical Sketches and Family Records. (1872) reprint 1994.
Cloth. $78.00. 756 pp. .... Vendor G0259

Hemenway, Abby Maria, ed. **Vermont Historical Gazetteer, Vol. III:** Orleans & Rutland Cos. (1877) reprint 1994.
Cloth. $119.50. 1,245 pp. .... Vendor G0259

History of Chittenden, with Illustrations & Biographical Sketches of Some of Its Prominent Men & Pioneers. (1886) reprint 1993.
Cloth. $89.00. 867 pp. .... Vendor G0259

Hollister, Hiel. **Pawlet for One Hundred Years**. (1867) reprint 1995.
Cloth. $36.00. 272 pp. .... Vendor G0259

Jenks, Margaret R. **Benson, Hubbardton and Sudbury Cemetery Inscriptions, Rutland County, Vermont**. 1993. Indexed. Illus.
Paper. $16.50. xiv + 103 pp. .... Vendor G0599

Jenks, Margaret R. **Brandon Cemetery Inscriptions, Rutland County, Vermont**. 1994. Indexed. Illus.
Paper. $25.50. xvi + 180 pp. .... Vendor G0599

Jenks, Margaret R. **Castleton Cemetery Inscriptions, Rutland County, Vermont**. 1989. Rev. ed. 1996. Indexed. Illus.
Paper. $18.00. x + 97 pp. .... Vendor G0599

Jenks, Margaret R. **Chittenden, Mendon, Pittsfield and Sherburne Cemetery Inscriptions, Rutland County, Vermont**. 1992. Indexed. Illus.
Paper. $15.50. xii + 94 pp. .... Vendor G0599

Jenks, Margaret R. **Clarendon and Shrewsbury Cemetery Inscriptions, Rutland County, Vermont**. 1992. Indexed. Illus.
Paper. $18.50. xii + 129 pp. .... Vendor G0599

Jenks, Margaret R. **Danby and Mount Tabor Cemetery Inscriptions, Rutland County, Vermont**. 1988. Rev. ed. 1993. Indexed. Illus.
Paper. $14.50. xii + 79 pp. .... Vendor G0599

Jenks, Margaret R. **Fair Haven and West Haven Cemetery Inscriptions, Rutland County, Vermont**. 1990. Rev. ed. 1994. Indexed. Illus.
Paper. $25.00. xvi + 209 pp. .... Vendor G0599

Jenks, Margaret R. **Middletown Springs and Ira Cemetery Inscriptions, Rutland County, Vermont**. (1983) reprint 1996. Indexed. Illus.
Paper. $11.50. 58 pp. .... Vendor G0599

Jenks, Margaret R. **Pawlet Cemetery Inscriptions, Rutland County, Vermont**. (1985) reprint 1996. Indexed. Illus.
Paper. $16.50. xvi + 90 pp. .... Vendor G0599

Jenks, Margaret R. **Pittsford and Proctor Cemetery Inscriptions, Rutland County, Vermont**. 1992. Indexed. Illus.
Paper. $25.50. xiv + 193 pp. .... Vendor G0599

Jenks, Margaret R. **Poultney Cemetery Inscriptions, Rutland County, Vermont**. 1983. Rev. ed. 1996. Indexed. Illus.
Paper. $18.00. xii + 103 pp. .... Vendor G0599

Jenks, Margaret R. **Rutland Cemetery Inscriptions, Rutland County, Vermont**. 1995. Indexed. Illus.
Paper. $45.00. xiv + 381 pp. .... Vendor G0599

Jenks, Margaret R. **Tinmouth Cemetery Inscriptions, Rutland County, Vermont**. 1985. Indexed. Illus.
Paper. $11.50. xii + 21 pp. .... Vendor G0599

Jenks, Margaret R. **Wallingford and Mount Holly Cemetery Inscriptions, Rutland County, Vermont**. 1992. Indexed. Illus.
Paper. $18.50. xiv + 150 pp. .... Vendor G0599

Jenks, Margaret R. **Wells Cemetery Inscriptions, Rutland County, Vermont**. 1981. Rev. ed. 1993. Indexed. Illus.
Paper. $10.50. xvi + 40 pp. .... Vendor G0599

Jenks, Margaret R. **West Rutland Cemetery Inscriptions, Rutland County, Vermont**. 1994. Indexed. Illus.
Paper. $18.50. xiv + 107 pp. .... Vendor G0599

Joslin, Frisbie, and Ruggles. **History of the Town of Poultney,** from Its Settlement to the Year 1875, with Family & Biographical Sketches & Incidents. (1875) reprint 1992.
Cloth. $41.00. 369 pp. .... Vendor G0259

Thorpe, Walter. **History of Wallingford**. (1911) reprint 1995.
Cloth. $32.50. 222 pp. .... Vendor G0259

Williams, J. C. **History & Map of Danby**. (1869) reprint 1993.
Cloth. $42.50. 391 pp. .... Vendor G0259

Washington County

Dewey, William T., and James F. Dewey. **Marriage Records of Barre and of Berlin, Washington County, Vermont.** Originally published in the *Vermont Antiquarian.* Reprinted. Indexed.
   The records of Barre are for 1793-1850 while those of Berlin are for 1791-1876.
Paper. $8.00. 60 pp. .... Vendor G0561

Dewey, William T. **Marriages in Montpelier, Vermont, 1791-1852**. 1984. Indexed.
Paper. $7.00. 56 pp. .... Vendor G0561

Gregory, John. **Centennial Proceedings & Historical Incidents of the Early Settlers of Northfield,** with Biographical Sketches. (1878) reprint 1993.
Cloth. $38.00. 320 pp. .... Vendor G0259

Hemenway, Abby Maria, ed. **History of Barre.** From Vermont Historical Gazetteer, Volume IV. (1882) reprint 1994.
Paper. $6.00. 30 pp. .... Vendor G0259

Hemenway, Abby Maria, ed. **History of Berlin.** From Vermont Historical Gazetteer, Volume IV. (1882) reprint 1994.
Paper. $5.00. 21 pp. .... Vendor G0259

Hemenway, Abby Maria, ed. **History of Cabot.** From Vermont Historical Gazetteer, Volume IV. (1882) reprint 1994.
Paper. $11.00. 54 pp. .... Vendor G0259

Hemenway, Abby Maria, ed. **Vermont Historical Gazetteer, Vol. IV:** (Washington Co.) Including a County Chapter & the Histories of the Towns . . . By "Native & Resident Historians." (1882) reprint 1994.
Cloth. $92.50. 932 pp. .... Vendor G0259

History of Calais. From Vermont Historical Gazetteer, Volume IV. (1882) reprint 1994.
Paper. $11.00. 55 pp. .... Vendor G0259

History of Marshfield. From Vermont Historical Gazetteer, Volume IV. (1882) reprint 1994.
Paper. $5.00. 25 pp. .... Vendor G0259

History of Middlesex. From Vermont Historical Gazetteer, Volume IV. (1882) reprint 1994.
Paper. $5.50. 26 pp. .... Vendor G0259

History of Northfield. From Vermont Historical Gazetteer, Volume IV. Incl. East Montpelier. (1882) reprint 1994.
Paper. $17.50. 101 pp. .... Vendor G0259

History of Plainfield. From Vermont Historical Gazetteer, Volume IV. Incl. East Montpelier. (1882) reprint 1994.
Paper. $5.00. 21 pp. .... Vendor G0259

History of Roxbury. From Vermont Historical Gazetteer, Volume IV. Incl. East Montpelier. (1882) reprint 1994.
Paper. $6.50. 33 pp. .... Vendor G0259

History of Waterbury. From Vermont Historical Gazetteer, Volume IV. Incl. East Montpelier. (1882) reprint 1994.
Paper. $12.00. 60 pp. .... Vendor G0259

History of Worcester. From Vermont Historical Gazetteer, Volume IV. Incl. East Montpelier. (1882) reprint 1994.
Paper. $6.00. 29 pp. .... Vendor G0259

Jones, M. B. **History of the Town of Waitsfield, 1782-1908,** with Family Genealogies. (1909) reprint 1987.
Cloth. $57.00. 534 pp. .... Vendor G0259

Research Pub. Co., comp. **Marriages of Montpelier (through 1852), Burlington (through 1833), Berlin (through 1876)**. (1903) reprint 1993.
Paper. $18.00. 92 pp. .... Vendor G0259

Thompson, D. P. **History of Montpelier,** from the Time It Was Chartered in 1781 to 1860, with Biographical Sketches of Its Most Noted Deceased Citizens. (1860) reprint 1993.
Cloth. $36.00. 312 pp. .... Vendor G0259

Walton, Eliakim P. **History of Montpelier.** From Vermont Historical Gazetteer, Volume IV. Incl. East Montpelier. (1882) reprint 1994.
Cloth. $39.50. 352 pp. .... Vendor G0259

Windham County

Burnham, Henry. **History of Brattleboro.** From Vermont Historical Gazetteer, Volume V. Edited by Abby Maria Hemenway. (1891) reprint 1994.
Cloth. $27.50. 191 pp. .... Vendor G0259

Child, Hamilton. **Index of Gazetteer of Windham County, Vermont**. (1884) reprint 1987.
Paper. $12.00. 205 pp. .... Vendor G0691

Foster, A. **History of Putney.** From Vermont Historical Gazetteer, Vol. V. (1891) reprint 1994.
Paper. $11.00. 53 pp. .... Vendor G0259

Green, J. J., C. Burnham, and J. H. Merrifield. **1774-1874: Centennial Proceedings and Other Historical Facts and Incidents, Relating to Newfane, the County Seat of Windham County.** (1877) reprint 1995.
Cloth. $35.00. 256 pp. .... Vendor G0259

Hayes, Lyman S. **History of the Town of Rockingham,** Including the Villages of Bellows Falls, Saxtons River, Rockingham, Cambridgeport & Bartonsville, 1753-1907, with Family Genealogies. (1907) reprint 1995.
Cloth. $87.00. 850 pp. .... Vendor G0259

Hemenway, Abby Maria, ed. **Vermont Historical Gazetteer, Vol. V:** The Towns of Windham County. (1891) reprint 1994.
Cloth. $115.00. 1,204 pp. .... Vendor G0259

History of Brookline. From Vermont Historical Gazetteer, Volume V. (1891) reprint 1994.
Paper. $6.00. 27 pp. .... Vendor G0259

History of Guilford. From Vermont Historical Gazetteer, Vol. V. (1891) reprint 1994.
Paper. $16.00. 80 pp. .... Vendor G0259

History of Marlboro. From Vermont Historical Gazetteer, Vol. V. (1891) reprint 1994.
Paper. $5.50. 22 pp. .... Vendor G0259

History of Newfane. From Vermont Historical Gazetteer, Volume V. (1891) reprint 1994.
Paper. $7.00. 36 pp. .... Vendor G0259

History of Vernon. From Vermont Historical Gazetteer, Volume V. (1891) reprint 1994.
Paper. $11.00. 54 pp. .... Vendor G0259

History of Westminster. From Vermont Historical Gazetteer, Volume V. (1891) reprint 1994.
Paper. $19.50. 110 pp. .... Vendor G0259

History of Whitingham. From Vermont Historical Gazetteer, Volume V. (1891) reprint 1994.
Paper. $8.00. 40 pp. .... Vendor G0259

Mansfield, D. L. **History of Dummerston.** From Vermont Historical Gazetteer, Vol. V. (1891) reprint 1994.
Cloth. $29.50. 216 pp. .... Vendor G0259

Palmer, Francis A. **History of the Town of Grafton.** (1954) reprint 1993.
Cloth. $21.00. 120 pp. .... Vendor G0259

Stevens, Ken. **A Complete Listing of Gravestone Inscriptions in Putney, Vermont.** 1994. Indexed.
Paper. $16.50. iv + 111 pp. .... Vendor G0599

Windsor County

Aldrich, Lewis Cass, and Frank R. Holmes, eds. **History of Windsor County,** with Illustrations & Biographical Sketches of Some of Its Prominent Men & Pioneers. (1891) reprint 1993.
Cloth. $97.50. 1,005 pp. .... Vendor G0259

Davis, Gilbert A. **Centennial Celebration, Together with an Historical Sketch of Reading, Windsor Co.,** and Its Inhabitants from the First Settlement of the Town to 1874. (1874) reprint 1996.
Cloth, $29.50. Paper, $19.50. 169 pp. .... Vendor G0259

Davis, Gilbert A. **History of Reading, Windsor Co.** 2nd ed. (1903) reprint 1987.
Cloth. $43.00. 375 + 12 pp. .... Vendor G0259

Goddard, M. E., and Henry V. Partridge. **History of Norwich,** with Portraits & Illustrations. (1905) reprint 1994.
Cloth. $35.00. 276 pp. .... Vendor G0259

Hubbard, C. H., and J. Dartt. **History of the Town of Springfield,** with a Genealogical Record. (1895) reprint 1990.
Cloth. $64.50. 618 pp. .... Vendor G0259

Lovejoy, E. M. W. **History of Royalton, with Family Genealogies, 1769-1911**. (1911) reprint 1991.
Cloth. $105.00. 1,146 pp. .... Vendor G0259

Newton, William Monroe. **History of Barnard,** with Family Genealogies, 1761-1927. 2 vols. (1927) reprint 1996.
Volume I: History.
Volume II: Genealogies.
Cloth. $42.00/Vol. I. $54.00/Vol. II. $89.00/set. 368 + 511 pp. .... Vendor G0259

Tucker, William Howard. **History of Hartford, July 4, 1761-April 4, 1889**. (1889) reprint 1992.
Cloth. $52.50. 488 pp. .... Vendor G0259

Vail, Henry Hobart. **Pomfret, Vermont, in Two Volumes.** Edited by Emma Chandler White. (1930) reprint 1993.
Cloth. $39.00/vol., $69.50/set. 338 + 327 pp. .... Vendor G0259

Warner, Rufus S. **Record of Deaths in the Town of Ludlow, Vermont from 1790-1901 Inclusive**. 1995.
Paper. $27.00. .... Vendor G0691

⤜ Virginia ⤛

(see also West Virginia)

Statewide and Regional References

Abbot, William W. **A Virginia Chronology 1585-1783.** "To pass away the time." (1957) reprint 1994. Illus.
Paper. $10.00. 78 pp. .... Vendor G0011

Abercrombie, Janice Luck, and Richard Slatten. **Virginia Revolutionary "Publick" Claims.** 3 vols. Indexed.
    The entire set of seventy county booklets (see listings under individual counties), in three volumes, with a single comprehensive index at the end of Volume 3.
Cloth. $200.00. 1,131 pp. .... Vendor G0632

Alvord, Clarence Walworth, and Lee Bidgood. **The First Explorations of the Trans-Allegheny Region by the Virginians, 1650-1674.** (1912) reprint 1996. Indexed. Illus.
Paper. $24.00. 275 pp. .... Vendor G0011

Atlas of Virginia Topographical.
This present-day atlas provides the researcher with the detail needed to conduct a proper search. It is the size of a Rand McNally atlas of the entire U.S. 11" x 15½".
$16.95. .... Vendor G0611

Atlases & Gazetteers: Virginia. Illus.
Paper. $16.95. 80 pp. .... Vendor G0632

Axelson, Edith F. **A Guide to Episcopal Church Records in Virginia**. 1988.
A major reference tool for every genealogical researcher who deals with the Church of England in the colonial period and the successor Protestant Episcopal Church.
Paper. 15.95. vi + 136 pp. .... Vendor G0632

Axelson, Edith F., comp. **Virginia Postmasters and Post Offices, 1789-1832**. 1991. Indexed.
Paper. $20.00. 248 pp. .... Vendor G0632

Barton, R. T. **The Reports of . . . Randolph and . . . Barradall on Decisions of the General Court of Virginia, 1728-1741.** 2 vols. (1909) reprint 1996. Indexed.
Paper. $59.95/set. 764 pp. in all. .... Vendor G0632

Bell, Landon C. **The Old Free State.** A Contribution to the History of Lunenburg County and Southside Virginia. 2 vols. (1927) reprint 1995. Indexed.
Paper. $95.00. 623 + 644 pp. .... Vendor G0011

Bentley, Elizabeth Petty. **Index to the 1810 Census of Virginia**. (1980) reprint 1996.
Paper. $29.00. 366 pp. .... Vendor G0011

Billings. **The Old Dominion in the Seventeenth Century: A Documentary History of Virginia, 1606-1689**. 1975.
This convenient collection of 17th-century Virginia documentary source materials reconstructs the history of Virginia using the observations and legal records of the colonists themselves.
Paper. $14.95. 324 pp. .... Vendor G0611

Bockstruck, Lloyd DeWitt. **Virginia's Colonial Soldiers**. 1990. Indexed.
Cloth. $30.00. 443 pp. .... Vendor G0010

Boddie, John Bennett. **Colonial Surry [Virginia]**. (1948) reprint 1992. Indexed.
A collection of genealogical data from important name lists for Colonial Surry, which once encompassed almost the entire southern part of Virginia (i.e., fourteen present-day Virginia counties).
Cloth. $25.00. 249 pp. .... Vendor G0011

Boddie, John Bennett. **Southside Virginia Families, Volume I**. (1955) reprint 1996. Indexed. Illus.
Paper. $31.50. 380 pp. .... Vendor G0011

Boddie, John Bennett. **Southside Virginia Families, Volume II**. (1956) reprint 1996. Indexed. Illus.
Paper. $29.50. 304 pp. .... Vendor G0011

Boddie, John Bennett. **Virginia Historical Genealogies**. (1954) reprint 1996. Indexed. Illus.
Paper. $32.50. 384 pp. .... Vendor G0011

Boogher, William F. **Gleanings of Virginia History.** An Historical and Genealogical Collection, Largely from Original Sources. (1903) reprint 1995. Indexed.
Paper. $35.00. 443 pp. .... Vendor G0011

The British Public Record Office: History, Description, Record Groups, Finding Aids, and Materials for American History, with Special Reference to Virginia. (1960) reprint 1984.
Paper. $7.95. 178 pp. .... Vendor G0553

Brock, R. A. **Virginia and Virginians.** Reprint.
    A reprint of his 1880s biographical sketches. This volume contains the counties of Elizabeth City, Warwick, Nansemond, Nottoway, Prince Edward, and Halifax.
Paper. $7.50. .... Vendor G0549

Brock, Robert Alonzo. **Huguenot Emigration to Virginia. . .** With an Appendix of Genealogies Presenting Data of the Fontaine, Maury, Dupuy, Trabue, Marye, Chastain, Cocke, and Other Families. (1886) reprint 1995. Indexed.
Paper. $23.00. 255 pp. .... Vendor G0011

Brock, Robert Alonzo, and Virginia A. Lewis. **Virginia and Virginians.** 2 vols. (1888?) reprint 1996.
Cloth. $65.00. 813 pp. in all. .... Vendor G0011

Brown, Stuart E., Jr. **Pocahontas** [In the Words of Her Contemporaries]. (1989) reprint 1995. Illus.
Paper. $9.95. 36 pp. .... Vendor G0011

Brumbaugh, Gaius Marcus. **Revolutionary War Records: Virginia.** Virginia Army and Navy Forces with Bounty Land Warrants for Virginia Military District of Ohio, and Virginia Military Scrip; from Federal and State Archives. (1936) reprint 1995. Indexed. Illus.
Cloth. $45.00. 707 pp. .... Vendor G0010

Burgess, Louis A. **Virginia Soldiers of 1776,** Compiled from Documents . . . in the Virginia Land Office. 3 vols. (1927, 1929) reprint 1994. Indexed.
Paper. $125.00. 1,514 pp. .... Vendor G0011

Butler, Stuart Lee. **A Guide to Virginia Militia Units in the War of 1812.** 1988. Indexed. Illus.
Paper. $22.00. 340 pp. .... Vendor G0632

Butler, Stuart Lee, comp. **Virginia Soldiers in the United States Army, 1800-1815.** 1986. Indexed.
Paper. $17.00. 188 pp. .... Vendor G0632

Campbell, James Brown. **Across the Wide Missouri: The Diary of a Journey from Virginia to Missouri in 1819 and Back Again in 1822.**
Paper. $19.95. .... Vendor G0632

Casey, Joseph J. **Personal Names in Hening's Statutes at Large of Virginia and Shepherd's Continuation.** (1896) reprint 1995.
Paper. $17.50. 159 pp. .... Vendor G0011

VIRGINIA GENEALOGY

SOME PROMINENT VIRGINIA FAMILIES
Louise Pecquet du Bellet
Of all the compilations of Virginia genealogies this is undoubtedly one of the most comprehensive. In the preparation of the work the author drew on letters, diaries, manuscripts, books, newspapers, reminiscences, and original records. Intended at first as a history of the descendants of Edward Jaqulin and Martha Cary, the book soon became a compendium of Virginia families, comprising hundreds of separate genealogies and tracing descendants through six, seven, and eight generations. The genealogies are well and fully augmented by will extracts, obituary notices, manuscript entries, parish vestry and register notations, marriage notices, newspaper excerpts, gravestone transcriptions, and a great variety of biographical matter.
4 vols. 1,715 pp. in all, illus., paper. (1907), repr. 1994. #1530. $135.00

HISTORY OF SOUTHWEST VIRGINIA, 1746–1786; WASHINGTON COUNTY, 1777–1870 With a re-arranged Index and an added Table of Contents
Lewis Preston Summers
This is the definitive history of Southwest Virginia, the area originally comprising Botetourt, Fincastle, and Washington counties and now embracing nineteen present-day counties of Virginia and seventeen of West Virginia. Numerous lists of genealogical importance are scattered throughout the text and especially the appendices, where researchers will discover several thousand ancestors linked to Washington County during the 100 years commencing with the American Revolution. In addition, a separate section is devoted to biographical sketches of more than 100 prominent citizens and includes inset portrait illustrations.
912 pp., illus., indexed, paper. (1903, 1971), repr. 1995. #5675. $65.00

GENEALOGICAL RECORDS OF BUCKINGHAM COUNTY, VIRGINIA
Edythe Rucker Whitley
This is one of the few collections of genealogical source records on Buckingham County ever published. Records abstracted include the tax lists of 1764, 1773, 1774, and 1800; military records of the Revolution and the War of 1812; land grants; a few scattered marriage records; and records of the settlement known as Planterstown. Highlighting the work is a collection of family sketches.
162 pp., indexed, paper. (1984), repr. 1996. #6349. $19.00

THE FIRST EXPLORATIONS OF THE TRANS-ALLEGHENY REGION BY THE VIRGINIANS, 1650–1674
Clarence Walworth Alvord & Lee Bidgood
The explorations of Virginia's colonial hinterland to its convergence with the Ohio River valley, undertaken by a group of intrepid 17th-century Virginia pioneers, are among the least understood accomplishments of our history. Within these pages are printed the sources of information concerning the western explorations of these Virginians, and they leave no doubt about the events. Authors Alvord and Bidgood recount the stories of the various expeditions, demonstrating how the interplay of economic motive and love of adventure conspired to lay the groundwork for colonial Virginia's claim on much of the Ohio territory.
275 pp., illus., indexed, paper. (1912), repr. 1996. #9028. $24.00

VIRGINIA VALLEY RECORDS Genealogical and Historical Materials of Rockingham County, Virginia and Related Regions
John W. Wayland
This volume is largely a source-book of genealogical and historical materials compiled from public records of the counties of Rockingham, Augusta, Greenbrier, Wythe, and Montgomery. Contents include Rockingham Marriages, 1795–1825; Rockingham Landowners, 1789; Augusta County Church Records, 1756–1844; Men in Service Against the Indians, 1774; Rockingham Militia, 1788; Early Settlers in East Rockingham; Extracts from Augusta Court Records; and Rockingham Wills. The book also includes sketches of a number of families in the area.
491 pp., map, indexed, paper. (1930), repr. 1996. #6180. $36.50

HISTORY OF AUGUSTA COUNTY, VIRGINIA
J. Lewis Peyton
The book at hand is the standard work on the county, and it is essentially a narrative account of Augusta from its aboriginal beginnings and Spotswood's discovery of the Valley of Virginia through the Civil War. Genealogists will value the book for its genealogical and biographical sketches of the following pioneering Augusta County families found in the Appendix to the volume: Baldwin, Bell, Campbell, Christian, Crawford, Fleming, Hanger, Hughes, Johnson, Koiner, Lee, Lewis, McCue, McDowell, McCulloch, Madison, Mathews, Peyton, Poe, Porterfield, Preston, Sheffey, Stuart, Tate, Waddell, Wayt, Wetzel, and Zane.
428 pp., indexed, paper. (Second ed., 1953), repr. 1996. #9270. $36.00

CLEARFIELD COMPANY
200 EAST EAGER STREET, BALTIMORE, MD 21202
1-800-296-6687

Cerny, Johni, and Gary J. Zimmerman, comps. **Before Germanna.** 12 vols. 1990. Indexed.

Vol. 1: Johann Michael Willheit, Anna Maria Hengsteler, 55 pp.
Vol. 2: Clore, Kaifer, Thomas, 58 pp.
Vol. 3: Blankenbaker, Fleshman, Slucter, 45 pp.
Vol. 4: Weaver, Utz, Flog, 57 pp.
Vol. 5: Sheible, Peck, Milker, Smith, Holt, 59 pp.
Vol. 6: Broyles, Paulitz, Moyer, Motz, 46 pp.
Vol. 7: Aylor, Castler, Maspiel, Reiner, 72 pp.
Vol. 8: Snyder, Amburger, Kerker, Kapler, 72 pp.
Vol. 9: Zimmerman, Yowell, Mercklin, Wegman, and Leatherer Families, 71 pp.
Vol. 10: Yager, Stolts, Crees, Beyerbach, 69 pp.
Vol. 11: Christler, Baumgartner, Deer, Dieter, Lotspeich, 73 pp.
Vol. 12: Wayland, Albrect, Cook, 50 pp.

Paper. $52.95/set. $5.95/vol. 59 pp. .... Vendor G0552

Chalkley, Lyman. **Chronicles of the Scotch-Irish Settlement of Virginia, Extracted from the Original Court Records of Augusta Co., 1745-1800.** 3 vols. (1912) reprint 1997.
Contact vendor for information. 623 + 652 + 712 pp. .... Vendor G0010

Clark, Jewell T., and Elizabeth Terry Long, comps. **A Guide to Church Records in the Archives Branch, Virginia State Library and Archives.** Reprint 1988.
Paper. $10.00. x + 271 pp. .... Vendor G0553

Clemens, William Montgomery. **Virginia Wills Before 1799.** A Complete Abstract Register of All Names Mentioned in over 600 Recorded Wills. (1924) reprint 1986.
Cloth. $10.00. 107 pp. .... Vendor G0010

Cocke, Charles Francis. **Parish Lines: Diocese of Southern Virginia**. (1964) reprint 1996.
Paper. $15.00. 287 pp. .... Vendor G0553

Cocke, Charles Francis. **Parish Lines: Diocese of Southwestern Virginia**. (1960) reprint 1980.
Paper. $10.00. 196 pp. .... Vendor G0553

Cocke, Charles Francis. **Parish Lines: Diocese of Virginia**. (1967) reprint 1978.
Paper. $10.00. xv + 321 pp. .... Vendor G0553

Committee of State Library. **Colonial Records of Virginia**. (1874) reprint 1992.
Cloth. $17.50. 106 pp. .... Vendor G0011

Craven, Wesley Frank. **The Virginia Company of London, 1606-1624**. (1957) reprint 1995. Illus.
Paper. $10.00. 70 pp. .... Vendor G0011

Crozier, William Armstrong. **Virginia Colonial Militia, 1651-1776** Vol. II of the Virginia County Records Series. (1905) reprint 1986. Indexed.
Cloth. $15.00. 144 pp. .... Vendor G0010

Crozier, William Armstrong. **Virginia County Records, Vol. VI—Miscellaneous County Records**. (1909) reprint 1994. Indexed.
Paper. $27.50. 326 pp. .... Vendor G0011

Crozier, William Armstrong. **Virginia County Records, Vol. VII—Miscellaneous County Records**. (1909) reprint 1994. Indexed.
Paper. $21.00. 218 pp. .... Vendor G0011

Crozier, William Armstrong. **Virginia County Records, Vol. IX—Miscellaneous County Records**. (1911) reprint 1997. Indexed.
Contact vendor for information. 151 pp. .... Vendor G0011

Crozier, William Armstrong. **Virginia County Records, Vol. X—Miscellaneous County Records**. (1912) reprint 1997.
Contact vendor for information. 95 pp. .... Vendor G0011

Crozier, William Armstrong. **Virginia County Records, Vol. I (New Series)—Westmoreland County**. (1913) reprint 1997. Indexed.
Contact vendor for information. 110 pp. .... Vendor G0011

Crumrine, Boyd. **Virginia Court Records in Southwestern Pennsylvania.** Records of the District of West Augusta and Ohio and Yohogania Counties, Virginia 1775-1780. (1902, 1905) reprint 1997. Indexed. Illus.
   The minute books of the old Virginia courts herein transcribed cover the District of West Augusta and Yohogania and Ohio counties during the period when Virginia claimed and exercised jurisdiction over what are now the Pennsylvania counties of Washington, Greene, Fayette, Westmoreland, and Allegheny.
Contact vendor for information. 542 pp. .... Vendor G0011

Currer-Briggs, Noel. **English Adventurers and Virginian Settlers.** 2 vols. 1969.
   Material relating to 17th-century emigrants from East Anglia to Virginia.
Paper. £30.00. .... Vendor G0579

des Cognets, Louis, Jr. **English Duplicates of Lost Virginia Records**. (1958) reprint 1990. Indexed.
Cloth. $25.00. 380 pp. .... Vendor G0010

Dickinson, Bill. **Diggin' for Roots in Old Virginia**. 1995. Indexed.
Paper. $24.95. 175 pp. .... Vendor G0011

Dilts, Bryan Lee, comp. **1890 Virginia Veterans Census Index.** 2nd ed. 1986. Illus.
Cloth. $19.00. 29 pp. .... Vendor G0552

Doran, Michael F. **Atlas of County Boundary Changes in Virginia: 1634-1895**. 1987.
Paper. $19.95. viii + 61 pp. .... Vendor G0632

du Bellet, Louise Pecquet. **Some Prominent Virginia Families.** 2 vols. in 4. (1907) reprint 1994. Illus.
Paper. $135.00. 1,715 pp. in all. .... Vendor G0011

Duke. **Don't Carry Me Back: Narratives by Former Virginia Slaves**. 1996.
   Slave narratives provide first-hand documentary on the slave experience in Virginia.
Paper. $19.95. 264 pp. .... Vendor G0611

Duvall, Lindsay O., ed., and Beverley Fleet, comp. **The Virginia Company of London, 1607-1624, Vol. 3**. (1950) reprint 1983. Indexed.
Paper. $17.50. 118 pp. .... Vendor G0610

Eckenrode, Hamilton J. **List of the Colonial Soldiers of Virginia**. (1917) reprint 1996.
Paper. $12.00. 91 pp. .... Vendor G0011

Eckenrode, Hamilton J., comp. **Virginia Soldiers of the American Revolution.** 2 vols. (1912-13) reprint 1989.
Cloth. $25.00. 488 + 335 pp. .... Vendor G0553

Egerton, Douglas R. **Gabriel's Rebellion: The Virginia Slave Conspiracies of 1800-1802**. 1993.
   The dramatic story of two related Virginia slave revolts in 1800 and 1802.
Paper. $13.95. 262 pp. .... Vendor G0611

Elliott, Katherine B. **Emigrations to Other States from Southside Virginia.** 2 vols. (1966) reprint 1983. Indexed.
Paper. $25.00/vol. 138 + 156 pp. .... Vendor G0610

Ely, William. **The Big Sandy Valley.** A History of the People and Country. (1887) reprint 1993. Indexed. Illus.
   The Big Sandy Valley, which is today situated mostly in Eastern Kentucky, encompasses all or part of sixteen counties in Kentucky, Virginia, and West Virginia.
Paper. $38.50. 500 pp. .... Vendor G0011

Everett, Alexander H. **Life of Patrick Henry**.
Paper. $15.00. .... Vendor G0549

Executive Journals of the Council of Colonial Virginia: Volume 1, 1680-1699. Edited by H. R. McIlwaine. (1925) reprint 1976.
Cloth. $24.95. xi + 587 pp. .... Vendor G0553

Executive Journals of the Council of Colonial Virginia: Volume 2, 1699-1705. Edited by H. R. McIlwaine. (1927) reprint 1976.
Cloth. $24.95. xi + 492 pp. .... Vendor G0553

Executive Journals of the Council of Colonial Virginia: Volume 3, 1705-1721. Edited by H. R. McIlwaine. (1928) reprint 1976.
Cloth. $24.95. vii + 679 pp. .... Vendor G0553

Executive Journals of the Council of Colonial Virginia: Volume 4, 1721-1739. Edited by H. R. McIlwaine. (1930) reprint 1978.
Cloth. $24.95. lvii + 555 pp. .... Vendor G0553

Executive Journals of the Council of Colonial Virginia: Volume 6, 1754-1775 (Volume 5, 1739-1754, is out of print). Edited by Benjamin J. Hillman. 1966.
Cloth. $24.95. xii + 768 pp. .... Vendor G0553

Family History Library. **Research Outline: Virginia**.
Leaflet. $.25. 16 pp. .... Vendor G0629

Felldin, Jeanne Robey. **Index to the 1820 Census of Virginia**. 1981.
Cloth. $30.00. 486 pp. .... Vendor G0010

The First Laws of the State of Virginia. (1785) reprint 1982.
Cloth. $62.50. 235 pp. .... Vendor G0118

Fleet, Beverley. **Virginia Colonial Abstracts.** 3 vols. (1937-1949) reprint 1988. Indexed.
Cloth. $50.00/vol. 2,087 pp. total. .... Vendor G0010

Foley, Louise Pledge Heath. **Early Virginia Families Along the James River. Vol. II,** Charles City County-Prince George County. (1978) reprint 1990. Indexed. Illus.
Cloth. $25.00. x + 201 pp. .... Vendor G0010

Foley, Louise Pledge Heath. **Early Virginia Families Along the James River. Vol. III,** James City County-Surry County. 1990. Indexed. Illus.
Cloth. $25.00. vii + 159 pp. .... Vendor G0010

Gannett, Henry. **A Gazetteer of Virginia and West Virginia.** 2 vols. in 1. (1904) reprint 1994.
Paper. $26.50. 323 pp. in all. .... Vendor G0011

Genealogical Research at the Virginia State Library. 1994.
Free. 16 pp. .... Vendor G0553

Genealogies of Virginia Families. From Tyler's Quarterly Historical and Genealogical Magazine. 5 vols. 1981. Indexed. Illus.
Vol. I: Albidgton-Gerlache. 894 pp.
Vol. II: Gildart-Pettus. 939 pp.
Vol. III: Pinkethman-Tyler. 892 pp.
Vol. IV: Walker-Yarkley. 896 pp.
Cloth. $45.00/vol., $180.00/set. 3,621 pp. in all. .... Vendor G0010

Genealogies of Virginia Families. From the William and Mary College Quarterly. 5 vols. 1982. Indexed. Illus.
Vol. I: Adams-Clopton. 944 pp.
Vol. II: Cobb-Hay. 990 pp.
Vol. III: Heale-Muscoe. 903 pp.
Vol. IV: Neville-Terrill. 893 pp.
Vol. V: Thompson-Yates. 1,010 pp.
Cloth. $45.00/vols. I & III-V. Contact vendor for information regarding Vol. II. 4,740 pp. in all. .... Vendor G0010

Gill, Harold B., Jr. **Apprentices of Virginia, 1623-1800**. 1989.
   A comprehensive listing of apprentices and their artisan masters for Virginia's colonial era to 1800.
Paper. $16.95. 304 pp. .... Vendor G0570

Gray, Gertrude E. **Virginia Northern Neck Land Grants, 1694-1742. [Vol. I]**. (1987) reprint 1988. Indexed.
Contact vendor for information. 184 pp. .... Vendor G0010

Gray, Gertrude E. **Virginia Northern Neck Land Grants, 1742-1775. [Vol. II]**. (1988) reprint 1993. Indexed.
Cloth. $25.00. 282 pp. .... Vendor G0010

Gray, Gertrude E. **Virginia Northern Neck Land Grants, 1775-1800. [Vol. III]**. 1993. Indexed.
Cloth. $28.50. 293 pp. .... Vendor G0010

Gray, Gertrude E. **Virginia Northern Neck Land Grants, 1800-1862. [Vol. IV]**. 1993. Indexed.
Cloth. $28.50. 311 pp. .... Vendor G0010

Greer, George Cabell. **Early Virginia Immigrants, 1623-1666**. (1912) reprint 1989.
Cloth. Contact vendor for information. 376 pp. .... Vendor G0010

Greer, George Cabell. **Early Virginia Immigrants, 1623-1666**. (1912) reprint 1993.
Cloth. $39.50. 376 pp. .... Vendor G0259

Gwathmey, John H. **Historical Register of Virginians in the Revolution**. (1938) reprint 1996.
Cloth. $45.00. 872 pp. .... Vendor G0010

Hall, Wilmer L., ed. **Journals of the Senate of Virginia: October Session, 1792**. 1949.
Cloth. $10.00. 151 pp. .... Vendor G0553

Hamlin, Charles Hughes. **They Went Thataway**. 3 vols. in 1. (1964-66) reprint 1995. Indexed.
   Provides substantive evidence of the migration of individuals and families to Virginia or from Virginia to other states, countries, or territories.
Paper. $38.50. 440 pp. in all. .... Vendor G0011

Hamlin, Charles Hughes. **Virginia Ancestors and Adventurers**. 3 vols. in 1. (1967-1973) reprint 1995. Indexed.
Paper. $32.50. 412 pp. in all. .... Vendor G0011

Hatch, Charles E., Jr. **The First Seventeen Years: Virginia, 1607-1624**. (1957) reprint 1994. Illus.
Paper. $15.00 . 124 pp. .... Vendor G0011

Hayden, Horace Edwin. **Virginia Genealogies**. A Genealogy of the Glassell Family of Scotland and Virginia, Also of the Families of Ball, Brown, Bryan, Conway, Daniel, Ewell, Holladay, Lewis, Littlepage, Moncure, Peyton, Robinson, Scott, Taylor, Wallace, and Others of Virginia and Maryland. (1891) reprint 1996. Indexed.
Paper. $49.95. 777 pp. .... Vendor G0011

Haydon, Robert. **Thomas Haydon—England to Virginia—1657**. (1995) reprint 1996. Indexed. Illus.
The life and times of Thomas Haydon circa 1640 to 1717. The development of social structure of Virginia from 1657 to 1717.
Cloth. $39.00. 105 pp. .... Vendor G0372

Heavener, Rev. Ulysses S. A. **German New River Settlement: Virginia**. (1929) reprint 1992. Indexed.
Paper. $12.50. 94 pp. .... Vendor G0011

Heisey, John W. **Virginia Genealogy Guide**.
Paper. $12.00. 42 pp. .... Vendor G0574

Hendrick, Burton J. **The Lees of Virginia.** Biography of a Family. (1935) reprint 1996. Indexed. Illus.
Paper. $39.95. 455 pp. .... Vendor G0011

Hiden, Martha W. **How Justice Grew.** Virginia Counties: An Abstract of Their Formation. (1957) reprint 1994. Indexed. Illus.
Paper. $12.00. 101 pp. .... Vendor G0011

The Historical Records Survey of Virginia/Work Projects Adm. **Guide to the Manuscript Collections of the Virginia Baptist Historical Society, Supplement No. 1: Index to Obituary Notices in *The Religious Herald*, Richmond, Virginia 1828-1938**. (1940) reprint 1996.
Paper. $33.50. 386 pp. .... Vendor G0011

The Historical Records Survey of Virginia/Work Projects Adm. **Guide to the Manuscript Collections of the Virginia Baptist Historical Society, Supplement No. 2: Index to Marriage Notices in *The Religious Herald*, Richmond, Virginia 1828-1938**. In Two Volumes. (1941) reprint 1996.
Paper. $56.50. 371 + 316 pp. .... Vendor G0011

The Historical Records Survey of Virginia/Work Projects Adm. **Index to Marriage Notices in the Southern Churchman, 1835-1941.** In Two Volumes. 2 vols. in 1. (1942) reprint 1996.
Paper. $49.95. 316 + 327 pp. .... Vendor G0011

Hogg, et al. **Virginia Cemeteries: A Guide to Resources**. 1989.
Survey of most VA cemetery records, published and unpublished, and those in progress. What's available, and where. Useful reference.
Paper. $14.95. 311 pp. .... Vendor G0611

Holbrook, Jay Mack. **Virginia's Colonial Schoolmasters**. 1966.
Documented account of all known schoolmasters from 1660-1776, tells when and where they taught. Over 300 identified.
Microfiche. $6.00 238 pp. on 1 fiche. .... Vendor G0148

Hopkins, William Lindsay, comp. **Some Wills from the Burned Counties of Virginia**.
Paper. $30.00. .... Vendor G0632

Hopkins, William Lindsay, comp. **Virginia Revolutionary War Land Grant Claims, 1783-1850 (Rejected)**. 1988. Indexed.
Paper. $35.00. iv + 293 pp. .... Vendor G0632

Howe, Henry. **Historical Collections of Virginia.** With an Added Index of Names. (1845) reprint 1993. Indexed. Illus.
Paper. $42.50. 568 pp. .... Vendor G0011

Hummel, Ray O., Jr., ed. **A List of Places Included in 19th Century Virginia Directories.** (1960) reprint 1981.
Paper. $7.95. 153 pp. .... Vendor G0553

Index to the Virginia Genealogist, Volumes 1 to 20.
    In the nearly 1,000 pages of this index, there are over 175,000 references relating to Virginia and West Virginia data. With the exception of Swem's *Virginia Historical Index*,this is the most comprehensive index to Virginia material ever published.
Cloth. $50.00. .... Vendor G0081

Index to the Virginia Revolutionary "Publick" Claims. 1992.
    A complete index to all the names and places mentioned in all seventy of the "Publick" Claims booklets listed below under the individual counties.
Paper. $20.00. xii + 271 pp. .... Vendor G0632

Isaac. **The Transformation of Virginia, 1740-1790**. 1982.
    Describes and analyzes the dramatic confrontations—primarily religious and political—that transformed Virginia in the second half of the 18th century.
Cloth. $37.50. 451 pp. .... Vendor G0611

Jester, Annie Lash, and Martha Woodroof Hiden. **Adventurers of Purse and Person: Virginia, 1607-1624/5.** 3rd ed. Revised and edited by Virginia M. Meyer and John Frederick Doman. 1956. Rev. ed. 1987.
    A remarkable record of the earliest Virginia settlers with extensive footnotes leading the reader to the original sources.
Cloth. $85.00. 827 pp. .... Vendor G0611

Jester, Annie Lash. **Domestic Life in Virginia in the Seventeenth Century**. (1957) reprint 1994. Indexed. Illus.
Paper. $12.00. 91 pp. .... Vendor G0011

Jillson, Willard Rouse. **The Big Sandy Valley.** A Regional History Prior to the Year 1850. (1923) reprint 1994. Indexed. Illus.
    Deals with the region (mostly in Eastern Kentucky), which today encompasses all or part of sixteen counties in Kentucky, Virginia, and West Virginia.
Paper. $18.00. 183 pp. .... Vendor G0011

Jones, William Macfarlane. **The Douglas Register,** Being a Detailed Register of Births, Marriages and Deaths . . . as Kept by the Rev. William Douglas, from 1750 to 1797. [With:] An Index of Goochland Wills and Notes on the French Huguenot Refugees who Lived in Manakin-Town. (1928) reprint 1997.
Paper. $32.50. 408 pp. .... Vendor G0011

Journals of the Council of the State of Virginia: Volume 1, 1776-1777. Edited by H. R. McIlwaine. 1931.
Cloth. $19.95. viii + 605 pp. .... Vendor G0553

Journals of the Council of the State of Virginia: Volume 2, 1777-1781. Edited by H. R. McIlwaine. 1932.
Cloth. $19.95. vii + 572 pp. .... Vendor G0553

Journals of the Council of the State of Virginia: Volume 3, 1781-1786. Edited by Wilmer L. Hall. 1952.
Cloth. $19.95. x + 699 pp. .... Vendor G0553

Journals of the Council of the State of Virginia: Volume 4, 1786-1788. Edited by George H. Reese. 1967.
Cloth. $19.95. x + 403 pp. .... Vendor G0553

Journals of the Council of the State of Virginia: Volume 5, 1788-1791. Edited by Sandra Gioia Treadway. 1982.
Cloth. $19.95. xi + 464 pp. .... Vendor G0553

Journals of the Senate of Virginia: November Session, 1793. Edited by George H. Reese and Patricia Hickin. 1972.
Cloth. $10.00. vii + 110 pp. .... Vendor G0553

Journals of the Senate of Virginia: November Session, 1794. Edited by Wilmer L. Hall. 1951.
Cloth. $10.00. 105 pp. .... Vendor G0553

Journals of the Senate of Virginia: November Session, 1795. Edited by Thomas J. Headlee, Jr. 1976.
Cloth. $10.00. vi + 113 pp. .... Vendor G0553

Journals of the Senate of Virginia: November Session, 1796. Edited by Thomas J. Headlee, Jr. 1976.
Cloth. $10.00. v + 107 pp. .... Vendor G0553

Journals of the Senate of Virginia: Session of 1797/98. Edited by Thomas J. Headlee, Jr. 1976.
Cloth. $10.00. v + 88 pp. .... Vendor G0553

Journals of the Senate of Virginia: Session of 1798/99. Edited by Cynthia A. Miller. 1977.
Cloth. $10.00. v + 92 pp. .... Vendor G0553

Journals of the Senate of Virginia: Session of 1802/03. Edited by George H. Reese and Patricia Hickin. 1973.
Cloth. $10.00. vi + 131 pp. .... Vendor G0553

Kentucky Historical Society. **Certificate Book of the Virginia Land Commission, 1779-1780,** The Register for 1923. 1923.
The original records of Kentucky County, Virginia, 1776-1780, were lost in a fire in the 19th century, which makes this book quite important because it contains the names of most of the pioneer settlers of the state of Kentucky.
Cloth. $35.00. 344 pp. .... Vendor G0610

Liahona Research. **Virginia Marriages, Early to 1800**. 1990. Illus.
Cloth. $145.00. 1,148 pp. .... Vendor G0552

M'Anally, D. R. **The Life & Times of Rev. Samuel Patton**. Reprint 1996. Indexed.
Not just a biography but also a history of Holston Conference of the Methodist Church in 1853.
$28.50 (perfect bound). 374 pp. .... Vendor G0549

McCary, Ben C. **Indians in Seventeenth-Century Virginia**. (1957) reprint 1995. Indexed. Illus.
Paper. $12.00. 102 pp. .... Vendor G0011

McCary, Ben C. **John Smith's Map of Virginia.** With a Brief Account of Its History. (1957) reprint 1995. Illus.
Paper. $9.50. 8 pp. .... Vendor G0011

McGinnis, Carol. **Virginia Genealogy, Sources and Resources**. (1993) reprint 1994. Indexed.
Cloth. $35.00. 505 pp. .... Vendor G0010

McIlwaine, H. R. **Index to Obituary Notices** in the *Richmond Enquirer* from May 9, 1804, through 1828, and the *Richmond Whig* from January 1824 through 1838. (1923) reprint 1996.
Paper. $11.00. 87 pp. .... Vendor G0011

McIlwaine, H. R., ed. **Legislative Journals of the Council of Colonial Virginia. 1918-1919.** 2nd ed. in 1 vol. 1979.
Cloth. $50.00. xii + 1,646 pp. .... Vendor G0553

McIlwaine, H. R., ed. **Minutes of the Council and General Court of Colonial Virginia**. 1924. 2nd ed. 1979.
Cloth. $29.95. xviii + 668 pp. .... Vendor G0553

McWhorter, Lucullus V. **The Border Settlers of Northwestern Virginia, from 1768 to 1795,** Embracing the Life of Jesse Hughes and Other Noted Scouts of the Great Woods of the Trans-Allegheny. (1915) reprint 1996. Illus.
Paper. $37.50. 519 pp. .... Vendor G0011

Meade, Bishop William. **Old Churches, Ministers and Families of Virginia. [With] Digested Index and Genealogical Guide.** 2 vols. (1857, 1910) reprint 1995. Indexed.
Cloth. $70.00. 1,100 pp. total. .... Vendor G0010

Middleton. **Tobacco Coast: A Maritime History of Chesapeake Bay in the Colonial Era**. Reprint 1984.
    The history of how the Chesapeake Bay shaped the society and economy of an entire region. Its physical dominance created an "essential unity" of lands sharing its shores, despite the political decisions that created the separate colonies of Maryland and Virginia.
Paper. $16.95. 508 pp. .... Vendor G0611

Nottingham, Stratton. **Soldiers and Sailors of the Eastern Shore of Virginia in the Revolutionary War**. 1995. Indexed.
Paper. $10.00. 142 pp. .... Vendor G0140

Nugent, Nell Marion. **Cavaliers and Pioneers: Abstracts of Virginia Land Patents and Grants, 1623-1666**. Vol. I. (1934) reprint 1991. Indexed.
Cloth. $40.00. xxxv + 767 pp. .... Vendor G0010

Nugent, Nell Marion (abstracted by). **Cavaliers and Pioneers: Abstracts of Virginia Land Patents and Grants:** Volume One, 1623-1666. (1934) reprint 1992.
Cloth. $30.00. $75.00/3-vol. set (see next 2 listings). xxxv +
767 pp. .... Vendor G0553

Nugent, Nell Marion (abstracted by). **Cavaliers and Pioneers: Abstracts of Virginia Land Patents and Grants:** Volume Two, 1666-1695. Indexed by Claudia B. Grundman. (1977) reprint 1992.
Cloth. $30.00. $75.00/3-vol. set (see listings for Vols. 1 & 3). xi +
609 pp. .... Vendor G0553

Nugent, Nell Marion (abstracted by). **Cavaliers and Pioneers: Abstracts of Virginia Land Patents and Grants:** Volume Three, 1695-1732. (1979) reprint 1992.
Cloth. $30.00. $75.00/3-vol. set (see listings for Vols. 1 & 2). ix +
578 pp. .... Vendor G0553

Nugent, Nell Marion (abstracted by). **Cavaliers and Pioneers: Abstracts of Virginia Land Patents and Grants:** Supplement, Northern Neck Grants No. 1, 1690-1692. 1980.
Paper. $4.95. iii + 18 pp. .... Vendor G0553

Nugent, Nell Marion. **Cavaliers and Pioneers: Abstracts of Virginia Land Patents and Grants, IV**. 1994.
Land patent records are an invaluable genealogical and historical resource for researchers of early Virginia. This continuation of Nell Marion Nugent's work begins with Patent Book 15 and covers the years 1732-1741.
Cloth. $30.00. 393 pp. .... Vendor G0582

Nugent, Nell Marion. **Cavaliers and Pioneers: Abstracts of Virginia Land Patents and Grants, V**. 1994.
Includes the years 1741-1750.
Cloth. $30.00. 477 pp. .... Vendor G0582

Nugent, Nell Marion. **Cavaliers and Pioneers: Abstracts of Virginia Land Patents and Grants, VI**. 1997.
Includes the years 1749-1763.
Contact vendor for information. .... Vendor G0582

Nugent, Nell Marion. **Cavaliers and Pioneers: Abstracts of Virginia Land Patents and Grants, VII**. 1997.
Volume VII of this classic work concludes the series.
Contact vendor for information. .... Vendor G0582

Pendleton, William C. **History of Tazewell County & Southwest Virginia, 1748-1920**. (1920) reprint 1994.
Cloth. $69.50. 700 pp. .... Vendor G0259

Pendleton, William C. **History of Tazewell County and Southwest Virginia**. 1920. Reprinted with index 1989. Indexed. Illus.
Cloth. $33.00. 720 pp. .... Vendor G0649

Perry. **The Formation of a Society on Virginia's Eastern Shore, 1615-1655**. 1990. Indexed.
A remarkably well-researched historical study of the first settlers. Although not intended as a genealogical study, it includes much family information from primary records. Completely indexed and documented.
Cloth. $34.95. 253 pp. .... Vendor G0611

Peters, Joan W. **Local Sources for African-American Family Historians: Using County Court Records and Census Returns**. 1993. Indexed. Illus.

Local Sources—covers the primary record base, using a local Virginia county as an illustration, found in a judicious use of census returns and court records including the often-overlooked entries found in local County Court Minute Books. The techniques found in this volume can be applied anywhere researchers find county courts. In addition, there are courthouse record forms and pre-1850 federal census forms to help African-American family historians trace their ancestry.

Paper. $24.00. 142 pp. .... Vendor G0074

Pierce, Alycon Trubey. **Selected Final Pension Payment Vouchers, 1818-1864: Richmond & Wheeling (Virginia)**. 2 vols. Indexed.

Paper. $49.95. 789 pp. .... Vendor G0632

Plunkett. **Afro-American Sources in Virginia: A Guide to Manuscripts**. 1990.

An extremely valuable collection of sources for African-American research.

Cloth. $35.00. 323 pp. .... Vendor G0611

Precision Indexing. **Virginia 1870 Census Index.** 4 vols. 1989. Illus.

Cloth. $395.00. .... Vendor G0552

Putnam, Martha A. **Quaker Records of Southeast Virginia**. 1996. Indexed.

Paper. $6.50. 77 pp. .... Vendor G0140

Quisenberry, Anderson Chenault. **Revolutionary Soldiers in Kentucky: Also a Roster of the Virginia Navy**. (1896) reprint 1992.

Hard-cover. $27.50. 248 pp. .... Vendor G0610

Quisenberry, Anderson Chenault. **Revolutionary Soldiers in Kentucky: Also a Roster of the Virginia Navy**. (1896) reprint 1996. Indexed.

Paper. $22.00. 206 pp. .... Vendor G0011

Ray, Suzanne Smith, Lyndon H. Hart III, and J. Christian Kolbe, comps. **A Preliminary Guide to Pre-1904 County Records in the Virginia State Library and Archives**. 1987.

Paper. $12.00. xxv + 61 pp. .... Vendor G0553

Roanoke Island Prisoners—Feb. 1862.

A listing of the prisoners taken at the Battle of Roanoke Island from VA and NC.

Paper. $11.50. .... Vendor G0549

Robertson. **Civil War Virginia: Battleground for a Nation**. 1991.

A history of Virginia and the Civil War.

Paper. $8.95. 197 pp. .... Vendor G0611

Robinson, Morgan P. **Virginia Counties:** Those Resulting from Virginia Legislation. (1916) reprint 1992. Indexed. Illus.

Cloth. $25.00. 283 pp. .... Vendor G0010

Robinson, W. Stitt. **Mother Earth**—Land Grants in Virginia, 1607-1699. (1957) reprint 1996. Illus.

Paper. $9.00. 77 pp. .... Vendor G0011

Rose, Christine. **Abstracts of Early Virginia Rose Estates to 1850**. 1972.
Paper. Contact vendor for information. 48 pp. .... Vendor G0474

Rose, Christine. **The Brothers Rev. Robert Rose and Rev. Charles Rose of Colonial Virginia and Scotland**. 1985. Indexed.
Cloth. Contact vendor for information. xvi + 318 pp. .... Vendor G0474

Rountree. **The Powhatan Indians of Virginia: Their Traditional Culture**. 1989.
Useful for anyone studying early 17th-century Virginia and the Powhatans.
Paper. $13.95. 221 pp. .... Vendor G0611

Rouse, Parke Jr. **When the Yankees Came: Civil War and Reconstruction on the Virginia Peninsula**. 1977.
An inside view to the Civil War and the hard times that followed for the Virginia Peninsula area. Shown through the eyes of George Ben West (1839-1917).
Paper. $15.00. 199 pp. .... Vendor G0611

Saffell, William T. R. **Records of the Revolutionary War.** Third Edition. [Bound with:] Index to Saffell's List of Virginia Soldiers in the Revolution, by J. T. McAllister. (1894, 1913) reprint 1996.
Paper. $45.00. 598 pp. .... Vendor G0011

Salmon, Emily J., and Edward D. C. Campbell, Jr., eds. **The Hornbook of Virginia History: A Ready-Reference Guide to the Old Dominion's People, Places, and Past.** 4th ed. 1994. Illus.
Cloth, $29.95. Paper, $19.95. ix + 324 pp. .... Vendor G0553

Sanchez-Saavedra, E. M. **A Guide to Virginia Military Organizations in the American Revolution, 1774-1787**. 1978.
Cloth. $24.95. ix + 226 pp. .... Vendor G0553

Schreiner-Yantis, Netti, and Florene Love. **1787 Census of Virginia, 3 vols.** 1987. Indexed.
Since the 1790 Federal Census of Virginia was destroyed (the work which has been used as a substitute is actually some state census reports taken between 1782 and 1785 that include less than half the counties), this work is of extreme value. It is made up of the 1787 Personal Property Tax Lists.
Cloth. $200.00. 2,022 pp. .... Vendor G0081

Schreiner-Yantis, Netti. **A Supplement to the 1810 Census of Virginia**. 1971. Indexed.
When the British burned the Capitol during the War of 1812, they destroyed part of the Virginia census enumerations of 1810. Bentley's *Index to the 1810 Census of Virginia* is an index to the portion that survived. This book contains the tax lists of each county whose census was destroyed. It includes all the genealogical data to be found in the original lists and an original map of each of the eighteen counties subsequently formed within those boundaries.
Paper. $22.00. 320 pp. .... Vendor G0081

Schuricht, Herrmann. **The German Element in Virginia.** 2 vols. in 1. (1898-1900) reprint 1989. Indexed.
Cloth. $23.95. 433 pp. in all. .... Vendor G0011

Schweitzer, George K. **Virginia Genealogical Research**. 1995. Illus.
History of the state, types of records (Bible through will), record locations, research techniques, listings of county records.
Paper. $15.00. 188 pp. .... Vendor G0569

Shumway, Burgess McK. **California Ranchos: Patented Private Land Grants Listed by County.** Edited by Michael and Mary Burgess. (1941) reprint 1988. Indexed.
Some of the earliest American families to migrate to California originated from Virginia or were of Virginia descent. This volume gives a listing of the Spanish and Mexican grants and the subsequent patents granted by the U.S. authorities.
Paper. $19.95. 144 pp. .... Vendor G0632

Sibley, F. Ray, Jr. **The Confederate Order of Battle, the Army of Northern Virginia.** 1995.
A meticulous examination of the organization of the Confederate army during each of its combat operations. 8½" x 11".
Cloth. $80.00. 480 pp. .... Vendor G0611

Sifakis. **Compendium of the Confederate Armies of Virginia**. 1992.
Describes each regiment, the officers, and lists the battles in which they fought.
Cloth. $29.95. 285 pp. .... Vendor G0611

Smith. **Virginia Revolutionary Militia.**
Paper. $12.00. 70 pp. .... Vendor G0574

Smith, Annie Laurie Wright. **The Quit Rents of Virginia, 1704**. (1957) reprint 1987.
Paper. $7.50. 114 pp. .... Vendor G0010

Southern California Genealogical Society. **Searching in Virginia.**
Paper. $.75. 4 pp. .... Vendor G0656

Spratt, Thomas M. **Men in Gray Interments, Volume I.**
A record of Confederate dead buried in Virginia.
Paper. $35.00. ix + 471 pp. .... Vendor G0632

Spratt, Thomas M. **Men in Gray Interments, Volume II.**
Paper. $35.00. iv + 443 pp. .... Vendor G0632

Spratt, Thomas M. **Men in Gray Interments, Volume III.**
Paper. $35.00. iv + 489 pp. .... Vendor G0632

Spratt, Thomas M. **Men in Gray Interments, Volume IV.**
Paper. $35.00. iv + 319 pp. .... Vendor G0632

Spratt, Thomas M. **Men in Gray Interments, Volume V.**
Paper. $35.00. iv + 335 pp. .... Vendor G0632

Stanard, William G., and Mary Newton Stanard. **The Colonial Virginia Register:** A List of Governors . . . and Other Higher Officials . . . of the Colony of Virginia. (1902) reprint 1989. Indexed.
Cloth. $22.00. 249 pp. .... Vendor G0011

Stanard, William G. **Some Emigrants to Virginia.** Memoranda in Regard to Several

Hundred Emigrants to Virginia During the Colonial Period Whose Parentage is Shown
or Former Residence Indicated by Authentic Records. 2nd ed. (1915) reprint 1996.
Paper. $10.00. 94 pp. .... Vendor G0011

Stewart, R. A., comp. **Index to Printed Va. Genealogies**. (1930) reprint 1991.
   About 6,000 family names with over 18,000 individual references.
Contact vendor for information. 265 pp. .... Vendor G0011

Stewart, Robert Armistead. **The History of Virginia's Navy of the Revolution**. (1934)
reprint 1993. Indexed.
Cloth. $18.50. 279 pp. .... Vendor G0011

Summers, Lewis Preston. **Annals of Southwest Virginia, 1769-1800**. 1 vol. bound in
2. (1920) reprint 1996. Indexed. Illus.
Cloth. $100.00. 1,757 pp. .... Vendor G0010

Summers, Lewis Preston. **Annals of Southwest Virginia, 1769-1800**. 2 vols. (1929)
reprint 1992. Indexed. Illus.
Cloth. $100.00. 1,780 pp. .... Vendor G0610

Summers, Lewis Preston. **History of Southwest Virginia, 1746-1786; Washington
County, 1777-1870 with a Re-arranged Index and an Added Table of Contents**.
(1903, 1971) reprint 1995. Indexed. Illus.
Paper. $65.00. 912 pp. .... Vendor G0011

Summers, Lewis Preston. **History of Southwest Virginia 1746-1786, and Washing-
ton County, 1777-1870**. (1903) reprint 1989.
   An early history of Virginia and counties that are now West Virginia.
Cloth. $37.95. 921 pp. .... Vendor G0611

Swem, E. G., John M. Jennings, and James A. Servies. **A Selected Bibliography of
Virginia, 1607-1699**. (1957) reprint 1994. Illus.
Paper. $10.00. 80 pp. .... Vendor G0011

Swem, E. G. **Virginia Historical Index**. 2 vols in 4. 1965.
   Volume 1: Part 1 A-C, Part 2 D-K. xx + 1,118 pp. in all.
   Volume 2: Part 1 L-P, Part 2 Q-Z. xiv + 1,181 pp. in all.
Contact vendor for information. .... Vendor G0648

T.L.C. Genealogy. **Virginia in 1740: A Reconstructed Census**. 1993. Indexed.
   A statewide, alphabetical list of 25,477 Virginia residents in 1740. Each entry gives
name, county, and source record. Sources include deeds, wills, tax lists, marriages,
order books, etc. An indispensable aid for finding Virginia ancestors. Can even help
when your ancestor was from a burned-record county.
Paper. $25.00. 308 pp. .... Vendor G0609

T.L.C. Genealogy. **Virginia in 1760: A Reconstructed Census**. 1996. Indexed.
   This book, which is based on primary records (order books, deeds, wills, tax lists,
etc.), is an alphabetical list of Virginia inhabitants, their county of residence, and the
source of the information about them. There are 46,768 names, of which there are
6,126 unique surnames and 24,308 different people. Included are people from every
county that existed in VA in 1760. Names are keyed to page numbers in each of
eighty-nine references (most of our references are previously unpublished), so that
copies of the original documents can easily be examined.
Paper. $35.00. 375 pp. .... Vendor G0609

Taylor, Philip Fall,. **Kentucky Land Warrants, for the French and Indian Revolutionary Wars:** A Calendar of Warrants for Land in Kentucky, Granted for Service in the French and Indian Wars; and Land Bounty Land Warrants Granted for Military Service in the War for Independence. (1913) reprint 1917. Indexed.

Gives the researcher for both Kentucky and Virginia a much-needed source of information on early settlers. Contains the names of approximately 6,075 men who served in the Revolution from Virginia.

Hard-cover. $30.00. 164 pp. + index. .... Vendor G0610

Thorndale, William, and William Dollarhide. **County Boundary Map Guides to the U.S. Federal Censuses, 1790-1920: Virginia, 1790-1920.** 1987.

$5.95. .... Vendor G0552

The Three Charters of the Virginia Company of London. With Seven Related Documents: 1606-1621. With an Introduction by Samuel M. Bemiss. (1957) reprint 1994.

Paper. $15.00. 128 pp. .... Vendor G0011

Torrence, Clayton. **The Edward Pleasants Valentine Papers** [Abstracts of 17th- and 18th-Century Virginia Records Relating to 34 Families]. 4 vols. (1927) reprint 1979. Indexed.

Cloth. $80.00. 2,768 pp. .... Vendor G0011

Torrence, Clayton. **Virginia Wills and Administrations, 1632-1800.** (1930) reprint 1995.

Cloth. $30.00. x + 483 pp. .... Vendor G0010

Tucker, Norma. **Colonial Virginians and Their Maryland Relatives.** A Genealogy of the Tucker Family and Also Families of Allen, Blackistone, Chandler, Ford, Gerard, Harmor, Hume, Monroe, Skaggs, Smith, Stevesson, Stone, Sturman, Thompson, Ward, and Yowell. (1994) reprint 1996. Indexed.

Paper. $25.00. 270 pp. .... Vendor G0011

United States Bureau of the Census. **1790 Census of Virginia.** Heads of Families at the First Census of the U.S. Taken in the Year 1790: Records of Enumerations: 1782-1785. 1995. Indexed.

Hard-cover. $32.50. 189 pp. .... Vendor G0610

United States Bureau of the Census. **Heads of Families at the First Census of the United States Taken in the Year 1790: Virginia.**

Cloth, $35.00. Paper, $20.00. .... Vendor G0552

United States Bureau of the Census. **Heads of Families at the First Census of the United States Taken in the Year 1790: Virginia.** Records of the State Enumerations: 1782 to 1785. (1907) reprint 1992. Indexed. Illus.

Contact vendor for information. 189 pp. .... Vendor G0010

Vernon, Robert, comp. **A Bibliography of Abstracts and Compilations of Virginia City and County Records.** 1993.

Paper. $14.95. vi + 107 pp. .... Vendor G0632

Virginia Genealogical Society. **Death Notices from Richmond, Virginia Newspapers, 1821-1840.** 1996. Indexed.

Records of deaths prior to 1853 were not kept but are found in isolated church

papers, family Bibles, or newspapers. Death notices in the Richmond newspapers were not limited to the immediate vicinity but are a statewide reference.
Contact vendor for information. .... Vendor G0582

Virginia Genealogical Society. **Index to Hayden's Virginia Genealogies**. 1977.
    Complete full-name index, compiled in cooperation with the Virginia Historical Society, to Horace Edwin Hayden's *Virginia Genealogies*.
Paper. $12.50. .... Vendor G0582

Virginia Genealogical Society. **Marriage Notices from Richmond, Virginia Newspapers, 1821-1840**. 1983.
    Although marriages were recorded in Virginia prior to 1853, parents were not listed unless the bride or groom was under-age. These notices provide additional details for marriages recorded elsewhere. In some cases, they provide the only record of the nuptials.
Paper. $20.00. 238 pp. .... Vendor G0582

Virginia Genealogical Society. **Marriages from Richmond, Virginia Newspapers, 1841-1853**. 1997.
    A continuation of this valuable series.
Contact vendor for information. .... Vendor G0582

Virginia Genealogical Society. **Some Marriages in the Burned Record Counties of Virginia**. (1972) reprint 1993. Indexed.
    Based on a search of the few original sources available for Hanover, Dinwiddie, Charles City, Nansemond, Elizabeth City, Buckingham, Stafford, King and Queen, and Gloucester counties.
Paper. $18.50. 146 pp. .... Vendor G0610

Virginia Genealogical Society. **Virginia Revolutionary War State Pensions**. (1980) reprint 1992. Indexed.
Cloth. $22.50. 192 pp. .... Vendor G0610

Virginia Tax Records from The Virginia Magazine of History and Biography, the William and Mary College Quarterly and Tyler's Quarterly. 1983. Indexed.
Cloth. $40.00. 663 pp. .... Vendor G0010

Virginia Will Records from The Virginia Magazine of History and Biography, the William and Mary College Quarterly and Tyler's Quarterly. (1982) reprint 1993. Indexed.
Cloth. $45.00. 984 pp. .... Vendor G0010

Virginia: The New Dominion: A History from 1607. 1971.
    A history of the state.
Paper. $18.50. 629 pp. .... Vendor G0611

Vogt, John (designed by). **Chart on the Formation of Virginia Counties**.
Chart. $3.00. .... Vendor G0632

Vogt, John, and T. William Kethley, Jr. **Marriage Records in the Virginia State Library: A Researcher's Guide**. 2nd ed. 1988.
Paper. $14.00. .... Vendor G0632

Vogt, John, and T. William Kethley, Jr. **Will and Estate Records in the Virginia State Library: A Researcher's Guide**. 1987. Illus.
Paper. $12.00. 186 pp. .... Vendor G0632

Walker, Thomas, Dr. **Journal of an Exploration**.
    This is the journal kept by Dr. Walker as he explored the vast reaches of the wilderness of western Virginia, West Virginia, and Kentucky during the 1750s.
Paper. $8.00. 70 pp. .... Vendor G0549

Wallace, Lee A., Jr., ed. **The Orderly Book of Captain Benjamin Taliaferro, 2nd Virginia Detachment, Charleston, South Carolina, 1780**. 1980.
Cloth. $15.00. ix + 185 pp. .... Vendor G0553

Wardell, P. G. **Timesaving Aid to Virginia-West Virginia Ancestors (A Genealogical Index of Surnames from Published Sources)**. 1990. Indexed.
Paper. $36.00. iv + 429 pp. .... Vendor G0632

Ware, Lowry. **Associate Reformed Presbyterian Death & Marriage Notices 1843-1863**. 1993. Indexed.
Cloth. $25.00. 209 pp. .... Vendor G0602

Washburn, Wilcomb E. **Virginia Under Charles I and Cromwell, 1625-1660**. (1957) reprint 1993. Illus.
Paper. $9.50. 64 pp. .... Vendor G0011

Wayland, John W. **Virginia Valley Records** Genealogical and Historical Materials of Rockingham County, Virginia and Related Regions. (1930) reprint 1996. Indexed. Illus.
Paper. $36.50. 491 pp. .... Vendor G0011

Wertenbaker, Thomas J. **Bacon's Rebellion, 1676**. (1957) reprint 1994. Illus.
Paper. $9.50. 60 pp. .... Vendor G0011

Wertenbaker, Thomas J. **The Government of Virginia in the Seventeenth Century**. (1957) reprint 1994. Illus.
Paper. $9.50. 61 pp. .... Vendor G0011

Wertenbaker, Thomas J. **The Planters of Colonial Virginia**. (1922, 1958) reprint 1997. Indexed.
Paper. $24.50. 260 pp. .... Vendor G0011

White, Miles, Jr. **Early Quaker Records in Virginia**. (1902, 1903) reprint 1989. Indexed.
Paper. $6.00. 64 pp. .... Vendor G0010

Whitelaw, Ralph T. **Virginia's Eastern Shore**. 2 vols. Reprinted 1989. Indexed. Illus. Book #1147.
Cloth. $89.50. 757 pp. each. .... Vendor G0082

Williams, Mike K. **Virginians in Tennessee 1850**.
Cloth. $25.00. .... Vendor G0549

Wilson, Samuel M. **Catalogue of Revolutionary Soldiers and Sailors of the Commonwealth of Virginia** To Whom Land Bounty Warrants Were Granted . . . (1913) reprint 1996.
Paper. $12.00. 84 pp. .... Vendor G0011

Withers, Alexander Scott. **Chronicles of Border Warfare,** or a History of the Settlement by the Whites, of Northwestern Virginia, and of the Indian Wars and Massacres in that Section of the State with Reflections, Anecdotes, Etc. Edited and annotated by Reuben Gold Thwaites. (1895) reprint 1994. Indexed.
Paper. $37.50. 467 pp. .... Vendor G0011

Withers, Alexander Scott. **Chronicles of Border Warfare.** Edited and annotated by Reuben Gold Thwaites. (1831) reprint 1989.
   History of the settlement of northern Virginia and of the Indian wars and massacres in that section of the state.
Paper. $14.95. .... Vendor G0660

Withington, Lothrop. **Virginia Gleanings in England.** Abstracts of 17th- and 18th-Century English Wills and Administrations Relating to Virginia and Virginians. 1980. Indexed. Illus.
Cloth. $35.00. 745 pp. .... Vendor G0010

Worrall, Jay, Jr. **The Friendly Virginians**. 1994. Indexed. Illus.
   Depicts the rise and progress of Virginia's Quakers since 1655.
Cloth. $29.95. 632 pp. .... Vendor G0632

Worrell, Anne Lowry. **Over the Mountain Men,** Their Early Court Records in Southwest Virginia. (1934) reprint 1996.
Paper. $7.50. 69 pp. .... Vendor G0010

Wulfeck, Dorothy Ford. **Marriages of Some Virginia Residents, 1607-1800**. (1961-1967) reprint 1995. Indexed.
Cloth. $120.00. 7 vols. in 2. 2,259 pp. total. .... Vendor G0010

Wust. **The Virginia Germans**. 1969.
   A fascinating study of these German immigrants.
Paper. $16.50. 310 pp. .... Vendor G0611

Yurechko, John Otto. **Virginia Genealogies Along and Near the Lower Rappahannock River, 1607-1799**. (1995, Long-Allen families updated 1996) reprint 1996. Indexed.
Paper. $28.00. 351 pp. .... Vendor G0140

Accomack County

Abercrombie, Janice Luck, and Richard Slatten. **Accomack Co., VA "Publick" Claims**. Indexed.
Paper. $5.00. 6 pp. .... Vendor G0632

Horsman, Mrs. Barbara Knott. **Reading Backwards On My Knott Heritage**. 1994. Indexed. Illus.
Cloth. $30.00. 432 pp. .... Vendor G0115

Lyons, Sherri H., comp. **Accomack County, Virginia Early Marriage Records, Volume I, 1735-1799**. 1996. Indexed.
Spiral binding. $21.27. 31 pp. .... Vendor G0672

Lyons, Sherri H., comp. **Accomack County, Virginia Early Marriage Records, Volume 2 1800-1850**. 1996.
Spiral binding. $21.27. 71 pp. .... Vendor G0672

Nottingham, Stratton. **Certificates and Rights, Accomack County, Virginia, 1663-1709**. (1929) reprint 1997. Indexed.
Contact vendor for information. 91 pp. .... Vendor G0011

Nottingham, Stratton. **The Marriage License Bonds of Accomack County, Virginia,** from 1774 to 1806. (1927) reprint 1997. Indexed.
Contact vendor for information. 49 pp. .... Vendor G0011

Schreiner-Yantis, Netti, and Florene Love. **1787 Census of Accomack County, Virginia**. 1987. Indexed.
   Information is from the 1787 Personal Property Tax Lists.
Paper. $6.00. 48 pp. .... Vendor G0081

Wise, Jennings Cropper. **Ye Kingdome of Accawmacke or the Eastern Shore of Virginia in the 17th Century**. (1911) reprint 1997. Indexed.
Contact vendor for information. 406 pp. .... Vendor G0011

Albemarle County

1790 Albemarle County, Virginia Census.
Paper. $3.50. .... Vendor G0549

Abercrombie, Janice Luck, and Richard Slatten. **Albemarle Co., VA "Publick" Claims**. Indexed.
Paper. $8.75. 70 pp. .... Vendor G0632

Davis, Rev. Bailey Fulton. **The Deeds of Amherst County, Virginia, 1761-1852, Books A-K and Albemarle County, Virginia, 1748-1807 (Books 1-3)**. (1950) reprint 1989. Indexed.
Cloth. $42.50. 560 pp. .... Vendor G0610

Schreiner-Yantis, Netti, and Florene Love. **1787 Census of Albemarle County, Virginia**. 1987. Indexed.
   Information is from the 1787 Personal Property Tax Lists.
Paper. $4.50. 40 pp. .... Vendor G0081

Vogt, John, and T. William Kethley, Jr. **Albemarle County, Virginia Marriages, 1780-1853.** 3 vols. 1991. Indexed.
Paper. $44.95/set. 862 pp. .... Vendor G0632

Weisiger, Benjamin B., III. **Albemarle County, VA Court Papers, 1744-1783**. 1987. Indexed.
Paper. $10.00. 86 pp. .... Vendor G0632

Woods, Rev. Edgar. **Albemarle County in Virginia**. (1901) reprint 1997. Indexed.
Contact vendor for information. 412 pp. .... Vendor G0011

Alexandria

Pippenger, Wesley E. **Tombstone Inscriptions of Alexandria: Vol. 1**. 1992. Indexed. Illus.

Includes First Presbyterian (1809), First Presbyterian Graveyard (1773), Trinity United Methodist Church (1808), Home of Peach (1860), Agudas Achim (1933), and Penny Hill (c. 1796) cemeteries.
Paper. $15.00. 208 pp. .... Vendor G0140

Pippenger, Wesley E. **Tombstone Inscriptions of Alexandria: Vol. 2**. 1992. Indexed. Illus.

Includes Freedmen's, or Contraband, Cemetery (1864), Union Cemetery of the Methodist Epis. Church South, Methodist Protestant Cemetery.
Paper. $18.50. 248 pp. .... Vendor G0140

Pippenger, Wesley E. **Tombstone Inscriptions of Alexandria: Vol. 3**. 1992. Indexed. Illus.

Includes Black Baptist Cemetery, Quaker Cemetery, Shuters Hill Cemetery, Christ Church Episcopal Cemetery, Douglas Memorial Cemetery, Lebanon Union Church Cemetery, and Oakland Baptist Church Cemetery.
Paper. $18.50. 228 pp. .... Vendor G0140

Pippenger, Wesley E. **Tombstone Inscriptions of Alexandria: Vol. 4**. 1993. Indexed. Illus.

Bethel Cemetery.
Paper. $32.50. 504 pp. .... Vendor G0140

Powell, Mary G. **The History of Old Alexandria.** From July 13, 1749–May 24, 1861. With a new index by Wesley E. Pippenger. (1928) reprint 1995. Indexed.
Paper. $26.00. 366 pp. .... Vendor G0140

Schreiner-Yantis, Netti, and Florene Love. **1787 Census of Alexandria Town, Virginia**. 1987. Indexed.
Information is from the 1787 Personal Property Tax Lists.
Paper. $2.75. 20 pp. .... Vendor G0081

Stetson, Charles W. **Four Mile Run Land Grants**. (1935) reprint 1994. Indexed.
History of the Northern Neck grants for the present-day Alexandria and Loudoun and Fairfax counties.
Paper. $10.00. 145 pp. .... Vendor G0140

Wright, F. Edward. **Early Church Records of Alexandria City and Fairfax County, Virginia**. 1996. Indexed.
Paper. $20.00. 255 pp. .... Vendor G0140

Alleghany County

1860 Alleghany County, Virginia Census.
Paper. $20.00. .... Vendor G0549

Alleghany County, Virginia Marriages, 1822-1854. Indexed.
Paper. $20.00. Approx. 120 pp. .... Vendor G0632

Martin, Nora B. **The Federal Census of 1870 for Alleghany County, Virginia**. Indexed. Illus.
Paper. $12.95. 122 pp. .... Vendor G0632

Martin, Nora B. **The Federal Censuses of 1830, 1840, and 1850 for Alleghany County, VA**. Indexed. Illus.
Paper. $12.95. 118 pp. .... Vendor G0632

Amelia County

1790 Amelia County, Virginia Census.
Paper. $3.50. .... Vendor G0549

Abercrombie, Janice Luck, and Richard Slatten. **Amelia Co., VA "Publick" Claims**.
Paper. $14.00. 107 pp. .... Vendor G0632

Amelia County, Virginia Court Order Book 1, 1735-1746.
Paper. $30.00. 297 pp. .... Vendor G0632

Journals of Stirling Ford, M.D. 1829-1831, Amelia County, Virginia.
Paper. $15.00. 160 pp. .... Vendor G0632

McConnaughey, Gibson Jefferson, comp. **Amelia County, Virginia Deeds 1735-1743: Bonds 1735-1741 (Deed Book 1)**.
Paper. $20.00. 115 pp. .... Vendor G0632

McConnaughey, Gibson Jefferson, comp. **Amelia County, Virginia Deeds 1742-1747 (Deed Book 2)**.
Paper. $17.50. 99 pp. .... Vendor G0632

McConnaughey, Gibson Jefferson, comp. **Amelia County, Virginia Deeds 1747-1753 (Deed Books 3 & 4)**.
Paper. $25.00. 161 pp. .... Vendor G0632

McConnaughey, Gibson Jefferson, comp. **Amelia County, Virginia Deeds 1753-1759 (Deed Books 5 & 6)**.
Paper. $25.00. 130 pp. .... Vendor G0632

McConnaughey, Gibson Jefferson, comp. **Amelia County, Virginia Deeds, 1759-1765 (Deed Books 7 & 8)**.
Paper. $30.00. 183 pp. .... Vendor G0632

McConnaughey, Gibson Jefferson, comp. **Amelia County, Virginia Deeds 1766-1773 (Deed Books 9, 10 & 11)**.
Paper. $30.00. 137 pp. .... Vendor G0632

McConnaughey, Gibson Jefferson, comp. **Amelia County, Virginia Deeds 1773-1778 (Deed Books 12, 13 & 14)**.
Paper. $30.00. 149 pp. .... Vendor G0632

McConnaughey, Gibson Jefferson, comp. **Amelia County, Virginia Wills 1735-1761: Bonds 1735-1754 (Will Book I)**.
Paper. $20.00. 87 pp. .... Vendor G0632

McConnaughey, Gibson Jefferson, comp. **Amelia County, Virginia Wills 1761-1771 (Will Box 2X)**.
Paper. $20.00. 63 pp. .... Vendor G0632

McConnaughey, Gibson Jefferson, comp. **Amelia County, Virginia Wills 1771-1780 (Will Book 2)**.
Paper. $20.00. 108 pp. .... Vendor G0632

McConnaughey, Gibson Jefferson. **Ghosts at Haw Branch Plantation, Amelia County, Virginia**.
Paper. $5.00. 26 pp. .... Vendor G0632

McConnaughey, Gibson Jefferson, comp. **Miscellaneous Records of Amelia County, Virginia 1735-1865**.
Paper. $30.00. 187 pp. .... Vendor G0632

McConnaughey, Gibson Jefferson, comp. **Unrecorded Deeds and Other Documents of Amelia County, Virginia, 1750-1902**.
Paper. $30.00. 183 pp. .... Vendor G0632

Old Homes and Buildings of Amelia County, Virginia, Volume 2.
Hard-cover. $25.00. 234 pp. .... Vendor G0632

Schreiner-Yantis, Netti, and Florene Love. **1787 Census of Amelia County, Virginia**. 1987. Indexed.
Information is from the 1787 Personal Property Tax Lists.
Paper. $5.00. 44 pp. .... Vendor G0081

T.L.C. Genealogy. **Amelia County, Virginia Court Orders, 1746-1751: An Every-Name Index**. 1995. Indexed.
Paper. $15.00. 110 pp. .... Vendor G0609

T.L.C. Genealogy. **Amelia County, Virginia Deeds, 1759-1765**. 1990. Indexed.
Paper. $12.00. 188 pp. .... Vendor G0609

T.L.C. Genealogy. **Amelia County, Virginia Deeds, 1765-1768**. 1990. Indexed.
Paper. $10.00. 71 pp. .... Vendor G0609

T.L.C. Genealogy. **Amelia County, Virginia, Tax Lists, 1736-1764: An Every-Name Index**. 1993. Indexed.
Paper. $15.00. 217 pp. .... Vendor G0609

Watson, Walter A. **Notes On Southside Virginia**. (1925) reprint 1990. Indexed.
Contains important genealogical materials on Nottoway and Amelia counties.
Cloth. $23.50. 346 pp. .... Vendor G0011

Williams, Kathleen Booth. **Marriages of Amelia County, Virginia 1735-1815**. (1961) reprint 1966. Indexed.
Paper. $18.50. 165 pp. .... Vendor G0011

Wise, Bel Hubbard. **Amelia County, Virginia Will Book 3, 1780-1786**.
Paper. $18.00. .... Vendor G0549

Wise, Bel Hubbard. **Amelia County, Virginia Will Book 4, 1786-1792**.
Paper. $14.50. .... Vendor G0549

Wise, Bel Hubbard. **Amelia County, Virginia Will Book 5, 1792-1799**.
Paper. $20.00. .... Vendor G0549

Amherst County

Abercrombie, Janice Luck, and Richard Slatten. **Amherst Co., VA "Publick" Claims**.
Paper. $6.75. 50 pp. .... Vendor G0632

Davis, Rev. Bailey Fulton. **The Deeds of Amherst County, Virginia, 1761-1852, Books A-K and Albemarle County, Virginia, 1748-1807 (Books 1-3)**. (1950) reprint 1989. Indexed.
Cloth. $42.50. 560 pp. .... Vendor G0610

Davis, Rev. Bailey Fulton. **The Deeds of Amherst County, Virginia, 1808-1852, Books L-R, Vol. 2**. 1985. Indexed.
Cloth. $42.50. 384 pp. .... Vendor G0610

Davis, Rev. Bailey Fulton. **The Deeds of Amherst County, Virginia, 1808-1852, Books S-Z, Vol. 3**. 1985. Indexed.
Cloth. $37.50. 420 pp. .... Vendor G0610

Schreiner-Yantis, Netti, and Florene Love. **1787 Census of Amherst County, Virginia**. 1987. Indexed.
  Information is from the 1787 Personal Property Tax Lists.
Paper. $6.00. 48 pp. .... Vendor G0081

Sweeny, William Montgomery. **Marriage Bonds and Other Marriage Records of Amherst County, Virginia 1763-1800**. (1937) reprint 1997. Indexed.
Paper. $14.00. 102 pp. .... Vendor G0011

Arlington County

Arlington Genealogical Club. **Graveyards of Arlington County, Virginia**. Indexed.
Paper. $18.00. 144 pp. .... Vendor G0627

Augusta County

Abercrombie, Janice Luck, and Richard Slatten. **Augusta Co., VA "Publick" Claims**.
Paper. $5.00. 38 pp. .... Vendor G0632

Harrison, J. Houston. **Settlers by the Long Grey Trail.** Some Pioneers to Old Augusta County, Virginia, and Their Descendants, of the Family of Harrison and Allied Lines. (1935) reprint 1994. Indexed. Illus.
Paper. $47.50. 665 pp. .... Vendor G0011

Kaylor, Peter C. **Abstract of Land Grant Surveys of Augusta and Rockingham Counties, Virginia, 1761-1791**. (1930) reprint 1991. Indexed.
Cloth. $21.50. 150 pp. .... Vendor G0011

Maxwell, Fay. **Virginia, Augusta County Rev. John Craig, D.D., Baptismal Records 1740-1749**. 1975. Indexed.
ISBN 1-885463-28-6. Scotch-Irish Father-Child name lists; many came into Ohio.
Paper. $6.75. 21 pp. .... Vendor G0135

Peyton, J. Lewis. **History of Augusta County, Virginia**. (2nd ed. 1953) reprint 1996. Indexed.
Paper. $36.00. 428 pp. .... Vendor G0011

Reese, Margaret C. **Abstract of Augusta County, Virginia Death Registers, 1853-1896**. 1983. Indexed.
Paper. $14.95. vii + 236 pp. .... Vendor G0632

Schreiner-Yantis, Netti, and Florene Love. **1787 Census of Augusta County, Virginia**. 1987. Indexed.
Information is from the 1787 Personal Property Tax Lists.
Paper. $6.50. 56 pp. .... Vendor G0081

Southern California Genealogical Society. **Borden and Beverly Patents of Orange and Augusta Counties, VA**.
Also contains two fold-out, oversized maps.
Paper. $3.50. 17 pp. .... Vendor G0656

Vogt, John, and T. William Kethley, Jr. **Augusta County Marriages, 1748-1850**. 1986. Indexed. Illus.
Paper. $20.00. ix + 414 pp. .... Vendor G0632

Waddell, Jos. A. **Annals of Augusta County, Virginia, from 1726 to 1871**. 2nd ed. (1901) reprint 1995. Indexed. Illus.
Paper. $35.00. 555 pp. .... Vendor G0011

Weaver, Dorothy Lee, scr. **The Federal Census of 1850 for Augusta County, VA**. 1991. Indexed.
Paper. $24.95. 404 pp. .... Vendor G0632

Bath County

Bruns, Jean R. **Abstracts of the Wills and Inventories of Bath County, Virginia, 1791-1842.** Will Books 1-4. (1995) reprint 1996. Indexed.
Paper. $25.00. 282 pp. .... Vendor G0011

Cleek, George Washington. **Early Western Augusta Pioneers,** Including the Families of Cleek, Gwin, Lightner, and Warwick and Related Families of Bratton, Campbell, Carlile, Craig, Crawford, Dyer, Gay, Givens, Graham, Harper, Henderson, Hull, Keister, Lockridge, McFarland, and Moore. (1957) reprint 1995. Indexed.
Paper. $37.50. 492 pp. .... Vendor G0011

Morton, Oren F. **Annals of Bath County, Virginia**. (1917) reprint 1996. Indexed.
Paper. $25.00. 208 pp. .... Vendor G0011

Bedford County

1850 Bedford County, Virginia Census.
Paper. $30.00. .... Vendor G0549

Abercrombie, Janice Luck, and Richard Slatten. **Bedford Co., VA "Publick" Claims**.
Paper. $7.75. 64 pp. .... Vendor G0632

Bedford County, Virginia Index to Wills from 1754-1830. Published by Heritage Papers.
Paper. $5.00. 16 pp. .... Vendor G0632

Chilton, Ann. **Bedford County, Virginia Birth Register Vol. 1, 1853-1856**. Indexed.
Paper. $27.50. .... Vendor G0549

Chilton, Ann. **Bedford County, Virginia Birth Register Vol. 2, 1856-1866**. Indexed.
$35.00 (perfect bound). 220 pp. .... Vendor G0549

Chilton, Ann. **Bedford County, Virginia Deed Book A-1, 1754-1762**. Indexed.
Paper. $11.50. .... Vendor G0549

Chilton, Ann. **Bedford County, Virginia Deed Book B-2, 1761-1766**. Indexed.
Paper. $10.00. .... Vendor G0549

Chilton, Ann. **Bedford County, Virginia Deed Book C-3, 1766-1771**. Indexed.
Paper. $10.00. .... Vendor G0549

Chilton, Ann. **Bedford County, Virginia Will Books 1-2**.
Paper. $18.50. .... Vendor G0549

Chilton, Ann. **Bedford County, Virginia Will Book 3**.
Paper. $10.00. .... Vendor G0549

Chilton, Ann. **Remnants of War 1861-1865**.
Paper. $22.50. .... Vendor G0549

Chilton, Ann. **Revolutionary War Pensions of Bedford County, Virginia**.
Paper. $12.50. .... Vendor G0549

Dennis, Earle S., and Jane E. Smith. **Marriage Bonds of Bedford County, Virginia, 1755-1800** (reprinted with) Bedford County, Virginia: Index of Wills, from 1754 to 1830. (1932, 1917) reprint 1989. Indexed.
Paper. $7.00. 99 pp. .... Vendor G0010

Neighbors, Marvin U. **Bedford County, Virginia Death Records 1853-1860, 1868-1880**. Indexed.
Paper. $35.00. .... Vendor G0549

Schreiner-Yantis, Netti, and Florene Love. **1787 Census of Bedford County, Virginia**. 1987. Indexed.
   Information is from the 1787 Personal Property Tax Lists.
Paper. $4.00. 36 pp. .... Vendor G0081

T.L.C. Genealogy. **Bedford County, Virginia Deeds, 1761-1766**. 1991. Indexed.
Paper. $11.00. 92 pp. .... Vendor G0609

Wright, F. Edward. **Quaker Records of South River Monthly Meeting, 1756-1800**.
1993.
Paper. $5.00. 74 pp. .... Vendor G0140

Berkeley County

Abercrombie, Janice Luck, and Richard Slatten. **Berkeley Co., VA "Publick" Claims**.
Paper. $5.00. 30 pp. .... Vendor G0632

Keesecker, Guy L. **Marriage Records of Berkeley County, Virginia 1781-1854**.
(1969) reprint 1995.
Paper. $24.00. 268 pp. .... Vendor G0011

Bland County

Brock, R. A. **Bland County, Virginia Biographies**. Indexed.
  A reprint of the 1880s edition of these biographies.
Paper. $5.00. .... Vendor G0549

Botetourt County

Abercrombie, Janice Luck, and Richard Slatten. **Botetourt Co., VA "Publick" Claims**.
Paper. $6.75. 49 pp. .... Vendor G0632

Boyd-Rush, Dorothy A. **Registers of Free Negroes, Botetourt Co., VA, 1802-1836**.
1993.
Paper. $10.95. Approx. 75 pp. .... Vendor G0632

Chilton, Ann. **Botetourt County, Virginia Will Book A, 1770-1801**.
Paper. $16.00. .... Vendor G0549

Prillaman, Helen R. **Places Near the Mountains [Botetourt and Roanoke Counties, Virginia]**. From the community of Amsterdam, Virginia up the road to Catawba, on the waters of the Catawba and Tinker Creeks, along the Carolina Road as it approached Big Lick and other areas, primarily North Roanoke. (1985) reprint 1996. Indexed. Illus.
Paper. $49.95. 397 pp. .... Vendor G0011

Schreiner-Yantis, Netti, and Florene Love. **1787 Census of Botetourt County, Virginia**. 1987. Indexed.
  Information is from the 1787 Personal Property Tax Lists.
Paper. $5.00. 44 pp. .... Vendor G0081

Schreiner-Yantis, Netti. **A List of Taxable Property . . . Formerly the Upper District of Botetourt and Now the Lower of Montgomery for the Year of 1790**.

From the District of John Robinson. Part of Botetourt was annexed to Montgomery County in 1789—this comprises that region. It can be used in conjunction with "Montgomery County—Circa 1790" to determine area covered.
Paper. $2.25. .... Vendor G0081

Vogt, John, and T. William Kethley, Jr. **Botetourt Co., VA Marriages, 1770-1853.** 2 vols. 1987. Indexed. Illus.
Paper. $24.95/set. 600 pp. .... Vendor G0632

Worrell, Anne Lowry. **Early Marriages, Wills, and Some Revolutionary War Records: Botetourt County, Virginia.** (1958) reprint 1996.
Paper. $7.50. 69 pp. .... Vendor G0010

Bristol

Holston Territory Genealogical Society. **Families of Washington County and Bristol, Virginia 1776-1996.** Indexed. Illus.
Handsome 9" x 12", hardbound book, featuring almost 900 family genealogies, family histories, and photos. Other important chapters include information on communities, education, churches, and military. Surname index.
Cloth. $63.00. 392 pp. .... Vendor G0087

Brunswick County

Abercrombie, Janice Luck, and Richard Slatten. **Brunswick Co., VA "Publick" Claims.**
Paper. $7.50. 58 pp. .... Vendor G0632

Fothergill, Augusta B. **Marriage Records of Brunswick County, Virginia, 1730-1852.** (1953) reprint 1995. Indexed.
Paper. $18.00. 153 pp. .... Vendor G0011

Knorr, Catherine Lindsay. **Marriage Bonds and Ministers' Returns of Brunswick County, Virginia, 1750-1810.** (1953) reprint 1982. Indexed. Illus.
Cloth. $18.50. 146 pp. .... Vendor G0610

Schreiner-Yantis, Netti, and Florene Love. **1787 Census of Brunswick County, Virginia.** 1987. Indexed.
Information is from the 1787 Personal Property Tax Lists.
Paper. $4.50. 40 pp. .... Vendor G0081

T.L.C. Genealogy. **Brunswick County, Virginia Court Orders, 1732-1737.** 1992. Indexed.
Paper. $15.00. 76 pp. .... Vendor G0609

T.L.C. Genealogy. **Brunswick County, Virginia Court Order Books, 1737-1749: An Every-Name Index.** 1992. Indexed.
Paper. $12.00. 111 pp. .... Vendor G0609

T.L.C. Genealogy. **Brunswick County, Virginia Deeds, 1740-1744.** 1991. Indexed.
Paper. $11.00. 75 pp. .... Vendor G0609

T.L.C. Genealogy. **Brunswick County, Virginia Deeds, 1745-1749**. 1991. Indexed.
Paper. $11.00. 96 pp. .... Vendor G0609

T.L.C. Genealogy. **Brunswick County, Virginia Wills, 1739-1750**. 1991. Indexed.
Paper. $14.00. 76 pp. .... Vendor G0609

Vogt, John, and T. William Kethley, Jr. **Brunswick County Marriages, 1750-1853**.
1988. Illus.
Paper. $17.00. 296 pp. .... Vendor G0632

Wynne, Frances Holloway. **Register of Free Negros and of Dower Slaves, Brunswick
County, Virginia 1803-1850**. 1985. Indexed.
Cloth. $37.75. 219 pp. .... Vendor G0040

Buckingham County

Abercrombie, Janice Luck, and Richard Slatten. **Buckingham Co., VA "Publick"
Claims**.
Paper. $5.00. 37 pp. .... Vendor G0632

Grundset, Eric G. **Buckingham County, Virginia Surveyor's Plat Book, 1762-1858**.
2nd ed. 1996. Indexed. Illus.
Paper. $12.00. 92 pp. .... Vendor G0011

Kidd, Randy. **Buckingham County, Virginia 1860 U.S. Census**. 1994. Indexed.
Paper. $17.95. vi + 169 pp. .... Vendor G0632

Kidd, Randy, and Jeanne Stinson. **Lost Buckingham County, Virginia Marriages**.
1992. Indexed. Illus.
Paper. $20.00. xii + 251 pp. .... Vendor G0632

Schreiner-Yantis, Netti, and Florene Love. **1787 Census of Buckingham County,
Virginia**. 1987. Indexed.
   Information is from the 1787 Personal Property Tax Lists.
Contact vendor for information. 32 pp. .... Vendor G0081

Stinson, Jeanne. **Buckingham Co., VA Board of Supervisors Minute Book 1870-
1887**. 1994. Indexed.
Paper. $12.95. Approx. 100 pp. .... Vendor G0632

Stinson, Jeanne. **Buckingham Co., VA Extant Poll Lists (1788, 1840, 1841 & 1848)**.
1994. Indexed.
Paper. $12.95. vi + 136 pp. .... Vendor G0632

Stinson, Jeanne. **Buckingham Co., VA Undetermined Chancery Files Index**. 1994.
Indexed.
Paper. $12.95. vi + 121 pp. .... Vendor G0632

Stinson, Jeanne. **Early Buckingham County, Virginia, Legal Papers, Volume One:
1765-1806**. 1993. Indexed. Illus.
Paper. $20.00. vi + 110 pp. .... Vendor G0632

Ward, Roger G. **Buckingham County, Virginia Land Tax Summaries & Implied Deeds, Volume 1: 1782-1814**. 1993. Indexed.
Paper. $20.00. 343 pp. .... Vendor G0632

Ward, Roger G. **Buckingham County, Virginia Land Tax Summaries & Implied Deeds, Volume 2: 1815-1840**. 1994. Indexed.
Paper. $20.00. vi + 300 pp. .... Vendor G0632

Ward, Roger G. **Buckingham County, Virginia Land Tax Summaries & Implied Deeds, Volume 3: 1841-1870**. 1995. Indexed.
Paper. $20.00. vi + 342 pp. .... Vendor G0632

Ward, Roger G. **Buckingham County, Virginia Natives Who Died Elsewhere, 1853-1896**. 1995. Indexed.
Paper. $14.95. 133 pp. .... Vendor G0632

Warren, Mary Bondurant, comp. **Buckingham Co., VA Church and Marriage Records, 1764-1822**. 1993. Indexed. Illus.
Paper. $12.50. 87 pp. .... Vendor G0632

Warren, Mary Bondurant, and Eve B. Weeks. **Virginia's District Courts, 1789-1809: Records of the Prince Edward District:** Buckingham, Charlotte, Cumberland, Halifax, and Prince Edward Counties. 1991. Indexed. Illus.
Cloth. $28.50. 497 pp. .... Vendor G0632

Weisiger, Benjamin B., III. **Buckingham County, Virginia 1850 U.S. Census**. 1984. Indexed.
Paper. $12.95. 151 pp. .... Vendor G0632

Weisiger, Benjamin B., III. **Burned County Data, 1809-1848 (As Found in the Virginia Contested Election Files)**. 1986. Indexed.
   The following counties are included: Hanover, Buckingham, Charles City, Gloucester, New Kent, James City, and Caroline.
Paper. $15.00. 100 pp. .... Vendor G0632

Whitley, Edythe Rucker. **Genealogical Records of Buckingham County, Virginia**. (1984) reprint 1996. Indexed.
Paper. $19.00. 162 pp. .... Vendor G0011

Woodson, Robert F., and Isobel B. Woodson. **Virginia Tithables from Burned Record Counties (Buckingham, Gloucester, Hanover, James City, and Stafford)**. (1970) reprint 1982.
Paper. $20.00. 122 pp. .... Vendor G0610

Campbell County

Abercrombie, Janice Luck, and Richard Slatten. **Campbell Co., VA "Publick" Claims**.
Paper. $5.00. 28 pp. .... Vendor G0632

Baker, L. M. H., and H. L. Williamson. **Campbell County Marriages, 1782-1810**. (1971) reprint 1980.
Paper. $18.50. 185 pp. .... Vendor G0259

Brock, R. A. **Campbell County Biographies**. Indexed.
  A reprint of his 1880s edition.
Paper. $7.50. .... Vendor G0549

Christian, William Asbury. **Lynchburg & Its People**. (1900) reprint 1995.
Cloth. $49.00. 463 pp. .... Vendor G0259

Davis, Rev. Bailey Fulton. **Lynchburg, Virginia and Nelson County, Virginia Wills, Deeds and Marriages**. (1964, 1968) reprint 1985. Indexed.
Cloth. $30.00. 252 pp. .... Vendor G0610

Early, Ruth Hairston. **Campbell Chronicles and Family Sketches,** Embracing the History of Campbell County, Virginia 1782-1926. (1927) reprint 1994. Indexed. Illus.
Paper. $39.95. 578 pp. .... Vendor G0011

Schreiner-Yantis, Netti, and Florene Love. **1787 Census of Campbell County, Virginia**. 1987. Indexed.
  Information is from the 1787 Personal Property Tax Lists.
Paper. $3.50. 32 pp. .... Vendor G0081

T.L.C. Genealogy. **Campbell County, Virginia Deeds, 1782-1784**. 1991. Indexed.
Paper. $9.00. 52 pp. .... Vendor G0609

T.L.C. Genealogy. **Campbell County, Virginia Deeds, 1784-1790**. 1991. Indexed.
Paper. $14.00. 112 pp. .... Vendor G0609

T.L.C. Genealogy. **Campbell County, Virginia Deeds, 1790-1796**. 1991. Indexed.
Paper. $15.00. 141 pp. .... Vendor G0609

T.L.C. Genealogy. **Campbell County, Virginia Wills, 1782-1800**. 1991. Indexed.
Paper. $14.00. 129 pp. .... Vendor G0609

Caroline County

Abercrombie, Janice Luck, and Richard Slatten. **Caroline Co., VA "Publick" Claims**.
Paper. $13.00. 100 pp. .... Vendor G0632

Collins, Herbert Ridgeway. **Cemeteries of Caroline County, Virginia.** 2 vols. 1995. Indexed.
Paper. $15.00/vol. 208 pp. .... Vendor G0140

Hopkins, William Lindsay. **Caroline County Court Records, 1742-1833 and Marriages, 1782-1810**. Indexed.
Paper. $30.00. 197 pp. .... Vendor G0632

Schreiner-Yantis, Netti, and Florene Love. **1787 Census of Caroline County, Virginia**. 1987. Indexed.
  Information is from the 1787 Personal Property Tax Lists.
Paper. $5.00. 44 pp. .... Vendor G0081

T.L.C. Genealogy. **Caroline County, Virginia Chancery Court Deeds, 1758-1845**. 1990. Indexed.
Paper. $12.00. 84 pp. .... Vendor G0609

T.L.C. Genealogy. **Caroline County, Virginia Land Tax Lists, 1787-1799**. 1991. Indexed.
Paper. $14.00. 175 pp. .... Vendor G0609

Weisiger, Benjamin B., III. **Burned County Data, 1809-1848 (As Found in the Virginia Contested Election Files)**. 1986. Indexed.
  The following counties are included: Hanover, Buckingham, Charles City, Gloucester, New Kent, James City, and Caroline.
Paper. $15.00. 100 pp. .... Vendor G0632

Wingfield, Marshall. **A History of Caroline County, Virginia,** from Its Formation in 1727 to 1924 to Which Is Appended "A Discourse of Virginia" by Edward Maria Wingfield, First Governor of the Colony of Virginia. (1924) reprint 1997. Indexed. Illus.
Contact vendor for information. 528 pp. .... Vendor G0011

Charles City County

Abercrombie, Janice Luck, and Richard Slatten. **Charles City Co., VA "Publick" Claims**.
Paper. $5.00. 30 pp. .... Vendor G0632

Schreiner-Yantis, Netti, and Florene Love. **1787 Census of Charles City County, Virginia**. 1987. Indexed.
  Information is from the 1787 Personal Property Tax Lists.
Paper. $2.75. 20 pp. .... Vendor G0081

Weisiger, Benjamin B., III. **Burned County Data, 1809-1848 (As Found in the Virginia Contested Election Files)**. 1986. Indexed.
  The following counties are included: Hanover, Buckingham, Charles City, Gloucester, New Kent, James City, and Caroline.
Paper. $15.00. 100 pp. .... Vendor G0632

Weisiger, Benjamin B., III. **Charles City County, Virginia Court Orders, 1687-1695 (with a Fragment of a Court Order Book for the Year 1680)**. 1980. Indexed.
Paper. $22.95. 249 pp. .... Vendor G0632

Weisiger, Benjamin B., III. **Charles City County, Virginia, 1725-1731**. 1984. Indexed.
  Abstracts of a book carried off by Union troops in the Civil War and returned in the 1970s.
Paper. $10.00. 63 pp. .... Vendor G0632

Weisiger, Benjamin B., III. **Charles City County, Virginia, Records, 1737-1774**. 1986. Indexed.
Paper. $20.00. 201 pp. .... Vendor G0632

Charlotte County

Abercrombie, Janice Luck, and Richard Slatten. **Charlotte Co., VA "Publick" Claims**.
Paper. $5.00. 33 pp. .... Vendor G0632

Knorr, Catherine Lindsay. **Marriage Bonds and Ministers' Returns of Charlotte County, Virginia, 1764-1815**. 1985. Indexed.
Cloth. $17.50. 170 pp. .... Vendor G0610

Schreiner-Yantis, Netti, and Florene Love. **1787 Census of Charlotte County, Virginia**. 1987. Indexed.
   Information is from the 1787 Personal Property Tax Lists.
Paper. $3.50. 32 pp. .... Vendor G0081

T.L.C. Genealogy. **Charlotte County, Virginia Deeds, 1771-1777**. 1990. Indexed.
Paper. $12.00. 120 pp. .... Vendor G0609

T.L.C. Genealogy. **Charlotte County, Virginia Wills, 1765-1791**. 1991. Indexed.
Paper. $19.00. 218 pp. .... Vendor G0609

Warren, Mary Bondurant, and Eve B. Weeks. **Virginia's District Courts, 1789-1809: Records of the Prince Edward District:** Buckingham, Charlotte, Cumberland, Halifax, and Prince Edward Counties. 1991. Indexed. Illus.
Cloth. $28.50. 497 pp. .... Vendor G0632

Wise, Bel H. **Charlotte County, Virginia Will Book 1, 1765-1791**. Indexed.
Paper. $18.50. 82 pp. .... Vendor G0549

Wise, Bel H. **Charlotte County, Virginia Will Book 2, 1791-1805**. Indexed.
Paper. $18.50. 80 pp. .... Vendor G0549

Chesterfield County

Abercrombie, Janice Luck, and Richard Slatten. **Chesterfield Co., VA "Publick" Claims**.
Paper. $7.50. 57 pp. .... Vendor G0632

Knorr, Catherine Lindsay. **Marriage Bonds and Ministers' Returns of Chesterfield County, Virginia 1771-1815**. (1958) reprint 1992. Indexed. Illus.
Cloth. $20.00. 170 pp. .... Vendor G0610

Schreiner-Yantis, Netti, and Florene Love. **1787 Census of Chesterfield County, Virginia**. 1987. Indexed.
   Although called the "1787 Census," this book is actually a combination of the 1786 Personal Property Tax Lists, one 1788 tax list, and ten Legislative Petitions (with signatures). The 1787 lists for this county are missing, so these items have been used to make up as much as possible the names of those persons who would have appeared in those lists.
Paper. $7.00. 64 pp. .... Vendor G0081

T.L.C. Genealogy. **Chesterfield County, Virginia Court Orders, 1749-1752**. 1991. Indexed.
Paper. $15.00. 140 pp. .... Vendor G0609

Weisiger, Benjamin B., III. **Chesterfield County, VA Deeds, 1749-1756**. 1986. Indexed.
Paper. $12.95. 109 pp. .... Vendor G0632

Weisiger, Benjamin B., III. **Chesterfield County, VA Deeds, 1756-1764**. 1989. Indexed.
Paper. $12.95. 113 pp. .... Vendor G0632

Weisiger, Benjamin B., III. **Chesterfield County, VA Deeds, 1764-1768**. 1991. Indexed.
Paper. $12.95. 74 pp. .... Vendor G0632

Weisiger, Benjamin B., III. **Chesterfield County, VA Marriages, 1816-1853**. 1981. Indexed.
Paper. $19.95. 201 pp. .... Vendor G0632

Weisiger, Benjamin B., III. **Chesterfield County, VA Wills, 1749-1774**. 1979. Indexed.
Paper. $17.00. 213 pp. .... Vendor G0632

Weisiger, Benjamin B., III. **Chesterfield County, VA, 1850 U.S. Census**. 1988. Indexed.
Paper. $17.95. 204 pp. .... Vendor G0632

Weisiger, Benjamin B., III. **Chesterfield County, Virginia Wills, 1774-1802.** Rev. ed. (1979) reprint 1982. Indexed.
Paper. $27.95. 327 pp. .... Vendor G0632

Clarke County

Morris, Mary Thomason. **Connections and Partings: Abstracts of Marriage, Divorce, Death, and Legal Notices Regarding Clarke County, Virginia 1857-1884 from Newspaper Accounts**. Indexed.
Paper. $16.95. 210 pp. .... Vendor G0632

Vogt, John, and T. William Kethley, Jr. **Clarke County Marriages, 1836-1850**. 1983. Indexed.
Paper. $6.00. vii + 62 pp. .... Vendor G0632

Culpeper County

Abercrombie, Janice Luck, and Richard Slatten. **Culpeper Co., VA "Publick" Claims**.
Paper. $11.00. 82 pp. .... Vendor G0632

Green, R. T. **Culpeper County Genealogical and Historical Notes,** Embracing a Revised and Enlarged Edition of Dr. Philip Slaughter's History of St. Mark's Parish. (1900) reprint 1992.
Cloth. $35.00. 120 + 160 pp. .... Vendor G0010

Knorr, Catherine Lindsay. **Marriages of Culpeper County, Virginia, 1781-1815**. (1954) reprint 1982. Indexed. Illus.
Cloth. $18.50. 136 pp. .... Vendor G0610

Schreiner-Yantis, Netti, and Florene Love. **1787 Census of Culpeper County, Virginia**. 1987. Indexed.
Information is from the 1787 Personal Property Tax Lists.
Paper. $7.50. 68 pp. .... Vendor G0081

Slaughter, Rev. Philip. **A History of St. Mark's Parish, Culpeper County, Virginia.** With Notes of Old Churches and Old Families. (1877) reprint 1994. Illus. Paper. $21.00. 210 pp. .... Vendor G0011

Vogt, John, and T. William Kethley, Jr. **Culpeper County Marriages, 1780-1853.** 1986. Indexed. Illus. Paper. $17.00. ix + 257 pp. .... Vendor G0632

Cumberland County

Abercrombie, Janice Luck, and Richard Slatten. **Cumberland Co., VA "Publick" Claims.** Paper. $8.75. 71 pp. .... Vendor G0632

Elliott, Katherine B. **Cumberland County, Virginia, Marriage Records, 1749-1840.** (1969) reprint 1983. Indexed. Cloth, $27.50. Paper, $22.50. 198 pp. .... Vendor G0610

Proceedings of the Committees of Safety of Cumberland and Isle of Wight Counties, Virginia, 1775-1776. 1919. Cloth. $5.00. 54 pp. .... Vendor G0553

Reynolds, Katherine. **Abstracts of Wills of Cumberland County, Virginia, Will Book 1 & 2, 1749-1792.** 1984. Indexed. Cloth. $17.50. 104 pp. .... Vendor G0610

Schreiner-Yantis, Netti, and Florene Love. **1787 Census of Cumberland County, Virginia.** 1987. Indexed.
  Information is from the 1787 Personal Property Tax Lists.
Paper. $3.25. 28 pp. .... Vendor G0081

T.L.C. Genealogy. **Cumberland County, Virginia Deeds, 1749-1752.** 1990. Indexed. Paper. $9.00. 60 pp. .... Vendor G0609

Warren, Mary Bondurant, and Eve B. Weeks. **Virginia's District Courts, 1789-1809: Records of the Prince Edward District:** Buckingham, Charlotte, Cumberland, Halifax, and Prince Edward Counties. 1991. Indexed. Illus. Cloth. $28.50. 497 pp. .... Vendor G0632

Dinwiddie County

Abercrombie, Janice Luck, and Richard Slatten. **Dinwiddie Co., VA "Publick" Claims.** Paper. $6.75. 51 pp. .... Vendor G0632

Chamberlayne, Churchill Gibson. **Births from the Bristol Parish Register of Henrico, Prince George, and Dinwiddie Counties, Virginia, 1720-1798.** (1898) reprint 1996. Indexed. Paper. $16.00. 133 pp. .... Vendor G0011

Chamberlayne, Churchill Gibson. **The Vestry Book and Register Briston Parish, Virginia, 1720-1789.** 1898. Indexed.

Bristol Parish covers the area later comprised of Dinwiddie, Henrico, and Prince George counties.

Hard-cover. $40.00. 428 pp. .... Vendor G0610

Hopkins, William Lindsay. **Bath Parish Register (Births, Deaths, Marriages), 1827-1897 and St. Andrews Parish Vestry Book, 1732-1797**. 1989. Indexed.

Paper. $24.00. 130 pp. .... Vendor G0632

Schreiner-Yantis, Netti, and Florene Love. **1787 Census of Dinwiddie County & Petersburg Town**. 1987. Indexed.

Information is from the 1787 Personal Property Tax Lists.

Paper. $5.00. 44 pp. .... Vendor G0081

Slaughter, Rev. Philip, D.D. **A History of Bristol Parish, with Genealogies of Families Connected Therewith and Historical Illustrations**. 1879. Indexed.

Bristol Parish covers the area later comprised of Dinwiddie, Henrico, and Prince George counties.

Cloth. $32.50. 238 pp. + index. .... Vendor G0610

T.L.C. Genealogy. **Dinwiddie County, Virginia, Surveyor's Platt Book (1755-1796) and Court Orders (1789-1791): An Every-Name Index**. 1995. Indexed.

Paper. $10.00. 65 pp. .... Vendor G0609

Virginia Genealogical Society. **Virginia Marriages in Rev. John Cameron's Register and Bath Parish Register (1827-1897)**. 1963. Indexed.

Marriages included are from the areas of Dinwiddie, Prince George, and Nottoway counties.

Paper. $10.00. 56 pp. .... Vendor G0610

Elizabeth City County

Abercrombie, Janice Luck, and Richard Slatten. **Elizabeth City Co., VA "Publick" Claims**.

Paper. $5.00. 17 pp. .... Vendor G0632

Chapman, Blanche Adams. **Wills and Administrations of Elizabeth City County, Virginia 1688-1800**. With Other Genealogical and Historical Items. (1941, 1980) reprint 1995. Indexed.

Paper. $20.00. 198 pp. .... Vendor G0011

Schreiner-Yantis, Netti, and Florene Love. **1787 Census of Elizabeth City County, Virginia**. 1987. Indexed.

Information is from the 1787 Personal Property Tax Lists.

Paper. $2.50. 16 pp. .... Vendor G0081

Essex County

Abercrombie, Janice Luck, and Richard Slatten. **Essex Co., VA "Publick" Claims**.

Paper. $5.00. 31 pp. .... Vendor G0632

Schreiner-Yantis, Netti, and Florene Love. **1787 Census of Essex County, Virginia**. 1987. Indexed.
Information is from the 1787 Personal Property Tax Lists.
Paper. $3.25. 28 pp. .... Vendor G0081

Wilkerson, Eva Eubank. **Index to Marriages of Old Rappahannock and Essex Counties, Virginia, 1655-1900**. (1953) reprint 1997.
Paper. $25.00. 256 pp. .... Vendor G0011

Wright, Sue. **Essex County, Virginia 1850 U.S. Census**. 1995. Indexed.
Paper. $14.50. 95 pp. .... Vendor G0471

Wright, Sue. **Essex County, Virginia 1860 U.S. Census**. 1995. Indexed.
Paper. $14.50. 107 pp. .... Vendor G0471

Fairfax County

Abercrombie, Janice Luck, and Richard Slatten. **Fairfax Co., VA "Publick" Claims**.
Paper. $5.00. 23 pp. .... Vendor G0632

Fairfax Genealogical Society. **Fairfax County, Virginia Gravestones Volume I, Northern Section: Great Falls, McLean, Oakton, Vienna and Surrounding Areas**. 1994. Indexed. Illus.
Fairfax Genealogical Society is compiling and publishing a series of volumes of extracts from gravestones in cemeteries and family burial grounds located in Fairfax County, including names, dates, and family relationships found on gravestones. The project will be completed with publication of a separate master index to all volumes. FGS members receive a discount; write for further information.
Paper. $22.00. 336 pp. .... Vendor G0543

Fairfax Genealogical Society. **Fairfax County, Virginia Gravestones Volume II, Southern Section: Burke, Clifton, Fairfax Station, Springfield and Surrounding Areas**. 1995. Indexed. Illus.
Includes area maps. See description under listing for Volume I.
Paper. $17.00. 216 pp. .... Vendor G0543

Fairfax Genealogical Society. **Fairfax County, Virginia Gravestones Volume III, Central Section: Annandale, Fairfax City, Falls Church and Surrounding Areas**. 1996. Indexed. Illus.
Includes area maps. See description under listing for Volume I.
Paper. $37.00. 628 pp. .... Vendor G0543

Fairfax Genealogical Society. **Fairfax County, Virginia Gravestones Volume IV, Western Section: Centreville, Chantilly, Herndon, Reston and Surrounding Areas**.
See description under listing for Volume I.
Contact vendor for information. .... Vendor G0543

Fairfax Genealogical Society. **Fairfax County, Virginia Gravestones Volume V, Eastern Section: Alexandria, Fort Belvoir, Lorton and Surrounding Areas**.
See description under listing for Volume I.
Contact vendor for information .... Vendor G0543

Hiatt, Marty, and Craig R. Scott. **Fairfax County, Virginia Implied Marriages**. 1994. Indexed.
Paper. $22.50. xiv + 345 pp. .... Vendor G0632

Johnson, William Page, II. **Brothers and Cousins: Confederate Soldiers & Sailors of Fairfax County, Virginia**. Indexed. Illus.
Paper. $20.00. xviii + 249 pp. .... Vendor G0632

King, Junie Estelle Stewart. **Abstracts of Wills and Inventories, Fairfax County, Virginia, 1742-1801**. (1936) reprint 1996. Indexed.
Paper. $7.50. 61 pp. .... Vendor G0010

McKay, H. B. **Fairfax Land Suit**.
Spiral binding. $21.00. 168 pp. .... Vendor G0758

Ring, Constance, comp. **Index to Fairfax County, Virginia Wills and Fiduciary Records 1742-1855**. 1995. Indexed.
Paper. $21.00. 204 pp. .... Vendor G0669

Schreiner-Yantis, Netti, and Florene Love. **1787 Census of Fairfax County, Virginia**. 1987. Indexed.
　Information is from the 1787 Personal Property Tax Lists.
Paper. $4.00. 36 pp. .... Vendor G0081

Stetson, Charles W. **Four Mile Run Land Grants**. (1935) reprint 1994. Indexed.
　History of the Northern Neck grants for the present-day Alexandria and Loudoun and Fairfax counties.
Paper. $10.00. 145 pp. .... Vendor G0140

Wright, F. Edward. **Early Church Records of Alexandria City and Fairfax County, Virginia**. 1996. Indexed.
Paper. $20.00. 255 pp. .... Vendor G0140

Fauquier County

Abercrombie, Janice Luck, and Richard Slatten. **Fauquier Co., VA "Publick" Claims**.
Paper. $6.75. 49 pp. .... Vendor G0632

Alcock, John P. **Fauquier Families, 1759-1799: Comprehensive Indexed Abstracts of Tax and Tithable Lists, Marriage Bonds and Minute, Deed and Will Books Plus Other 18th Century Records of Fauquier County, Virginia**. 1994. Indexed.
Paper. $39.95. 445 pp. .... Vendor G0632

Buck, Dee Ann. **Fauquier County, Virginia Births, 1853-1896**.
Spiral binding. $30.00. 259 pp. .... Vendor G0758

Buck, Dee Ann. **Fauquier County, Virginia Deaths, 1853-1896**.
Spiral binding. $25.00. 184 pp. .... Vendor G0758

Buck, Dee Ann. **Fauquier County, Virginia Marriages, 1854-1880**.
Spiral binding. $27.50. 244 pp. .... Vendor G0758

Buck, Dee Ann. **Fauquier County, Virginia Marriages, 1881-1896**.
Spiral binding. $25.00. 176 pp. .... Vendor G0758

Gott, John K. **Abstracts of Fauquier County, Virginia.** Wills, Inventories, and Accounts, 1759-1800. (1976) reprint 1994. Indexed.
Paper. $28.00. 348 pp. .... Vendor G0011

Groome, Harry C. **Fauquier During the Proprietorship.** A Chronicle of the Colonization and Organization of a Northern Neck County. (1927) reprint 1989. Indexed. Illus.
Contact vendor for information. 255 pp. .... Vendor G0011

King, Junie Estelle Stewart. **Abstracts of Wills, Administrations, and Marriages of Fauquier County, Virginia, 1759-1800**. (1939) reprint 1986. Indexed.
Paper. $7.50. 101 pp. .... Vendor G0010

Schreiner-Yantis, Netti, and Florene Love. **1787 Census of Fauquier County, Virginia**. 1987. Indexed.
    Information is from the 1787 Personal Property Tax Lists.
Paper. $7.00. 64 pp. .... Vendor G0081

Fayette County

Shuck, Larry G., scr. **Fayette County, West Virginia Death Records, 1866-1899**. 1994. Indexed.
Paper. $17.95. Approx. 220 pp. .... Vendor G0632

Fincastle County

Harwell, Richard Barksdale, ed. **The Committees of Safety of Westmoreland and Fincastle: Proceedings of the County Committees, 1774-1776**. (1956) reprint 1974.
Paper. $7.95. 127 pp. .... Vendor G0553

Worrell, Anne Lowry. **A Brief of Wills and Marriages in Montgomery and Fincastle Counties, Virginia, 1733-1831**. (1932) reprint 1996.
Paper. $7.50. 56 pp. .... Vendor G0010

Floyd County

1850 Census, Floyd County, Virginia.
Paper. $25.00. .... Vendor G0549

Neighbors, Marvin U. **Floyd County, Virginia Marriages 1840-1863**.
Paper. $10.00. .... Vendor G0549

Robertson, Donna J. **Tombstone Inscriptions of Floyd County, Virginia**. 1993. Indexed.
Paper. $27.95. 297 pp. .... Vendor G0545

Fluvanna County

Abercrombie, Janice Luck, and Richard Slatten. **Fluvanna Co., VA "Publick" Claims**.
Paper. $5.00. 34 pp. .... Vendor G0632

Hailey, Nell. **Fluvanna County Death Records, 1853-1896**. Indexed.
Paper. $17.95. vi + 296 pp. .... Vendor G0632

Schreiner-Yantis, Netti, and Florene Love. **1787 Census of Fluvanna County, Virginia**. 1987. Indexed.
Information is from the 1787 Personal Property Tax Lists.
Paper. $2.75. 20 pp. .... Vendor G0081

T.L.C. Genealogy. **Fluvanna County, Virginia Deeds, 1777-1783**. 1991. Indexed.
Paper. $10.00. 77 pp. .... Vendor G0609

Vogt, John, and T. William Kethley, Jr. **Fluvanna County Marriages, 1781-1849**.
1984. Indexed. Illus.
Paper. $10.95. ix + 103 pp. .... Vendor G0632

Franklin County

1850 Franklin County, Virginia Census.
Paper. $39.50. .... Vendor G0549

Chiarito, Marian Dodson, scr. **Entry Record Book [1], 1737-1770** (Land Entries in the Present Virginia Counties of Halifax, Pittsylvania, Henry, Franklin, and Patrick).
1984. Indexed.
Paper. $45.95. 432 pp. .... Vendor G0632

Chiarito, Marian Dodson, scr. **Entry Record Book [2], 1770-1796** (Land Entries in the Present Virginia Counties of Pittsylvania, Henry, Franklin, and Patrick). 1988.
Indexed.
   Pittsylvania was formed from Halifax County in 1767. The map included with the book gives names of most of the early watercourses, and makes possible the location of land entries, adjoining landowners, and other points of interest.
Paper. $23.95. 138 pp. .... Vendor G0632

Schreiner-Yantis, Netti, and Florene Love. **1787 Census of Franklin County, Virginia**. 1987. Indexed.
Information is from the 1787 Personal Property Tax Lists.
Paper. $4.50. 40 pp. .... Vendor G0081

Southern California Genealogical Society. **Settlement Map of Franklin County, Virginia, with Every-name Index**.
Also contains fold-out, oversized map.
Paper. $7.50. 6 pp. .... Vendor G0656

T.L.C. Genealogy. **Franklin County, Virginia Wills, 1786-1812**. 1991. Indexed.
Paper. $18.00. 162 pp. .... Vendor G0609

Wingfield, Marshall. **Franklin County, Virginia: A History**. (1964) reprint 1996. Indexed.
Paper. $28.50. 319 pp. .... Vendor G0011

Wingfield, Marshall. **Marriage Bonds of Franklin County, Virginia 1786-1858.** With a New Index of Brides, Parents, and Sureties. (1939) reprint 1995. Indexed.
Paper. $24.00. 299 pp. .... Vendor G0011

Wingfield, Marshall. **An Old Virginia Court,** Being a Transcript of the Records of the First Court of Franklin County, Virginia, 1786-1789. With Biographies of the Justices and Stories of Famous Cases, Annotated, Glossarized and Indexed. (1948) reprint 1996. Indexed.
Paper. $24.00. 258 pp. .... Vendor G0011

Wingfield, Marshall. **Pioneer Families of Franklin County, Virginia**. (1964) reprint 1996. Indexed.
Paper. $31.50. 373 pp. .... Vendor G0011

Frederick County

Abercrombie, Janice Luck and Richard Slatten. **Frederick Co., VA "Publick" Claims**.
Paper. $6.25. 45 pp. .... Vendor G0632

Buck, Dee Ann. **Frederick County, Virginia Marriages, 1853-1880**.
Spiral binding. $28.00. 223 pp. .... Vendor G0758

Cartmell, T. K. **Shenandoah Valley Pioneers and Their Descendants:** A History of Frederick County, Virginia from Its Formation in 1738 to 1908. Compiled Mainly from Original Records of Old Frederick County, now Hampshire, Berkeley, Shenandoah, Jefferson, Hardy, Clarke, Warren, Morgan and Frederick. Indexed Edition. (1908, 1963) reprint 1995. Indexed.
Paper. $57.50. vii + 572 pp. .... Vendor G0011

Davis, Eliza Timberlake. **Frederick County, Virginia, Marriages 1771-1825**. (1941) reprint 1996. Indexed.
Paper. $16.00. 129 pp. .... Vendor G0011

Greene, Katherin Glass. **Winchester & Its Beginnings, 1743-1814**. (1926) reprint 1993.
Cloth. $47.50. 441 pp. .... Vendor G0259

Hopewell Friends. **Hopewell Friends History, 1734-1934, Frederick County, Virginia.** Records of Hopewell Monthly Meetings and Meetings Reporting to Hopewell. (1936) reprint 1993. Indexed. Illus.
Cloth. $38.50. 671 pp. .... Vendor G0010

Hutton, James V., Jr. **The Federal Census of 1850 for Frederick Co., VA**. 1987. Indexed.
Paper. $19.95. xii + 369 pp. .... Vendor G0632

Hutton, James V., Jr. **Tell Me of a Land That's Fair**. 1987.
   The author has written an essay on the occasion of the 250th celebration of Frederick County's formation (1738-1988).
Paper. $5.00. 52 pp. .... Vendor G0632

Kangas, M. N., and D. E. Payne. **Frederick County, Virginia, Wills & Administrations, 1795-1816**. (1983) reprint 1995. Indexed.
Contact vendor for information. 144 pp. .... Vendor G0011

King, Junie Estelle Stewart. **Abstracts of Wills, Inventories, and Administration Accounts of Frederick County, Virginia, 1743-1800**. (1961) reprint 1996. Indexed.
Paper. $7.50. 88 pp. .... Vendor G0010

Lathrop, J. M., and B. N. Griffing. **Hammond's Edition of the 1885 Atlas of Frederick County, Virginia.** Revised Compilation Based on 1885 Surveys. 1996. Indexed. Illus.
Paper. $32.70 (VA residents add tax). 72 pp. .... Vendor G0670

O'Dell. **Pioneers of Old Frederick County, Virginia**. 1995.
 This monumental work identifies the early land holdings of several hundred settlers in the area. Each patent, grant, deed, will, court suit, or other source mentioned is identified in the extensive footnote citations, and the location of the tracts is keyed to a series of sixteen maps. Extremely useful for this area.
Cloth. $49.50. 623 pp. .... Vendor G0611

Schreiner-Yantis, Netti, and Florene Love. **1787 Census of Frederick County & Winchester Town**. 1987. Indexed.
 Information is from the 1787 Personal Property Tax Lists.
Paper. $7.50. 68 pp. .... Vendor G0081

Vogt, John, and T. William Kethley, Jr. **Frederick County Marriages, 1738-1859**. 1984. Indexed. Illus.
Paper. $20.00. ix + 461 pp. .... Vendor G0632

Fredericksburg

Embrey, Alvin T. **History of Fredericksburg, Virginia**. (1937) reprint 1994. Indexed. Illus.
Paper. $22.00. 202 pp. .... Vendor G0011

Giles County

Giles County Historical Society. **Giles County, Virginia History—Families.** 6th printing. 1982. Indexed. Illus.
One of the most popular in the County Heritage Book series. Rich, hand-rubbed maroon cover and embossed seal, 8½" x 11", hardbound. More than 500 family histories, genealogies, and family photos. Also includes chapters on military history, schools, churches, towns, and villages. County records include land grants, taxes, births, deaths, marriages, and cemetery records. Every-name index.
Cloth. $63.50. Contact vendor for information on second vol. in this series. 440 pp.
Vendor G0087

Schreiner-Yantis, Netti. **1810 Census of Giles County**.
All or part of present-day counties of Giles and Craig counties, Virginia, and Monroe, Mercer, Summers, Wyoming, Raleigh, and Fayette counties, West Virginia were in Giles in 1810 and 1815. There were 3,745 people living in Giles County in 1810. This booklet gives all census data as shown in the original manuscript.
Paper. $2.50. .... Vendor G0081

Schreiner-Yantis, Netti. **1815 Tax List & Abstracts of 310 Early Deeds & Surveys, Giles County**. Indexed.
This unique tax list mentions such items as carpets, bookcases, window curtains, clocks, watches, mirrors, and mills—besides the usual horses, cattle, and slaves. Approximate places of residence of the taxpayers are given. Map shows 1815 boundaries as well as natural features. All names of witnesses, etc., that are in the abstracts are included in the index, which has approximately 2,000 entries.
Paper. $3.25. .... Vendor G0081

Vogt, John, and T. William Kethley, Jr. **Giles County Marriages, 1806-1850**. 1985. Indexed. Illus.
Paper. $12.95. vii + 147 pp. .... Vendor G0632

Gloucester County

Abercrombie, Janice Luck, and Richard Slatten. **Gloucester Co., VA "Publick" Claims**.
Paper. $5.00. 35 pp. .... Vendor G0632

Bodie, Charles, and William Seiner. **A Guide to Gloucester County, Virginia, Historical Manuscripts, 1651-1865**. 1976.
Paper. $7.95. xvii + 109 pp. .... Vendor G0553

Branch, J. B., comp. **Epitaphs of Gloucester and Mathews Cos., in Tidewater Virginia, Through 1865**. (1959) reprint 1995.
Paper. $21.00. 168 pp. .... Vendor G0259

Chamberlayne, C. G., ed. **Vestry Book of Petsworth Parish, Gloucester County, Virginia, 1677-1793**. (1933) reprint 1979.
Paper. $15.00. xv + 429 pp. .... Vendor G0553

Mason, Polly Cary. **Records of Colonial Gloucester County, Virginia.** A Collection of Abstracts from Original Documents Concerning the Lands and People of Colonial Gloucester County. 2 vols. in 1. (1946-48) reprint 1994. Indexed. Illus.
Paper. $39.95. 146 + 150 pp. .... Vendor G0011

Matheny, Emma R., and Helen K. Yates. **Kingston Parish Register,** Gloucester and Mathews Counties, Virginia, 1749-1827. (1963) reprint 1996. Indexed.
Paper. $18.00. 167 pp. .... Vendor G0011

Schreiner-Yantis, Netti, and Florene Love. **1787 Census of Gloucester County, Virginia**. 1987. Indexed.
    Information is from the 1787 Personal Property Tax Lists.
Paper. $4.50. 40 pp. .... Vendor G0081

Weisiger, Benjamin B., III. **Burned County Data, 1809-1848 (As Found in the Virginia Contested Election Files)**. 1986. Indexed.
    The following counties are included: Hanover, Buckingham, Charles City, Gloucester, New Kent, James City, and Caroline.
Paper. $15.00. 100 pp. .... Vendor G0632

Woodson, Robert F., and Isobel B. Woodson. **Virginia Tithables from Burned Record Counties (Buckingham, Gloucester, Hanover, James City, and Stafford)**. (1970) reprint 1982.
Paper. $20.00. 122 pp. .... Vendor G0610

Goochland County

Abercrombie, Janice Luck, and Richard Slatten. **Goochland Co., VA "Publick" Claims**.
Paper. $6.75. 52 pp. .... Vendor G0632

Foley, Louise Pledge Heath. **Early Virginia Families Along the James River.** Volume I: Henrico County—Goochland County. (1974) reprint 1996. Indexed. Illus. Paper. $18.50. 162 pp. .... Vendor G0011

Hopkins, William Lindsay. **St. James Northam Parish Vestry Book, 1744-1850.** 1987. Indexed. Paper. $17.00. 129 pp. .... Vendor G0632

Jones, William Macfarlane. **The Douglas Register,** Being a Detailed Register of Births, Marriages and Deaths . . . as Kept by the Rev. William Douglas, from 1750 to 1797. [With:] An Index of Goochland Wills and Notes on the French Huguenot Refugees who Lived in Manakin-Town. (1928) reprint 1997. Paper. $32.50. 408 pp. .... Vendor G0011

Schreiner-Yantis, Netti, and Florene Love. **1787 Census of Goochland County, Virginia.** 1987. Indexed. Information is from the 1787 Personal Property Tax Lists. Paper. $4.00. 36 pp. .... Vendor G0081

T.L.C. Genealogy. **Goochland County, Virginia Court Order Books, 1728-1735: An Every-Name Index.** 1992. Indexed. Paper. $12.00. 102 pp. .... Vendor G0609

T.L.C. Genealogy. **Goochland County, Virginia Court Orders, 1735-1737.** 1991. Indexed. Paper. $15.00. 134 pp. .... Vendor G0609

T.L.C. Genealogy. **Goochland County, Virginia Deeds, 1741-1745.** 1990. Indexed. Paper. $12.00. 104 pp. .... Vendor G0609

Weisiger, Benjamin B., III. **Goochland Co., Virginia, Wills & Deeds, 1728-1736.** 1983. Indexed. Paper. $12.95. 105 pp. .... Vendor G0632

Weisiger, Benjamin B., III. **Goochland County, Virginia, Wills & Deeds, 1736-1742.** 1984. Indexed. Paper. $12.95. 76 pp. .... Vendor G0632

Weisiger, Benjamin B., III. **Goochland County, Virginia, Wills, 1742-1749.** 1984. Indexed. Paper. $12.95. 88 pp. .... Vendor G0632

Williams, Kathleen Booth. **Marriages of Goochland County, Virginia, 1733-1815.** (1960) reprint 1996. Indexed. Paper. $17.00. 148 pp. .... Vendor G0011

Grayson County

1860 Grayson County, Virginia.
Paper. $16.50. .... Vendor G0549

Douthat, James L. **Grayson County, Virginia Will Book 1, 1796-1839**.
Paper. $14.00. .... Vendor G0549

Nuckolls, Benjamin Floyd. **Pioneer Settlers of Grayson County, Virginia**. With a New Index. (1914) reprint 1997. Indexed.
Contact vendor for information. 219 pp. .... Vendor G0011

Schreiner-Yantis, Netti. **1810 Tax List of Grayson County, Virginia**.
Included in *A Supplement to the 1810 Census of Virginia*.
Paper. $2.00. .... Vendor G0081

Greenbrier County

Abercrombie, Janice Luck, and Richard Slatten. **Greenbrier Co., VA "Publick" Claims**.
Paper. $5.00. 20 pp. .... Vendor G0632

Shuck, Larry. **Greenbrier County Records, Volume 8:** Birth Records of Greenbrier County, [W.] Virginia, 1853-1898. 2 vols. 1995. Indexed.
Paper. $29.95. iv + 614 pp. .... Vendor G0632

Greene County

Vogt, John, and T. William Kethley, Jr. **Greene County Marriages, 1838-1850**. 1984. Indexed.
Paper. $6.00. viii + 44 pp. .... Vendor G0632

Greensville County

Abercrombie, Janice Luck, and Richard Slatten. **Greensville Co., VA "Publick" Claims**.
Paper. $5.00. 21 pp. .... Vendor G0632

Knorr, Catherine Lindsay. **Marriages of Greensville County, Virginia, 1781-1825**. (1955) reprint 1983. Indexed. Illus.
Cloth. $15.00. 106 pp. .... Vendor G0610

Schreiner-Yantis, Netti, and Florene Love. **1787 Census of Greensville County, Virginia**. 1987. Indexed.
Information is from the 1787 Personal Property Tax Lists.
Paper. $3.00. 24 pp. .... Vendor G0081

Vogt, John, and T. William Kethley, Jr. **Greensville County Marriages, 1781-1853**. 1989. Indexed.
Paper. $17.95. xi + 156 pp. .... Vendor G0632

Halifax County

1790 Halifax County, Virginia Census.
Paper. $6.00. .... Vendor G0549

1820 Halifax County, Virginia Census.
Paper. $7.50. .... Vendor G0549

Abercrombie, Janice Luck, and Richard Slatten. **Halifax Co., VA "Publick" Claims**.
Paper. $7.75. 61 pp. .... Vendor G0632

Bouldin, Powhatan. **The Old Trunk.** Reprinted 1990 by the Clarkton Press. (1896) reprint 1990. Indexed.
   Originally inspired by documents dating to colonial times found in an old trunk by the author; of particular genealogical value to those whose ancestors lived in Southside Virginia. A complete index of names and marriage records for some people mentioned has been added in the reprinting.
Paper. $10.95. 84 pp. .... Vendor G0632

Carrington, Wirt Johnson. **A History of Halifax County [Virginia]**. (1924) reprint 1995. Indexed. Illus.
Paper. $39.95. 525 pp. .... Vendor G0011

Carrington, Wirt Johnson. **A History of Halifax County, Virginia**. 1924. Indexed.
Hard-cover. $42.50. Approx. 560 pp. .... Vendor G0610

Chiarito, Marian Dodson, scr. **1850 Census of Halifax County, Virginia**. 1982. Indexed.
Paper. $20.00. 270 pp. .... Vendor G0632

Chiarito, Marian Dodson, scr. **Entry Record Book [1], 1737-1770** (Land Entries in the Present Virginia Counties of Halifax, Pittsylvania, Henry, Franklin, and Patrick). 1984. Indexed.
Paper. $45.95. 432 pp. .... Vendor G0632

Chiarito, Marian Dodson, scr. **Entry Record Book [2], 1770-1796** (Land Entries in the Present Virginia Counties of Pittsylvania, Henry, Franklin, and Patrick). 1988. Indexed.
   Pittsylvania was formed from Halifax County in 1767. The map included with the book gives names of most of the early watercourses, and makes possible the location of land entries, adjoining landowners, and other points of interest.
Paper. $23.95. 138 pp. .... Vendor G0632

Chiarito, Marian Dodson, scr. **Halifax County, Virginia, Deed Book 1, 1752-1759**. 1988. Indexed.
Paper. $9.95. 64 pp. .... Vendor G0632

Chiarito, Marian Dodson, scr. **Halifax County, Virginia Deed Books 2, 3, 4, 5 & 6, 1759-1767**. 1989. Indexed.
Paper. $28.95. 224 pp. .... Vendor G0632

Chiarito, Marian Dodson, scr. **Halifax County, Virginia, Deed Book 7, 1767-1770.** 1990. Indexed.
Paper. $12.95. 66 pp. .... Vendor G0632

Chiarito, Marian Dodson, scr. **Halifax County, Virginia, Plea Book 1, 1752-1755.** 1990. Indexed.
Paper. $23.95. 146 pp. .... Vendor G0632

Chiarito, Marian Dodson, scr. **Halifax County, Virginia, Will Book 0, 1752-1773.** 1982. Indexed.
Paper. $14.95. 88 pp. .... Vendor G0632

Chiarito, Marian Dodson, scr. **Halifax County, Virginia, Will Book 1, 1773-1783.** 1984. Indexed.
Paper. $17.95. 136 pp. .... Vendor G0632

Chiarito, Marian Dodson, scr. **Halifax County, Virginia Will Book 2, 1783-1792.** 1989. Indexed.
Paper. $20.95. 136 pp. .... Vendor G0632

Chiarito, Marian Dodson, scr. **List of Voters for Elections of Burgesses, 1764-1769.** 1986. Indexed.
Paper. $6.95. 44 pp. .... Vendor G0632

Chiarito, Marian Dodson, scr. **Marriages of Halifax County, Virginia, 1801-1830.** 1985. Indexed.
Paper. $23.95. 183 pp. .... Vendor G0632

Chiarito, Marian Dodson, scr. **Vestry Book of Antrim Parish, Halifax Co., Virginia, 1752-1817.** 1983. Indexed.
Paper. $23.95. 160 pp. .... Vendor G0632

Knorr, Catherine Lindsay. **Marriage Bonds and Ministers' Returns of Halifax County, Virginia, 1756-1800.** (1957) reprint 1995. Indexed. Illus.
Cloth. $18.50. 142 pp. .... Vendor G0610

Schreiner-Yantis, Netti, and Florene Love. **1787 Census of Halifax County, Virginia.** 1987. Indexed.
    Information is from the 1787 Personal Property Tax Lists.
Paper. $5.00. 44 pp. .... Vendor G0081

Schreiner-Yantis, Netti. **1810 Tax List of Halifax County, Virginia.**
    Included in *A Supplement to the 1810 Census of Virginia.*
Paper. $2.00. .... Vendor G0081

T.L.C. Genealogy. **Halifax County, Virginia Court Orders, 1755-1758 (Plea Book No. 2, Part 1).** 1992. Indexed.
Paper. $16.00. 166 pp. .... Vendor G0609

T.L.C. Genealogy. **Halifax County, Virginia Deeds, 1767-1772.** 1989. Indexed.
Paper. $12.00. 117 pp. .... Vendor G0609

T.L.C. Genealogy. **Halifax County, Virginia Deed Book 9 (1773-1775).** 1990. Indexed.
Paper. $10.00. 98 pp. .... Vendor G0609

T.L.C. Genealogy. **Halifax County, Virginia Deed Book 10 (1775-1778)**. 1991. Indexed.
Paper. $10.00. 94 pp. .... Vendor G0609

T.L.C. Genealogy. **Halifax County, Virginia Deeds, 1778-1784**. 1992. Indexed.
Paper. $14.00. 186 pp. .... Vendor G0609

T.L.C. Genealogy. **Halifax County, Virginia Deeds, 1784-1790**. 1994. Indexed.
Paper. $20.00. 240 pp. .... Vendor G0609

T.L.C. Genealogy. **Halifax County, Virginia Deed Book 15 (1790-1793)**. 1996. Indexed.
Paper. $15.00. 151 pp. .... Vendor G0609

T.L.C. Genealogy. **Halifax County, Virginia Wills, 1792-1797**. 1991. Indexed.
Paper. $16.00. 131 pp. .... Vendor G0609

Warren, Mary Bondurant, scr. **Halifax County, Virginia Tithables and Voters, 1755-1780**. 1990. Indexed. Illus.
Paper. $10.00. 44 pp. .... Vendor G0632

Warren, Mary Bondurant, and Eve B. Weeks. **Virginia's District Courts, 1789-1809: Records of the Prince Edward District:** Buckingham, Charlotte, Cumberland, Halifax, and Prince Edward Counties. 1991. Indexed. Illus.
Cloth. $28.50. 497 pp. .... Vendor G0632

Hampshire County

Abercrombie, Janice Luck, and Richard Slatten. **Hampshire Co., VA "Publick" Claims**.
Paper. $5.00. 37 pp. .... Vendor G0632

Sage, Clara McCormick, and Laura Sage Jones. **Early Records, Hampshire County, Virginia**. (1939) reprint 1990. Indexed.
Cloth. $25.00. 170 pp. .... Vendor G0010

T.L.C. Genealogy. **Hampshire County, [West] Virginia Personal Property Tax Lists, 1782-1799**. 1990. Indexed.
Paper. $16.00. 308 pp. .... Vendor G0609

Hanover County

Abercrombie, Janice Luck, and Richard Slatten. **Hanover Co., VA "Publick" Claims**.
Paper. $14.50. 116 pp. .... Vendor G0632

Chamberlayne, C. G., ed. **Vestry Book of St. Paul's Parish, Hanover County, Virginia, 1706-1786**. (1940) reprint 1989.
Paper. $15.00. xx + 672 pp. .... Vendor G0553

Cocke, William Ronald. **Hanover County [VA] Taxpayers (St. Paul's Parish), 1782-1815**. (1956) reprint 1990. Indexed.
Cloth. $12.00. 158 pp. .... Vendor G0011

Inman, Joseph F., and Isobel B. Inman. **Hanover County, Virginia, 1850 United States Census**. 1974. Indexed.
Paper. $17.50. 210 pp. .... Vendor G0610

Schreiner-Yantis, Netti, and Florene Love. **1787 Census of Hanover County, Virginia**. 1987. Indexed.
Information is from the 1787 Personal Property Tax Lists.
Paper. $4.50. 40 pp. .... Vendor G0081

Slatten, Richard, ed. **Hanover County, Virginia Superior Court Records, Vol. 1: Superior Court of Law, 1809-1826; 1815-1826.** Transcribed and indexed by Janice Luck Abercrombie. 2 vols. 1987. Indexed.
Paper. $20.00. 257 pp. .... Vendor G0632

Slatten, Richard, ed. **Hanover County, Virginia Superior Court Records, Vol. 2: Superior Court of Law and Chancery, 1831-1838.** Transcribed and indexed by Janice Luck Abercrombie. 1987. Indexed.
Paper. $20.00. 172 pp. .... Vendor G0632

Weisiger, Benjamin B., III. **Burned County Data, 1809-1848 (As Found in the Virginia Contested Election Files)**. 1986. Indexed.
The following counties are included: Hanover, Buckingham, Charles City, Gloucester, New Kent, James City, and Caroline.
Paper. $15.00. 100 pp. .... Vendor G0632

Woodson, Robert F., and Isobel B. Woodson. **Virginia Tithables from Burned Record Counties (Buckingham, Gloucester, Hanover, James City, and Stafford)**. (1970) reprint 1982.
Paper. $20.00. 122 pp. .... Vendor G0610

Harrison County

Morris, Earle, ed. **Harrison Co., Va., West Virginia Marriage Records, 1874-1850**. 1981. Indexed.
List of ministers, parents when available.
Cloth. $20.00. 287 pp. .... Vendor G0531

Henrico County

Abercrombie, Janice Luck, and Richard Slatten. **Henrico Co., VA "Publick" Claims**.
Paper. $5.00. 23 pp. .... Vendor G0632

Chamberlayne, Churchill Gibson. **Births from the Bristol Parish Register of Henrico, Prince George, and Dinwiddie Counties, Virginia, 1720-1798**. (1898) reprint 1996. Indexed.
Paper. $16.00. 133 pp. .... Vendor G0011

Chamberlayne, Churchill Gibson. **The Vestry Book and Register Briston Parish, Virginia, 1720-1789**. 1898. Indexed.

Bristol Parish covers the area later comprised of Dinwiddie, Henrico, and Prince George counties.

Hard-cover. $40.00. 428 pp. .... Vendor G0610

Fleet, Beverley. **Henrico County, Virginia, Records, Vol. 21**. (1944) reprint 1984. Indexed.

Paper. $15.00. 104 pp. .... Vendor G0610

Foley, Louise Pledge Heath. **Early Virginia Families Along the James River.** Volume I: Henrico County—Goochland County. (1974) reprint 1996. Indexed. Illus.

Paper. $18.50. 162 pp. .... Vendor G0011

Lindsay, Joycey H. **Marriages of Henrico County, Virginia, 1680-1808**. (1983) reprint 1995. Indexed.

Paper. $15.00. vi + 96 pp. + index. .... Vendor G0610

Schreiner-Yantis, Netti, and Florene Love. **1787 Census of Henrico County & Richmond City, Virginia**. 1987. Indexed.

Information is from the 1787 Personal Property Tax Lists.

Paper. $6.00. 48 pp. .... Vendor G0081

Slaughter, Rev. Philip, D.D. **A History of Bristol Parish, with Genealogies of Families Connected Therewith and Historical Illustrations**. 1879. Indexed.

Bristol Parish covers the area later comprised of Dinwiddie, Henrico, and Prince George counties.

Cloth. $32.50. 238 pp. + index. .... Vendor G0610

T.L.C. Genealogy. **Henrico County, Virginia Court Order Book, 1737-1746: An Every-Name Index**. 1992. Indexed.

Paper. $12.00. 101 pp. .... Vendor G0609

Virginia Genealogical Society. **Richmond City and Henrico County, Virginia, 1850 U.S. Census**. 1981. Indexed.

Paper. $20.00. 505 pp. .... Vendor G0610

Weisiger, Benjamin B., III. **Colonial Wills of Henrico County, Virginia, 1677-1737**. 1976. Indexed.

Paper. $20.00. 214 pp. .... Vendor G0632

Weisiger, Benjamin B., III. **Colonial Wills of Henrico County, Virginia, 1737-1781,** with Addenda. 1977. Rev. ed. 1985. Indexed.

Paper. $20.00. 233 pp. .... Vendor G0632

Weisiger, Benjamin B., III. **Henrico County, Virginia Deeds, 1677-1705**. 1986. Indexed.

Paper. $20.00. 188 pp. .... Vendor G0632

Weisiger, Benjamin B., III. **Henrico County, Virginia Deeds, 1706-1737**. (1985) reprint 1995. Indexed.

Paper. $20.00. 256 pp. .... Vendor G0632

Weisiger, Benjamin B., III. **Henrico County, Virginia Deeds, 1737-1750**. 1985. Indexed.

Paper. $20.00. 142 pp. .... Vendor G0632

Henrico Parish

Brock, Dr. R. A. **The Vestry Book of Henrico Parish, 1730-1773**. (1904) reprint 1995. Indexed.
Hard-cover. $32.50. 204 pp. + index. .... Vendor G0610

Moore, J. Staunton. **The Annals and History of Henrico Parish,** Diocese of Virginia, and St. John's P.E. Church. (1904) reprint 1996. Indexed. Illus.
Paper. $45.00. 578 pp. .... Vendor G0011

Henry County

1820 Henry County, Virginia Census.
Paper. $5.00. .... Vendor G0549

1850 Henry County, Virginia Census.
Paper. $25.00. .... Vendor G0549

Abercrombie, Janice Luck, and Richard Slatten. **Henry Co., VA "Publick" Claims**.
Paper. $7.25. 53 pp. .... Vendor G0632

Adams, Lela C. **Henry County, Virginia, Feb 1776-July 1784, Abstracts of Deed Books 1 & 2**. (1975) reprint 1992. Indexed.
Paper. $20.00. 188 pp. .... Vendor G0610

Adams, Lela C. **Henry County, Virginia, August 1784-June 1792, Abstracts of Deed Books 3 & 4**. (1978) reprint 1984. Indexed.
Paper. $18.50. 136 pp. .... Vendor G0610

Adams, Lela C. **Henry County, Virginia, October 1792-December 1805, Abstracts of Deed Books 5 & 6**. (1978) reprint 1984. Indexed.
Paper. $18.50. 136 pp. .... Vendor G0610

Adams, Lela C. **Henry County, Virginia, Will Abstracts, Vol. I and Vol. II, 1777-1820**. 1984. Indexed.
Cloth. $17.50. 120 pp. .... Vendor G0610

Adams, Lela C. **Tax Lists of Henry County, Virginia, 1778-1780**. (1973) reprint 1989.
Paper. $12.50. 34 pp. .... Vendor G0610

Chiarito, Marian Dodson, scr. **Entry Record Book [1], 1737-1770** (Land Entries in the Present Virginia Counties of Halifax, Pittsylvania, Henry, Franklin, and Patrick). 1984. Indexed.
Paper. $45.95. 432 pp. .... Vendor G0632

Chiarito, Marian Dodson, scr. **Entry Record Book [2], 1770-1796** (Land Entries in the Present Virginia Counties of Pittsylvania, Henry, Franklin, and Patrick). 1988. Indexed.
   Pittsylvania was formed from Halifax County in 1767. The map included with the book gives names of most of the early watercourses, and makes possible the location of land entries, adjoining landowners, and other points of interest.
Paper. $23.95. 138 pp. .... Vendor G0632

Dodd, Virginia Anderton. **Henry County, Virginia, Marriage Bonds, 1778-1849**. (1953) reprint 1997. Indexed.
Contact vendor for information. 132 pp. .... Vendor G0011

Hill, J. P. A. **History of Henry County,** with Biographical Sketches of Its Most Prominent Citizens & Genealogical History of Half a Hundred of Its Oldest Residents. (1925) reprint 1993.
Contact vendor for information. 329 pp. .... Vendor G0011

Hill, Judith Parks America. **History of Henry County, Virginia**. (1925) reprint 1995. Indexed.
Cloth. $38.00. 332 pp. + index. .... Vendor G0610

Pedigo, Virginia G., and Lewis G. Pedigo. **History of Patrick and Henry Counties, Virginia**. (1933) reprint 1990. Indexed. Illus.
Cloth. $27.00. 400 pp. .... Vendor G0011

Schreiner-Yantis, Netti, and Florene Love. **1787 Census of Henry County, Virginia**. 1987. Indexed.
   Information is from the 1787 Personal Property Tax Lists.
Paper. $3.50. 32 pp. .... Vendor G0081

Schreiner-Yantis, Netti. **1810 Tax List of Henry County, Virginia**.
   Included in *A Supplement to the 1810 Census of Virginia.*
Paper. $2.00. .... Vendor G0081

Highland County

Cleek, George Washington. **Early Western Augusta Pioneers,** Including the Families of Cleek, Gwin, Lightner, and Warwick and Related Families of Bratton, Campbell, Carlile, Craig, Crawford, Dyer, Gay, Givens, Graham, Harper, Henderson, Hull, Keister, Lockridge, McFarland, and Moore. (1957) reprint 1995. Indexed.
Paper. $37.50. 492 pp. .... Vendor G0011

Morton, Oren F. **A History of Highland County, Virginia**. With a New 112-Page Index to Names. (1911) reprint 1997. Indexed. Illus.
Contact vendor for information. 532 pp. .... Vendor G0011

Isle of Wight County

Abercrombie, Janice Luck, and Richard Slatten. **Isle of Wight Co., VA "Publick" Claims**.
Paper. $5.00. 33 pp. .... Vendor G0632

Boddie, John Bennett. **Seventeenth Century Isle of Wight County, Virginia**. (1938) reprint 1994. Indexed. Illus.
Cloth. $40.00. 756 pp. .... Vendor G0010

Boddie, John Bennett. **Seventeenth Century Isle of Wight County, Virginia. A History of the County of the Isle of Wight, Virginia, During the 17th Century, Including Abstracts of the County Records**. 1938. Indexed. Illus.
Cloth. $45.00. 756 pp. .... Vendor G0610

Chapman, Blanche Adams. **Marriages of Isle of Wight County, Virginia, 1628-1800.** With a New Index. (1933) reprint 1997. Indexed.
Contact vendor for information. 124 pp. .... Vendor G0011

Chapman, Blanche Adams. **Wills and Administrations of Isle of Wight County, Virginia, 1647-1800.** With an Improved Index. (1938, 1975) reprint 1996. Indexed.
Paper. $32.00. 370 pp. .... Vendor G0011

Chapman, Blanche Adams. **Wills and Administrations of Isle of Wight County, 1647-1800.** (1938) reprint 1994. Indexed.
Paper. $30.00. 347 pp. .... Vendor G0140

Chapman, Blanche Adams. **Wills and Administrations of Isle of Wight County, Virginia, 1647-1800.** 1938. Reprint on microfiche. Indexed.
Order no. 681, $14.00. 152 pp. .... Vendor G0478

Hopkins, William Lindsay, scr. **Isle of Wight County, Virginia Deeds, 1647-1719, Court Orders, 1693-1695 and Guardian Accounts, 1740-1767.** Reprint 1995. Indexed.
Paper. $30.00. .... Vendor G0632

Hopkins, William Lindsay, scr. **Isle of Wight County, Virginia Deeds, 1720-1736, and Deeds, 1741-1749.** Reprint 1994. Indexed.
Paper. $30.00. 156 pp. .... Vendor G0632

Hopkins, William Lindsay, scr. **Isle of Wight County, Virginia Deeds, 1750-1782.** 1995. Indexed.
Paper. $30.00. v + 209 pp. .... Vendor G0632

Proceedings of the Committees of Safety of Cumberland and Isle of Wight Counties, Virginia, 1775-1776. 1919.
Cloth. $5.00. 54 pp. .... Vendor G0553

Schreiner-Yantis, Netti, and Florene Love. **1787 Census of Isle of Wight County, Virginia.** 1987. Indexed.
Information is from the 1787 Personal Property Tax Lists.
Paper. $3.50. 32 pp. .... Vendor G0081

T.L.C. Genealogy. **Isle of Wight County, Virginia, Deeds, 1736-1741.** 1992. Indexed.
Paper. $12.00. 115 pp. .... Vendor G0609

James City County

Abercrombie, Janice Luck, and Richard Slatten. **James City Co., VA "Publick" Claims.**
Paper. $5.00. 26 pp. .... Vendor G0632

Blackmon, Jean E., scr. **James City County, Virginia Land Tax Records, 1782-1813.** 1991. Indexed.
Paper. $29.95. Approx. 330 pp. .... Vendor G0632

Duvall, Lindsay O. **James City County, Va., 1634-1659, Vol. 4.** (1957) reprint 1978. Indexed.
Paper. $17.50. 96 pp. .... Vendor G0610

Map of "James City," Virginia 1607-1608.
Map. $2.50. .... Vendor G0549

Schreiner-Yantis, Netti. and Florene Love. **1787 Census of James City County & Williamsburg City, Virginia**. 1987. Indexed.
Information is from the 1787 Personal Property Tax List for James City County, but this year's list is missing for Williamsburg. Instead, the 1784, 1786, and 1788 lists are transcribed for this work. The names of all white males over 21 years are missing from the Williamsburg list, as are the number of 16-21 year olds in the household. The names of all the slaves are given in the 1784 and 1786 lists of Williamsburg.
Paper. $3.50. 32 pp. .... Vendor G0081

Schreiner-Yantis, Netti. **1810 Tax List of James City County, Virginia**.
Included in *A Supplement to the 1810 Census of Virginia*.
Paper. $2.00. .... Vendor G0081

Weisiger, Benjamin B., III. **Burned County Data, 1809-1848 (As Found in the Virginia Contested Election Files)**. 1986. Indexed.
The following counties are included: Hanover, Buckingham, Charles City, Gloucester, New Kent, James City, and Caroline.
Paper. $15.00. 100 pp. .... Vendor G0632

Woodson, Robert F., and Isobel B. Woodson. **Virginia Tithables from Burned Record Counties (Buckingham, Gloucester, Hanover, James City, and Stafford)**. (1970) reprint 1982.
Paper. $20.00. 122 pp. .... Vendor G0610

King and Queen County

Abercrombie, Janice Luck, and Richard Slatten. **King & Queen Co., VA "Publick" Claims**.
Paper. $8.25. 66 pp. .... Vendor G0632

Bagby, Rev. Alfred. **King and Queen County, Virginia**. (1908) reprint 1990. Indexed. Illus.
Cloth. $23.50. 402 pp. .... Vendor G0011

Chamberlayne, C. G., ed. **Vestry Book of Stratton Major Parish, King and Queen County, Virginia, 1729-1783**. (1933) reprint 1980.
Paper. $15.00. xxi + 257 pp. .... Vendor G0553

Schreiner-Yantis, Netti, and Florene Love. **1787 Census of King & Queen County, Virginia**. 1987. Indexed.
Information is from the 1787 Personal Property Tax Lists.
Paper. $3.50. 32 pp. .... Vendor G0081

King George County

Abercrombie, Janice Luck, and Richard Slatten. **King George Co., VA "Publick" Claims**.
Paper. $5.00. 27 pp. .... Vendor G0632

Harris, Nancy E. **King George County, Virginia 1720-1990**. (1990) reprint 1994. Indexed. Illus.
Paper. $40.00. 424 pp. .... Vendor G0011

King, George H. S. **King George County, Virginia, Will Book A-I: 1721-1752, and Miscellaneous Notes**. (1978) reprint 1985. Indexed. Illus.
Cloth. $35.00. 352 pp. .... Vendor G0610

King, George H. S. **King George County, Virginia, 1777-1798, The Register of Saint Paul's Parish, 1715-1776. Stafford County 1715-1776, Arranged Alphabetically by Surnames in Chronological Order**. (1960) reprint 1985. Illus.
Cloth. $27.50. 192 pp. .... Vendor G0610

Klein, Margaret C. **Tombstone Inscriptions of King George County, Virginia**. (1979) reprint 1994. Indexed.
Paper. $10.00. 84 pp. .... Vendor G0011

Lee, Elizabeth Nuckols, scr. **King George County, Virginia Marriages, Volume I, Marriage Bonds Book 1, 1786-1850 (Including Ministers' Returns)**. 1995. Indexed.
Paper. $12.95. ix + 77 pp. .... Vendor G0632

Lee, Elizabeth Nuckols, scr and T. William Kethley, Jr. **King George County, Virginia, Marriages: Volume II, Implied Marriages**. 1995. Indexed.
Paper. $19.95. ix + 138 pp. .... Vendor G0632

Nicklin, John B. C. **St. Paul's Parish Register** (Stafford-King George Counties, Virginia) 1715-1798. (1962) reprint 1995.
Paper. $8.50. 78 pp. .... Vendor G0011

Schreiner-Yantis, Netti, and Florene Love. **1787 Census of King George County, Virginia**. 1987. Indexed.
   Information is from the 1787 Personal Property Tax Lists.
Paper. $3.00. 24 pp. .... Vendor G0081

King William County

Abercrombie, Janice Luck, and Richard Slatten. **King William Co., VA "Publick" Claims**.
Paper. $7.50. 58 pp. .... Vendor G0632

Clarke, Peyton Neale. **Old King William Homes and Families.** An Account of Some of the Old Homesteads and Families of King William County, Virginia, from Its Earliest Settlement. (1897) reprint 1995. Indexed. Illus.
Paper. $21.50. 211 pp. .... Vendor G0011

Schreiner-Yantis, Netti, and Florene Love. **1787 Census of King William County, Virginia**. 1987. Indexed.
   Information is from the 1787 Personal Property Tax Lists.
Paper. $3.00. 24 pp. .... Vendor G0081

Schreiner-Yantis, Netti. **1810 Tax List of King William County, Virginia**.
Included in *A Supplement to the 1810 Census of Virginia*.
Paper. $2.00. .... Vendor G0081

Lancaster County

Abercrombie, Janice Luck, and Richard Slatten. **Lancaster Co., VA "Publick" Claims**.
Paper. $5.00. 30 pp. .... Vendor G0632

Duvall, Lindsay O. **Lancaster County, Va., Court Order and Deeds, 1656-1680: Vol. 2**. (1978) reprint 1989. Indexed.
Paper. $17.50. 112 pp. .... Vendor G0610

Lee, Ida J. **Abstracts Lancaster County, Virginia Wills 1653-1800**. (1959) reprint 1995.
Paper. $23.00. 240 pp. .... Vendor G0011

Lee, Ida J. **Lancaster County, Virginia, Marriage Bonds, 1652-1850**. (1965) reprint 1997.
Contact vendor for information. 71 pp. .... Vendor G0011

Nottingham, Stratton. **The Marriage License Bonds of Lancaster County, Virginia from 1701 to 1848**. (1927) reprint 1996. Indexed.
Paper. $13.50. 106 pp. .... Vendor G0011

Schreiner-Yantis, Netti, and Florene Love. **1787 Census of Lancaster County, Virginia**. 1987. Indexed.
Information is from the 1787 Personal Property Tax Lists.
Paper. $2.75. 20 pp. .... Vendor G0081

Lee County

1850 Lee County, Virginia Census.
Paper. $29.50. .... Vendor G0549

Duckworth, Reda T. **Lee County, Virginia Deed Book Records: Vol. 1, 1793-1804**. Indexed.
Paper. $15.00. .... Vendor G0549

Duckworth, Reda T. **Lee County, Virginia Deed Book Records: Vol. 2, 1805-1812**. Indexed.
Paper. $15.00. .... Vendor G0549

Duckworth, Reda T. **Lee County, Virginia Deed Book Records: Vol. 3, 1813-1820**. Indexed.
Paper. $15.00. .... Vendor G0549

Schreiner-Yantis, Netti. **1810 Tax List of Lee County, Virginia**.
Included in *A Supplement to the 1810 Census of Virginia*.
Paper. $2.00. .... Vendor G0081

Vogt, John, and T. William Kethley, Jr. **Lee County Marriages, 1830-1836**. 1984. Indexed. Illus.
Paper. $5.95. ix + 28 pp. .... Vendor G0632

Loudoun County

Abercrombie, Janice Luck, and Richard Slatten. **Loudoun Co., VA "Publick" Claims**.
Paper. $7.75. 64 pp. .... Vendor G0632

Blincoe, Don, Sr. **Loudoun County Militia Registers, 1793-1829**. 1993. Indexed.
Paper. $29.95. ix + 495 pp. .... Vendor G0632

Frain, Elizabeth R. **Union Cemetery, Leesburg, Loudoun County, Virginia, Plats A and B, 1784-1995**. 1995. Indexed.
Paper. $34.00. vii + 350 pp. .... Vendor G0669

Head, James W. **History and Comprehensive Description of Loudoun County, Virginia**. (1908) reprint 1989.
Cloth. $18.00. 186 pp. .... Vendor G0011

Hiatt, Marty, and Craig Roberts Scott. **Loudoun County, Virginia Chancery Suits, 1759-1915**. 1994. Indexed.
Paper. $20.00. 206 pp. .... Vendor G0632

Hiatt, Marty, and Craig Roberts Scott. **Loudoun County, Virginia Tithables, 1758-1786**. 3 vols. 1994. Indexed.
Paper. $54.95. 1,400 pp. .... Vendor G0632

Hopkins, Margaret Lail. **Index to the Tithables of Loudoun County, Virginia, and to Slaveholders and Slaves, 1758-1786**. 1991.
Cloth. $20.00. 156 pp. .... Vendor G0010

Jewell, Aurelia M. **Loudoun County, Virginia Marriage Bonds, 1762-1850**. (1962) reprint 1997. Indexed.
Contact vendor for information. 219 pp. .... Vendor G0011

King, Junie Estelle Stewart. **Abstracts of Wills, Inventories, and Administration Accounts of Loudoun County, Virginia, 1757-1800**. (1940) reprint 1996. Indexed.
Paper. $7.50. 85 pp. .... Vendor G0010

Mower, Jerry, and Tedi Jeen Mower. **St. James United Church of Christ Church Register (Ref. Church) Loudoun Co. Virginia ca. Sept. 17, 1789-August 23, 1823,** Translated from German to English. Indexed.
    The members of this church were largely German immigrants or the children of German immigrants. Some individuals who attended this church had lived in Frederick County, Maryland. Many members later moved to Bedford County, Pennsylvania. Anyone with Virginia, Maryland, or Pennsylvania ancestors of German origin should investigate this record.
Paper. $7.00. 53 pp. .... Vendor G0536

Schreiner-Yantis, Netti, and Florene Love. **1787 Census of Loudoun County, Virginia**. 1987. Indexed.
    Information is from the 1787 Personal Property Tax Lists.
Paper. $10.00. 84 pp. .... Vendor G0081

Schreiner-Yantis, Netti, and Florene Love. **1788 Tax Lists of Loudoun County, Virginia**. 1987. Indexed.
Paper. $10.00. .... Vendor G0081

Schreiner-Yantis, Netti. **1789 Tax Lists of Loudoun County, Virginia**. Indexed.
Contact vendor for information. .... Vendor G0081

Schreiner-Yantis, Netti. **Loudoun County, Virginia Tithable Lists for the Taxable Year 1784/5**. 1990.
 Seventeen separate lists; possibly each is a militia district. Loudoun County was the most populous county during this period and the division into separate lists is helpful in determining the locality in which taxpayers resided. Names of white tithes (males over 16 years) and names of Negro tithes are given.
Paper. $4.75. 40 pp. .... Vendor G0081

Stetson, Charles W. **Four Mile Run Land Grants**. (1935) reprint 1994. Indexed.
 History of the Northern Neck grants for the present-day Alexandria and Loudoun and Fairfax counties.
Paper. $10.00. 145 pp. .... Vendor G0140

Stevenson, Brenda E. **Life in Black and White: Family and Community in the Slave South**. 1996.
 This book provides a panoramic portrait of family and community life in and around Loudoun County, Virginia, weaving the fascinating personal stories of planters and slaves, of free blacks and poor to middling whites, into a powerful portrait of southern society from the mid-18th century to the Civil War.
Cloth. 35.00. 457 pp. .... Vendor G0611

T.L.C. Genealogy. **Loudoun County, Virginia Minute Book, 1780-1783**. 1990. Indexed.
Paper. $12.00. 196 pp. .... Vendor G0609

Vogt, John, and T. William Kethley, Jr. **Loudoun County Marriages, 1760-1850**. 1985. Indexed. Illus.
Paper. $20.00. ix + 462 pp. .... Vendor G0632

Wertz, Mary Alice. **Marriages of Loudoun County, Virginia, 1757-1853**. (1985) reprint 1990. Indexed.
Cloth. $15.00. 231 pp. .... Vendor G0011

Louisa County

Abercrombie, Janice Luck, scr. **Free Blacks of Louisa County, VA: Bonds, Wills & Other Records**. 1993. Indexed.
Paper. $14.95. vi + 193 pp. .... Vendor G0632

Abercrombie, Janice Luck, and Richard Slatten. **Louisa Co., VA "Publick" Claims**.
Paper. $7.75. 73 pp. .... Vendor G0632

Gilmer, Col. J. F. **Map of Louisa County, Virginia (1863)**.
Map. $6.00. .... Vendor G0632

Hiatt, Marty, and Craig Roberts Scott, comps. **Louisa County, Virginia 1850 Federal Census**. 1995. Indexed.
Paper. $20.00. 201 pp. .... Vendor G0632

Kiblinger, William H., and Janice L. Abercrombie, comps. **Marriages of Louisa Co., VA, 1815-1861**. 1989. Indexed.
Cloth. $18.50. iv + 188 pp. .... Vendor G0632

Schreiner-Yantis, Netti, and Florene Love. **1787 Census of Louisa County, Virginia**. 1987. Indexed.
    Information is from the 1787 Personal Property Tax Lists.
Paper. $3.50. 32 pp. .... Vendor G0081

Schreiner-Yantis, Netti. **1810 Tax List of Louisa County, Virginia**.
    Included in *A Supplement to the 1810 Census of Virginia*.
Paper. $2.00. .... Vendor G0081

Williams, Kathleen Booth. **Marriages of Louisa County, Virginia, 1766-1815**. (1959) reprint 1989. Indexed.
Cloth. $17.95. 143 pp. .... Vendor G0011

Lunenburg County

Abercrombie, Janice Luck, and Richard Slatten. **Lunenburg Co., VA "Publick" Claims**.
Paper. $5.00. 27 pp. .... Vendor G0632

Bell, Landon C. **Cumberland Parish, Lunenburg County, Virginia 1746-1816 [and] Vestry Book 1746-1816**. (1930) reprint 1994. Indexed.
Paper. $45.00. 633 pp. .... Vendor G0011

Bell, Landon C. **Cumberland Parish, Lunenburg County, Virginia, 1746-1816 and Vestry Book 1746-1816**. (1930) reprint 1995. Indexed.
Cloth. $45.00. 633 pp. .... Vendor G0610

Bell, Landon C. **The Old Free State.** A Contribution to the History of Lunenburg County and Southside Virginia. 2 vols. (1927) reprint 1995. Indexed.
Paper. $95.00. 623 + 644 pp. .... Vendor G0011

Bell, Landon C. **Sunlight on the Southside.** Lists of Tithes, Lunenburg County, Virginia, 1748-1783. (1931) reprint 1991. Indexed. Illus.
Cloth. $37.50. 503 pp. .... Vendor G0011

Coke, Ben H. **Some Early Landowners in Southern Nottoway and Northern Lunenburg Counties, Virginia, and the Cocke Family . . .** 1996. Indexed. Illus.
Paper. $25.00. vi + 135 pp. .... Vendor G0632

Elliott, Katherine B. **Lunenburg County, Virginia, Early Wills, 1746-1765**. (1967) reprint 1983. Indexed.
Cloth, $27.50. Paper, $22.50. 178 pp. .... Vendor G0610

Matheny, Emma R., and Helen K. Yates. **Marriages of Lunenburg County, Virginia, 1746-1853**. (1967) reprint 1997. Indexed. Illus.
Contact vendor for information. 177 pp. .... Vendor G0011

Schreiner-Yantis, Netti, and Florene Love. **1787 Census of Lunenburg County, Virginia**. 1987. Indexed.
   Information is from the 1787 Personal Property Tax Lists.
Paper. $3.50. 32 pp. .... Vendor G0081

T.L.C. Genealogy. **Lunenburg County, Virginia Court Orders, 1746-1748**. 1991. Indexed.
Paper. $15.00. 219 pp. .... Vendor G0609

T.L.C. Genealogy. **Lunenburg County, Virginia Court Orders, 1752-1762: An Every-Name Index to Order Books 2 1/2 A, 2 1/2 B, 3, 4, 5, 6, 7, & 8**. 1995. Indexed.
Paper. $20.00. 160 pp. .... Vendor G0609

T.L.C. Genealogy. **Lunenburg County, Virginia Deeds, 1746-1752**. 1990. Indexed.
Paper. $12.00. 98 pp. .... Vendor G0609

T.L.C. Genealogy. **Lunenburg County, Virginia Deeds, 1752-1757**. 1990. Indexed.
Paper. $12.00. 137 pp. .... Vendor G0609

T.L.C. Genealogy. **Lunenburg County, Virginia Deeds, 1757-1761**. 1990. Indexed.
Paper. $12.00. 143 pp. .... Vendor G0609

T.L.C. Genealogy. **Lunenburg County, Virginia Deed Books 7 & 8 (1761-1764)**. 1990. Indexed.
Paper. $12.00. 134 pp. .... Vendor G0609

T.L.C. Genealogy. **Lunenburg County, Virginia Deed Book 9 (1763-1764)**. 1990. Indexed.
Paper. $9.00. 66 pp. .... Vendor G0609

T.L.C. Genealogy. **Lunenburg County, Virginia Deeds, 1764-1771**. 1990. Indexed.
Paper. $12.00. 126 pp. .... Vendor G0609

T.L.C. Genealogy. **Lunenburg County, Virginia Deeds, 1771-1777**. 1990. Indexed.
Paper. $12.00. 114 pp. .... Vendor G0609

T.L.C. Genealogy. **Lunenburg County, Virginia Deeds, 1777-1784**. 1991. Indexed.
Paper. $12.00. 142 pp. .... Vendor G0609

T.L.C. Genealogy. **Lunenburg County, Virginia Deeds, 1784-1787**. 1990. Indexed.
Paper. $10.00. 79 pp. .... Vendor G0609

T.L.C. Genealogy. **Lunenburg County, Virginia Deeds, 1787-1790**. 1991. Indexed.
Paper. $9.00. 78 pp. .... Vendor G0609

T.L.C. Genealogy. **Lunenburg County, Virginia Deeds, 1790-1795**. 1992. Indexed.
Paper. $12.00. 147 pp. .... Vendor G0609

T.L.C. Genealogy. **Lunenburg County, Virginia, Deed Books 1-16 (1746-1795): An Every-Name Index**. 1992. Indexed.
Paper. $15.00. 204 pp. .... Vendor G0609

T.L.C. Genealogy. **Lunenburg County, Virginia Land Patents, 1746-1916**. 1990. Indexed.
Paper. $12.00. 169 pp. .... Vendor G0609

T.L.C. Genealogy. **Lunenburg County, Virginia Personal Property Tax Lists, 1782 & 1785**. 1992. Indexed.
Paper. $10.00. 82 pp. .... Vendor G0609

T.L.C. Genealogy. **Lunenburg County, Virginia Will Book 2 (1760-1778)**. 1991. Indexed.
Paper. $16.00. 145 pp. .... Vendor G0609

Vogt, John, and T. William Kethley, Jr. **Lunenburg County Marriages, 1750-1853**. 1988. Indexed. Illus.
Paper. $12.00. xii + 174 pp. .... Vendor G0632

Lynchburg

Baber, Lucy H. M., Louise A. Blunt, and Marion A. L. Collins. **Marriages and Deaths from Lynchburg, Virginia Newspapers, 1794-1836**. (1980) reprint 1993.
Paper. $23.00. 266 pp. .... Vendor G0011

Madison County

Vogt, John, and T. William Kethley, Jr. **Madison County Marriages, 1792-1850**. 1984. Indexed.
Paper. $12.95. vii + 156 pp. .... Vendor G0632

Mason County

Eldridge, Carrie. **Mason County, Virginia Marriages, 1806-1850**. Illus.
Paper. $12.95. 49 pp. .... Vendor G0632

Mathews County

Branch, J. B., comp. **Epitaphs of Gloucester and Mathews Cos., in Tidewater Virginia, Through 1865**. (1959) reprint 1995.
Paper. $21.00. 168 pp. .... Vendor G0259

Matheny, Emma R., and Helen K. Yates. **Kingston Parish Register,** Gloucester and Mathews Counties, Virginia, 1749-1827. (1963) reprint 1996. Indexed.
Paper. $18.00. 167 pp. .... Vendor G0011

Mecklenburg County

Abercrombie, Janice Luck, and Richard Slatten. **Mecklenburg Co., VA "Publick" Claims**.
Paper. $7.75. 65 pp. .... Vendor G0632

Elliott, Katherine B. **Mecklenburg County, Virginia, Early Settlers, Vol. 1**. (1964) reprint 1983. Indexed.
Cloth, $30.00. Paper, $25.00. 240 pp. .... Vendor G0610

Elliott, Katherine B. **Mecklenburg County, Virginia, Early Settlers, Vol. 2**. (1965) reprint 1983. Indexed.
Cloth, $30.00. Paper, $25.00. 266 pp. .... Vendor G0610

Elliott, Katherine B. **Mecklenburg County, Virginia, Early Wills, 1765-1795**. (1963) reprint 1983. Indexed.
Cloth, $30.00. Paper, $25.00. 246 pp. .... Vendor G0610

Elliott, Katherine B. **Mecklenburg County, Virginia, Marriage Records, 1765-1810**. (1963) reprint 1984. Indexed.
Cloth, $27.50. Paper, $22.50. 190 pp. .... Vendor G0610

Elliott, Katherine B. **Mecklenburg County, Virginia, Marriage Records, 1811-1853**. (1962) reprint 1983. Indexed.
Cloth, $28.50. Paper, $24.00. 236 pp. .... Vendor G0610

Elliott, Katherine B. **Mecklenburg County, Virginia, Revolutionary War Records**. (1964) reprint 1983. Indexed.
Cloth, $30.00. Paper, $25.00. 230 pp. .... Vendor G0610

Nottingham, Stratton. **Marriages of Mecklenburg County [Virginia] from 1765 to 1810**. (1928) reprint 1996. Indexed.
Paper. $10.00. 71 pp. .... Vendor G0011

Schreiner-Yantis, Netti, and Florene Love. **1787 Census of Mecklenburg County, Virginia**. 1987. Indexed.
    Information is from the 1787 Personal Property Tax Lists. Mecklenburg County is one of the most informative of all the county enumerations.
Paper. $9.00. 84 pp. .... Vendor G0081

Schreiner-Yantis, Netti. **1810 Tax List of Mecklenburg County, Virginia**.
    Included in *A Supplement to the 1810 Census of Virginia*.
Paper. $2.00. .... Vendor G0081

T.L.C. Genealogy. **Mecklenburg County, Virginia Deeds, 1765-1771**. 1990. Indexed.
Paper. $12.00. 157 pp. .... Vendor G0609

T.L.C. Genealogy. **Mecklenburg County, Virginia Deeds, 1771-1776**. 1991. Indexed.
Paper. $14.00. 171 pp. .... Vendor G0609

T.L.C. Genealogy. **Mecklenburg County, Virginia Deeds, 1777-1779**. 1994. Indexed.
Paper. $15.00. 117 pp. .... Vendor G0609

T.L.C. Genealogy. **Mecklenburg County, Virginia Deeds, 1779-1786**. 1991. Indexed.
Paper. $14.00. 165 pp. .... Vendor G0609

Vogt, John, and T. William Kethley, Jr. **Mecklenburg Co. Marriages, 1765-1853**.
1989. Indexed. Illus.
Paper. $17.95. ix + 302 pp. .... Vendor G0632

Middlesex County

Abercrombie, Janice Luck, and Richard Slatten. **Middlesex Co., VA "Publick" Claims**.
Paper. $5.00. 14 pp. .... Vendor G0632

Hopkins, William Lindsay, scr. **Middlesex County, Virginia Wills, Inventories and Accounts, 1673-1812**. 1989. Indexed.
Paper. $34.95. vi + 252 pp. .... Vendor G0632

Hopkins, William Lindsay. **Middlesex County, Virginia Wills, Inventories, and Other Court Papers, 1673-1812**. 1989. Indexed.
Paper. $34.95. 252 pp. .... Vendor G0140

The National Society of the Colonial Dames of America in the State of Virginia. **The Parish Register of Christ Church, Middlesex Co., Virginia, from 1625 to 1812**.
(1897) reprint 1988. Indexed.
Cloth. $37.50. 360 pp. .... Vendor G0610

The Parish Register of Christ Church, Middlesex County, Virginia from 1653 to 1812. (1897) reprint 1997. Indexed.
Contact vendor for information. 341 pp. .... Vendor G0011

Schreiner-Yantis, Netti, and Florene Love. **1787 Census of Middlesex County, Virginia**. 1987. Indexed.
  Information is from the 1787 Personal Property Tax Lists.
Paper. $2.50. 38 pp. .... Vendor G0081

Schreiner-Yantis, Netti. **1810 Census and 1810 Tax List of Middlesex County**.
   Not just an index. Gives all census data as found in the 1810 census and all infor-
mation in 1810 Personal Property Tax List, then compares the two.
Paper. $2.50. .... Vendor G0081

T.L.C. Genealogy. **Middlesex County, Virginia, Deed Book 1 (1687-1750) and
Miscellaneous Records (1752-1831)**. 1993. Indexed.
Paper. $12.00. 67 pp. .... Vendor G0609

Virginia Genealogical Society. **Marriages of Middlesex County, Virginia, 1740-
1852**. (1965) reprint 1976. Indexed.
Contact vendor for information 124 pp. .... Vendor G0610

Wright, Sue. **Middlesex County, Virginia 1850 U.S. Census**. 1995. Indexed.
Paper. $12.50. 56 pp. .... Vendor G0471

Wright, Sue. **Middlesex County, Virginia 1860 U.S. Census**. 1995. Indexed.
Paper. $12.50. 58 pp. .... Vendor G0471

Monongalia County

1790 Monongalia County, Virginia (WV) Census.
Paper. $2.50. .... Vendor G0549

Abercrombie, Janice Luck, and Richard Slatten. **Monongalia Co., VA "Publick"
Claims**.
Paper. $5.00. 16 pp. .... Vendor G0632

Montgomery County

Abercrombie, Janice Luck, and Richard Slatten. **Montgomery Co., VA "Publick"
Claims**.
Paper. $5.00. 21 pp. .... Vendor G0632

Brock, R. A. **Montgomery County, Virginia Biographies**.
   A reprint of his 1880s edition of sketches in the area.
Paper. $10.00. .... Vendor G0549

Crush, Judge C. W. **Montgomery County, Virginia: The First 100 Years.** With
Index by Frances Ingmire. 1994. Indexed.
Paper. $29.95. ii + 209 pp. .... Vendor G0632

Dickenson, Richard B. **Entitled! Free Papers in Appalachia Concerning Antebellum Freeborn Negroes and Emancipated Blacks of Montgomery County, Virginia.** Edited and indexed by Varney R. Nell.
   Freeborn Negroes and emancipated blacks identified from 1830, 1840, 1850, 1860,
and 1867 censuses and 1866 Marriage Register of Montgomery County.
Cloth. $18.50. 102 pp. .... Vendor G0627

Douthat, James L. **Early Settlers of Montgomery County, Virginia, 1810-1850
Census**. Indexed.
Paper. $20.00. .... Vendor G0549

Douthat, James L. **Montgomery County, Virginia Deed Book 1, 1773-1789**.
Paper. $17.50. .... Vendor G0549

Douthat, James L. **Montgomery County, Virginia Will Book 1, 1786-1809**.
Paper. $12.50. .... Vendor G0549

Schreiner-Yantis, Netti, and Florene Love. **1787 Census of Montgomery County, Virginia**. 1987. Indexed.
Information is from the 1787 Personal Property Tax Lists.
Paper. $6.00. 48 pp. .... Vendor G0081

Schreiner-Yantis, Netti. **1788 Tax List of Montgomery County, Virginia**. 1972.
About 1,700 taxpayers listed. This list is very important as it names every tithable male 21 years of age or over. Many sons are named who are living in their father's households. White males between 16 and 21 years are enumerated by number, not name, in another column. The number of slaves and horses owned are also shown.
Paper. $3.75. .... Vendor G0081

Schreiner-Yantis, Netti. **1790 Tax List of the Portion of Montgomery Which Had Been Annexed from Botetourt in 1789**. Indexed.
This list also shows all tithable males over 21 by name and enumerates white males in a household between 16 and 21 years. The approximate location of taxpayers within the county is indicated in most cases.
Paper. $2.25. .... Vendor G0081

Schreiner-Yantis, Netti. **Montgomery County, Virginia Circa 1790**. Indexed.
Near the end of the 18th century, Montgomery County, Virginia was a vast domain. This territory is now divided into twenty-two Virginia and West Virginia counties (Virginia: Bland, Carroll, Craig, Floyd, Giles, Grayson, Montgomery, Pulaski, Roanoke, Smythe, Tazewell, Wythe; West Virginia: Boone, Fayette, Kanawha, Logan, McDowell, Mercer, Mingo, Raleigh, Summers, Wyoming). Although a large number of people resided there, a very limited quantity of records are available concerning them. The first two federal census enumerations for the county were destroyed. Only two types of records were kept with care and consistency—the land records and the tax records. This book contains heretofore unpublished material from these sources.
Cloth, $17.50. Paper, $12.50. 124 pp. .... Vendor G0081

Worrell, Anne Lowry. **A Brief of Wills and Marriages in Montgomery and Fincastle Counties, Virginia, 1733-1831**. (1932) reprint 1996.
Paper. $7.50. 56 pp. .... Vendor G0010

Nansemond County

Abercrombie, Janice Luck, and Richard Slatten. **Nansemond Co., VA "Publick" Claims**.
Paper. $6.75. 50 pp. .... Vendor G0632

Hall, Wilmer L., ed. **Vestry Book of the Upper Parish of Nansemond County, Virginia, 1743-1793**. (1949) reprint 1981.
Paper. $15.00. lxxiv + 328 pp. .... Vendor G0553

Hopkins, William Lindsay, scr. **Suffolk Parish Vestry Book, 1749-1784 and Newport Parish Vestry Book, 1724-1772**. 1988. Indexed.
Paper. $27.95. iv + 210 pp. .... Vendor G0632

Norfleet, Fillmore. **Bible Records of Suffolk and Nansemond County, Virginia,** Together with Other Statistical Data. (1963) reprint 1996. Indexed.
Paper. $22.00. 220 pp. .... Vendor G0011

Schreiner-Yantis, Netti, and Florene Love. **1787 Census of Nansemond County, Virginia**. 1987. Indexed.
   Nansemond County is one of the counties for which the 1787 Personal Property Tax Lists are missing. [All PP Tax lists prior to 1814 are missing for this county.] Contemporary records have been used to obtain the names of those who were resident in the county.
Paper. $5.00. 44 pp. .... Vendor G0081

Nelson County

Davis, Rev. Bailey Fulton. **Lynchburg, Virginia and Nelson County, Virginia Wills, Deeds and Marriages**. (1964, 1968) reprint 1985. Indexed.
Cloth. $30.00. 252 pp. .... Vendor G0610

Vogt, John, and T. William Kethley, Jr. **Nelson County Marriages, 1808-1850**. 1985. Indexed.
Paper. $12.95. viii + 129 pp. .... Vendor G0632

New Kent County

Abercrombie, Janice Luck, and Richard Slatten. **New Kent Co., VA "Publick" Claims**.
Paper. $5.00. 31 pp. .... Vendor G0632

National Society of the Colonial Dames of America in the State of Virginia. **The Parish Register of St. Peter's, New Kent County, Virginia, 1680 to 1787**. (1904) reprint 1996. Indexed.
Paper. $22.00. 206 pp. .... Vendor G0011

National Society of the Colonial Dames of America in the State of Virginia. **The Vestry Book of St. Peter's, New Kent County, Va from 1682-1758**. (1905) reprint 1995. Indexed.
Paper. $22.50. 242 pp. .... Vendor G0011

Schreiner-Yantis, Netti, and Florene Love. **1787 Census of New Kent County, Virginia**. 1987. Indexed.
   Information is from the 1787 Personal Property Tax Lists.
Paper. $3.00. 24 pp. .... Vendor G0081

T.L.C. Genealogy. **New Kent County, Virginia Land Tax Lists, 1782-1790**. 1992. Indexed.
Paper. $12.00. 82 pp. .... Vendor G0609

Weisiger, Benjamin B., III. **Burned County Data, 1809-1848 (As Found in the Virginia Contested Election Files)**. 1986. Indexed.
   The following counties are included: Hanover, Buckingham, Charles City, Gloucester, New Kent, James City, and Caroline.
Paper. $15.00. 100 pp. .... Vendor G0632

Norfolk County

Abercrombie, Janice Luck, and Richard Slatten. **Norfolk Co., VA "Publick" Claims**.
Paper. $5.00. 33 pp. .... Vendor G0632

McIntosh, Charles F. **Brief Abstract of Lower Norfolk Co. & Norfolk Co. Wills,
1637-1710**. (1914) reprint 1994.
Cloth. $23.00. 223 pp. .... Vendor G0259

McIntosh, Charles Fleming. **(Brief Abstract of) Lower Norfolk County & Norfolk
County Wills, 1637-1710**. 1914.
Paper. $14.00. 226 pp. .... Vendor G0140

McIntosh, Charles Fleming. **Brief Abstracts of Norfolk County Wills, 1710-1753**. 1922.
Paper. $21.00. 347 pp. .... Vendor G0140

McIntosh, Charles Fleming. **Brief Abstracts of Norfolk County Wills, 1710-1753**.
(1922) reprint 1982. Indexed.
Paper. $30.00. 344 pp. .... Vendor G0610

McIntosh, Charles Fleming. **Lower Norfolk County and Norfolk County Wills,
1637-1710**. (1914) reprint 1982. Indexed.
Paper. $30.00. 224 pp. .... Vendor G0610

Schreiner-Yantis, Netti, and Florene Love. **1787 Census of Norfolk County & Norfolk City, Virginia**. 1987. Indexed.
  Information is from the 1787 Personal Property Tax Lists.
Paper. $6.00. 48 pp. .... Vendor G0081

Walter, Alice Granbery. **Lower Norfolk County, Virginia Court Records: Books
"A" and "B," 1637-1651/2**. 2 vols. in 1. (1978, 1994) reprint 1995. Indexed. Illus.
Paper. $36.50. 263 + 205 pp. .... Vendor G0011

Walter, Alice Granbery. **Virginia Land Patents of the Counties of Norfolk, Princess
Anne & Warwick**. From Patent Books "0" & "6", 1666 to 1679. (1972) reprint 1993.
Indexed.
Paper. $10.00. 75 pp. .... Vendor G0011

Wingo, Elizabeth B. **Collection of Unrecorded Wills of Norfolk County, Virginia,
1711-1800**. (1961) reprint 1984. Indexed.
Contact vendor for information. 148 pp. .... Vendor G0610

Wingo, Elizabeth B. **Marriages of Norfolk County, Virginia, Vol. 1, 1706-1792**.
(1961) reprint 1984. Indexed.
Paper. $25.00. 92 pp. .... Vendor G0610

Wingo, Elizabeth B. **Marriages of Norfolk County, Virginia, Vol. 2, 1788, 1793-
1817**. 1963. Indexed.
Paper. $25.00. 170 pp. .... Vendor G0610

Wingo, Elizabeth B., and W. Bruce Wingo. **Norfolk County, Virginia, Tithables,
1730-1750**. 1979. Indexed.
Paper. $22.50. 258 pp. .... Vendor G0610

Wingo, Mrs. William B., comp. **Guardian Bonds of Norfolk County, Virginia, 1750-1800**. 1993. Indexed.
Paper. $17.95. viii + 105 pp. .... Vendor G0632

Wingo, Mrs. William B., comp. **Norfolk Co., VA Will Book 1, 1755-1772**.
Paper. $20.50. 155 pp. .... Vendor G0632

Northampton County

Abercrombie, Janice Luck, and Richard Slatten. **Northampton Co., VA "Publick" Claims**.
Paper. $5.00. 11 pp. .... Vendor G0632

The Marriage License Bonds of Northampton County, Virginia from 1706 to 1854. (1929) reprint 1994. Indexed.
Paper. $15.00. 135 pp. .... Vendor G0011

Marshall, James Handley. **Abstracts of Wills & Administrations of Northampton County, Virginia 1632-1802**. 1994. Indexed.
   Book #1446.
Cloth. $59.50. 736 pp. .... Vendor G0082

Mihalyka, Jean Merritt, comp. **Gravestone Inscriptions in Northampton County, Virginia.** Edited by Alice B. Deal. Rev. ed. 1984.
Paper. $12.50. xxxiii + 106 pp. .... Vendor G0553

Schreiner-Yantis, Netti, and Florene Love. **1787 Census of Northampton County, Virginia**. 1987. Indexed.
   Information is from the 1787 Personal Property Tax Lists.
Paper. $3.25. 28 pp. .... Vendor G0081

Schreiner-Yantis, Netti. **1810 Tax List of Northampton County, Virginia**.
   Included in *A Supplement to the 1810 Census of Virginia*.
Paper. $2.00. .... Vendor G0081

Wise, Jennings Cropper. **Ye Kingdome of Accawmacke or the Eastern Shore of Virginia in the 17th Century**. (1911) reprint 1997. Indexed.
Contact vendor for information. 406 pp. .... Vendor G0011

Northumberland County

Abercrombie, Janice Luck, and Richard Slatten. **Northumberland Co., VA "Publick" Claims**.
Paper. $5.00. 22 pp. .... Vendor G0632

Duvall, Lindsay O. **Northumberland County, Va., 1678-1713, Vol. 1**. (1952) reprint 1978. Indexed.
Paper. $20.00. 160 pp. .... Vendor G0610

Nottingham, Stratton. **The Marriage License Bonds of Northumberland Co., Va . . . 1783-1850**. (1929) reprint 1994. Indexed.
Paper. $13.50. 132 pp. .... Vendor G0011

Nottingham, Stratton. **Marriage License Bonds of Northumberland County, Virginia from 1783 to 1850**. (1929) reprint 1993. Indexed.
Paper. $10.00. 140 pp. .... Vendor G0140

Schreiner-Yantis, Netti, and Florene Love. **1787 Census of Northumberland County, Virginia**. 1987. Indexed.
Information is from the 1787 Personal Property Tax Lists.
Paper. $3.50. 32 pp. .... Vendor G0081

Nottoway County

Coke, Ben H. **Some Early Landowners in Southern Nottoway and Northern Lunenburg Counties, Virginia, and the Cocke Family . . .** 1996. Indexed. Illus.
Paper. $25.00. vi + 135 pp. .... Vendor G0632

Virginia Genealogical Society. **Virginia Marriages in Rev. John Cameron's Register and Bath Parish Register (1827-1897)**. 1963. Indexed.
Marriages included are from the areas of Dinwiddie, Prince George, and Nottoway counties.
Paper. $10.00. 56 pp. .... Vendor G0610

Watson, Walter A. **Notes On Southside Virginia**. (1925) reprint 1990. Indexed.
Contains important genealogical materials on Nottoway and Amelia counties.
Cloth. $23.50. 346 pp. .... Vendor G0011

Orange County

Abercrombie, Janice Luck, and Richard Slatten. **Orange Co., VA "Publick" Claims**.
Paper. $8.25. 68 pp. .... Vendor G0632

Grymes, J. Randolph, Jr. **The Fanny Hume Diary of 1862: A Year in Wartime Orange, VA**. 1994. Indexed.
Paper. $15.00. 235 pp. .... Vendor G0632

Klein, Margaret C. **Tombstone Inscriptions of Orange County, Virginia**. (1979) reprint 1995. Indexed.
Paper. $15.00. 132 pp. .... Vendor G0011

Knorr, Catherine Lindsay. **Marriages of Orange County, Virginia, 1747-1810**. (1959) reprint 1982. Indexed. Illus.
Cloth. $17.50. 132 pp. .... Vendor G0610

Little, Barbara Vines. **Orange Co., VA Order Book One, 1734-1739: Part One, 1734-1736**. 1990. Indexed.
Paper. $15.00. iv + 114 pp. .... Vendor G0632

Schreiner-Yantis, Netti, and Florene Love. **1787 Census of Orange County, Virginia**. 1987. Indexed.
Information is from the 1787 Personal Property Tax Lists.
Paper. $3.50. 32 pp. .... Vendor G0081

Schreiner-Yantis, Netti. **1810 Tax List of Orange County, Virginia**.
Included in *A Supplement to the 1810 Census of Virginia*.
Paper. $2.00. .... Vendor G0081

Scott, William W. **A History of Orange County, Virginia**. (1907) reprint 1996.
Indexed. Illus.
Paper. $33.50. 292 pp. .... Vendor G0011

Southern California Genealogical Society. **Borden and Beverly Patents of Orange and Augusta Counties, VA**.
Also contains two fold-out, oversized maps.
Paper. $3.50. 17 pp. .... Vendor G0656

T.L.C. Genealogy. **Orange County, Virginia, Court Orders, 1734-1741**. 1994.
Indexed.
Paper. $20.00. 116 pp. .... Vendor G0609

Vogt, John, and T. William Kethley, Jr. **Orange County Marriages, 1747-1850**. 1991.
Indexed.
Paper. $20.00. xiv + 320 pp. .... Vendor G0632

Page County

1840 Page County, Virginia Census.
Paper. $5.00. .... Vendor G0549

Page County, VA Land Tax Registers 1858-1859 [Facsimile edition]. With Introduction and Index by Chester E. Ramey, III. 1995. Indexed.
Paper. $22.50. 113 pp. .... Vendor G0632

Spratt, Thomas M., comp. **Page County, Virginia Men in Gray**. 1994. Indexed.
Paper. $24.95. Approx. 400 pp. .... Vendor G0632

Vogt, John, and T. William Kethley, Jr. **Page County Marriage Bonds, 1831-1850**.
1983. Indexed.
Paper. $7.95. viii + 57 pp. .... Vendor G0632

Patrick County

1850 Patrick County, Virginia Census.
Paper. $20.00. .... Vendor G0549

Adams, Lela C. **Marriages of Patrick County, Virginia, 1791-1850**. (1972) reprint 1984. Indexed.
Paper. $20.00. 165 pp. .... Vendor G0610

Adams, Lela C. **Patrick County, Virginia, 1791-1823, Abstracts of Wills, Inventories & Accounts**. (1972) reprint 1983. Indexed.
Paper. $17.50. 110 pp. .... Vendor G0610

Adams, Lela C. **Patrick County, Virginia, 1791-August 1800, Abstracts of Order Book No. "O"**. 1984. Indexed.
Paper. $20.00. 130 pp. .... Vendor G0610

Chiarito, Marian Dodson, scr. **Entry Record Book [1], 1737-1770** (Land Entries in the Present Virginia Counties of Halifax, Pittsylvania, Henry, Franklin, and Patrick). 1984. Indexed.
Paper. $45.95. 432 pp. .... Vendor G0632

Chiarito, Marian Dodson, scr. **Entry Record Book [2], 1770-1796** (Land Entries in the Present Virginia Counties of Pittsylvania, Henry, Franklin, and Patrick). 1988. Indexed.
Pittsylvania was formed from Halifax County in 1767. The map included with the book gives names of most of the early watercourses, and makes possible the location of land entries, adjoining landowners, and other points of interest.
Paper. $23.95. 138 pp. .... Vendor G0632

James, Anne W. **Patrick County, Virginia Death Register: 1853-1870**. Indexed.
Paper. $25.00. .... Vendor G0549

Pedigo, Virginia G., and Lewis G. Pedigo. **History of Patrick and Henry Counties, Virginia**. (1933) reprint 1990. Indexed. Illus.
Cloth. $27.00. 400 pp. .... Vendor G0011

Schreiner-Yantis, Netti. **1810 Tax List of Patrick County, Virginia**.
With detailed 1821 John Wood map, showing roads, waterways, and some residences and businesses, by owner's name. (Included in *A Supplement to the 1810 Census of Virginia*.)
Paper. $2.50. .... Vendor G0081

T.L.C. Genealogy. **Patrick County, Virginia, Deed Book No. 1, 1791-1801**. (1996) reprint 1997.
Paper. $20.00. .... Vendor G0609

Pittsylvania County

1790 Pittsylvania County, Virginia Census.
Paper. $5.00. .... Vendor G0549

1820 Pittsylvania County, Virginia Census.
Paper. $7.50. .... Vendor G0549

1850 Pittsylvania County, Virginia Census.
Paper. $27.50. .... Vendor G0549

Abercrombie, Janice Luck, and Richard Slatten. **Pittsylvania Co., VA "Publick" Claims**.
Paper. $6.25. 43 pp. .... Vendor G0632

Abstracts of Pittsylvania County, Virginia Wills, 1767-1820. 1986. Indexed.
Cloth. $37.50. 408 pp. .... Vendor G0610

Brock, R. A. **Pittsylvania County, Virginia Biographies**.
A reprint of his 1880s edition of sketches in the area.
Paper. $7.50. .... Vendor G0549

Chiarito, Marian Dodson, scr. **Entry Record Book [1], 1737-1770** (Land Entries in
the Present Virginia Counties of Halifax, Pittsylvania, Henry, Franklin, and Patrick).
1984. Indexed.
Paper. $45.95. 432 pp. .... Vendor G0632

Chiarito, Marian Dodson, scr. **Entry Record Book [2], 1770-1796** (Land Entries in
the Present Virginia Counties of Pittsylvania, Henry, Franklin, and Patrick). 1988.
Indexed.
  Pittsylvania was formed from Halifax County in 1767. The map included with the
book gives names of most of the early watercourses, and makes possible the location
of land entries, adjoining landowners, and other points of interest.
Paper. $23.95. 138 pp. .... Vendor G0632

Chiarito, Marian Dodson, scr. **Old Survey Book 1, 1746-1782, Pittsylvania County,
Virginia**. 1988. Indexed.
Paper. $33.95. 400 pp. .... Vendor G0632

Chiarito, Marian Dodson, scr. **Old Survey Book 2, 1797-1829, Pittsylvania County,
Virginia**. 1988. Indexed.
Paper. $12.95. 102 pp. .... Vendor G0632

Clement, Maud C. **The History of Pittsylvania County, Virginia**. (1929) reprint
1987. Indexed. Illus.
Cloth. $21.50. 340 pp. .... Vendor G0010

Knorr, Catherine Lindsay. **Marriage Bonds and Ministers' Returns of Pittsylvania
County, Virginia, 1767-1805**. (1956) reprint 1982. Indexed.
Paper. $17.50. 136 pp. .... Vendor G0610

Payne, Lucille C., and Neil G. Payne. **Pittsylvania County, Virginia, Deed Books 1,
2 & 3, 1765-1774**. 1991, 1992. Indexed.
Paper. $25.00. 218 pp. .... Vendor G1991

Schreiner-Yantis, Netti, and Florene Love. **1787 Census of Pittsylvania County,
Virginia**. 1987. Indexed.
  Information is from the 1787 Personal Property Tax Lists.
Paper. $5.00. 44 pp. .... Vendor G0081

Schreiner-Yantis, Netti. **1810 Tax List of Pittsylvania County, Virginia**.
  Approximately 2,500 names with number of white tithables, slaves over 12 years,
and horses. A number of relationships and places of residence are given. Map of
county showing rivers and creeks. (Included in *A Supplement to the 1810 Census of
Virginia*.)
Paper. $2.50. 20 pp. .... Vendor G0081

T.L.C. Genealogy. **Pittsylvania County, Virginia Deed Book 4 (1774-1778)**. 1991.
Indexed.
Paper. $12.00. 114 pp. .... Vendor G0609

T.L.C. Genealogy. **Pittsylvania County, Virginia Deeds, 1791-1794**. 1991. Indexed.
Paper. $12.00. 103 pp. .... Vendor G0609

Williams, Mike K. **Confederate Soldiers of Pittsylvania County, Virginia & Danville**.
Paper. $12.50. .... Vendor G0549

Williams, Mike K. **Marriages of Pittsylvania County, Virginia 1831-1861**. Indexed.
Paper. $25.00. 110 pp. .... Vendor G0549

Williams, Mike K. **Marriages of Pittsylvania County, Virginia 1862-1875**.
Paper. $37.50. .... Vendor G0549

Williams, Mike K. **Wills of Pittsylvania County, Virginia 1820-1845**. Indexed.
$10.00 (perfect bound). 46 pp. .... Vendor G0549

Powhatan County

Abercrombie, Janice Luck, and Richard Slatten. **Powhatan Co., VA "Publick" Claims**.
Paper. $6.00. 40 pp. .... Vendor G0632

Knorr, Catherine Lindsay. **Marriage Bonds and Ministers' Returns of Powhatan County, Virginia, 1777-1830**. (1957) reprint 1983. Indexed. Illus.
Cloth. $15.00. 96 pp. .... Vendor G0610

Schreiner-Yantis, Netti, and Florene Love. **1787 Census of Powhatan County, Virginia**. 1987. Indexed.
Information is from the 1787 Personal Property Tax Lists.
Paper. $3.00. 24 pp. .... Vendor G0081

Vogt, John, and T. William Kethley, Jr. **Powhatan County Marriages, 1777-1850**. 1985. Indexed.
Paper. $12.95. viii + 143 pp. .... Vendor G0632

Weisiger, Benjamin B., III. **Powhatan County, Virginia Wills, 1777-1795**. 1986. Indexed.
Contact vendor for information. 70 pp. .... Vendor G0632

Prince Edward County

Abercrombie, Janice Luck, and Richard Slatten. **Prince Edward Co., VA "Publick" Claims**.
Paper. $6.25. 43 pp. .... Vendor G0632

Knorr, Catherine Lindsay. **Marriage Bonds and Ministers' Returns of Prince Edward County, Virginia, 1754-1810**. (1950) reprint 1982. Indexed. Illus.
Cloth. $15.00. 108 pp. .... Vendor G0610

Schreiner-Yantis, Netti, and Florene Love. **1787 Census of Prince Edward County, Virginia**. 1987. Indexed.
Information is from the 1787 Personal Property Tax Lists.
Paper. $3.50. 32 pp. .... Vendor G0081

T.L.C. Genealogy. **Prince Edward County, Virginia Deed Book 1 (1754-1759)**. 1990. Indexed.
Paper. $10.00. 71 pp. .... Vendor G0609

T.L.C. Genealogy. **Prince Edward County, Virginia Deed Book 2 (1759-1765)**. 1990. Indexed.
Paper. $10.00. 74 pp. .... Vendor G0609

T.L.C. Genealogy. **Prince Edward County, Virginia Wills, 1754-1776**. 1991. Indexed.
Paper. $14.00. 91 pp. .... Vendor G0609

Warren, Mary Bondurant, and Eve B. Weeks. **Virginia's District Courts, 1789-1809: Records of the Prince Edward District:** Buckingham, Charlotte, Cumberland, Halifax, and Prince Edward Counties. 1991. Indexed. Illus.
Cloth. $28.50. 497 pp. .... Vendor G0632

Prince George County

Abercrombie, Janice Luck, and Richard Slatten. **Prince George Co., VA "Publick" Claims**.
Paper. $5.00. 18 pp. .... Vendor G0632

Chamberlayne, Churchill Gibson. **Births from the Bristol Parish Register of Henrico, Prince George, and Dinwiddie Counties, Virginia, 1720-1798**. (1898) reprint 1996. Indexed.
Paper. $16.00. 133 pp. .... Vendor G0011

Chamberlayne, Churchill Gibson. **The Vestry Book and Register Briston Parish, Virginia, 1720-1789**. 1898. Indexed.
  Bristol Parish covers the area later comprised of Dinwiddie, Henrico, and Prince George counties.
Hard-cover. $40.00. 428 pp. .... Vendor G0610

Duvall, Lindsay O. **Prince George County, VA 1666-1719, Vol. 6**. (1962) reprint 1978. Indexed.
Paper. $17.50. 80 pp. .... Vendor G0610

Schreiner-Yantis, Netti, and Florene Love. **1787 Census of Prince George County, Virginia**. 1987. Indexed.
  Information is from the 1787 Personal Property Tax Lists.
Paper. $3.25. 28 pp. .... Vendor G0081

Slaughter, Rev. Philip, D.D. **A History of Bristol Parish, with Genealogies of Families Connected Therewith and Historical Illustrations**. 1879. Indexed.
  Bristol Parish covers the area later comprised of Dinwiddie, Henrico, and Prince George counties.
Cloth. $32.50. 238 pp. + index. .... Vendor G0610

Virginia Genealogical Society. **Virginia Marriages in Rev. John Cameron's Register and Bath Parish Register (1827-1897)**. 1963. Indexed.

Marriages included are from the areas of Dinwiddie, Prince George, and Nottoway counties.
Paper. $10.00. 56 pp. .... Vendor G0610

Weisiger, Benjamin B., III. **Prince George County, Virginia Miscellany, 1711-1814**. 1986. Indexed.
Paper. $17.00. 121 pp. .... Vendor G0632

Weisiger, Benjamin B., III. **Prince George County, Virginia Records, 1733-1792**. 1975. Indexed.
Paper. $19.95. 228 pp. .... Vendor G0632

Weisiger, Benjamin B., III. **Prince George County, Virginia Wills & Deeds, 1710-1713**. 1992. Indexed.
Paper. $12.95. 49 pp. .... Vendor G0632

Weisiger, Benjamin B., III. **Prince George County, Virginia Wills & Deeds, 1713-1728**. 1973. Indexed.
Paper. $19.95. 184 pp. .... Vendor G0632

Prince William County

Abercrombie, Janice Luck, and Richard Slatten. **Prince William Co., VA "Publick" Claims**.
Paper. $5.00. 20 pp. .... Vendor G0632

Schreiner-Yantis, Netti, and Florene Love. **1787 Census of Prince William County, Virginia**. 1987. Indexed.
  Information is from the 1787 Personal Property Tax Lists.
Paper. $4.00. 36 pp. .... Vendor G0081

Princess Anne County

Abercrombie, Janice Luck, and Richard Slatten. **Princess Anne Co., VA "Publick" Claims**.
Paper. $5.00. 20 pp. .... Vendor G0632

Schreiner-Yantis, Netti, and Florene Love. **1787 Census of Princess Anne County, Virginia**. 1987. Indexed.
  Information is from the 1787 Personal Property Tax Lists.
Paper. $3.50. 32 pp. .... Vendor G0081

Walter, Alice Granbery. **Genealogical Abstracts of Princess Anne County, Va. from Deed Books & Minute Books 6 & 7, 1740-1762**. (1975) reprint 1996. Indexed.
Paper. $25.00. 134 pp. .... Vendor G0011

Walter, Alice Granbery. **Virginia Land Patents of the Counties of Norfolk, Princess Anne & Warwick.** From Patent Books "0" & "6", 1666 to 1679. (1972) reprint 1993. Indexed.
Paper. $10.00. 75 pp. .... Vendor G0011

Wingo, Elizabeth B. **Marriages of Princess Anne County, Virginia, Vol. 2, 1799-1821.** (1968) reprint 1983. Indexed.
Contact vendor for information. 98 pp. + index. .... Vendor G0610

Pulaski County

Brock, R. A. **Pulaski County, Virginia Biographies.**
A reprint of his 1880s edition of sketches in the area.
Paper. $7.50. .... Vendor G0549

Douthat, James L. **Early Settlers of Pulaski County, Virginia.** Indexed.
Paper. $15.00. .... Vendor G0549

Douthat, James L. **Pulaski County, Virginia Will Books 1-2, 1840-1870.**
Paper. $12.50. .... Vendor G0549

Glynn, Victoria. **Pulaski County, Virginia Deaths 1853-1870.**
Paper. $22.50. .... Vendor G0549

Murphy, Malita W. **Gates to Glory.**
Cemetery records of over 8,000 burials in some thirty-three different cemeteries in the county.
Paper. $20.00. .... Vendor G0549

Pulaski County, Virginia Births 1853-1870.
Paper. $16.50. .... Vendor G0549

Vogt, John, and T. William Kethley, Jr. **Pulaski County Marriages, 1687-1695.** 1984. Indexed.
Paper. $5.00. viii + 36 pp. .... Vendor G0632

Rappahannock County

Dennis, Robert T. **Wakefield Manor, Rappahannock Co., VA 1734-1992.** 1993. Indexed. Illus.
Paper. $15.00. vi + 65 pp. .... Vendor G0632

Vogt, John, and T. William Kethley, Jr. **Rappahannock County Marriages, 1833-1850.** 1984. Indexed. Illus.
Paper. $7.95. viii+ 75 pp. .... Vendor G0632

Wilkerson, Eva Eubank. **Index to Marriages of Old Rappahannock and Essex Counties, Virginia, 1655-1900.** (1953) reprint 1997.
Paper. $25.00. 256 pp. .... Vendor G0011

Richmond City

Reedy, A. W., and A. L. Riffe, IV. **Marriage Bonds, 1797-1853: Richmond City.** 1939.
Paper. $19.00. 158 pp. .... Vendor G0259

Schreiner-Yantis, Netti, and Florene Love. **1787 Census of Henrico County & Richmond City, Virginia.** 1987. Indexed.
Information is from the 1787 Personal Property Tax Lists.
Paper. $6.00. 48 pp. .... Vendor G0081

Tyler-Macgraw, Marie. **At the Falls: Richmond, Virginia, & Its People.** 1994. Illus.
With marvelous pictures and illustrations, the author develops a history of a rich and complex city in American history. 8½" x 11".
Paper. $19.95. 361 pp. .... Vendor G0611

Virginia Genealogical Society. **Marriages and Deaths from Richmond, Virginia, Newspapers, 1780-1820.** (1983) reprint 1987. Indexed.
Cloth. $37.50. 286 pp. .... Vendor G0610

Virginia Genealogical Society. **Richmond City and Henrico County, Virginia, 1850 U.S. Census.** 1981. Indexed.
Paper. $20.00. 505 pp. .... Vendor G0610

Ward and Greer. **Richmond During the Revolution, 1775-1783.** 1977.
Reconstructs the strategic role of Richmond in the Revolution and describes everyday life in the city during that time.
Cloth. $26.00. 205 pp. .... Vendor G0611

Weisiger, Benjamin B., III. **City of Richmond, VA Wills, 1782-1810.** 1932. Indexed.
Paper. $12.95. 55 pp. .... Vendor G0632

Richmond County

Abercrombie, Janice Luck, and Richard Slatten. **Richmond Co., VA "Publick" Claims.**
Paper. $5.00. 20 pp. .... Vendor G0632

Headley, Robert K., Jr. **Wills of Richmond County, Virginia, 1699-1800.** (1983) reprint 1995. Indexed.
Contact vendor for information. 220 pp. .... Vendor G0011

King, George H. S. **Marriages of Richmond County, Virginia, 1668-1853.** (1964) reprint 1985. Indexed. Illus.
Cloth. $28.50. 312 pp. .... Vendor G0610

King, George H. S. **The Registers of North Farnham Parish, 1663-1814, and Lunenburg Parish, 1783-1800, Richmond County, Virginia.** (1966) reprint 1985. Indexed. Illus.
Cloth. $28.50. 240 pp. .... Vendor G0610

Schreiner-Yantis, Netti, and Florene Love. **1787 Census of Richmond County, Virginia**. 1987. Indexed.
Information is from the 1787 Personal Property Tax Lists.
Paper. $3.00. 24 pp. .... Vendor G0081

T.L.C. Genealogy. **Richmond County, Virginia Court Orders, 1721-1752: An Every-Name Index**. 1996. Indexed.
Paper. $20.00. 172 pp. .... Vendor G0609

T.L.C. Genealogy. **Richmond County, Virginia Deeds and Bonds, 1721-1734**. 1991. Indexed.
Paper. $14.00. 155 pp. .... Vendor G0609

T.L.C. Genealogy. **Richmond County, Virginia Deeds, 1734-1741**. 1991. Indexed.
Paper. $14.00. 101 pp. .... Vendor G0609

T.L.C. Genealogy. **Richmond County, Virginia Deeds, 1741-1750**. 1992. Indexed.
Paper. $14.00. 107 pp. .... Vendor G0609

Roanoke County

1840 Census.
Paper. $10.00. .... Vendor G0549

Brock, R. A. **Roanoke County, Virginia Biographies**.
A reprint of his 1880s edition of sketches in the area.
Paper. $5.00. .... Vendor G0549

Neighbors, Marvin U. **Roanoke County, Virginia Deaths 1853-1881**.
Paper. $27.50. .... Vendor G0549

Prillaman, Helen R. **Places Near the Mountains [Botetourt and Roanoke Counties, Virginia]**. From the community of Amsterdam, Virginia up the road to Catawba, on the waters of the Catawba and Tinker Creeks, along the Carolina Road as it approached Big Lick and other areas, primarily North Roanoke. (1985) reprint 1996. Indexed. Illus.
Paper. $49.95. 397 pp. .... Vendor G0011

Vogt, John, and T. William Kethley, Jr. **Roanoke County, Marriages, 1838-1850**. 1984. Indexed. Illus.
Paper. $7.95. viii + 54 pp. .... Vendor G0632

Rockbridge County

1850 Rockbridge County, Virginia Census.
Paper. $35.00. .... Vendor G0549

Abercrombie, Janice Luck, and Richard Slatten. **Rockbridge Co., VA "Publick" Claims**.
Paper. $5.00. 24 pp. .... Vendor G0632

Brown, James Moore. **The Captives of Abb's Valley**. New edition of 1942 book by Robert Bell Woodworth. Indexed.
The story of the capture of Mary Moore by the Shawnee Indians, her subsequent return to Virginia and marriage to Rev. Samuel Brown. Contains the genealogy of the Moore/Brown family and related families of Tazewell and Rockbridge counties.
Cloth. $34.50. 392 pp. .... Vendor G0549

Douthat, James L. **Rockbridge County, Virginia Deed Book B, 1788-1793**. Indexed.
Paper. $18.50. .... Vendor G0549

Kirkpatrick, Dorthie, and Edwin Kirkpatrick. **Rockbridge County Births, 1853-1877**.
2 vols. 1988. Indexed.
Paper. $25.95. viii + 734 pp. .... Vendor G0632

Kirkpatrick, Dorthie, and Edwin Kirkpatrick. **Rockbridge County Marriages, 1778-1850**. 1985. Indexed.
Paper. $19.95. ix + 443 pp. .... Vendor G0632

McClure, Rhonda R. **Abstracts of Rockbridge County, Virginia Circuit Court Will Book 1, 1809-1874**.
Paper. $10.00. .... Vendor G0549

Morton, Oren F. **A History of Rockbridge County, Virginia**. (1920) reprint 1997.
Indexed. Illus.
Contact vendor for information. 574 pp. .... Vendor G0011

Perkins, Louise M. **Rockbridge County, Virginia Marriages 1851-1885**.
Paper. $48.50. 475 pp. .... Vendor G0549

Ruley, Angela M. **Rockbridge County, Virginia Death Registers, 1853-1870, 1912-1917**. Indexed.
Paper. $29.95. vi + 504 pp. .... Vendor G0632

Schreiner-Yantis, Netti, and Florene Love. **1787 Census of Rockbridge County, Virginia**. 1987. Indexed.
Information is from the 1787 Personal Property Tax Lists.
Paper. $4.00. 36 pp. .... Vendor G0081

Rockingham County

Abercrombie, Janice Luck, and Richard Slatten. **Rockingham Co., VA "Publick" Claims**.
Paper. $6.25. 45 pp. .... Vendor G0632

Kaylor, Peter C. **Abstract of Land Grant Surveys of Augusta and Rockingham Counties, Virginia, 1761-1791**. (1930) reprint 1991. Indexed.
Cloth. $21.50. 150 pp. .... Vendor G0011

Ritchie, Patricia Turner. **Index to the 1880 Rockingham County, Virginia Census**.
Indexed.
Paper. $14.00. iv + 178 pp. .... Vendor G0632

Rockingham County in the World War, 1917-1918. Published by Rockingham Post No. 27, The American Legion. (1931) reprint 1993. Indexed. Illus.
Paper. $9.95. 128 pp. .... Vendor G0632

Schreiner-Yantis, Netti, and Florene Love. **1787 Census of Rockingham County, Virginia.** 1987. Indexed.
 Information is from the 1787 Personal Property Tax Lists.
Paper. $6.00. 48 pp. .... Vendor G0081

Spratt, Thomas M., comp. **Rockingham Co., VA Men in Gray.** 2 vols. 1995. Indexed.
Paper. $35.95/set. xix + 615 pp. .... Vendor G0632

Strickler, Harry M. **Old Tenth Legion Marriages:** Marriages in Rockingham County, Virginia, from 1778 to 1816. (1928) reprint 1986. Indexed.
Cloth. $11.50. 128 pp. .... Vendor G0011

Vogt, John, and T. William Kethley, Jr. **Rockingham County Marriages, 1778-1850.** 1984. Indexed. Illus.
Paper. $17.95. ix + 433 pp. .... Vendor G0632

Russell County

1870 Russell County, Virginia Census.
Paper. $30.00. .... Vendor G0549

Colley, Tom. **Russell County, Virginia Deed Book 1, 1787-1795.** 1995. Indexed.
Paper. $20.00. 101 pp. .... Vendor G0632

Colley, Tom. **Russell County, Virginia Deed Book 2, 1795-1798.** 1995. Indexed.
Paper. $20.00. 117 pp. .... Vendor G0632

Colley, Tom. **Russell County, Virginia Deed Book 3, 1798-1806.** 1995. Indexed.
Paper. $20.00. 233 pp. .... Vendor G0632

Colley, Tom. **Russell County, Virginia Deed Book 4, 1806-1814.** 1996. Indexed.
Paper. $25.00. 302 pp. .... Vendor G0632

Fugate, Mary D. **Implied Marriages of Russell County, Virginia.** Indexed.
Paper. $14.95. vi + 112 pp. .... Vendor G0632

Nix, Lois. **Russell Co. Abstr. of Deeds, from Deed Book I, 1781-1795.** 1985.
Paper. $7.00. 34 pp. .... Vendor G0259

Schreiner-Yantis, Netti, and Florene Love. **1787 Census of Russell County, Virginia.** 1987. Indexed.
 Information is from the 1787 Personal Property Tax Lists.
Paper. $2.75. 20 pp. .... Vendor G0081

Schreiner-Yantis, Netti. **1810 Tax List of Russell County, Virginia.**
 Included in *A Supplement to the 1810 Census of Virginia.*
Paper. $2.00. .... Vendor G0081

Scott County

Addington, Robert M. **History of Scott County, Virginia.** (1932) reprint 1994. Indexed. Illus.
Paper. $30.00. 378 pp. .... Vendor G0011

Fugate, Mary D. **Scott County Marriages, 1815-1853.** 1989. Indexed.
Paper. $12.95. x + 109 pp. .... Vendor G0632

Scott County Heritage Book Committee. **Scott County, VA and Its People 1814-1991.** 3rd printing. Indexed. Illus.
Attractive 9" x 12" hardbound book, featuring more than 700 family genealogies and family photos. Topics include military, towns, churches, schools, and a photo album. Surname index.
Cloth. $59.50. 382 pp. .... Vendor G0087

Shenandoah County

Abercrombie, Janice Luck, and Richard Slatten. **Shenandoah Co., VA "Publick" Claims.**
Paper. $5.00. 26 pp. .... Vendor G0632

Ashby, Bernice M. **Shenandoah County Marriage Bonds, 1772-1850.** (1967) reprint 1996. Indexed.
Paper. $36.50. 518 pp. .... Vendor G0011

Buck, Dee Ann. **Shenandoah County, Virginia Marriages, 1854-1880.**
Spiral binding. $32.50. 272 pp. .... Vendor G0758

Schreiner-Yantis, Netti, and Florene Love. **1787 Census of Shenandoah County, Virginia.** 1987. Indexed.
Information is from the 1787 Personal Property Tax Lists.
Contact vendor for information. 52 pp. .... Vendor G0081

Spratt, Thomas M., comp. **Shenandoah County, Virginia Men in Gray.** 2 vols. 1992. Indexed.
Paper. $35.95. xix + 902 pp. .... Vendor G0632

Vogt, John, and T. William Kethley, Jr. **Shenandoah County Marriage Bonds, 1772-1850.** 1984. Indexed.
Paper. $17.95. ix + 417 pp. .... Vendor G0632

Smyth County

1870 Smyth County, Virginia Census.
Paper. $25.00. .... Vendor G0549

Brock, R. A. **Smyth County, Virginia Biographies.**
A reprint of his 1880s edition of sketches in the area.
Paper. $7.50. .... Vendor G0549

Douthat, James L. **Smyth County, Virginia Will Book 1, 1832-1844**.
Paper. $10.00. .... Vendor G0549

Vogt, John, and T. William Kethley, Jr. **Smyth County Marriages, 1832-1850**. 1984.
Indexed.
Paper. $7.95. viii + 89 pp. .... Vendor G0632

Wilson, Goodbridge. **Smyth County History & Traditions**. (1937) reprint 1994.
Cloth. $45.00. 397 pp. .... Vendor G0259

Southampton County

Abercrombie, Janice Luck, and Richard Slatten. **Southampton Co., VA "Publick"**
Claims.
Paper. $5.00. 25 pp. .... Vendor G0632

Chapman, Blanche Adams. **Wills and Administrations of Southampton County,**
Virginia, 1749-1800. (1947, 1958) reprint 1980. Indexed.
Cloth. $17.50. 208 pp. .... Vendor G0010

Knorr, Catherine Lindsay. **Marriage Bonds and Ministers' Returns of Southampton**
County, Virginia, 1750-1810. (1955) reprint 1982. Indexed. Illus.
Cloth. $18.50. 152 pp. .... Vendor G0610

Schreiner-Yantis, Netti, and Florene Love. **1787 Census of Southampton County,**
Virginia. 1987. Indexed.
   Information is from the 1787 Personal Property Tax Lists.
Paper. $4.50. 40 pp. .... Vendor G0081

Spotsylvania County

Abercrombie, Janice Luck, and Richard Slatten. **Spotsylvania Co., VA "Publick"**
Claims.
Paper. $7.25. 52 pp. .... Vendor G0632

Crozier, William Armstrong. **Spotsylvania County Records**. Vol. I of the Virginia
County Records Series. (1905) reprint 1990. Indexed.
Cloth. $35.00. 576 pp. .... Vendor G0010

Knorr, Catherine Lindsay. **Marriage Bonds and Ministers' Returns of**
Fredericksburg, Virginia, 1782-1850 (and Tombstone Inscriptions from St. George
Cemetery, 1752-1920). 1954. Indexed. Illus.
Contact vendor for information. 116 pp. .... Vendor G0610

Schreiner-Yantis, Netti, and Florene Love. **1787 Census of Spotsylvania County &**
Fredericksburg City, Virginia. 1987. Indexed.
   Information is from the 1787 Personal Property Tax Lists.
Paper. $4.00. 36 pp. .... Vendor G0081

Stafford County

Abercrombie, Janice Luck, and Richard Slatten. **Stafford Co., VA "Publick" Claims**.
Paper. $6.25. 45 pp. .... Vendor G0632

Boogher, William F. **Old Stafford County, Virginia: Overwharton Parish Register, 1720-1760**. (1899) reprint 1995. Illus.
Paper. $20.00. 210 pp. .... Vendor G0011

King, George H.S. **The Register of Overwharton Parish, Stafford County, Virginia, 1723-1758,** and Sundry Historical and Genealogical Notes. (1961) reprint 1985. Indexed. Illus.
Cloth. $30.00. 296 pp. .... Vendor G0610

Nicklin, John B. C. **St. Paul's Parish Register** (Stafford-King George Counties, Virginia) 1715-1798. (1962) reprint 1995.
Paper. $8.50. 78 pp. .... Vendor G0011

Schreiner-Yantis, Netti, and Florene Love. **1787 Census of Stafford County, Virginia**. 1987. Indexed.
　Information is from the 1787 Personal Property Tax Lists.
Paper. $4.00. 36 pp. .... Vendor G0081

Vogt, John, and T. William Kethley, Jr. **Stafford County, Virginia Tithables: Quit Rents, Personal Property Taxes and Related Lists and Petitions, 1723-1790**. With Introduction by Michael Burgess. 2 vols. 1990. Indexed.
Paper. $30.00/set. xi + 612 pp. .... Vendor G0632

Woodson, Robert F., and Isobel B. Woodson. **Virginia Tithables from Burned Record Counties (Buckingham, Gloucester, Hanover, James City, and Stafford)**. (1970) reprint 1982.
Paper. $20.00. 122 pp. .... Vendor G0610

Suffolk County

Norfleet, Fillmore. **Bible Records of Suffolk and Nansemond County, Virginia,** Together with Other Statistical Data. (1963) reprint 1996. Indexed.
Paper. $22.00. 220 pp. .... Vendor G0011

Surry County

Abercrombie, Janice Luck, and Richard Slatten. **Surry Co., VA "Publick" Claims**.
Paper. $5.00. 19 pp. .... Vendor G0632

Boddie, John Bennett. **The Albemarle Parish Register of Surry and Sussex Counties, Virginia,** Births, Deaths and Sponsors, 1717-1778. (1858) reprint 1992. Indexed.
Cloth. $22.00. 167 pp. .... Vendor G0011

Boddie, John Bennett. **Colonial Surry [Virginia]**. (1948) reprint 1992. Indexed.
　A collection of genealogical data from important name lists for Colonial Surry,

which once encompassed almost the entire southern part of Virginia (i.e., fourteen present-day Virginia counties).
Cloth. $25.00. 249 pp. .... Vendor G0011

Davis, Eliza Timberlake. **Surry County Records,** Surry County, Virginia, 1652-1684. (195-, 1980) reprint 1997. Indexed.
Paper. $17.50. 156 pp. .... Vendor G0011

Davis, Eliza Timberlake. **Wills and Administrations of Surry County, Virginia 1671-1750**. (1955, 1980) reprint 1996. Indexed.
Paper. $20.00. 184 pp. .... Vendor G0011

Hart, Lyndon H., III. **Surry County Wills, Estate Accounts and Inventories, 1730-1800**. (1983) reprint 1984. Indexed.
Paper. $25.00. 182 pp. .... Vendor G0610

Hopkins, William Lindsay, scr. **Surry County, Virginia Deeds, 1684-1733 and Other Court Papers**. Reprint 1994. Indexed.
Paper. $30.00. iv + 203 pp. .... Vendor G0632

Hopkins, William Lindsay, scr. **Surry County, Virginia Deeds and Estate Accounts, 1734-1755**. Reprint 1994. Indexed.
Paper. $30.00. iv + 163 pp. .... Vendor G0632

Hopkins, William Lindsay, scr. **Surry County, Virginia Deeds and Estate Accounts, 1756-1787**. 1995. Indexed.
Paper. $30.00. iv + 182 pp. .... Vendor G0632

Knorr, Catherine Lindsay. **Marriage Bonds and Ministers' Returns of Surry County, Virginia, 1768-1825**. (1960) reprint 1982. Indexed. Illus.
Cloth. $16.00. 124 pp. .... Vendor G0610

The National Society Colonial Dames of America in the Commonwealth of Virginia. **Register of Albemarle Parish, Surry & Sussex Counties, 1739-1788.** Edited by Gertrude Richards. (1958) reprint 1984. Indexed. Illus.
Cloth. $32.50. 275 pp. + index. .... Vendor G0610

Schreiner-Yantis, Netti, and Florene Love. **1787 Census of Surry County, Virginia**. 1987. Indexed.
Information is from the 1787 Personal Property Tax Lists.
Paper. $6.00. 48 pp. .... Vendor G0081

T.L.C. Genealogy. **Surry County, Virginia, Court Orders, 1741-1751: An Every-Name Index**. 1992. Indexed.
Paper. $12.00. 106 pp. .... Vendor G0609

T.L.C. Genealogy. **Surry County, Virginia Deed Book 4 (1742-1747)**. 1991. Indexed.
Paper. $15.00. 95 pp. .... Vendor G0609

Virginia Genealogical Society. **Surry County Register of Free Negroes**. 1995.
The register of free Negroes, kept from 1794-1862, gives description, age, free-born or emancipated. In some cases, multiple family generations can be traced. Some marriage records are included.
Paper. $30.00. 339 pp. .... Vendor G0582

Sussex County

Abercrombie, Janice Luck, and Richard Slatten. **Sussex Co., VA "Publick" Claims**. Paper. $5.00. 28 pp. .... Vendor G0632

Boddie, John Bennett. **The Albemarle Parish Register of Surry and Sussex Counties, Virginia,** Births, Deaths and Sponsors, 1717-1778. (1858) reprint 1992. Indexed. Cloth. $22.00. 167 pp. .... Vendor G0011

Hopkins, William Lindsay, scr. **Sussex County, Virginia Deed Books A-E, 1754-1779**. Reprint 1995. Indexed.
Paper. $30.00. .... Vendor G0632

Hopkins, William Lindsay, scr. **Sussex County, Virginia Will Books A-F, 1754-1806**. Reprint 1994. Indexed.
Paper. $30.00. iv + 188 pp. .... Vendor G0632

Knorr, Catherine Lindsay. **Marriages of Sussex County, Virginia, 1754-1810**. (1952) reprint 1982. Indexed. Illus.
Cloth. $16.00. 118 pp. .... Vendor G0610

The National Society Colonial Dames of America in the Commonwealth of Virginia. **Register of Albemarle Parish, Surry & Sussex Counties, 1739-1788.** Edited by Gertrude Richards. (1958) reprint 1984. Indexed. Illus.
Cloth. $32.50. 275 pp. + index. .... Vendor G0610

Schreiner-Yantis, Netti, and Florene Love. **1787 Census of Sussex County, Virginia**. 1987. Indexed.
   Information is from the 1787 Personal Property Tax Lists.
Paper. $3.50. 32 pp. .... Vendor G0081

T.L.C. Genealogy. **Sussex County, Virginia Wills, 1754-1764**. 1991. Indexed.
Paper. $15.00. 131 pp. .... Vendor G0609

Tazewell County

1850 Tazewell County, Virginia Census.
Paper. $20.00. .... Vendor G0549

1860 Tazewell County, Virginia Census.
Paper. $20.00. .... Vendor G0549

1880 Tazewell County, Virginia Census.
Paper. $30.00. .... Vendor G0549

Brown, James Moore. **The Captives of Abb's Valley.** New edition of 1942 book by Robert Bell Woodworth. Indexed.
   The story of the capture of Mary Moore by the Shawnee Indians, her subsequent return to Virginia and marriage to Rev. Samuel Brown. Contains the genealogy of the Moore/Brown family and related families of Tazewell and Rockbridge counties.
Cloth. $34.50. 392 pp. .... Vendor G0549

Bundy, Nellie White. **Sketches of Tazewell County, Virginia**.
Paper. $4.00. 64 pp. .... Vendor G0549

Douthat, James L. **Tazewell County, Virginia Survey Book 1, 1801-1824**. Indexed.
$17.50 (perfect bound). 90 pp. .... Vendor G0549

Haga, Pauline. **Tazewell County, Virginia Marriage Records 1-2, 1800-1853**.
Indexed.
Paper. $15.00. .... Vendor G0549

Haga, Pauline. **Tazewell County, Virginia Marriage Records 3, 1854-1866**.
Paper. $10.00. .... Vendor G0549

Harman, John Newton, Sr. **Annals of Tazewell County.** 2 vols. in 1. Indexed.
 Long out of print, this extremely valuable two-volume set by John Newton Harman, Sr. is at last reprinted. Approximately 35,000 entries appear in the new index. Note: Although *Archives of the Pioneers of Tazewell County, Virginia* (see listing below under "Schreiner-Yantis, Netti") and this work contain similar types of records, there are less than 20 pages of duplication.
Cloth. $48.00. 1,134 pp. .... Vendor G0081

Leslie, Louise. **Tazewell County.** With new index. (1982) reprint 1995. Illus.
 A general survey of the county. Includes history, stories, important events, people making significant contributions to Tazewell County, and much more.
Cloth. $43.00. 786 pp. .... Vendor G0649

Pendleton, William C. **History of Tazewell County & Southwest Virginia, 1748-1920**. (1920) reprint 1994.
Cloth. $69.50. 700 pp. .... Vendor G0259

Pendleton, William C. **History of Tazewell County and Southwest Virginia**. 1920.
Reprinted with index 1989. Indexed. Illus.
Cloth. $33.00. 720 pp. .... Vendor G0649

Schreiner-Yantis, Netti. **1810 Tax List of Tazewell County, Virginia**.
 Included in *A Supplement to the 1810 Census of Virginia*.
Paper. $2.00. .... Vendor G0081

Schreiner-Yantis, Netti. **1820 Census of Tazewell County, Virginia**. 1970.
 The population of Tazewell County in 1820 was 3,981. This booklet gives all genealogical data as shown in the original census manuscripts. Also included is a map showing boundaries in 1820 and indicating the counties that have been created from the area since that time. Alphabetized.
Paper. $2.50. .... Vendor G0081

Schreiner-Yantis, Netti. **1830 Census of Tazewell County, Virginia**. 1971.
 The population of Tazewell County had increased to 5,748 by 1830. All genealogical census data has been transcribed in this booklet. The map that is included shows that there was a boundary change between 1820 and 1830. Alphabetized.
Paper. $2.50. .... Vendor G0081

Schreiner-Yantis, Netti. **Archives of the Pioneers of Tazewell County, Virginia**.
1973. Indexed.

This work is an assemblage of a great many of the public records created by the people living in this county before 1820. County, state, and federal records are included. A section entitled "Descendants of the Pioneers" includes lineages for as many as six or seven generations, and there is a study of the immigration and emigration routes, illustrated by maps and discussed in detail.
Cloth. $40.00. 344 pp. .... Vendor G0081

Tazewell County Historical Society. **1850 Tazewell County, Virginia Census**. Indexed.
Paper. $28.00. 103 pp. .... Vendor G0649

Tazewell County Historical Society. **1860 U.S. Federal Census, Tazewell County, Virginia**. 1989. Indexed.
Paper. $28.00. 220 pp. .... Vendor G0649

Tazewell County Historical Society. **1880 Tazewell County, Virginia Census**. Indexed.
Paper. $33.00. 138 pp. .... Vendor G0649

Tazewell County Historical Society. **An Album of Tazewell County, Virginia**. (1989) reprint 1990. Illus.
   Old photos, most before 1925, of Tazewell County; people, places, structures, and events.
Cloth. $33.00. 208 pp. .... Vendor G0649

Tazewell County Historical Society. **Another Album of Tazewell County, Virginia, Part I**. (1991) reprint 1993. Illus.
   Old photos, most before 1925, of Tazewell County; people.
Cloth. $33.00. 280 pp. .... Vendor G0649

Tazewell County Historical Society. **Another Album of Tazewell County, Virginia, Part II**. 1991. Illus.
   Old photos, most before 1925, of Tazewell County; places, structures, events, and groups.
Cloth. $33.00. 278 pp. .... Vendor G0649

Tazewell County Historical Society. **Reprints of the Tazewell County Historical Society Newsletters, 1989-1994** (each year is bound separately).
Paper. $14.00 each. 80 pp./yr. .... Vendor G0649

Tazewell County Historical Society. **Still Another Album of Tazewell County, Virginia**. 1992. Illus.
   Old photos, most before 1925, of Tazewell County; people, places, structures, and events.
Cloth. $33.00. 346 pp. .... Vendor G0649

Wilson, Thurman Robert, and Ruth Boyd Wilson. **Tazewell County Cemeteries, Vol. I, Western**. 1992. Indexed. Illus.
Paper. $28.00. 108 pp. .... Vendor G0649

Wilson, Thurman Robert, and Ruth Boyd Wilson. **Tazewell County Cemeteries, Vol. 2, West-Central**. 1994. Indexed. Illus.
Paper. $28.00. 106 pp. .... Vendor G0649

Wilson, Thurman Robert and Ruth Boyd Wilson. **Tazewell County Cemeteries, Vol. III, East-Central Region**. 1995. Indexed. Illus.
Paper. $28.00. 105 pp. .... Vendor G0649

Wilson, Thurman Robert, and Ruth Boyd Wilson. **Tazewell County Death Register**. 1993. Indexed.
Paper. $28.00. 74 pp. .... Vendor G0649

Witten, Jack. **Frog Level.** Compiled by Mary Witten. Published by Clinch Valley Printing Company. 1996. Indexed. Illus.
   A compilation of columns from the *Clinch Valley News*.
Cloth. $33.00. 183 pp. .... Vendor G0649

Truro Parish

Slaughter, Philip. **History of Truro Parish in Virginia.** Edited with Notes and Addenda by Edward L. Goodwin. (1907) reprint 1995. Indexed.
Paper. $17.50. 169 pp. .... Vendor G0011

Warren County

Buck, Dee Ann. **Warren County, Virginia Births, 1853-1895**.
Spiral binding. $23.00. 181 pp. .... Vendor G0758

Buck, Dee Ann. **Warren County, Virginia Marriages, 1854-1880**.
Spiral binding. $15.50. 105 pp. .... Vendor G0758

Henry, Louise. **Warren County, Virginia, Mortality Schedules, 1850, 1860, 1870**. 1994. Indexed.
Paper. $12.95. 59 pp. .... Vendor G0632

Vogt, John, and T. William Kethley, Jr. **Warren County Marriages, 1836-1850**. 1983. Indexed. Illus.
Paper. $7.95. vii + 48 pp. .... Vendor G0632

Warwick County

Abercrombie, Janice Luck, and Richard Slatten. **Warwick Co., VA "Publick" Claims**.
Paper. $5.00. 13 pp. .... Vendor G0632

Schreiner-Yantis, Netti, and Florene Love. **1787 Census of Warwick County, Virginia**. 1987. Indexed.
   Information is from the 1787 Personal Property Tax Lists.
Paper. $2.00. 12 pp. .... Vendor G0081

Walter, Alice Granbery. **Virginia Land Patents of the Counties of Norfolk, Princess Anne & Warwick.** From Patent Books "0" & "6", 1666 to 1679. (1972) reprint 1993. Indexed.
Paper. $10.00. 75 pp. .... Vendor G0011

Washington County

1830 Washington County, Virginia Census.
Paper. $7.50. .... Vendor G0549

1840 Washington County, Virginia Census.
Paper. $7.50. .... Vendor G0549

Brock, R. A. **Washington County, Virginia Biographies**.
A reprint of his 1880s edition of sketches in the area.
Paper. $12.00. .... Vendor G0549

Clark, Gerald H. **The Militia of Washington County, Virginia 1777-1835**.
Paper. $30.00. .... Vendor G0549

Douthat, James L. **Washington County, Virginia Civil War Records**.
Paper. $15.00. .... Vendor G0549

Fleet, Beverley. **Washington County, Virginia Records, Vol 34**. (1949) reprint 1985.
Indexed.
Paper. $15.00. 96 pp. + index. .... Vendor G0610

Hiatt, Marty, and Craig Roberts Scott. **Washington County, VA Marriages: Ministers' Returns, 1776-1859**. 1995. Indexed.
Paper. $25.00. 315 pp. .... Vendor G0632

Holston Territory Genealogical Society. **Families of Washington County and Bristol, Virginia 1776-1996**. Indexed. Illus.
Handsome 9" x 12", hardbound book, featuring almost 900 family genealogies, family histories, and photos. Other important chapters include information on communities, education, churches, and military. Surname index.
Cloth. $63.00. 392 pp. .... Vendor G0087

The Reverend Daniel H. Carr's Journal, 1884-1890.
Paper. $5.00. .... Vendor G0549

Schreiner-Yantis, Netti, and Florene Love. **1787 Census of Washington County, Virginia**. 1987. Indexed.
Information is from the 1787 Personal Property Tax Lists.
Paper. $3.25. 28 pp. .... Vendor G0081

Summers, Lewis Preston. **History of Southwest Virginia, 1746-1786; Washington County, 1777-1870 with a Re-arranged Index and an Added Table of Contents**. (1903, 1971) reprint 1995. Indexed. Illus.
Paper. $65.00. 912 pp. .... Vendor G0011

Summers, Lewis Preston. **History of Southwest Virginia 1746-1786, and Washington County, 1777-1870**. (1903) reprint 1989.
An early history of Virginia and counties that are now West Virginia.
Cloth. $37.95. 921 pp. .... Vendor G0611

Washington County, Virginia Water Ways.
An 11" x 17" map of the county, showing the major communities and water ways.
Map. $2.50 .... Vendor G0549

Westmoreland County

Abercrombie, Janice Luck, and Richard Slatten. **Westmoreland Co., VA "Publick" Claims**.
Paper. $5.00. 21 pp. .... Vendor G0632

Crozier, William Armstrong. **Virginia County Records, Vol. I (New Series)— Westmoreland County**. (1913) reprint 1997. Indexed.
Contact vendor for information. 110 pp. .... Vendor G0011

Fleet, Beverley. **Westmoreland County, Virginia, Records, Vol. 23**. (1945) reprint 1985. Indexed.
Paper. $15.00. 104 pp. + index. .... Vendor G0610

Fothergill, Augusta B. **Wills of Westmoreland County, Virginia, 1654-1800**. (1925) reprint 1990. Indexed.
Cloth. $17.50. 229 pp. .... Vendor G0011

Fothergill, Augusta B. **Wills of Westmoreland County, Virginia, 1654-1800**. (1925) reprint 1982. Indexed.
Paper. Contact vendor for information. 238 pp. .... Vendor G0610

Harwell, Richard Barksdale, ed. **The Committees of Safety of Westmoreland and Fincastle: Proceedings of the County Committees, 1774-1776**. (1956) reprint 1974.
Paper. $7.95. 127 pp. .... Vendor G0553

Nottingham, Stratton. **The Marriage License Bonds of Westmoreland County, Virginia from 1786 to 1850**. (1928) reprint 1995. Indexed.
Paper. $12.00. 97 pp. .... Vendor G0011

Schreiner-Yantis, Netti, and Florene Love. **1787 Census of Westmoreland County, Virginia**. 1987. Indexed.
Information is from the 1787 Personal Property Tax Lists.
Paper. $3.25. 28 pp. .... Vendor G0081

Williamsburg

Crozier, William Armstrong. **Williamsburg Wills,** Vol. III of Virginia County Records. (1906) reprint 1995. Indexed.
Paper. $12.00. 77 pp. .... Vendor G0011

Goodwin, W. A. R. **Historical Sketch of Bruton Church, Williamsburg, Virginia**. (1903) reprint 1997. Indexed.
Contact vendor for information. 183 pp. .... Vendor G0011

Wythe County

1860 Wythe County, Virginia Census.
Paper. $20.00. .... Vendor G0549

1880 Wythe County, Virginia Census.
Paper. $20.00. .... Vendor G0549

Brock, R. A. **Wythe County, Virginia Biographies**.
Paper. $10.00. .... Vendor G0549

Douthat, James L. **Early Wythe Settlers**.
Paper. $25.00. .... Vendor G0549

Douthat, James L. **Wythe County, Virginia Civil War Records**.
Paper. $15.00. .... Vendor G0549

Douthat, James L. **Wythe County, Virginia Tax 1790-1800**. Indexed.
Paper. $15.00. .... Vendor G0549

Douthat, James L. **Wythe County, Virginia Will Books 1-2, 1790-1822**. Indexed.
Paper. $12.50. .... Vendor G0549

Schreiner-Yantis, Netti. **1800 Tax Lists and Abstracts of Deeds [1796-1800] of Wythe County, Virginia**. (1971) reprint 1979. Indexed.
   Over 1,700 individuals paid taxes in this county in 1800. There were two tax districts (both of which are included in this work). A map showing the districts, as well as natural features, is included. Parts or all of present-day counties—Bland, Boone, Giles, Mercer, McDowell, Mingo, Pulaski, Smyth, Tazewell, Wyoming , and Wythe— were within Wythe County's borders in 1800.
Paper. $4.00. 40 pp. .... Vendor G0081

Vogt, John, and T. William Kethley, Jr. **Wythe County Marriages, 1790-1850**. 1985. Indexed. Illus.
Paper. $14.95. ix + 224 pp. .... Vendor G0632

York County

Abercrombie, Janice Luck, and Richard Slatten. **York Co., VA "Publick" Claims**.
Paper. $5.00. 27 pp. .... Vendor G0632

Bell, Landon C. **Charles Parish, York County, Virginia: History and Registers. Births, 1648-1789, Deaths, 1665-1787**. (1932) reprint 1996.
Paper. $15.00. xii + 285 pp. .... Vendor G0553

Duvall, Lindsay O. **York County, Va., Wills, Deeds, and Orders, 1657-1659, Vol. 5**. (1961) reprint 1978. Indexed.
Paper. $17.50. 94 pp. .... Vendor G0610

Schreiner-Yantis, Netti, and Florene Love. **1787 Census of York County & York Town, Virginia**. 1987. Indexed.
   The 1787 Personal Property Tax Lists for York County are missing. However, both the 1786 and the 1788 tax lists are in this booklet.
Paper. $3.25. 28 pp. .... Vendor G0081

T.L.C. Genealogy. **York County, Virginia, Orders, Wills, & Inventories, 1733-1734**. 1992. Indexed.
Paper. $14.00. 117 pp. .... Vendor G0609

Weisiger, Benjamin B., III. **York County, VA Records, 1659-1662**. 1989. Indexed. Paper. $17.95. 188 pp. .... Vendor G0632

Weisiger, Benjamin B., III. **York County, VA Records, 1665-1672**. 1987. Indexed. Paper. $20.00. 281 pp. .... Vendor G0632

Weisiger, Benjamin B., III. **York County, VA Records, 1676-1676**. 1991. Indexed. Contact vendor for information. 216 pp. .... Vendor G0632

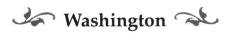

Washington

Statewide and Regional References

Banvard, Theodore James Fleming. **Goodenows Who Originated in Sudbury, Massachusetts 1638 A.D.** 1994. Indexed. Illus. Cloth. $78.50. 952 pp. .... Vendor G0116

Eastern Washington Genealogical Society. **Bible Records**. Indexed. Illus. Contact vendor for information. 145 pp. .... Vendor G0733

Family History Library. **Research Outline: Washington**. Leaflet. $.25. 8 pp. .... Vendor G0629

Southern California Genealogical Society. **Sources of Genealogical Help in Washington**. Paper. $2.25. 14 pp. .... Vendor G0656

Thorndale, William, and William Dollarhide. **County Boundary Map Guides to the U.S. Federal Censuses, 1790-1920: Washington, 1850-1920**. 1987. $5.95. .... Vendor G0552

Washington Interment Association and Washington State Funeral Directors Association. **A Directory of Cemeteries and Funeral Homes in Washington State**. Indexed. Paper. $45.00. 414 pp. .... Vendor G0552

Clark County

Clark County Genealogical Society. **Clark County, Washington Cemeteries, Volumes 7 and 8, Evergreen Memorial Gardens Cemetery**. 1994. Indexed. Paper. $42.50/set. Contact vendor about availability of other volumes. 960 pp. .... Vendor G0717

Clark County Genealogical Society. **Clark County, Washington Cemeteries, Volumes 9, 10 and 11, Park Hill Cemeteries**. 1995. Indexed. Paper. $62.00/set. 1,267 pp. .... Vendor G0717

Clark County Genealogical Society. **Clark County, Washington Marriages Volume Eleven**. 1995. Indexed.
Paper. $20.50. 383 pp. .... Vendor G0717

Clark County Genealogical Society. **Clark County, Washington Marriages Volume Twelve**. 1995. Indexed.
Paper. $20.50. 276 pp. .... Vendor G0717

Clark County Genealogical Society. **Clark County, Washington Marriages Volume Thirteen**. 1995.
Paper. $20.50. 276 pp. .... Vendor G0717

Pacific County

Martin, Irene. **A Newspaper Index and Guide for Genealogy in Wahkiakum County and Naselle Area of Pacific County, Washington**.
Paper. $13.25. .... Vendor G0718

Pierce County

Baccus, Janet Nixon. **Roy Area, Pierce County, Washington, An Historical Overview**. 1995. Indexed. Illus.
Over 400 pages with an every name index including the names of farms, creeks, rivers, lakes, organizations, churches, etc.; 112 identified photos.
Paper. $51.90. 426 pp. .... Vendor G0456

San Juan County

Whatcom Genealogical Society. **1860 Federal Census of Whatcom County, Washington Territory**. Transcribed by Earle H. Christensen. ca. 1980. Indexed.
Includes San Juan Islands and present Skagit County.
Paper. $2.50. 10 pp. .... Vendor G0503

Whatcom Genealogical Society. **1870 Federal Census of Whatcom County, Washington Territory**. Transcribed by Donna Stuart Ewing and Zelda Harlan Stout. ca. 1980. Indexed.
Includes San Juan Islands and present Skagit County.
Paper. $4.00. 25 pp. .... Vendor G0503

Whatcom Genealogical Society. **Will Book I, San Juan County, Washington Territory**. Transcribed by Thomas R. Branigar. ca. 1983. Indexed.
Paper. $2.50. 17 pp. .... Vendor G0503

Skagit County

Ackerman, Dolores Dunn, and Earle H. Christensen. **1885 Territorial Auditor's Census of Skagit County, Washington Territory**. 1986. Indexed.
Paper. $7.50. 60 pp. .... Vendor G0503

Whatcom Genealogical Society. **1860 Federal Census of Whatcom County, Washington Territory**. Transcribed by Earle H. Christensen. ca. 1980. Indexed.
Includes San Juan Islands and present Skagit County.
Paper. $2.50. 10 pp. .... Vendor G0503

Whatcom Genealogical Society. **1870 Federal Census of Whatcom County, Washington Territory**. Transcribed by Donna Stuart Ewing and Zelda Harlan Stout. ca. 1980. Indexed.
Includes San Juan Islands and present Skagit County.
Paper. $4.00. 25 pp. .... Vendor G0503

Whatcom Genealogical Society. **Tenth (1880) Census of the United States, Whatcom County, Washington Territory**. ca. 1980. Indexed.
Includes present Skagit County.
Paper. $7.50. 67 pp. .... Vendor G0503

Spokane County

Eastern Washington Genealogical Society. **Spokane County, Washington Early Birth Records 1890-1906**.
$30.00. 425 pp. .... Vendor G0733

Roberts, Ann, comp. **Spokane County Cemetery**. 1989. Indexed. Illus.
Paper. $12.95. 105 pp. .... Vendor G0552

Wahkiakum County

Martin, Irene. **A Newspaper Index and Guide for Genealogy in Wahkiakum County and Naselle Area of Pacific County, Washington**.
Paper. $13.25. .... Vendor G0718

Whatcom County

Whatcom Genealogical Society. **1860 Federal Census of Whatcom County, Washington Territory**. Transcribed by Earle H. Christensen. ca. 1980. Indexed.
Includes San Juan Islands and present Skagit County.
Paper. $2.50. 10 pp. .... Vendor G0503

Whatcom Genealogical Society. **1870 Federal Census of Whatcom County, Washington Territory**. Transcribed by Donna Stuart Ewing and Zelda Harlan Stout. ca. 1980. Indexed.
Includes San Juan Islands and present Skagit County.
Paper. $4.00. 25 pp. .... Vendor G0503

Whatcom Genealogical Society. **1871-1885-1887 Territorial Auditor's Censuses for Whatcom County, Washington Territory**. ca. 1980. Indexed.
Paper. $15.00. 185 pp. .... Vendor G0503

Whatcom Genealogical Society. **1900 U.S. Census, Whatcom County, Washington.**
2 vols. 1979. Indexed.

Not just an index but a listing of 24,000+ names with genealogical data.

Paper. $25.00. 490 pp. .... Vendor G0503

Whatcom Genealogical Society. **1910 U.S. Census, Whatcom County, Washington.**
4 vols. 1987. Indexed.

Paper. $50.00. Also available on microfiche, $20.00. 932 pp. .... Vendor G0503

Whatcom Genealogical Society. **Cemetery Records of Watcom County, Series 1.**
5 vols.

Vol. 1—Greenacres Memorial Park and Lummi Island Cemetery. 1973. 171 pp.

Vol. 2—Bayview, Congregation Beth Israel, Mount Calvary, and Buchanan Cemeteries. 1973. 174 pp.

Vol. 3—Enterprise, Haynie, Mountain View, Ten-Mile, Woodlawn, and Zion Lutheran Cemeteries. 1975. 191 pp.

Vol. 4—Compiled by Earle H. Christensen. Blaine, Blaine Masonic, Greenwood, Hillsdale, Lakeside, Lynden, Monumenta, Nooksack, Perry, Point Roberts, St. Anne's, and Sumas Cemeteries. 1975. 199 pp.

Vol. 5—Compiled by Earle H. Christensen. Covers twenty-three additional small cemeteries and deaths where burial site is unknown. Includes index to all smaller cemeteries in the five vols. 1976. 228 pp.

Paper. $12.50/vol. $60.00/set. .... Vendor G0503

Whatcom Genealogical Society. **Cemetery Records of Whatcom County, Series 2, Vol. 1:** A Listing of Persons Whose Remains Were Shipped in Another Place for Burial, or Who Died Elsewhere But Had Connections with Whatcom County. 1993. Indexed.

Paper. $20.00. 288 pp. .... Vendor G0503

Whatcom Genealogical Society. **Index to Lottie Roeder Roth's** *History of Whatcom County*. 1983. Indexed.

More than 22,000 names in this index to Roth's 2-vol. *History of Whatcom County* published in 1926. Incorporated in 1994 reprint of *History of Whatcom County*.

Paper. $10.00. 73 pp. .... Vendor G0503

Whatcom Genealogical Society. **Marriage Records of Whatcom County, Washington, 1890-1893**. 1986. Indexed.

Paper. $7.50. 82 pp. .... Vendor G0503

Whatcom Genealogical Society. **Marriage Records of Whatcom County, Washington, 1893-1898**. 1986. Indexed.

Paper. $7.50. 51 pp. .... Vendor G0503

Whatcom Genealogical Society. **Marriage Records of Whatcom County, Washington, 1898-1902**. 1986. Indexed.

Paper. $7.50. 91 pp. .... Vendor G0503

Whatcom Genealogical Society. **Tenth (1880) Census of the United States, Whatcom County, Washington Territory**. ca. 1980. Indexed.

Includes present Skagit County.

Paper. $7.50. 67 pp. .... Vendor G0503

Whatcom Genealogical Society. **Territorial Auditor's 1889 Census, Whatcom County, Washington Territory**. ca. 1980. Indexed.
Paper. $15.00. 126 pp. .... Vendor G0503

Whatcom Genealogical Society. **Whatcom Genealogical Society Members' Surname Index Book, Volume 4, 1993**. 1993. Indexed.
Almost 4,000 names and data submitted by fifty-three members.
Paper. $4.00. 56 pp. .... Vendor G0503

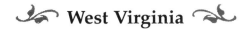 West Virginia

Statewide and Regional References

Allegheny Regional Family History Society. **ARFHS Ancestor Charts, Volume 1**.
Paper. $15.00. .... Vendor G0662

Allegheny Regional Family History Society. **Getting Started in Genealogy**.
Paper. $4.00. .... Vendor G0662

Allegheny Regional Family History Society. **Where to Write for Vital Records**.
Paper. $3.00. .... Vendor G0662

Atlas of West Virginia, 55 county maps.
Includes detailed maps of individual counties, all the back roads, streams, lakes, towns, etc. 11" x 16".
$14.95. .... Vendor G0611

Bittinger, Emmert Foster. **Allegheny Passage**. 1990. Indexed. Illus.
Book #1166.
Cloth. $45.00. 880 pp. .... Vendor G0082

Butcher, Bernard L. **Genealogical and Personal History of the Upper Monongahela Valley, West Virginia**. 2 vols. (1912) reprint 1994. Indexed.
Paper. $80.00. 1,037 pp. in all [pp. 363-1399]. .... Vendor G0011

Callahan, James M. **Genealogical & Personal History of the Upper Monongahela Valley**. 3 vols. (1912) reprint 1994.
Cloth. $49.50/vol., $135.00/set. 1,399 pp. .... Vendor G0259

Creswell, Stephen, ed. **We Will Know What War Is: The Civil War Diary of Sirene Bunten**. 1993.
The diary begins on the first day of 1863, spans the war years, and ends in the 1870s. In 1901 Sirene Bunten picked up her diary one last time and made a final entry. In her diary we see what war was like for many West Virginians. The diary's postwar entries show the rural life lived by a young West Virginia woman.
Paper. $8.00. .... Vendor G0660

DeHass, Wills. **History of the Early Settlement and Indian Wars of Western Virginia**. (1851) reprint 1989. Illus.
An early history of what is now West Virginia.
Paper. $14.95. .... Vendor G0660

Dilts, Bryan Lee, comp. **1890 West Virginia Veterans Census Index**. 2nd ed. 1993. Illus.
Cloth. $33.00. 85 pp. .... Vendor G0552

Dyer, M. H. **Dyer's Index to Land Grants in West Virginia**. (1895) reprint 1992.
Cloth. $89.00. 948 pp. .... Vendor G0259

Ely, William. **The Big Sandy Valley**. A History of the People and Country. (1887) reprint 1993. Indexed. Illus.
The Big Sandy Valley, which is today situated mostly in Eastern Kentucky, encompasses all or part of sixteen counties in Kentucky, Virginia, and West Virginia.
Paper. $38.50. 500 pp. .... Vendor G0011

Family History Library. **Research Outline: West Virginia**.
Leaflet. $.25. 11 pp. .... Vendor G0629

Gannett, Henry. **A Gazetteer of Virginia and West Virginia**. 2 vols. in 1. (1904) reprint 1994.
Paper. $26.50. 323 pp. in all. .... Vendor G0011

Genealogies of West Virginia Families. (1901-5) reprint 1992. Indexed.
Contact vendor for information. 286 pp. .... Vendor G0011

History of the Great Kanawha Valley, with Family History and Biographical Sketches. 2 vols. (1891) reprint 1994.
Volume I: History.
Volume II: Biography.
Cloth. $62.50. 308 + 307 pp. .... Vendor G0259

Hulbert, Archer Butler. **The Ohio River: A Course of Empire**. (1906) reprint 1996.
The history of the territory along the Ohio, especially Pittsburgh, Wheeling, Marietta, Cincinnati, and Louisville.
Cloth. $45.00. 378 pp. .... Vendor G0259

An Inventory of the Records of the West Virginia University Library (Archives Section) at Morgantown, West Virginia.
A vast number of manuscript records for the West Virginia counties are located at the West Virginia University Library. Many of the original county court record books have been deposited there because of lack of space in the courthouses. Numerous private collections containing such documents as diaries, journals, and account books are there. For those who have West Virginia ancestors, this inventory of the University's holdings is an invaluable book.
Paper. $2.00. .... Vendor G0081

Jillson, Willard Rouse. **The Big Sandy Valley**. A Regional History Prior to the Year 1850. (1923) reprint 1994. Indexed. Illus.
Deals with the region (mostly in Eastern Kentucky), which today encompasses all or part of sixteen counties in Kentucky, Virginia, and West Virginia.
Paper. $18.00. 183 pp. .... Vendor G0011

Johnson, David E. **History of Middle New River Settlements & Contiguous Territory**. (1906) reprint 1993.
Cloth. $57.00. 500 + xxxi pp. .... Vendor G0259

Johnston, Ross B. **West Virginia Estate Settlements:** An Index to Wills, Inventories, Appraisements, Land Grants, and Surveys to 1850. (1955-1963) reprint 1988.
Cloth. $15.00. 176 pp. .... Vendor G0010

Johnston, Ross B. **West Virginians in the American Revolution**. (1939-47) reprint 1995.
Paper. $25.00. 320 pp. .... Vendor G0011

Lewis, Virgil A. **The Soldiery of West Virginia** in the French and Indian War; Lord Dunmore's War; the Revolution; the Later Indian Wars; the Whiskey Insurrection; the Second War with England; the War with Mexico. And Addenda Relating to West Virginians in the Civil War. (1911) reprint 1996.
Paper. $25.00. 227 pp. .... Vendor G0011

McFarland, Kenneth T. H. **Early West Virginia Wills, Volume I**.
Paper. $14.95. 167 pp. .... Vendor G0536

Myers, Sylvester. **Myers' History of West Virginia**. 2 vols. (1915) reprint 1993.
  Volume I: History.
  Volume II: County Histories and Biographies.
Cloth. $52.50/vol., $99.50/set. 560 + 480 pp. .... Vendor G0259

Precision Indexing. **West Virginia 1870 Census Index**. 1990.
Cloth. $175.00. .... Vendor G0552

Reddy, Anne Waller. **West Virginia Revolutionary Ancestors** Whose Services Were Non-military and Whose Names, Therefore, Do Not Appear in Revolutionary Indexes of Soldiers and Sailors. (1930) reprint 1997.
Paper. $12.00. 93 pp. .... Vendor G0011

Rice and Brown. **West Virginia: A History**. 1993.
  From its earliest settlement until 1992.
Cloth. $32.00. 344 pp. .... Vendor G0611

Scott, Carol A. **Marriage and Death Notices of Wheeling, Western Virginia, and the Tri-State Area**. 3 vols.
  Extracted paid marriage and death notices from major newspapers published in Wheeling, WV. The newspapers carried notices of the people from West Virginia, western Pennsylvania, and southeastern Ohio. Volume I covers records from 1818 to 1857. Volume II covers records from 1858 to 1865. Volume III covers 1866 through 1870.
Paper. $9.50/vol. 90 + 104 + 110 pp. .... Vendor G0536

Sims, Edgar B. **Sim's Index to Land Grants in the State of West Virginia**. (1952) reprint 1992. Indexed.
  Contains all grants issued and is an outstanding finding aid for people in what is now West Virginia.
Cloth. $65.00. 1,024 pp. .... Vendor G0081

Southern California Genealogical Society. **Sources of Genealogical Help in West Virginia**.
Paper. $1.50. 5 pp. .... Vendor G0656

Summers, Lewis Preston. **History of Southwest Virginia 1746-1786, and Washington County, 1777-1870**. (1903) reprint 1989.
  An early history of Virginia and counties that are now West Virginia.
Cloth. $37.95. 921 pp. .... Vendor G0611

Thorndale, William, and William Dollarhide. **County Boundary Map Guides to the U.S. Federal Censuses, 1790-1920: West Virginia, 1790-1920**. 1987.
$5.95. .... Vendor G0552

Wardell, P. G. **Timesaving Aid to Virginia-West Virginia Ancestors (A Genealogical Index of Surnames from Published Sources)**. 1990. Indexed.
Paper. $36.00. 429 pp. .... Vendor G0632

Western Pennsylvania Genealogical Society. **Marriages & Deaths from Pittsburgh Dispatch 1858-1860**. 1993.
  Over 4,500 names listed from a time before vital records were recorded in PA. Names from all over western PA, Ohio, West Virginia.
Paper. $15.00. .... Vendor G0615

Barbour County

Allegheny Regional Family History Society. **Barbour County, WV Cemetery Headstone Readings, Volume 1**.
Paper. $15.00. .... Vendor G0662

Allegheny Regional Family History Society. **Barbour County, WV Cemetery Headstone Readings, Volume 2**.
Paper. $15.00. .... Vendor G0662

Maxwell, Hu. **History of Barbour County,** from Its Earliest Exploration & Settlement to the Present Time. (1899) reprint 1993.
Cloth. $54.50. 518 pp. .... Vendor G0259

Berkeley County

Aler, F. Vernon. **Aler's History of Martinsburg & Berkeley Co**. (1888) reprint 1993.
Cloth. $48.50. 452 pp. .... Vendor G0259

Norris, J. E. **History of the Lower Shenandoah Valley Counties of Frederick, Berkeley, Jefferson and Clarke**. (1890, 1972) reprint 1996. Indexed. Illus.
Paper. $55.00. 925 pp. .... Vendor G0011

Schreiner-Yantis, Netti, and Florene Love. **1787 Census of Berkeley County**. 1987. Indexed.
  Information is from the 1787 Personal Property Tax Lists.
Paper. $8.00. 76 pp. .... Vendor G0081

Boone County

Boone County Genealogical Society. **Kith and Kin of Boone County, West Virginia Volume XXI**. Indexed.
Paper. $13.00. Contact vendor for other books in series. 133 pp. .... Vendor G0766

Brooke County

McFarland, Kenneth T. H. **Will Abstracts of Brooke County, (West) Virginia**.
Brooke County was formed out of Ohio County and, until the formation of Hancock Couny in 1848, it comprised the northern half of the Virginia Panhandle.
Paper. $9.50. 88 pp. .... Vendor G0536

Cabell County

Cabell County, [W] Virginia Deed Book 1, 1808-1814. 1985. Indexed.
Paper. $11.00. 55 pp. .... Vendor G0632

Cabell County, [W] Virginia Deed Book 2, 1814-1819. 1986. Indexed. Illus.
Paper. $13.50. 66 pp. .... Vendor G0632

Cabell County, [W] Virginia Deed Book 3 (vols. 1 & 2), 1819-1824. 1988. Indexed.
Paper. $15.00. 94 pp. .... Vendor G0632

Cabell County, [W] Virginia Deed Book 4, 1824-1831. 1990. Indexed. Illus.
Paper. $13.50. 64 pp. .... Vendor G0632

Cabell County, [W] Virginia Deed Book 5, 1830-1835. 1993. Indexed. Illus.
Paper. $13.50. 59 pp. .... Vendor G0632

Cabell County, [W] Virginia Marriages, 1809-1850. 1989. Indexed. Illus.
Paper. $11.00. 47p. .... Vendor G0632

Cabell County, [W] Virginia Minute Book 1, 1809-1815: Abstracts of the Combined "First" Minute and Law Order Books. Indexed. Illus.
Paper. $13.50. 57 pp. .... Vendor G0632

Cabell County, [W] Virginia Will Book 1, 1820-1848. 1989. Indexed. Illus.
Paper. $14.95. 89 pp. .... Vendor G0632

Eldridge, Carrie. **Cabell County, [W] Virginia Minute Book, 3 1826-1835**. 1994. Illus.
Paper. $27.00. iv + 323 pp. .... Vendor G0632

A Gazetteer of Extinct Towns in Cabell County, West Virginia. 1982. Rev. ed. 1990. Illus.
Paper. $7.95. 21 pp. .... Vendor G0632

Lost Records of the "Washington Aqueduct Project" (Fall of 1853): Records found in Cabell Co., W. Virginia. Illus.
Paper. $13.50. 69 pp. .... Vendor G0632

Schreiner-Yantis, Netti. **1810 Tax List of Cabell County, Virginia. [Included in "A Supplement to the 1810 Census of Virginia.].**
Paper. $2.00. .... Vendor G0081

Schreiner-Yantis, Netti. **1815 Tax List of Cabell County, Virginia**. Indexed. Illus.
     Present-day counties of Cabell, Wayne, Lincoln, Mingo, Logan, and part of Boone were in Cabell in 1815. This booklet includes a facsimile of a map drafted by John Wood in 1820. The map is very detailed, showing mills, ferries, taverns, and salt works with the owners, names given. A second map showing the counties that have been created from the 1820 Cabell territory is given. (There is also an index to John Wood's map.)
Paper. $3.25. .... Vendor G0081

Clarke County

Norris, J. E. **History of the Lower Shenandoah Valley Counties of Frederick, Berkeley, Jefferson and Clarke**. (1890, 1972) reprint 1996. Indexed. Illus.
Paper. $55.00. 925 pp. .... Vendor G0011

Fayette County

Haga, Pauline. **Fayette County, West Virginia Marriages 1830-1870**. Indexed.
$25.00 .... Vendor G0549

Shuck, Larry G. **Fayette County, (W) VA Marriages, 1832-1853 and 1865-1903**. Indexed.
Paper. $29.95. 315 pp. .... Vendor G0536

Shuck, Larry G., scr. **The Federal Census of 1850 for Fayette County (W.) Virginia**. 1991. Indexed.
     This book is an accurate and thorough transcription of the first census for Fayette County, West Virginia, in which all members of each household were listed individually by name. Contains over 1,000 unique surname entries.
Paper. $12.95. iv + 127 pp. .... Vendor G0632

Shuck, Larry G., scr. **The Federal Census of 1870 for Fayette County (W.) Virginia**. 1991. Indexed.
Paper. $17.95. iv + 224 pp. .... Vendor G0632

Frederick County

Norris, J. E. **History of the Lower Shenandoah Valley Counties of Frederick, Berkeley, Jefferson and Clarke**. (1890, 1972) reprint 1996. Indexed. Illus.
Paper. $55.00. 925 pp. .... Vendor G0011

Greenbrier County

1790 Greenbrier, Virginia [WV] Census.
Paper. $3.50. .... Vendor G0549

Dayton, Ruth Woods. **Greenbrier [W. Va.] Pioneers and Their Homes**. (1942) reprint 1997. Indexed. Illus.
Paper. $36.50. 383 pp. .... Vendor G0011

Haga, Pauline. **Greenbrier County, West Virginia Wills 1780-1865**. Indexed.
$20.00 .... Vendor G0549

Schreiner-Yantis, Netti, and Florene Love. **1787 Census of Greenbrier County**. 1987.
Indexed.
Information is from the 1787 Personal Property Tax Lists.
Paper. $8.00. 28 pp. .... Vendor G0081

Schreiner-Yantis, Netti. **1810 Tax List of Greenbrier County, Virginia**.
Included in *A Supplement to the 1810 Census of Virginia*.
Paper. $2.00. .... Vendor G0081

Shuck, Larry, scr. **Greenbrier County Records, Volume 1:** Early Survey Records,
1780-1799; Early Court Minutes 1780-1801 [1811]; Magistrate's Memoranda, 1817-1819; Court Record Books, 1828-1835; District Court Records, 1792-1797; Deeds,
Sweet Springs Courthouse, 1789-1808. 1988. Illus.
Paper. $22.00. viii + 457 pp. .... Vendor G0632

Shuck, Larry, scr. **Greenbrier County Records, Volume 2:** Personal Property Tax
Lists, 1782/83, 1786/88, 1792, 1796, 1799, 1805, 1815. 1989. Indexed.
Paper. $22.00. 302 pp. .... Vendor G0632

Shuck, Larry, scr. **Greenbrier County Records, Volume 3:** U.S. Federal Population
Schedules, 1820, 1830, 1840, and 1850. 1990.
Paper. $22.00. xii + 421 pp. .... Vendor G0632

Shuck, Larry, scr. **Greenbrier County Records, Volume 4:** Marriages of Greenbrier
County, [W] Virginia, 1782-1900. 3 vols. 1991.
Paper. $49.95. 997 pp. .... Vendor G0632

Shuck, Larry, scr. **Greenbrier County Records, Volume 5:** Greenbrier County, [W.]
Virginia, Deeds & Wills; Early Miscellaneous Deeds, 1750-52, 1754, 1769, 1783-84;
Deed Books 1-5, 1780-1814; Will Book 1, 1777-1833. 1993. Indexed.
Paper. $22.00. iv + 399 pp. .... Vendor G0632

Stinson, Helen S., scr. **Greenbrier County Records, Volume 7:** Greenbrier County,
[W.] Virginia, Land Entry Book, 1780-1786. 1994. Indexed.
Paper. $24.95. xxii + 297 pp. .... Vendor G0632

Hampshire County

1790 Hampshire County, Virginia (WV) Census.
Paper. $6.00. .... Vendor G0549

Casilear, Connie Jean. **Hampshire County (Virginia) West Virginia Births 1865-1889**. 1996.
Paper. $23.00. 183 pp. .... Vendor G0480

Casilear, Connie Jean. **Hampshire County (Virginia) West Virginia Deaths 1866-1894**. 1996.
Paper. $23.00. 172 pp. .... Vendor G0480

Casilear, Connie Jean. **Hampshire County (Virginia) West Virginia Marriages 1865-1899**. 1996.
Paper. $34.00. 282 pp. .... Vendor G0480

Casilear, Connie Jean. **Hampshire County (Virginia) West Virginia Will Abstracts 1758-1899**. 1996.
Paper. $18.00. 125 pp. .... Vendor G0480

Horton, Vicki Bidinger. **Hampshire County, Virginia (now West Virginia) Minute Book Abstracts, 1788-1802**. (1993) reprint 1995. Indexed.
Paper. $15.00. 135 pp. .... Vendor G0011

Maxwell, Hu, and H. L. Swisher. **History of Hampshire County,** from Its Earliest Settlement to the Present [1897]. (1897) reprint 1995.
Cloth. $75.00. 744 pp. .... Vendor G0259

Pugh, Maud. **Capon Valley. Its Pioneers and Their Descendants, 1698 to 1940**. (1948) reprint 1995. Illus.
Paper. $28.50. 350 pp. .... Vendor G0011

Schreiner-Yantis, Netti, and Florene Love. **1787 Census of Hampshire County**. 1987. Indexed.
   Information is from the 1787 Personal Property Tax Lists.
Paper. $4.00. 36 pp. .... Vendor G0081

Hancock County

Thayer, George, and Mary Thayer. **Hancock County, W.V. Cemeteries**.
Paper. $15.00. 205 pp. .... Vendor G0536

Thayer, George, and Mary Thayer. **Hancock County, W.V. Deaths (1865-1899) & Births (1857-1896)**.
Paper. $20.00. 189 pp. .... Vendor G0536

Hardy County

Schreiner-Yantis, Netti, and Florene Love. **1787 Census of Hardy County**. 1987. Indexed.
   Information is from the 1787 Personal Property Tax Lists.
Paper. $3.25. 28 pp. .... Vendor G0081

Schreiner-Yantis, Netti. **1810 Tax List of Hardy County, Virginia**.
   Included in *A Supplement to the 1810 Census of Virginia*.
Paper. $2.00. .... Vendor G0081

Harrison County

1790 Harrison County, Virginia (WV) Census.
Paper. $3.50. .... Vendor G0549

Eldridge, Carrie. **A Gazetteer of Communities in Harrison County, West Virginia,** with Extinct Towns. 1992. Illus.
Paper. $7.95. 23 pp. .... Vendor G0632

Haines, Jeffrey L. **Harrison County, West Virginia Will Book Index, 1788-1924.** 1993. Indexed.
Paper. $12.50. 65 pp. .... Vendor G0163

Haymond, Henry. **History of Harrison County,** from the Early Days of Northwestern Virginia to the Present. (1910) reprint 1995.
Cloth. $48.00. 451 pp. .... Vendor G0259

Schreiner-Yantis, Netti, and Florene Love. **1787 Census of Harrison County.** 1987. Indexed.
Information is from the 1787 Personal Property Tax Lists.
Paper. $2.50. 16 pp. .... Vendor G0081

Jefferson County

Brown, Stuart E., Jr. **The Guns of Harpers Ferry.** (1968) reprint 1996. Indexed. Illus.
Paper. $17.50. 158 pp. .... Vendor G0011

Norris, J. E. **History of the Lower Shenandoah Valley Counties of Frederick, Berkeley, Jefferson and Clarke.** (1890, 1972) reprint 1996. Indexed. Illus.
Paper. $55.00. 925 pp. .... Vendor G0011

Lewis County

Smith, Edward C. **History of Lewis County.** (1920) reprint 1993.
Cloth. $47.00. 427 pp. .... Vendor G0259

Logan County

Schreiner-Yantis, Netti. **1830 Census of Logan County, Virginia (now WV).** Indexed.
There were 3,680 individuals living in Logan County in 1830. All data concerning them—as recorded in the 1830 Federal Census Enumerations—is included in this booklet. A chart showing the lineage of Logan County will help in planning further research on residents who had been living in the area before Logan County was formed. There is a map illustrating the boundaries as they were to be found at the time the 1830 census was taken.
Paper. $2.50. .... Vendor G0081

Marion County

Haines, Jeffrey L. **Marion County, West Virginia Will Book Index, 1842-1924**. 1992. Indexed.
Paper. $12.50. 40 pp. .... Vendor G0163

Marshall County

Powell, Scott. **History of Marshall County, from Forest to Field**. A Story of Early Settlement & Development of Marshall Co., with Incidents of Early Life. (1925) reprint 1993.
Cloth. $39.50. 334 pp. .... Vendor G0259

Mason County

Hesson, Julie Chapin, with Sherman Gene Gesson and Jane J. Russell. **Mason County, West Virginia Marriages, 1806-1915**. 1997. Indexed.
Paper. $25.00. 289 pp. .... Vendor G0011

McDowell County

McDowell County Historical Society. **Heritage of McDowell County, West Virginia, 1858-1995**. Surname index. 1995.
Cloth. $64.00. 294 pp. .... Vendor G0649

Mercer County

Haga, Pauline. **Mercer County, West Virginia Deaths 1853-1882**.
Paper. $27.50. 110 pp. .... Vendor G0549

Hayes, Sallie. **Mercer County, West Virginia Marriages 1854-1901**.
Paper. $35.00. .... Vendor G0549

Holdren, Betsy M. **1860 Mercer County, (West) Virginia Census**.
Paper. $22.50. 247 pp. .... Vendor G0549

Schreiner-Yantis, Netti, and Lewis Bailey. **1840 Census and 1838 Land Tax List of Mercer County, Virginia (now WV)**. 1977.
    Mercer County was created in 1837 from Giles and Tazewell. The tax list includes the number of acres in each tract an individual owned and tells how far, and in what direction, from the courthouse it was located. If a tract was being taxed for the first time, it tells how the land was obtained, i.e., "Deeded by ___," "Granted 18 May 1837," etc.
Paper. $3.00. 17 pp. .... Vendor G0081

Schreiner-Yantis, Netti. **1850 Census of Mercer County, Virginia**. 1971. Indexed.
The first federal census that identified every individual by name, and gave the age and place of birth of each, was the 1850 census. All this data, plus that concerning occupations, has been transcribed. The slave schedules were recorded separately in the original census. Information from these has been transferred in order that those interested may see whether the families they are researching owned slaves. A map of the county is included. Every resident is included in the index.
Paper. $7.00. 52 pp. .... Vendor G0081

Monongalia County

Core, Earl L. **The Monongalia Story**. 5 vols.
Volume I: Prelude. 484 pp. Contains a general description of the county and a record of more than 1,000 early settlers.
Volume II: The Pioneers. 595 pp. Presents the history from the establishment of the county in 1776 up to 1826.
Volume III: Discord. 796 pp. Relates the story of the next fifty years, up to the Civil War.
Volume IV: Industrialization. 667 pp. Covers the period between 1876 and 1926.
Volume V: Sophistication. Gives the history of the county from 1926 to 1976.
Cloth. $35.00/vol. .... Vendor G0660

Haines, Jeffrey L. **Monongalia County, West Virginia Will Book Index, 1796-1923**. 1993. Indexed.
Paper. $12.50. 45 pp. .... Vendor G0163

Schreiner-Yantis, Netti, and Florene Love. **1787 Census of Monongalia County [Including the Extant 1787 Property Tax Lists, and All Lists for 1786 & 1788; Also Fourteen Legislative Petitions]**. 1987. Indexed.
Information from two of three 1787 Personal Property Tax Lists.
Paper. $4.00. 36 pp. .... Vendor G0081

Monroe County

1810 Monroe County, West Virginia Census.
Paper. $7.50. .... Vendor G0549

1850 Monroe County, West Virginia Census.
Paper. $15.00. .... Vendor G0549

Morton, Oren F. **A History of Monroe County, West Virginia**. (1916) reprint 1988. Indexed. Illus.
Cloth. $25.00. 510 pp. .... Vendor G0010

Shuck, Larry G. **Monroe County (W)VA Abstracts**. Indexed.
Paper. $19.95. 187 pp. .... Vendor G0536

Nicholas County

Brown, William Griffee. **History of Nicholas County.** (1954) reprint 1994.
Cloth. $47.00. 425 pp. .... Vendor G0259

Ohio County

Bowen, J. B. **The Wheeling Directory and Advertiser.** Indexed.
Alphabetically arranged names, addresses, and occupations of heads of families and occupations. Businesses included. Also includes a history of Wheeling from the time it was laid out in 1793 to 1839.
Paper. $9.95. 144 pp. .... Vendor G0536

Canmer, Gibson Lamb, ed. **History of Wheeling City and Ohio County,** and Representative Citizens. (1902) reprint 1995.
Cloth. $85.00. 853 pp. .... Vendor G0259

Schreiner-Yantis, Netti, and Florene Love. **1787 Census of Ohio County.** 1987. Indexed.
Information is from the 1787 Personal Property Tax Lists.
Paper. $3.00. 24 pp. .... Vendor G0081

Scott, Carol A. **A Listing of Letters Found in the Wheeling, WV Post Office.**
List of names and dates of letters remaining in the Post Office in the town of Wheeling, July 1818 through Dec. 1822.
Paper. $5.00. 34 pp. .... Vendor G0536

Scott, Carol A. **Marriage and Death Notices of Wheeling, Western Virginia, and the Tri-State Area.** 3 vols.
Extracted paid marriage and death notices from major newspapers published in Wheeling, WV. The newspapers carried notices of the people from West Virginia, western Pennsylvania, and southeastern Ohio. Volume I covers records from 1818 to 1857. Volume II covers records from 1858 to 1865. Volume III covers 1866 through 1870.
Paper. $9.50/vol. 90 + 104 + 110 pp. .... Vendor G0536

Pendleton County

1840 Pendleton County, West Virginia Census.
Paper. $5.00. .... Vendor G0549

Morton, Oren F. **A History of Pendleton County, West Virginia.** (1910) reprint 1996. Illus.
Paper. $35.00. 493 pp. .... Vendor G0011

Preston County

King, E. T. **Genealogy of Some Early Families in Grant & Pleasant District, Preston Co.** (1933) reprint 1990.
The main families treated are Christopher, Connor, Cunningham, King, Methany, Ryan, Street, Thorpe, Walls, Wheeler, and Wolf. There are also sections on church, Bible, and cemetery records.
Cloth. $29.50. 233 pp. .... Vendor G0259

King, Edward T. **Genealogy of Some Early Families in Grant and Pleasant Districts, Preston County, W. Va.** (1933) reprint 1994. Indexed.
Paper. $22.50. 233 pp. .... Vendor G0011

Peter, M. L. **Aurora Community, Preston Co.** With Genealogies. (1950) reprint 1993.
Paper. $9.00. 44 pp. .... Vendor G0259

Powell, Harold F. **Index to S. T. Wiley's History of Preston County** (see below). 1971.
Paper. $3.00. .... Vendor G0660

Sisler, Janice Cale. **In Remembrance, Tombstone Readings of Preston County, West Virginia Volume 1**. 1995. Indexed.
Paper. $24.50. 247 pp. .... Vendor G0719

Wiley, S. T. **History of Preston County**. 1882.
Cloth. $55.00. 529 pp. .... Vendor G0259

Wiley, S. T. **History of Preston County**. (1968) reprint 1993.
Cloth. $35.00. 500+ pp. .... Vendor G0660

Raleigh County

Haga, Pauline. **Early Births of Raleigh County, West Virginia 1853-1870**. Indexed.
Paper. $22.50. .... Vendor G0549

Haga, Pauline. **Early Marriages of Raleigh County (WV) 1850-1870**. Indexed.
Paper. $18.00. .... Vendor G0549

Haga, Pauline. **Raleigh County, West Virginia Deaths 1869-1914**. Indexed.
Paper. $12.50. .... Vendor G0549

Haga, Pauline. **Raleigh County, West Virginia Early Deaths 1853-1875**.
Paper. $15.00. .... Vendor G0549

Haga, Pauline. **Raleigh County, West Virginia Marriages 1871-1890**.
Paper. $20.00. .... Vendor G0549

WPA. **Raleigh County, West Virginia Veterans' Burial Records**. Indexed.
Paper. $18.00. .... Vendor G0549

Randolph County

Allegheny Regional Family History Society. **Randolph County, WV Cemetery Headstone Readings, Volume 1**.
Paper. $15.00. .... Vendor G0662

Maxwell, Hu. **History of Randolph Co.,** from Its Earliest Exploration & Settlement to the Present Time. (1898) reprint 1993.
Cloth. $55.00. 531 pp. .... Vendor G0259

Maxwell, Hu. **History of Randolph County**. (1898) reprint 1991. Indexed. Illus.
   A history of the county from its earliest settlement in 1898.
Paper. $20.00. 531 pp. .... Vendor G0660

Russell, John. **Mill Creek Memories**. 1995. Illus.
   The history of Mill Creek, West Virginia.
Paper. $7.00. .... Vendor G0660

Schreiner-Yantis, Netti, and Florene Love. **1787 Census of Randolph County**. 1987. Indexed.
   Information is from the 1787 and 1788 Personal Property Tax Lists. Both years' lists are intact, and both are included here—each being arranged a second time by the date of receiving lists.
Paper. $2.50. 16 pp. .... Vendor G0081

Ritchie County

Lowther, Minnie Kendall. **Ritchie County History—In History and Romance**. 1990. Indexed.
   Includes an index of over 5,000 neames.
Cloth. $25.00. Approx. 470 pp. .... Vendor G0660

Roane County

Bishop, William H. **Roane County, West Virginia Families,** Excerpted from History of Roane County, West Virginia from the Time of Its Exploration to A.D. 1927. (1927) reprint 1995.
Paper. $21.50. [431-704] pp. .... Vendor G0011

Summers County

1880 Summers County, West Virginia Census.
Paper. $25.00. .... Vendor G0549

Haga, Pauline. **Summers County, West Virginia Deaths 1872-1890, Volume 1**.
Paper. $20.00. .... Vendor G0549

Haga, Pauline. **Summers County, West Virginia Deaths 1891-1900, Volume 2**.
Paper. $24.50. 100 pp. .... Vendor G0549

Haga, Pauline. **Summers County, West Virginia Marriages 1871-1883**.
Paper. $10.00. .... Vendor G0549

Haga, Pauline. **Summers County, West Virginia Wills 1871-1900**.
Paper. $22.00. .... Vendor G0549

Tucker County

Fansler, Homer Floyd. **History of Tucker County**. (1962) reprint 1990. Indexed.
Illus.
Cloth. $35.00. 700+ pp. .... Vendor G0660

Maxwell, Hu. **History of Tucker County**. (1884) reprint 1993.
   Focuses on lumber, travelers, the Civil War, and brief biographies of the settlers,
towspeople, and historical figures of Tucker County.
Cloth. $35.00. .... Vendor G0660

Upshur County

Cutright, William Bernard. **The History of Upshur County, West Virginia** from Its
Earliest Exploration and Settlement to the Present Time. (1907) reprint 1996. Illus.
Paper. $49.95. 607 pp. .... Vendor G0011

Webster County

Dodrill, William C. **Moccasin Tracks and Other Imprints** (sketches relating to pioneer history of Webster Co. & pioneer families). (1915) reprint 1995.
Cloth. $37.50. 298 pp. .... Vendor G0259

Wyoming County

Haga, Pauline. **Wyoming County, West Virginia Marriages 1854-1890, Vol. 1**.
$22.50 (perfect bound). 118 pp. .... Vendor G0549

Haga, Pauline. **Wyoming County, West Virginia Marriages 1890-1902, Vol. 2**.
$20.00 (perfect bound). 94 pp. .... Vendor G0549

Wisconsin

Statewide and Regional References

Banvard, Theodore James Fleming. **Goodenows Who Originated in Sudbury, Massachusetts 1638 A.D.** 1994. Indexed. Illus.
Cloth. $78.50. 952 pp. .... Vendor G0116

Doering, Anita Tylor. **Guide to Local History and Genealogy Resources 1995**.
　Summarizes resources found in the Winding Rivers, Wisconsin Library System. Includes information on libraries and historical societies in Buffalo, Jackson, Juneau, LaCrosse, Monroe, Trempealeau, and Vernone counties (also, more brief information on Houston, Olmstead, and Winona counties, Minnesota).
Spiral binding. $13.00. Approx. 200 pp. .... Vendor G0722

Estabrook, McGregor, and Holway. **Wisconsin Volunteers War of the Rebellion 1861-1865**. 1885-1899. Reprint on microfiche.
　Organized alphabetically.
Order no. 138, $22.00. 1,137 pp. .... Vendor G0478

Family History Library. **Research Outline: Wisconsin**.
Leaflet. $.25. 9 pp. .... Vendor G0629

A Few Good Men of Wisconsin. (1878) reprint 1995. Indexed.
　Over 5,000 men taken who settled early Wisconsin. Taken from Historical Atlas of Wisconsin 1878.
Paper. $18.00. 192 pp. .... Vendor G0195

Folsom, W. H. C. **Fifty Years in the Northwest,** with an Introduction and Appendix Containing Reminiscences, Incidents and Notes. (1888) reprint 1994.
　A history of the settlement of Wisconsin and Minnesota, with town and county histories, and biographies of pioneers.
Cloth. $77.00. 763 pp. .... Vendor G0259

Gregory, John G., and Thomas J. Cunningham. **West Central Wisconsin: A History**. 4 vols. (1933) reprint 1994.
Cloth. $57.50/vol., $210.00/set. 2,460 pp. .... Vendor G0259

Herrick, Linda. **Wisconsin Genealogical Research**. 1996.
Paper. $17.00. 64 pp. .... Vendor G0195

Historical Atlas of Wisconsin 1878. (1878) reprint 1995.
Paper. $23.00. 108 pp. .... Vendor G0195

History of Northern Wisconsin, Containing an Account of Its Settlement, Growth, Development & Resources; an Extensive Sketch of Its Counties, Cities, Towns & Villages; Biographical Sketches, Portraits of Prominent Men & Early Settlers, Etc. (1881) reprint 1995.
Cloth. $119.00. 1,218 pp. .... Vendor G0259

History of Wisconsin, Comprising Sketches of Counties, Towns, Events, Institutions & Persons, Arranged in Cyclopedic Form. (1906) reprint 1992.
Cloth. $44.50. 417 pp. .... Vendor G0259

Levi, Kate, and Albert Faust. **Early German Immigrants in Wisconsin.** (1898, 1909) reprint 1996. Indexed.
Paper. $11.00. 48 pp. .... Vendor G0195

Smith, Clifford N. **Immigrants to America (Mainly Wisconsin) from the Former Recklinghausen District (Nordrhein-Westfalen, Germany) Around the Middle of the Nineteenth Century.** German-American Genealogical Research Monograph Number 15. 1983.
    ISBN 0-915162-12-1.
Paper. $20.00. iv + 28 pp. .... Vendor G0491

Strong, Moses M. **History of the Territory of Wisconsin,** from 1836 to 1848. Preceded by an Account of Some Events . . . Previous to 1836. (1870) reprint 1994.
Cloth. $67.00. 637 pp. .... Vendor G0259

Thorndale, William, and William Dollarhide. **County Boundary Map Guides to the U.S. Federal Censuses, 1790-1920: Wisconsin, 1820-1920.** 1987.
$5.95. .... Vendor G0552

Titus, William A., ed. **History of the Fox River Valley,** Lake Winnebago and the Green Bay Region. 3 vols. in 2. (1930) reprint 1995.
    Volume I & II, History.
    Volume III, Biography.
Cloth. $87.50/Vol. I & II. $69.00/Vol. III. $145.00/set. 853 + 683 pp. Vendor G0259

Uncapher, Wendy, and Linda Herrick. **Wisconsin: Its Counties, Townships, Villages.** 1994. Indexed.
    County maps divided by township. List of all past and present towns.
Paper. $21.00. 96 pp. .... Vendor G0195

Williams, Nancy Greenwood, C.G.R. **First Ladies of Wisconsin: The Governors' Wives.** 1991. Indexed. Illus.
    The only single source.
Cloth. $20.00 + p&h. 300 pp. .... Vendor G0199

Adams County

Stafford, Linda Berg. **The Tangney & Day Families of Adams County, Wisconsin.** 1993. Indexed. Illus.
Cloth. $50.00. 692 pp. .... Vendor G0032

Clark County

Heath, Jim, and Kathie Heath, comps. **Clark County, Wisconsin Cemeteries Volume 1, Townshipos of Dewhurst, Henfren, Hewitt, Levis, Mentor, Seif, Sherwood, Weston.** 1996. Indexed. Illus.
Spiral binding. $18.00. 65 pp. .... Vendor G0720

Columbia County

History of Columbia County, Containing an Acct. of Its Settlement, Growth & Resources . . . & Biographical Sketches. (1880) reprint 1993.
Cloth. $105.00. 1,095 pp. .... Vendor G0259

Crawford County

History of Crawford & Richland Counties, Together with Sketches of Their Towns & Villages . . . and Biographies of Representative Citizens, with a History of Wisconsin. With 1981 index to Richland Co. Section. (1884) reprint 1996.
Cloth. $125.00. 1,308 + 36 pp. .... Vendor G0259

Dane County

History of Dane County, Containing an Account of Its Settlement, Growth, Development, Etc . . . & Biographical Sketches. (1880) reprint 1993.
Cloth. $119.50. 1,289 pp. .... Vendor G0259

Keyes, Elisha W., ed. **History of Dane County.** 2 vols. (1906) reprint 1992.
    Volume I: History.
    Volume II: Biographical & Genealogical.
Cloth. $43.50/Vol. I. $$97.50/Vol. II. $132.00/set. 423 + 974 pp. .... Vendor G0259

Madison, Dane County, & Surrounding Towns, Being a History & Guide. (1877) reprint 1993.
Cloth. $68.50. 664 pp. .... Vendor G0259

Uncapher, Wendy, scr. **Rockdale Lutheran Cemetery, Rockdale, WI.** 1995. Indexed.
Paper. $8.00. 8 pp. .... Vendor G0195

Dodge County

History of Dodge County, Containing . . . Its Early Settlement . . . Biographical Sketches, etc. (1880) reprint 1995.
Cloth. $79.00. 766 pp. .... Vendor G0259

Hubbell, Homer B. **Dodge County, Wis., Past & Present**. 2 vols. (1913) reprint 1994.
Volume I: History.
Volume II: Biography.
Cloth. $47.50/vol., $89.50/set. 432 + 494 pp. .... Vendor G0259

Douglas County

Mershart, Ronald V. **Pioneers of Superior Wisconsin**. 1996. Indexed.
Paper. $27.95. 80 pp. .... Vendor G0583

Dunn County

Curtiss-Wedge, F., G. O. Jones, et al., comps. **History of Dunn County**. With Biographical Sketches. (1925) reprint 1995.
Cloth. $95.00. 966 pp. .... Vendor G0259

Fond du Lac County

History of Fond du Lac County, Containing a History of . . . Its Early Settlement . . . and Biographical Sketches. . . . (1880) reprint 1994.
Cloth. $105.00. 1,063 pp. .... Vendor G0259

McKenna, Maurice, ed. **Fond du Lac County: Past & Present**. 2 vols. (1912) reprint 1995.
Volume I: History.
Volume II: Biography.
Cloth. $45.00/Vol. I. $75.00/Vol. II. $109.00/set. 399 + 715 pp. .... Vendor G0259

Green County

History of Green County, Together with Sketches of Its Towns & Villages . . . and Biographies of Representative Citizens. (1884) reprint 1995.
Cloth. $109.00. 1,158 pp. .... Vendor G0259

Green Lake County

Portrait & Biographical Album of Green Lake, Marquette & Waushara Counties. (1890) reprint 1994.
Cloth. $89.50. 850 pp. .... Vendor G0259

Jackson County

Eddy, Sue, Jim Heath, and Kathie Heath, comps. **Jackson County, Wisconsin Cemeteries Volume 1, Riverside Cemetery**. 1995. Indexed. Illus.
Spiral binding. $18.00. 65 pp. .... Vendor G0720

Jefferson County

History of Jefferson County, Its Early Settlement, Growth . . . Etc; an Extensive & Minute Sketch of Its Cities, Towns & Villages . . . Biographical Sketches, Portraits of Prominent Men & Early Settlers . . . . (1879) reprint 1995.
Cloth. $75.00. 733 pp. .... Vendor G0259

Prairie Farmer Directory of Jefferson Co. 1927. (1927) reprint 1995.
Paper. $12.50. 64 pp. .... Vendor G0195

Uncapher, Wendy, comp. **Lake Ripley Cemetery, Cambridge, WI**. 1994. Indexed.
Paper. $10.00. 28 pp. .... Vendor G0195

Uncapher, Wendy, scr. **Oakland Township Cemeteries, Jefferson Co., WI**. 1995.
Indexed.
Paper. $10.00. 26 pp. .... Vendor G0195

Uncapher, Wendy, scr. **Sumner Township Cemeteries, Jefferson Co., WI**. 1996.
Indexed.
Paper. $10.50. 30 pp. .... Vendor G0195

Kenosha County

History of Racine & Kenosha Counties, Containing a History of Each County, Its Early Settlement, Growth, Etc . . . & Biographical Sketches. (1879) reprint 1994.
Cloth. $75.00. 738 pp. .... Vendor G0259

Lafayette County

History of Lafayette County, Containing an Account of Its Settlement . . . an Extensive & Minute Sketch of Its Cities, Towns & Villages . . . Biographical Sketches, Portraits of Prominent Men & Early Settlers . . . (1881) reprint 1995.
Cloth. $82.00. 800 pp. .... Vendor G0259

Lincoln County

Jones, George O., et al. **History of Lincoln, Oneida & Vilas Counties**. (1924) reprint 1994.
Cloth. $79.50. 787 pp. .... Vendor G0259

Manitowoc County

Falge, Dr. Louis. **History of Manitowoc County**. 2 vols. (1911-12) reprint 1994.
Cloth. $109.50. 463 + 675 pp. .... Vendor G0259

Marquette County

Portrait & Biographical Album of Green Lake, Marquette & Waushara Counties. (1890) reprint 1994.
Cloth. $89.50. 850 pp. .... Vendor G0259

Milwaukee Area

Vargas, Mark A., ed. **Guide to Genealogical Collections in the Milwaukee Metropolitan Area**. 1995. Indexed. Illus.
Paper. $15.00 individuals/$35.00 institutions. 185 pp. .... Vendor G0510

Milwaukee County

T.L.C. Genealogy. **Milwaukee County, Wisconsin Censuses of 1846 & 1847**. 1991. Indexed.
Paper. $12.00. 104 pp. .... Vendor G0609

Monroe County

Richards, Randolph A. **History of Monroe County: Past & Present,** Including an Account of the Cities, Towns & Villages of the County. (1912) reprint 1995.
Cloth. $95.00. 946 pp. .... Vendor G0259

Oneida County

Jones, George O., et al. **History of Lincoln, Oneida & Vilas Counties**. (1924) reprint 1994.
Cloth. $79.50. 787 pp. .... Vendor G0259

Outagamie County

Bubolz, Gordon A., ed. **The Land of the Fox: A Saga of Outagamie County**. (1949) reprint 1994.
Cloth. $36.00. 302 pp. .... Vendor G0259

Racine County

History of Racine & Kenosha Counties, Containing a History of Each County, Its Early Settlement, Growth, Etc . . . & Biographical Sketches. (1879) reprint 1994. Cloth. $75.00. 738 pp. .... Vendor G0259

Richland County

History of Crawford & Richland Counties, Together with Sketches of Their Towns & Villages . . . and Biographies of Representative Citizens, with a History of Wisconsin. With 1981 index to Richland Co. Section. (1884) reprint 1996. Cloth. $125.00. 1,308 + 36 pp. .... Vendor G0259

Miner, James H. **History of Richland County**. With 1988 Index. (1906) reprint 1996. Cloth. $77.50. 698 + 50 pp. .... Vendor G0259

Rock County

History of Rock County, Containing a History of Each County, Its Early Settlement, Growth, Etc . . . & Biographical Sketches. (1879) reprint 1994. Cloth. $89.50. 897 pp. .... Vendor G0259

Kjendlie, Donna Long, comp. **Luther Valley Confirmation Extractions 1850s-1934.** 1991. Indexed. Paper. $17.00. 175 pp. .... Vendor G0195

Kjendlie, Donna Long. **Rock Co., WI Birth Book 4 thru 1875**. 1993. Indexed. Paper. $13.00. 55 pp. .... Vendor G0195

Rock County Farm Directory 1928. (1928) reprint 1994. Paper. $12.50. 80 pp. .... Vendor G0195

Uncapher, Wendy, and Linda Herrick, comps. **Barrett School, Center Twp. Rock Co., WI**. 1994.
    Some school records 1866 to 1943.
Paper. $10.50. 52 pp. .... Vendor G0195

Sauk County

History of Sauk County, Containing a History of Each County, Its Early Settlement, Growth, Etc . . . & Biographical Sketches. (1880) reprint 1994. Cloth. $85.00. 825 pp. .... Vendor G0259

Trempeleau County

Curtiss-Wedge, Franklyn, comp. **History of Trempeleau County**. Edited by Eben Pierce. (1917) reprint 1993. Cloth. $92.00. 922 pp. .... Vendor G0259

Vilas County

Jones, George O., et al. **History of Lincoln, Oneida & Vilas Counties**. (1924) reprint 1994.
Cloth. $79.50. 787 pp. .... Vendor G0259

Van Noy, Rosamond. **Cemeteries of Vilas County, WI, Vol. I**. Headstones transcribed 1995 by Rosamond Van Noy, Conover, WI. 1995. Indexed. Illus.
   Arbor Vitae, Boulder Junction, Conover, Phelps, Land O Lakes, Sayner, Star Lake, and St. Germain cemeteries, 2,555 names indexed. Military records included.
Paper. $33.00. 139 pp. .... Vendor G0245

Van Noy, Rosamond. **Cemeteries of Vilas County, WI, Vol. II**. Headstones transcribed 1995/96 by Rosamond Van Noy, Conover, WI. 1996. Indexed. Illus.
   Eagle River, Eagle River Catholic, Lac Du Flambeau, Manitowish Waters, Presque Isle, Winchester cemeteries, 4,524 names indexed. Military records included. Obituaries noted and available/past five years.
Paper. $55.00. 231 pp. .... Vendor G0245

Walworth County

Cravath, Prosper, and Spencer Steele. **Early Annals of Whitewater, 1837-1867**. Edited by Albert Salisbury. (1906) reprint 1995.
Cloth. $37.50. 283 pp. .... Vendor G0259

History of Walworth County, Containing an Account of Its Settlement . . . Its Cities, Towns and Villages . . . and Biographical Sketches. (1882) reprint 1994.
Cloth. $98.00. 967 pp. .... Vendor G0259

Waukesha County

Waukesha County Genealogical Society. **Obituary Index—1859 to 1920, The Waukesha Freeman Newspaper, Waukesha County, Wisconsin**.
Spiral binding. $24.95 314 pp. + appendix .... Vendor G0721

Waupaca County

Wakefield, J. **History of Waupaca County**. (1890) reprint 1995.
Cloth. $32.00. 219 pp. .... Vendor G0259

Waushara County

Portrait & Biographical Album of Green Lake, Marquette & Waushara Counties. (1890) reprint 1994.
Cloth. $89.50. 850 pp. .... Vendor G0259

Winnebago County

Cunningham, G. A. **History of Neenah,** Being a Complete Historical Sketch from the "Early Days" to [1878], with Interesting Incidents & Personal Reminiscences. (1878) reprint 1995.
Cloth. $39.00. 254 + 53 pp. .... Vendor G0259

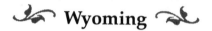

Wyoming

Statewide and Regional References

Dilts, Bryan Lee. **1910 Wyoming Census Index: Heads of Households and Other Surnames in Households**. 2nd ed. 1992.
Cloth. $47.00. 245 pp. .... Vendor G0552

Family History Library. **Research Outline: Wyoming**.
Leaflet. $.25. 7 pp. .... Vendor G0629

Saltiel, E. H., and George Barnett, comps. **History & Business Directory of Cheyenne** & Guide to Mining Regions of the Rocky Mountains. (1868) reprint 1993.
Cloth. $22.50. 114 pp. .... Vendor G0259

Southern California Genealogical Society. **Sources of Genealogical Help in Wyoming**.
Paper. $1.50. 8 pp. .... Vendor G0656

Thorndale, William, and William Dollarhide. **County Boundary Map Guides to the U.S. Federal Censuses, 1790-1920: Wyoming, 1860-1920**. 1987.
$5.95. .... Vendor G0552

Laramie County

Saltiel, E. H., and George Barnett, comps. **History & Business Directory of Cheyenne** & Guide to Mining Regions of the Rocky Mountains. (1868) reprint 1993.
Cloth. $22.50. 114 pp. .... Vendor G0259

Author Index

Abbeville County Heritage Book Committee, 172
Abbot, William W., 278
Abercrombie, Janice Luck, 278, 299-300, 302, 304, 306-318, 320-321, 323-324, 326-327, 329-330, 332-340, 343-350, 352, 354-356, 358-360, 362-364, 366, 369, 371-372
Aberle, Monseigneur George P., 38
Abler, ___, 95
Absher, Mrs. W. O., 34-35, 37
Ackerman, Dolores Dunn, 374
Acklen, Jeannette Tillotson, 187
Adams, Andrew N., 272
Adams, Lela C., 332, 351-352
Adams, Raymond D., 143
Addington, Robert M., 362
Africa, J. Simpson, 118, 129
Albert, George D., 153
Alcock, John P., 318
Aldrich, L. C., 271
Aldrich, Lewis Cass, 53, 269, 277
Aler, F. Vernon, 380
Alexander, J. B., 26
Alexander, Nancy, 15
Alexander, Susan R., 57
Alexander, Virginia, 172, 182
Alexander, Virginia Wood, 225
Allegheny Regional Fam-

ily History Society, 377, 380, 390
Allen, Penelope Johnson, 187, 236, 240
Allen, Ruth, 119
Allen, V. C., 227, 231
Allen, W. C., 23
Allison, John, 187
Alvord, Clarence Walworth, 278, 281
Anson County Heritage Book Committee, 12
Apsley, Marmie, 83
Arlington Genealogical Club, 304
Armstrong, Zella, 187
Arnold, H. V., 38
Arnold, James N., 155-156, 159-161
Ashby, Bernice M., 362
Ashmead, Henry G., 122, 125, 126
Ashtabula County Genealogical Society, 47
Auld, Joseph, 270
Austin, John Osborne, 156
Axelson, Edith F., 279

Babcock, Charles A., 150
Baber, Lucy H. M., 342
Baccus, Janet Nixon, 374
Bachar, Jacqueline Miller, 63, 74
Bagby, Alfred, 335
Bahmer, William J., 51
Bailey, ___, 188
Bailey, Dana R., 187
Bailey, J. D., 184
Bailey, Lewis, 386
Bailey, Lloyd R., 13, 27, 37, 38
Baker, Julie P., 77

Baker, L. M. H., 310
Baker, Russell P., 188
Baker, T. Lindsay, 77
Balderston, Marion, 90
Baldwin, Agnes Leland, 162
Bamman, Gale Williams, 188
Banvard, Theodore James Fleming, 84, 90, 245, 373, 392
Bareis, George F., 54
Barnes, ___, 48, 58, 62, 65, 72, 74
Barnes, Robert, 106, 154
Barnett, George, 400
Barrett, ___, 1, 11
Barth, Margaret, 112
Bartlesville Genealogical Society, 84
Bartlett, John R., 156
Bartley, Scott A., 267
Barton, R. T., 279
Batcheller, Birney C., 272
Bates, Marlene S., 154
Bates, Samuel P., 91, 129
Battle, J. H., 123, 141
F. A. Battley & Company, 246
Baughman, A. J., 46, 70
Bausman, J. H., 114
Baxter, Samuel A., 46
Bayles, Richard M., 159-160
Bean, T. W., 140
Beard, Jane A., 246
Beardsley, D. B., 58
Beers & Co., J. H., 116
Beers', D. G., 153
Beers', S. N., 153
Begley, Paul R., 163
Bell, Carol Willsey, 39, 66

Wright, Sue, 317, 345
Wulfeck, Dorothy Ford, 299
Wust, ___, 299
Wynne, Frances Holloway, 19, 36, 309

Xakellis, Martha J., 134

Yates, Helen K., 324, 341-342
Yearns, ___, 11
Yinger, Hilda E., 66-67
Yoder, Don, 106
Young, ___, 95
Young, Connie Copeland, 230

Young, Pauline, 171-172
Younger, Lillye, 206
Yurechko, John Otto, 299

Zelinsky, ___, 95
Zenglein, Dieter, 76
Zimmerman, Gary J., 282

Title Index

Collin County, Texas, Cemetery Inscriptions. Volume I, 257

Collin County, Texas, Cemetery Inscriptions. Volume II, 257

Collin County, Texas, Families, 257

Colonial and Revolutionary Families of Pennsylvania, 99

Colonial and Revolutionary History of Upper South Carolina, 167

Colonial and State Records of North Carolina, The, 2

Colonial Bertie County, North Carolina, Deed Books A-H, 1720-1757, 13

Colonial Records of North Carolina [Second Series], Volume I: North Carolina Charters and Constitutions, 1578-1698, 3

Colonial Records of North Carolina [Second Series], Volume II: North Carolina Higher-Court Records, 1670-1696, 3

Colonial Records of North Carolina [Second Series], Volume III: North Carolina Higher-Court Records, 1697-1701, 3

Colonial Records of North Carolina [Second Series], Volume IV: North Carolina Higher-Court Records, 1702-1708, 3

Colonial Records of North Carolina [Second Series], Volume V: North Carolina Higher-Court Minutes, 1709-1723, 3

Colonial Records of North Carolina [Second Series], Volume VI: North Carolina Higher-Court Minutes, 1724-1730, 3

Colonial Records of North Carolina [Second Series], Volume VII: Records of the Executive Council, 1664-1734, 3

Colonial Records of North Carolina [Second Series], Volume VIII: Records of the Executive Council, 1735-1754, 3

Colonial Records of North Carolina [Second Series], Volume IX: Records of the Executive Council, 1755-1775, 3

Colonial Records of Virginia, 282

Colonial Surry [Virginia], 279, 364

Colonial Virginia Register, The, 294

Colonial Virginians and Their Maryland Relatives, 296

Colonial Wills of Henrico County, Virginia, 1677-1737, 331

Colonial Wills of Henrico County, Virginia, 1737-1781, 331

Colony of North Carolina, 1736-1764: Abstracts of Land Patents, Volume 1, 5

Columbia County, Oregon Marriage Records, 1855-1900, 86

Columbus: Its History, Resources & Progress, with Numerous Illustrations, 55

Comanche County, OK Marriage Records, Books 1 and 2, Aug. 1901-25 Feb. 1906, 81

Commemorative & Biographical Records of the Counties of Harrison & Carroll, 49, 58

Commemorative Biographical Record of Washington County, 151

Commemorative Biographical Record of Wayne County, 76

Commemorative Historical & Biographical Record of Wood County, 76

Committees of Safety of Westmoreland and Fincastle, The: Proceedings of the County Committees, 1774-1776, 319, 371

Compendium of History & Biography of North Dakota, 38

Compendium of the Confederate Armies: North Carolina, 10

Compendium of the Confederate Armies: South Carolina and Georgia, 169

Compendium of the Confederate Armies: Tennessee, 192

Compendium of the Confederate Armies: Texas, 248

Compendium of the Confederate Armies of Virginia, 294

Compilation of the Original Lists of Protestant Immigrants to South Carolina, 1763-1773, A, 169

Compiled Index to Elected and Appointed Officials of the Republic of Texas, 1836-1846, 249

Complete History of Fairfield County, 1795-1876, A, 54

Complete Listing of Gravestone Inscriptions in Putney, Vermont, A, 276

Complete Records of Emmanuel Evangelical Lutheran Church, Freeport, Armstrong, PA, 1875-1920, 112

Index to Advertisers